Ohio's Regulars in the War of 1812

Eric Eugene Johnson

Society of the War of 1812
in the
State of Ohio

HERITAGE BOOKS
2014

HERITAGE BOOKS
AN IMPRINT OF HERITAGE BOOKS, INC.

Books, CDs, and more—Worldwide

For our listing of thousands of titles see our website
at
www.HeritageBooks.com

Published 2014 by
HERITAGE BOOKS, INC.
Publishing Division
5810 Ruatan Street
Berwyn Heights, Md. 20740

Copyright © 2014 Society of the War of 1812 in the State of Ohio

Heritage Books by the Society of the War of 1812 in the State of Ohio:
American Prisoners of War Held at Bermuda, Cape of Good Hope and Jamaica During the War of 1812
American Prisoners of War Held at Barbados, Newfoundland and New Providence During the War of 1812
American Prisoners of War Held at Quebec During the War of 1812, 8 June 1813–11 December 1814
American Prisoners of War Held at Halifax, During the War of 1812, Volume I and II
Ohio and the War of 1812: A Collection of Lists, Musters and Essays
Ohio's Regulars in the War of 1812

All rights reserved. No part of this book may be reproduced or transmitted in any form or by any means, electronic or mechanical, including photocopying, recording or by any information storage and retrieval system without written permission from the author, except for the inclusion of brief quotations in a review.

International Standard Book Numbers
Paperbound: 978-0-7884-5574-2
Clothbound: 978-0-7884-6007-4

The Contents

Introduction 1
The Regiments 5
The Scorecard 13
The Officers 19
The Enlisted Men 41
Bibliography 175

The Introduction

The War of 1812 is largely forgotten by the American public today except for academia, military historians, and people who are researching their family trees. There is a genre of War of 1812 research that is largely overlooked today, that is, identifying the men who served in the U.S. Army during this war.

Academia concentrates on the causes and the effects of this war. The military historians will write a history of a particular battle or campaign, highlighting only the key players, not the individual soldiers. Family historians will research militia records for their ancestors, but many fail to look in army records for the same individuals.

My 'expertise' in the War of 1812 is with Major General William Henry Harrison's Army of the Northwest. Even in this narrow field of American military history, I have concentrated on the logistics of this army, that is, how the army was formed, how it was organized, and how it was supplied. I leave the battles for others to research and write about. I am also particularly interested in the role that the State of Ohio and its citizens played during this conflict.

Originally, I had been asked to re-publish a corrective version of the *Roster of Ohio Soldiers in the War of 1812*, first published by Ohio's Adjutant-General Department in 1916. This book has more errors in it than Swiss cheese has holes. The Ohio Historical Society in Columbus, Ohio, has the original militia rosters that were used in this book. The compiler or compiler(s) of this *Roster* left out all personal information. This includes who died and where, who was promoted, and who was sick or wounded. Most of these events have dates. All the militia companies were organized into three regiments in this book. A normal militia regiment only had eight companies of soldiers not the hundreds that are listed in these three regiments. This book does beg to be re-published correctly.

After nearly twenty years of researching the Army of the Northwest, I felt that were was a need to publish a book listing the Ohioans who served in the U.S. Army. Many Ohioans served a tour of duty with the state militia in 1812 and then joined the army in 1813. A plus side of this endeavor is the fact that the army kept far better records of its men than the Ohio militia maintained for its own soldiers.

The Army of the Northwest is very unique when compared to the other armies that were raised during this war. This army was reorganized a number of times which created a major problem in researching individual men. A single man who enlisted for five years in 1812 could have been assigned to three or four different regiments within the three year period for this war. He would also have had even more company commanders than what would be normal in the other American armies.

As an example, John Chunn was commissioned a captain in the 2nd Battalion of the 17th Regiment of U.S. Infantry in April 1812. The 1st Battalion was raised in Kentucky while the second was raised in Ohio. In June, the 2nd Battalion was split off to become the 19th Regiment of U.S. Infantry. In May 1814, the 19th Infantry was disbanded and its soldiers were transferred to the new 17th Infantry. Finally, the 17th Infantry was disbanded in May 1815 and its soldiers were transferred to the new 3rd Infantry. Captain Chunn served in four regiments during this war, all within the Army of the Northwest.

Two other re-organizations occurred within General Harrison's army. After the Battle of the Thames River in October 1813, General Harrison was ordered to take half of his troops to New York State to join the Army of the North. The general re-organized his troops, leaving any soldier who was a prisoner of war on parole status or who was sick, wounded or injured, and then he proceeded with his healthier troops to New York. All of the companies were reorganized accordingly. Also in May of 1814 the 2nd Regiment of U.S. Rifles was raised at Fort Detroit using a cadre of officers and men from the regiments within General Harrison's army. This created another re-organization. Most regiments in the U.S. Army maintained their identities throughout the war until 17 May 1815 when all army regiments were re-organized into eight infantry regiments, one rifle regiment and one dragoon regiment plus a Corps of Artillery.

Re-organizations created other problems. On 12 May 1814, the 26th and the 27th Regiments of U.S. Infantry (both raised in Ohio) were disbanded and its soldiers transferred to the new 19th Infantry. At the same time, the 46th Regiment of U.S. Infantry was re-designated as the new 26th Infantry while the 47th

Regiment of U.S. Infantry became the new 27th Infantry. Knowing the names of the company commanders in the new 26th and 27th Infantries greatly helped in determining if a soldier was from Ohio, Vermont or New York.

Likewise, the 3rd Regiment of U.S. Infantry was headquartered in Georgia during the war and then merged into the new 1st Infantry on 17 May 1815. This information helped in sorting out which soldiers were Ohioans which were Georgians. Luckily, I had done my homework on the re-organizations long before I started compiling this book.

The Plan of Action

As stated, the army kept far better records than the militia. The army, however, did not annotate on the enlistment records the residences of its soldiers, only where they were born and where they enlisted. In this book, there will be men who crossed the Ohio River from Kentucky and enlisted in the U.S. Army at Cincinnati. They will be listed as Ohioans unless I had found other sources stating that they were from Kentucky.

I established a 5-part criterion to order to identify Ohioans who served in the U.S. Army:

> One, if the soldier was born in the state (enlistment records).
> Two, if the soldier was married in Ohio during the war (pension indexes).
> Three, if the soldier enlisted in Ohio during the war (enlistment records).
> Four, if the soldier belonged to an Ohio raised regiment (enlistment records).
> Five, if the soldier died in Ohio and was buried in this state (various sources).

I felt that the last criterion was important. The 24th Regiment of U.S. Infantry, raised in Tennessee, and the 28th Regiment of U.S. Infantry, raised in Kentucky, both served in Ohio, and as such, men from these states died and where buried in Ohio. In my opinion, these men are forever Ohioans and should be honored as such.

Concerning item four: the 26th and 27th Regiments of Infantry plus the two companies of U.S. Rangers were raised in Ohio, so it is safe to assume that all men were Ohioans. The 19th Regiment of U.S. Infantry was raised in Ohio, Indiana and Michigan, but the majority of men were Ohioans. There may be men listed in this book who were actually from either Indiana or Michigan.

The 17th Regiment of U.S. Infantry plus a company of light dragoons, two companies of artillery, and companies from the 1st and 2nd Regiments of Rifles recruited in Ohio, Michigan, Indiana, Kentucky, Pennsylvania and Tennessee, before and during the war. Men may have been misidentified because of the lack of good source material.

Many Ohioans have been missed and are not included in this book. The 1st, 2nd and 7th Infantries plus the Artillery Regiment all recruited in Ohio before the war and on the enlisted records for these men, the birth and enlistment places were normally not recorded. Some of the sources that I used listed men by last name and first initial. If I did not find any supporting information from the enlistment records, pension indexes and land bounty warrants, I excluded them from this book.

Besides determining the criteria of those soldiers who were Ohioans, I needed to identify the source material that I would be using for this book. I first created a database and entered the names of the army officers that I had previously found who were from Ohio. I then collected the names of Ohioans from books in my personal library and from army rosters and musters that I had copied over the years. These records included muster rosters, enlistment rosters, discharge rosters, and other types of army documents.

I then decided to use the *U.S. Army, Register of Enlistments, 1798-1914*, the *War of 1812 Pension Application Files Index, 1812-1815*, and the *U.S. War Bounty Land Warrants, 1789-1858* files which are on Ancestry.com. At this point I realized that the purpose of this book was to identify Ohioans who served during the war and not to reconstruct a complete military service record for each individual man.

At the time that I was researching this book, the complete set of pension records were only available at the National Archives in Washington, DC, and they were not the Internet. I would have had to move to

Washington and set up residence at the National Archives in order to review each pension record. As such, I determined that the pension index, which had the basic information that I needed for each individual was sufficient for this book.

The *Register of Enlistments in the U.S. Army, 1798-1914* is an extract of personnel information from the land forces of the United States obtained from documents generated by the U.S. Army. These documents include enlistment records, recruiting reports, discharge records, commissioning records, muster rosters, inspection reports, morning reports, court-martial records, etc.

The first section of *Register of Enlistments* covers the period from 1798 to 17 May 1815. This section of the book is also called the *Records of the Men Enlisted in the U.S. Army Prior to the Peace Establishment, May 17, 1815*. It contains 7,360 pages with approximately 10 to 20 men listed on each page. The majority of these pages were generated during the War of 1812. I went through this section twice reading each name and determining each man's residence.

I then tackled the 76,126 records of the *War of 1812 Pension Application Files Index, 1812-1815* file. As I did with the Register of Enlistments, I entered into my database the Ohioans who I found in this index and copied their personal information.

Finally, I reviewed the *U.S. War Bounty Land Warrants, 1789-1858* file. This file contained 27,433 warrants that were issued to soldiers under the Congressional Acts of 1812, 1814 and 1842. The majority of these warrants were issued to soldiers between 1817 and 1819. I did not use the *U.S. General Land Office Records, 1796-1907* file in my research. The military bounty land warrants issued under the Acts of 1850 and 1855 are included in this last file but the vast majority of these warrants are for militia men not U.S. soldiers. This file's primary purpose was to index civilian purchases of federal lands. The military warrants were a small portion of this file.

Conclusion

As stated, the purpose of this book is to identify Ohio residents who served in the U.S. Army during the War of 1812 and not to create a detailed service record for each individual man. There are mistakes! Due to misspelling of surnames, missing records, and other factors, some men are missing, some men are listed twice, and some men are not properly identified. Overall, this book should be used to identify soldiers and to point out what records are available for each individual.

Researching this book started out as a fun project and evolved quickly into an obsession. By the time that I was reading each land warrant, I found that I had been transported back in time to the War of 1812. As I was reading each warrant, I started to see the faces of these men. I saw fathers and sons enlisting together. I saw brothers enlisting. I saw the faces of the heirs who were listed on the warrants because their loved ones had died during the war. I hope this book will honor the memory of those Ohioans who fought in this war while serving as members of the U.S. Army.

Eric E. Johnson
1 March 2014

Ohio's Regulars the War of 1812

The Regiments

The Army of the Northwest served with distinction throughout the War of 1812. The army is famous for its defeats at Detroit and at the River Raisin as well as its victory over the British Army at the Battle of the Thames River. Men from this army would also fight at Lundy's Lane, at Chippewa and at New Orleans. The army was made up of woodsmen, farmers and laborers from the present day states of Alabama, Indiana, Illinois, Kentucky, Michigan, Missouri, Mississippi, Ohio, Pennsylvania, Tennessee, West Virginia and Virginia.

Three future presidents from two different countries were soldiers in the Army of the Northwest. William Henry Harrison and Zachary Taylor were officers in this army and they would later become presidents of the United States. Few people realized that Samuel Houston was a sergeant in the Army of the Northwest and he would later become the first president of the Republic of Texas. Richard M. Johnson of Kentucky would later serve as a vice president of the United States. Many other men would become famous as governors and senators in the years following this war.

Most people see only a watered-down version of the history of this army in the books written on the war. What they know is that Brigadier General William Hull formed the first army and then he surrendered this force to the British at Detroit on 16 August 1812, and then Major General William Henry Harrison would form a second army and he would defeat the British at the Battle of the Thames River on 5 October 1813.

In actuality, the Army of the Northwest had four commanders and its area of responsibilities included nearly half of the area of the United States according to its boundaries in 1812. This area was the Northwest Territory plus Kentucky and the Territory of Missouri. The Territory of Missouri included most of the original land from the Louisiana Purchase minus the State of Louisiana.

The army had thousands of soldiers and employees who operated the numerous forts, camps, barracks, depots, hospitals and command centers stretching from Pittsburgh, Pennsylvania, to well beyond St. Louis, Missouri, and then from Detroit, Michigan, to Nashville, Tennessee. The main supply line for this army started at Philadelphia, Pennsylvania, and ended at the forts along the lower Missouri Valley. It took an army of men and women to support and to supply the army of soldiers.

The army was created on 25 May 1812 when Brigadier General William Hull took command of a mixed force of Ohio militia and the 4th Regiment of U.S. Infantry. On 17 May 1815 the army was disbanded when most of its regular infantry regiments from this army merged to form the new 3rd Regiment of U.S. Infantry. This regiment is now the 3rd Infantry Regiment and is the oldest regiment on active duty with the U.S. Army. The 3rd Infantry is nicknamed "The Old Guard" and its mission is to "conduct ceremonies, memorial affairs, and special events to demonstrate the excellence of the United States Army to the world." The regiment is a ceremonial regiment, which conducts state funerals, honor guards, honor guards at the Tomb of the Unknown Soldier, drill teams and Fife and Drum Corps.

In May 1812, the country was following a course that could only lead towards war with Great Britain. The initial army was formed to protect Fort Detroit and the Territory of Michigan from a possible invasion by the British. But in reality it was being staged so that when the war was declared, the army could immediately invade Upper Canada, as the Province of Ontario was called in 1812. War would be declared on 16 June 1812 and all of the best-laid plans ended when General Hull surrendered to the British on 16 August 1812.

The army would be reformed and go on to win victories at Fort Meigs and Fort Stephenson. After the Battle of the Thames River half of the army would be sent to New York to bolster the main American army, which was located there.

The end of the War of 1812 did not occur on 24 December 1814 when the Treaty of Ghent was signed between Great Britain and the United States. Due to the slowness of ship travel it would not be until early February 1815 before the United States would find out that the treaty had been signed and a couple of more months until our furthest military outposts were notified.

The war ended on 17 February 1815 when the United States exchanged a signed treaty with Great Britain. Had there been better communication lines between Europe and America in December 1814 both sides would have probably agreed to a cease-fire right after the treaty was signed, which would have prevented the Battle of New Orleans from ever occurring. By the provisions in the treaty, the war actually ended on 17 June 1815.

The last battle of the war was fought on 24 May 1815 near the site of Fort Howard, Territory of Illinois (now Wisconsin), when a company of U.S. Rangers engaged the enemy.[1] The land war started in the Old Northwest Territory and the land war would end in the Old Northwest Territory.

The Raising of the Regiments

At the start of the war, the army had the 1st Regiment of U.S. Infantry and a couple of companies of artillery stationed in the northwest. The 7th Regiment of U.S. Infantry had been authorized in 1808 and it was not yet at full strength. A couple of rifle companies were also in the process of being raised from within Kentucky and Ohio.

In the first six months of 1812, the 17th and 19th Regiments of U.S. Infantry were formed along with a company of light dragoons (cavalry), one artillery company and seven rangers companies. Another artillery company from Pennsylvania was transferred to Ohio. During 1813, three more infantry regiments were raised in the northwest. These were the 26th, 27th and 28th Regiments of U.S. Infantry. The 24th Regiment of U.S. Infantry and a company of artillery were transferred from Tennessee.

On 12 May 1814 the Army of the Northwest went through a major reorganization of its regiments. The 17th Infantry and the 19th Infantry merged to form the new 17th Regiment of U.S. Infantry while the 26th and the 27th Regiments of U.S. Infantry merged to form the new 19th Regiment of U.S. Infantry.

Six ensigns from the 17th Infantry were transferred to the 24th Regiment of U.S. Infantry while two ensigns from the 17th Infantry and four ensigns from the 19th Infantry were transferred to the 28th Regiment of U.S. Infantry. Both the 17th and 19th Infantries, as reorganized, were new regiments having all new regimental commanders and field grade officers.

Most of the men from the 26th Infantry who had been transferred to New York were re-assigned to the 25th Regiment of U.S. Infantry. The 26th Infantry had been organized using one-year enlistments and the men were nearing their discharge dates. Only a few of the men re-enlisted and actually served with the 25th Infantry. A few men from the 17th and 19th Infantries were also re-assigned to the 25th Infantry. Finally, a small number of men from the 17th, the 19th and the 26th Infantries were re-assigned to the Light Dragoon Regiment and the Rifle Regiment.

The majority of these men were left behind in late 1814 when the 17th and 19th Infantries were withdrawn from New York State to take up winter quarters in Erie, PA. The men had been recovering in hospitals from wounds, injuries or sickness; or had been prisoners of war or on special assignments from the companies. It was easier to re-assign these men to other regiments in New York State rather than to gather them up and march them to Pennsylvania.

Enlistment lengths for the army varied during the war. Before the war, enlistments ran for five years and then it was changed to 'five years' or 'during the war' after the war started. When enlistments began to fall off, men were given the options to enlist for 18 months. The nineteen new regiments and the ten ranger companies of 1813 were permitted to have one-year enlistments. The one year and the 18-month enlistees were not entitled to bonuses or military land bounties for their services. Many of these men with shorter enlistments had their enlistments changed so that they would qualify for these benefits.

Surprisingly, new recruits were rarely assigned as replacements in existing companies. When the number of recruits reached 100 they would be organized into new companies. As the existing companies

---

[1] Heitman, Francis B., **Historical Register and Dictionary of the United States Army From Its Organization, September 29, 1789, to March 2, 1903**, Volume II, (Genealogical Publishing Company, Baltimore, Maryland: 1994), part II, chronological list of battles, page 394.

in the field dwindled down in size, companies would merge and the access officers were either discharged or sent home to recruit more men.

Most infantry regiments did form ten companies during the war but at any given time there may have been only four to six companies actually serving in the field. There was at least one company always being formed at the regiment's recruiting headquarters. Some recruits waited months before being assigned to a new company.

1st Regiment of U.S. Infantry
29 September 1789 – 17 May 1815

The 1st Regiment of U.S. Infantry was organized under the act of 3 June 1784 to serve for twelve months but yearly resolutions by Congress maintained the regiment's existence until 29 September 1789 when the regiment became the Regiment of Infantry. Under the act of 3 March 1791 the regiment became the 1st Regiment of Infantry. Under the act of 5 May 1792 the regiment became the 1st Sublegion. Under the act of 1 November 1796, the regiment became the 1st Regiment of Infantry. The regiment was restructured under the act of 26 June 1812. Under the act of 3 March 1815 the regiment was consolidated with the 17th, 19th, 24th, 28th and 39th Regiments of Infantry to form the 3rd Regiment of Infantry on 17 May 1815.

The regiment's recruiting headquarters was at New Brunswick, New Jersey, while the regiment's field headquarters was at Fort Belle Fontaine in the Territory of Missouri. The regiment was authorized to recruit men for 'during the war' and 5-year enlistments.

In 1814, three companies from the 1st Infantry were transferred to the Army of the North in New York where these detachments fought at the Battle of Fort Erie. The regiment never operated as a full regiment during the war.

The regiment did recruit in Ohio before and during the war. Captain Thomas Ramsey of the Rifle Regiment raised his company from the Cincinnati area. Early in the war, the captain was ordered to report with his company to St. Louis, Missouri. Upon reaching the new duty station, all of Ramsey's enlisted men were transferred to the various companies of the 1st Infantry, and then he and his officers were ordered back to Cincinnati to recruit more men. Captain Ramsey would recruit another company at Cincinnati and then be assigned to the New York theatre. The captain would distinguish himself during the Battle of Fort Erie.

The 1st Infantry did have a large number of Ohioans within its ranks but most of the men have not yet been identified.

7th Regiment of U.S. Infantry
12 April 1808 to 17 May 1815

The 7th Regiment of U.S. Infantry was organized under the act of 12 April 1808, the regiment was restructured under the act of 26 June 1812. Under the act of 3 March 1815 the regiment was consolidated with the 2nd, 3rd and 44th Regiments of Infantry to form the 1st Regiment of Infantry on 17 May 1815. Recruiting headquarters were established in Kentucky at Eddyville and Hopkinsville. The regiment offered 'during the war' and 5-year enlistments.

Recruiting was very slow before the war, so the regiment sent its recruiters into Ohio, Tennessee, and the Territory of Indiana. The regiment had recruiting stations in Cincinnati and Lebanon, Ohio, and during the war it still sent its officers into Ohio searching for recruits.

One reoccurring problem with both the 1st and 7th Infantries was when the recruiting officers were sent to Ohio, the recruits that they enlisted were sent to the recruiting depots at Chillicothe and Zanesville for processing. The recruits were then reassigned to either the 17th or the 19th Infantries. This was probably pay back to what happened to Captain Thomas Ramsey at St. Louis.

Eight companies from this regiment were transferred to New Orleans before the war and this regiment fought hard during the Battle of New Orleans. The remaining two companies, under Major Zachary Taylor, operated out of Fort Belle Fontaine in the Territory of Missouri throughout the war. Most Ohioans who served in the 7th Infantry have not been identified.

17th Regiment of U.S. Infantry
First Organization

11 January 1812 to 12 May 1814

The 17th Regiment of U.S. Infantry was organized under the Congressional Act of 11 January 1812 as part of a ten-regiment buildup of the army prior to the beginning of the War of 1812. The regiment was authorized for a maximum period of five years and it was to be raised in Kentucky, Ohio, and in the Territories of Indiana and Michigan.

The regiment was structured into two battalions of nine 110-man companies. A lieutenant colonel commanded each of the battalions while a colonel served as the regimental commander. The 1st battalion was raised in Kentucky while the 2nd battalion was scheduled to have been raised in Ohio, Indiana and Michigan.

The 17th Infantry was reorganized under the Congressional Act of 26 July 1812 and restructured into ten 102-man companies. The regiment's authorized manning was set at 1,070 men. The 2nd battalion was split off to become the 19th Regiment of U.S. Infantry. Enlistments were authorized for five years, during the war, and 18 months.

17th Regiment of U.S. Infantry
Second Organization

12 May 1814 to 17 May 1815

The second 17th Regiment of U.S. Infantry was authorized under the act of 3 March 1814 then the 17th and 19th Regiments of U.S. Infantry merged to form this new regiment on 12 May 1814. The "17" designation was reused for this new regiment. The new regiment was made up of men from Kentucky, Ohio, and the Territories of Indiana and Michigan. Under the act of 3 March 1815 the regiment was consolidated with the 1st, 19th, 24th, 28th and 39th Regiments of Infantry to form the 3rd Regiment of Infantry on 17 May 1815.

Enlistments were authorized for five years, during the war, and 18 months. Regimental headquarters was established at Chillicothe, Ohio, and the regiment maintained three recruiting depots at Chillicothe, Zanesville, Ohio, and Lexington, Kentucky.

19th Regiment of U.S. Infantry
First Organization

26 June 1812 to 12 May 1814

The 19th Regiment of U.S. Infantry was authorized under the Congressional Act of 26 June 1812 for a period of not more than five years. The regiment was initially formed from the 2nd battalion of the 17th Regiment of U.S. Infantry. The regiment was authorized to have ten companies of 102 men each with a headquarters' staff for a total manning of 1,070 men. The officers and men were recruited from Ohio and from the Territories of Indiana and Michigan.

Enlistments were authorized for five years, during the war, and 18 months. The regimental headquarters was established at Chillicothe, Ohio, and the regiment maintained two recruiting depot at Chillicothe, and Zanesville, Ohio.

19th Regiment of U.S. Infantry
Second Organization

12 May 1814 to 17 May 1815

The second 19th Regiment of U.S. Infantry was authorized under the act of 3 March 1814 then the 26th and 27th Regiments of U.S. Infantry merged to form this second regiment on 12 May 1814. None of the officers from the first 19th Infantry were transferred to the second 19th Infantry. The 26th and 27th Regiments of U.S. Infantry were raised in Ohio under the act of 29 January 1813.

Enlistments were authorized for five years, during the war, and 18 months. Regimental headquarters was established at Zanesville, Ohio, and the regiment maintained two recruiting depots at Chillicothe, Ohio, and Zanesville.

26th Regiment of U.S. Infantry
29 January 1813 to 12 May 1814

The 26th Regiment of U.S. Infantry was organized under an Act of Congress on 29 January 1813 as the first of 19 new infantry regiments that were to be raised for one year. The 26th Infantry was authorized to have ten 102-man companies plus a headquarters' staff for a total strength of 1,091 men. The regiment would be raised from within the 1st, 2nd and 5th Divisions of the Ohio Militia, which constituted the western half of Ohio.

On 28 January 1814 the regiment's authorization was changed to five years or less. At the same time enlistments were approved for five years or during the war. The regimental headquarters and the main recruiting center were established at Chillicothe, Ohio.

27th Regiment of U.S. Infantry
29 January 1813 to 12 May 1814

The 27th Regiment of U.S. Infantry was organized under the Congressional Act of 29 January 1813. This new regiment was part of a nineteen-regiment build up of the army during the War of 1812. It was authorized for one year and all initial enlistments were for twelve months. The regiment would be raised from within the 3rd and 4th Divisions of the Ohio Militia, which constituted the eastern half of Ohio.

On 28 January 1814 the regiment's authorization was changed to five years or less. At the same time enlistments were approved for five years or during the war and the one-year enlistments were eliminated. The regimental headquarters and the main recruiting center were established at Zanesville, Ohio. The regiment operated as part of the Army of the Northwest in the 8th Military District.

2nd Regiment of U.S. Artillery
11 January 1812 to 12 May 1814

The 2nd Regiment of U.S. Artillery was organized under the act of 11 January 1812 to service for a period of not more than five years. The regiment consisted of two battalions of ten companies. Enlistments were set at five years, 18 months and 'during the war.'

On 12 May 1814, under the act of 30 March 1814, the regiment was consolidated with the 1st and 3rd Regiments of U.S. Artillery to form the Corps of U.S. Artillery. Three companies from the 2nd Artillery were assigned to the Army of the Northwest.

Captain Daniel Cushing raised a company for 2nd Artillery from within Ohio. He recruited most of his men from western Ohio while 1st Lieutenant Joseph H. Larwill recruited the remaining men from eastern Ohio. A few men were recruited from Kentucky.

Captain Stanton Sholes raised his company from western Pennsylvania primarily from Beaver County. His company was assigned to the Army of the Northwest on 3 May 1813. Captain Sholes did recruit men from Ohio during the summer of 1813 while his company was stationed at Cleveland, Ohio.

Captain Joseph Philips raised an artillery company for the 2nd Artillery in Tennessee. The company was stationed at Fort Massac in the Territory of Illinois. It is doubtful that any Ohioans served in this company.

2nd Regiment of U.S. Light Dragoons
11 January 1812 to 12 May 1814

The 2nd Regiment of U.S. Light Dragoons was authorized under the act of 11 January 1812 to serve for a period not to exceed five years. The regiment consisted of twelve companies. Enlistments were set at five years but changed to five years or 18 months on 8 April 1812. On 12 December 1812 'during the war' enlistments were authorized.

Major James V. Ball of Virginia was ordered by the Secretary of War on 16 September 1812 to report to Brigadier General William H. Harrison in order to organize a squadron of dragoons for the Army of the Northwest. Captain Samuel Hopkins of Kentucky raised a company of dragoons for the 2nd Dragoons and the company was assigned to Major Ball's squadron. There were a few men from Ohio who were recruited for this company.

1st Regiment of U.S. Rifles
12 April 1808 to 17 May 1815

The 1st Regiment of U.S. Rifles was organized under the act of 12 April 1808 as the Regiment of U.S. Rifle to serve for a period of not more than five years. On 24 December 1811 the regiment became a part of the permanent peace establishment. Under the act of 3 March 1815 the regiment was consolidated with the 2nd, 3rd, and 4th Regiment of U.S. Rifles to become the Regiment of U.S. Rifles. The regiment was discharged under the act of 1 June 1821.

Enlistments were authorized for five years or during the war. Recruiting headquarters were located at Shepherdstown, Virginia, and Savannah, Georgia. Four companies were raised by the Army of the Northwest. Captain James McDonald and Captain Thomas Ramsey were Ohioans and the majority of the men in their companies were Ohioans.

2nd Regiment of U.S. Rifles
10 February 1814 to 17 May 1815

The 2nd Regiment of U.S. Rifles was organized under the act of 10 February 1814 for a period of not more than five years. The regiment was raised in Kentucky, Ohio, Tennessee and the Territory of Indiana. Recruiting headquarters were established at Chillicothe, Ohio, Lexington, Kentucky, and Nashville, Tennessee. Enlistments were authorized for five years or during the war.

It appears that only three companies were raised by this regiment before the war ended. Captain Batteal Harrison was from Ohio. Under the act of 3 March 1815 the regiment was consolidated with the 1st, 3rd, and 4th Regiment of U.S. Rifles to become the Regiment of U.S. Rifles on 17 May 1815.

United States Rangers
2 January 1812 to 15 June 1815

Six companies of U.S. Rangers were organized under the act of 2 January 1812 for one year and by the act of 1 July 1812 an additional company was authorized under the same provisions and restrictions. The act of 25 February 1813 authorized ten additional companies for one year in lieu of one of the regiments of infantry authorized by the act of 29 January 1813. The act of 2 August 1813 more fully defined the organization of these ten additional companies, and by the act of 27 January 1814 the ten companies were retained in service to 15 June 1815, when discharged under the act of 3 March 1815.

Captain James Manary raised the 1st Company of Rangers from Ohio while Captain William Perry raised the 2nd Company of Ranges from Ohio. Both Manary and Perry were dismissed from the service after one year. Captain Samuel McCormick raised a new 1st Company of Rangers from Ohio while the 2nd Company of Rangers was re-assigned to the Territory of Michigan under the command of Captain John H. Audrain.

Ohio's Regulars the War of 1812

The Scorecard

This chapter will explain the data fields, abbreviations, terms and phrases used in creating the 'service record' of each officer and enlisted personnel listed in the following two chapters.

Data Field	Explanation
Rank	The highest known military rank is listed for each soldier. The ranks of third lieutenant and ensign were discontinued in the army after the War of 1812.

Officer ranks:

Major General
Brigadier General
Colonel
Lieutenant Colonel
Major
Captain
First Lieutenant
Second Lieutenant
Third Lieutenant
Ensign or Cornet

The lowest officer's rank in the infantry, rifles, and artillery was an ensign while a cornet was the lowest officer's rank in the light dragoons.

Enlisted ranks:

Sergeant Major
Quartermaster Sergeant
Fife Major
Sergeant
Corporal
Private
Recruit

Equal in rank to privates were: musicians, artificers, saddlers, farriers, blacksmiths and drivers of artillery. Musicians were found in all branches of the army while artificers were used in the artillery instead of privates. The other ranks were used in the artillery and light dragoons regiments.

Regiment — The names of the regiments are abbreviated:

1st Infantry = 1st Regiment of U.S. Infantry
7th Infantry = 7th Regiment of U.S. Infantry
17th Infantry = 17th Regiment of U.S. Infantry
19th Infantry = 19th Regiment of U.S. Infantry
24th Infantry = 24th Regiment of U.S. Infantry
26th Infantry = 26th Regiment of U.S. Infantry (Ohio)
26th Infantry (new) = 26th Regiment of U.S. Infantry (Vermont)
27th Infantry = 27th Regiment of U.S. Infantry
28th Infantry = 28th Regiment of U.S. Infantry
1st Artillery = 1st Regiment of U.S. Artillery
2nd Artillery = 2nd Regiment of U.S. Artillery
1st Rifles = 1st Regiment of U.S. Rifles
2nd Rifles = 2nd Regiment of U.S. Rifles
2nd Light Dragoons = 2nd Regiment of U.S. Dragoons

Other regiment(s) — If a soldier was transferred to another regiment or regiments, the name of the additional regiments are listed in this field.

Company — The company's commander name

Up until 1816 the army identified a company by the company commander's

The Scorecard

name and started using alpha characters: A through K (J not used).

Age	Age of the soldier at the time of his enlistment or commissioning
Height	Height of the soldier in feet and inches.
Birth Place	The enlistment rosters list the birth of a soldier by state or country, county and city.
Trade	Civilian trade of a soldier at the time of enlistment.
Commissioning date	Date that an officer was commissioned into the army.
Enlistment date	Date that an enlisted man entered service.
Enlistment Place	The place of enlistment by state, county and city.
Enlistment Period	There were four enlistment periods which a soldier could select. All soldiers could choose to re-enlist once their initial enlistment period ended. Those soldiers who enlisted "during the war" were discharged at the end of the War of 1812.

18 Mos = 18 months
1 Yr = 1 year
5 Yrs = 5 years
War = "during the war"

All officers had "during the war" enlistments. In the spring of 1815, officers were selected to be retained for peacetime duty while the remaining officers were released from duty.

By whom	The recruiting officer's name.
Discharged	The date of discharge and location with other comments.
Died or Killed	Date of death and known location while serving in the army with additional comments.
Pension	I-9999 – Invalid IC-9999 – Invalid's Certificate IF-9999 – Invalid's File IO-9999 – Invalid's Original MC-9999 – Minor's Certificate MO-9999 – Minor's Original SC-9999 – Survivor's Certificate SF-9999 – Survivor's File SO-9999 – Survivor's Original WC-9999 – Widow's Certificate WF-9999 – Widow's File WO-9999 – Widow's Original

Bounty Number   BLW 123456-160-12

BLW = Bounty land warrant number
-160- or -320- = number of acres issued for the warrant
-12 or -14 or -42 or -50 or -55 = Years of the Land Bounty Acts

(Arkansas), (Illinois), (Missouri), or other = State in which the warrant was assigned

Comments   Any additional comments for a soldier.

Abbreviations

Standard U.S. Postal Service abbreviations are used for U.S. states plus
LC = Lower Canada (now Quebec)
UC = Upper Canada (now Ontario)
NS = Nova Scotia

Capt. = Captain
Lt. = Lieutenant
Ens. = Ensign

Enlistment records

MoRet or MRet - Monthly Returns
M.R. - Morning Reports or Muster Rolls
R.R. - Recruiting Returns
D.R. - Descriptive Rolls
G.O. - General Orders
S.O. – Special Orders
I.R. - Inspection Returns
CoBook or C.B. - Company book
S.A.M.R. – Semi-Annual Muster Rolls
S.A.I.R. – Semi-Annual Inspection Returns
P.R. - Payroll Reports
O.B. - Orders Book or Orderly Book
C.M. – Court-Martial
Correspondences

Terms and phases

Battle of Bridgewater
   Another name for the Battle of Lundy's Lane.

Discharged by writ of habeas corpus
   If an under aged soldier had enlisted without his father's permission, the father could go to the county courthouse and obtain a "writ of habeas corpus" and the army would then discharge the soldier.

Heirs obtained half pay for five years in lieu of military bounty land
Early in the war, the heirs of soldiers who had died (or were killed) during the war and who had enlisted for one-year or 18-months, could elect to receive the soldiers' half-month pay for five years or receive 160 acres of land. This was changed so that the heirs only received the half pay. The heirs of soldiers who enlisted for five years or during the war always received either 160 or 320 acres of land. 320 acres of land was issued to soldiers who enlisted or re-enlisted after 1 February 1814.

Land bounty to "name of heirs" heirs at law of "name of soldier"
This phase lists the name of the heir or heirs (by law) who received the land bounty of a deceased soldier.

Served aboard the US "name of ship" on the Lake Erie Squadron
This phase identifies the ship in which the soldier served as a officer, sailor or marine during the Battle of Lake Erie on 10 September 1813.

Discharged after furnishing a substitute
A soldier could be released early from his enlistment period if he supplied his own substitute.

Surgeon's Certificate of Disability
An army surgeon could issue a "Surgeon's Certificate of Disability" to a wounded, sick or injured soldier and this would released the soldier from the service. The soldier's enlistment would end and he was still entitled to all his back pay, bonuses and land bounties.

Executed
This term identifies a soldier who was executed for desertion or other crimes by a firing squad.

Breveted
Officers could be promoted to the next highest rank by brevet, that is, they would wear the insignia of the next officer's rank without an increase in pay.

Deserted
This term denotes soldiers who left their regiments and who did not return to duty. When found, some men were executed for this crime, while others returned to duty and received either a punishment or extended enlistment period. In early 1815, many soldiers simply left their regiments without permission and returned home. These men were not entitled to their enlistment benefits.

Pioneer
A pioneer was a soldier who was delegated to clear a path for a regiment, normally in a wooded area. These soldiers wore a leather apron and used axes to clear a road.

Prisoners of War

Prisoner of War (Halifax, NS)
An American soldier who was held at the British prisoner of war camp at Halifax, Nova Scotia.

Prisoner of War (Montreal, LC)
An American soldier who was held at the British prisoner of war camp at Montreal, Quebec.

Prisoner of War (Quebec, LC)
An American soldier who was held at the British prisoner of war camp at Quebec City, Quebec.

Prisoner of War on Parole, captured at Detroit, MI, 16 Aug 1812
An American soldier who was captured by the British at Detroit on 16 August 1812, and then released 'on parole' and then permitted to return home. These men signed an agreement that they would not take up arms against Great Britain unless they were exchanged for a British prisoner of war during the Prisoner of War exchange between the United States and Great Britain.

Exchanged
An American prisoner of war who was exchanged for a British prisoner of war.

Ohio's Black soldiers

Only four African-American Ohioans have been identified in this research. William Bradbury, Titus Folbert and Andrew Matthews enlisted in the new 26th Regiment of U.S. Infantry in Philadelphia, PA. Samuel Looks enlisted as a musician in the 2nd Regiment of U.S. Rifles at Chillicothe, OH.

Detachment Commanders

Many pension records list Lieutenants Featherstone, Goode, Gray and McElvain as company commanders. These officers were never company commanders but they were 'commanders' of discharge detachments. Simply, they were assigned the duty of escorting a group of soldiers who were being discharged from the army to a processing out center. These detachments were made up of soldiers from a number of different regiments.

Second Lieutenant John Goode
Second Lieutenant John McElvain
Third Lieutenant William Featherstone
Second Lieutenant. James Gray

The Scorecard

The Officers

Ohio's Regulars in the War of 1812

Abbott, James
Born – Pennsylvania
Residence – Ohio
Commissioned 3rd lieutenant, 26th Infantry, 20 May 1813
Recruiting at Franklinton, OH, Aug 1813
Resigned 1 Mar 1814
Died 1819

Albright, Peter
Born – Pennsylvania
Residence – Chillicothe, OH
Commissioned ensign, 1st Rifles, 1 Aug 1813
Assigned to Capt. Hamilton's Company
Promoted 3rd Lieutenant, 17 Mar 1814
Promoted 2nd Lieutenant, 6 Oct 1814
Assigned to Capt. Ramsey's Company, 15 Feb 1814
Transferred to Capt. Gray's Company, 28 Feb 1815
Honorable discharge 15 Jun 1815

Anderson, Charles M.
Born – Delaware
Residence – Ohio
Commissioned captain, 1st Artillery, 25 Mar 1812
Died 2 Jul 1812

Anderson, Jacob
Residence – Ohio
Private and sergeant, 7th Infantry, 24 Apr 1812- Apr 1813
Prisoner of War on parole status, captured at Detroit, MI, 16 Aug 1812.
Commissioned 3rd lieutenant, 19th Infantry, 6 Apr 1813
Promoted 2nd lieutenant, 20 Sep 1813
Transferred to 17th Infantry, 12 May 1814
Honorable discharge 15 Jun 1815

Anderson, Robert
Residence – Butler County, Ohio
Commissioned 1st lieutenant, 26th Infantry, 20 May 1812
Recruiting at Cincinnati, Newton and Brookfield, OH, Jun-Jul 1813
Served aboard the US Schooner Ariel during the Battle of Lake Erie.
Ordered to Newark, UC, Aug 1813
Assigned to Capt. Swearingen's Company at Sackets Harbor, NY, Dec 1813
Returned to recruiting in OH, Mar 1814
Recruiting at Lebanon and Cincinnati, Apr-Mar 1814
Honorable discharge 1 Jun 1814

Applegate, James
Residence – Trumbull County, Ohio
Commission captain, 27th Infantry, 20 May 1813
Recruiting at Zanesville, OH, Jun-Oct 1813
Recruiting at Warren, OH
Resigned 16 Oct 1813

Armstrong, Daniel D.
Residence – Cincinnati, OH
Commissioned ensign, 19th Infantry, 12 Mar 1812
Resigned 18 Nov 1812

Armstrong, William
Born – Pennsylvania
Residence – Ohio
Commissioned ensign, 1st Rifles, 19 Jan 1813
Promoted 3rd lieutenant, 12 Mar 1813
Assigned to Capt. Hay's Company, Oct 1813
Promoted 2nd lieutenant, 24 Jan 1814
Assigned to Capt. Wadsworth's Company, Feb 1815
Promoted 1st lieutenant, 1 Oct 1816
Promoted captain, 31 Jul 1818
Transferred to 6th Infantry, 1 Jun 1821
Died 11 Feb 1827

Avery, John C.
Residence – Ohio
Commissioned 3rd lieutenant, 26th Infantry, 20 May 1813
Recruiting at Cincinnati, OH, Jun-Nov 1813
Ordered to Frankfort, KY, with British prisoners of war
Recruiting at Cincinnati, OH, Jan 1814
On furlough, Feb 1814
Recruiting at Lebanon, OH, Feb 1814 and then at Cincinnati.
Honorable discharge 1 Jun 1814
Died 1 Feb 1850

Baird, William
Residence – Ohio
Commissioned 1st lieutenant, 26th Infantry, 20 May 1813
Served in Capt. Puthuff's company
Transferred to 19th Infantry, 12 May 1814
Recruiting at Zanesville, OH, Jul-Dec 1814, Jan-Feb 1815
Recruiting at Urbana and Cincinnati, OH
Promoted captain, 29 Jun 1814
Honorable discharge 15 Jun 1815

Baskerville, Edward B.
Residence – Ohio
Commissioned ensign, 19th Infantry, 12 Mar 1812
Dismissed 9 Nov 1813

Benedict, Ebenezer
Residence – Washington County, Ohio

The Officers

Commissioned 1st lieutenant, 27th Infantry, 20 May 1813
Recruiting at Zanesville, OH, Sep-Dec 1813, Jan-May 1814
Recruiting at Warren, OH
Honorable discharge 1 Jun 1814
Pension: Wife Irenea Barnum, WO-427, WC-1178; married 14 Feb 1802 in Danbury, Fairfield County, CT; soldier died on 25 Feb 1866 in Belpre, OH
Bounty: BLW 6178-160-50

Blair, James
Born – Pennsylvania
Residence – Ohio
Commissioned 2nd Lieutenant, 27th Infantry, 20 May 1813
Served aboard the US Sloop Trippe during the Battle of Lake Erie.
Transferred to 19th Infantry, 12 May 1814
Assigned to Capt. Gill's Company
Recruiting at Steubenville, OH, May 1815
Promoted 1st lieutenant, 27 May 1914
Honorable discharge 15 Jun 1815

Booker, Samuel
Residence – St. Clairsville, OH
Commissioned 1st lieutenant, 19th Infantry, 12 Mar 1812
Promoted captain, 20 Sep 1813
Honorable discharge 1 Jun 1814

Booten, John
Residence – Ohio
Commissioned 3rd lieutenant, 27th Infantry, 20 May 1813
Recruiting at Zanesville, OH, Dec 1813-Jan 1814
Transferred to 19th Infantry, 12 May 1814
Recruiting in Ohio, Jun 1814 to Feb 1815
Promoted 2nd lieutenant, 13 Sep 1814
Honorable discharge 15 Jun 1815

Bradford, Harry C.
Residence – Ohio
Commissioned surgeon's mate, 24th Infantry, 9 Aug 1813
Promoted surgeon, 12 Jul 1814
Resigned 14 Apr 1815

Brady, Josiah
Residence – Ohio
Commissioned 1st lieutenant, 26th Infantry, 20 May 1813
Recruiting at Lebanon, OH, Jun 1813
Recruiting at Bethel, OH, Jun-Aug 1813
Recruiting at Lebanon, OH, Feb-May 1814
Recruiting at Denham's Town (Bethel, OH)
Negatived by Senate 2 Aug 1813

Brown, John
Residence – Ohio
Commissioned 2nd lieutenant, 26th Infantry, 20 May 1813
Assigned to Capt. Kesling's company, Sackets Harbor, NY
Recruiting at Lebanon, OH, Apr-May 1814
Recruiting at Portsmouth, OH
Honorable discharge 1 Jun 1814

Bryan, George S.
Residence – Ohio
Commissioned 2nd lieutenant, 26th Infantry, 1 Jun 1813
Recruiting at Lebanon, OH, Jun-Aug 1813
Assigned to Capt. Kesling's company, Sackets Harbor, NY
Resigned 15 Aug 1813

Bryan, Peter
Residence – Ohio
Commissioned ensign, 19th Infantry, 31 Mar 1814
Transferred to 28th Infantry, 12 May 1814
Promoted 2nd lieutenant, 21 Jul 1814
Recruiting in Kentucky, Jul-Dec 1814, Jan 1815
Resigned 31 Jan 1815

Bushnell, Andrew
Residence – Ohio
Commissioned 3rd Lieutenant, 27th Infantry, 20 May 1813
Recruiting at Warren, OH, Feb 1814
Transferred to 19th Infantry, 12 May 1814
Promoted 2nd Lieutenant, 27 May 1814
Wounded at the Battle of Fort Erie, UC, 15 Aug 1814
Promoted 1st Lieutenant, 11 Nov 1814
Recruiting at Warren, OH, Dec 1814, Jan-Feb 1815
Honorable discharge 15 Jun 1815
Pension: Old War IF- 26588, served as a lieutenant in Capt. J. Chunn's Company, U.S. Infantry

Buttles, Avery
Residence – Ohio
Prisoner of War on parole status, captured at Detroit, MI, 16 Aug 1812
Commissioned 2nd lieutenant, 27th Infantry, 20 May 1813
Recruiting at Zanesville, OH, Apr-May 1814
Recruiting at Columbus, OH
Honorable discharge 1 Jun 1814

Cairns, Joseph

Residence – Muskingum County, Ohio
Captain, Ohio Volunteers, 1812-1813
Prisoner of War on parole status, captured at Detroit, MI, 16 Aug 1812
Prisoner of war, captured at Detroit, MI
Commissioned captain, 27th Infantry, 20 May 1813
Recruiting at Zanesville, OH, May-Jun 1813
Dismissed 18 Feb 1814

Camp, William G.
Residence – Ohio
Sergeant, 19th Infantry, 3 Feb 1813 to Mar 1814
Commissioned ensign, 2nd Rifles, 17 Mar 1814
Wounded 25 Jul 1814 during Battle of Fort Erie, UC, while attached to 21st Infantry
Promoted 3rd lieutenant, 1 Oct 1814
Honorable discharge 15 Jun 1815
Commissioned 2nd lieutenant, 5th Infantry, 13 Feb 1818
Regimental quartermaster, 1 Aug 1819 to 1 Jun 1821
Honorable discharge 1 Jun 1821
Pension: Old War IF-24497; served as an ensign
Bounty: BLW 24782-160-12 (Arkansas)

Campbell, Caleb B.
Residence – Ohio
Commissioned ensign, 19th Infantry, 24 Oct 1813
Transferred to 25th Infantry, 27 Aug 1814
Promoted 2nd lieutenant, 1 Oct 1814
Transferred to 6th Infantry, 17 May 1815
Resigned 10 Sep 1816

Campbell, James
Residence – Westminster, Ohio
Commissioned 1st lieutenant, 19th Infantry, 6 Jul 1812
Present at Fort Meigs, OH, Sep 1813
Present at Sackets Harbor, NY, Mar 1814
Recruiting in Ohio
Transferred to 17th Infantry, 12 May 1814
Honorable discharge 15 Jun 1815

Carney, David L.
Residence – Ohio
Commissioned 3rd lieutenant, 19th Infantry, 6 Apr 1813
Recruiting at Chillicothe, OH, Feb-Apr 1814
Transferred to 17th Infantry, 12 May 1814
Recruiting at Cincinnati, OH, May 1814
Promoted 2nd lieutenant, 9 Jul 1814
Recruiting at Newport, KY, Dec 1814, Jan 1815
Honorable discharge 15 Jun 1815

Carr, Robert
Residence – Ohio
Commissioned 3rd lieutenant, 19th Infantry, 6 Apr 1813
Honorable discharge 1 Jun 1814

Carroll, John
Residence - Ohio
Commissioned 2nd lieutenant, 27th Infantry, 20 May 1813
Recruiting at Zanesville, Dec 1813-May 1814
Recruiting at Steubenville
Transferred to 19th Infantry, 12 May 1814
Recruiting at Steubenville, Jun-Jul 1814
Ordered to Erie, PA, Capt. Trimble's Company, Feb 1815
Promoted 1st lieutenant, 15 Jul 1815
Honorable discharge 15 Jun 1815
Pension: Old War IF-13018; served as a lieutenant in the 27th Infantry

Cass, Charles Lee
Born - New Hampshire
Residence - Ohio
Commissioned 1st lieutenant, 27th Infantry, 20 May 1813
Recruiting at Zanesville, Aug-Sep 1813
Recruiting at Newark, Feb 1814
Recruiting at Cambridge, Mar-Apr 1814
Transferred to 19th Infantry, 12 May 1814
Sick at Williamsville, NY, Aug 1814
Sick at Buffalo, NY, Sep 1814
Recruiting at Zanesville, Dec 1814-Jan 1815
Honorable discharge, 15 Jun 1815
Reinstated 2 Dec 1815 with 3rd Infantry
Promoted captain, 31 Dec 1818
Transferred to 5th Infantry, 1 Jun 1821
Resigned 1 May 1814
Died 4 Jan 1842

Cass, Lewis
Born – New Hampshire
Residence – Muskingum County, Ohio
Colonel, 3rd Ohio Volunteer Regiment, 1812
Prisoner of war, captured at Detroit, MI, 16 Aug 1812
Commissioned colonel, 27th Infantry, 20 Feb 1813
Promoted brigadier general, 8th Military District, 12 Mar 1813
Commanded a brigade in the Army of the Northwest, Apr 1813
Resigned 1 May 1814
Died 17 Jun 1866
Bounty: BLW 27030-160-50
Note: 2nd territorial governor of Michigan; 14th U.S. Secretary of War; 22nd U.S. Secretary of State

Chunn, John T.

Residence – Ohio
Commissioned Captain, 19th Infantry, 14 Apr 1812
Transferred 17th Infantry, 12 May 1814
Brevet major, 15 Aug 1814, for distinguished service in the defense of Fort Erie, UC.
Transferred 3rd Infantry, 17 May 1815
Honorable discharged 1 Jun 1821

Cissna, Charles
Residence – Ohio
Commissioned ensign, 26th Infantry, 20 May 1813
Recruiting at Chillicothe, OH, Jun 1813-Jul 1814
Transferred to 19th Infantry, 12 May 1814
Promoted 3rd lieutenant, 16 Jun 1814
Serving in New York
Brevet 2nd lieutenant, 15 Aug 1814, for distinguished service in defense of Fort Erie, UC.
Wounded during the Battle of Fort Erie, UC, 15 Aug 1814
Serving at Erie, PA, Dec 1814
Promoted 2nd lieutenant, 12 Oct 1814
Honorable discharge 15 Jun 1815
Died 7 Mar 1827
Pension: Old War IF-26594, served as a lieutenant

Clarkson, Charles S.
Residence – Ohio
Commissioned assistant district paymaster, 21 Sep 1814
Honorable discharge 15 Jun 1815
Pension: Wife Charlotte Dunlap, SO-22508, SC-16822; married 2 Nov 1815 in Cumberland County, PA; served as a sergeant in Capt. William Garand's Company, KY militia and was an assistant district paymaster in the US Army; lived in St. Louis County, MO
Bounty: BLW 26115-160-50
Comments: Assistant District Paymaster in 8th Military District.

Clendenin, David
Residence – Ohio
Commissioned assistant district paymaster, 19 Apr 1814
Resigned 18 Dec 1814

Cochran, John
Residence – Pickaway County, OH
Commissioning date: 25 Apr 1812
Discharge date: 22 Apr 1815 resigned
Pension: Wife Mary O'Harra, SO-25252, SC-11222; married 26 May 1816, soldier died circa 1878; wife died on 14 Dec 1864; served as an ensign and a third lieutenant in the recruiting service of the 19th Infantry and in Capt. Holt's Company, 17th Infantry, lived in Pickaway County, OH
Bounty: BLW 391-160-50

Cole, Leonard
Residence – Ohio
Commissioned ensign, 26th Infantry, 7 Aug 1813
Recruiting at Franklinton, OH, Aug 1813
Ordered to join regiment at Sackets Harbor, NY, Sep 1813, but was sick in Detroit, MI
Recruiting at West Union, OH, Jan-Feb 1814
Honorable discharge 12 May 1814
Pension: Wife Harriet McDonald, WC-29404; married 16 Dec 1840 in Fleming County, KY; soldier died 10 May 1852 in Bracken County, KY; wife died 24 Feb 1881 in Lewis County, KY; served in Capt. Lockhart's Company, 26th Infantry; lived in Bracken County, KY; widow lived in Lewis County, KY

Coleman, Samuel (Colman)
Residence - Ohio
Commissioned 2nd lieutenant, 27th Infantry, 20 May 1813
Recruiting at Detroit, MI, Apr-May 1814
Transferred to 19th Infantry, 12 May 1814
Ordered to Ohio for recruiting, May 1814
Promoted 1st lieutenant, 6 Jul 1814
Recruiting in Ohio, Jul-Feb 1815
Honorable discharge 15 Jun 1815
Prisoner of war

Collins, Jeremiah
Residence – Ohio
Commissioned 2nd lieutenant, 20 May 1813
Recruiting at Lancaster, OH, Apr 1813
Recruiting at Zanesville, OH, Aug-Dec 1813, Jan-Feb 1814
Recruiting at Lancaster, OH
Honorable discharge 1 Jun 1814

Collins, Joel
Residence – Butler County, Ohio
Commissioned captain, 26th Infantry, 20 May 1813
Recruiting in Ohio, Jun-Sep 1813
Transferred to 19th Infantry, 12 May 1814
Ordered to Lower Sandusky, OH, Oct 1813
Commanding at Fort Malden, UC, Dec 1814
Honorable discharge 15 Jun 1815

Crawford, Bratton
Residence – Ohio
Commissioned 2nd lieutenant, U.S. Rangers, 5 Aug 1813
Assigned to Capt. Manary's Company
Honorable discharge 15 Jun 1815

Cushing, Daniel
Residence – Ohio
Commissioned captain, 2nd Artillery, 2 Jul 1812
Recruiting at Lebanon, OH, Jan 1814
Transferred to Corps of Artillery, 12 May 1814
Drowned 24 Mar 1815
Pension: Old War IF-13391, wife Margaret, served as a captain in the U.S. Army

Cutler, Enos
Born – Massachusetts
Residence – Hamilton County, Ohio
Commissioned 1st lieutenant, 7th Infantry, 3 May 1808
Promoted captain, 3 Sep 1810
Major, assistant adjutant general, 15 Feb 1813
Major, assistant inspector general, 18 Mar 1813
Promoted major and transferred to 38th Infantry, 1 May 1814
Retained 17 May 1815 as captain, 4th Infantry, with brevet of major from 1 May 1814
Promoted major, 10 Feb 1818
Promoted lieutenant colonel and transferred to 3rd Infantry, 28 Apr 1826
Transferred to 5th Infantry, 31 Jan 1829
Promoted colonel and transferred to 4th Infantry, 21 Sep 1836
Resigned 30 Nov 1839
Died 14 Jul 1860

Danielson, Timothy E.
Residence – Marietta, Ohio
Commissioned 2nd lieutenant, 24th Infantry, 12 May 1812
Promoted 1st lieutenant, 26 Jun 1813
Died Sep 1813

Davidson, Robert (possible Ohio Militia)
Captain, 27th Infantry
Recruiting at Newark, OH, May 1813

Delerae, Alexander
Residence – Butler County, Ohio
Commissioned 1st lieutenant, 20 May 1813
Recruiting at Franklinton, OH, May-Sep 1813
Recruiting at Lebanon, OH, Oct 1813
Recruiting at Lebanon, OH, May 1814
Resigned 14 May 1814

Dougherty, William
Residence – Ohio
Commissioned 3rd lieutenant, 2nd Rifles, 17 Mar 1814
Recruiting at Zanesville, OH, May-Jul 1814
Regimental paymaster, 25 Oct 1814 to Jun 1815
Honorable discharge 15 Jun 1815

Drennan, Samuel
Residence – Ohio
Commissioned 1st lieutenant, 27th Infantry, 20 May 1813
Recruiting at Canton, OH, Dec 1813, Jan-Mar 1814
Honorable discharge 1 Jun 1814

Eagan, John
Residence – Ohio
Lieutenant, 3rd Ohio Volunteers, 1812-1813
Prisoner of war, captured at Detroit, MI, 16 Aug 1812
Commissioned 2nd lieutenant, 27th Infantry, 20 May 1813
Resigned 27 Apr 1814

Edwards, Abraham
Born – New Jersey
Residence – Dayton, Ohio
Commissioned surgeon's mate, 8 Jun 1804
Resigned 1 Jun 1810
Commissioned captain, 17th Infantry, 12 Mar 1812
Prisoner of war, captured at Detroit, MI, 16 Aug 1812
Major DQMG 15 Mar 1814
Honorable discharge 15 Jun 1815

Elliott, Wilson
Residence – Warren, Ohio
Commissioned captain, 19th Infantry, 12 Mar 1812
Recruiting at Warren, OH, Jul-Aug 1812
Commanding company
Recruiting service, 1814
Honorable discharge 1 Jun 1814

Finley, James B.
Residence – Ohio
Commissioned ensign, 19th Infantry, 30 Mar 1814
Transferred to 28th Infantry, 12 May 1814
Promoted 3rd lieutenant, 14 May 1814
Promoted 2nd lieutenant, 19 Jul 1814
Honorable discharge 15 Jun 1815
Pension: Wife Mary E. Moon, WO-14608, WC-9248; served as a lieutenant in the 28th Inf; first wife was Mary Theresa Brown; married Mary on 31 Mar 1840 in Philadelphia, PA; soldier died on 14 May 1851 in South Bend, IN; widow died on 17 Aug 1888; she lived in Elkton, Cecil County, MD, and later South Bend, St. Joseph County, IN
Bounty: BLW 1404-160-50

Fisk, Abraham James
Born – Ohio
Residence – Ohio

Commissioned 2nd lieutenant, 27th Infantry, 10 Aug 1813
Prisoner of war, broke his parole & escaped
Served in Capt. William MacDonald's company
Wounded during the Battle of Fort Erie, 25 Jul 1814
Transferred to 19th Infantry, 12 May 1814
Resigned 30 Sep 1814

Flinn, James
Residence – Adams County, Ohio
Commissioned ensign, U.S. Rangers, 13 Mar 1812
Assigned to Capt. McCormick's Company
Promoted 2nd lieutenant, 5 Jul 1812
Promoted 1st lieutenant, 1 Oct 1813
Left service in 1814

Fobes, Caleb G.
Residence – Ohio
Commissioned 2nd lieutenant, 24th Infantry, 12 Sep 1812
Assigned to Capt. Rodgers' Company, Dec 1813
Promoted 1st lieutenant, 15 Aug 1813
Recruiting at Fayetteville, TN, Apr-Aug 1814
Died 24 Apr 1815, probably at Mobile, AL

Frederick, Henry
Residence – New Lisbon, Ohio
Commissioned 2nd lieutenant, 19th Infantry, 12 Mar 1812
Promoted 1st lieutenant, 15 Aug 1813
Prisoner of War at Quebec, LC, captured at Fort Niagara, NY, 19 Dec 1813; exchanged 4 May 1814
Honorable discharge 1 Jun 1814
Prisoner of war

Gano, Aaron G.
Born – Ohio
Residence – Ohio
Graduate U.S. Military Academy
Commissioned 3rd lieutenant, Corps of Artillery, 2 Mar 1815
Resigned 1 Oct 1817
Died 2 Dec 1854
Note: Ohio's third West Point graduate having entered the academy on 8 Jan 1814

Gill, William
Residence – Belmont County, Ohio
Captain, 3rd Ohio Volunteers
Prisoner of War, captured at Detroit, MI, on 16 Aug 1812.
Commissioned captain, 27th Infantry, 20 May 1813
Recruiting at St. Clairsville, OH, May-Jul 1813
Transferred to 19th Infantry, 12 May 1814
Recruiting at Zanesville, OH, Jul-Sep 1814
Commanding company
Honorable discharge 15 Jun 1815

Gillfillan, John
Residence – Ohio
Commissioned ensign, 7th Infantry, 13 Jun 1814
Recruiting at Hopkinsville, KY, Aug-Dec 1814
Promoted 3rd lieutenant, 19 Jun 1814
Assigned to Capt. Miller's Company, Apr 1815
Honorable discharge 15 Jun 1815

Gilman, Elias
Residence – Ohio
Lieutenant, Ohio Volunteers, 1812-1813
Prisoner of War, captured at Detroit, MI, on 16 Aug 1812
Commissioned 1st lieutenant, 27th Infantry, 20 May 1813
Recruiting at Lancaster and Newark, OH
Regimental paymaster, 9 Jun 1813-May 1814
Resigned 18 May 1814

Gilman, Samuel
Commissioned first lieutenant, 27th Infantry, 20 May 1813
Discharged 18 May 1814

Gilmore, Andrew
Residence – Ohio
Commissioned ensign, 2nd Rifles, 17 Mar 1814
Promoted 3rd lieutenant, 26 May 1814
Recruiting at Portsmouth, OH, May-Jul 1814
Assigned to Capt. Harrison's Company, Ft. Malden, UC, Mar 1815
Honorable discharge 15 Jun 1815

Goode, John
Born – Virginia
Residence – Ohio
Commissioned 3rd lieutenant, 26th Infantry, 20 May 1813
Recruiting duties, Jun 1813-Jun 1814
Transferred to 19th Infantry, 12 May 1814
Recruiting duties, Jul 1814
Assigned to Capt. Talbott's Company, Erie, PA, Feb-May 1815
Promoted 2nd lieutenant, 4 Aug 1814
Honorable discharge 15 Jun 1815

Granger, Orrin
Residence – Ohio
Commission 3rd lieutenant, 27th Infantry, 20 May 1813
Transferred to 19th Infantry, 12 May 1814
Promoted 2nd lieutenant, 6 Jul 1814

Recruiting at Franklinton, OH, Aug-Dec 1814, Jan-Feb 1815
Honorable discharge 15 Jun 1815

Gregory, Nehemiah
Residence, Athens County, Ohio
Commission 1st lieutenant, 27th Infantry, 20 May 1813
Recruiting at Zanesville, OH, Jan-May 1814
Transferred to 19th Infantry, 12 May 1814
Recruiting in Ohio, Jun-Sep 1814, Feb 1815
Promoted captain, 11 Nov 1814
Honorable discharge 15 Jun 1815

Griswold, Henry William
Born – Ohio
Residence – Ohio
Graduate U.S. Military Academy
Commissioned 3rd lieutenant, Corps of Artillery, 2 Mar 1815
Promoted 2nd lieutenant, 1 May 1817
Promoted 1st lieutenant, 12 Dec 1818
Transferred to 1st Artillery, 1 Jun 1821
Regiment adjutant, 25 Sep 1822 to 11 Oct 1831
Breveted captain, 12 Dec 1828 for 10 years faithful service in one grade
Promoted captain, 26 Apr 1832
Died 23 Oct 1834
Note: Ohio's second West Point graduate having entered the academy on 28 Jul 1813

Guthridge, William
Commissioned ensign, 26th Infantry, 20 May 1813
Discharged 1 Jun 1814

Gwynne, David
Born – Maryland
Residence – Franklinton, Ohio
Commission 1st lieutenant, 19th Infantry, 12 Mar 1812
Regimental paymaster from 1 Oct 1812 to 30 Mar 1813
Promoted captain, 30 Mar 1813
Present at Camp Middle Sister, UC, 22 Sep 1813
Present at Detroit, MI, 13 Oct 1813
Promoted major and transferred to 2nd Rifles, 21 Feb 1814
Recruiting in Kentucky, Jun-Dec 1814
Honorable discharge, 15 Jun 1815
Major, paymaster, 29 Apr 1816
Resigned 29 Apr 1830
Died 1849

Hall, John
Residence – Butler County, Ohio
Commissioned 3rd lieutenant, 26th Infantry, 20 May 1813
Recruiting at Rossville, Jun-Sep 1813
Assigned to Capt. Kesling's Company, Sackets Harbor, NY, 31 Dec 1813
Ordered to recruiting service, 12 Dec 1813
Recruiting at Hamilton, OH, Apr-May 1814
Transferred to 19th Infantry, 12 May 1814
Recruiting at Hamilton, OH, Jun-Jul 1814
Assigned to Capt. Talbott's Company, Erie, PA, 28 Feb 1815
Promoted 2nd lieutenant, 15 Aug 1814
Appointed quartermaster, 9 Apr 1815
Honorable discharge 15 Jun 1815

Hall, William
Residence – Ohio
Commissioned ensign, 27th Infantry, 20 May 1813
Honorable discharge 1 Jun 1814

Halm, John
Residence – Ohio
Commissioned 3rd lieutenant, 27th Infantry, 20 May 1813
Honorable discharge 1 Jun 1814

Hamm, John
Residence – Ohio
Commissioned surgeon, 27th Infantry, 16 Apr 1813
Transferred to 19th Infantry, 12 May 1814
Resigned 6 Jul 1814

Harper, James A.
Residence – Trumbull County, Ohio
Commissioned captain, 27th Infantry, 20 May 1813
Recruiting at Zanesville, OH, Jun-Sep 1814
Recruiting at Cuyahoga County, OH
Recruiting at Harpersfiled, OH, Apr-May 1814
Honorable discharge 1 Jun 1814

Harrison, Batteal
Residence – St. Clairsville, Ohio
Commissioned ensign, 19th Infantry, 12 Mar 1812
Promoted 2nd lieutenant, 20 Mar 1812
Assigned to Capt. Elliott's Company
Promoted 1st lieutenant, 15 Aug 1813
Promoted captain and transferred to 2nd Rifles, 17 Mar 1814
Commanding company
Honorable discharge 15 Jun 1815

Harrison, William Henry
Born – Virginia
Residence – Ohio
Commissioned ensign, 1st Infantry, 16 Aug 1791
Promoted lieutenant, 2 Jun 1792

Transferred to 1st Sub-Legion, 4 Sep 1792
Transferred to 1st Infantry, 1 Nov 1796
Promoted captain, 15 May 1797
Resigned 1 Jun 1798
Commissioned brigadier general, 22 Aug 1812
Promoted major general, 2 Mar 1813
Commanding 8th Military District
Resigned 31 May 1814
President of United States, 4 Mar 1841
Died 4 Apr 1841
Bounty: BLW 1112-160-50

Harvey, John
Residence – Ohio
Commissioned ensign, 28th Infantry, 31 Mar 1814
Promoted 3rd lieutenant, 14 May 1814
Recruiting at Olympian Springs, KY, Jul 1814
Greenup Courthouse, KY, Jul 1814
Promoted 2nd lieutenant, 21 Jul 1814
Greenup Courthouse, KY, Sep-Dec 1814, Jan 1815
Resigned 31 Jan 1815

Hawkins, Thomas L.
Born – Kentucky
Residence - Kentucky
Commissioned first lieutenant, 8th Military District, 6 Aug 1813
Discharged 31 Jan 1816
Assistant Deputy Commissary Ordnance from 6 Aug 1813
Pension: Wife Ann Broderick, WO-548, WC-2202, married on 15 Nov 1814 in Franklinton, OH; soldier died on 28 Apr 1862 in Vinton County, IA; served as a first lieutenant in the Ordnance Department of the US Army; lived in Sandusky County, OH; widow lived in Benton County, IA
Bounty: BLW 2288-160-50

Hays, Michael C.
Residence – Ohio
Commissioned 1st lieutenant, 1st Rifles, 3 May 1808
Recruiting at Chillicothe, OH, Mar 1809
Promoted captain, 1 Jun 1811
Commanding recruits at Knoxville, TN, Jul 1813
Resigned 30 Nov 1813

Hedges, James
Residence – Ohio
Commissioned 2nd lieutenant, 2nd Dragoons, 12 Mar 1812
Wounded during the Battle of Mississinewa, IN, on 18 Dec 1812
Commissioned captain and transferred to 26th Infantry (formally the 48th Infantry), 21 Apr 1814
Recruiting at Harrisburg, PA, Jul-Sep 1814

Recruiting at Philadelphia, PA, Jan 1815
Honorable discharge 15 Jun 1815

Herron, James
Residence – Zanesville, OH
Commissioned captain, 19th Infantry, 12 Mar 1812
Commanding company
Recruiting at Zanesville, OH
Transferred to 17th Infantry, 12 May 1814
Recruiting at Warren, OH, Aug 1814
Recruiting at Louisville, OH, Sep 1814
Recruiting at Chillicothe, OH, Dec 1814, Jan 1815
Honorable discharge 15 Jun 1815

Hill, Alexander
Residence – Washington County, OH
Commissioned captain, 27th Infantry, 20 May 1813
Recruiting at Zanesville
Recruiting at Marietta May-Nov 1813
Ordered to Detroit 1 Dec 1813
Transferred to 19th Infantry, 12 May 1814
Resigned 11 Nov 1814

Hoffmann, Adam E.
Born – Germany
Residence – Ohio
Commissioned 2nd lieutenant, 19th Infantry, 6 Apr 1813
Recruiting at Hillsborough, OH, Mar 1814
Transferred to 17th Infantry, 12 May 1814
Served in Capt. Chunn's company
Promoted 1st lieutenant, 1 Oct 1814
Resigned 4 Jan 1815
Reinstated to 1st Infantry, 13 Aug 1819
Honorable discharge 1 Jun 1821

Hopkins, John
Residence – Ohio
Commissioned 2nd lieutenant, U.S. Rangers, 20 Jan 1812
Assigned to Capt. Manary's Company
Promoted to 1st lieutenant, 5 Aug 1813
Honorable discharge 15 Jun 1815
Pension: SO-10007, SC-13270, served in Captain William Perry's Company, US Rangers, and in the Ohio militia as a lieutenant

Howell, Lewis
Residence – Ohio
Commissioned 1st lieutenant, 19th Infantry, 12 Mar 1812
Resigned 20 Mar 1813

Hughes, Joseph L.
Residence – Ohio
Appointed chaplain, 20 May 1813

Resigned 5 Aug 1813

Hunt, Jesse
Residence - Ohio
Commissioned 22 Sep 1812
District Paymaster for Ohio
Discharged 15 June 1815
Died 24 Aug 1835

Huntington, Samuel
Residence – Painesville, Ohio
Commissioned colonel, 8th Military District, 3 Oct 1812
Served as the district paymaster
Resigned 3 Mar 1815
Pension: Old War Minor File 15311 Rejected; served as a paymaster in the US Army
Comment: 2nd governor of Ohio

Huston, William
Residence – Ohio
Commissioned 2nd lieutenant, 26th Infantry, 20 May 1813
Recruiting at Lebanon, OH, May 1814
Recruiting at Manchester
Honorable discharge 1 Jun 1814

Jackson, George W.
Residence – Zanesville, Ohio
Commissioned 1st lieutenant, 19th Infantry, 12 Mar 1812
Served in Capt. Langham's company
Promoted captain, 15 Aug 1813
Recruiting at Zanesville, Feb 1814
Recruiting at Chillicothe, Mar 1814
Transferred to 17th Infantry, 12 May 1814
Recruiting at Chillicothe, May 1814
Resigned 9 July 1814
Pension: SO-30,145, SC-21654; served in Capt. Langham's Company, 17th and 19th US Infantries as a 1st Lieutenant and Captain

Jenkinson, Joseph
Residence – Butler County, Ohio
Major, Ohio Volunteers, 1812
Commissioned major, 26th Infantry, 19 Feb 1813
Honorable discharge 1 Jun 1814

Jesup, Thomas Sidney
Born – Virginia
Residence – Ohio
Commissioned 2nd lieutenant, 7th Infantry, 3 May 1808
Promoted 1st lieutenant, 1 Dec 1809
Prisoner of war, captured at Detroit, MI, 16 Aug 1812
Promoted captain, 20 Jan 1813
Promoted major and transferred to 19th Infantry, 6 Apr 1813
Transferred to 25th Infantry, 18 Apr 1814
Transferred to 1st Infantry, 17 May 1815
Promoted lieutenant colonel and transferred to 3rd Infantry, 30 Apr 1817
Colonel AG, 27 Mar 1818
Brigadier general QM, 8 May 1818
Brevet lieutenant colonel, 5 Jul 1814, for distinguished and meritorious service in the Battle of Chippewa, UC
Brevet colonel, 25 Jul 1814, for distinguished and meritorious service in the Battle of Niagara, UC
Promoted major general, 8 May 1828, for 10 years faithful service in one grade
Died 10 Jun 1860

Johns, Abijah
Residence – Ohio
Commissioned ensign, 26th Infantry, 20 May 1813
Recruiting in Ohio, Jun-Jul 1813
Assigned to Capt. Kesling's Company
Recruiting in Ohio, Apr-Aug 1814
Transferred to 19th Infantry, 12 May 1814
Resigned 1 Sep 1814

Jolly, John
Residence – Ohio
Commissioned ensign, 19th Infantry, 19 Jul 1813
Recruiting at Xenia, OH, Feb 1814
Recruiting at Chillicothe, OH, Mar-Apr 1813
Struck off 10 May 1814

Kercheval, Samuel
Residence – Ohio
Commissioned 2nd lieutenant, 7th Infantry, 10 Feb 1812
Promoted 1st lieutenant, 6 Apr 1813
Died 20 Jun 1813

Kesling, George
Residence – Ohio
Commissioned captain, 26th Infantry, 20 May 1813
Recruiting at Lebanon, OH, May –Jun 1813
Recruiting for Light Dragoons
Assigned command of company at Sackets Harbor, NY
Ordered to recruiting service in Ohio, Mar 1814
Transferred to 19th Infantry, 12 May 1814
Recruiting at Lebanon, OH, May 1814
Recruiting at Chillicothe, OH, Aug-Dec 1814
Recruiting at Lebanon, OH, Jan-Feb 1815
Honorable discharge 15 Jun 1815

Knox, John

Residence – Ohio
Commissioned ensign, U.S. Rangers, 6 Jul 1812
Promoted 2nd lieutenant, 1 Oct 1813
Promoted 1st lieutenant, 30 May 1814
Assigned to Capt. McCormick's Company, Oct-Nov 1814
Honorable discharge 15 Jun 1815

Langham, Angus Lewis
Born – Virginia
Residence – Chillicothe, Ohio
Commissioned ensign, 1st Rifles, 3 May 1808
Resigned 15 Apr 1809
Commission captain, 19th Infantry, 12 Mar 1812
Fought at the Battle of the River Raisin, 22 Jan 1813
Promoted major, 10th Infantry, 15 Aug 1813
Honorable discharge 15 Jun 1815
Reinstated 2 Dec 1815 as captain, 7th Infantry, with brevet of major from 15 Aug 1813
Resigned 15 Oct 1815
Died 28 Aug 1834

Langham, Elias T.
Born – Virginia
Residence – Ohio
Commissioned ensign, 19th Infantry, 12 Mar 1812
Promoted 3rd lieutenant, 1 Apr 1813
Promoted 2nd lieutenant, 6 Apr 1813
Promoted 1st lieutenant and transferred to 2nd Rifles, 17 Mar 1814
Recruiting at Chillicothe, OH, Jun-Jul 1814
Recruiting at Cincinnati, OH
Assigned to Capt. Harrison's Company, Fort Malden, UC
Honorable discharge 15 Jun 1815
Died 3 Apr 1830

Larwell, Joseph H.
Residence – Canton, Ohio
Commissioned 1st lieutenant, 2nd Artillery, 12 Mar 1812
Assigned to Capt. Cushing's Company
Transferred to Corps of Artillery, 12 May 1814
Resigned 29 Jul 1814
Pension: Wife Nancy, SC-14730; served in Capt. Cushing's Company, 2nd Artillery as a first lieutenant.

Leavitt, William
Residence – Ohio
Sergeant, Capt. Elliott's Company
Appointed quartermaster sergeant
Commissioned 3rd Lieutenant, 19th Infantry, 6 Apr 1813
Recruiting at Warren, OH, Feb 1814
Recruiting at Chillicothe, OH, Mar-May 1814
Recruiting at Canton, OH
Honorable discharge 1 Jun 1814

Leslie, Jacob C.
Residence – Ohio
Commissioned 2nd lieutenant, 26th Infantry, 20 May 1813
Assigned to Capt. Kesling's Company
Recruiting at Lebanon, OH, May-Aug 1814
Transferred to 19th Infantry, 12 May 1814
Recruiting at Xenia, OH
Resigned 13 Sep 1814

Lindsay, Andrew
Residence – Ohio
Commissioned 3rd lieutenant, 1st Rifles, 29 Jun 1813
Assigned to Capt. Graham's Company, Oct 1813
Resigned 10 Feb 1814

Lindsley, Stephen
Residence – Ohio
Appointed chaplain, 16th Infantry, 29 Jul 1813
Honorable discharge 15 Jun 1815

Lockhart, Josiah
Residence – Ohio
Commissioned captain, 26th Infantry, 20 May 1813
Recruiting at West Union, OH, Jun-Aug 1813
Recruiting at Portsmouth, OH
Honorable discharge 1 Jun 1814

Looker, Alison C.
Residence – Ohio
Commissioned ensign, 19th Infantry, 19 Jul 1813
Promoted 3rd lieutenant, 15 Aug 1813
Recruiting at Brookville, IN
Promoted 2nd lieutenant and transferred to 2nd Rifles, 17 Mar 1814
Assigned to Capt. Harrison's Company, Mar 1815
Assigned to Capt. Desha's Company, Apr 815
Honorable discharge 15 Jun 1815
Died 10 Aug 1824

Lucas, John
Born – Virginia
Residence – Ohio
Commission captain, 26th Infantry, 20 May 1813
Recruiting at Portsmouth, OH, Jun-Dec 1813, Jan-Feb 1814
Recruiting at Lebanon, OH, Apr-May 1814
Recruiting at Jefferson, Pickaway Plains, OH
Honorable discharge 1 Jun 1814

Lucas, Robert
Born – Virginia
Residence – Portsmouth, Ohio

Commissioned captain, 19th Infantry, 14 Mar 1812
Prisoner of war, captured at Detroit, MI, 16 Aug 1812
Resigned 10 Feb 1813
Commissioned lieutenant colonel, U.S. Rangers, 20 Feb 1813
Resigned 30 Jun 1813
Brigadier general, Ohio militia, 1812-1815
Died 7 Feb 1853
Note: 12th governor of Ohio and 1st territorial governor of Iowa

McArthur, Duncan
Born – New York
Residence – Chillicothe, Ohio
Colonel, 1st Ohio Volunteers, 7 May 1812
Prisoner of War, captured at Detroit, MI, exchanged
Commissioned colonel, 26th Infantry, 20 Feb 1813
Promoted brigadier general, 12 Mar 1813
Commander, 1st Brigade, Northwest Army
Commanding 8th Military District, 1814-1815
Honorable discharge 15 Jun 1815
Died 28 Apr 1839
Note: 11th governor of Ohio

McClain, Joseph
Residence – Ohio
Commissioned 2nd lieutenant, 26th Infantry, 20 May 1813
Recruiting at Lebanon, OH, Aug-Sep 1813
Recruiting at Hillsborough, OH, Oct 1813
Recruiting at Lebanon, OH, Apr-May 1814
Recruiting at Hillsborough, OH
Transferred to 2nd Rifles, 17 Mar 1814
Recruiting at Hillsborough, OH, May-Jul 1814
Promoted 1st lieutenant, 28 May 1814
Resigned 30 Sep 1814

McClelland, Michael
Residence – Ohio
Commissioned 2nd lieutenant, 7th Infantry, 10 Feb 1812
Promoted 1st lieutenant, 20 Jan 1813
Promoted captain, 24 May 1814
Killed 23 Dec 1814 in first Battle of New Orleans, LA

McCormick, Samuel
Residence – Ohio
Commissioned ensign, 7th Infantry, 3 May 1808
Promoted 2nd lieutenant, 1 Nov 1809
Resigned 1 Dec 1810
Commissioned 1st lieutenant, U.S. Rangers, 17 Mar 1812
Promoted captain, 7 Aug 1813
Honorable discharge 15 Jun 1815

Died 1851

McDonald, James
Born – Virginia
Residence – Ohio
Commissioned captain, 1st Rifles, 3 May 1808
Promoted major, 1 Aug 1812
Promoted lieutenant colonel, 24 Jan 1814
Breveted colonel, 17 Sep 1814, for distinguished and meritorious conduct in the sortie from Fort Erie, UC.
Promoted colonel and transferred to 4th Rifles, 17 Sep 1814
Transferred to 7th Infantry, 17 May 1815
Resigned 30 Apr 1817
Died 1830

McDonald, John
Residence – Ohio
Commissioned captain, 26th Infantry, 20 May 1813
Recruiting at Hillsborough, Washington & Greenfield, OH, Jun-Aug 1813
Resigned 7 Aug 1813

McElvain, John
Residence – Ohio
Commissioned 3rd lieutenant, 26th Infantry, 20 May 1813
Transferred to 19th Infantry, 12 May 1814
Promoted 2nd lieutenant, 20 Aug 1814
Honorable discharge 15 Jun 1815

McFadden, Neil
Born – Ireland
Residence – Ohio
Prisoner of War on Parole, captured at Detroit, MI, 16 Aug 1812
Commissioned ensign, 27th Infantry, 20 May 1813
Recruiting at Zanesville, OH, Feb 1814
Transferred to 19th Infantry, 12 May 1814
Recruiting at Zanesville, OH, Jun-Dec 1814, Jan-Feb 1815
Promoted 3rd Lieutenant, 20 Aug 1814
Honorable discharge 15 Jun 1815

McFarland, Daniel
Residence – Ohio
Commissioned 1st lieutenant, 26th Infantry, 20 May 1813
Honorable discharge 1 Jun 1814

McGuire, James
Residence – Ohio
Commissioned ensign, 19th Infantry, 15 Aug 1813
Assigned to Capt, Elliott's Company, Nov 1813
Transferred to 17th Infantry, 12 May 1814

The Officers

Resigned 15 Jul 1814

McKeehan, Samuel
Residence – Ohio
Surgeon in Ohio Volunteers in 1813
Commissioned surgeon, 18th Infantry, 29 Jul 1813
Resigned 18 Jan 1815

McKnight, Thomas R.
Residence – Ohio
Commissioned ensign, 19th Infantry, 14 Jul 1813
Served in Capt. Adair's company
Recruiting at New Lisbon, OH
Promoted 3rd lieutenant, 7 Mar 1814
Transferred to 17th Infantry, 12 May 1814
Honorable discharge 15 Jun 1815

McLeod, Collin
Residence – Ohio
Commissioned 2nd lieutenant, 26th Infantry, 20 May 1813
Assigned to Capt. Puthuff's Company
Transferred to 19th Infantry, 12 May 1814
Transferred to 3rd Infantry, 17 May 1815
Resigned 31 Dec 1818

McMillan, William
Residence – Ohio
Commission lieutenant colonel, 17th Infantry, 12 Mar 1812
Prisoner of war, 27 Feb 1814
Honorable discharge 1 Jun 1814

MacDonald, William (Senior)
Born – Pennsylvania
Residence – Ohio
Commissioned 1st lieutenant, 26th Infantry, 20 May 1813
Recruiting at Urbana, OH, Nov-Dec 1813, Jan 1814
Recruiting at Lebanon, OH, Apr 1814
Recruiting at Lower Sandusky, OH
Transferred to 19th Infantry, 12 May 1814
Commission captain, 11 Nov 1814
Transferred to 3rd Infantry, 17 May 1815
Major, assistant inspector general, 29 Apr 1816 to 17 Oct 1820
Dismissed 17 Oct 1820
Breveted major 25 Jul 1814 for distinguished service at Niagara Falls, UC

MacDonald, William (Junior)
Born – Pennsylvania
Residence – Ohio
Commissioned 3rd lieutenant, 26th Infantry, 30 Jun 1813
Recruiting at Williamsburgh, OH, Jan-Dec 181

Recruiting at Chillicothe, OH, Jan-Feb 1815
Recruiting at Urbana, OH
Honorable discharge 1 Jun 1814

Maltbie, Benjamin
Residence – Ohio
Commissioned 1st lieutenant, 26th Infantry, 7 Aug 1813
Recruiting at Lebanon, OH, Aug-Dec 1813, Jan-Apr 1814
Resigned 9 May 1814

Manary, James Sr
Residence – Ross County, Ohio
Commissioned captain, U.S. Rangers, 5 Aug 1813
Honorable discharge 15 Jun 1815

Manary, James Jr
Residence – Ross County, Ohio
Commissioned 1st Lieutenant, U.S. Rangers, 6 Jul 1812
Served in Capt. Manary's company
Honorable discharge 15 Jun 1815

Martin, Absalom
Residence – Belmont County, Ohio
Commission captain, 27th Infantry, 20 May 1813
Recruiting at Zanesville, OH, May-Jun 1813
Recruiting at Zanesville, OH and Guernsey County, OH
Honorable discharge 1 Jun 1814

Marvin, Charles
Residence – Ohio
Commissioned surgeon's mate, 19th Infantry, 12 Mar 1812
Resigned 30 Nov 1813
Commissioned surgeon, 26th Infantry, 15 Apr 1814
Transferred to 1st Rifles, 21 May 1814
Honorable discharge 15 Jun 1815

Meek, Alexander A.
Residence – Ohio
Commissioned 2nd lieutenant, 2nd Artillery, 8 May 1812
Assigned to Capt. Cushing's Company
Resigned 31 May 1813
Died 16 Oct 1821

Meek, John
Residence – Ohio
Commissioned ensign, 7th Infantry, 10 Feb 1812
Promoted 2nd lieutenant, 20 Jan 1813
Promoted 1st lieutenant, 19 Apr 1814
Resigned 30 Sep 1814
Military storekeeper of ordnance, 10 Jul 1838

Removed 30 Jun 1814[1]
Received by resolution of Congress, 13 Feb 1835, the testimonial of a sword for being engaged in the defense of Fort Stephenson, OH

Meldrum, John
Residence – Ohio
Commissioned ensign, 26th Infantry, 7 Aug 1813
Assigned to Capt. Swearingen's Company
Recruiting at Lebanon, OH, May 1814
Recruiting at Detroit, MI
Honorable discharge 1 Jun 1814

Milford, John
Residence – Ohio
Commissioned 2nd lieutenant, 27th Infantry, 20 May 1813
Honorable discharge 1 Jun 1814

Miller, Edward W.
Residence – Ohio
Commissioned 3rd lieutenant, 2nd Rifles, 17 Mar 1814
Recruiting at Chillicothe, OH, May-Jul 1814
Assigned to Capt. Harrison's company, Mar-Apr 1815
Honorable discharge 15 Jun 1815

Miller, John
Born – Ohio
Residence – Steubenville, Ohio
Commissioned lieutenant colonel, 17th Infantry, 12 Mar 1812
Promoted colonel and transferred to 19th Infantry, 6 Jul 1812
Transferred to 17th Infantry, 12 May 1814
Transferred to 3rd Infantry, 17 May 1815
Resigned 10 Feb 1818
Died 18 Mar 1846
Note: 4th governor of Missouri

Miller, Joseph
Residence – Ohio
Commission captain, 8th Military District, 1 Sep 1813
Served as the Assistant Deputy Quartermaster General
Died 1814

Milligan, John
Residence – Jefferson County, Ohio
Commissioned ensign, 19th Infantry, 12 Mar 1812
Promoted 2nd lieutenant, 15 Aug 1813
Recruiting at Chillicothe, OH, Mar-May 1814
Recruiting at Marietta, OH
Honorable discharge 1 Jun 1814

Pension: Served in Captains Elliott's and Herron's Companies, 19th Infantry as an ensign and as a second lieutenant
Bounty: BLW 606-160-50

Monroe, Thomas J. C.
Commission garrison surgeon's mate, 6th Infantry, 12 Sep 1811
Discharged 15 Jun 1815

Moore, Hugh
Residence – Cincinnati, Ohio
Commissioned captain, 19th Infantry, 12 Mar 1812
Recruiting in Cincinnati, OH, 1814
Resigned 12 Oct 1814

Moore, John
Residence – Ohio
Commission captain, 26th Infantry, 20 May 1813
Recruiting in Ohio, Jun-Dec 1813, Jan-May 1814
Honorable discharge 1 Jun 1814

Moore, Robert
Residence – Ohio
Commissioned surgeon, 19th Infantry, 6 Jul 1814
Honorable discharge 15 Jun 1815

Morgan, John E.
Residence – Jefferson County, OH
Commissioned ensign, 19th Infantry, 12 Mar 1812
Resigned 4 Dec 1812

Morris, David
Residence – Ohio
Commissioned 2nd lieutenant, 19th Infantry, 8 May 1812
Resigned 20 Jan 1813

Morrison, Robert
Residence – Belmont County, Ohio
Prisoner of War, captured at Detroit, MI. on 16 Aug 1812
Major, 3rd Ohio Volunteers, 1812
Commission major, 27th Infantry, 9 Apr 1813
Promoted lieutenant colonel, 29 Jun 1813
Died 12 Dec 1813 at Detroit, MI

Munson, Jeremiah R.
Residence – Muskingum County, Ohio
Major, 3rd Ohio Volunteers, 1812
Prisoner of War on Parole, captured at Detroit, MI, 16 Aug 1812
Commission major, 27th Infantry, 18 Mar 1813
Recruiting at Zanesville, OH, May-Dec 1813
Honorable discharge 1 Jun 1814

The Officers

Murray, Harvey
Residence – Ohio
Commissioned 2nd lieutenant, 1st Rifles, 17 Oct 1812
Died 4 Sep 1813

Nearing, Asahael
Born – Connecticut
Residence – Connecticut
Commissioned captain, 19th Infantry, 6 Jul 1812
Killed 30 Sep 1813 at Fort Meigs, OH.

Neeley, Nicholas
Residence – Ohio
Sergeant, 19th Infantry
Commissioned ensign, 6 Jul 1814
Wounded during the Battle of Fort Erie, UC, 17 Sep 1814
Promoted 3rd lieutenant, 1 Oct 1814
Recruiting at Washington, OH
Honorable discharge 15 Jun 1815

Neville, Robert
Residence – Ohio
Commissioned 3rd lieutenant, 26th Infantry, 20 May 1813
Assigned to Capt. Puthuff's Company, Dec 1813
Recruiting, Jan 1814
Transferred to 19th Infantry, 12 May 1814
Resigned 16 Jun 1814

Niswanger, Christian
Born – Germany
Residence – Ohio
Commissioned ensign, 19th Infantry, 19 Jul 1813
Promoted 3rd lieutenant, 7 Mar 1814
Honorable discharge 1 Jun 1814

Nixon, James
Residence – Ohio
Prisoner of War on Parole, captured at Detroit, MI, 16 Aug 1812
Commissioned 3rd lieutenant, 20 May 1813
Transferred to 19th Infantry, 12 May 1814
Promoted 2nd lieutenant, 29 Jun 1814
Promoted 1st lieutenant, 11 Nov 1814
Honorable discharge 15 Jun 1815
Prisoner of war on parole

Noel, John
Residence – Ohio
Commissioned ensign, 26th Infantry, 20 May 1813
Recruiting at Portsmouth, OH, Feb 1814
Recruiting at Lebanon, OH, Apr-May 1814
Recruiting at Waynesville, OH
Honorable discharge 1 Jun 1814

Northup, Henry
Residence – Muskingum County, Ohio
Lieutenant, 3rd Ohio Volunteers, 1812
Prisoner of War on Parole, captured at Detroit, MI, 16 Aug 1812
Commissioned captain, 27th Infantry, 20 May 1813
Recruiting at Zanesville, OH, Jul-Dec 1813, Jan-May 1814
Transferred to 19th Infantry, 12 May 1814
Recruiting at Zanesville, OH, Jun-Aug 1814
Resigned 11 Nov 1814

Norton, Carlos A.
Residence – Ohio
Commission 1st lieutenant, 26th Infantry, 20 May 1813
Transferred to 19th Infantry, 12 May 1814
Resigned 6 Jul 1814

Patterson, Alexander
Residence – Jefferson County, Ohio
Commissioned 3rd lieutenant, 27th Infantry, 20 May 1813
Recruiting at Zanesville, Aug 1813-Jul 1814
Transferred to 19th Infantry, 12 May 1814
Ordered to Fort Erie, UC, Aug-Dec 1814
Left wounded at General Hospital, Williamsville, NY, 14 Aug 1814
Promoted 2nd lieutenant, 15 Aug 1814
Ordered to Erie, PA, Capt. Trimble's Company, Feb 1815
Absent May 1815 - disabled by severe wounds received in action, sent home to Jefferson County
Honorable discharge 15 Jun 1815

Patterson, John
Residence – Ohio
Commissioned ensign, 27th Infantry, 20 May 1813
Recruiting at Detroit, MI
Transferred to 19th Infantry, 12 May 1814
Wounded during the Battle of Fort Erie, UC, on 14 Aug 1814
Promoted 3rd Lieutenant, 15 Aug 1814
Honorable discharge 15 Jun 1815

Paull, George
Residence – Belmont County, Ohio
Major, Pennsylvania Volunteers, 1790
Commission lieutenant colonel, 27th Infantry, 9 Apr 1813
Promoted colonel, 29 Jun 1813
Transferred to 19th Infantry, 12 May 1814
Recruiting at Zanesville, OH, May-Jun 1814
Recruiting superintendent, Jul-Oct 1814
Resigned 31 Oct 1814

Perrine, James
    Residence – Ohio
    Commissioned surgeon's mate, 19th Infantry, 29 Jun 1814
    Honorable discharge 15 Jun 1815
    Pension: Wife Lucy N., WC-35203, served as a surgeon's mate in the 19th Infantry

Perry, William
    Residence – Ohio
    Captain, U.S. Rangers
    Commissioned 1812
    Discharged 1813

Phillips, Asher
    Residence – Dayton, Ohio
    Commissioned ensign, 19th Infantry, 12 Mar 1812
    Prisoner of war at Quebec, LC, captured 16 Aug 1812 at Detroit, MI
    Promoted 2nd lieutenant, 20 May 1813
    Transferred to 17th Infantry, 12 May 1814
    Assigned to Capt. Holder's Company
    Transferred to 3rd Infantry, 17 May 1815
    Promoted 1st lieutenant, 17 May 1816
    Regimental paymaster, 26 Aug 1815 to 1 Jun 1821
    Major paymaster, 1 Jun 1821
    Resigned 17 Jan 1834
    Died 20 May 1843

Pickett, James C.
    Residence – Ohio
    Midshipman, U.S. Navy, 4 Jun 1812
    Commissioned 3rd lieutenant, 2nd Artillery, 14 Aug 1813
    Served in Capt. Cushing's company
    Promoted 2nd lieutenant, 19 Apr 1814
    Transferred to Corps of Artillery, 12 May 1814
    Honorable discharge 15 Jun 1815
    Captain, assistant deputy quartermaster general, 16 Jun 1818
    Honorable discharge 1 Jun 1821
    Pension: SC-14327; served in Captain Cushing's Company, US Artillery, as a second lieutenant
    Died 10 Jul 1872

Pigman, John G.
    Residence – Coshocton County, Ohio
    Prisoner of War on Parole, captured at Detroit, MI, 16 Aug 1812
    Commissioned ensign, 27th Infantry, 20 May 1813
    Honorable discharge 1 Jun 1814

Pinney, Abner P.
    Residence – Ohio
    Commissioned 1st lieutenant, 27th Infantry, 20 May 1813
    Recruiting at Zanesville, OH, Jun-Dec 1813, Feb-Apr 1814
    Recruiting at Worthington, OH
    Transferred to 19th Infantry, 12 May 1814
    Resigned 27 May 1814

Potter, John C.
    Residence - Ohio
    Commissioned 3rd lieutenant, 26th Infantry, 19 Apr 1814
    Transferred to 24th Infantry, 29 Jul 1814
    Promoted 2nd lieutenant, 17 Oct 1814
    Attached to command at Fort Gratiot, MI, Dec 1814
    Honorable discharge 15 Jun 1815

Price, Clarkson
    Residence – Ohio
    Commissioned 2nd lieutenant, 26th Infantry, 20 May 1813
    Recruiting at Montgomery, Hamilton Cty, OH, May-Dec 1813, Jan-May 1814
    Recruiting at Lebanon, OH, May 1814
    Honorable discharge 1 Jun 1814

Price, Philip P.
    Residence – Cincinnati, Ohio
    Commissioned 2nd lieutenant, 19th Infantry, 12 Mar 1812
    Recruiting at Dayton, OH
    Promoted 1st lieutenant, 30 Mar 1813
    Transferred to 17th Infantry, 12 May 1814
    Recruiting at Dayton, OH
    Recruiting in Kentucky
    Resigned 1 Oct 1814
    Pension: Wife Mary R., WO-1723, WC-1354; served as a lieutenant in Capt. Hugh Moore's Company, 19th Infantry and in Capt. H. H. Hickman's Company
    Bounty: BLW 17433-160-50

Prosser, William
    Residence – Ohio
    Commissioned ensign, 7th Infantry, 10 Feb 1812
    Promoted 2nd lieutenant, 10 Feb 1812
    Assigned to Capt. Oldham's Company
    Promoted 1st lieutenant, 21 Feb 1814
    Died 28 Sep 1814 at Camp Tchifonti, LA

Puthuff, William Henry
    Residence – Ohio
    Adjutant, Ohio Volunteers, 1812-1813
    Commissioned captain, 26th Infantry, 20 May 1813
    Recruiting at Chillicothe, OH, Jun-Jul 1813

Promoted major and transferred to 2nd Rifles, 21 Feb 1814
Honorable discharge 15 Jun 1815
Died Nov 1824

Ramsey, Thomas
Born – Pennsylvania
Residence – Ohio
Commissioned 2nd lieutenant, 1st Rifles, 27 Jan 1809
Recruiting at Cincinnati, OH, Apr 1809
Promoted 1st lieutenant, 31 Jul 1810
Recruiting at Cincinnati, OH, Mar 1812
Promoted captain, 30 Nov 1812
Commanding company at Fort Erie, UC
Wounded in action during Battle of Fort Erie, 17 Sep 1814
Recruiting at Cincinnati, OH, Feb 1814
Honorable discharge 15 Jun 1815
Reinstated 2 Dec 1815
Killed in a duel by Capt. Wylie Martin near St. Louis, MO, 6 Aug 1818

Rees, Jonathan
Residence – Ohio
Commissioned 2nd lieutenant, 19th Infantry, 12 Mar 1812
Promoted 1st lieutenant, 30 Mar 1813
Wounded in action at Fort Meigs, OH, 5 May 1813
Recruiting at Circleville, OH
Transferred to 17th Infantry, 12 May 1814
Recruiting in Ohio
Honorable discharge 15 Jun 1815
Died 23 Feb 1834
Pension: Old War IF-25772, served in Captain Nearings' Company, 19th Infantry as a second lieutenant and in Captain Pritchard's Company, 17th U.S. Infantry as a first lieutenant
Bounty: BLW 18621-160-50

Reeves, John D.
Residence – Ross County, Ohio
Commissioned 2nd lieutenant, 19th Infantry, 1 May 1812
Assigned to Capt. Graham's Company
Resigned 11 May 1813

Reeves, Nathan L.
Commissioned ensign, 27th Infantry, 20 May 1813
Recruiting at Zanesville, OH, Jan-Mar 1814
Recruiting at Portage County, OH
Transferred to 19th Infantry, 12 May 1814
Promoted 3rd lieutenant, 6 Jul 1814
Promoted 2nd lieutenant, 1 Nov 1814
Ordered to Erie, PA, Capt. Trimble's Company, Feb 1815
Honorable discharge 15 Jun 1815

Reinstated Rifle Regiment, 19 Sep 1818
Resigned 11 Mar 1819

Reyburn, William M.
Born – Maryland
Residence – Ohio
Commissioned ensign, U.S. Rangers, 1 Oct 1813
Promoted 3rd lieutenant, 30 May 1814
Honorable discharge 15 Jun 1815

Richardson, Robert D.
Born – Virginia
Residence - Ohio
Commissioned captain, 8th Military District, 5 Aug 1813
Served as the deputy commissary ordnance officer
Retained as captain of ordnance, 8 Feb 1815
Transferred to 7th Infantry, 1 Jun 1821
Transferred to 1st Infantry, 24 Sep 1821
Discharged 1 Jun 1822

Richardson, Thomas R.
Residence – Ohio
Commissioned 2nd lieutenant, 7th Infantry, 10 Feb 1812
Promoted 1st lieutenant, 10 Feb 1812
Killed on 11 Oct 1813 in a duel

Riddle, John
Ensign, 27th Infantry
Recruiting at Zanesville, OH, Jul-Dec 1813, Jan-May 1814
Recruiting at St. Clairsville, OH

Riddle, Thomas
Born – Pennsylvania
Residence – Ohio
Commissioned ensign, 27th Infantry, 20 May 1813
Recruiting at St. Clairsville, OH, Feb 1814
Transferred to 19th Infantry, 12 May 1814
Recruiting at Zanesville, OH, Jun-Sep 1814, Jan-Feb 1815
Promoted 3rd lieutenant, 13 Sep 1814
Honorable discharge 15 Jun 1815

Riley, Isaac M.
Residence – Ohio
Commissioned ensign, 7th Infantry, 8 May 1812
Promoted 3rd lieutenant, 12 Mar 1813
Promoted 2nd lieutenant, 22 Jan 1814
Recruiting at Steubenville, OH, Feb 1814
Promoted 1st lieutenant, 24 May 1814
Recruiting at Hopkinsville, KY, May-Oct 1814
Assigned to Capt. Vail's Company, Dec 1814
Honorable discharge 15 Jun 1815

Robinson, Israel A.
Ensign, 27th Infantry
Recruiting at Zanesville, OH, Feb 1814
Recruiting at Salem, Ashtabula County, OH, Feb-May 1814
Pension: Wife Delia, WO-6506, WC-2463; served in Capt. James Harper's Company, 27th Infantry as an ensign

Rogers, Levi
Residence – Ohio
Commission surgeon, 19th Infantry, 28 Jan 1813
Dismissed 30 Sep 1813
Died 4 Apr 1815

Rowland, Thomas
Residence – Columbiana County, Ohio
Captain, Ohio Volunteers, 1812
Commission major, 27th Infantry, 29 Jun 1813
Recruiting at Zanesville, OH, May-Aug 1813
Recruiting at Detroit, MI, Mar-May 1814
Transferred to 19th Infantry, 12 May 1814
Recruiting at Zanesville, OH, Dec 1814, Jan-Feb 1815
Honorable discharge 15 Jun 1815
Died Aug 1848

Rue, Benjamin S.
Residence – Ohio
Commissioned ensign, 17th Infantry, 30 Mar 1814
Transferred to 24th Infantry, 12 May 1814
Promoted 3rd lieutenant, 14 May 1814
Recruiting at Nashville, TN, Aug-Oct 1814
Recruiting at Springfield, TN
Honorable discharge 15 Jun 1815

Sanderson, George
Residence – Fairfield County, Ohio
Commission captain, 27th Infantry, 20 May 1813
Recruiting at Zanesville, OH, May-Jul 1813
Recruiting at Lancaster, OH
Honorable discharge 1 Jun 1814
Pension: SO-2322, SC-21222; served as a captain in Colonel Cass's regiment, OH Militia
Bounty: BLW 81-160-50

Seaman, Ebenezer
Residence – Ohio
Commissioned ensign, U.S. Rangers, 5 Aug 1813
Assigned to Capt. Manary's Company
Honorable discharge 15 Jun 1815
Pension: Wife Lillis, WO-3057, WC-1202; served in James Manary's Company, US Rangers, and in Captain Thomas Lloyd's Company, Ohio militia

Servess, William G.
Residence – Ohio
Commissioned 3rd lieutenant, U.S. Rangers, 1 Oct 1813
Promoted 2nd lieutenant, 30 May 1814
Assigned to Capt. McCormick's Company
Prisoner of War (Quebec, LC), captured at Fort Erie, UC, 30 Aug 1814; released on 13 March 1815; wounded in battle
Honorable discharge 15 Jun 1815
Pension: Wife Margaret, Old War WF-17741 Rejected; served in Capt. McCormick's Company, US Rangers, as a lieutenant

Seward, Mason
Residence – Ohio
Sergeant, 19th Infantry
Commissioned 3rd lieutenant, 6 Apr 1812
Promoted 2nd lieutenant, 20 Nov 1813
Honorable discharge 1 Jun 1814
Re-instated as ensign, 17th Infantry, 5 Jul 1814
Promoted 2nd lieutenant, 25th Infantry, 11 Feb 1815
Honorable discharge 15 Jun 1815

Shane, Abraham
Residence – Tuscarawas County, Ohio
Commissioned 1st lieutenant, 27th Infantry, 20 May 1813
Recruiting at New Philadelphia, OH, Jun-Dec 1813, Jan-May 1814
Honorable discharge 1 Jun 1814

Shanks, Thomas
Born – Vermont
Residence – Ohio
Commissioned ensign, 26th Infantry, 7 Aug 1813
Served in Capt. Talbott's company
Died 1814

Shannon, James
Residence – Ohio
Commissioned ensign, 27th Infantry, 20 May 1813
Assigned to Capt. Gill's Company
Transferred to 19th Infantry, 12 May 1814
Promoted 3rd lieutenant, 27 May 1814
Promoted 2nd lieutenant, 30 Sep 1814
Honorable discharge 15 Jun 1815

Shannon, John
Commissioned ensign, 27th Infantry, 20 May 1813
Discharged 12 May 1814

Shannon, Samuel
Residence – Ohio
Commissioned 1st lieutenant, 27th Infantry, 20 May 1813
Recruiting at Zanesville, OH, May-Jul 1813

Recruiting at Steubenville, OH
Regimental paymaster, 24 Jul 1813 to 12 May 1814
Transferred to 19th Infantry, 12 May 1814
Resigned 15 Jul 1814
Pension: Wife Louisa, WO-37982, WC-33503; served as a lieutenant and paymaster in Major T. Rowland's Company, 19th and 27th Infantries, lived in Indiana

Shannon, Thomas
Commissioned ensign, 19th Infantry, 12 May 1814
Discharged 27 May 1814

Shaung, William H.
Residence – Ohio
Commissioned ensign, 19th Infantry, 30 Mar 1814
Transferred to 17th Infantry, 12 May 1814
Recruiting at Athens, OH, May 1814
Recruiting at Cambridge, OH, Aug-Sep 1814
Recruiting at Lancaster, OH, Nov-Dec 1814
Recruiting at Xenia, OH, Jan-Feb 18115
Promoted 3rd lieutenant, 1 Oct 1814
Honorable discharge 15 Jun 1815

Shields, Thomas C.
Residence – Ohio
Commissioned 2nd lieutenant, 27th Infantry, 20 May 1813
Transferred to 19th Infantry, 12 May 1814
Promoted 1st lieutenant, 20 Aug 1814
Honorable discharge 15 Jun 1815

Simmonds, John
Residence – Ohio
Commissioned ensign, 19th Infantry, 19 Jul 1813
Promoted 3rd lieutenant, 7 Mar 1814
Recruiting at Franklinton, OH, Apr-Aug 1814
Transferred to 17th Infantry, 12 May 1814
Resigned 13 Aug 1814
Commissioned 2nd lieutenant, 3rd Infantry, 2 Mar 1815
Honorable discharge 15 Jun 1815

Simons, John H.
Residence – Ohio
Commissioned ensign, 27th Infantry, 20 May 1813
Recruiting at Eaton, OH, Feb 1814
Recruiting at Franklinton, OH, Mar-Apr 1814
Transferred to 19th Infantry, 12 May 1814
Promoted 3rd lieutenant, 29 Jun 1814
Recruiting at Lancaster, OH
Promoted 2nd lieutenant, 11 Nov 1814
Honorable discharge 15 Jun 1815

Sloo, John Roe
Born – Kentucky
Residence – Ohio
Graduate U.S. Military Academy
Commissioned 3rd lieutenant, Corps of Artillery, 2 Mar 1815
Promoted 2nd lieutenant, 20 Apr 1817
Resigned 30 Apr 1818
Died 1837
Note: Ohio's first West Point graduate having entered the academy on 25 Jun 1813

Smith, Daniel Jr
Residence – Ohio
Appointed surgeon's mate, 2nd Rifles, 17 May 1814
Honorable discharge 15 Jun 1815

Smith, Robert
Residence – Ohio
Commissioned ensign, 26th Infantry, 20 May 1813
Recruiting at Franklinton, OH, Oct 1813
Transferred to 19th Infantry, 12 May 1814
Recruiting at Sandwich, UC, May 1814
Recruiting at Springfield, OH, Aug 1814
Promoted 3rd lieutenant, 15 Aug 1814
Recruiting at Xenia, OH, Dec 1814-Jan-Feb 1815
Honorable discharge 15 Jun 1815

Spencer, Anderson
Residence – Butler County, Ohio
Commissioned 2nd lieutenant, 26th Infantry, 20 May 1813
Recruiting at Hamilton, OH, May-Jul 1813
Recruiting at Franklinton, OH, Aug 1813
Honorable discharge 1 Jun 1814

Spencer, John
Residence – Licking County, Ohio
Captain, 3rd Ohio Volunteers, 1812-1813
Prisoner of War on Parole, captured at Detroit, MI, 16 Aug 1812
Commissioned captain, 27th Infantry, 20 May 1813
Recruiting at Newark, OH, May-Dec 1813, Jan-May 1814
Honorable discharge 1 Jun 1814

Spenck, Peter Jr
Residence – Ohio
Commission surgeon's mate, 26th Infantry, 26 Apr 1813
Transferred to 19th Infantry, 12 May 1814
Resigned 15 Jun 1814

Stall, George W.
Born – Germany
Residence – Ohio
Commissioned ensign, 19th Infantry, 12 Mar 1812
Promoted 2nd lieutenant, 6 Apr 1813

Recruiting at Hamilton, OH, Feb-Apr 1814
Transferred to 17th Infantry, 12 May 1814
Promoted 1st lieutenant, 1 Oct 1814
Assigned to Capt. Holt's Company, Feb 1815
Honorable discharge 15 Jun 1815
Reinstated 2nd lieutenant, 3rd Infantry, 4 Sep 1817
Died 6 Feb 1819

Steele, David
Residence – Ohio
Commissioned 3rd lieutenant, U.S. Rangers, 5 Aug 1813
Assigned to Capt. Manary's Company
Honorable discharge 15 Jun 1815

Stephenson, John
Residence – Ohio
Commissioned 2nd lieutenant, U.S. Rangers, 20 Jan 1812
Resigned 15 May 1813

Stockton, John
Residence – Ohio
Commissioned ensign, 19th Infantry, 31 Dec 1812
Promoted 2nd lieutenant, 15 Aug 1813
Recruiting at Lancaster, OH, Feb-Mar 1814
Promoted 1st lieutenant and transferred to 2nd Rifles, 17 Mar 1814
Recruiting at Lancaster, OH, May-Jul 1814
Assigned to Capt. O'Fallons' Company, Mar 1815
Honorable discharge 15 Jun 1815
Died 29 Oct 1822

Stockton, Robert
Residence – Ohio
Commissioned 2nd lieutenant, 26th Infantry, 20 May 1813
Recruiting at Chillicothe, OH, Oct-Dec 1813,
Transferred to 19th Infantry, 12 May 1814
Promoted 1st lieutenant, 29 Jun 1814
Assigned to Fort Erie, UN, Aug 1814
Struck off 13 Mar 1815

Stoddard, Amos
Born – Connecticut
Residence – Ohio
Commissioned captain, 2nd Artillery and Engineers, 4 Jun 1798
Transferred to Artillery Regiment, 1 Apr 1802
Promoted major, 30 Jun 1807
Transferred to 1st Artillery, 12 Mar 1812
Served as deputy quartermaster general, 16 Jul to Dec 1812
Died 11 May 1813 of wounds received in siege of Fort Meigs, OH.

Struthers, Alexander
Residence – Ohio
Commission 1st lieutenant, 27th Infantry, 20 may 1813
Died 18 Dec 1813

Stubbs, James R.
Born – Kentucky
Residence – Ohio
Graduate U.S. Military Academy
Breveted 2nd lieutenant, Light Artillery, 11 Dec 1815
Resigned 15 Nov 1817
Captain ADQMG, 30 Nov 1819
Honorable discharge 1 Jun 1821
Died 4 Aug 1832
Note: Ohio's fourth West Point graduate having entered the academy on 8 Jan 1814

Swearingen, James
Commissioned colonel quartermaster general, 17 May 1813
Discharged 15 Jun 1815

Swearingen, James Strode
Born – Virginia
Residence – Ohio
Commissioned 2nd lieutenant, Artillery Regiment, 25 Jan 1803
Promoted 1st lieutenant, 16 May 1806
Promoted captain, 13 Jan 1811
Artillery Regiment redesigned 1st Artillery, 12 Mar 1812
Transferred to Corps of Artillery, 12 May 1814
DQMG 17 Mar 1813
Colonel QM 21 Mar 1814
Honorable discharge 15 Jun 1815
Died 3 Feb 1864

Swearingen, John
Born - Virginia
Residence - Ohio
Commissioned 3rd lieutenant, 26th Infantry, 20 May 1813
Recruiting at Chillicothe, OH, Dec 1813, Jan 1814
Ordered to the Army, Mar 1814
Recruiting at Lower Sandusky, OH, Apr 1814
Transferred to 19th Infantry, 12 May 1814
Promoted 2nd lieutenant, 2nd Rifles, 17 Mar 1814
Recruiting at Circleville, OH, May-Jul 1814
Promoted 1st lieutenant, 21 Jul 1814
Assigned to Capt. Harrison's Company, Mar 1815
Commanding at Malden, UC
Honorable discharge 15 Jun 1815

Swearingen, Samuel

Born - Virginia
Residence - Ross County, Ohio
Commission captain, 26th Infantry, 20 May 1813
Recruiting at Chillicothe, OH, Jun-Jul 1813
Recruiting at Franklinton, OH, Aug 1813
Ordered to Sackets Harbor, NY
Ordered to recruiting service
Resigned 9 Apr 1814
Died 27 Dec 1832

Symmes, John Cleves
Born – New Jersey
Residence – Ohio
Commissioned ensign, 1st Infantry, 26 Mar 1802
Promoted 2nd lieutenant, 1 May 1804
Promoted 1st lieutenant, 29 Jul 1807
Promoted captain, 20 Jan 1813
Participated in Battle of Bridgewater, UC, 25 Jul 1814
Participated in sortie from Fort Erie, UC, 17 Sep 1814
Served as the assistant deputy quartermaster
Honorable discharge 15 Jun 1815
Died 28 May 1829

Talbott, Josiah G. (John G.)
Residence – Ohio
Commissioned 3rd lieutenant, 26th Infantry, 20 May 1813
Recruiting duties, Jun 1813
Recruiting at Franklinton, OH, Nov 1813
Recruiting at Troy, OH, Dec 1813
Recruiting at Dayton, OH, Jan-Apr 1814
Recruiting at Xenia, OH, May 1814
Honorable discharge 1 Jun 1814
Pension: Wife Nancy, WC-1883; served in Capt. Talbott's Company, 26th Infantry

Talbott, Richard C.
Residence – Ohio
Commission captain, 26th Infantry, 20 May 1813
Recruiting at Xenia, OH, May-Dec 1813
Recruiting at Lebanon, OH, Apr-Jul 1814
Transferred to 19th Infantry, 12 May 1814
Honorable discharge 1 Jun 1814

Tiffin, Clayton
Residence – Ohio
Commissioned surgeon's mate, 17th Infantry, 11 Mar 1814
Honorable discharge 15 Jun 1815
Pension: Wife Belilla M., WO-42835, WC-33845; served as a surgeon's mate in the 17th Infantry

Tod, George
Residence – Youngstown, Ohio
Commissioned major, 17th Infantry, 12 Mar 1812
Transferred to 19th Infantry, 6 Jul 1812
Promoted lieutenant colonel and transferred to 17th Infantry, 13 Mar 1814
Honorable discharge 15 Jun 1815

Townsley, William
Residence – Ohio
Commissioned 2nd lieutenant, 1st Rifles, 15 May 1812
Promoted 1st lieutenant, 1 Aug 1812
Captain, assistant deputy quartermaster general, 11 Jan 1814
Resigned 30 Apr 1814

Trimble, Cary A.
Born – Kentucky
Residence – Ohio
Commission 1st lieutenant, 26th Infantry, 20 May 1813
Recruiting at Hillsborough, Washington & Greenfield, OH, Jun 1813
Served in Capt. Kesling's Company
Prisoner of War (Quebec, LC), captured at Fort Niagara, NY, 19 Dec 1813; exchanged 4 May 1814. Ordered to join regiment, 18 May 1814
Transferred to 19th Infantry, 12 May 1814
Recruiting at Chillicothe, OH, Jul-Aug 1814
Promoted captain, 20 Aug 1814
Honorable discharge 15 Jun 1815
Died 10 Sep 1821

Trimble, David
Born – Kentucky
Residence – Ohio
Commissioned 3rd lieutenant, 1st Infantry, 17 Mar 1814
Promoted 2nd lieutenant, 19 Apr 1814
Resigned 14 May 1814

Trimble, William A.
Born – Kentucky
Residence – Highland County, Ohio
Major, Ohio Volunteers, 1812-1813
Commissioned major, 26th Infantry, 18 Mar 1813
Recruiting at Lebanon, OH, Apr 1814
Transferred to 19th Infantry, 12 May 1814
Promoted lieutenant colonel, 30 Nov 1814
Transferred to 8th Infantry, 17 May 1815
Resigned 1 Mar 1819
Died 13 Dec 1821
Breveted lieutenant colonel, 17 Sep 1814, for gallant conduct in the sortie from Fort Erie, UC. Wounded 17 Sep 1814 during the sortie

Tullass, John J.

Residence – Ohio
Commissioned ensign, 27th Infantry, 7 Aug 1813
Recruiting at Zanesville, OH, Sep-Nov 1813, Feb 1814
Recruiting at Newark, OH
Honorable discharge 1 Jun 1814

Turney, David
Born – Kentucky
Residence – Ohio
Commissioned surgeon's mate, 19th Infantry, 31 Dec 1812
Promoted surgeon and transferred to 2nd Rifles, 21 Feb 1814
Honorable discharge 15 Jun 1815
Commission assistant surgeon of volunteers, 7 Jul 1846
Promoted surgeon of volunteers, 13 Jul 1847
Honorable discharge 26 Oct 1848

Van Horne, Isaac Jr
Residence – Muskingum County, Ohio
Commission captain, 27th Infantry, 20 May 1813
Transferred to 19th Infantry, 12 May 1814
Killed 4 Aug 1814 in the attack on Fort Mackinac, MI

Van Horne, Thomas B.
Residence – Warren County, Ohio
Major, Ohio Volunteers, 1812
Commissioned lieutenant colonel, 26th Infantry, 9 Apr 1813
Recruiting at Lebanon, OH, May-Dec 1813
Transferred to 19th Infantry, 12 May 1814
Honorable discharge 15 Jun 1815
Pension: Wife Elizabeth; served as a lieutenant colonel in the 19th and 26th Infantries
Bounty: BLW 5322-160-50

Wadsworth, Edward
Residence – Ohio
Commissioned 2nd lieutenant, 1st Rifles, 15 May 1812
Promoted 1st lieutenant, 1 Aug 1812
Assigned to Capt. Hay's Company, Oct 1813
Promoted captain, 16 Jul 1814
Wounded during the Battle of Fort Erie, UC, on 3 Aug 1814
Honorable discharge 15 Jun 1815
Pension: Old War IF-10266, captain in the US Rifles
Died 6 Aug 1835

Warner, Wynkoop
Residence – Belmont County, Ohio
Prisoner of War on Parole, captured at Detroit, MI, 16 Aug 1812 (3rd Ohio Volunteers)
Commissioned 1st lieutenant, 27th Infantry, 20 May 1813
Recruiting at Detroit, MI, Apr-May 1814
Transferred to 19th Infantry, 12 May 1814
Recruiting at Zanesville, OH, Jun-Sep 1814
Recruiting at New Lebanon and Cleveland
Assigned to Capt. Gill's Company
Honorable discharge 15 Jun 1815

Watson, Joseph
Residence – Ohio
Commissioned 2nd lieutenant, 19th Infantry, 25 Jul 1812
Served as a district paymaster
Discharged 15 Jun 1815

Watson, Simon Zelotus
Residence - Ohio
Commissioned major, Topographical Engineers, 20 Aug 1813
Died 1 Feb 1814

Watson, William
Born – New York
Residence – Ohio
Commission ensign, 26th Infantry, 20 May 1813
Recruiting at Hillsborough, Washington & Greenfield, OH
Honorable discharge 1 Jun 1814

Westfall, Newton E.
Residence – Indiana
Commissioned 1st lieutenant, 1st Infantry, 3 Jan 1812
Discharged 15 Jun 1815
Pension: Wife Anna Eliza Frazer, WO-1812, WC-504; married 12 or 14 Mar 1814 in Marietta, OH; solider died 27 May 1883 in Sacket Harbor, NY; served in Capt. Johnson's Company, 1st Infantry as a lieutenant; widow lived in Suffork County, NY in 1871
Bounty: BLW 201-160-50
Died: 27 May 1883

Will, George
Born – Virginia
Residence – Ohio
Private, corporal, sergeant, sergeant major, 2nd Infantry, Aug 1792 to Aug 1797
Commissioned 1st lieutenant, 16th Infantry, 20 May 1813
Transferred to 19th Infantry, 12 May 1814
Recruiting at Zanesville, OH, Jun-Jul 1814
Recruiting at Adelphia, OH
Promoted captain, 4 Aug 1814
Recruiting at Adelphia, OH, Feb 1815
Honorable discharge 15 Jun 1815

Died 27 Mar 1845

Wills, John S.
    Residence - Ohio
    Appointed judge advocate, 7 May 1813
    Honorable discharge 15 Jun 1815

Williams, Biram
    Residence – Ohio
    Commission ensign, 19th Infantry, 15 Apr 1814
    Transferred to 28th Infantry, 12 May 1814
    Promoted 3rd lieutenant, 13 Jul 1814
    Recruiting at Olympian Springs, KY, Jul-Dec 1814
    Recruiting at Crab Orchard, KY, Jan 1815
    Honorable discharge 15 Jun 1815

Williby, John
    Residence – Ohio
    Commissioned ensign, 27th Infantry, 20 May 1813
    Recruiting at Zanesville, OH, Oct-Dec 1813, Jan-May 1814
    Recruiting at New Lisbon, OH
    Honorable discharge 1 Jun 1814

Wood, Christopher
    Residence - Ohio
    Commission captain, 26th Infantry, 20 May 1813
    Recruiting at Urbana, OH, Jun-Dec 1813, Jan 1814
    Recruiting at Troy, OH, Feb 1814
    Recruiting at Urbana, OH, Apr 1814
    Honorable discharge 1 Jun 1814

Young, Robert
    Residence – Ohio
    Commissioned ensign, 26th Infantry, 20 May 1813
    Recruiting at Franklinton, OH, Jun-Dec 1813, Jan-Aug 1814
    Transferred to 19th Infantry, 12 May 1814
    Promoted 3rd lieutenant, 4 Aug 1814
    Assigned to Capt. Talbott's Company, 28 Feb 1815
    Regimental paymaster, 30 Nov 1814 to Jun 1815
    Honorable discharge 15 Jun 1815
    Pension: Served as an ensign in the 19th Infantry
    Bounty: BLW 169-160-50

The Enlisted Men

Ohio's Regulars in the War of 1812

Aanole, John - 19th Infantry - Enlistment date: 6 Jul 1812 - Enlistment place: St. Clairsville - Enlistment period: 5 Yrs - By whom: Samuel Booker.

Abbott, George - Private - 19th Infantry - Company: Joel Collins - Age: 21 - Height: 6' - Born: Pennsylvania - Trade: Laborer - Enlistment date: 17 Mar 1814 - Enlistment place: Detroit - Enlistment period: War - By whom: Samuel Coleman - Discharged: 20 Jul 1815 at Detroit - Bounty: BLW 14983-160-12 (Illinois).

Abbott, Joel - Private - 19th Infantry - Company: Angus Langham - Other regiments: 17th Infantry then 3rd Infantry - Pension: SO-21396; served in Captains Chunn and C. L. Cass Companies, 3rd Infantry.

Abbott, Joseph - Private - 26th Infantry - Company: George Kesling - Other regiments: 19th Infantry then 2nd Light Dragoons - Age: 18 - Height: 5' 7" - Born: New York - Enlistment date: 28 May 1813 - Enlistment place: Cincinnati - Comments: Re-enlisted on 20 Aug 1814.

Abbott, Samuel - Private - 26th Infantry - Company: Samuel Swearingen - Other regiment: 25th Infantry - Enlistment date: 8 May 1813 - Enlistment period: 1 Yr - Discharged: 8 May 1814.

Abrams, Deshaze - Sergeant - 19th Infantry - Died: 16 Aug 1814 at Fort Erie, UC.

Acy, Archibald - Private - 19th Infantry - Age: 24 - Height: 5' 5" - Born: Delaware - Enlistment date: 9 Aug 1814 - Enlistment place: Canton.

Adams, Alexander - Private - 26th Infantry - Company: Samuel Swearingen - Enlistment date: 13 Jul 1813 - Enlistment period: 1 Yr - Discharged: 20 Jun 1814.

Adams, David - Private - 2nd Rifles - Company: Batteal Harrison - Other regiments: Rifle Regiment then 5th Infantry - Age: 22 - Height: 5' 10" - Born: Kentucky or Virginia - Trade: Farmer - Enlistment date: 16 Aug 1814 - Enlistment place: Portsmouth - Enlistment period: 5 Yrs - By whom: Andrew Gilmore - Discharged: 1 Jun 1815 - Bounty: BLW 22683-160-12 (Arkansas).

Adams, Elijah - Sergeant - 27th Infantry - Company: Alexander Hill - Other regiment: 19th Infantry - Age: 24 - Height: 5' 5 3/4" - Born: NY, Saratoga County, Milton - Trade: Laborer - Enlistment date: 27 Apr 1814 - Enlistment place: Clinton County - Enlistment period: War - Discharged: 6 Jun 1815 at Chillicothe - Bounty: BLW 5125-160-12 (Illinois).

Adams, Hugh - Private - 26th Infantry - Company: Samuel Swearingen - Enlistment date: 9 May 1813 - Enlistment period: 1 Yr - Died: 19 Dec 1813.

Adams, James - Private - 19th Infantry - Company: Richard Talbott - Age: 31 - Height: 5' 11" - Born: Virginia - Trade: Paper maker - Enlistment date: 17 Jul 1814 - Enlistment place: Darke County - Enlistment period: War - By whom: Richard Talbott - Discharged: 31 May 1815 at Chillicothe - Bounty: BLW 26153-160-12 (Arkansas).

Agnew, Samuel - Musician - 17th Infantry - Company: Henry Crittenden - Other regiment: 3rd Infantry - Age: 17 - Height: 5' 1 1/2" - Born: Ohio - Enlistment date: 29 May 1814 - Enlistment place: Chillicothe - Enlistment period: 5 Yrs - By whom: Adam Hoffman.

Ainsworth, Andrew - Private - 26th Infantry - Company: George Kesling - Other regiment: 25th Infantry - Enlistment date: 20 Jun 1813 - Enlistment period: 1 Yr - Discharged: 20 Jun 1814 - Pension: Wife Margaret Conover, SC-2488, SO-1760; married 16 Nov 1816 in Warren County, OH; soldier died on 13 May 1885 in Hillsborough, IN; served in Capt. Kesling's Company, 26th Infantry; lived in Fountain County, IN - Bounty: BLW 2141-160-50.

Aiso, Morris - Private - 17th Infantry - Age: 22 - Height: 5' 6" - Born: Pennsylvania - Trade: Farmer - Enlistment date: 5 Jun 1814 - Enlistment period: War - By whom: William Shang.

Alberry, John - Private - 19th Infantry - Age: 19 - Height: 6' 2 1/2" - Born: MD, Allegeny County - Enlistment date: 22 Jul 1812 - Enlistment place: Zanesville - Enlistment period: 18 Mos.

Albright, Peter - Private - 1st Rifles - Company: Thomas Hamilton - Age: 26 - Height: 5' 6" - Born: PA, Philadelphia County - Trade: Printer - Enlistment date: 15 Apr 1812 - Enlistment place: Chillicothe - Enlistment period: 5 Yrs - By whom: John Swearingen - Bounty: BLW 15897-160-12 (Illinois) - Comments: Transferred to Capt. Thomas Ramsey's Company, 1st Rifles.

Aldridge, Thomas - Private - 17th Infantry - Company: Angus Langham - Age: 37 - Height: 5' 10 1/4" - Born: RI, Providence County, Smithfield - Trade: Carpenter - Enlistment date: 15 Jul 1813 - Enlistment place: Portsmouth - Enlistment period: War - By whom: Hugh May - Discharged: 9 Jun 1815 at Chillicothe - Bounty: BLW 24217-160-12 (Arkansas).

Aleshire, William - Sergeant - 19th Infantry - Company: Joel Collins - Age: 22 - Height: 5' 7" - Born: Virginia - Trade: Shoemaker - Enlistment date: 10 Mar 1814 - Enlistment place: Detroit - Enlistment period: War - By whom: Wynkoop Warner - Bounty: BLW 9840-160-12 (Illinois).

Alexander, Ezekiel - Private - 27th Infantry - Company: William Gill - Other regiment: 19th Infantry - Age: 19 - Height: 5' 9" - Born: Virginia - Trade: Blacksmith - Enlistment date: 18 Apr 1814 - Enlistment place: New

Lisbon - Enlistment period: War - By whom: John Williby - Discharged: 5 Jun 1815 at Chillicothe - Bounty: BLW 3457-160-12 (Illinois).

Alexander, Joseph - Private - 27th Infantry - Company: James Applegate - Enlistment date: 20 May 1813 - Discharged: 24 Nov 1813 - Pension: Wife Eleanor Miller (2nd wife), Old War IF-12056, WO-42050, SC-33155; married on 2 May 1830 in Millersburg, Holmes County, OH; soldier died in 1852 in Scott, Kosciusko County, IN; widow died on 12 Mar 1885 in Adams County, NE - Bounty: BLW 14148-160-50.

Alexander, William - Private - 26th Infantry - Company: Benjamin Watson - Other regiment: 25th Infantry - Age: 25 - Height: 5' 10 3/4" - Born: PA, Dauphin County - Trade: Farmer - Enlistment date: 6 Aug 1813 - Enlistment place: Ohio - Enlistment period: War - By whom: Isaac Reiley - Discharged: 17 May 1815 at Sackets Harbor, NY.

Allabough, John - Private - 26th Infantry - Company: George Kesling - Enlistment date: 2 Jun 1813 - Enlistment period: 1 Yr - Died: 27 Sep 1813.

Allaways, Joseph - Private - 26th or 27th Infantry - Company: Joel Collins - Other regiment: 19th Infantry - Age: 19 - Height: 6' - Born: New Jersey - Trade: Laborer - Enlistment date: 15 Mar 1814 - Enlistment place: Detroit - Enlistment period: War - By whom: Wynkoop Warner - Discharged: 20 Jul 1815 at Detroit - Bounty: BLW 12682-160-12 (Arkansas) - Comments: Re-enlisted.

Allen, Hutchins - Private - 19th Infantry - Company: Richard Talbott - Age: 32 - Height: 5' 5" - Born: New Jersey - Trade: Farmer - Enlistment date: 30 Nov 1813 - Enlistment place: Clermont County, Williamsburg - Enlistment period: 1 Yr - By whom: William McDonald Jr - Discharged: 30 Nov 1814 at Cleveland - Pension: Wife Keziah South, WO-2792, WC-4271; married on 10 May 1810 in Clermont County, OH; soldier died on 12 May 1868 in Brown County, OH; widow died circa 1876; served in Capt. Talbott's Company, 19th Infantry; lived in Brown County, OH - Bounty: BLW 4750-160-50.

Allen, John - Private - 26th Infantry - Company: George Kesling - Other regiment: 25th Infantry - Enlistment date: 6 Jun 1813 - Enlistment period: 1 Yr - Discharged: 6 Jun 1814.

Alley, Peter - Private - 26th Infantry - Company: Samuel Swearingen - Other regiment: 25th Infantry - Enlistment date: 18 Jun 1813 - Enlistment period: 1 Yr - Discharged: 18 Jun 1814.

Allways, Joseph - Private - 27th Infantry - Company: George Sanderson - Enlistment date: 22 Jun 1813.

Ambler, Peter - Private - 19th Infantry - Company: William Gill - Age: 25 - Height: 5' 8" - Born: Virginia - Trade: Farmer - Enlistment date: 5 Jun 1814 - Enlistment place: New Lisbon - Enlistment period: War - By whom: Wynkoop Warner - Discharged: 5 Jun 1815 at Chillicothe - Bounty: BLW 6902-160-12 (Illinois).

Amerine, John - Sergeant - 17th Infantry - Company: William Adair - Pension: Wife Catherine, SO-12438, SC-7903; served as a sergeant in Capt. William Adair's Company, 17th Infantry; married in Mar 1815 in Belmont County, OH - Bounty: BLW 10348-160-50.

Anderson, Alexander - Private - 26th Infantry - Company: Samuel Swearingen - Enlistment date: 17 Jul 1813 - Enlistment period: 1 Yr.

Anderson, John - Private - 19th Infantry - Company: Harris Hickman - Other regiment: 17th Infantry - Age: 26 - Height: 5' 9" - Born: PA, Bedford County - Trade: Laborer - Enlistment date: 8 Apr 1814 - Enlistment place: Marietta - Enlistment period: War - By whom: John Miligan - Discharged: 9 Jun 1815 at Chillicothe - Bounty: BLW 6594-160-12 (Illinois).

Anderson, Joseph - Private - 27th Infantry - Company: George Sanderson - Enlistment date: 27 Apr 1813.

Anderson, Thomas - Private - 26th Infantry - Company: Samuel Swearingen - Comments: Prisoner of War captured at Fort Niagara, NY, 19 Dec 1813, exchanged 28 Apr 1814; served aboard the US Ariel on the Lake Erie Squadron.

Anderson, William - Private - 19th Infantry - Born: VA, Pendleton County - Enlistment date: 16 Jun 1814 - Enlistment place: Worthington.

Anderson, William - Private - 27th Infantry - Company: George Sanderson - Enlistment date: 29 May 1813.

Anderson, William - Private - 26th Infantry - Company: William Puthuff - Enlistment date: 9 Aug 1813 - Enlistment period: 1 Yr - Died: 19 Dec 1813 at Detroit.

Andrews, Robert - Private - 17th Infantry - Company: Caleb Holder - Age: 36 - Height: 5' 10 1/4" - Born: Virginia - Trade: Laborer - Enlistment date: 6 Sep 1814 - Enlistment period: War - By whom: George Stall - Discharged: 30 Jun 1815 at Detroit - Bounty: BLW 20677-160-12 (Missouri) - Cancelled; BLW 24534-160-12 (Arkansas) - Comments: Second land bounty to Isaac Andrews & other heirs at law of Robert Andrews.

Anway, George - Private - 19th Infantry - Company: Carey Trimble - Other regiment: 17th Infantry - Age: 26 - Height: 5' 10" - Born: New Jersey - Trade: Farmer - Enlistment date: 30 May 1814 - Enlistment place: Chillicothe - Enlistment period: War - By whom: Charles Cissna - Discharged: 6 Jun 1815 at Chillicothe - Bounty: BLW 6774-160-12 (Illinois).

Archer, Earl P. - Private - 2nd Rifles - Company: Batteal Harrison - Age: 40 - Height: 5' 6" - Born: CT, Hebron or Hartford - Trade: Farmer - Enlistment date: 27 Sep 1814 - Enlistment place: Gallipolis or Rutland Twp - Enlistment period: 5 Yrs - By whom: Edward Miller - Discharged: 4 Feb 1816 at Detroit on Surgeon's Certificate of Disability.

Argo, Morris - Private - 17th Infantry - Company: David Holt - Age: 22 - Height: 5' 6" - Born: Pennsylvania - Trade: Laborer - Enlistment date: 5 Jun 1814 - Enlistment place: Cambridge - Enlistment period: War - By whom: Ensign Strong - Discharged: 4 Jun 1815 at Chillicothe - Bounty: BLW 3724-160-12 (Illinois).

Armour, Robert - Private - 19th Infantry - Company: Wilson Elliott - Other regiment: 17th Infantry - Age: 31 - Height: 5' 9" - Born: Pennsylvania - Trade: Farmer - Enlistment date: 10 May 1813 - Enlistment place: Cincinnati - Enlistment period: War - By whom: Philip Price - Discharged: 18 Apr 1815 at Chillicothe - Bounty: BLW 23469-160-12 (Arkansas) - Comments: Prisoner of War exchanged on 11 May 1814

Armstrong, Archibald - Corporal - 2nd Artillery - Company: Daniel Cushing - Enlistment date: 16 Dec 1812 - Enlistment period: 5 Yrs - Died: 3 Dec 1813.

Armstrong, James - Private - 27th Infantry - Company: Alexander Hill - Other regiment: 19th Infantry - Age: 37 - Height: 6' - Born: Ireland, County Fermangh, McGiersbury - Trade: Laborer - Enlistment date: 27 Feb 1814 - Enlistment period: War - By whom: Henry Northrup - Discharged: 5 Jun 1815 at Chillicothe - Bounty: BLW 8908-160-12 (Illinois).

Armstrong, Stephen - Corporal - 19th Infantry - Company: George Kesling - Age: 39 - Height: 6' - Born: Connecticut - Trade: Farmer - Enlistment date: 1 Feb 1815 - Enlistment place: Lebanon - Enlistment period: War - By whom: George Kesling - Discharged: 27 Mar 1815 at Zanesville - Bounty: BLW 489-320-14.

Armstrong, William - Private - 27th Infantry - Age: 22 - Height: 6' 7" - Born: Pennsylvania - Enlistment date: 10 Jun 1814 - Enlistment place: Newark - By whom: John Spencer.

Arnett, Seth - Private - 26th Infantry - Company: George Kesling - Enlistment date: 30 May 1813 - Enlistment period: 1 Yr - Discharged: 31 May 1814.

Arnhart, John - Private - 26th Infantry - Company: George Kesling - Other regiment: 25th Infantry - Age: 21 - Height: 5' 7" - Born: PA, Northampton County - Trade: Blacksmith - Enlistment date: 25 Apr 1813 - Enlistment period: 1 Yr - Discharged: 20 Apr 1814.

Arnold, George - Private - 17th Infantry - Age: 28 - Height: 5' 11" - Born: Virginia - Trade: Farmer - Enlistment date: 17 Aug 1814 - Enlistment place: Coshocton County - Enlistment period: 5 Yrs - By whom: John Reeves.

Arnold, John - Private - 19th Infantry - Company: Angus Langham - Bounty: BLW 27250-160-42 - Comments: Land bounty to Samuel Arnold, Hannah Durbin & Honor Durbin, brother and sisters, only heirs at law of John Arnold.

Arnold, John - Private - 2nd Artillery - Company: Daniel Cushing - Age: 26 - Height: 5' 8" - Born: MD, Allegeny County - Enlistment date: 6 Jul 1812 - Enlistment place: St. Clairsville - Enlistment period: 5 Yrs.

Arnold, Samuel - Private - 17th Infantry - Company: Harris Hickman - Age: 35 - Height: 5' 6" - Born: MD, Frederick County, Westminster - Trade: Farmer - Enlistment date: 17 Oct 1813 - Enlistment place: Harrison County, Cadiz - Enlistment period: War - By whom: John Milligan - Discharged: 9 Jun 1815 at Chillicothe - Bounty: BLW 6536-160-12 (Illinois).

Arnold, William - Private - 27th Infantry - Company: Alexander Hill.

Arthurs, John - Private - 19th Infantry - Company: John Chunn - Other regiment: 17th Infantry - Age: 48 - Height: 5' 11" - Born: PA, York County - Trade: Barber - Enlistment date: 10 May 1813 - Enlistment place: Cincinnati - Enlistment period: War - By whom: Philip Price - Discharged: 7 Jun 1815 at Chillicothe - Bounty: BLW 3725-160-12 Cancelled; BLW 4424-160-12 (Illinois).

Arwin, Joseph - Private - 2nd Artillery - Company: Daniel Cushing - Enlistment date: 23 Sep 1812 - Died: Oct 1813.

Ashes, James - Private - 19th Infantry - Company: Wilson Elliott.

Ashly, Jeremiah - Private - 19th Infantry - Company: James Herron - Enlistment date: 3 Oct 1812 - Enlistment period: 18 Mos.

Atcheson, Michael - Private - 24th Infantry - Company: Ensign Thomas Young - Other regiment: 8th Infantry - Age: 27 - Height: 6' 1" - Born: Ohio - Trade: Farmer - Enlistment date: 11 Aug 1814 - Enlistment place: MO, St. Louis - Enlistment period: 5 Yrs - By whom: Francis Valle - Discharged: 11 Aug 1819 - Comments: Re-enlisted.

Atkins, John - Private - 27th Infantry - Company: George Sanderson - Enlistment date: 30 May 1813 - Enlistment period: 1 Yr - Discharged: 30 May 1814 - Pension: Wife Sally Meeker, WC-11972 SC-11905; married on 30 Jan 1817 at Harpersfield, OH, soldier died on 7 Feb 1873 in Thompson, OH, widow died on 23 Mar 1895, served in Captain George Sanderson's Company, 27th Infantry - Bounty: BLW 3912-160-50.

Atkins, Samuel - Private - 19th Infantry - Company: Isaac Van Horn - Enlistment date: 15 Jun 1813 - Enlistment period: 1 Yr - Discharged: 14 Jun 1814 - Pension: Wife Hannah Lane, SO-10957, SC-15269, WO-10290 Rejected; served as a private in Capt. Isaac Van Horn's Company, 19th Infantry; married on 22 Aug 1817 in Groton, Tompkins County, NY; soldier died on 25 Apr 1873 in Chatham, Medina County, OH; wife died about 1 Sept 1885 in Homersville, OH - Bounty: BLW 6483-160-50.

Atkinson, Stephen - Private - 19th Infantry - Company: John Chunn - Other regiment: 17th Infantry.

Austin, William - Private - 2nd Light Dragoons - Company: Samuel Hopkins - Age: 32 - Height: 5' 11" - Born: MA, Sheffield - Trade: Farmer - Enlistment date: 28 Jul 1813 - Enlistment place: Cleveland - Enlistment period: 18 Mos - By whom: Samuel Hopkins - Discharged: 28 Jan 1815.

Ayers, Peter - Private - 26th Infantry - Company: George Kesling - Other regiment: Light Dragoons Regiment - Enlistment date: 25 May 1813 - Enlistment period: 1 Yr.

Ayrs, Morris - Private - 17th Infantry - Company: David Holt - Age: 22 - Height: 5' 6" - Born: Pennsylvania - Trade: Laborer - Enlistment date: 5 Jun 1814 - Enlistment place: Cambridge - Enlistment period: War - By whom: Ensign Strong - Discharged: 4 Jun 1815 at Chillicothe.

Babcock, Henry - Private - 19th Infantry - Company: Joel Collins - Age: 29 - Height: 6' - Born: New York - Trade: Laborer - Enlistment date: 7 Mar 1814 - Enlistment place: Detroit - Enlistment period: War - By whom: Wynkoop Warner - Discharged: 20 Jul 1815 at Detroit- Bounty: BLW 19284-160-12 (Missouri).

Bachum, John - Private - 26th Infantry - Company: William Puthuff - Enlistment date: 5 Apr 1813 - Enlistment period: 1 Yr.

Badgley, Abraham - Drummer - 27th Infantry - Company: Alexander Hill - Other regiment: 19th Infantry - Age: 18 - Height: 4' 10 1/2" - Born: VA, Hardy County (now WV) - Enlistment date: 2 May 1814 - Enlistment place: Athens County - Enlistment period: War - By whom: Nehemiah Gregory - Discharged: 5 Jun 1815 at Chillicothe - Pension: Wife Mary Grogan, SO-2986, SC-1702; married on 15 Feb 1821 in Lee Creek, Wood County, WV, served in William Gill's Company, 19th Infantry - Bounty: BLW 9897-160-12.

Bagdley, David - Private - 1st Rifles - Company: Thomas Ramsey - Age: 21 - Height: 5' 10" - Born: NY, Cayuga County - Trade: Laborer - Enlistment date: 20 Feb 1814 - Enlistment place: Cincinnati - Enlistment period: 5 Yrs - By whom: Thomas Ramsey - Discharged: 7 Jun 1815 at Buffalo, NY- Pension: Old War IF-12202 - Bounty: BLW 11760-160-12 (Illinois).

Bailey, Benjamin - 27th Infantry - Company: George Sanderson - Pension: Wife Elizabeth (2nd wife), WC-35205; married on 20 Jan 1867 in Athens County, OH; soldier died on 11 Feb 1872, wife died on 6 Jun 1894; served in Capt. Sanderson's Company, 27th Infantry; lived in Athens County, OH; first wife Ruth Cross.

Bailey, Benjamin - Private - 17th Infantry - Company: David Holt - Age: 19 - Height: 5' 8" - Born: Ohio - Trade: Laborer - Enlistment date: 15 Jun 1814 - Enlistment place: Chillicothe - Enlistment period: War - By whom: Lieutenant Huffman.

Bailey, Charles - Private - 19th Infantry - Company: John Chunn.

Bailey, Cyrus - Corporal - 27th Infantry - Company: Alexander Hill - Other regiment: 19th Infantry - Age: 18 - Height: 5' 8" - Born: CT, Middlesex County, Middletown - Trade: Farmer - Enlistment date: 11 May 1814 - Enlistment place: Zanesville - Enlistment period: War - By whom: Henry Northrup - Discharged: 6 Jun 1815 at Chillicothe - Pension: Wife Permelia Edie, WC-19485, SC-9730, SO-19544; married on 12 May 1838 in St. Clair County, MI, soldier died on 29 Mar 1872 in Mt. Hope, IN, served in Capt. John McElvanin's Company, 19th Infantry - Bounty: BLW 8023-160-12 (Illinois).

Bailey, Jacob - Private - 19th Infantry - Age: 26 - Height: 5' 10" - Born: New York - Enlistment date: 18 Apr 1814 - Enlistment place: Franklin County - Enlistment period: War - By whom: John Simons - Comments: Deserted 7 May 1814.

Bailey, James - Private - 26th Infantry - Company: Nimrod Moore - Comments: Served aboard the US Brig Niagara on the Lake Erie Squadron.

Bailey, Joshua - Private - 19th Infantry - Company: Joel Collins - Age: 19 - Height: 5' 7" - Born: Maryland - Trade: Carpenter - Enlistment date: 28 Jun 1813 - Enlistment place: Detroit - Enlistment period: War - By whom: John Patterson - Discharged: 19 Jul 1815 - Bounty: BLW 27712-160-42.

Bailey, Robert - Private - 19th Infantry - Company: George Kesling - Age: 23 - Height: 5' 9" - Born: Virginia - Trade: Farmer - Enlistment date: 23 Dec 1814 - Enlistment place: Zanesville - Enlistment period: War - By whom: Lieutenant Cass - Discharged: 27 Mar 1815 at Zanesville - Bounty: BLW 464-320-14 (Illinois).

Baine, William - Private - 19th Infantry - Company: Joel Collins - Enlistment date: 13 Oct 1814 - Discharged: 15 Jul 1815 - Pension: Wife Martha Mann, SO-6572, SC-13801; married on Jul 1824 in Butler County, OH - Bounty: BLW 19570-80-50; BLW 11038-80-55.

Ohio's Regulars in the War of 1812

Bair, Adam - Private - 27th Infantry - Company: Alexander Hill - Other regiment: 19th Infantry - Bounty: BLW 26660-160-12 (Arkansas) - Comments: Land bounty to John Bair & Henry Bair, only heirs at law of Adam Bair.

Baird, Jacob - Private - 19th Infantry - Company: George Kesling - Age: 18 - Height: 5' 8" - Born: MD, Baltimore County - Trade: Farmer - Enlistment date: 17 Jan 1815 - Enlistment place: Lebanon - Enlistment period: War - By whom: George Kesling.

Baird, John - Private - 19th Infantry - Company: George Kesling - Age: 24 - Height: 5' 8" - Born: New York - Trade: Farmer - Enlistment date: 12 Jan 1814 - Enlistment place: New Lisbon - Enlistment period: War - By whom: Samuel Coleman - Comments: Deserted 1 Feb 1815.

Baker, Daniel - Private - 27th Infantry - Company: George Sanderson - Enlistment date: 24 May 1813 - Pension: Wife Mary McNamee, WC-6134; married 23 Dec 1813 Fairfield County, OH, soldier died 15 Mar 1855 in Rushville, OH, served in Captain George Sanderson's Company, OH Militia, lived in Fairfield County, OH.

Baker, Jacob - Private - 19th Infantry - Company: Martin Hawkins - Other regiments: 17th Infantry then 3rd Infantry - Age: 34 - Height: 5' 9" - Born: Virginia - Trade: Farmer - Enlistment date: 7 Mar 1814 - Enlistment place: Detroit - Enlistment period: 5 Yrs - By whom: George Atchison - Discharged: 7 Mar 1819 at Fort Howard, WI.

Baker, Jeptha - Private - Rangers - Company: Samuel McCormick - Age: 22 - Height: 5' 6" - Born: Pennsylvania - Trade: Wagon maker - Enlistment date: 24 Nov 1813 - Enlistment period: 1 Yr - Discharged: 17 Nov 1814 at Fort Malden, UC, on Surgeon's Certificate of Disability.

Baker, Joseph - Private - 26th Infantry - Company: George Kesling - Enlistment date: 26 May 1813.

Baker, William - Private - 17th Infantry - Company: Caleb Holder - Other regiment: 3rd Infantry - Age: 35 - Height: 5' 8 1/2" - Born: MA, Suffolk County, Boston - Trade: Shoemaker - Enlistment date: 6 Aug 1814 - Enlistment place: Steubenville - Enlistment period: 5 Yrs - By whom: William Featherstone.

Baldridge, Ely - Private - 26th Infantry - Company: Richard Talbott - Other regiment: 19th Infantry - Age: 23 - Height: 5' 9" - Born: Carolina - Trade: Farmer - Enlistment date: 13 Oct 1813 - Enlistment place: Franklin County - Enlistment period: 1 Yr - By whom: Robert Young - Discharged: 13 Oct 1814.

Baldwin, James - Private - 2nd Rifles - Company: Batteal Harrison - Other regiment: Rifle Regiment - Age: 36 - Height: 5' 10" - Born: Pennsylvania - Trade: Laborer - Enlistment date: 24 May 1814 - Enlistment place: Lancaster - Enlistment period: 5 Yrs - By whom: John Stockton - Discharged: 24 May 1819 - Bounty: BLW 27044-160-12 (Arkansas) - Comments: Discharged at Fort Crawford, IL; land bounty to David Baldwin, son & other heirs at law of James Baldwin.

Baldwin, Thomas - Private - Rangers - Company: Samuel McCormick - Enlistment date: 7 Nov 1812 - Died: 1814 - Pension: Old War WF-10390, Old War WF 12287 Rejected; served as a private in Captain McCormick's Company, US Rangers, widow not named - Comments: Wounded by the enemy on 16 Jul 1814, on furlough in Ohio, died.

Ball, Adam A. - Corporal - 19th Infantry - Company: David Holt - Other regiment: 17th Infantry - Age: 20 - Height: 5' 5 1/2" - Born: Maryland - Enlistment date: 7 Apr 1814 - Enlistment place: Marietta - Enlistment period: War - By whom: John Milligan - Died: 7 Jan 1815 - Bounty: BLW 24687-160-12 (Arkansas) - Comments: Died at Williamsville, NY; buried in the War of 1812 Cemetery in Cheektowaga, Erie County, NY; land bounty to Dinah Bryam, only heir at law of Adam Ball.

Ball, Edward - Private - 19th Infantry - Company: Wilson Elliott - Age: 43 - Height: 5' 11" - Born: VA, Fauquier County - Enlistment date: 2 Sep 1812 - Enlistment period: 18 Mos - Pension: Wife Letitia, Old War WF-10390: served in the 19th Infantry - Bounty: BLW 14756-160-50.

Ballard, Evan - Private - 19th Infantry - Bounty: BLW 5581-160-12 (Illinois).

Ballard, Lindsey L. - Private - 19th Infantry - Company: Carey Trimble - Died: 1 Mar 1815 - Bounty: BLW 18140-160-12 (Illinois) - Comments: Died in New York; buried in the War of 1812 Cemetery in Cheektowaga, Erie County, NY; land bounty to Anderson Ballard & other heirs at law of Lindsey L. Ballard.

Banfield, Enoch - Private - 17th Infantry - Age: 27 - Height: 5' 8" - Born: New Hampshire - Trade: Laborer - Enlistment date: 18 Dec 1814 - Enlistment place: Adams County, West Union - Enlistment period: War - By whom: James Campbell - Discharged: 18 Apr 1815 at Chillicothe - Bounty: BLW 490-320-14.

Bannon, John - Private - 19th Infantry - Company: James Herron - Enlistment date: 2 Oct 1812 - Enlistment period: 18 Mos.

Barbadoes, Andrew - Private - 17th Infantry - Company: Benjamin Sanders - Other regiment: 3rd Infantry - Age: 28 - Height: 5' 5" - Born: New Spain - Trade: Tailor - Enlistment date: 10 Jul 1814 - Enlistment place: Chillicothe - Enlistment period: 5 Yrs - By whom: George Stall.

Barker, John - Private - 19th Infantry - Company: Carey Trimble - Other regiment: 17th Infantry - Age: 21 -

The Enlisted Men

Height: 5' 10 1/2" - Born: New York - Trade: Farmer - Enlistment date: 18 Apr 1814 - Enlistment place: Columbiana County, Salem - Enlistment period: War - By whom: Ensign Robinson - Discharged: 6 Jun 1815 at Chillicothe - Bounty: BLW 2885-160-12 (Illinois).

Barker, John - Private - 27th Infantry - Company: Alexander Hill - Other regiment: 19th Infantry - Pension: Old War IF-12229, served as a private in Capt. Alexander Hill's Company, 19th Infantry.

Barker, Joseph - Private - 26th Infantry - Enlistment date: 26 May 1813 - Enlistment period: 1 Yr.

Barlow, William A. - Sergeant - 19th Infantry - Company: James Herron - Enlistment date: 8 Jun 1813.

Barnes, Baldwin - Private - 19th Infantry - Company: Wilson Elliott.

Barr, Charles - 19th Infantry - Died: 8 Jul 1814, executed at Chillicothe.

Barr, Isaac - Private - 17th Infantry - Age: 18 - Height: 6' - Born: Pennsylvania - Trade: Carpenter - Enlistment date: 8 Jul 1814 - Enlistment period: War - By whom: William Featherstone.

Barrett, John - Private - 2nd Artillery - Company: Daniel Cushing - Height: 5' 5 3/4" - Born: NJ, Burlington County - Enlistment date: 10 Jul 1812 - Enlistment place: Canton - Comments: Deserted.

Bartholomew, Abram - Private - 27th Infantry - Company: George Sanderson - Enlistment date: 31 May 1813.

Bartholomew, Daniel I. - Corporal - 27th Infantry - Company: George Sanderson - Enlistment date: 8 May 1813.

Bartholomew, John J. - Private - 27th Infantry - Company: George Sanderson - Enlistment date: 17 Jun 1813 - Enlistment period: 1 Yr - Discharged: 17 Jun 1814 - Pension: Wife Susan Shears, SO-19143, SC-18939; married in Jun 1822 in Ashtabula County, OH, served in Captain George Sanderson's Company, 27th Infantry, lived in Harpersfield, OH, and in Bureau County, IL - Bounty: BLW 10459-160-50.

Bartholomew, Samuel - Private - 27th Infantry - Company: George Sanderson - Enlistment date: 8 Jun 1813.

Bartlett, John W. - Private - 28th Infantry - Company: Nimrod Moore - Enlistment date: 27 May 1813 - Enlistment period: 1 Yr - Died: 15 Oct 1813 at Fort Seneca (now Old Fort, OH).

Bartlett, William - Corporal - 19th Infantry - Company: James Herron - Enlistment date: 26 Oct 1812 - Enlistment period: 18 Mos.

Bash, Jacob - Private - 28th Infantry - Company: George Stockton - Age: 21 - Height: 5' 9" - Born: Maryland or Cleveland - Trade: Carpenter - Enlistment date: 16 Oct 1814 - Enlistment place: Cleveland - Enlistment period: War - By whom: Thomas Edmondson - Discharged: 30 Jun 1815 at Detroit.

Bates, William - Private - 2nd Rifles - Company: Batteal Harrison - Age: 26 - Height: 5' 9" - Born: Pennsylvania - Trade: Laborer - Enlistment date: 19 Oct 1814 - Enlistment period: War - By whom: William Pritchard - Discharged: 30 Jun 1815 at Detroit- Bounty: BLW 4563-160-12 (Arkansas).

Batteese – see Delaurier, John Baptist

Baxter, Thomas - Corporal - 19th Infantry - Company: William Gill - Enlistment date: 28 Apr 1814 - Enlistment period: War - Discharged: 31 May 1815 - Pension: Wife Prudence Howard (1st wife), SC-9345; married in 1814; 2nd wife Elizabeth Shafter, married in Feb 1840, 1st wife died in 1836; served in Capt. Ephraim Brown's Company, OH militia and in Capt. Gill's Company, 19th Infantry; lived in Henry and Hancock Counties, IN; died about 1877 - Bounty: BLW 12166-160-12 (Illinois); BLW 4074-160-50.

Beach, William - Private - 19th Infantry - Company: William Gill.

Beam, Jacob - Private - 26th Infantry - Company: Samuel Swearingen - Other regiment: 25th Infantry - Enlistment date: 3 May 1813 - Enlistment period: 1 Yr - Discharged: 3 May 1814.

Beam, Phillip - Private - 26th Infantry - Company: George Kesling - Pension: Wife Mary, WO-9302; served in Capt. George Kesling's Company, 26th Infantry

Beamer, Levi - Private - 19th Infantry - Bounty: BLW 381-320-14 (Illinois).

Bear, Adam - Private - 19th Infantry - Company: Carey Trimble - Other regiment: 17th Infantry - Enlistment date: 28 Feb 1814 - Enlistment period: War - Died: 3 Dec 1814 at Williamsville, NY; buried in the War of 1812 Cemetery in Cheektowaga, Erie County, NY.

Beard, Jacob - Private - 19th Infantry - Age: 18 - Height: 5' 8" - Born: Maryland - Trade: Farmer - Enlistment date: 17 Jan 1815 - Enlistment period: War - By whom: George Kesling - Discharged: 27 Mar 1815 at Zanesville - Bounty: BLW 463-320-14 (Illinois).

Beatly, John - Private - 26th Infantry - Company: George Kesling - Other regiment: 25th Infantry - Enlistment date: 15 May 1813 - Enlistment period: 1 Yr - Discharged: 15 May 1814.

Beatty, George - Private - 19th Infantry - Company: Abraham Edwards - Enlistment date: 29 Mar 1813 - Enlistment period: 5 Yrs - Died: 31 Dec 1813 - Bounty: BLW 18884-160-12 (Arkansas) - Comments: Died on or about 31 Dec 1813; land bounty to William Beatty, brother & heirs at law of George Beatty.

Beatty, John - Private - 27th Infantry - Company: George Sanderson - Enlistment date: 15 Apr 1813.

Beebe, Sheldon - Private - 27th Infantry - Company: George Sanderson - Enlistment date: 28 Apr 1813 - Enlistment period: 1 Yr - Discharged: 29 Apr 1814 - Pension: Wife Temperance Denman, WO-40260, WC-31027;

married on 21 January 1815 in Franklin County, Ohio, soldier died on 18 December 1864 at Carey, Ohio, widow died circa 1881, served in Captain George Sanderson's Company, 27th Infantry, lived in Wyandot County, Ohio - Bounty: BLW 2542-160-50.

Beemer, Charles J. - Private - 17th Infantry - Company: Caleb Holder - Age: 31 - Height: 5' 10 1/2" - Born: Germany - Trade: Tanner - Enlistment date: 15 Jan 1814 - Enlistment period: War - By whom: William Featherstone - Discharged: 30 Jun 1815 at Detroit - Bounty: BLW 8661-160-12 (Arkansas).

Beers, Benjamin - Private - 17th Infantry - Company: Henry Crittenden - Other regiment: 3rd Infantry - Age: 24 - Height: 5' 10" - Born: RI, Providence County - Trade: Farmer - Enlistment date: 15 Jan 1813 - Enlistment place: Zanesville - Enlistment period: 5 Yrs - By whom: James Herron - Comments: Re-enlisted.

Bell, Simon - Private - 26th Infantry - Company: George Kesling - Enlistment date: 15 May 1813 - Enlistment period: 1 Yr - By whom: George Kesling.

Bell, Thomas - Private - 19th Infantry - Pension: Wife Nancy May, Old War WF-12424; served as a private in the 19th Infantry

Bell, William - Musician - 17th Infantry - Company: Henry Crittenden - Other regiment: 3rd Infantry - Age: 15 - Height: 4' 10" - Born: East Jersey - Trade: Farmer - Enlistment date: 15 May 1814 - Enlistment period: 5 Yrs - By whom: George Stall - Discharged: 15 May 1819.

Benedict, Alvin - Private - 19th Infantry - Company: William Gill - Other regiments: 17th Infantry then 3rd Infantry - Age: 23 - Height: 5' 7" - Born: NY, Saratoga County, Ballstown - Trade: Laborer - Enlistment date: 13 Oct 1814 - Enlistment place: Delaware County - Enlistment period: 5 Yrs - By whom: William Gill - Comments: Deserted 15 Jun 1816.

Benjamin, Daniel - Private - 27th Infantry - Company: George Sanderson - Enlistment date: 27 Apr 1813.

Bennett, Archibald - Private - 19th Infantry - Company: James Herron - Enlistment date: 28 Aug 1812 - Enlistment period: 18 Mos.

Bennett, George - Private - 17th Infantry - Company: John Chunn - Age: 20 - Height: 5' 7" - Born: England - Trade: Laborer - Enlistment date: 5 Jan 1814 - Enlistment place: Franklin County, Franklinton - Enlistment period: War - By whom: John Cochran - Discharged: 25 Jul 1815 at Fort Meigs, OH - Pension: Wife Eliza, WO-40891, WC-31646; private in Capt. John T. Chunn's Company, 17th Infantry; first wife Mary Frankeburger; married Eliza in February 1855 in Princeton, IL; soldier died in 1866 in Bureau County, IL; widow died about 1888 - Bounty: BLW 24905-160-12 (Arkansas).

Bennett, Joshua - Private - 19th Infantry - Company: Richard Graham - Age: 22 - Height: 5' 8" - Born: New York - Trade: Blacksmith - Discharged: 30 Aug 1813 - Pension: Old War IF-25998, served as a private in Captain Richard Graham's Company, 19th Infantry - Comments: Discharged at Seneca Town, OH, on Surgeon's Certificate of Disability, lost an arm at Fort Meigs, 5 May 1813.

Bennett, Paul - Private - 19th Infantry - Company: James Herron - Enlistment date: 1 Sep 1812 - Enlistment period: 18 Mos.

Bennett, William - Private - 27th Infantry - Company: Isaac Van Horne - Enlistment date: 6 Jun 1813 - Discharged: 6 Jun 1814 - Pension: Wife Margaret Slusher, WO-29259, WC-23573, SO-18419, SC-11487, married on 18 Jan 1817 in Washington County, PA, soldier died on 10 Dec 1874 in Guernsey County, OH, widow died on 16 May 1883 in Salesville, OH, served in Captain Isaac Van Horne's Company, 27th US Infantry, lived in Guernsey County, OH - Bounty: BLW 3290-160-50.

Bennett, William - Private - 19th Infantry - Company: George Kesling - Other regiment: 17th Infantry - Age: 19 - Height: 5' 8" - Born: Virginia - Trade: Laborer - Enlistment date: 5 May 1814 - Enlistment place: Lebanon - Enlistment period: War - By whom: Richard Talbott - Discharged: 27 Mar 1815 at Zanesville - Bounty: BLW 4499-160-12 (Illinois).

Benson, John - Private - 19th Infantry - Company: Carey Trimble - Age: 18 - Height: 5' 7" - Born: Pennsylvania - Trade: Farmer - Enlistment date: 26 Apr 1814 - Enlistment place: Chillicothe - Enlistment period: War - By whom: Charles Cissna - Discharged: 6 Jun 1815 at Chillicothe - Bounty: BLW 11113-160-12 (Illinois).

Benton, Edward - 1st Rifles - Company: Thomas Ramsey - Age: 17 - Height: 5' 5" - Born: Vermont - Trade: Laborer - Enlistment date: 8 Feb 1814 - Enlistment place: Cincinnati - Enlistment period: 5 Yrs - By whom: Thomas Ramsey - Comments: Deserted at hospital, Buffalo, NY, 10 Nov 1814.

Benton, William - Private - 26th Infantry - Company: William Puthuff - Enlistment date: 17 May 1813 - Enlistment period: 1 Yr.

Bercaw – see Burcaw

Berlew – see Burlew, Daniel

Bernett, Robert - Private - 19th Infantry - Company: Richard Talbott.

Berry, Joseph - Corporal - 27th Infantry - Company: Absalom Martin - Enlistment date: 29 Apr 1813 - Enlistment place: St. Clairsville - Enlistment period: 1 Yr - Discharged: 28 Apr 1814 - Pension: Wife Margaret Rouse, WO-11043, WC-30622; married on 27 February 1817 in Mount Pleasant, Jefferson County, OH, soldier died on 5 Aug 1859 in Warren County, OH, widow died on 13 January 1884 in Tama City, Tama County, IA, served in Capt. Absalom Martin's Company, 27th Infantry, lived in Guernsey County, OH, widow lived also in Tama City, Tama County, IA - Bounty: BLW 1695-160-50 - Comments: Served aboard the US Schooner Scorpion on the Lake Erie Squadron.

Berryman, John - Private - 27th Infantry - Company: George Sanderson - Enlistment date: 19 Jun 1813.

Bessey, David - Private - 26th Infantry - Company: William Puthuff - Enlistment date: 18 Apr 1813 - Enlistment period: 1 Yr.

Best, George - Private - 19th Infantry - Company: James Herron - Enlistment date: 30 Oct 1812 - Enlistment period: 5 Yrs.

Beverly, John - Private - 2nd Artillery - Company: Daniel Cushing - Other regiment: Corps of Artillery - Age: 37 - Height: 5' 10" - Born: South Carolina - Trade: Laborer - Enlistment date: 21 Dec 1814 - Enlistment period: War - Discharged: 25 Jul 1815 - Bounty: BLW 747-320-14 (Illinois) - Comments: Discharged at Lower Sandusky (now Fremont, OH).

Bickel, Simon - Private - 19th Infantry - Company: John Chunn - Other regiment: 17th Infantry - Pension: Wife Catharine, Old War W-5827.

Bidlack, John - Private - 19th Infantry - Company: John Chunn - Enlistment date: 9 Apr 1813 - Enlistment period: War - Died: 1 Mar 1814 - Bounty: BLW 26389-160-12 (Arkansas) - Comments: Died about 1 Mar 1814; land bounty to Elizabeth Gilbert, daughter & other heirs at law of John Bidlack.

Biggs, Daniel - Private - 27th Infantry - Company: Absalom Martin - Enlistment date: 9 Apr 1813 - Discharged: 17 Mar 1814 - Pension: Wife Elizabeth Barrows, SO-8238, SC-5509; served in Capt. Absalom Martin's Company, 27th Infantry, lived in Warren County, IN - Bounty: BLW 7566-160-50.

Biggs, Daniel - Private - 27th Infantry - Company: Joel Collins - Other regiment: 19th Infantry - Age: 21 - Height: 5' 4" - Born: Virginia - Trade: Shoemaker - Enlistment date: 18 Mar 1814 - Enlistment place: Detroit - Enlistment period: War - By whom: Samuel Coleman - Discharged: 20 Jul 1815 at Detroit - Bounty: BLW 17533-160-12 (Illinois) - Comments: Re-enlisted.

Biggs, Josiah - Private - 27th Infantry - Company: Absalom Martin - Other regiment: 19th Infantry - Age: 19 - Height: 5' 7" - Born: Virginia - Trade: Farmer - Enlistment date: 10 Mar 1814 - Enlistment place: Detroit - Enlistment period: War - By whom: Samuel Coleman - Discharged: 20 Jul 1815 at Detroit - Bounty: BLW 17779-160-12 (Illinois) - Comments: Served aboard the US Schooner Scorpion on the Lake Erie Squadron.; re-enlisted.

Biggs, Willis - Private - 24th Infantry - Company: James Campbell - Enlistment date: Apr 1813 - Enlistment period: 5 Yrs - Died: Oct 1813/1814 - Pension: Wife Mary, Old War WF-14301; served in Capt. Campbell's Company, 24th Infantry in 1812, resided in TN - Bounty: BLW 9049-160-12 (Arkansas) - Comments: Died probably at Fort Ball, OH (now Tiffin, OH); land bounty to James Biggs & other heirs at law of Willis Biggs.

Billings, Thomas - Private - 27th Infantry - Company: George Sanderson - Enlistment date: 3 Jun 1813.

Birch, Daniel - Private - 19th Infantry - Company: Richard Talbott - Age: 40 - Height: 5' 9" - Born: Pennsylvania - Trade: Farmer - Enlistment date: 23 Mar 1814 - Enlistment place: Franklin County - Enlistment period: War - By whom: Robert Young - Discharged: 5 Jun 1815 at Chillicothe - Bounty: BLW 16778-160-12 (Missouri).

Bird, Johnston - Private - 19th Infantry - Company: William Gill.

Birdino – see Burdinaw, Charles

Bishop, Daniel - Private - 27th Infantry - Born: VT, Bennington County, Sandersland - Enlistment date: 4 Apr 1814 - Enlistment place: Worthington.

Bishop, Jacob - Fifer - 26th Infantry - Company: William Puthuff - Enlistment date: 19 Arp 1813 - Enlistment period: 1 Yr.

Bixler, Henry - Private - 27th Infantry - Company: George Sanderson - Enlistment date: 27 May 1813.

Black, James - Private - 26th Infantry - Company: Samuel Swearingen - Other regiment: 25th Infantry - Enlistment date: 6 Jun 1813 - Enlistment period: 1 Yr - Comments: Deserted at Geneva, NY, on 22 Mar 1814.

Black, John - Private - 26th Infantry - Company: George Kesling - Enlistment date: 8 May 1813 - Enlistment period: 1 Yr.

Black, William - Private - 19th Infantry - Company: William Gill - Bounty: BLW 5859-160-12 (Illinois).

Blackburn, James - Corporal - 19th Infantry - Company: Richard Talbott - Age: 29 - Height: 5' 8" - Born: Virginia - Trade: Carpenter - Enlistment date: 10 Jun 1814 - Enlistment place: Franklin County - Enlistment period: War - By whom: John Goode - Discharged: 5 Jun 1815 at Chillicothe - Pension: Served in Capt. Talbott's Company, 19th Infantry; born in VA - Bounty: BLW 13765-160-12 (Missouri).

Blackstone, Ebenezer - Private - 19th Infantry - Company: James Herron - Other regiment: 17th Infantry - Enlistment date: 15 Aug 1812 - Enlistment period: 5 Yrs - Bounty: BLW 23465-160-12 - Comments: Land bounty to Kennard Blackstone, son & other heirs at law of Ebenezer Blackstone.

Blagg, Joseph - Private - 1st Rifles - Company: Thomas Ramsey - Other regiment: Rifle Regiment - Age: 18 - Height: 5' 8" - Born: VA, Green County - Trade: Farmer - Enlistment date: 29 May 1813 - Enlistment place: Clinton County - Enlistment period: 5 Yrs - By whom: James Findley - Discharged: 29 May 1818 at Bellefontaine, MO - Pension: Wife Mary Dick, WC-27829; married on 21 Jan 1823 in Jefferson County, TN; soldier died on 26 Feb 1858 in Nodaway County, MO; wife died on 16 Dec 1880 in Barnard, MO; served in the companies of Ramsey, Morgan and McIntosh in the US Rifles.

Blair, Asahel - Private - 19th Infantry - Company: David Holt - Other regiment: 17th Infantry - Age: 35 - Height: 5' 10" - Born: Massachusetts - Enlistment date: 4 May 1814 - Enlistment place: Trumbull County, Warren - Enlistment period: War - By whom: Wilson Elliott - Died: 13 Nov 1814 at Buffalo, NY - Pension: Wife Anna Pulsifer, Old War Pension WF-10935, private in 19th Infantry; land bounty to Arlina Blair, daughter and heirs at law of Asahel Blair - Bounty: BLW 8831-160-12.

Blair, Daniel - Private - 19th Infantry - Company: Angus Langham - Age: 26 - Height: 5' 7" - Born: NJ, Morris County - Enlistment date: 16 Jul 1812 - Enlistment place: St. Clairsville - Enlistment period: 18 Mos.

Blake, Henry T. - Drummer - 27th Infantry - Company: Isaac Van Horne - Other regiment: 19th Infantry - Age: 23 - Height: 5' 11" - Born: Massachusetts - Trade: Baker - Enlistment date: 21 Mar 1814 - Enlistment place: Detroit - Enlistment period: War - By whom: Wynkoop Warner - Discharged: 20 Jul 1815 at Detroit - Pension: Old War IF-6661, served as a musician in Capt. Isaac Van Horne's Company, 19th Infantry - Bounty: BLW 4096-160-12 (Arkansas) - Comments: Prisoner of War on Parole, captured at Detroit, MI, 16 Aug 1812; re-enlisted.

Blake, Nehemiah - Private - 27th Infantry - Company: Joseph Cairns - Enlistment date: 12 Apr 1812 - Enlistment period: 1 Yr - Discharged: 12 Apr 1813 - Pension: SO-12465, SC-11614, served in Capt. Joseph Cairne's Company, 27th Infantry lived in Louisa County, IA - Bounty: BLW 3330-160-50 - Comments: Prisoner of War on Parole, captured at Detroit, MI, 16 Aug 1812.

Blake, Thomas J. - Private - 27th Infantry - Company: Isaac Van Horne - Pension: Old War IF-6669; served in Capt. Van Horn's company, 1st Dragoons, in 1813.

Blakeman, Nathan - Sergeant - 19th Infantry - Company: James Herron - Other regiment: 17th Infantry - Enlistment date: 16 Dec 1812 - Enlistment period: 18 Mos - Comments: Re-enlisted.

Blanchard, Benjamin - Private - 19th Infantry

Blanchard, Enoch - Sergeant - 2nd Artillery - Company: Daniel Cushing - Age: 26 - Height: 5' 9" - Born: VT, Windham County, Brattleboro - Trade: Farmer - Enlistment date: 3 Feb 1813 - Enlistment place: Lebanon - Enlistment period: War - By whom: Alexander Meek - Discharged: 8 May 1815 - Bounty: BLW 26872-160-12 (Arkansas).

Blanchard, Labin - Private - 19th Infantry - Company: James Herron - Enlistment date: 3 Oct 1812 - Enlistment period: 18 Mos.

Blanchard, Moses - Musician - 2nd Artillery - Company: Daniel Cushing.

Blaney, David L. - Private - 27th Infantry - Company: Joseph Cairns - Comments: Served aboard the US Sloop Trippe on the Lake Erie Squadron.

Bledsoe, Jacob - Private - 19th Infantry - Company: William MacDonald - Died: 15 Oct 1814 at Williamsville, NY (hospital), buried in the War of 1812 Cemetery in Cheektowaga, Erie County, NY.

Blue, Frederick - Private - 19th Infantry - Company: William Gill - Other regiment: 17th Infantry - Age: 27 - Height: 5' 11" - Born: NY, New York County - Trade: Joiner - Enlistment date: 18 Apr 1814 - Enlistment place: Chillicothe - Enlistment period: 5 Yrs - By whom: Charles Cissna - Discharged: 18 Apr 1819 - Pension: Old War IF-12507 Rejected; served in the 17th Infantry in 1812.

Bogard, John - Private - 2nd Rifles - Company: Wyle Martin - Age: 19 - Height: 5' 10" - Born: Kentucky - Trade: Laborer - Enlistment date: 19 Aug 1814 - Enlistment place: Scioto County - Enlistment period: 5 Yrs - By whom: Abner Harrison - Discharged: 19 Aug 1819 - Bounty: BLW 23033-160-12 (Arkansas) - Comments: Discharged at Martin's Cantonment, AK (a military headquarters).

Bolden, Samuel L. - Private - 2nd Artillery - Company: Daniel Cushing - Other regiment: Corps of Artillery - Age: 40 - Height: 5' 10" - Born: New Jersey - Trade: Blacksmith - Enlistment date: 20 May 1814 - Enlistment period: War - Discharged: 28 Jul 1815 at Lower Sandusky (now Fremont, OH).

Bolser, Henry - Private - 2nd Artillery - Company: Daniel Cushing - Other regiment: Corps of Artillery - Age: 25 - Height: 5' 10" - Born: Pennsylvania - Trade: Blacksmith - Enlistment date: 4 Feb 1814 - Enlistment place: Lebanon - Enlistment period: 5 Yrs - By whom: Daniel Cushing - Discharged: 4 Feb 1816 at Detroit -

Comments: Discharged after furnishing a substitute (John Dennin).

Bonnel – see Bunnell, Paul

Bonner, Arthur - Private - 17th Infantry - Company: Caleb Holder - Other regiment: 3rd Infantry - Age: 57 - Height: 5' 11" - Born: MD, Harford County - Trade: Farmer - Enlistment date: 10 Sep 1813 - Enlistment place: Cincinnati - Enlistment period: 18 Mos - By whom: Philip Price - Discharged: 9 Nov 1815 - Comments: Discharged at Newport, KY, in consequence of old age.

Bonner, William - Corporal - 2nd Artillery - Company: Daniel Cushing - Other regiment: Corps of Artillery - Age: 21 - Height: 5' 6" - Born: KY, Cynthiana County, Harrison - Trade: Farmer - Enlistment date: 25 Apr 1812 - Enlistment place: Chillicothe - Enlistment period: 5 Yrs - By whom: Lieutenant Kercheval - Discharged: 25 Apr 1817 - Comments: Served aboard the US Sloop Trippe on the Lake Erie Squadron.

Bonvill, Lewis - Private - 19th Infantry - Company: James Herron.

Boodle, John - Private - 26th Infantry - Enlistment date: 20 May 1813 - Enlistment period: 1 Yr.

Boone, John - Private - 19th Infantry - Company: James Herron - Other regiment: 17th Infantry - Enlistment date: 6 Aug 1812 - Enlistment period: 18 Mos - Discharged: 13 Aug 1813 - Pension: Wife Margaret Cooper, WO-11632, WC-9419; married on 25 Jan 1816 in Adams County, OH; soldier died on 2 Dec 1841/42; widow died on 25 Oct 1884; served in Lt. Campbell's Company, 17th Infantry; lived in Adams County, OH - Bounty: BLW 2591-160-50.

Boose, Michael R. - 26th Infantry - Other regiment: 25th Infantry - Enlistment date: 25 Apr 1813 - Discharged: 28 Feb 1814 - Pension: Wife Julia A. Atkins, SO-11010, SC-6761, WO-12781, WC-18836; private in Capt. Bartholomew Fryatt's Company, OH Militia; Capt. Puthuff's Company, 26th Infantry; and Capt. George Howard's Company, 25th Infantry; first wife Wheeler, married on 21 Aug 1851 in Lafayette, IN; soldier died on 4 Feb 1878, Clarks Hill, Tippecanoe County, IN; widow died about 1892 - Bounty: BLW 2324-160-50.

Boothe, Charles - Private - 19th Infantry - Company: Asabael Nearing - Enlistment date: 30 Jan 1813 - Enlistment period: War - Died: 31 Aug 1813 probably at Lower Sandusky (now Fremont, OH), about 31 Aug 1813 - Pension: Heirs obtained half pay for five years in lieu of military bounty land.

Boothe, John - Private - 17th Infantry - Company: David Holt - Age: 21 - Height: 5' 9" - Born: Virginia - Trade: Hatter - Enlistment date: 12 Jun 1814 - Enlistment period: War - By whom: William Shang - Bounty: BLW 18001-160-12 (Illinois).

Boston, John - Private - 26th Infantry - Company: Samuel Swearingen - Other regiment: 25th Infantry - Enlistment date: 8 May 1813 - Enlistment period: 1 Yr - Died: 2 May 1814 at Batavia, NY.

Boucher, John - Private - 19th Infantry - Company: William Gill.

Bounds, Thomas - Private - 19th Infantry - Company: Wilson Elliott - Other regiment: 17th Infantry.

Bourn, William - Private - 19th Infantry - Enlistment date: 10 Apr 1813 - Enlistment place: Cincinnati - Enlistment period: 18 Mos.

Bow, Curtis - 19th Infantry - Died: 8 Jul 1814, executed at Chillicothe.

Bowen, William - Private - 19th Infantry - Company: Wilson Elliott.

Bowman, Enoch - Corporal - 2nd Artillery - Company: Daniel Cushing - Died: 1 Dec 1813, probably at Detroit.

Bowman, Gilbert - Private - 26th Infantry - Company: Samuel Swearingen - Enlistment date: 23 May 1813 - Enlistment period: 1 Yr - Died: 8 Nov 1813 - Comments: Served aboard the US Schooner Ariel on the Lake Erie Squadron; died at Fort Schlosser, NY.

Bowman, John - Private - 27th Infantry - Company: Alexander Hill.

Bowman, John - Private - 2nd Rifles - Company: Batteal Harrison - Other regiment: Rifle Regiment - Age: 28 - Height: 5' 9" - Born: VA, Shenandoah County - Trade: Farmer - Enlistment date: 28 May 1814 - Enlistment place: Highland County, Hillsboro - Enlistment period: 5 Yrs - By whom: Joseph McClain - Discharged: 28 May 1819 at Martin's Cantonment - Bounty: BLW 22545-160-12 (Arkansas).

Boyd, Cornelius - Private - 17th Infantry - Company: Harris Hickman - Age: 29 - Height: 5' 10 1/2" - Born: PA, Cumberland County - Trade: Laborer - Enlistment date: 15 Oct 1813 - Enlistment place: Harrison County, Cadiz - Enlistment period: War - By whom: John Milligan

Boyd, Francis - Private - 19th Infantry - Age: 27 - Height: 5' 10 1/2" - Born: Maryland - Enlistment date: 31 Mar 1814 - Enlistment place: Lebanon - Enlistment period: 18 Mos - By whom: Adam Hoffman.

Boyd, Francis - 2nd Rifles - Age: 27 - Height: 5' 8 3/4" - Born: MD, Cecil County - Trade: Saddler - Enlistment date: 25 May 1814 - Enlistment place: Chillicothe - Enlistment period: 5 Yrs - By whom: Batteal Harrison - Discharged: 22 Sep 1815 at Detroit inability, abscess in jaw.

Boyler, Thomas - Private - 27th Infantry - Company: George Sanderson - Enlistment date: 16 Apr 1813 - Bounty: BLW 4945-160-12.

Bradbury, William - Corporal - 26th Infantry (new) - Company: William Bezeau - Age: 25 - Height: 5' 10" - Born:

Ohio - Trade: Farmer - Enlistment date: 19 Oct 1814 - Enlistment place: PA, Philadelphia County - Enlistment period: 5 Yrs - By whom: William Bezeau - Discharged: 27 Mar 1815 at Philadelphia, PA (Colored).

Braden, James - Private - 27th Infantry - Company: George Sanderson - Enlistment date: 23 Jul 1813.

Bradley, Edward - Private - 19th Infantry - Company: George Kesling - Age: 18 - Height: 5' 8" - Born: Kentucky - Trade: Blacksmith - Enlistment date: 21 Feb 1815 - Enlistment place: Cincinnati - Enlistment period: War - By whom: William Baird - Discharged: 27 Mar 1815 at Zanesville.

Bradley, William - Private - 19th Infantry - Company: Joel Collins - Age: 24 - Height: 5' 10" - Born: Pennsylvania - Trade: Laborer - Enlistment date: 16 Mar 1814 - Enlistment place: Detroit - Enlistment period: War - By whom: Warner - Discharged: 19 Jul 1815 - Bounty: BLW 10012-160-12.

Brady, Eli - Private - 27th Infantry - Company: Joel Collins - Other regiment: 19th Infantry - Age: 27 - Height: 5' 9" - Born: Virginia - Trade: Shoemaker - Enlistment date: 7 Jul 1813 - Bounty: BLW 5545-160-12 (Illinois) - Comments: Re-enlisted at Detroit on 31 Mar 1814 for during the war enlistment with Lieutenant Warner.

Brady, Henry - Private - 27th Infantry - Company: Joseph Carins - Enlistment date: 2 Jun 1813 - Enlistment period: 1 Yr - Discharged: 1 Jun 1814 - Pension: Wife Mary A., SO-8986, SC-12586, WO-43913, WC-34278; served as a private in Capt. Joseph Carin's Company, 27th Infantry; first wife was Hannah Dunn; married on 29 Mar 1865 in Indianapolis, IN; soldier died on 2 Jun 1885 in Marion County, IN; widow died about 1905 - Bounty: BLW 2301-160-50.

Brady, James - Private - 19th Infantry - Company: William Gill.

Bramblet, Elkana - Private - 26th Infantry - Company: George Kesling - Other regiment: 25th Infantry - Enlistment date: 5 May 1813 - Enlistment period: 1 Yr - Discharged: 5 May 1814.

Brannon, Henry - Private - 26th Infantry - Company: Samuel Swearingen - Enlistment date: 10 Jul 1813 - Enlistment period: 1 Yr - Pension: Old War IF-12718 Rejected; served as a private in the 3rd Company, Light Infantry, 26th Infantry during the War of 1812.

Brascott – see Brently, Benjamin

Brears, Benjamin - Private - 19th Infantry - Company: John Chunn - Other regiment: 3rd Infantry - Bounty: BLW 21397-160-12 (Missouri).

Breckinridge, Alexander - Private - 19th Infantry - Company: George Kesling - Other regiment: 3rd Infantry - Age: 26 - Height: 5' 11" - Born: Pennsylvania - Trade: Farmer - Enlistment date: 14 Nov 1814 - Enlistment place: Franklin County, Franklinton - Enlistment period: 5 Yrs - By whom: Orren Granger - Comments: Deserted at Franklinton, OH, on 24 Sep 1815.

Brently, Benjamin - Private - 26th Infantry - Company: William Puthuff - Enlistment date: 12 May 1813 - Enlistment period: 1 Yr - Discharged: 11 May 1814 - Pension: Wife Ellendor Richards, SO-11720, SC-6820; served as a private in Capt. W. H. Puthoff's Company, 26th Infantry; married on 20 Nov 1864 in Rensselaer, Jasper County, IN, lived in Champaign County, OH, in 1850; lived in Jasper County, IN, in 1871 - Bounty: BLW 4870-160-50.

Brewer, Enoch - Private - 19th Infantry - Company: William Gill - Age: 19 - Height: 6' 1" - Born: North Carolina - Trade: Farmer - Enlistment date: 27 Sep 1814 - Enlistment place: Canton - Enlistment period: War - By whom: Wynkoop Warner - Comments: Deserted at Zanesville, OH, 28 Nov 1814.

Brewer, Enoch - Private - 26th Infantry - Company: Samuel Swearingen - Enlistment date: 13 Jul 1813 - Enlistment period: 1 Yr - Comments: Deserted at Upper Sandusky, OH, 8 Aug 1813.

Brewer, William - Private - 19th Infantry - Company: George Kesling - Age: 18 - Height: 5' 6" - Born: Virginia - Trade: Blacksmith - Enlistment date: 10 Jan 1814 - Enlistment place: Xenia - Enlistment period: War - By whom: Lieutenant Smith - Discharged: 27 Mar 1815 at Zanesville - Bounty: BLW 336-320-14.

Briant – see Bryant, Charles E.

Bridges, William - Private - 19th Infantry - Company: John McElvain - Enlistment date: 4 Jun 1814 - Discharged: 6 Jun 1815 - Pension: Wife Elizabeth Kelly, WO-13949, WC-24631; married 10 Feb 1825 in Pike County, OH; soldier died on 25 May 1854 in Green County, WI; widow died circa 1892; served in Lt. McElvine's Company, 19th Infantry; lived in Green County, WI - Bounty: BLW 6041-160-12 (Arkansas).

Brierly, Robert - Private - 17th Infantry - Company: William Adair - Enlistment date: 21 May 1814 - Discharged: 4 Jun 1815 - Pension: Wife Jane, WO-26764, WC-20886; served as a private in Lt. Hawkins' Detachment, 17th Infantry; married on 18 Mar 1832 in Gallia County, OH; soldier died on 20 Mar 1864 in Bracken County, KY; widow died on 24 Dec 1891; lived in Gallipolis, OH, in 1857 and 1858, and Racine, Meigs County, OH, in 1878 - Bounty: BLW 6122-160-12.

Bright, George - Corporal - 19th Infantry - Company: Wilson Elliott - Age: 27 - Height: 6' - Born: VA, Augusta County - Enlistment date: 2 Aug 1812 - Enlistment period: 18 Mos.

The Enlisted Men

Briney, John - Private - 2nd Artillery - Company: Daniel Cushing.

Brison, George - Private - 26th Infantry - Company: Joel Collins - Enlistment date: 25 Apr 1813 - Enlistment period: 1 Yr - By whom: Robert Smith - Comments: Deserted 15 Oct 1813.

Bromwell, John - Private - 27th Infantry - Company: William Gill - Comments: Served aboard the US Brig Niagara on the Lake Erie Squadron.

Brooks, James - Private - 27th Infantry - Company: Alexander Hill - Other regiment: 19th Infantry - Bounty: BLW 5860-160-12 (Illinois).

Brosius, Jacob - Private - 27th Infantry - Company: Alexander Hill - Other regiment: 19th Infantry.

Browden, James - Private - Rangers - Company: Samuel McCormick - Enlistment date: 6 Dec 1813 - Enlistment period: 1 Yr - Discharged: 6 Dec 1814.

Brown, Abner - Private - 19th Infantry - Company: John Chunn.

Brown, Frederick - Private - 19th Infantry - Company: Carey Trimble - Age: 21 - Height: 5' 6" - Born: North or South Carolina - Trade: Farmer - Enlistment date: 21 Apr 1814 - Enlistment place: Chillicothe - Enlistment period: War - By whom: Charles Cissna - Discharged: 6 Jun 1815 at Chillicothe - Bounty: BLW 6592-160-12 (Illinois).

Brown, Gilbert - Private - 26th Infantry - Company: William Puthuff - Enlistment date: 22 May 1813 - Enlistment period: 1 Yr.

Brown, Henry - Private - Rangers - Company: James Manary - Enlistment date: 16 Mar 1812 - Enlistment period: 1 Yr - Discharged: 16 Mar 1813 - Pension: Wife Jane Gormly, WO-10312, WC-5560; served as a private in Capt. James Manary's Company, US Rangers; married on 22 Nov 1814 at Big Walnut Creek, Pickaway County, OH; soldier died on 8 Nov 1858 in Armysburg, IN; widow died about 1879 in Rockville, IN - Bounty: BLW 22376-160-50.

Brown, Hugh - Private - 17th Infantry - Company: David Holt - Age: 25 - Height: 5' 6 1/2" - Born: PA, Northumberland County - Trade: Shoemaker - Enlistment date: 25 Jun 1814 - Enlistment place: New Lisbon - Enlistment period: War - By whom: Thomas McKnight - Discharged: 4 Jun 1815 at Chillicothe- Bounty: BLW 9995-160-13 (Illinois).

Brown, Jacob - Private - 17th Infantry - Age: 49 - Height: 5' 10" - Born: Germany - Trade: Laborer - Enlistment date: 17 Jan 1815 - Enlistment place: Cincinnati - Enlistment period: War - By whom: Russell Reese - Discharged: 10 Jul 1815 at Chillicothe - Bounty: BLW 373-320-14 (Illinois).

Brown, James - Private - 27th Infantry - Company: George Sanderson - Enlistment date: 27 Apr 1813 - Comments: Prisoner of War on Parole, captured at Detroit, MI, 16 Aug 1812.

Brown, James - Private - 19th Infantry - Company: Richard Talbott - Pension: Wife Mary or Polly, WO-25662; served as a private in Capt. Talbert's Company, 19th Infantry and Captains Howell'and Ross Companies, OH militia.

Brown, John - Private - 19th Infantry - Company: William Adair - Other regiment: 17th Infantry - Died: 11 Jan 1815 - Pension: Old War IF-26549; served as a private in Lt. Steward's 17th and 19th Infantries - Bounty: BLW 18312-160-12 (Illinois) - Comments: Died in New York; buried in the War of 1812 Cemetery in Cheektowaga, Erie County, NY.

Brown, John - 19th Infantry - Company: Richard Talbott - Pension: Wife Mary or Polly, WO-25662; served in Captain Howell's and Captain Ross' Companies, OH Militia, and in Captain Talbert's Company, 19th Infantry.

Brown, John - Corporal - 27th Infantry - Company: William Gill - Other regiment: 19th Infantry - Comments: Served aboard the US Sloop Trippe on the Lake Erie Squadron.

Brown, Joseph - Private - 19th Infantry - Company: William Gill - Bounty: BLW 20215-160-12 (Missouri).

Brown, Solomon - Private - 19th Infantry - Company: James Herron - Enlistment date: 13 Oct 1812 - Enlistment period: 18 Mos.

Brown, William - Private - 3rd Infantry - Company: Gray - Pension: Old War IF-6742.

Brown, William - 19th Infantry - Company: William Gill.

Browne, David - Private - 24th Infantry - Died: 10 Aug 1813, probably at Fort Meigs.

Brownlee, David - 27th Infantry - Company: James Applegate - Pension: SO-24853, served in Capt. Applegate's Company, 27th Infantry.

Bruce, Achilles - Private - 1st Rifles - Company: Thomas Ramsey - Age: 22 - Height: 5' 11" - Born: Virginia - Trade: Laborer - Enlistment date: 11 Jan 1814 - Enlistment place: Cincinnati - Enlistment period: 5 Yrs - By whom: Thomas Ramsey - Bounty: BLW 20743-160-12 (Missouri).

Bruff, James - Private - 26th Infantry - Company: Samuel Swearingen - Other regiment: Light Dragoons Regiment - Enlistment date: 13 Jul 1813 - Discharged: 20 Jul 1814 - Pension: Wife Matilda Coker, SC-11524; married on 8 Oct 1818 in Livingston County, KY; soldier died circa 1883; served in Capt. Swearingen's Company, 26th Infantry; lived in Union County, IL - Bounty: BLW 9038-160-50.

Brunson, Alfred - Sergeant - 27th Infantry - Company: Isaac Van Horne - Enlistment date: 22 May 1813 - Enlistment period: 1 Yr - Discharged: 22 May 1814 - Pension: Wife Eunice Burr, SO-25208 Rejected; served as a sergeant in Capt. Van Horn's Company, 27th Infantry; married on 3 Apr 1861 in Sextonville, Richland County, WI; second wife Caroline S. Birge then Malinda Richards; soldier died on 3 Aug 1882; soldier lived in Crawford County, WI - Bounty: BLW 13143-160-50.

Brusus, Jacob - Private - 19th Infantry - Company: John McElvain - Pension: Old War IF-9720; served in Lt. Featherstone's Company, 19th Infantry in 1814 - Bounty: BLW 2034-160-42 (Illinois).

Bryan, Aaron - Private - 19th Infantry - Company: Joel Collins - Age: 30 - Height: 5' 9" - Born: Pennsylvania - Trade: Laborer - Enlistment date: 2 Mar 1814 - Enlistment place: Detroit - Enlistment period: War - By whom: Wynkoop Warner.

Bryan, Cornelius - Private - 19th Infantry - Age: 37 - Height: 5' 10 1/2" - Born: VA, Rockingham County - Enlistment date: 1 Jul 1812 - Enlistment period: 5 Yrs.

Bryan, Daniel - Private - 19th Infantry - Age: 19 - Height: 5' 8 1/2" - Born: OH, Fairfield County - Enlistment date: 7 Sep 1814 - Enlistment place: Canton.

Bryan, Farren W. - Private - 19th Infantry - Company: Richard Talbott - Age: 21 - Height: 5' 8" - Born: Pennsylvania - Trade: Ship's carpenter - Enlistment date: 11 May 1814 - Enlistment place: Cincinnati - Enlistment period: War - By whom: Robert Anderson.

Bryant, Charles E. - Sergeant - 17th Infantry - Company: Harris Hickman - Age: 20 - Height: 5' 6 1/4" - Born: VA, Brook County - Trade: Carpenter - Enlistment date: 20 Mar 1814 - Enlistment place: Chillicothe - Enlistment period: War - By whom: Batteal Harrison - Discharged: 9 Jun 1815 at Chillicothe - Bounty: BLW 3179-160-12.

Buchanan, John - Private - 2nd Artillery - Company: Daniel Cushing.

Buck, Benjamin - Private - 1st Rifles - Company: Thomas Ramsey - Age: 22 - Height: 5' 8" - Born: VT, Bennington County - Trade: Carpenter - Enlistment date: 12 May 1814 - Enlistment place: Cincinnati - Enlistment period: War - By whom: Thomas Ramsey - Died: 30 May 1815 at Conjocta Creek, NY, of sickness.

Buck, James - Private - 19th Infantry - Company: George Kesling - Enlistment date: 25 Jun 1814 - Enlistment period: War - Killed: 15 Aug 1814 at Fort Erie, UC - Bounty: BLW 25752-160-12 (Arkansas) - Comments: Land bounty to John Buck, father & only heir at law of James Buck.

Buck, John - Private - 19th Infantry - Bounty: BLW 5236-160-12 (Illinois).

Buck, Joseph - Private - 17th Infantry - Company: David Holt - Age: 16 - Height: 5' 4" - Born: Ohio - Trade: Farmer - Enlistment date: 9 Jun 1814 - Enlistment period: War - By whom: Benjamin Griffith - Bounty: BLW 6042-160-12 (Arkansas).

Buckles, Robert - Private - 19th Infantry - Company: James Herron - Enlistment date: 6 Oct 1812 - Enlistment period: 18 Mos.

Buckley, Cornelius - Private - 19th Infantry - Company: William Gill - Other regiment: 17th Infantry then 3rd Infantry - Age: 37 - Height: 5' 7" - Born: Ireland, County Cork - Trade: Farmer - Enlistment date: 5 Aug 1814 - Enlistment place: Chillicothe - Enlistment period: 5 Yrs - By whom: Charles Cissna - Comments: Deserted 6 May 1816.

Buckley, Ebenezer - Private - 27th Infantry - Company: William Gill - Other regiment: 19th Infantry - Age: 26 - Height: 5' 7" - Born: Connecticut - Trade: Joiner - Enlistment date: 4 May 1814 - Enlistment period: War - By whom: John Reeves - Discharged: 5 Jun 1815 at Chillicothe - Bounty: BLW 19457-160-12 (Illinois).

Buckover, Peter - Private - 19th Infantry - Company: John Chunn - Other regiment: 17th Infantry - Comments: Prisoner of War, exchanged 25 Apr 1814.

Buley, Nathan - Private - 19th Infantry - Bounty: BLW 22696-160-12 (Arkansas).

Bullard, John - Musician - 24th Infantry - Company: Robert Desha - Other regiment: 7th Infantry - Age: 13 - Height: 5' 7 1/2" - Born: Ohio - Trade: Farmer - Enlistment date: 25 Jun 1812 - Enlistment place: West Tennessee - Enlistment period: 5 Yrs - By whom: Avery Clark.

Bullman, Jonathan - Private - 19th Infantry - Company: Wilson Elliott - Other regiment: 17th Infantry - Age: 39 - Height: 5' 8" - Born: NJ, Morris County - Enlistment date: 18 Aug 1812 - Enlistment period: 18 Mos - Comments: Re-enlisted.

Bumgardner, Christian - Private - 17th Infantry - Company: Caleb Holder - Age: 21 - Height: 5' 9 1/2" - Born: Germany - Trade: Soldier - Enlistment date: 14 Aug 1814 - Enlistment place: Steubenville - Enlistment period: War - By whom: William Featherstone - Discharged: 11 Jul 1815 at Chillicothe - Bounty: BLW

3482-160-12 (Illinois).

Bumgardner, Nicholas - Private - 27th Infantry - Company: Alexander Hill.

Bumgardner, Peter - Private - 26th Infantry - Pension: Wife Frances, Old War IF-12911; served as a private in the 26th Infantry.

Bunnell, Brasilla - Private - 26th Infantry - Company: George Kesling - Other regiment: 19th Infantry - Age: 20 - Height: 5' 7" - Born: Kentucky - Trade: Farmer - Enlistment date: 7 May 1813 - Enlistment period: 1 Yr - Comments: Re-enlisted at Sandwich, UC, 14 Apr 1814, during the war enlistment.

Bunnell, Paul - Private - 17th Infantry - Age: 44 - Height: 6' - Born: New Jersey - Trade: Sawyer - Enlistment date: 1 Feb 1815 - Enlistment period: War - By whom: James Campbell - Discharged: 18 Apr 1815 - Bounty: BLW 1058-320-14 (Arkansas) - Comments: Discharged at Chillicothe; land bounty to Elizabeth Caldwell, daughter & other heirs at law of Paul Bonnel.

Bunnell, William - Private - 19th Infantry - Company: William MacDonald - Enlistment date: 27 Jun 1813 - Discharged: 27 Jul 1814 - Pension: SO-17315, SC-17424, served in Lt. William McDonald's Company, 19th Infantry lived in Jasper County, IN, and in Harrison County, MO - Bounty: BLW 6183-160-50.

Burcaw, Gilbert - Private - 26th Infantry - Company: George Kesling - Other regiment: Light Dragoons Regiment - Enlistment date: 22 Apr 1813 - Enlistment period: 1 Yr - Pension: Wife Elizabeth, Old War W-12283; served as a private in the 26th Infantry.

Burcaw, Peter - Private - 26th Infantry - Company: George Kesling - Other regiment: Light Dragoons Regiment - Enlistment date: 19 Apr 1813 - Enlistment period: 1 Yr - Comments: Prisoner of War on Parole, captured at Detroit, MI, 16 Aug 1812.

Burdinaw, Charles - Private - 27th Infantry - Company: George Sanderson - Other regiment: 19th Infantry - Age: 41 - Height: 5' 10" - Born: Vermont - Trade: Laborer - Enlistment date: 16 Mar 1814 - Enlistment place: Detroit - Enlistment period: War - By whom: Wynkoop Warner - Discharged: 20 Jul 1815 at Detroit - Pension: Old War IF-12454; served in Capt Shephard's Company, OH militia, Captains Hill, Spencer and Sanuderson's Companies, 27th Infantry; and Captains Collins and Holmes Companies, 19th Infantry - Bounty: BLW 3809-160-12 (Illinois) - Comments: Re-enlisted.

Burgess, Henry - Private - 28th Infantry - Company: Benjamin Mosbey - Enlistment date: 17 Jun 1813 - Enlistment period: 1 Yr - Died: 5 Sep 1813 at Fort Seneca (now Old Fort, OH).

Burch – see Birch, Daniel

Burk, Edward - Private - 1st Rifles - Company: Thomas Ramsey - Age: 24 - Height: 5' 7" - Born: VA, Rockbridge County - Trade: Farmer - Enlistment date: 4 May 1814 - Enlistment place: Cincinnati - Enlistment period: War - By whom: Thomas Ramsey - Discharged: 20 Aug 1815 - Comments: Prisoner of War (Quebec, LC), captured at Fort Erie, UC, 17 Sep 1814; sent to Halifax, NS, 8 Nov 1814; released 10 Apr 1815, discharged at New London, CT.

Burk, John - Private - 19th Infantry - Company: John McElvain.

Burlew, Daniel - Private - 2nd Rifles - Company: Batteal Harrison - Age: 33 - Height: 5' 9" - Born: MD, Baltimore County - Trade: Carpenter - Enlistment date: 22 May 1814 - Enlistment place: Cincinnati - Enlistment period: War - By whom: Edward Miller - Discharged: 30 Jun 1815 at Detroit - Bounty: BLW 12165-160-12 (Illinois).

Burnet, Nehemiah - Private - 19th Infantry - Age: 21 - Height: 6' 1 1/2" - Born: PA, Luzerne County - Enlistment date: 24 Jun 1812 - Enlistment period: 5 Yrs - Comments: Deserted.

Burns, Francis - Private - 26th Infantry - Company: Samuel Swearingen - Other regiment: 25th Infantry - Age: 23 - Height: 5' 8 1/2" - Enlistment date: 29 Jul 1813 - Enlistment period: 1 Yr - Discharged: 21 Jun 1814 - Comments: Served aboard the US Schooner Ariel on the Lake Erie Squadron.

Burns, James - Private - 19th Infantry - Company: William Gill - Bounty: BLW 6970-160-12 (Illinois).

Burr, Aaron - Sergeant - 17th Infantry - Company: David Holt - Died: 19 Aug 1813 - Bounty: BLW 19673-160-12 (Illinois) - Comments: Land bounty to Philip Burr, father and heir at law of Aaron Burr.

Burris, John - 27th Infantry - Company: Joseph Cairns - Pension: Old War IF-12872 Rejected, served as a private in Capt. Cairne's Company, 27th Infantry.

Burriss, Bassell - Private - 28th Infantry - Company: Joseph Belt - Enlistment date: 5 May 1813 - Enlistment period: 1 Yr - Died: 2 Sep 1813 at Fort Seneca (now Old Fort, OH).

Burriss, John - Private - 19th Infantry - Company: Joel Collins - Bounty: BLW 9598-160-12 (Missouri).

Burroughs, Thomas Newton - Musician - 26th Infantry - Company: Nimrod Moore - Enlistment date: 17 Jun 1813 - Enlistment period: 1 Yr - Discharged: 28 Jun 1814 - Pension: Wife Ann D., SO-6620, SC-7457, WO-19927, SC-17623; served as a musician in Capt. Moore's Company, 26th Infantry; first wife Rebecca; soldier died on 18 Aug 1846 in Cincinnati, OH; widow died on 12 Nov 1874 in Ripley County, IN - Bounty: BLW

5959-160-50.
- **Burt, John S.** - Private - 1st Rifles - Company: Thomas Ramsey - Age: 23 - Height: 5' 5" - Born: New York - Trade: Shoemaker - Enlistment date: 25 Jun 1814 - Enlistment place: Greenville - Enlistment period: War - By whom: Thomas Ramsey - Discharged: 5 Jun 1815 at Buffalo, NY - Bounty: BLW 6044-160-.
- **Burton, Charles** - Private - 26th Infantry - Company: Joel Collins - Enlistment date: 7 Jul 1813 - Enlistment period: 1 Yr - Died: 5 Jan 1814, probably at Detroit.
- **Burton, Daniel** - Sergeant - 17th Infantry - Company: Harris Hickman - Age: 19 - Height: 5' 9 1/2" - Born: MA, Hampshire County, Vorage - Trade: Farmer - Enlistment date: 27 Oct 1812 - Enlistment place: Warren County - Enlistment period: War - By whom: William Leavitt - Discharged: 9 Jun 1815 at Chillicothe - Bounty: BLW 2660-160-12 (Illinois).
- **Bush, George** - Corporal - 17th Infantry - Company: Harris Hickman - Age: 20 - Height: 5' 10" - Born: VA, Harrison County - Trade: Farmer - Enlistment date: 30 Mar 1814 - Enlistment place: Chillicothe - Enlistment period: War - By whom: Batteal Harrison - Discharged: 9 Jun 1815 at Chillicothe - Bounty: BLW 11570-160-12 (Illinois).
- **Bush, Jacob** - Private - 19th Infantry - Company: Cary Trimble - Enlistment date: 19 Feb 1814 - Discharged: 19 Feb 1815 - Pension: Wife Julia Prosser, SO-4629, SC-19938; served as a private in Capt. C. A. Trimble's Company, 19th Infantry; married in Newark, OH; soldier died about 1881; lived in Licking County, OH - Bounty: BLW 17555-160-50.
- **Bussey, John** - Private - 27th Infantry - Company: George Sanderson - Enlistment date: 26 Apr 1813.
- **Butler, Asaph** - Private - 27th Infantry - Comments: Prisoner of War on Parole, captured at Detroit, MI, 16 Aug 1812.
- **Byard, John** - Private - 17th Infantry - Company: David Holt - Age: 35 - Height: 6' 1" - Born: Pennsylvania - Trade: Laborer - Enlistment date: 29 Apr 1814 - Enlistment period: War - By whom: George Bryant
- **Byron, John** - Private - 27th Infantry - Comments: Prisoner of War on Parole, captured at Detroit, MI, 16 Aug 1812.
- **Byrum, William** - Private - 19th Infantry - Age: 20 - Height: 5' 9 1/2" - Born: Maryland - Enlistment date: 7 Apr 1814 - Enlistment place: Marietta - By whom: John Milligan.
- **Cadarette, Joseph** - Private - 19th Infantry - Company: Joel Collins - Other regiment: 3rd Infantry - Age: 22 - Height: 4' 11" - Born: Michigan - Trade: Laborer - Enlistment date: 30 May 1814 - Enlistment place: Detroit - Enlistment period: 5 Yrs - By whom: John Meldrum - Comments: Re-enlisted at Fort Howard, IL, on 12 May 1819.
- **Cady, Samuel** - Private - 27th Infantry - Company: George Sanderson - Enlistment date: 12 May 1813 - Enlistment period: 1 Yr - Discharged: 12 May 1814 - Pension: Wife Jane Wagoner, WO-44382, WC-34945; married on 26 March 1834 in Franklin County, OH, soldier died on Dec 1851 in Franklin County, OH, widow died on 7 Jul 1895 in Black Lick, OH, 1st wife Sally Nickerson, served as a private in Captain George Sanderson's Company, 27th Infantry lived in Franklin County, OH - Bounty: BLW 3566-160-50.
- **Cady, William** - Private - 27th Infantry - Company: George Sanderson - Enlistment date: 12 May 1813 - Died: 20 Nov 1813.
- **Cahill, Isaac** - Private - 19th Infantry - Company: William Gill - Other regiment: 3rd Infantry - Age: 21 - Height: 5' 4" - Born: KY, Fleming County, Madison - Trade: Farmer - Enlistment date: 11 Aug 1814 - Enlistment place: Xenia - Enlistment period: 5 Yrs - By whom: Jacob Leslie - Discharged: 11 Aug 1819 at Fort Howard, WI.
- **Cain, Daniel** - Private - 27th Infantry - Company: Joel Collins - Other regiments: 19th Infantry then 3rd Infantry - Age: 22 - Height: 5' 10" - Born: VA, Harrison County - Trade: Farmer - Enlistment date: 2 Jan 1813 - Enlistment place: Detroit - Enlistment period: 5 Yrs - By whom: Samuel Coleman - Discharged: 24 Mar 1819 - Pension: Wife Eliza (2nd wife), WC-34533, SC-1210; married on 17 Jan 1861 in Worth County, MO; soldier died on 7 Apr 1883; wife died circa 1888; served in Capt. Gill's Company, 27th Infantry Capt. Collins' Company, 19th Infantry and Capt. George Gray's Company, 3rd Infantry; lived in Fillmore County, NB and Clark County, IA; widow lived in Worth County, MO; first wife was Hannah.- Bounty: BLW 23789-160-12 - Comments: Re-enlisted.
- **Cain, John** - Private - 19th Infantry - Company: Angus Langham - Other regiment: 17th Infantry - Age: 30 - Height: 5' 8" - Born: NJ, Trenton County - Trade: Shoemaker - Enlistment date: 4 Jul 1812 - Enlistment place: Zanesville - Enlistment period: 5 Yrs - By whom: James Herron - Discharged: 4 Jul 1817 at Fort Howard, WI.
- **Cairns, Richard** - Private - 27th Infantry - Comments: Prisoner of War on Parole, captured at Detroit, MI, 16 Aug 1812.

The Enlisted Men

Calder, Daniel - Private - 19th Infantry - Company: Wilson Elliott - Age: 27 - Height: 5' 8 1/2" - Born: Scotland - Enlistment date: 6 Jul 1812 - Enlistment place: New Lisbon - Enlistment period: 5 Yrs - By whom: Henry Frederick - Bounty: BLW 25092-160-12 (Arkansas) - Comments: Died probably at Fort Meigs; land bounty to John Calder, brother & only heir at law of Daniel Calder.

Caldwell, Andrew - Corporal - 17th Infantry - Company: Angus Langham - Age: 32 - Height: 5' 11" - Born: Kentucky - Enlistment date: 29 May 1814 - By whom: John Cochran.

Caldwell, James - Private - 17th Infantry - Company: Caleb Holder - Age: 18 - Height: 5' 5 1/2" - Born: PA, Washington County - Trade: Weaver - Enlistment date: 21 Jul 1814 - Enlistment period: War - By whom: William Featherstone - Discharged: 11 Jul 1815 at Chillicothe - Bounty: BLW 9890-160-12 (Illinois).

Calhoun, Samuel - Private - 2nd Rifles - Company: Batteal Harrison - Age: 38 - Height: 5' 4" - Born: Ireland - Trade: Laborer - Enlistment date: 13 Jul 1814 - Enlistment place: Cincinnati - Enlistment period: War - By whom: Elias Langham - Discharged: 30 Jun 1815 at Detroit.

Call, Charles - Sergeant - 17th Infantry - Company: John Chunn - Age: 19 - Height: 6' 2 1/2" - Born: NC, Rowan, Salisbury - Trade: Farmer - Enlistment date: 5 May 1813 - Enlistment period: War - By whom: Charles Querey - Discharged: 7 Jun 1815 at Chillicothe - Pension: Wife Margaret Ashley, WO-19314, WC-10117, SO-19197, SC-18850, SC-19725; married on 18 Feb 1816 in Scioto County, OH, soldier died on 29 Jan 1875, widow died on 6 Mar 1884, served in Lt. Mason Seward's Company, 17th Infantry, lived in Scioto County, OH - Bounty: BLW 18931-160-12.

Cameron, William - Private - 17th Infantry - Age: 21 - Height: 5' 6 3/4" - Born: Scotland - Enlistment date: 4 Jan 1815 - Enlistment place: Adams County, West Union - Enlistment period: 5 Yrs - By whom: James Campbell.

Camp, John - Private - 17th Infantry - Company: John Chunn - Age: 26 - Height: 5' 8 3/4" - Born: Maryland - Trade: Clock maker - Enlistment date: 15 Sep 1814 - Enlistment period: War - By whom: William Featherstone - Discharged: 11 Jul 1815 at Chillicothe - Bounty: BLW 24828-160-12 (Arkansas).

Campbell, Alexander - Private - 2nd Artillery - Company: Daniel Cushing.

Campbell, James - Private - 19th Infantry - Company: Wilson Elliott - Enlistment date: 21 Jul 1812 - Enlistment period: 5 Yrs - By whom: James Campbell - Killed: 5 May 1813 - Bounty: BLW 25233-160-12 (Arkansas) - Comments: Land bounty to Rachael Campbell & other heirs at law of James Campbell.

Campbell, John - Private - 26th Infantry - Company: Samuel Swearingen - Other regiment: 25th Infantry - Enlistment date: 16 May 1813 - Enlistment period: 1 Yr - Discharged: 16 May 1814.

Campbell, John - Private - 2nd Artillery - Company: Daniel Cushing.

Campbell, Joseph Jr - Private - 19th Infantry - Age: 17 - Height: 5' 5" - Born: VA, Shenandoah County - Enlistment date: 18 Jul 1812 - Enlistment place: St. Clairsville - Enlistment period: 5 Yrs.

Campbell, Joseph Sr - Private - 19th Infantry - Company: Angus Langham - Age: 43 - Height: 5' 10" - Born: Ireland - Enlistment date: 18 Jul 1812 - Enlistment place: St. Clairsville - Enlistment period: 5 Yrs - Killed: 5 May 1813 - Pension: Wife Catherine, Old War Pension WF-10393, private in US infantry during the War of 1812 - Bounty: BLW 27617-160-42 - Comments: Land bounty to Mary Beggs and Nancy Coles, daughters and only heirs at law of Joseph Campbell.

Campbell, Samuel - Private - 17th Infantry - Company: Harris Hickman - Enlistment date: 12 Oct 1813 - Enlistment period: War - By whom: Isaac Rieley - Died: Feb 1815 at Williamsville, NY (General Hospital), of natural death.

Canary, Thomas - Private - 26th Infantry - Company: Joel Collins - Enlistment date: 9 Oct 1813 - Enlistment period: 1 Yr.

Cane, John - Sergeant - 26th Infantry - Company: George Kesling - Other regiment: 25th Infantry - Enlistment date: 28 Apr 1813.

Caneley, Peter - Private - 27th Infantry - Company: George Sanderson - Enlistment date: 1 Jun 1813.

Cannop, James - Private - 2nd Rifles - Company: Batteal Harrison - Other regiment: Rifle Regiment - Age: 21 - Height: 5' 6" - Born: Wales - Trade: Brick maker - Enlistment date: 15 Jul 1814 - Enlistment place: Chillicothe - Enlistment period: 5 Yrs - By whom: Batteal Harrison - Comments: Deserted 18 Aug 1816.

Cantwell, Thomas - Private - 17th Infantry - Company: Caleb Holder - Age: 30 - Height: 5' 6 1/2" - Born: Pennsylvania - Trade: Farmer - Enlistment date: 18 Jun 1814 - Enlistment period: War - By whom: Jonathan Rees - Discharged: 30 Jun 1815 at Detroit - Bounty: BLW 5004-160-12 (Illinois).

Canway, Jacob - Private - 27th Infantry - Company: George Sanderson - Enlistment date: 19 Apr 1813.

Canway, Lewis - Private - 27th Infantry - Company: George Sanderson - Enlistment date: 28 Apr 1813 - Died: 27 Oct 1813.

Cape, Thomas - Private - 2nd Rifles - Company: Benjamin Johnson - Age: 23 - Height: 5' 8" - Born: SC,

Buncombe County, Greenville - Trade: Farmer - Enlistment date: 3 Aug 1812 - Enlistment place: Knox County - Enlistment period: 5 Yrs - By whom: James Campbell - Discharged: 3 Aug 1817 at Fort Crawford, IL - Bounty: BLW 23317-16012 (Arkansas).

Capson, Thomas - Private - 19th Infantry - Pension: Wife Huldah, Old War WF-10585; served as a private in the 19th Infantry.

Carl, John B. - Private - 17th Infantry - Company: Caleb Holder - Age: 27 - Height: 5' 6 1/2" - Born: New Jersey - Trade: Hatter - Enlistment date: 22 Jul 1814 - Enlistment place: Zanesville - Enlistment period: War - By whom: James Campbell - Discharged: 18 Apr 1815 at Chillicothe - Bounty: BLW 8364-160-12 (Illinois).

Carleton, Almon - Private - 27th Infantry - Company: George Sanderson - Enlistment date: 17 Jun 1813 - Died: 28 Nov 1813.

Carlisle, James - Corporal - 26th Infantry - Company: George Kesling - Other regiment: 25th Infantry - Enlistment date: 11 May 1813 - Enlistment period: 1 Yr - Discharged: 11 May 1814.

Carlisle, Joseph - Private - 27th Infantry - Age: 21 - Height: 5' 7" - Born: Kentucky - Enlistment date: 16 May 1814 - Enlistment place: Zanesville - Enlistment period: War - By whom: Neal McFadden - Comments: Deserted.

Carlisle, Robert - Private - 19th Infantry - Company: Richard Talbott - Age: 21 - Height: 5' 11" - Born: Virginia or Pennsylvania - Trade: Farmer - Enlistment date: 19 Apr 1814 - Enlistment place: Washington County - Enlistment period: War - By whom: John Goode - Discharged: 5 Jun 1815 at Chillicothe - Bounty: BLW 24626-160-12 (Arkansas).

Carlisle, William - Private - 26th Infantry - Company: William Puthuff - Enlistment date: 18 Apr 1813 - Enlistment period: 1 Yr.

Carnes, Michael - Private - 26th Infantry - Company: John McDonald - Enlistment date: 20 May 1813 - Enlistment period: 1 Yr - Discharged: 20 May 1814 - Pension: Wife Rhoda Heath, WO-11648, WC-23232; married on 11 Apr 1814 in Bellefontaine, OH; soldier died on Apr 1851 in Bellefontaine, OH; wife died on 26 Sep 1890; served in Capt. McDonald's Company, 26th Infantry; lived in Logan County, OH - Bounty: BLW 27186-160-55.

Carns, Jacob - Private - 26th Infantry - Company: George Kesling - Enlistment date: 11 May 1813 - Enlistment period: 1 Yr.

Carpenter, Daniel - Private - 27th Infantry - Age: 18 - Height: 5' - Born: Ohio - Enlistment date: 26 Apr 1814 - Enlistment place: Zanesville.

Carpenter, Jesse - Private - 2nd Rifles - Company: Batteal Harrison - Age: 27 - Height: 5' 7" - Born: VA, Harrison County - Trade: Laborer - Enlistment date: 6 Sep 1814 - Enlistment place: Gallipolis - Enlistment period: War - By whom: Edward Miller - Discharged: 30 Jun 1815 at Detroit - Pension: Wife Margaret Cottrell, WO-38491, WC-30979; married in 1814; soldier died 1840/1843 in Braxton County, WV; wife died 24 Nov 1880; served in Captain Batteal Harrison's Company, 2nd Rifles; widow lived in Clay County, WV - Bounty: BLW 25017-160-12.

Carr, Charles B. - Private - 17th Infantry - Bounty: BLW 8364-160-42 (Illinois).

Carrington, Nicholas - Private - 2nd Rifles - Company: Batteal Harrison - Age: 29 - Height: 5' 11" - Born: VA, Fairfax County - Trade: Farmer - Enlistment date: 9 Jun 1814 - Enlistment place: Zanesville - Enlistment period: War - By whom: William Dougherty - Discharged: 30 Jun 1815 at Detroit.

Carroll, John - Private - 17th Infantry - Company: Caleb Holder - Age: 15 - Height: 5' 3" - Born: PA, Cumberland County - Trade: Farmer - Enlistment date: 2 Nov 1813 - Enlistment period: War - By whom: Isaac Reiley - Discharged: 30 Jun 1815 - Bounty: BLW 15849-160-12 (Illinois) - Comments: Discharged at Detroit.

Carroll, Philip - Private - 2nd Artillery - Company: Stanton Sholes - Enlistment date: 25 May 1813 - Enlistment period: 5 Yrs - Died: 10 Dec 1813 at Detroit.

Carson, Jacob - Corporal - 19th Infantry - Company: Wilson Elliott.

Carson, Reuben R. - Private - 19th Infantry - Company: Wilson Elliott - Enlistment date: 24 Aug 1812 - Discharged: 23 Feb 1814 - Pension: Wife Margaret Williams, SO-28937, SC-20953; served as a private in Capt. James Herron's Company, 19th Infantry; married 28 Jul 1822 in Champaign County, OH; lived in Scio, Linn County, OR - Bounty: BLW 113647-160-55.

Carson – see Ceasar, Thomas

Carson, W. B. - Private - 19th Infantry - Company: Wilson Elliott - Comments: Waiter to Dr. Mervin..

Carter, Charles - Private - 19th Infantry - Company: William Gill - Other regiment: 3rd Infantry - Age: 25 - Height: 5' 10" - Born: CT, Litchfield County - Trade: Farmer - Enlistment date: 4 Jul 1814 - Enlistment place: Canton - Enlistment period: 5 Yrs - By whom: Thomas Riddle - Discharged: 20 Jul 1819.

Carter, Daniel C. - Private - 17th Infantry - Company: Caleb Holder - Age: 37 - Height: 5' 9" - Born: Connecticut - Trade: Carpenter - Enlistment date: 28 Aug 1814 - Enlistment place: Cincinnati - Enlistment period: 5 Yrs -

The Enlisted Men

By whom: George Stall - Discharged: 27 Sep 1815 - Pension: Old War IF-26990; served as a private in Capt. Holder's Company, 17th Infantry - Bounty: BLW 9476-160-12 (Illinois) - Comments: Discharged at Detroit on Surgeon's Certificate of Disability.

Carter, Robert - Private - 1st Rifles - Company: Thomas Ramsey - Age: 16 - Height: 5' - Born: VA, Winchester - Trade: Laborer - Enlistment date: 8 Jan 1814 - Enlistment place: Cincinnati - Enlistment period: War - By whom: Peter Albright - Discharged: 12 Jun 1815 at Buffalo, NY.

Carver, William - Private - Rangers - Company: William Perry - Samuel McCormick - Enlistment date: 14 Apr 1812 - Discharged: 30 Jun 1814 - Pension: Wife Martha Clarke, SO-13570, SC-15716; served as a private in Captains William Perry and Samuel McCormick companies, OH Militia (US Rangers); married in Garrard County, KY; lived in Gallatin County, KY - Bounty: BLW 7715-160-50.

Cary, David - Private - Rangers - Company: Samuel McCormick - Age: 23 - Height: 5' 9" - Born: New Jersey - Trade: Farmer - Enlistment date: 31 Oct 1813 - Enlistment period: 1 Yr - Discharged: 31 Oct 1814 - Comments: Discharged at Fort Malden, UC.

Cary, John - Private - Rangers - Company: Samuel McCormick - Enlistment date: 14 Nov 1813 - Discharged: 14 Nov 1815.

Case, Augustus - Sergeant - 27th Infantry - Company: William Gill - Enlistment date: 16 Apr 1813 - Enlistment period: 1 Yr - Discharged: 19 Apr 1814 - Pension: Wife Lucinda Curtis, SO-4639, SC-2333; served as a sergeant in Capt. William Gill's Company, 27th Infantry; married on 31 May 1814 in Marietta, OH; soldier died on 20 Oct 1884 - Bounty: BLW 9420-160-50.

Case, Henry - Private - 27th Infantry - Company: George Sanderson - Other regiment: 19th Infantry - Enlistment date: 28 Apr 1813 - Died: 11 Jan 1815 - Pension: Heirs obtained half pay for five years in lieu of military bounty land.

Case, Nathan - Private - 27th Infantry - Company: George Sanderson - Enlistment date: 29 Apr 1813.

Casey, Archibald - Private - 27th Infantry - Comments: Prisoner of War on Parole, captured at Detroit, MI, 16 Aug 1812.

Cash, John - Private - 17th Infantry - Age: 23 - Height: 5' 8" - Born: Virginia - Trade: Laborer - Enlistment date: 6 Jan 1814 - Enlistment place: Xenia - Enlistment period: War - By whom: Ensign Shay - Discharged: 25 Jul 1815 at Fort Meigs, OH - Pension: SO-10488, SC-17010; soldier died on 29 Mar 1877 in Shenandoah County, VA; served as a private in the 17th Infantry - Bounty: BLW 548-160-12.

Cass, Ira - Private - 27th Infantry - Comments: Prisoner of War on Parole, captured at Detroit, MI, 16 Aug 1812.

Cassady, Michael - Private - 19th Infantry - Discharged: 26 Sep 1814.

Cassel, Thomas - Private - 19th Infantry.

Castle, George - Private - 19th Infantry - Company: Carey Trimble - Enlistment date: 2 Mar 1814 - Enlistment period: War - By whom: John Booten - Killed: 17 Sep 1814 during the Battle of Fort Erie, UC - Bounty: BLW26882-160-12 (Arkansas) - Comments: Land bounty to Eleazer Castle, son & other heirs at law of George Castle.

Cathers, Alexander - Private - 2nd Rifles - Company: Benjamin Desha - Age: 37 - Height: 5' 9 3/4" - Born: Ireland - Trade: Weaver - Enlistment date: 12 Dec 1814 - Enlistment place: Cincinnati - Enlistment period: 5 Yrs - By whom: William Pritchard.

Catterline, Harris - Drummer - 19th Infantry - Company: Richard Talbott - Age: 20 - Height: 5' 10" - Born: Pennsylvania - Trade: Laborer - Enlistment date: 23 Mar 1814 - Enlistment place: Lebanon - Enlistment period: War - By whom: Robert Young - Discharged: 5 Jun 1815 at Chillicothe - Bounty: BLW 3144-160-12 (Illinois).

Cavaller, Thomas - Sergeant - 19th Infantry - Company: Wilson Elliott - Other regiment: 17th Infantry - Age: 30 - Height: 5' 9" - Born: Connecticut - Enlistment date: 9 Jul 1812 - Enlistment place: Trumbull County, Warren - Enlistment period: 5 Yrs - By whom: Wilson Elliott - Died: 29 Oct 1813 - Bounty: BLW 26355-160-12 (Arkansas) - Comments: Served aboard the US Schooner Porcupine on the Lake Erie Squadron; land bounty to John B. Cavaller, son & other heirs at law of Thomas Cavaller.

Ceasar, Thomas - Private - 1st Infantry - Company: Simon Owens - Other regiment: 28th then 3rd Infantry - Age: 23 - Height: 5' 9" - Born: KY, Garrett County - Trade: Farmer - Enlistment date: 19 Feb 1814 - Enlistment place: Cincinnati - Enlistment period: 5 Yrs - By whom: Laurence Taliaferro - Died: 2 Mar 1816 at Detroit.

Cecil, Henry B. - Sergeant - 19th Infantry - Company: Martin Hawkins - Other regiment: 17th Infantry - Age: 31 - Height: 5' 10" - Born: MD, Frederick County, Frederick - Trade: Laborer - Enlistment date: 4 Apr 1814 - Enlistment place: Detroit - Enlistment period: War - By whom: George Atchison - Discharged: 9 Jun 1815 at Chillicothe - Bounty: BLW 5718-160-12.

Cessna, William - Fifer - 2nd Artillery - Company: Daniel Cushing - Comments: Deserted at Fort Meigs, OH, on 7

Aug 1813.

Chadwick, Thomas - Private - 27th Infantry - Company: Absalom Martin - Comments: Prisoner of War, exchanged 25 Apr 1814.

Chalfin, Robert - Private - 17th Infantry - Age: 23 - Height: 5' 10" - Born: Virginia - Trade: Carpenter - Enlistment date: 22 Jun 1814 - Enlistment place: Cincinnati - Enlistment period: War - By whom: David Carney - Bounty: BLW 8020-160-12.

Chamberlain, Benjamin - Private - 2nd Rifles - Company: Batteal Harrison - Age: 39 - Height: 5' 9" - Born: At sea - Trade: Laborer - Enlistment date: 1 Aug 1814 - Enlistment place: Cincinnati - Enlistment period: War - By whom: Elias Langham - Discharged: 30 Jun 1815 at Detroit.

Chamberlain, Emanuel - Private - 1st Rifles - Company: Thomas Ramsey - Other regiment: 1st Infantry then 3rd Infantry - Age: 19 - Height: 5' 6" - Born: PA, Allegheny County - Trade: Farmer - Enlistment date: 20 Dec 1811 - Enlistment place: Cincinnati - Enlistment period: 5 Yrs - By whom: Thomas Ramsey - Discharged: 20 Dec 1816.

Chamberlain, John D. - Wagon master - 8th Military District - Company: Quartermaster Department - Enlistment date: May 1813 - Discharged: Sep 1813 – Pension: SO-6938, SC-6853; served as a wagon master in the Quartermaster Department, US Army; married 9 Aug 1817 in Chester, Meigs County, OH; soldier died about 1879; lived in Waterford and Marietta, Washington County, OH - Bounty: BLW 58021-160-55.

Chambers, Benjamin - Private - 26th Infantry - Company: George Kesling - Other regiment: Light Dragoons Regiment - Enlistment date: 17 May 1813 - Enlistment period: 1 Yr.

Chambers, Henry - Private - 17th Infantry - Company: John Chunn - Age: 24 - Height: 5' 5" - Born: North Carolina - Trade: Saddler - Enlistment date: 20 Dec 1813 - Enlistment place: Butler County, Hamilton - Enlistment period: War - By whom: George Stall - Discharged: 7 Jun 1815 at Chillicothe - Bounty: BLW 7418-160-12 (Illinois).

Chambers, Jonathan - Private - 17th Infantry - Company: Martin Hawkins - Age: 22 - Height: 5' 9" - Born: NY, New York County - Trade: Nailer - Enlistment date: 10 Aug 1813 - Enlistment place: Portsmouth - Enlistment period: War - By whom: Hugh May - Discharged: 30 Jun 1815 at Detroit - Bounty: BLW 24390-160-12 (Arkansas).

Champ, Nathaniel - Sergeant - 17th Infantry - Company: Angus Langham - Age: 21 - Height: 6' - Born: VA, Hardy County (now WV) - Trade: Farmer - Enlistment date: 7 Jun 1813 - Enlistment place: Circleville - Enlistment period: War - By whom: Ensign Harrison - Discharged: 9 Jun 1815 at Chillicothe - Bounty: BLW 7380-160-12 (Illinois).

Champaigne, Lambert - Private - 19th Infantry - Company: Joel Collins - Other regiment: 3rd Infantry - Age: 18 - Height: 5' 6" - Born: MI, Wayne County, Detroit - Trade: Laborer - Enlistment date: 6 May 1814 - Enlistment place: Detroit - Enlistment period: 5 Yrs - By whom: John Meldrum - Comments: Re-enlisted 18 Jan 1819.

Champygne, Louis - Private - 19th Infantry - Company: Joel Collins - Other regiment: 3rd Infantry - Age: 23 - Height: 5' 8" - Born: MI, Wayne County, Detroit - Trade: Fiddler - Enlistment date: 4 May 1814 - Enlistment place: Detroit - Enlistment period: 5 Yrs - By whom: John Meldrum - Discharged: 30 Jun 1814 - Comments: Discharged after furnishing a substitute (Dennis Marr).

Chance, Henry - Sergeant - 12th Infantry - Company: James Paxton - Age: 20 - Height: 5' 10" - Born: Ohio - Trade: Laborer - Enlistment date: 20 Apr 1812 - Enlistment place: VA, Martinsburg - Enlistment period: 5 Yrs - By whom: Lewis Willis - Discharged: 8 Jun 1815 at Buffalo, NY, or Fort Erie, UC, for general disability - Bounty: BLW 20210-160-12 (Missouri).

Chaney, Richard - Musician - 2nd Artillery - Company: Daniel Cushing - Other regiment: Corps of Artillery - Age: 21 - Height: 5' 8 1/4" - Born: DC, Washington City - Trade: Laborer - Enlistment date: 19 Sep 1812 - Enlistment place: Chillicothe - Enlistment period: 5 Yrs - By whom: Samuel Kercheval - Discharged: 4 Dec 1815 - Bounty: BLW 26417-160-12 (Arkansas) - Comments: Discharged after furnishing a substitute (Burnett T. Hobson).

Chapman, Solomon - Sergeant - 19th Infantry - Company: Wilson Elliott - Age: 22 - Height: 5' 9 1/2" - Born: PA, Cumberland County - Enlistment date: 6 Jul 1812 - Enlistment place: Trumbull County, Warren - Enlistment period: 18 Mos.

Chase, William - Private - 26th Infantry - Company: Samuel Swearingen - Enlistment date: 20 Jun 1813 - Enlistment period: 1 Yr - Died: 5 Dec 1813, probably at Sackets Harbor, NY.

Chenaworth, Elijah - Private - 19th Infantry - Discharged: 6 Dec 1814.

Chick, Nathaniel - Sergeant - 19th Infantry - Company: James Herron - Enlistment date: 11 Aug 1812 - Enlistment period: 18 Mos - Discharged: 27 Jun 1814 - Comments: Prisoner of War (Quebec, LC), captured at Fort

Niagara, NY, 19 Dec 1813; exchanged 4 May 1814.

Childers, Abraham - Private - 17th Infantry - Age: 24 - Height: 5' 9 1/2" - Born: KY, Bourbon County - Trade: Mason - Enlistment date: 13 Feb 1815 - Enlistment period: 5 Yrs - By whom: John Reeves - Died: 30 Dec 1813.

Childers, James - Private - 26th Infantry - Company: William Puthuff - Enlistment date: 26 May 1813 - Enlistment period: 1 Yr.

Childers, Joseph - Private - 26th Infantry - Company: George Kesling - Enlistment date: 2 May 1813 - Enlistment period: 1 Yr - Comments: Prisoner of War on Parole, captured at Detroit, MI, 16 Aug 1812.

Childress, Joseph - Private - 19th Infantry - Company: George Stockton - Other regiment: 3rd Infantry - Age: 21 - Height: 5' 11" - Born: PA, Cumberland County - Trade: Farmer - Enlistment date: 14 Apr 1814 - Enlistment place: Washington County - Enlistment period: 5 Yrs - By whom: Lieutenant Beard - Comments: Deserted at Detroit, on 25 April 1816.

Childress, Squire - Private - 24th Infantry - Company: John Rodgers - Enlistment date: 24 Aug 1812 - Enlistment period: 18 Mos - By whom: John Rogers - Died: 14 Jul 1813 at Sandusky (now Fremont, OH).

Chiles, Isaac - Corporal - 19th Infantry - Company: Angus Langham - Other regiment: 17th Infantry then 3rd Infantry - Age: 44 - Height: 5' 8 1/4" - Born: NJ, Burlington County - Trade: Brick layer - Enlistment date: 10 Jun 1812 - Enlistment place: Zanesville - Enlistment period: 5 Yrs - By whom: James Herron - Comments: Died probably at Fort Dearborn, IL (now Chicago, IL), on 30 Jun 1817.

Chinoweth, Elijah - Private - 26th Infantry - Other regiment: 19th Infantry - Pension: Old War IF-26590, served in Captain Collins' Company, 26th Infantry.

Chipps, John - Private - 19th Infantry - Company: George Kesling - Enlistment date: 2 Jun 1814 - Enlistment period: War - Died: 10 Sep 1814 - Bounty: BLW 24909-160-12 (Arkansas) - Comments: Land bounty to Simeon Chipps & other heirs at law of John Chipps.

Cholffin, Robert - Private - 17th Infantry - Company: Henry Crittenden - Age: 23 - Height: 5' 10" - Born: Virginia - Trade: Carpenter - Enlistment date: 22 Jun 1814 - Enlistment period: War - By whom: David Carney - Discharged: 9 Jun 1815 at Chillicothe.

Cissna, Stephen - Private - 19th Infantry - Company: William Gill - Age: 21 - Height: 5' 7 1/2" - Born: PA, Allegheny County, Pittsburgh - Trade: Farmer - Enlistment date: 25 Jul 1814 - Enlistment place: Chillicothe - Enlistment period: War - By whom: Carey Trimble - Discharged: 5 Jun 1815 at Chillicothe - Bounty: BLW 6726-160-12 (Illinois).

Cissna, William - Sergeant - 26th Infantry - Company: Samuel Swearingen - Other regiment: 25th Infantry - Enlistment date: 18 Apr 1813 - Enlistment period: 1 Yr - Discharged: 18 Apr 1814.

Clanbers, Benjamin - Private - 19th Infantry - Age: 23 - Height: 5' 5" - Born: New Jersey - Enlistment date: 29 Nov 1814 - Enlistment place: Cincinnati.

Clapper, Henry - Private - 19th Infantry - Enlistment date: 14 Feb 1814 - Discharged: 13 Feb 1815 - Pension: Wife Mary Smith, SO-21462, SC-19836; married August 1815, Canton, OH, served as a private in the 19th Infantry; lived in Blackford County, IN - Bounty: Register 204876 1/2 55 Rejected.

Clapper, Lewis - Private - 27th Infantry - Company: Alexander Hill.

Clark, Ambrose - Private - 17th Infantry - Company: John Chunn - Age: 26 - Height: 6' 1/2" - Born: Virginia - Trade: Carpenter - Enlistment date: 28 Oct 1813 - Enlistment place: Butler County, Hamilton - Enlistment period: War - By whom: George Stall - Discharged: 18 May 1815 at Newport, KY - Bounty: BLW 11438-160-12 (Illinois).

Clark, Amos B. - Private - 27th Infantry - Company: Absalom Martin - Other regiment: 19th Infantry - Age: 19 - Height: 5' 5" - Born: Pennsylvania - Trade: Laborer - Enlistment date: 2 Jun 1813 - Enlistment period: 1 Yr - War - Discharged: 19 Jun 1815 at Detroit - Pension: Wife Catherine Hardman, WO-42168, WC-35180; married on 22 Mar 1826 in Belmont County, OH; soldier died on 30 Dec 1869 in Elmwood, IL; wife died on 22 Jan 1892 in Evansville, IN; served in Capt Absalom Martin's Company, 27th Infantry and in Capt Joel Collin's Company, 19 Infantry; lived in Chautauqua County, NY and Jefferson County, OH; wife lived in Peoria County, IL and Rock County, WI - Bounty: BLW 26903-160-12 (Arkansas), BLW 17704-160-50 - Comments: Re-enlisted 15 Mar 1814 at Detroit for war by Lieutenant Coleman.

Clark, Chaney - Private - 27th Infantry - Company: George Sanderson - Enlistment date: 27 Apr 1813.

Clark, Isaac - Private - Rangers - Company: William Perry - Discharged: 15 Sep 1812.

Clark, James - Private - 17th Infantry - Company: Caleb Holder - Age: 20 - Height: 5' 8" - Born: Vermont - Trade: Farmer - Enlistment date: 8 Sep 1814 - Enlistment period: War - By whom: William Featherstone - Discharged: 30 Jun 1815 at Detroit - Bounty: BLW 8662-160-12 (Illinois) t.

Clark, James - Private - 19th Infantry - Company: James Herron - Enlistment date: 13 Sep 1812 - Enlistment period: 5 Yrs.

Clark, John - Corporal - 19th Infantry - Company: William Gill - Age: 24 - Height: 5' 8" - Born: Pennsylvania - Trade: Farmer - Enlistment date: 2 Aug 1814 - Enlistment place: Athens - Enlistment period: War - By whom: Nehemiah Gregory - Discharged: 5 Jun 1815 at Chillicothe - Pension: Wife Mary Pearce, WO-24444, WC-17267; married in Jan 1817 in Fayette County, PA; soldier died on 23 Jul 1870 in Russellville, OH; wife died circa 1882; served in Captain William Gill's Company, 19th Infantry; lived in Brown County, OH - Bounty: BLW 13674-160-12 (Illinois) .

Clark, Jonathan - Private - 1st Rifles - Company: Thomas Ramsey - Age: 20 - Height: 5' 11" - Born: NJ, Somerset County - Trade: Blacksmith - Enlistment date: 27 Nov 1813 - Enlistment place: Cincinnati - Enlistment period: 5 Yrs - By whom: Thomas Ramsey - Discharged: 1 Aug 1815 at Buffalo, NY - Comments: Wounded during the Battle of Fort Erie, UC, on 17 Sep 1814.

Clark, Joseph - Private - 27th Infantry - Company: George Sanderson - Enlistment date: 18 May 1813.

Clark, Samuel - Private - 17th Infantry - Age: 23 - Height: 5' 8" - Born: Connecticut - Enlistment date: 3 May 1814 - Enlistment period: War - By whom: George Bryant.

Clark, Samuel - Private - 27th Infantry - Company: Isaac Van Horne - Enlistment date: 17 May 1813 - Enlistment period: 1 Yr - Discharged: 16 May 1814 - Pension: Wife Nancy Feazel, Old War IF-26596, Old War IC-1547, WO-11545, SC-6671; served as a private in Capt. Isaac Van Horn's Company, 27th Infantry; married on 5 Mar 1815 in Wayne County, OH; died on 23 Jun 1850 in Medina County, OH; widow died on 11 Jul 1886; lived in Medina and Wayne Counties, OH - Bounty: BLW 6304-160-50.

Clark, Stephen B. - Corporal - 19th Infantry - Company: Carey Trimble - Other regiment: 17th Infantry - Age: 22 - Height: 5' 8" - Born: PA, Bedford County - Trade: Farmer - Enlistment date: 29 Mar 1814 - Enlistment place: Ross County, Adelphi - Enlistment period: War - By whom: George Will - Discharged: 6 Jun 1815 at Chillicothe - Bounty: BLW 5577-160-12.

Clark, Thomas - Private - 19th Infantry - Company: Angus Langham - Comments: Prisoner of War, captured at Frenchtown, MI.

Clark, Thomas - Private - 17th Infantry - Age: 31 - Height: 5' 9" - Born: NY, Van Rensselaer County, Pittsfield - Trade: Carpenter - Enlistment date: 1 Dec 1814 - Enlistment place: Cincinnati - Enlistment period: War - By whom: Lieutenant Rees - Discharged: 11 Jul 1815 at Chillicothe - Bounty: BLW 24249-160-12 (Arkansas).

Clark, William - Private - 1st Infantry - Company: Horatio Stark - Age: 23 - Height: 5' 7" - Born: VA, Fauquier County - Trade: Carpenter - Enlistment date: 14 Feb 1814 - Enlistment place: Cincinnati - By whom: Laurence Taliaferro.

Clark, William - Private - 2nd Rifles - Company: Batteal Harrison - Age: 22 - Height: 5' 10 3/4" - Born: PA, Northumberland County - Trade: Blacksmith - Enlistment date: 19 Jul 1814 - Enlistment place: Cincinnati - Enlistment period: War - By whom: Elias Langham - Discharged: 30 Jun 1815 at Detroit.

Clark, William - Private - 26th Infantry - Company: Joel Collins - Enlistment date: 14 Sep 1813 - Enlistment period: 1 Yr - Died: 21 Dec 1813, probably at Detroit.

Clarke, John S. - Private - Rangers - Company: Samuel McCormick - Enlistment date: 1 Nov 1813 - Discharged: 1 Nov 1814.

Clary, Zachariah - Private - 19th Infantry - Company: George Kesling - Age: 34 - Height: 5' 11" - Born: MD, Frederick County - Trade: Tailor - Enlistment date: 29 Sep 1814 - Enlistment place: Franklin County, Franklinton - Enlistment period: 5 Yrs - By whom: Orren Granger.

Cleland, Martin - Private - 19th Infantry - Company: George Kesling - Other regiment: 3rd Infantry - Age: 18 - Height: 5' 8" - Born: Pennsylvania - Trade: Farmer - Enlistment date: 5 Feb 1815 - Enlistment place: Xenia - Enlistment period: 5 Yrs - By whom: Robert Smith - Comments: Deserted at Springfield, OH, 19 Sep 1815.

Clendenning, John - Private - 17th Infantry - Company: David Holt - Age: 34 - Height: 5' 9 1/2" - Born: PA, Franklin County - Trade: Farmer - Enlistment date: 30 Jun 1814 - Enlistment place: Franklin County, Franklinton - Enlistment period: War - By whom: John Cochran - Discharged: 4 Jun 1815 at Chillicothe - Bounty: BLW 13663-160-12 (Illinois).

Clifford, George - Private - 19th Infantry - Company: Asabael Nearing - Enlistment date: 19 Jan 1813 - Enlistment period: 5 Yrs - Died: 11 Aug 1813 - Bounty: BLW 18738-160-12 (Missouri) - Comments: Died at Fort Meigs; land bounty to James Clifford, brother et al, heirs at law of George Clifford.

Clifford, John - Private - 19th Infantry - Company: Joel Collins - Age: 38 - Height: 5' 7" - Born: Ireland - Trade: Laborer - Enlistment date: 8 May 1814 - Enlistment place: Upper Canada, Sandwich - Enlistment period: War - By whom: Collin McLeod - Discharged: 20 Jul 1815 at Detroit - Bounty: BLW 8929-160-12.

Clifford, John - Private - 26th Infantry - Company: Samuel Swearingen - Other regiment: 25th Infantry - Enlistment date: 17 May 1813 - Enlistment period: 1 Yr - Comments: Served aboard the US Schooner

Scorpion on the Lake Erie Squadron; Prisoner of War (Quebec, LC), captured at Fort Niagara, NY, 19 Dec 1813; exchanged 4 May 1814.

Clintock, (-----) - Private - 19th Infantry - Died: 13 Sept 1814.

Clutier, Romain - Private - 19th Infantry - Company: Joel Collins - Other regiment: 3rd Infantry - Age: 17 - Height: 5' - Born: Michigan - Trade: Laborer - Enlistment date: 19 May 1814 - Enlistment place: Detroit - Enlistment period: 5 Yrs - By whom: John Meldrum - Discharged: 19 May 1819 at Fort Howard, WI.

Clutter, Samuel - Private - 19th Infantry - Company: John Chunn.

Coburn, John - Private - 19th Infantry - Company: George Kesling - Age: 31 - Height: 5' 6" - Born: Massachusetts - Trade: Farmer - Enlistment date: 22 Feb 1815 - Enlistment place: Cincinnati - Enlistment period: War - By whom: William Baird.

Cochran, Andrew - Private - 19th Infantry - Company: Angus Langham - Pension: Wife Jane, Old War IF-12774; served in Capt. Langham's Company, 19th Infantry - Bounty: BLW 16515-160-50.

Cochran, George - Private - 17th Infantry - Company: Caleb Holder - Other regiment: 3rd Infantry - Age: 34 - Height: 5' 6" - Born: VA, Hampshire County (now WV) - Trade: Laborer - Enlistment date: 12 Mar 1813 - Enlistment place: Chillicothe - Enlistment period: 5 Yrs - By whom: William Featherstone - Discharged: 11 Mar 1818 - Comments: Discharged at Michilimackinac, MI.

Cochran, Robert - Private - 19th Infantry - Age: 26 - Height: 6' - Born: Pennsylvania - Enlistment date: 26 Apr 1814 - Enlistment place: Warren County, Waynesville - Enlistment period: War.

Cochran, William - Private - 19th Infantry - Company: Carey Trimble - Pension: Served as a private in Capt. Shepherd's Company, OH Militia, and as a private in Capt. Trimble's Company, 19th Infantry - Bounty: BLW 1900-160-50.

Cogshall, Daniel - Sergeant - 26th Infantry - Company: Samuel Swearingen - Other regiment: 25th Infantry - Enlistment date: 18 Jun 1813 - Enlistment period: 1 Yr - Discharged: 18 Jun 1814 - Pension: Wife Rebecca, WO-43390, WC-33925; served as a private in Capt. Howard's Company, 25th Infantry; married on 7 Oct 1838 in Gallia County, OH; soldier died on 21 Mar 1863 in Bath, Mason County, IL; widow died about 1888; lived in Gallia County, OH, and Hancock County, IL - Bounty: BLW 8913-160-50.

Coisin, Thomas - Private - 19th Infantry - Died: 30 Sep 1814 at Fort Erie, UC.

Coldwell, Edward - Private - 19th Infantry - Company: Asabael Nearing - Enlistment date: 2 Jan 1813 - Enlistment period: 18 Mos - Died: 25 May 1813.

Cole, Chester P. - Private - 27th Infantry - Company: George Sanderson - Enlistment date: 12 May 1813 - Enlistment period: 1 Yr - Discharged: 10 May 1814 - Pension: Wife Sophia Losure, WC-17734, SO-6953, SC-7027; married on 17 Dec 1837 in Wooster, Wayne County, OH, soldier died on 23 Jun 1872 in Copley, OH, widow died about 1882, served in Capt. George Sanderson's Company, 27th Infantry lived in Copley, Summit County, OH - Bounty: BLW 57-160-50.

Cole, Robert - Private - 17th Infantry - Company: Caleb Holder - Age: 36 - Height: 5' 5 1/2" - Born: Delaware - Trade: Carpenter - Enlistment date: 7 Sep 1814 - Enlistment place: Cincinnati - Enlistment period: 5 Yrs - By whom: George Stall - Discharged: 26 Sep 1815 at Detroit on Surgeon's Certificate of Disability - Bounty: BLW 14910-160-12 (Illinois).

Collins, David - Private - 26th Infantry - Company: George Kesling - Other regiment: 2nd Rifles - Enlistment date: 23 Apr 1813Collins, David - Private - 26th Infantry - Company: William Puthuff - Enlistment date: 9 Aug 1813 - Enlistment period: 1 Yr - Died: 24 Dec 1813 at Detroit.

Collins, Holdon K. - Private - 27th Infantry - Company: George Sanderson - Enlistment date: 5 Jun 1813.

Collins, James - Private - 19th Infantry - Other regiment: 17th Infantry - Age: 25 - Height: 5' 9" - Born: VA, Monongahela County - Trade: Mechanic - Enlistment date: 20 Apr 1814 - Enlistment place: Circleville - Enlistment period: War - By whom: John Reeves - Discharged: 25 Jul 1815 - Comments: Discharged at Lower Sandusky (now Fremont, OH).

Collins, James - Corporal - 17th Infantry - Other regiment: 3rd Infantry - Age: 29 - Height: 5' 8" - Born: Virginia - Trade: Farmer - Enlistment date: 13 Jan 1815 - Enlistment period: 5 Yrs - By whom: William Shang - Discharged: 29 Feb 1820 at Fort Howard, WI - Bounty: BLW 956-320-14.

Collins, James - Private - 17th Infantry - Age: 19 - Height: 6' - Born: Virginia - Enlistment date: 15 Jan 1815 - Enlistment place: Xenia - Enlistment period: 5 Yrs - By whom: Ensign Shay - Bounty: BLW 26222-160-12 (Arkansas).

Collins, John - Corporal - 27th Infantry - Company: George Sanderson - Enlistment date: 12 Apr 1813.

Collins, John - Private - 17th Infantry - Age: 32 - Height: 5' 6" - Born: Maryland - Enlistment date: 17 May 1814 - Enlistment place: Zanesville - By whom: James Herron.

Collins, John - Sergeant - 26th Infantry - Company: Joel Collins - Other regiment: 19th Infantry - Age: 21 - Height:

5' 8 1/2" - Born: New York - Trade: Distiller - Enlistment date: 18 Dec 1813 - Enlistment period: 1 Yr - War - Discharged: 20 Jul 1815 at Detroit - Pension: Wife Margaret Hall, SO-9650, SC-4789; married in July 1815 in Detroit, MI, soldier died on 22 Jan 1875, widow died in 1855, served as a sergeant in Captain Joel Collins' Company, 19th Infantry; lived in Grand Rapids, Kent County, MI - Bounty: BLW 9172-160-12 (Illinois) - Comments: Re-enlisted.

Collins, John - Private - 19th Infantry - Company: William Gill - Age: 30 - Height: 5' 8" - Born: Ireland - Trade: Weaver - Enlistment date: 2 Aug 1814 - Enlistment place: Urbana - Enlistment period: War - By whom: William Baird - Discharged: 5 Jun 1815 at Chillicothe - Bounty: BLW 4826-160-12 (Illinois).

Collins, Lewis - Private - 17th Infantry - Company: Richard Hightower - Enlistment date: 8 Jul 1812 - Enlistment period: 18 Mos - Died: 17 Sep 1813 - Bounty: BLW 26502-160-12 (Arkansas) - Comments: Died at Fort Meigs; land bounty to Richard G. Collins, son & only heir at law of Lewis Collins.

Collins, Samuel - Corporal - 26th Infantry - Company: William Puthuff - Enlistment date: 18 Apr 1813 - Enlistment period: 1 Yr.

Comer, Emanuel - Private - 17th Infantry - Company: David Holt - Other regiment: 3rd Infantry - Age: 22 - Height: 5' 8" - Born: Virginia - Trade: Laborer - Enlistment date: 17 Feb 1814 - Enlistment place: Portsmouth or Gallipolis - Enlistment period: 5 Yrs - By whom: Jacob Anderson - Discharged: 17 Feb 1819.

Compton, Calvin - Private - 19th Infantry - Company: George Kesling - Age: 30 - Height: 5' 9" - Born: NY, Washington County, Westfield - Trade: Farmer - Enlistment date: 3 Jan 1815 - Enlistment place: New Lisbon - Enlistment period: War - By whom: Samuel Coleman - Comments: Deserted 25 Jan 1815.

Compton, John - Private - 2nd Rifles - Company: Batteal Harrison - Age: 36 - Height: 5' 8" - Born: NJ, Monmouth County - Trade: Carpenter - Enlistment date: 16 May 1814 - Enlistment place: Chillicothe - Enlistment period: War - By whom: Batteal Harrison - Discharged: 30 Jun 1815 at Detroit - Bounty: BLW 6040-160-42 (Illinois).

Condon, James - Private - 17th Infantry - Company: Harris Hickman - Age: 32 - Height: 5' 6 1/4" - Born: MD, Baltimore County - Trade: Weaver - Enlistment date: 1 Mar 1814 - Enlistment place: New Lisbon - Enlistment period: War - By whom: Thomas McKnight - Discharged: 9 Jun 1815 at Chillicothe - Bounty: BLW 6254-160-12.

Coney, Joseph - Private - 19th Infantry - Company: George Kesling - Age: 31 - Height: 5' 6" - Born: Carolina - Trade: Farmer - Enlistment date: 4 Feb 1815 - Enlistment place: Cincinnati - Enlistment period: War - By whom: William Baird - Discharged: 27 Mar 1815 at Zanesville.

Conley, James T. - Private - 26th Infantry - Company: William Puthuff - Enlistment date: 16 Jun 1814 - Enlistment period: 1 Yr.

Conley, Michael - Private - 17th Infantry - Bounty: BLW 26724-160-12 (Arkansas) - Comments: Land bounty to John Conley, son & other heirs at law of Michael Conley.

Conner – see Connor, John

Conner, William - 19th Infantry - Pension: Wife Elizabeth Chapman, WC-34089, married on 30 Nov 1820 in Delaware County, IN, solider died on 8 Aug 1855 Hamilton County, IN, served in Patterson Bain's Company, 19th US Infantry, lived in Hamilton County, IN, widow lived also in Marion County, IN.

Connett, Henry - Private - 19th Infantry - Company: William Gill - Age: 18 - Height: 5' 3" - Born: New Jersey - Trade: Laborer - Enlistment date: 26 May 1814 - Enlistment period: War - Discharged: 5 Jun 1815 at Chillicothe - Pension: Wife Anna Butt, SO-13820, SC-9026; married on 31 Dec 1818 in Hamilton County, OH; served as a private in Capt. Gill's Company, 19th Infantry; lived in Caldwell County, MO - Bounty: BLW 8048-160-12 (Illinois).

Connor, John - Private - 17th Infantry - Company: Martin Hawkins - Other regiment: 3rd Infantry - Age: 27 - Height: 5' 10" - Born: PA, Northumberland County - Trade: Farmer - Enlistment date: 21 Jan 1813 - Enlistment place: Chillicothe - Enlistment period: 5 Yrs - By whom: Asabael Nearing - Discharged: 21 Jan 1818 - Comments: Discharged at Fort Howard, WI.

Conture, Wizer - Private - 26th Infantry - Company: William Puthuff - Enlistment date: 1 Aug 1813 - Enlistment period: 1 Yr.

Cooder, Jonathan - Private - 19th Infantry - Company: James Herron - Enlistment date: 3 Dec 1812 - Enlistment period: 5 Yrs.

Cook, Charles - Private - 17th Infantry - Company: Harris Hickman - Age: 35 - Height: 5' 7 1/2" - Born: CT, New Haven County, Wallingsford - Trade: Farmer - Enlistment date: 19 Jun 1814 - Enlistment place: Butler County, Hamilton - Enlistment period: War - By whom: George Stall - Discharged: 9 Jun 1815 at Chillicothe - Bounty: BLW 6590-160-42 (Illinois).

Cook, Jacob - Sergeant - 19th Infantry - Company: Angus Langham - Other regiments: 17th Infantry then 3rd

The Enlisted Men

Infantry - Age: 26 - Height: 6' - Born: MA, Berkshire County, Louden - Trade: Carpenter - Enlistment date: 4 May 1812 - Enlistment place: Detroit - Enlistment period: 5 Yrs - By whom: Harris Hickman - Comments: Discharged at Fort Howard, WI; died in 1817.

Cook, Solomon - Private - 17th Infantry - Company: Henry Crittenden - Age: 20 - Height: 5' 8" - Born: VT, Rutland County - Trade: Laborer - Enlistment date: 13 Mar 1813 - Enlistment place: Franklin County, Franklinton - Enlistment period: War - By whom: Stephen Lee - Discharged: 9 Jun 1815 at Chillicothe - Pension: Wife Hannah Reagan, SO-8304, SC-9455, married on 9 Apr 1818 in Clark County, OH; soldier died on 22 Jul 1881 in Akadia, Hamilton County, OH; served as a private in Captain Henry Crittenden's and Lieutenant James Gray's Companies, 17th Infantry; lived in Tipton County, IN - Bounty: BLW 6039-160-12 (Illinois).

Cook, Stephen - Private - 27th Infantry - Company: George Sanderson - Enlistment date: 5 Jul 1813 - Died: 8 Nov 1813.

Cook, Thomas - Private - Rangers - Company: Samuel McCormick - Enlistment date: 1 Nov 1813 - Discharged: 22 Oct 1814.

Cooling, Thomas - Private - 2nd Rifles - Company: Batteal Harrison - Age: 21 - Height: 5' 6" - Born: England - Trade: Stocking weaver - Enlistment date: 3 Jul 1814 - Enlistment place: Chillicothe or Circleville - Enlistment period: War - By whom: John Swearingen - Discharged: 30 Jun 1815 at Detroit.

Cooper, Enoch - Private - 26th Infantry - Died: 13 Nov 1813.

Cooper, Justis - Private - 19th Infantry - Age: 28 - Height: 5' 11" - Born: New Jersey - Enlistment date: 5 Jul 1814 - Enlistment place: Xenia.

Cooper, Moses - Private - 19th Infantry - Company: Caleb Holder - Other regiment: 17th Infantry - Age: 27 - Height: 6' 3 1/2" - Born: VA, Greenbrier County - Trade: Farmer - Enlistment date: 13 May 1814 - Enlistment place: Springfield - Enlistment period: War - By whom: Abijah Johns - Discharged: 30 Jun 1815 at Detroit- Bounty: BLW 2519-160-12 (Illinois).

Cooper, Moses - Private - 2nd Rifles - Age: 28 - Height: 6' 1/2" - Born: Virginia - Enlistment date: 27 Jun 1814 - Enlistment place: Cincinnati.

Cooper, Samuel - Private - 27th Infantry - Company: Alexander Hill - Other regiment: 19th Infantry - Age: 22 - Height: 5' 10" - Born: PA, Washington County - Trade: Joiner - Enlistment date: 27 May 1814 - Enlistment place: Ashtabula County, Harpersfield - Enlistment period: War - By whom: James Harper - Discharged: 5 Jun 1815 at Chillicothe - Bounty: BLW 2886-160-12 (Illinois).

Cooper, Samuel - Private - 2nd Rifles - Company: Batteal Harrison - Age: 24 - Height: 5' 7 1/2" - Born: Pennsylvania - Trade: Laborer - Enlistment date: 24 Aug 1814 - Enlistment place: Cincinnati - Enlistment period: War - By whom: Elias Langham - Discharged: 30 Jun 1815 - Comments: Discharged at Detroit.

Copeland, Willis - Private - 17th Infantry - Company: Henry Crittenden - Other regiment: 3rd Infantry - Age: 43 - Height: 5' 6" - Born: Pennsylvania - Trade: Carpenter - Enlistment date: 25 Feb 1814 - Enlistment period: 5 Yrs - By whom: George Stall - Discharged: 1 Aug 1817 at Fort Harrison, IN, on Surgeon's Certificate of Disability.

Cornwell, David - Private - 19th Infantry - Company: Harris Hickman - Other regiment: 17th Infantry - Age: 30 - Height: 5' 10" - Born: NJ, Cumberland County - Trade: Laborer - Enlistment date: 22 Apr 1814 - Enlistment place: Lebanon - Enlistment period: War - By whom: Adam Hoffman - Discharged: 9 Jun 1819 at Chillicothe - Bounty: BLW 14858-160-12 (Illinois).

Corser, William - Private - 19th Infantry - Other regiment: 2nd Rifles - Age: 33 - Height: 5' 8" - Born: NH, Monmouth - Enlistment date: 16 Apr 1814 - Enlistment place: Clermont County, Hillsborough - By whom: John McClain.

Corwin, Oliver - Private - 19th Infantry - Company: David Holt - Other regiments: 17th Infantry then 3rd Infantry - Age: 26 - Height: 5' 8" - Born: NY, New York County - Trade: Laborer - Enlistment date: 29 Apr 1814 - Enlistment place: Chillicothe - Enlistment period: War - By whom: James Campbell - Discharged: 29 Apr 1819 at Fort Howard, WI - Bounty: BLW 25195-160-12 (Arkansas).

Cory, Abraham - Private - 26th Infantry - Company: Samuel Swearingen - Enlistment date: 3 Jul 1813 - Enlistment period: 1 Yr - Died: 21 Oct 1813.

Cotterell, Daniel - Private - 1st Rifles - Company: Thomas Ramsey - Age: 35 - Height: 5' 7" - Born: Virginia - Trade: Stone mason - Enlistment date: 21 Apr 1814 - Enlistment place: Columbiana County, Middleton - Enlistment period: War - By whom: Peter Albright - Discharged: 5 Jun 1815 at Buffalo, NY - Bounty: BLW 14749-160-12).

Cottles, Daniel - Private - 19th Infantry - Company: Carey Trimble - Other regiments: 17th Infantry then 3rd Infantry - Age: 18 - Height: 5' 8" - Born: England - Trade: Farmer - Enlistment date: 13 Mar 1814 - Enlistment place: Franklin County, Franklinton - Enlistment period: War - By whom: John McElvain -

Discharged: 31 Mar 1815 - Bounty: BLW 6667-160-12 (Illinois) - Comments: Re-enlisted 1 Apr 1815 at Erie, PA, for 5 years.

Cottrell – see Cotterell, Daniel

Countis, John - Private - 26th Infantry - Company: Samuel Swearingen - Other regiment: 25th Infantry - Enlistment date: 30 May 1813 - Enlistment period: 1 Yr - Discharged: 30 May 1814.

Courtney, Michael S. - Private - 19th Infantry - Company: Harris Hickman - Other regiment: 17th Infantry - Age: 18 - Height: 5' 2" - Born: PA, Mayson - Trade: Laborer - Enlistment date: 2 Apr 1814 - Enlistment place: Adams County - Enlistment period: War - By whom: Stephen Lee - Discharged: 9 Jun 1815 at Chillicothe - Pension: Wife Leah, SO-25271, SC-11161; served as a private in Capt. Hickman's and Lt. W. Featherston's Companies, 17th Infantry; married on 21 Apr 1830 in Pendleton County, KY; lived in Crawford County, IN. - Bounty: BLW 4502-160-12.

Courtney, Nicholas - Private - 17th Infantry - Company: David Holt - Age: 21 - Height: 5' 7" - Born: Virginia - Trade: Farmer - Enlistment date: 30 May 1814 - Enlistment place: New Lisbon - Enlistment period: War - By whom: Thomas McKnight - Discharged: 4 Jun 1815 at Chillicothe - Pension: Wife Susannah Boerstler, WO-16240, WC-10840, SO-18235, SC-8645; married on 13 Apr 1854 in Canfield, Mahoning County, OH; soldier died on 7 Jun 1877 in Ellsworth, OH; wife died on 4 Apr 1891; served as a private in Lt. Goode's detachment, 17th Infantry; lived in Ellsworth, Mahoning County, OH - Bounty: BLW 2884-160-12 (Illinois).

Covington, Benjamin - Private - 17th Infantry - Age: 44 - Height: 5' 10" - Born: New Jersey - Enlistment date: 12 Jan 1815 - Enlistment place: Adams County, West Union - Enlistment period: 5 Yrs - By whom: James Campbell - Comments: Deserted at West Union, OH.

Cox, John - Private - 27th Infantry - Company: Alexander Hill - Other regiment: 19th Infantry - Age: 22 - Height: 5' 1 1/2" - Born: PA, Somerset County - Enlistment date: 23 Feb 1814 - Enlistment place: Marietta - Enlistment period: War - By whom: Nehemiah Gregory - Died: 12 Jul 1814 - Bounty: BLW 24967-160-12 (Arkansas) - Comments: Drown, fell overboard on vessel from Cleveland, OH, to Erie, PA; land bounty to Jacob Cox, brother & other heirs at law of John Cox.

Cox, Otho - Private - 26th Infantry - Company: George Kesling - Other regiment: 25th Infantry - Enlistment date: 29 Jul 1813 - Discharged: 29 Jul 1814 at Buffalo, NY.

Cox, Robert M. - Private - 19th Infantry - Company: Angus Langham - Enlistment date: 31 Jul 1812 - Enlistment period: 18 Mos - Discharged: 31 Jan 1814 - Pension: Wife Elizabeth Johnson, WO-1232, WC-7531; served as a private in Capt. Edwards' Company, 19th Infantry; married on 15 Nov 1815 in Mt. Pleasant, Hamilton County, OH; soldier died on 3 Jul 1847 in Butler County, OH; widow died on 27 Jul 1884 in Upshur, OH; lived in Preble County, OH - Bounty: BLW 9877-160-50.

Cox, William B. - Private - 26th Infantry - Company: Joel Collins - Enlistment date: 3 Aug 1813 - Enlistment period: 1 Yr.

Cozine, Samuel - Private - 19th Infantry - Company: John Chunn - Other regiment: 17th Infantry - Enlistment date: 7 Aug 1813 - Enlistment period: 18 Mos - War - Killed: 25 Jul 1814 - Bounty: BLW 26974-160-12 - Comments: Previously re-enlisted 7 Feb 1814 for War; land bounty to Elizabeth Cozine, mother & other heirs at law of Samuel Cozine.

Craegen, John - Private - 2nd Artillery - Company: Daniel Cushing.

Crage, James - Private - 26th Infantry - Company: Samuel Swearingen - Other regiment: 25th Infantry - Age: 18 - Height: 5' 7" - Enlistment date: 16 Jun 1813 - Enlistment period: 1 Yr - Discharged: 16 Jun 1814.

Craig, John - Private - 26th Infantry - Company: William Puthuff - Enlistment date: 23 May 1813 - Enlistment period: 1 Yr.

Craig, John - Corporal - 2nd Artillery - Company: Daniel Cushing - Other regiment: Corps of Artillery - Age: 17 - Height: 5' 6" - Born: PA, Washington County - Trade: Farmer - Enlistment date: 4 Sep 1812 - Enlistment place: Chillicothe - Enlistment period: 5 Yrs - By whom: Samuel Kercheval - Discharged: 2 Dec 1815 - Pension: Wife Priscilla Morgan, WO-18472, WC-19213; married on 16 Aug 1821 in Ross County, OH; soldier died on 26 Mar 1841; wife died on 18 Aug 1883; served in Captains Cushing, Morgan and Biddle Companies, US Art; lived in Ross County, OH - Bounty: BLW 11461-160-12 - Comments: Discharged after furnishing a substitute (Charles W. Hyde).

Craig, Samuel - Private - 19th Infantry - Company: Joel Collins - Age: 44 - Height: 5' 6" - Born: Maryland - Trade: Laborer - Enlistment date: 19 Mar 1814 - Enlistment place: Detroit - Enlistment period: War - By whom: Wynkoop Warner - Discharged: 20 Jul 1815 at Detroit - Bounty: BLW 4390-160-12 (Illinois).

Craig, Uriah - Private - 19th Infantry - Company: Wilson Elliott - Age: 38 - Height: 5' 10" - Born: Vermont - Enlistment date: 3 May 1814 - Enlistment place: Franklin County, Franklinton - Enlistment period: War - By whom: Hugh Moore.

The Enlisted Men

Crain, John - Private - 27th Infantry - Company: Isaac Van Horne - Enlistment date: 5 May 1813 - Enlistment period: 1 Yr - Discharged: 30 Apr 1814 - Pension: Wife Tabitha Pritchard, WO-27847, WC-20863; married on 3 Jan 1815 New Lisbon, Columbiana County, OH, soldier died on 13 June 1844 in Columbiana County, OH, widow died circa 1881, served in Capt. Isaac Van Horne's Company, 27th Infantry lived in Columbiana County, OH - Bounty: BLW 1419-160-50.

Cramer, Richard - Private - 19th Infantry - Age: 36 - Height: 5' 10 1/2" - Born: MD, Baltimore County - Enlistment date: 10 Jul 1812 - Enlistment place: St. Clairsville - Enlistment period: 5 Yrs - By whom: Samuel Booker.

Crandell, Wilson - Corporal - 1st Rifles - Company: Thomas Ramsey - Age: 18 - Height: 5' 7" - Born: NY, Cayuga County - Trade: Farmer - Enlistment date: 1 May 1814 - Enlistment place: Cincinnati - Enlistment period: 5 Yrs - By whom: Thomas Ramsey - Discharged: 1 May 1819 - Bounty: BLW 22613-160-12 (Arkansas) - Comments: Wounded during the Battle of Fort Erie, UC; discharged at St. Louis, MO.

Crandle, Abraham - Private - 2nd Rifles - Company: Batteal Harrison - Age: 38 - Height: 5' 6" - Born: NY, Duchess County - Trade: Shoemaker - Enlistment date: 25 May 1814 - Enlistment place: Cincinnati - Enlistment period: War - By whom: Edward Miller.

Crane – Crain, John

Cranmore, Obadiah - Fifer - 19th Infantry - Company: Henry Crittenden - Other regiment: 17th Infantry - Age: 15 - Height: 5' 2" - Born: New York - Trade: Farmer - Enlistment date: 12 Apr 1814 - Enlistment place: Circleville - Enlistment period: War - By whom: John Reeves - Discharged: 7 Jun 1815 at Chillicothe - Bounty: BLW 5862-160-12 (Illinois).

Crasser – see Crosser, Jacob

Crawford, Hugh - Private - 2nd Rifles - Company: Batteal Harrison - Age: 27 - Height: 5' 5 1/2" - Born: Ireland - Trade: Carpenter - Enlistment date: 9 Aug 1814 - Enlistment place: Cincinnati - Enlistment period: War - By whom: Elias Langham - Discharged: 30 Jun 1815 at Detroit.

Creamer, Hiram - Waiter - 19th Infantry - Company: William Gill - Enlistment date: 1 Jun 1814 - Comments: Waiter to Capt William Gill.

Creamer, Peter - Waiter - 19th Infantry - Company: William Gill - Enlistment date: 1 Jun 1814 - By whom: Wynkoop Warner.

Creery, John - Private - 26th Infantry - Company: George Kesling - Other regiment: 25th Infantry - Age: 31 - Height: 5' 9" - Enlistment date: 19 Apr 1813 - Enlistment period: 1 Yr - Discharged: 19 Apr 1814.

Creighton, Hugh - Private - 17th Infantry - Company: Caleb Holder - Other regiment: 3rd Infantry - Age: 29 - Height: 5' 11" - Born: Ireland, County Tyrone - Trade: Mason - Enlistment date: 15 Sep 1814 - Enlistment period: 5 Yrs - By whom: James Herron - Discharged: 15 Sep 1819 at Fort Dearborn, IL.

Creighton, Hugh - Private - 19th Infantry - Company: James Herron - Enlistment date: 21 Nov 1812 - Enlistment period: 5 Yrs - Comments: Prisoner of War (Quebec, LC), captured at Fort Niagara, NY, 19 Dec 1813; exchanged 4 May 1814.

Cremenes, Baldes - Private - 27th Infantry - Company: George Sanderson - Enlistment date: 19 Apr 1813.

Crissel, Samuel - Drummer - 17th Infantry - Company: John Chunn - Age: 18 - Height: 5' 4" - Born: MD, Harford County - Trade: Plasterer - Enlistment date: 15 Jul 1814 - Enlistment place: Lancaster - Enlistment period: War - By whom: Adam Hoffman - Discharged: 7 Jun 1815 at Chillicothe - Bounty: BLW 7098-160-12 (Illinois).

Crock, P. - Private - 24th Infantry - Company: Alexander Gray - Died: Before 18 Nov 1813.

Crone, Henry - Private - 19th Infantry - Company: Carey Trimble - Age: 38 - Height: 5' 5" - Born: NJ, Morris County - Trade: Carpenter - Enlistment date: 14 Jun 1814 - Enlistment place: Zanesville - Enlistment period: War - By whom: Neal McFadden - Discharged: 6 Jun 1815 at Chillicothe - Bounty: BLW 6038-160-12 (Illinois).

Crosby, David - Private - 27th Infantry - Company: George Sanderson - Enlistment date: 30 Jun 1813.

Cross, Israel - Private - 27th Infantry - Company: Alexander Hill - Other regiment: 19th Infantry - Age: 21 - Height: 5' 10 1/2" - Born: Maryland or Virginia - Trade: Farmer - Enlistment date: 21 May 1814 - Enlistment place: Athens - Enlistment period: War - By whom: Nehemiah Gregory - Discharged: 6 Jun 1815 at Chillicothe - Bounty: BLW 16414-160-12 (Illinois).

Cross, Nathan - Private - 27th Infantry - Company: Alexander Hill - Other regiment: 19th Infantry - Age: 19 - Height: 6' - Born: Virginia - Trade: Laborer - Enlistment date: 1 Feb 1814 - Enlistment place: Warren County - Enlistment period: War - By whom: John Reeves - Discharged: 12 Mar 1817 - Bounty: BLW 9212-160-12 (Illinois).

Crosser, Jacob - Private - 19th Infantry - Company: Asabeal Nearing - Other regiment: 17th Infantry - Age: 21 -

Height: 5' 8 1/2" - Born: Maryland - Enlistment date: 7 Jul 1812 - Enlistment place: Trumbull County, Warren - Enlistment period: 5 Yrs - Died: Oct 1813 - Bounty: BLW 25408-160-12 (Arkansas) - Comments: Land bounty to Henry Crosser, father & only heir at law of Jacob Crosser.

Crouch, John - Private - 2nd Rifles - Age: 25 - Height: 6 2 1/2" - Born: South Carolina - Enlistment date: 17 Jun 1814 Enlistment place: Cincinnati.

Crouch, Samuel - Private - 17th Infantry - Company: David Holt - Age: 27 - Height: 5' 10" - Born: NY, Washington County - Trade: Blacksmith - Enlistment date: 18 May 1814 - Enlistment place: Franklin County, Franklinton - Enlistment period: War - By whom: John Cochran.

Crow, Christian - Musician - 19th Infantry - Company: William Gill - Age: 44 - Height: 5' 6 3/4" - Born: PA, Lancaster County - Trade: Shoemaker - Enlistment date: 29 Mar 1814 - Enlistment place: Ross County, Adelphi or Chillicothe - Enlistment period: 5 Yrs - By whom: George Will - Discharged: 10 Nov 1815 at Detroit on Surgeon's Certificate of Disability, old age.

Crow, Edward - Corporal - 17th Infantry - Company: David Holt - Age: 20 - Height: 5' 6 1/2" - Born: MD, Baltimore County, Baltimore - Trade: Tanner - Enlistment date: 2 Mar 1814 - Enlistment place: Franklin County, Franklinton - Enlistment period: War - By whom: John Cochran - Discharged: 4 Jun 1815 at Chillicothe - Bounty: BLW 10778-160-12 (Illinois).

Crown, Henry - Private - 27th Infantry - Company: Alexander Hill.

Crum, Abraham - Private - 19th Infantry - Company: Wilson Elliott - Age: 21 - Height: 5' 9" - Born: VA, Loudoun County - Enlistment date: 1 Sep 1812.

Crumb, Abraham - Private - 26th Infantry - Company: Benjamin Watson - Other regiment: 25th Infantry then 6th Infantry - Age: 25 - Height: 5' 9" - Born: Virginia - Trade: Laborer - Enlistment date: 5 Jun 1812 - Enlistment place: Ohio - Enlistment period: 5 Yrs - By whom: Samuel Booker - Discharged: 12 Sep 1817 at Plattsburgh, NY.

Crumer, Peter - Private - 19th Infantry - Company: William Gill - Enlistment date: 1 Jun 1814.

Cue, Robert - Private - 19th Infantry - Company: Asabael Nearing - Age: 27 - Height: 5' 10 1/2" - Born: VA, Wheeling Island - Trade: Laborer - Enlistment date: 11 Feb 1813 - Enlistment period: 18 Mos - Discharged: 5 Sep 1813 at Seneca Town, OH, for rifle shot through right knee - Pension: Old War IF-10511.

Culbertson, Samuel - Private - 19th Infantry - Company: Carey Trimble - Age: 21 - Height: 6' 1" - Born: PA, Cumberland County - Trade: Laborer - Enlistment date: 9 May 1814 - Enlistment place: Franklin County, Franklinton - Enlistment period: War - By whom: Hugh Moore - Discharged: 6 Jun 1815 at Chillicothe - Bounty: BLW 13666-160-12 (Illinois).

Culins, George - Private - 27th Infantry - Company: Joseph Carins - Enlistment date: 1 Apr 1813 - Enlistment period: 1 Yr - Discharged: 31 Mar 1814 - Pension: Wife Mary Muckler, Old War WF-472, Old War IF-9841; SO-13050, SC-4419, WO-10786, SC-6131; served as a private in Capt. Joseph Carnes' Company, 27th Infantry; married on 11 Apr 1813 in Muskingum County, OH; soldier died on 9 Feb 1872 in Sonora, OH; widow died on 21 Aug 1884; lived in Zanesville, Muskingum County, OH - Bounty: BLW 7299-160-50 - Comments: Wounded during the Battle of the Thames River, UC.

Cullumber, Richard - Private - 26th Infantry - Company: George Kesling - Other regiment: 25th Infantry - Enlistment date: 9 Jun 1813 - Enlistment period: 1 Yr - Comments: Deserted 26 Apr 1814.

Cumpton, William - Private - Rangers - Company: Samuel McCormick - Enlistment date: 2 Nov 1813 - Enlistment period: 1 Yr - Discharged: 22 Nov 1814.

Cunningham, Benjamin - Private - 19th Infantry - Company: Wilson Elliott - Age: 26 - Height: 5' 10 1/2" - Born: NY, Orange County - Enlistment date: 20 Aug 1812 - Enlistment place: Trumbull County, Warren - Enlistment period: 5 Yrs - By whom: Wilson Elliott - Comments: Deserted 24 Mar 1814.

Cunningham, Ebenezer - Private - 27th Infantry - Company: Joseph Cairns - Enlistment date: 16 Jun 1813 - Enlistment place: Zanesville - Enlistment period: 1 Yr - Discharged: 18 Jun 1814 - Pension: Wife Sally Mogradge, WO-4662, WC-9508; married 25 Dec 1816 in Salem, Washington County, OH, soldier died on 27 November 1851 in Noble County, OH, widow died circa 1879, served as a private in Capt. Joseph Cairne's Company, 27th Infantry, lived in Morgan and Noble Counties, OH, widow lived also in Beverly, Washington County, OH - Bounty: BLW 4819-160-50 - Comments: Served aboard the US Brig Lawrence on the Lake Erie Squadron; discharged at Fort Shelby, MI.

Cunningham, Robert - Private - 19th Infantry - Company: Asabael Nearing - Enlistment date: 20 Feb 1813 - Enlistment period: War - Died: 16 May 1813 - Pension: Heirs obtained half pay for five years in lieu of military bounty land.

Cunningham, William - Private - 26th Infantry - Company: Joel Collins - Enlistment date: 5 Oct 1813 - Enlistment period: 1 Yr.

Curran, Robert - Private - 17th Infantry - Age: 33 - Height: 5' 7" - Born: Scotland - Trade: Silversmith - Enlistment date: 21 Dec 1814 - Enlistment place: Adams County, West Union - Enlistment period: War - By whom: James Campbell - Discharged: 18 Apr 1815 at Chillicothe - Bounty: BLW 796-320-14 (Arkansas).

Current, James - Sergeant - 19th Infantry - Company: Wilson Elliott - Other regiment: 25th Infantry - Age: 26 - Height: 5' 11" - Born: PA, Allegheny County - Enlistment date: 4 Aug 1812 - Enlistment place: Trumbull County, Warren - Enlistment period: 18 Mos - By whom: Wilson Elliot.

Curry, William - Private - 19th Infantry - Company: Angus Langham - Pension: Old War IF-26066, served in Lieutenant Featherston's Detachment, 19th Infantry.

Curry, William - Private - 17th Infantry - Company: Harris Hickman - Age: 36 - Height: 5' 10 1/2" - Born: PA, Westmoreland County - Trade: Reed maker - Enlistment date: 8 May 1814 - Enlistment place: Chillicothe - Enlistment period: War - By whom: John Stockton - Discharged: 9 Jun 1815 at Chillicothe - Bounty: BLW 3145-160-12 (Missouri).

Curtis, John - Private - 19th Infantry - Company: Carey Trimble - Other regiment: 17th Infantry - Age: 21 - Height: 5' 11" - Born: Pennsylvania - Trade: Farmer - Enlistment date: 28 May 1814 - Enlistment place: Urbana - Enlistment period: War - By whom: William Baird.

Daffen, George (Daffon) - Private - 26th Infantry - Company: Joel Collins - Other regiment: 19th Infantry - Age: 19 - Height: 5' 8" - Born: North Carolina - Trade: Laborer - Enlistment date: 21 Aug 1813 - Enlistment period: 1 Yr - War - Bounty: BLW 21051-160-12 (Missouri) - Comments: Re-enlisted until the end of the war at Sandwich, UC.

Dailey, Benjamin - 26th Infantry - Company: Benjamin Watson - Other regiment: 25th Infantry then 6th Infantry - Age: 19 - Height: 5' 3" - Born: OH, Hamilton County, Cincinnati - Trade: Carpenter - Enlistment date: 30 Jan 1813 - Enlistment place: Cincinnati - Enlistment period: 5 Yrs - By whom: Lieutenant Hawley - Comments: Probably transferred from the 26th Infantry.

Dailey, Benoni H. (or Benjamin) - Private - 27th Infantry - Company: George Sanderson - Enlistment date: 18 Jun 1813 - Enlistment period: 1 Yr - Discharged: 12 Jul 1813 - Pension: Wife Elizabeth, SO-3752, WO-43809, WC-35205; served as a private in Captain George Sanderson's Company, 27th Infantry; first wife Ruth Cross; married second time on 20 Jan 1867 in Carthage, Athens County, OH; soldier died on 11 Feb 1872 in Athens County, OH; widow died on 6 Jun 1894; lived in Athens County, OH - Bounty: BLW 7887-160-50.

Dailey, James - Private - 26th Infantry - Company: Joel Collins - Enlistment date: 22 Sep 1813 - Enlistment period: 1 Yr - Died: 12 Dec 1813 at Sandwich, UC (now Windsor, Ontario).

Dailey, Jehu (or John) - Corporal - 19th Infantry - Company: Angus Langham - Age: 25 - Height: 5' 8" - Born: MD, Baltimore County - Trade: Laborer - Enlistment date: 23 Feb 1814 - Enlistment place: New Lisbon - Enlistment period: War - By whom: Thomas McKnight - Discharged: 6 Jun 1815 - Bounty: BLW 1088-160-12 at Chillicothe - Comments: Prisoner of War, exchanged 28 Apr 1814.

Dailey, John S. - Private - 17th Infantry - Age: 40 - Height: 5' 9 1/4" - Born: New York - Trade: Cooper - Enlistment date: 14 Jul 1813 - Enlistment period: 5 Yrs - By whom: Philip Price - Discharged: 15 May 1815 at Newport, KY- Bounty: BLW 9472-160-12.

Dally, James M. - Private - 19th Infantry - Age: 25 - Height: 5' 10" - Born: PA, Cumberland County, Carlisle - Enlistment date: 10 Jul 1814 - Enlistment place: Urbana.

Dalson, James - Private - 19th Infantry - Enlistment date: 2 Jun 1813 - Enlistment place: Cincinnati - Enlistment period: War.

Danbury, Philip - Private - 19th Infantry - Company: Richard Talbott - Age: 18 - Height: 5' 4" - Born: New Jersey - Trade: Farmer - Enlistment date: 16 May 1814 - Enlistment place: Clermont County, Williamsburg - Enlistment period: War - By whom: William McDonald Jr - Discharged: 5 Jun 1815 at Chillicothe - Bounty: BLW 3171-170-12 (Illinois).

Danley, John - Private - 1st Rifles - Company: Thomas Ramsey - Age: 18 - Height: 5' 6" - Born: PA, Franklin County - Trade: Farmer - Enlistment date: 2 Jun 1814 - Enlistment place: Cincinnati - Enlistment period: 5 Yrs - By whom: Thomas Ramsey - Discharged: 2 Mar 1819 - Bounty: BLW 22393-160-12 (Arkansas) - Comments: Discharged at Fort Crawford, IL, and then re-enlisted.

Darnell, David - Corporal - 2nd Rifles - Company: Benjamin Johnson - Age: 25 - Height: 5' 8" - Born: NC, Mecklenburg County, Macklin - Trade: Farmer - Enlistment date: 1 Jan 1814 - Enlistment place: Ohio River - Enlistment period: War - By whom: Benjamin Desha - Discharged: 30 Jun 1815 at Detroit - Bounty: BLW 13008-160-12 (Illinois).

Darrell, Redman - Private - 26th Infantry - Company: George Kesling - Other regiment: 25th Infantry - Enlistment date: 10 Jun 1813 - Enlistment period: 1 Yr - Discharged: 10 Jun 1814.

Daugherty, Mathew - Private - 19th Infantry - Age: 18 - Height: 5' 7" - Born: PA, Cumberland County - Enlistment date: 10 Sep 1812 - Enlistment period: 18 Mos.

Daugherty, Zachariah - Private - 17th Infantry - Company: Caleb Holder - Age: 20 - Height: 5' 8" - Born: KY, Paris County - Trade: Farmer - Enlistment date: 3 Jul 1813 - Enlistment place: Cincinnati - Enlistment period: War - By whom: Philip Price - Discharged: 9 Jun 1815 at Chillicothe.

Daughy, Daniel - Private - 19th Infantry - Age: 31 - Height: 6' - Born: NJ, Sussex County - Enlistment date: 7 Jul 1812 - Enlistment period: 5 Yrs.

Davidson, William - Private - 19th Infantry - Other regiment: 3rd Infantry - Age: 23 - Height: 5' 7" - Born: MD, Baltimore County - Trade: Farmer - Enlistment date: 22 Jul 1814 - Enlistment place: New Lisbon - Enlistment period: 5 Yrs - By whom: Wynkoop Warner - Discharged: 22 Jul 1819 at Fort Howard, WI.

Davis, Anthony - Private - 19th Infantry - Age: 28 - Height: 5' 10: - Born: Lower Canada, Montreal - Enlistment date: 17 Mar 1814 - Enlistment place: Detroit - By whom: George Atchison.

Davis, Benjamin - Private - 19th Infantry - Company: James Herron - Other regiment: 25th Infantry - Age: 21 - Height: 6' 1" - Born: Pennsylvania - Enlistment date: 5 Sep 1812 - Enlistment period: 18 Mos - By whom: Benjamin Desha.

Davis, Daniel - Sergeant - 17th Infantry - Company: Henry Crittenden - Age: 23 - Height: 6' - Born: PA, Washington County, Burgess - Trade: Laborer - Enlistment date: 12 Mar 1814 - Enlistment place: Butler County, Hamilton - Enlistment period: War - By whom: George Stall - Discharged: 9 Jun 1815 at Chillicothe - Bounty: BLW 2415-160-12 (Illinois).

Davis, David - Private - Rangers - Company: Samuel McCormick - Enlistment date: 20 Dec 1813 - Discharged: 19 Dec 1814.

Davis, Elias - Private - 19th Infantry - Company: Carey Trimble - Other regiment: 3rd Infantry - Age: 25 - Height: 5' 9" - Born: New York - Trade: Laborer - Enlistment date: 13 Apr 1814 - Enlistment place: Franklin County, Franklinton - Enlistment period: War - By whom: John McElvain - Bounty: BLW 14628-160-12 (Illinois) - Comments: Discharged at Erie, PA, on 31 March 1815 and re-enlisted.

Davis, George C. - Sergeant - 17th Infantry - Company: Harris Hickman - Age: 22 - Height: 5' 8" - Born: KY, Scott County - Trade: Silversmith - Enlistment date: 2 Mar 1813 - Enlistment place: Franklin County, Franklinton - Enlistment period: War - By whom: John Cochran - Discharged: 9 Jun 1815 at Chillicothe - Bounty: BLW 25457-160-12 (Arkansas).

Davis, Jacob W. - Sergeant - 19th Infantry - Company: Wilson Elliott - Other regiment: 17th Infantry then 3rd Infantry - Age: 25 - Height: 6' - Born: VA, Loudoun County - Enlistment date: 25 Aug 1812 - Enlistment period: 5 Yrs - By whom: James Herron - Discharged: 30 Aug 1816 - Pension: Wife Hannah Darby, WO-12511, WC-26086, Old War IF1520 File 46031, Old War IC-1502; married circa 4 Jan 1818 in Gallia County, OH; soldier died in 1838 near Vincennes, IN; wife died before 11 Sep 1886; served in Capt. Elliott's Company, 19th Infantry and in Capt. Chunn's Company, 3rd Infantry; lived in Little York, IL, Warren County, IN and in White County, IL; wife lived in Buchanan County, MO; heirs obtained half pay for five years in lieu of military bounty land - Bounty: BLW 27847-160-12 - Comments: Discharged having furnished a substitute; wounded twice, once in right thigh in Battle of Mississinewa and the other wound in the right shoulder at the siege of Fort Meigs on 5 May 1813; land bounty to Margaret Bricker, Rebecca Jones, Emanuel Davis and Hiram Davis, the children and only heirs at law of Jacob Davis.

Davis, Jesse - Sergeant - 27th Infantry - Company: George Sanderson - Enlistment date: 20 May 1813.

Davis, John - Private - 19th Infantry - Company: Wilson Elliott - Bounty: BLW 14431-160-42 (Illinois).

Davis, John - Private - 17th Infantry - Company: Henry Crittenden - Other regiment: 3rd Infantry - Age: 15 - Height: 5' - Born: PA, Allegheny County, McKeesport - Trade: S. maker - Enlistment date: 15 Mar 1813 - Enlistment place: Zanesville - Enlistment period: 5 Yrs - By whom: James Herron - Killed: 22 Jul 1815, by lightning at Fort Knox, IN.

Davis, Richard - Private - Rangers - Company: Samuel McCormick - Enlistment date: 8 Dec 1813 - Enlistment period: 1 Yr - Discharged: 7 Dec 1814.

Davis, Silas - Private - 19th Infantry - Bounty: BLW 14626-160-12 (Illinois).

Davis, Spenser - Private - 26th Infantry - Company: William Puthuff - Enlistment date: 3 Apr 1813 - Enlistment period: 1 Yr.

Davis, Thomas - Private - 1st Rifles - Company: Thomas Ramsey - Age: 20 - Height: 5' 10" - Born: New Jersey - Trade: Shoemaker - Enlistment date: 3 Apr 1814 - Enlistment place: Cincinnati - Enlistment period: 5 Yrs - By whom: Thomas Ramsey - Discharged: 21 Sep 1814 - Bounty: BLW 4497-160-12 (Illinois) - Comments: Discharged at Urbana, OH, on Surgeon's Certificate of Disability for apoplectic fits.

Davis, William - Private - 19th Infantry - Company: William Gill - Age: 19 - Height: 5' 9" - Born: Virginia - Trade: Farmer - Enlistment date: 10 Aug 1814 - Enlistment period: War - By whom: Neal McFadden - Discharged:

The Enlisted Men

5 Jun 1815 at Chillicothe - Bounty: BLW 9636-160-42 (Illinois).

Davis, William - Private - 19th Infantry - Company: William Gill - Age: 21 - Height: 5' 7" - Born: Virginia - Trade: Laborer - Enlistment date: 27 Aug 1814 - Enlistment place: Urbana - Enlistment period: War - By whom: William Baird.

Davis, William - Private - 26th Infantry - Company: George Kesling - Other regiment: Light Dragoons Regiment - Enlistment date: 7 Jun 1813 - Enlistment period: 1 Yr - Discharged: 18 May 1814 - Comments: Prisoner of War on Parole, captured at Detroit, MI, 16 Aug 1812.

Davison, Jabe L. - Private - 17th Infantry - Age: 24 - Height: 5' 7" - Born: MA, Barnstable County - Trade: Laborer - Enlistment date: 8 Dec 1814 - Enlistment place: Adams County, West Union - Enlistment period: 5 Yrs - By whom: James Campbell.

Davison, Samuel - Private - 17th Infantry - Enlistment date: 16 Jan 1815 - Enlistment place: Adams County, West Union - Enlistment period: War.

Dawson, John - Private - 2nd Artillery - Company: Daniel Cushing - Other regiment: Corps of Artillery - Age: 20 - Height: 6' - Born: Virginia - Trade: Laborer - Enlistment date: 6 Jan 1815 - Enlistment period: War - Discharged: 25 Jul 1815 - Bounty: BLW 627-160-42 (Illinois) - Comments: Discharged at Lower Sandusky (now Fremont, OH).

Dealy, Jehu - Private - 27th Infantry - Company: Alexander Hill.

Dean, John - Private - 19th Infantry - Age: 34 - Height: 5' 8" - Born: CT, Litchfield County, Cornwall - Enlistment date: 27 Mar 1814 - Enlistment place: Ashtabula County, Harpersfield.

Dean, Joseph - Private - 27th Infantry - Company: Alexander Hill - Other regiment: 19th Infantry - Age: 34 - Height: 5' 8" - Born: Connecticut - Trade: Farmer - Enlistment date: 27 Mar 1814 - Enlistment place: Warren County - Enlistment period: War - By whom: Lieutenant Morse - Discharged: 12 Jun 1815 - Bounty: BLW 9195-160-12 (Illinois).

Dearborn, Nathan - Private - 19th Infantry - Company: Carey Trimble - Age: 25 - Height: 5' 10" - Born: New Hampshire - Trade: Laborer - Enlistment date: 3 Mar 1814 - Enlistment place: Franklin County, Franklinton - Enlistment period: 1 Yr - By whom: Hugh Moore.

Dearth, William - Private - 19th Infantry - Comments: Deserted at Morristown, OH; tried and acquitted at Pittsburgh, PA; deserted again on 29 Mar 1815.

Death, Asahel - Fifer - 17th Infantry - Company: Henry Crittenden - Enlistment date: 20 Jul 1813 - Enlistment period: 18 Mos - Discharged: 20 Jan 1815 - Pension: Wife Elizabeth Brister, WO-28633, WC-15875, SO-16801, SC-10183; married in Sep 1818 in Waterford, OH; soldier died on 4 Nov 1871 in McLean County, IL; wife died on 2 Jan 1879 Woodford County, IL; served as a musician in Capt. Crittenden's Company, 17th Infantry; lived in Morgan County, OH and McLean County, IL - Bounty: BLW 574-160-50.

Debent, Anthony - Private - 19th Infantry - Company: Henry Crittenden - Other regiment: 17th Infantry.

Decker, John - Private - 27th Infantry - Company: Isaac Van Horne - Comments: Served aboard the US Sloop Trippe on the Lake Erie Squadron.

Decker, John - Private - 17th Infantry - Company: David Holt - Age: 35 - Height: 5' 1" - Born: Germany - Trade: Farmer - Enlistment date: 25 May 1814 - Enlistment place: New Lisbon - Enlistment period: War - By whom: Thomas McKnight - Discharged: 4 Jun 1815 at Chillicothe - Bounty: BLW 15845-160-12 (Illinois).

Deeds, Abraham - Fifer - 27th Infantry - Company: George Sanderson - Enlistment date: 28 Apr 1813.

Degear, Conrad - Private - 2nd Artillery - Company: Daniel Cushing - Age: 18 - Height: 5' 5 3/4" - Enlistment date: 22 Aug 1812 - Enlistment period: 5 Yrs - Died: 2 Jun 1813.

Degear, John - Private - 1st Rifles - Company: Thomas Ramsey - Other regiment: 1st Infantry - Age: 19 - Height: 5' 6" - Born: New York - Trade: Laborer - Enlistment date: 23 Dec 1813 - Enlistment place: Cincinnati - Enlistment period: 5 Yrs - By whom: Thomas Ramsey - Discharged: 25 Dec 1818 - Bounty: BLW 23932-160-12 (Arkansas) - Comments: Wounded during the Battle of Fort Erie, UC.

Degroff, Joseph - Private - 26th Infantry - Company: Richard Talbott - Other regiment: 19th Infantry - Age: 32 - Height: 5' 11" - Born: New York - Trade: Laborer - Enlistment date: 18 Feb 1814 - Enlistment place: Montgomery County - Enlistment period: 1 Yr - By whom: Philip Price - Discharged: 17 Feb 1815 at Erie, PA.

Dehague, Joseph - Private - 2nd Rifles - Company: Batteal Harrison - Age: 67 - Height: 5' 5 1/2" - Born: France, Gascony - Trade: Ship's carpenter - Enlistment date: 27 Jun 1814 - Enlistment period: 5 Yrs - By whom: Elias Langham - Discharged: 22 Sep 1815 - Comments: Discharged at Detroit advanced age and general disability.

Dehaven, Peter - Private - 26th Infantry - Company: Samuel Swearingen.

Delaurier, John Baptist - Private - 27th Infantry - Company: George Sanderson - Other regiment: 28th Infantry -

Enlistment date: 28 May 1813 - Enlistment period: War - Discharged: 30 Jun 1815 - Pension: Wife Julia Hazel, SO-27828, SC-20025; married on 8 Jun 1819 in Detroit, MI; wife died in Jan 1862; served as a private in Capt George Sanderson's Company, 27th Infantry and in Capt George Stockton's Company, 28th Infantry; lived in West Sandwich Province in western Canada, and in Essex County, UC - Bounty: BLW 14937-160-12 - Comments: Prisoner of War on Parole, captured at Detroit, MI, 16 Aug 1812.

Demster, Noah - Private - 27th Infantry - Company: Alexander Hill - Age: 27 - Height: 5' 9 1/2" - Born: Maryland - Enlistment date: 23 Apr 1814 - Enlistment place: Steubenville.

Denman, Samuel - Private - 19th Infantry - Company: Carey Trimble - Other regiment: 17th Infantry - Enlistment date: 5 Jul 1814 - Enlistment period: 1 Yr - Died: 30 Dec 1814 - Comments: Died at Williamsville, NY.

Denman, Samuel - Private - 27th Infantry - Age: 44 - Height: 5' 6 1/2" - Born: New Jersey - Enlistment date: 25 Jan 1814 - Enlistment place: Newark - By whom: John Spencer.

Denning, James - Private - 17th Infantry - Company: Harris Hickman - Age: 40 - Height: 5' 8" - Born: Maryland - Trade: Farmer - Enlistment date: 23 Feb 1814 - Enlistment place: Butler County, Hamilton - Enlistment period: War - By whom: George Stall - Discharged: 9 Jun 1815 at Chillicothe - Bounty: BLW 9288-160-12 (Illinois).

Dennis, David - Private - 19th Infantry - Company: George Kesling - Age: 28 - Height: 5' 6" - Born: Pennsylvania - Trade: Potter - Enlistment date: 29 Nov 1814 - Enlistment place: Lancaster - Enlistment period: War - By whom: John Simons - Discharged: 27 Mar 1815 at Zanesville - Bounty: BLW 6204-160-12.

Dennis, John - Private - 27th Infantry - Age: 28 - Height: 5' 8 1/2" - Born: Pennsylvania - Enlistment date: 5 Apr 1814 - Enlistment place: New Lisbon.

Dennis, Samuel - Private - 27th Infantry - Comments: Prisoner of War on Parole, captured at Detroit, MI, 16 Aug 1812.

Dennis, William - Private - 27th Infantry - Company: Joseph Cairns - Enlistment date: 3 Apr 1813 - Enlistment period: 1 Yr - Discharged: 2 Apr 1814 - Pension: Wife Mary Newman, WO-36372, WC-25757; served as a private in Capt. Joseph Cairne's Company, 27th Infantry; married in Nov 1816 in Muskingum County, OH; soldier died on 7 Sep 1869 in Perry County, OH; widow on died 10 Mar 1881; lived in Perry County, OH - Bounty: BLW-8012-160-50.

Dennison, Joseph - Drummer - 19th Infantry - Company: Wilson Elliott - Other regiment: 17th Infantry then 3rd Infantry - Age: 14 - Height: 4' 5" - Born: PA, Bucks County - Trade: Carpenter - Enlistment date: 9 Apr 1812 - Enlistment place: Dayton - Enlistment period: 5 Yrs - By whom: David Gwynn - Comments: Deserted 7 or 17 May 1815.

Denny, Daniel - Private - 19th Infantry - Company: George Kesling - Other regiment: 3rd Infantry - Age: 20 - Height: 5' 9" - Born: Pennsylvania - Trade: Shoemaker - Enlistment date: 15 Feb 1815 - Enlistment place: Zanesville - Enlistment period: 5 Yrs - By whom: Charles Cass - Discharged: 15 Feb 1820 at Fort Dearborn, IL.

Denson, Samuel - Private - 17th Infantry - Age: 21 - Height: 5' 8 1/2" - Born: Maryland - Trade: Laborer - Enlistment date: 16 Jan 1815 - Enlistment period: War - By whom: James Campbell - Discharged: 11 Jul 1815 at Chillicothe - Bounty: BLW 9734-160-12 Cancelled (because he was entitled to 320 acres); BLW 403-320-14.

Depoister, Joseph - Private - 17th Infantry - Company: John Chunn - Other regiment: 3rd Infantry - Age: 21 - Height: 5' 11 1/4" - Born: NC, Roane County - Trade: Farmer - Enlistment date: 13 Nov 1813 - Enlistment period: 18 Mos - By whom: John Mershon - Discharged: 13 May 1815.

Derue, Benjamin - Sergeant - 26th Infantry - Company: William Puthuff - Enlistment date: 6 May 1813 - Enlistment period: 1 Yr - Died: 27 Jan 1814, probably at Detroit.

Devault, Edward - Private - 19th Infantry - Age: 18 - Height: 5' 7" - Born: MD, Prince Georges County - Enlistment date: 22 Jun 1812 - Enlistment period: 5 Yrs.

Devault, Isaac - Private - 27th Infantry - Company: Absalom Martin - Comments: Served aboard the US Schooner Scorpion on the Lake Erie Squadron; Prisoner of War (Quebec, LC), captured at Fort Niagara, NY, 19 Dec 1813; exchanged 4 May 1814.

Devers, John - Private - 26th Infantry - Company: Joel Collins - Other regiment: 19th Infantry - Age: 29 - Height: 5' 9" - Born: Maryland - Trade: Cooper - Enlistment date: 23 Sep 1813 - Enlistment period: 1 Yr - By whom: Alexander Delerae - Discharged: 20 Jul 1815 at Detroit - Bounty: BLW 7100-160-12 (Illinois) - Comments: Re-enlisted in the 19 Infantry on 21 Apr 1814, Lieutenant Delorac, during the war enlistment, Sandwich, UC.

Devling, Patrick - Corporal - 2nd Artillery - Company: Daniel Cushing.

Devore, Enos - Private - 27th Infantry - Company: George Sanderson - Other regiment: 19th Infantry - Age: 22 - Height: 5' 6" - Born: Virginia - Trade: Laborer - Enlistment date: 31 May 1813 - Enlistment period: War -

Discharged: 20 Jul 1815 at Detroit - Pension: Wife Mary Prior, SO-947, SC-947, Old War IC-1363, Old War IF-1363 File 3276, Duplicate Old War IF-27675; married on 8 Feb 1816 in Muskingum County, OH, served as a private in Captain Isaac Van Horne's Company, 19th US Infantry; lived in Perry and Muskingum Counties, also Dresden, OH - Bounty: BLW 6167-160-12 (Illinois) - Comments: Prisoner of War on Parole, captured at Detroit, MI, 16 Aug 1812.

Devore, Peter - Private - 19th Infantry - Company: William Gill - Age: 34 - Height: 5' 8" - Born: Jersey - Enlistment date: 12 Oct 1814 - Enlistment period: War - By whom: Wynkoop Warner - Discharged: 5 Jun 1815 at Chillicothe - Bounty: BLW 5191-160-12 (Illinois).

Dewese, Samuel - Private - 27th Infantry - Company: Isaac Van Horne - Enlistment date: 14 May 1813 - Enlistment period: 1 Yr - Discharged: 14 May 1814 - Pension: Wife Anna Switzer (2nd wife), WO-18515, WC-13630, SO-4535, SC-2168; married on 16 Nov 1828 in Stark County, OH; soldier died on 27 Dec 1876 in Weston, Wood County, OH; wife died on 22 Dec 1883; served as a private in Capt. Van Horne's Company, 27th Infantry; lived in Seneca and Wood Counties, OH; 1st wife was Sarah Boyer - Bounty: BLW 726-160-50.

Dewey, Lemuel - Private - 19th Infantry - Company: Wilson Elliott - Enlistment date: 10 Aug 1812 - Discharged: 13 Aug 1813 - Pension: Wife Sara Groat, SO-5616, SC-3181, WO-40268, WC-30619; served in Capt. Wilson Elliott's Company, US Artillery; married on 28 May 1817 in Western, Oneida County, NY; soldier died on 25 Jan 1880 in Waupaca, WI; widow died about 1882; lived in La Marine and Waupaca, WS - Bounty: BLW 23987-160-50.

Dexter, Stephen - Private - 26th Infantry - Company: Samuel Swearingen - Enlistment date: 16 Jul 1813 - Enlistment period: 1 Yr.

Dial, Daniel - Private - 27th Infantry - Company: Carey Trimble - Other regiment: 19th Infantry - Age: 25 - Height: 5' 7" - Born: Pennsylvania - Enlistment date: 3 Jan 1814 - Enlistment place: Newark - Enlistment period: 1 Yr - By whom: John Spencer - Discharged: 3 Jan 1815.

Dickey, John - Private - 19th Infantry - Company: John Chunn - Enlistment date: 9 May 1813 - Enlistment period: 5 Yrs - Died: Dec 1812 - Pension: Wife Nancy, Old War WF-12448; served as a private in the 19th Infantry - Comments: Died between 1 Sep and 31 Dec 1813, at Lower Sandusky, OH (Fremont, OH).

Dickinson, Richard - Waiter - 19th Infantry - Company: Asabael Nearing.

Didder, Samuel - 1st Rifles - Company: Thomas Ramsey - Age: 25 - Height: 6' 2" - Born: PA, Bedford County - Trade: Farmer - Enlistment date: 1 Aug 1814 - Enlistment place: Dayton - Enlistment period: War - By whom: Thomas Ramsey - Comments: Deserted 5 Aug 1814 at Camp Urbana, OH.

Digby, John - Private - 19th Infantry - Age: 18 - Height: 5' 10" - Born: OH, Hamilton County - Enlistment date: 29 Apr 1814 - Enlistment place: Lebanon - Enlistment period: 5 Yrs - By whom: Richard Talbott.

Dinkins, John - Private - 19th Infantry - Company: Joel Collins - Age: 20 - Height: 5' 7" - Born: Connecticut - Trade: Brick layer - Enlistment date: 15 Mar 1814 - Enlistment place: Detroit - Enlistment period: War - By whom: Wynkoop Warner - Discharged: 20 Jul 1815 at Detroit - Bounty: BLW 18492-160-12 - Comments: Re-enlisted.

Dixon, John - Corporal - 17th Infantry - Company: Harris Hickman - Age: 43 - Height: 6' 1" - Born: PA, Franklin County - Trade: Powder maker - Enlistment date: 23 Feb 1814 - Enlistment period: War - By whom: William Leavitt.

Dobson, Matthew - Private - 17th Infantry - Company: Henry Crittenden - Age: 27 - Height: 5' 8" - Born: OH, Muskingum County - Trade: Farmer - Enlistment date: 16 May 1813 - Enlistment place: Franklin County, Franklinton - Enlistment period: War - By whom: John Cochran - Discharged: 9 Jun 1815 at Chillicothe - Bounty: BLW 8665-160-12 (Illinois).

Dodds, Joseph - Private - 7th Infantry - Company: Zachary Taylor - Enlistment date: 2 Mar 1812 - Enlistment period: 5 Yrs - By whom: Thomas Ramsey - Killed: 4 Sep 1812 - Pension: Heirs obtained half pay for five years in lieu of military bounty land.

Dodemead, John - Sergeant - 19th Infantry - Enlistment date: 15 Apr 1812 - Enlistment period: 5 Yrs - Died: 1814 - Comments: Prisoner of War; discharged at Greenbush, NY; died on journey home.

Dodge, Hezekiah - Private - 2nd Artillery - Company: Daniel Cushing - Height: 5' 11" - Born: NY, Dutchess County Enlistment date: 25 Jul 1812 - Enlistment place: Canton.

Dollarhide, John - Private - 1st Rifles - Company: Thomas Ramsey - Age: 42 - Height: 5' 6" - Born: Ireland, County Cavan - Trade: Laborer - Enlistment date: 15 Nov 1813 - Enlistment place: Cincinnati - Enlistment period: War - By whom: Thomas Ramsey - Discharged: 5 Jun 1815 at Buffalo, NY.

Dolson, Nathan - Private - 17th Infantry - Age: 27 - Height: 5' 8" - Born: PA, Northumberland County - Trade: Laborer - Enlistment date: 16 May 1813 - Enlistment place: Franklin County, Franklinton - Enlistment period: War - By whom: John Cochran.

Don, Peter - Private - 27th Infantry - Age: 23 - Height: 5' 9" - Born: MI, Wayne County, Detroit - Enlistment date: 1 May 1814 - Enlistment place: Zanesville - Comments: Deserted 4 May 1814.

Donahue, David - Private - 19th Infantry - Company: Wilson Elliott - Age: 43 - Height: 6' 1" - Born: DE, New Castle County - Enlistment date: 4 Aug 1812.

Donahy, Samuel - Private - 2nd Artillery - Company: Daniel Cushing.

Donica, Samuel - Private - 2nd Artillery - Company: Daniel Cushing - Other regiment: Corps of Artillery - Age: 27 - Height: 5' 7" - Born: Virginia - Trade: Farmer - Enlistment date: 15 Jul 1812 - Enlistment place: Chillicothe - Enlistment period: 5 Yrs - By whom: Samuel Kercheval - Discharged: 18 Jul 1817 - Bounty: BLW 10561-160-12 (Illinois).

Donley, Joseph - Private - 26th Infantry - Company: George Kesling - Other regiment: 2nd Light Dragoons.

Donohoe, George - Private - 1st Rifles - Company: Thomas Ramsey - Age: 35 - Height: 5' 6" - Born: Ireland, County Cork - Trade: Laborer - Enlistment date: 20 Dec 1813 - Enlistment place: Cincinnati - Enlistment period: 5 Yrs - By whom: Thomas Ramsey - Discharged: 20 Dec 1818.

Dougherty, Daniel - Sergeant - 19th Infantry - Company: James Herron - Other regiments: 17th Infantry then 3rd Infantry - Age: 31 - Height: 6' - Born: NJ, Sussex County - Trade: Farmer - Enlistment date: 7 Jul 1812 - Enlistment place: Zanesville - Enlistment period: 5 Yrs - By whom: James Herron - Discharged: 2 Apr 1816 - Comments: Discharged after furnishing a substitute.

Dougherty, James - Private - 1st Rifles - Company: Thomas Ramsey - Age: 36 - Height: 5' 6" - Born: Ireland, County Donegal - Trade: Baker - Enlistment date: 3 Mar 1814 - Enlistment place: Cincinnati - Enlistment period: War - By whom: Thomas Ramsey - Died: 24 Aug 1814, drown in Lake Erie at Cleveland.

Dougherty, Levi - Private - 26th Infantry - Company: George Kesling - Other regiment: 2nd Light Dragoons - Enlistment date: 30 May 1813 - Enlistment period: 1 Yr.

Dougherty, Robert - Sergeant - 19th Infantry - Comments: Prisoner of War on Parole, captured at Detroit, MI, 16 Aug 1812.

Dougherty, William - Private - 17th Infantry - Age: 32 - Height: 5' 10" - Born: Pennsylvania - Trade: Blacksmith - Enlistment date: 5 Sep 1814 - Enlistment period: War - By whom: James Campbell.

Doughtey, Zachariah - Private - 17th Infantry - Company: Henry Crittenden - Age: 19 - Height: 5' 9 1/2" - Born: KY, Paris County - Trade: Farmer - Enlistment date: 3 Jul 1813 - Enlistment place: Cincinnati - Enlistment period: War - By whom: Lieutenant Price - Discharged: 9 Jun 1815 at Chillicothe - Bounty: BLW 23750-160-12.

Douglass, Alexander - Private - 26th Infantry - Company: Samuel Swearingen - Other regiment: 25th Infantry - Enlistment date: 28 Apr 1813 - Enlistment period: 1 Yr - Discharged: 29 Apr 1814.

Douglass, Andrew - Private - 26th Infantry - Company: Joel Collins - Enlistment date: 2 Oct 1813 - Enlistment period: 1 Yr.

Douglass, James - Sergeant - 19th Infantry - Company: William Gill - Age: 18 - Height: 5' 6" - Born: PA, York County - Trade: Cabinet maker - Enlistment date: 12 Feb 1814 - Enlistment period: 1 Yr - By whom: Richard Talbott Discharged: 10 Feb 1815.

Douglass, Jeremiah - Private - 17th Infantry - Company: John Chunn - Age: 40 - Height: 5' 10" - Born: England - Trade: Blacksmith - Enlistment date: 7 Nov 1813 - Enlistment period: War - By whom: George Stall - Pension: Old War IF-26077; served as a private in Capt. Chunn's Company, 17th Infantry - Bounty: BLW 11624-160-12 (Missouri) - Comments: Lost right arm.

Douthout, Jacob - Private - 26th Infantry - Company: George Kesling - Enlistment date: 11 May 1813 - Died: 9 Oct 1813.

Douty, Joseph - Private - 26th Infantry - Company: George Kesling - Enlistment date: 30 May 1813.

Dowing, Robert - Corporal - 1st Rifles - Age: 19 - Height: 5' 9" - Born: Virginia - Trade: Farmer - Enlistment date: 5 Apr 1812 - Enlistment place: Cincinnati - Enlistment period: 5 Yrs - By whom: Thomas Ramsey - Discharged: 1 Aug 1815 - Comments: Discharged at Buffalo, NY, wounded at Fort Erie on 17 Sep 1814 and unfit for duty.

Downey, William - Private - 2nd Light Dragoons - Company: Samuel Hopkins - Enlistment date: 9 Jun 1812 - Enlistment period: 5 Yrs - Died: 10 Jul 1813 at Pickaway Plains, OH.

Downs, Jesse - Private - 19th Infantry - Company: Angus Langham - Enlistment date: 29 Jul 1812 - Enlistment period: 18 Mos - Pension: Wife Charlotte, Old War IF-13820 Rejected; served as a private in Capt. A. Langham's Company - Comments: Prisoner of War, exchanged 25 Apr 1814.

Downs, Noah - Fifer - 19th Infantry - Company: Carey Trimble - Age: 23 - Height: 6' 1" - Born: Maryland - Trade: Farmer - Enlistment date: 22 Mar 1814 - Enlistment place: Chillicothe - Enlistment period: War - By whom: Charles Cissna - Discharged: 6 Jun 1815 at Chillicothe - Bounty: BLW 9471-160-12 (Illinois).

The Enlisted Men

Doyle, Benjamin - Private - 26th Infantry - Company: George Kesling - Other regiment: 25th Infantry - Enlistment date: 13 May 1813 - Discharged: 13 May 1814.

Drake, Jesse - Private - 17th Infantry - Company: Caleb Holder - Age: 38 - Height: 6' - Born: New York - Trade: Shoemaker - Enlistment date: 8 Jul 1814 - Enlistment period: War - By whom: William Featherstone - Bounty: BLW 27708-160-42.

Draper, Asa - Private - 27th Infantry - Company: George Sanderson - Enlistment date: 28 Jun 1813.

Drewer, Joseph - Fifer - 19th Infantry - Company: Wilson Elliott - Other regiment: 17th Infantry - Age: 17 - Height: 5' 6" - Born: VA, Kanawha County, Charleston (now WV) - Enlistment date: 30 Oct 1812 - By whom: John Reeves.

Drouillard, Joseph - Fifer - 19th Infantry - Company: George Stockton - Other regiment: 3rd Infantry - Enlistment date: 30 Oct 1812 - Discharged: 30 Oct 1815 - Pension: Wife Sarah Bowen, SO-27444, SC-18579; served as a fifer in Capt. George Stockton's Company, 3rd Infantry; married on 1 Sep 1820 in Rome, Lawrence County, OH; soldier died on 10 Mar 1895; lived in Gallia County, OH - Bounty: BLW 2001-160-50.

Duckwall, Henry - Private - 27th Infantry - Born: OH, Belmont County, St. Clairsville - Enlistment date: 23 Apr 1814 - Enlistment place: St. Clairsville - Enlistment period: War - By whom: Ensign Biddle.

Dugan, John - Corporal - 27th Infantry - Company: George Sanderson - Enlistment date: 10 Apr 1813 - Comments: Prisoner of War on Parole, captured at Detroit, MI, 16 Aug 1812.

Dugan, John - Private - Rangers - Company: Samuel McCormick - Enlistment date: 6 Dec 1813 - Enlistment period: 1 Yr - Discharged: 5 Dec 1814.

Duke, Peter L. - Private - 26th Infantry - Comments: Prisoner of War, sent to Fort Walcott.

Dukes, George - Private - 1st Rifles - Company: Thomas Ramsey - Age: 22 - Height: 6' - Born: PA, Bedford County - Trade: Blacksmith - Enlistment date: 1 Aug 1813 - Enlistment place: Cincinnati - Enlistment period: 5 Yrs - By whom: Thomas Ramsey - Discharged: 1 Aug 1818 - Bounty: BLW 19243-160-12 (Missouri).

Dumont, Peter Jr - Private - 1st Rifles - Company: Thomas Ramsey - Age: 33 - Height: 5' 6" - Born: NJ, Somerset County - Trade: Printer - Enlistment date: 24 Mar 1814 - Enlistment place: Cincinnati - Enlistment period: War - By whom: Thomas Ramsey - Discharged: 5 Jun 1815 at Buffalo, NY.

Duncan, Joseph - Private - 19th Infantry - Company: James Herron - Enlistment date: 16 Nov 1812 - Enlistment period: 5 Yrs.

Duncan, William - Corporal - Rangers - Company: Samuel McCormick - Enlistment date: 10 Nov 1813 - Enlistment period: 1 Yr - Discharged: 22 Nov 1814.

Duncan, William - Corporal - 19th Infantry - Company: Richard Talbott - Age: 21 - Height: 5' 9" - Born: Ohio - Trade: Laborer - Enlistment date: 25 Mar 1814 - Enlistment place: Lebanon - Enlistment period: War - By whom: Richard Talbott - Discharged: 5 Jun 1815 at Chillicothe - Pension: Served as a corporal in Capt. R. C. Talbott's Company, 19th Infantry - Bounty: BLW 13766-160-12 (Missouri).

Dunday, John - Private - 27th Infantry - Company: Isaac Van Horne - Other regiment: 19th Infantry - Enlistment date: 6 Jun 1813 - Enlistment period: 1 Yr - Discharged: 6 Jun 1814 - Pension: Wife Mary Seth, SO-24350, SC-16611; served as a private in Capt. Isaac Van Horn's Company, 19th and 27th Infantries; married on 4 Feb 1822 in Fowler, Trumbull County, OH; lived in Pierce County, WI, and Allamakee County, IA - Bounty: BLW 3013-160-50.

Dunevin, James L. - Musician - 19th Infantry - Company: James Herron - Enlistment date: 25 Jul 1812 - Enlistment period: 5 Yrs.

Dunham, Walter - Private - 27th Infantry - Company: George Sanderson - Enlistment date: 1 May 1813.

Dunlap, James - Private - 19th Infantry - Comments: Prisoner of War on Parole, captured at Detroit, MI, 16 Aug 1812.

Dunman, Samuel - Private - 19th Infantry - Company: William MacDonald - Died: 6 Jan 1815.

Dunn, John - Private - 1st Rifles - Company: Thomas Ramsey - Age: 32 - Height: 5' 10 1/2" - Born: New York - Trade: Cooper - Enlistment date: 23 Jan 1814 - Enlistment place: Cincinnati - Enlistment period: 5 Yrs - By whom: Thomas Ramsey - Comments: Deserted 3 Aug 1814 at Camp Springfield.

Dunseath, David - Sergeant - 1st Rifles - Company: Thomas Ramsey - Age: 19 - Height: 5' 8 1/2" - Born: PA, Westmoreland County - Trade: Store keeper - Enlistment date: 16 Nov 1813 - Enlistment place: Cincinnati - Enlistment period: 5 Yrs - By whom: Thomas Ramsey - Died: 16 Jan 1815 at Conjocquita Creek, NY - Bounty: BLW 25183-160-12 (Arkansas) - Comments: Land bounty to John Dunseth, brother & other heirs at law of David Dunseath.

Dunseath, David - Private - 19th Infantry - Enlistment date: 6 May 1813 - Enlistment place: Cincinnati - Enlistment period: 18 Mos.

Dupree, Francis - Private - 19th Infantry - Company: Martin Hawkins - Other regiment: 17th Infantry - Age: 25 - Height: 5' 10" - Born: Lower Canada, Montreal - Trade: Blacksmith - Enlistment date: 14 Apr 1814 - Enlistment place: Detroit - Enlistment period: 5 Yrs - By whom: George Atchison - Died: 12 Sep 1814 - Bounty: BLW 22001-160-12 (Arkansas) - Comments: Died of wounds received on board US Schooner Scorpion, while engaged with the enemy near Fort Mackinac, MI; land bounty to Louis Depree & other heirs at law of Francis Depree.

Dupree, John B. - Private - 19th Infantry - Company: Martin Hawkins - Other regiment: 17th Infantry then 3rd Infantry - Age: 23 - Height: 5' 9" - Born: MI, Wayne County, Detroit - Trade: Laborer - Enlistment date: 14 Apr 1814 - Enlistment place: Detroit - Enlistment period: 5 Yrs - By whom: George Atchison - Discharged: 14 Apr 1819.

Dutton, Jonas - Private - 2nd Artillery - Company: Daniel Cushing.

Duval, Presberry - Private - 19th Infantry - Age: 32 - Height: 5' 7 3/4" - Born: Rhode Island - Enlistment date: 4 Aug 1812 - Comments: Deserted.

Duvault, Edmond - 19th Infantry.

Dwyer, David - Private - 27th Infantry - Enlistment place: Newark - Comments: Deserted.

Dyer, Conrad - Private - 2nd Artillery - Company: Daniel Cushing - Age: 18 - Height: 5' 5 3/4" - Enlistment date: 22 Aug 1812.

Dyer, John - Sergeant - 19th Infantry - Company: Carey Trimble - Age: 24 - Height: 5' 9" - Born: Pennsylvania - Trade: Farmer - Enlistment date: 21 Mar 1814 - Enlistment place: Chillicothe - Enlistment period: War - By whom: Charles Cissna - Discharged: 6 Jun 1815 at Chillicothe - Bounty: BLW 6029-160-12 (Arkansas).

Dysart, Joseph - Private - 28th Infantry - Company: Nimrod Moore - Enlistment date: 17 Jun 1813 - Enlistment place: North Carolina - Enlistment period: 1 Yr - Died: 31 Dec 1813 at Bass Island, OH (Put-in-Bay, OH); on command while onboard the fleet.

Eagan, John - Private - 27th Infantry - Comments: Prisoner of War on Parole, captured at Detroit, MI, 16 Aug 1812.

Early, John - Private - 19th Infantry - Company: Harris Hickman - Other regiment: 17th Infantry - Age: 21 - Height: 5' 10 1/2" - Born: Ireland, County Down - Trade: Carpenter - Enlistment date: 6 Apr 1814 - Enlistment place: Chillicothe - Enlistment period: War - By whom: David Carney - Discharged: 9 Jun 1815 at Chillicothe - Bounty: BLW 6025-160-12 (Illinois).

Eastwood, Benjamin - Private - Rangers - Company: Samuel McCormick - Enlistment date: 1 Nov 1813 - Enlistment period: 1 Yr - Discharged: 22 Nov 1814.

Eaton – see Heaton, Samuel

Eckhart, William - Private - 19th Infantry - Company: William Gill - Other regiment: 3rd Infantry - Age: 23 - Height: 5' 3" - Born: NJ, Essex County - Trade: Shoemaker - Enlistment date: 2 Oct 1814 - Enlistment period: 5 Yrs - By whom: Lieutenant Huff - Discharged: 12 Jul 1819 - Comments: Discharged at Fort Howard, WI, re-enlisted.

Edgar, Martin - Private - 19th Infantry - Company: Angus Langham - Other regiment: 17th Infantry - Trade: Cooper.

Edging, Martin - Private - 19th Infantry - Company: John Chunn - Other regiment: 17th Infantry - Age: 32 - Height: 5' 11" - Born: MD, Cecil County, Easton - Enlistment date: 18 Jul 1812 - Enlistment place: St. Clairsville - Enlistment period: 5 Yrs - By whom: Samuel Booker - Comments: Prisoner of War (Halifax, NS), captured at Fort Erie, UC, 15 Aug 1814; released 8 Apr 1815.

Edington, Jonathan - 19th Infantry - Enlistment date: 25 Jul 1812 - Enlistment place: St. Clairsville.

Edmunson, William - Private - 19th Infantry - Age: 32 - Height: 5' 10" - Born: Ireland - Enlistment date: 6 Jul 1812 - Enlistment place: St. Clairsville - Enlistment period: 5 Yrs - By whom: Samuel Booker.

Edson, Luther - Corporal - 27th Infantry - Company: George Sanderson - Enlistment date: 26 Apr 1813 - Comments: Prisoner of War on Parole, captured at Detroit, MI, 16 Aug 1812.

Edwards, John - Private - 26th Infantry - Company: George Kesling - Other regiment: 25th Infantry - Enlistment date: 13 May 1813 - Enlistment period: 1 Yr - Discharged: 13 May 1814.

Edwin, John G. - Sergeant - 19th Infantry - Company: Martin Hawkins - Other regiment: 17th Infantry - Age: 28 - Height: 5' 7 1/2" - Born: PA, Philadelphia County - Enlistment date: 1 Apr 1814 - Enlistment place: Detroit - Enlistment period: War - By whom: George Atchison - Died: 19 Dec 1814 at Buffalo, NY.

Eling, James - Private - 17th Infantry - Company: Caleb Holder - Age: 23 - Height: 5' 7 1/2" - Born: Pennsylvania - Trade: Shoemaker - Enlistment date: 2 Jul 1814 - Enlistment place: Steubenville - Enlistment period: War - By whom: William Featherstone.

Ellerton, John - Corporal - 19th Infantry - Company: Angus Langham - Comments: Prisoner of War, captured at

The Enlisted Men

Frenchtown, MI on 22 Feb 1813..

Ellinger, Joseph - Private - 27th Infantry - Company: George Sanderson - Enlistment date: 16 Apr 1813 - Enlistment period: 1 Yr - Discharged: 19 Apr 1814.

Elliott, George - Sergeant - 19th Infantry - Company: William Gill - Other regiment: 3rd Infantry - Age: 22 - Height: 5' 11" - Born: Ireland, County Donegal - Trade: Blacksmith - Enlistment date: 28 Aug 1814 - Enlistment place: Steubenville - Enlistment period: 5 Yrs - By whom: James Blair - Discharged: 28 Aug 1819 at Fort Howard, WI.

Elliott, James - Private - 17th Infantry - Other regiment: 3rd Infantry - Age: 25 - Height: 5' 8" - Born: Virginia - Trade: Farmer - Enlistment date: 25 Dec 1814 - Enlistment place: Cincinnati - Enlistment period: 5 Yrs - By whom: John Reeves - Discharged: 25 Dec 1819 at Fort Mackinac, MI.

Elliott, John - Sergeant - 27th Infantry - Company: William Gill - Other regiment: 19th Infantry - Age: 37 - Height: 5' 7" - Born: PA, Franklin County - Trade: Joiner - Enlistment date: 8 Mar 1814 - Enlistment period: War - By whom: John Spencer - Discharged: 5 Jun 1815 at Chillicothe - Bounty: BLW 6166-160-12 (Illinois).

Elliott, Thomas - Private - 27th Infantry - Company: Absalom Martin - Enlistment date: 11 Aug 1813 - Enlistment period: 1 Yr - Discharged: 11 Aug 1814.

Elliott, William - Private - 27th Infantry - Company: Carey Trimble - Other regiment: 19th Infantry - Age: 40 - Height: 5' 9" - Born: Pennsylvania - Trade: Potter - Enlistment date: 16 Mar 1814 - Enlistment place: Warren County - Enlistment period: War - By whom: Ebenezer Benedict - Discharged: 6 Jun 1815 at Chillicothe - Bounty: BLW 3716-160-12 (Arkansas).

Ellison, James - Private - 19th Infantry - Company: Angus Langham - Other regiment: 17th Infantry - Age: 18 - Height: 5' 9" - Born: Ireland, County Tyrone - Trade: Farmer - Enlistment date: 31 Jul 1812 - Enlistment place: Cincinnati - Enlistment period: 5 Yrs - By whom: Hugh Moore - Discharged: 31 Jul 1817 - Comments: Prisoner of War; discharged at Fort Harrison, IN.

Elsey, William - Corporal - 1st Infantry - Company: Horatio Stark - Age: 27 - Height: 5' 9" - Born: Virginia - Trade: Shoemaker - Enlistment date: 11 Apr 1812 - Enlistment place: Chillicothe - Enlistment period: 5 Yrs - By whom: John Swearingen - Killed: 16 Jul 1813 by Indians.

Emery, James - Private - 19th Infantry - Company: Richard Talbott - Age: 20 - Height: 5' 6" - Born: England, Somerset County - Trade: Farmer - Enlistment date: 11 Jul 1814 - Enlistment place: Urbana - Enlistment period: War - By whom: William Baird - Discharged: 5 Jun 1815 at Chillicothe - Bounty: BLW 6666-160-12 (Illinois).

Emmit, Abraham - Private - 27th Infantry - Comments: Prisoner of War on Parole, captured at Detroit, MI, 16 Aug 1812.

Emmonds, John - Private - 17th Infantry - Company: Caleb Holder - Age: 37 - Height: 5' 8" - Born: Virginia - Trade: Tailor - Enlistment date: 14 Aug 1814 - Enlistment place: Cincinnati - Enlistment period: War - By whom: George Stall - Discharged: 30 Jun 1815 at Detroit - Bounty: BLW 21670-160-12 (Arkansas).

English, George - Private - 19th Infantry - Company: William Gill - Age: 23 - Height: 5' 9" - Born: Pennsylvania - Enlistment date: 3 Sep 1814 - Enlistment place: Zanesville - Enlistment period: War - By whom: Neal McFadden - Discharged: 11 Oct 1814 - Comments: Discharged by writ of habeas corpus at Zanesville, OH.

Enimans, Elisha - Private - 19th Infantry - Age: 23 - Height: 5' 11" - Born: NJ, Monmouth County - Enlistment date: 30 Jul 1812 - Enlistment period: 18 Mos.

Ernhart, Jacob - Private - 26th Infantry - Company: William Puthuff - Enlistment date: 27 Apr 1813 - Enlistment period: 1 Yr.

Evans, Edward - Private - 19th Infantry - Company: Wilson Elliott.

Evans, Edward - Private - 17th Infantry - Company: Harris Hickman - Age: 30 - Height: 5' 9" - Born: PA, Bucks County - Trade: Farmer - Enlistment date: 7 May 1814 - Enlistment place: Cincinnati - Enlistment period: War - By whom: George Stall - Discharged: 9 Jun 1815 at Chillicothe - Bounty: BLW 9269-160-12 (Illinois).

Evans, Isaac - Corporal - 26th Infantry - Company: William Puthuff - Enlistment date: 12 Apr 1813 - Enlistment period: 1 Yr - Discharged: 14 Apr 1814 - Pension: Wife Elizabeth Welsh, WO-24980, WC-11609; married on 14 Nov 1816 in Portsmouth, Scioto County, OH, soldier died on 4 Apr 1850 in Milan, OH; widow died on 11 Dec 1887 Fremont, OH; served as corporal in Capt. William H. Puthuff's Company, 26th Infantry; lived in Erie and Sandusky Counties, OH - Bounty: BLW 6253-160-50.

Evans, John - Private - 27th Infantry - Company: George Sanderson - Enlistment date: 14 Jun 1813.

Evans, Joseph - Private - 2nd Rifles - Company: Batteal Harrison - Age: 25 - Height: 5' 8 3/4" - Born: PA, Fayette County, Redstone - Trade: Laborer - Enlistment date: 31 May 1814 - Enlistment place: Cincinnati - Enlistment period: 5 Yrs - By whom: Edward Miller - Died: 31 May 1815.

Evans, Montgomery - Private - Rangers - Company: James Manary - Enlistment date: 6 Apr 1812 - Enlistment period: 1 Yr - Discharged: 22 Mar 1813 - Pension: Wife Sarah Warren, WO-5866, WC-2968; served as a private in Capt. Manary's Company, OH Militia; married on 30 Mar 1814 in Delaware County; soldier died on 16 Aug 1847 in Defiance, OH; lived in Defiance and Darke Counties, OH - Bounty: BLW 12870-160-50.

Evans, Robert - Corporal - 19th Infantry - Company: Richard Talbott - Age: 40 - Height: 5' 7" - Born: DE, New Castle County - Trade: School master - Enlistment date: 28 Apr 1814 - Enlistment place: Lebanon - Enlistment period: War - By whom: Richard Talbott - Discharged: 5 Jun 1815 at Chillicothe - Bounty: BLW 8012-160-12.

Everett, Isaac - Private - 26th Infantry - Company: William Puthuff - Enlistment date: 5 Jun 1813 - Enlistment period: 1 Yr - Died: 27 Dec 1813 at Sandwich, UC (now Windsor, Ontario).

Everett, Moses - Drummer - 26th Infantry - Company: Samuel Swearingen - Other regiment: 25th Infantry - Enlistment date: 12 Mar 1813 - Enlistment period: 1 Yr - Discharged: 30 Apr 1814.

Everhart, Samuel - Private - 2nd Artillery - Company: Daniel Cushing - Pension: Wife Elizabeth Luthers, Old War Invalid and Widow Rejected 14047; served as a private in Capt. Cushing's Company, 2nd Regiment, US Art.

Ewing, William M. - Quartermaster Sergeant - 19th Infantry - Company: George Kesling - Age: 22 - Height: 5' 8 1/2" - Born: Kentucky - Trade: Saddler - Enlistment date: 22 Oct 1814 - Enlistment place: Xenia - Enlistment period: 5 Yrs - By whom: Robert Smith - Discharged: 27 Mar 1815 at Zanesville - Bounty: BLW 706-320-14 (Illinois).

Ewings, James - Private - 2nd Rifles - Age: 37 - Height: 5' 8 1/3" - Born: Ireland - Trade: Weaver - Enlistment date: 9 May 1814 - Enlistment place: New Lisbon - Enlistment period: War - By whom: William Pritchard - Discharged: 30 Jun 1815 at Detroit.

Exline, Daniel - Private - 19th Infantry - Company: Carey Trimble - Age: 24 - Height: 5' 8" - Born: VA, Monongahela County (now West Virginia) - Trade: Farmer - Enlistment date: 21 Apr 1814 - Enlistment place: Athens - Enlistment period: War - By whom: Charles Cissna - Discharged: 6 Jun 1815 at Chillicothe - Bounty: BLW 6253-160-12 (Illinois).

Exline, Edward - Private - 19th Infantry - Company: Carey Trimble - Age: 25 - Height: 5' 5 1/2" - Born: Virginia - Trade: Farmer - Enlistment date: 3 Feb 1814 - Enlistment place: Chillicothe - Enlistment period: War - By whom: John Swearingen - Discharged: 6 Jun 1815 at Chillicothe - Bounty: BLW 6252-160-12 (Illinois).

Facer, Lewis (Farer) - Musician - 19th Infantry - Company: William Gill - Age: 25 - Height: 5' 11" - Born: Virginia - Trade: Farmer - Enlistment date: 6 May 1814 - Enlistment period: War - By whom: John Spencer - Discharged: 5 Jun 1815 at Chillicothe - Bounty: BLW 16915-160-12 (Illinois).

Faherty, Bartlett - Private - 28th Infantry - Company: Nimrod Moore - Enlistment date: 28 May 1813 - Enlistment period: 1 Yr - Died: 11 Nov 1813 at Fort Seneca (now Old Fort, OH).

Faid, John - Private - 27th Infantry - Company: George Sanderson - Enlistment date: 22 Apr 1813 - Discharged: 23 Nov 1813.

Faircloth, James - Private - 2nd Artillery - Company: Daniel Cushing - Died: 16 Mar 1813 at Fort Meigs.

Fairhurst, David - Private - 19th Infantry - Company: Angus Langham - Age: 23 - Height: 5' 11" - Born: VA, Loudoun County - Enlistment date: 10 Jul 1812 - Enlistment place: St. Clairsville - Enlistment period: 5 Yrs - By whom: Samuel Booker - Died: 17 May 1813 - Bounty: BLW 26942-160-12 (Arkansas) - Comments: Died from wounds; land bounty to David and John Fairhurst, sons and only heirs at law of David Fairhurst.

Falgner, Charles - Corporal - 2nd Artillery - Company: Daniel Cushing - Other regiment: Corps of Artillery - Age: 25 - Height: 5' 7" - Born: Virginia - Trade: Farmer - Enlistment date: 11 Jun 1814 - Enlistment period: War - Discharged: 4 Jul 1815 - Comments: Discharged at Fort Meigs, OH.

Faris, John - Private - 2nd Rifles - Company: Batteal Harrison - Other regiment: Rifle Regiment - Age: 22 - Height: 5' 3 1/2" - Born: Virginia - Trade: Laborer - Enlistment date: 19 Apr 1814 - Enlistment place: Chillicothe - Enlistment period: 5 Yrs - By whom: Batteal Harrison - Bounty: BLW 22392-160-12 (Arkansas) - Comments: Re-enlisted.

Farmer, M. Michael - Private - 26th Infantry - Company: George Kesling - Enlistment date: 11 May 1813 - Enlistment period: 1 Yr - By whom: George Kesling - Died: 9 Sep 1813.

Farmer, Singleton - Private - 26th Infantry - Company: William Puthuff - Other regiment: 25th Infantry - Enlistment date: 9 May 1813 - Discharged: 9 May 1814.

Farris, Joseph H. - Corporal - 19th Infantry - Company: Richard Talbott - Age: 21 - Height: 5' 6" - Born: New Jersey - Trade: Tanner - Enlistment date: 29 Apr 1814 - Enlistment place: Springfield (or Redding) - Enlistment period: War - By whom: Abijah Johns - Discharged: 5 Jun 1815 at Chillicothe - Bounty: BLW 27145-160-12.

Faulker, James - Private - 2nd Artillery - Company: Daniel Cushing.

The Enlisted Men

Faulkner, John - Private - 19th Infantry - Company: William Gill - Age: 31 - Height: 5' 7 1/2" - Trade: Gardener - Enlistment date: 12 Oct 1814 - Enlistment period: War - By whom: Nehemiah Gregory - Discharged: 5 Jun 1815 at Chillicothe - Bounty: BLW 6017-160-12.

Feddeman, Henry - Private - 2nd Artillery - Company: Daniel Cushing - Died: 28 Jun 1813 at Fort Meigs.

Felter, John D. - Private - 26th Infantry - Company: Samuel Swearingen - Other regiment: 25th Infantry - Age: 23 - Height: 5' 11" - Enlistment date: 8 Jul 1813 - Enlistment period: 1 Yr - Discharged: 21 Jun 1814.

Felton, James - 1st Rifles - Company: Thomas Ramsey - Age: 19 - Height: 5' 8" - Born: Pennsylvania - Trade: Farmer - Enlistment date: 9 Feb 1814 - Enlistment place: Cincinnati - Enlistment period: 5 Yrs - By whom: Thomas Ramsey - Comments: Deserted at Cincinnati on 11 Feb 1814.

Feltwet, Louis - 2nd Rifles - Company: Batteal Harrison - Age: 25 - Height: 5' 7 1/2" - Born: Lower Canada, Quebec - Trade: Laborer - Enlistment date: 2 Jul 1814 - Enlistment place: Chillicothe - Enlistment period: War - By whom: Batteal Harrison - Discharged: 30 Jun 1815 at Detroit.

Fennimore, William F. - Private - Rangers - Company: James Manary - Enlistment date: 14 Apr 1812 - Enlistment period: 1 Yr - Discharged: 21 Mar 1813 - Pension: Wife Mariah Hurst, WO-1703, WC-5416: served as a private in Capt. James Manary's Company, US Rangers, and in Capt. Alexander Manary's Company, OH militia; married on 23 Dec 1813 in Chillicothe, Ross County, OH; soldier died on 26 Dec 1870 in Peru, IN; lived in Miami County, IN, and Ross County, OH - Bounty: BLW 84333-40-50; BLW 2030-160-50 - Comments: Served from 28 July 1813 to 5 Sep 1813 in Capt. Alexander Manary's Company.

Fenton, Davidson - Private - 27th Infantry - Company: William Gill - Enlistment date: 14 Apr 1809 ?? - Enlistment period: 5 Yrs - By whom: Lieutenant Gilland - Comments: Prisoner of War, exchanged 25 Apr 1814.

Ferguson, James - Private - 2nd Artillery - Company: Daniel Cushing - Enlistment date: 11 Aug 1812 - Enlistment period: 5 Yrs - Died: 6 Aug 1813, probably at Detroit.

Ferguson, John - Private - 19th Infantry - Company: Asabael Nearing.

Ferguson, John D. - Private - 19th Infantry - Company: William Gill - Age: 36 - Height: 5' 10" - Born: VA, Berkeley County (now WV) - Trade: Farmer - Enlistment date: 21 Apr 1814 - Enlistment place: Springfield - Enlistment period: War - By whom: George Will - Discharged: 5 Jun 1815 at Chillicothe - Bounty: BLW 11108-160-12 (Arkansas).

Ferris, Thomas - Private - 27th Infantry - Pension: Old War IF-14124 Rejected, private in the 27th Infantry.

Fickle, Michael F. - Sergeant - 17th Infantry - Company: John Chunn - Other regiment: 3rd Infantry - Age: 24 - Height: 5' 8" - Born: KY, Washington County, Springfield - Trade: Shoemaker - Enlistment date: 14 Jan 1813 - Enlistment period: 5 Yrs - By whom: James Herron - Pension: Wife Elizabeth, WO-6570; served in Captains Cairns', Sanderson's and Gill's Companies, OH Militia - Bounty: BLW 27328-160-50 - Comments: Deserted 8 Mar 1816.

Fieldeman – see Feddeman, Henry

Fields, Daniel - Private - 26th Infantry - Company: George Kesling - Other regiment: 25th Infantry - Age: 21 - Height: 5' 8" - Enlistment date: 31 May 1813 - Discharged: 31 May 1814.

Fields, Jonathan - Private - 19th Infantry - Age: 26 - Height: 5' 10" - Born: Pennsylvania - Enlistment date: 14 Apr 1814 - Enlistment place: Lancaster - By whom: James Hazelton.

Filed, John H. - Private - 1st Infantry - Company: Simon Owens - Age: 36 - Height: 5' 7" - Born: New York - Trade: Blacksmith - Enlistment date: 19 Mar 1814 - Enlistment place: Cincinnati - Enlistment period: 5 Yrs - By whom: Laurence Taliaferro - Died: 20 Nov 1814 at Cayuga, NY, a natural death.

Filkall, Daniel - Private - 27th Infantry - Company: George Sanderson - Enlistment date: 1 May 1813.

Filler, Henry - Sergeant - 27th Infantry - Company: Joseph Cairns - Enlistment date: 19 Apr 1813 - Enlistment period: 1 Yr - Discharged: 21 Apr 1814 - Pension: Wife Elizabeth Snyder, WO-18577, WC-15395; married on 23 Dec 1815 in Frederick County, MD; soldier died on 27 Jul 1836 in Somerset, Perry County, OH; wife died about 1879; served as a sergeant in Captain Joseph Carines' Company, 27th Infantry; widow lived in Perry County, OH - Bounty: BLW 6087-160-50.

Finly, John - Private - 24th Infantry - Died: Jul 1813, probably at Fort Meigs..

Fires, Thomas - Private - 19th Infantry - Company: Richard Talbott - Age: 16 - Height: 5' 8 1/2" - Born: Virginia - Trade: Farmer - Enlistment date: 16 Apr 1814 - Enlistment place: Xenia - Enlistment period: War - By whom: Richard Talbott - Discharged: 5 Jun 1815 at Chillicothe - Pension: Wife Ann Lewis, SO-10250, SC-6208; served as a private in Capt. Talbott's Company, 19th Infantry; lived in Indiana - Bounty: BLW 8320-160-12 (Illinois).

Fish, Peter - Private - 19th Infantry - Company: William Gill - Age: 18 - Height: 5' 5 1/2" - Born: Maryland - Enlistment date: 17 Aug 1814 - Enlistment place: New Lisbon - Enlistment period: War - By whom: Wynkoop Warner.

Fish, Richard - Corporal - 26th or 27th Infantry - Company: Joel Collins - Other regiment: 19th Infantry - Age: 41 - Height: 5' 10" - Born: Maryland - Trade: Farmer - Enlistment date: 9 Jun 1814 - Enlistment place: Detroit - Enlistment period: War - By whom: John Patterson - Discharged: 20 Jul 1815 at Detroit- Bounty: BLW 15847-160-12 (Illinois) - Comments: Re-enlisted.

Fishback, John - Private - 27th Infantry - Company: Alexander Hill - Other regiment: 19th Infantry - Age: 33 - Height: 5' 8" - Born: New York - Trade: Farmer - Enlistment date: 21 Apr 1814 - Enlistment place: Newark - Enlistment period: 5 Yrs - By whom: John Spencer - Died: 26 Nov 1814 at Buffalo, NY - Pension: Heirs obtained half pay for five years in lieu of military bounty land.

Fisher, Brice - Private - 26th or 27th Infantry - Company: Joel Collins - Other regiment: 19th Infantry - Age: 35 - Height: 5' 10" - Born: Maryland - Trade: Farmer - Enlistment date: 21 May 1814 - Enlistment place: Detroit - Enlistment period: War - By whom: John Patterson - Discharged: 19 Jul 1815 at Detroit - Bounty: BLW 10748-160-12 (Illinois) - Comments: Re-enlisted.

Fisher, Frederick - Private - 24th Infantry - Company: Robert Butler - Enlistment date: 13 Jul 1812 - Enlistment period: 5 Yrs - By whom: Lieutenant Dean - Died: 2 Sep 1813 - Bounty: BLW 18201-160-12 (Missouri) - Comments: Died probably at Sandusky (now Fremont, OH); land bounty to Polly Moser, sister & other heirs at law of Frederick Fisher.

Fisher, John B. - Private - 17th Infantry - Company: Harris Hickman - Age: 32 - Height: 5' 9" - Born: Delaware - Trade: Paper maker - Enlistment date: 12 Mar 1812 - Enlistment period: War - By whom: Thomas McKnight - Discharged: 9 Jun 1815 at Chillicothe - Bounty: BLW 20573-160-12 (Missouri).

Fisher, Joseph - Private - 27th Infantry - Company: Alexander Hill - Other regiment: 19th Infantry - Age: 35 - Height: 5' 10" - Born: New Jersey - Enlistment date: 7 May 1814 - Enlistment place: Ashtabula County, Harpersfield - Enlistment period: War - Killed: 2 Sep 1814 during the Battle of Fort Erie, UC - Bounty: BLW 25658-160-12 (Arkansas) - Comments: Land bounty to John Fisher & other heirs at law of Joseph Fisher.

Fisher, Levin - Private - 19th Infantry - Company: Joel Collins - Age: 21 - Height: 5' 6" - Born: Maryland - Trade: Laborer - Enlistment date: 16 Mar 1814 - Enlistment place: Detroit - Enlistment period: War - By whom: Samuel Coleman - Discharged: 19 Jul 1815 at Detroit - Bounty: BLW 2955-160-12 (Arkansas).

Fisher, Peter - Private - 19th Infantry - Company: William Gill - Age: 34 - Height: 5' 4" - Born: PA, Lancaster County - Trade: Carpenter - Enlistment date: 29 Aug 1812 - Enlistment place: Chillicothe - Enlistment period: 18 Mos - War - By whom: Carey Trimble - Discharged: 5 Jun 1815 at Chillicothe - Bounty: BLW 24943-160-12 (Arkansas).

Fisher, Peter - Private - 26th Infantry - Company: George Kesling - Other regiment: 25th Infantry - Enlistment date: 30 May 1813 - Enlistment period: 1 Yr - Discharged: 30 May 1814.

Fisher, Samuel - Private - 27th Infantry - Company: Alexander Hill - Other regiment: 19th Infantry - Age: 25 - Height: 5' 10 1/2" - Born: Maryland - Trade: Blacksmith - Enlistment date: 22 Apr 1814 - Enlistment place: Steubenville - Enlistment period: War - By whom: John Carroll - Comments: Re-enlisted on 1 Apr 1815 at Erie, PA, for 5 years.

Fisher, Thomas - Sergeant - 19th Infantry - Company: Wilson Elliott - Age: 23 - Height: 5' 11" - Born: Pennsylvania Enlistment date: 20 Jul 1812 - Enlistment period: 18 Mos.

Fishwater, William - Private - 19th Infantry - Discharged: 4 Aug 1814.

Fitzgerald, Daniel - Private - 26th Infantry - Company: Samuel Swearingen - Other regiment: 25th Infantry - Enlistment date: 17 Jul 1813 - Enlistment period: 1 Yr - Discharged: 20 Jun 1814 - Comments: Discharged at Buffalo, NY.

Fitzgerald, Elijah - Private - 26th Infantry - Company: George Kesling - Other regiment: 25th Infantry - Enlistment date: 11 May 1813 - Enlistment period: 1 Yr - Discharged: 11 May 1814.

Fitzhenry, Miley - Private - 17th Infantry - Age: 42 - Height: 5' 5" - Born: Ireland - Enlistment date: 28 Sep 1813 - Enlistment period: War - By whom: George Stall.

Fitzpatrick, James - Private - 19th Infantry - Company: James Herron - Enlistment date: 4 Aug 1812 - Enlistment period: 18 Mos.

Fitzpatrick, Rees - Private - 19th Infantry - Company: George Kesling - Age: 27 - Height: 5' 10" - Born: Virginia - Trade: Farmer - Enlistment date: 17 Nov 1814 - Enlistment place: Lancaster - Enlistment period: War - By whom: John Simmons - Discharged: 27 Mar 1815 at Zanesville - Bounty: BLW 19943-160-12 (Missouri).

Fitzwater, Thomas - Rangers - Company: William Perry - Enlistment date: 16 Jun 1813 - Discharged: 30 Sep 1813 - Pension: Wife Ann Mitchell, SO-14856, SC-16185; served in Capt. Perry's Company, US Rangers; married on 27 Mar 1823 in Clermont County, OH; lived in Clermont County, OH - Bounty: BLW 43580-40-50; BLW 74786-120-55.

Flaherty, Sim - Private - 27th Infantry - Company: William Gill - Discharged: 10 Nov 1813 - Comments: Served aboard the US Sloop Trippe on the Lake Erie Squadron.

Fleming, Patrick - Private - 19th Infantry - Company: Carey Trimble - Other regiment: 17th Infantry - Enlistment date: 13 Feb 1814 - Enlistment period: War - By whom: Isaac Rieley - Died: 17 Nov 1814 - Comments: Died at 11 Mile Creek, NY; buried in the War of 1812 Cemetery in Cheektowaga, Erie County, NY.

Fleming, Robert - Private - 17th Infantry - Company: Caleb Holder - Other regiment: 3rd Infantry - Age: 35 - Height: 5' 7 3/4" - Born: Ireland - Trade: Laborer - Enlistment date: 30 Sep 1814 - Enlistment place: Cincinnati - Enlistment period: 5 Yrs - By whom: George Stall - Discharged: 30 Sep 1819 at Fort Mackinac, MI.

Fleming, William - Private - 17th Infantry - Company: John Chunn - Other regiment: 3rd Infantry - Age: 15 - Height: 4' 8" - Born: Virginia - Trade: Laborer - Enlistment date: 15 Feb 1814 - Enlistment place: Franklin County, Franklinton - Enlistment period: 5 yrs - By whom: John Cochran - Discharged: 15 Feb 1819 at Fort Dearborn, IL.

Flemming, David - Private - 19th Infantry - Company: John Chunn - Other regiment: 17th Infantry - Age: 40 - Height: 5' 4" - Born: Pennsylvania - Enlistment date: 13 Feb 1814 - Enlistment period: War - By whom: William Leavitt - Died: 14 Jan 1815 - Bounty: BLW 26102-160-12 (Arkansas) - Comments: Died at Williamsville, NY (General Hospital), of natural death; buried in the War of 1812 Cemetery in Cheektowaga, Erie County, NY; land bounty to John Flemming, son & other heirs at law of David Flemming.

Fletcher, David Jr - Private - Rangers - Company: Samuel McCormick - Enlistment date: 1 Dec 1813 - Enlistment period: 1 Yr - Discharged: 30 Nov 1814 - Pension: Old War IF-14215 Rejected; served in Captain Samuel McCormick's Company as a private.

Fletcher, Jacob - Private - 19th Infantry - Company: Richard Talbott - Other regiment: 3rd Infantry - Age: 21 - Height: 6' 1" - Born: Virginia - Trade: Distiller - Enlistment date: 16 Mar 1814 - Enlistment place: Dayton - Enlistment period: 5 Yrs - By whom: Lieutenant Malone.

Fletcher, William - Corporal - Rangers - Company: Samuel McCormick - Enlistment date: 1 Nov 1813 - Enlistment period: 1 Yr - Discharged: 22 Nov 1814.

Foeck, Joseph - 2nd Rifles - Age: 21 - Height: 5' 6 3/4" - Born: Pennsylvania - Enlistment date: 10 Mar 1814 - Enlistment place: New Lisbon.

Foens, Daniel B. - Sergeant - 19th Infantry - Other regiment: 17th Infantry - Bounty: BLW 5884-160-12 (Arkansas) - Comments: Prisoner of War, exchanged 25 Apr 1814.

Folbert, Titus - Private - 26th Infantry (new) - Company: William Bezeau - Age: 28 - Height: 5' 6" - Born: Ohio - Trade: Farmer - Enlistment date: 25 Jan 1815 - Enlistment place: PA, Philadelphia County - Enlistment period: War - By whom: William Bezeau - Comments: Colored man.

Foley, Bayliss - Private - 19th Infantry - Company: George Kesling - Age: 40 - Height: 5' 8" - Born: Virginia - Trade: School master - Enlistment date: 31 Aug 1814 - Enlistment place: Franklin County, Franklinton - Enlistment period: 5 Yrs - By whom: Orren Granger - Comments: Deserted 4 Sep 1814.

Follis, John - Private - 26th Infantry - Company: Joel Collins - Enlistment date: 27 Sep 1813 - Enlistment period: 1 Yr - By whom: Richard Talbott - Died: 13 Dec 1813 at Sandwich, UC (now Windsor, Ontario).

Forbes, William Jr. - Musician - 1st Rifles - Company: Thomas Ramsey - Age: 19 - Height: 5' 8 1/2" - Born: VA, Augusta County - Trade: Silversmith - Enlistment date: 13 Dec 1813 - Enlistment place: Cincinnati - Enlistment period: 5 Yrs - By whom: Thomas Ramsey - Died: 9 Nov 1814 - Bounty: BLW 8869-160-12 (Illinois) - Comments: Died at Buffalo, NY; land bounty to William Forbes, father and heir at law of William Forbes, Junior.

Force, Lewis - Private - 27th Infantry - Age: 20 - Height: 5' 8 3/4" - Born: Michigan - Enlistment date: 6 May 1814 - Enlistment place: Newark.

Ford, Ambrose A. - Sergeant - 27th Infantry - Company: Alexander Hill - Other regiment: 19th Infantry - Age: 23 - Height: 5' 8" - Born: MA, Hampshire County, Chesterfield - Trade: Carpenter - Enlistment date: 9 Apr 1814 - Enlistment place: Ashtabula County, Harpersfield - Enlistment period: War - By whom: James Harper.

Ford, Robert - Private - 26th Infantry - Company: William Puthuff - Other regiment: 25th Infantry - Enlistment date: 12 Apr 1813 - Discharged: 12 Apr 1814.

Forquier, Robert - Private - 2nd Artillery - Company: Daniel Cushing - Other regiment: Corps of Artillery - Age: 19 - Height: 5' 10" - Born: Kentucky - Trade: Farmer - Enlistment date: 28 Oct 1814 - Enlistment period: War - Discharged: 25 Jul 1815 at Lower Sandusky (now Fremont, OH).

Forrester, Peter - Private - 19th Infantry - Company: David Holt - Comments: Prisoner of War (Quebec, LC), captured at Fort Niagara, NY, 19 Dec 1813; exchanged 4 May 1814.

Forsythe, John - Private - 27th Infantry - Company: George Sanderson - Enlistment date: 28 Apr 1813.

Foster, Ira L. - Private - 27th Infantry - Company: Alexander Hill - Other regiment: 19th Infantry - Age: 20 -

Height: 5' 10" - Born: Vermont or Virginia - Trade: Farmer - Enlistment date: 19 May 1814 - Enlistment place: Athens - Enlistment period: War - By whom: Nehemiah Gregory - Discharged: 5 Jun 1815 at Chillicothe - Pension: Old War Invalid and Widow Rejected File 14261; served as a private in the 19th Infantry - Bounty: BLW 2536-160-12 (Illinois).

Foster, Samuel - Private - 26th Infantry - Company: George Kesling - Enlistment date: 9 Jun 1813 - Enlistment period: 1 Yr.

Fourston, John - Private - 19th Infantry - Age: 25 - Height: 5' 7" - Born: New Jersey - Enlistment date: 18 Apr 1814 - Enlistment place: Lancaster - By whom: James Hazelton.

Fover, Philip - Private - 19th Infantry - Company: James Herron - Enlistment date: 30 Oct 1812.

Fox, Christopher - 2nd Rifles - Age: 18 - Height: 5' 4 3/4" - Born: Pennsylvania - Enlistment date: 16 May 1814 - Enlistment place: New Lisbon - Enlistment period: War - By whom: William Pritchard - Comments: Discharged by writ of habeas corpus.

Fox, Joseph - Private - 19th Infantry - Company: Joel Collins - Age: 27 - Height: 5' 7" - Born: Maryland - Trade: Farmer - Enlistment date: 15 Apr 1814 - Enlistment period: War - Discharged: 20 Jul 1815 at Detroit.

Fox, Joseph - Private - 26th Infantry - Company: Joel Collins - Other regiment: 19th Infantry - Age: 43 - Height: 5' 7" - Born: New York - Trade: Farmer - Enlistment date: 23 Aug 1813 - Enlistment period: 1 Yr - Bounty: BLW 10242-160-12 (Illinois) - Comments: Re-enlisted on 13 Apr 1814 by Lieutenant Delorac, Sandwich, UC, during the war enlistment.

Fox, Martin - Private - 2nd Rifles - Company: Batteal Harrison - Age: 22 - Height: 5' 6 1/2" - Born: CT, Litchfield County, Colebrook - Trade: Farmer - Enlistment date: 27 Sep 1814 - Enlistment place: Gallipolis - Enlistment period: 5 Yrs - By whom: Edward Miller - Discharged: 27 Sep 1819 at Bellefontaine, MO - Bounty: BLW 23106-160-12 (Arkansas).

Frakes, Nathan - 19th Infantry - Died: 8 Jul 1814, executed at Chillicothe.

Francisco, John - Private - 2nd Rifles - Company: Batteal Harrison - Age: 29 - Height: 5' 10" - Born: LA, Orleans Parish, New Orleans - Trade: Barber - Enlistment date: 15 Jul 1814 - Enlistment place: Cincinnati - Enlistment period: War - By whom: Elias Langham - Discharged: 30 Jun 1815 at Detroit - Pension: Wife Triphena, Old War WF-14315 Rejected; served in Captain Crittenden's Company.

Franklin, James - Private - 19th Infantry - Company: Richard Talbott - Age: 24 - Height: 5' 6" - Born: Rhode Island - Enlistment date: 2 May 1814 - Enlistment place: Butler County, Hamilton - Enlistment period: War - By whom: John Hall.

Franks, John - Corporal - 27th Infantry - Company: Alexander Hill - Other regiment: 19th Infantry - Age: 30 - Height: 6' 1" - Born: Pennsylvania - Trade: Laborer - Enlistment date: 1 Mar 1814 - Enlistment place: Zanesville - Enlistment period: War - By whom: Henry Northrup - Discharged: 6 Jun 1815 at Chillicothe - Bounty: BLW 6165-160-12 (Illinois).

Frazier, James - Private - 26th Infantry - Company: Samuel Swearingen - Enlistment date: 18 Jun 1813 - Enlistment period: 1 Yr.

Frazier, Josiah - Private - 27th Infantry - Company: Isaac Van Horne - Other regiment: 19th Infantry - Enlistment date: 17 Jun 1813 - Enlistment period: 1 Yr - Discharged: 3 Jul 1814 - Pension: Wife Eveline, SO-8273, SC-5460; served as a private in Capt. Joseph Carines' Company, 27th Infantry Capt Isaac Van Horne's Company, 19th Infantry and Capt. B. Hackesey's Company, MD Militia; married Aug 1824 in Frederick County, MD; soldier died on 15 Jul 1875; lived in Frederick County, MD, and Poughkeepsie, Dutchess County, NY - Bounty: BLW 48619-40-50, BLW 41375-120-55, BLW 6950-160-50 - Comments: Re-enlisted.

Fredericks, Henry - Private - 19th Infantry - Company: Carey Trimble - Other regiment: 17th Infantry - Age: 27 - Height: 6' 1/2" - Born: PA, Northumberland County - Trade: Farmer - Enlistment date: 21 Apr 1814 - Enlistment place: Springfield or Adelphi - Enlistment period: War - By whom: George Will - Discharged: 6 Jun 1815 at Chillicothe - Bounty: BLW 6895-160-12 (Illinois).

Freeland, Thomas - 1st Rifles - Company: Thomas Ramsey - Age: 23 - Height: 5' 9" - Born: NJ, Bergen County - Trade: Blacksmith - Enlistment date: 29 Jan 1814 - Enlistment place: Cincinnati - Enlistment period: 5 Yrs - By whom: Thomas Ramsey - Comments: Deserted at Erie, PA, on 1 Sep 1814.

Freeman, Eli - Private - 26th Infantry - Company: Samuel Swearingen - Other regiment: Light Dragoons Regiment - Enlistment date: 25 Jul 1813 - Enlistment period: 1 Yr - Discharged: 13 Jul 1814.

Freeman, Joshua - Private - 17th Infantry - Company: Harris Hickman - Age: 19 - Height: 5' 6" - Born: KY, Nelson County - Trade: Laborer - Enlistment date: 23 Mar 1814 - Enlistment place: Portsmouth - Enlistment period: War - By whom: Hugh May - Discharged: 9 Jun 1815 at Chillicothe - Bounty: BLW 13907-160-12 (Illinois).

French, John - Sergeant - 19th Infantry - Company: Angus Langham - Age: 26 - Height: 5' 9" - Born: New

The Enlisted Men

Hampshire - Enlistment date: 1 Jul 1812 - Enlistment period: 5 Yrs - Died: 21 Oct 1812, murdered.

Friggle, Evens - Private - 26th Infantry - Company: Joel Collins - Other regiment: 19th Infantry - Discharged: 6 Sep 1814.

Frost, Hiram - Private - 19th Infantry - Age: 19 - Height: 5' 7" - Born: New York - Enlistment date: 7 Apr 1814 - Enlistment place: Chillicothe - Enlistment period: War.

Frost, Joseph - Private - 1st Rifles - Other regiment: 1st Infantry - Age: 28 - Height: 5' 7" - Born: NY, Dutchess County, Bickmantown - Trade: Farmer - Enlistment date: 29 Apr 1812 - Enlistment place: Cincinnati - Enlistment period: 5 Yrs - By whom: Thomas Ramsey - Discharged: 27 May 1816 - Comments: Doing duty in Captain Stark's Company, 1st Infantry 1812-1815; discharged at Detroit, MI, early by reason of an injury in the line of duty.

Fry, Henry - Private - 17th Infantry - Company: David Holt - Age: 25 - Height: 5' 4 3/4" - Born: PA, Northampton County - Enlistment date: 23 May 1814 - Enlistment place: New Lisbon - Enlistment period: War - By whom: Thomas McKnight - Died: 24 Oct 1814 at Fort Erie, UC.

Fry, Jacob - Private - 17th Infantry - Company: Henry Crittenden - Age: 35 - Height: 5' 5" - Born: PA, York County, Little York - Trade: Miller - Enlistment date: 22 Nov 1813 - Enlistment place: Chillicothe - Enlistment period: War - By whom: Richard Mitchell - Discharged: 9 Jun 1815 at Chillicothe - Bounty: BLW 11189-16012.

Fryer, Benjamin - Private - 26th Infantry - Company: George Kesling - Other regiment: 25th Infantry - Enlistment date: 12 May 1813 - Enlistment period: 1 Yr - Discharged: 12 May 1814 - Pension: Wife Catherine Jefferson, WO-10675, WC-6039; married on 18 Aug 1814 in Chillicothe, OH; soldier died on 3 Jan 1868 in Portsmouth, OH; served as a private in Lt. Brown's Company, 26th Infantry; lived in Portsmouth, Scioto County, OH - Bounty: BLW 4080-160-50.

Fryman, Frederick - Private - 19th Infantry - Company: Angus Langham - Age: 24 - Height: 6' 2" - Born: VA, Shenandoah County - Enlistment date: 7 Jul 1812 - Enlistment place: St. Clairsville - Enlistment period: 18 Mos - By whom: Samuel Booker - Died: 5 May 1813 - Bounty: BLW 27473-160-42 - Comments: Land bounty to John Fryman, senior, John Fryman, junior, Samuel Fryman, Frederick Fryman, George Fryman, David Fryman, Mary Ann Fryman, Margaret Fryman, George Fryman (son of Henry Fryman), Catherine Malett, John Winer, Frederick Winer, Maria Winer, Ann Rice, Mary Haus, Margaret Jackson and Mary Fryman, sole heirs at law of Frederick Fryman.

Fulk, Abram - Corporal - 19th Infantry - Company: James Herron - Enlistment date: 31 Oct 1812.

Fulk, Andrew - Private - 17th Infantry - Company: Harris Hickman - Age: 22 - Height: 5' 10 1/4" - Born: Virginia - Trade: Wheelwright - Enlistment date: 28 Mar 1814 - Enlistment place: Steubenville - Enlistment period: War - By whom: Lieutenant Mitchell - Discharged: 9 Jun 1815 at Chillicothe - Bounty: BLW 14817-160-12 (Illinois).

Fulk, Peter - Private - 27th Infantry - Company: George Sanderson - Enlistment date: 26 Apr 1813Fulton, Edward - Private - 19th Infantry - Age: 22 - Height: 5' 7" - Born: Pennsylvania - Enlistment date: 26 Jul 1812 - Enlistment period: 18 Mos.

Fultz, Jacob - Private - 1st Rifles - Company: Thomas Ramsey - Age: 22 - Height: 5' 9" - Born: Pennsylvania - Trade: Brick layer - Enlistment date: 8 Feb 1814 - Enlistment place: Cincinnati - Enlistment period: 5 Yrs - By whom: Thomas Ramsey - Discharged: 8 Feb 1819 at Bellefontaine, MO - Bounty: BLW 22580-160-12 (Arkansas).

Furlough, John - Private - 28th Infantry - Company: Nimrod Moore - Enlistment date: 8 Jun 1813 - Enlistment period: 1 Yr - Died: 31 Dec 1813 at Fort Seneca (now Old Fort, OH).

Futhey, Isaac - Private - 27th Infantry - Company: Caleb Holder - Other regiment: 17th Infantry - Age: 25 - Height: 5' 11 1/4" - Born: Pennsylvania - Trade: Blacksmith - Enlistment date: 5 Sep 1814 - Enlistment period: War - By whom: James Campbell - Discharged: 30 Jun 1815 at Detroit - Bounty: BLW 17664-160-12 (Illinois) - Comments: Prisoner of War on Parole, captured at Detroit, MI, 16 Aug 1812.

Gable, Abraham - Private - 17th Infantry - Company: David Holt - Age: 21 - Height: 5' 8" - Born: VA, Shenandoah County - Trade: Laborer - Enlistment date: 7 Mar 1813 - Enlistment place: Franklin County, Franklinton - Enlistment period: War - By whom: Stephen Lee - Discharged: 9 Jun 1815 at Chillicothe - Bounty: BLW 8907-160-12 (Illinois).

Gaither, Benjamin - Private - 19th Infantry - Company: Wilson Elliott - Enlistment date: 9 Jul 1812 - Enlistment period: 18 Mos.

Gallagher, George H. - Private - 17th Infantry - Company: Caleb Holder - Age: 26 - Height: 5' 7" - Born: Ireland - Enlistment date: 24 Aug 1814 - Enlistment place: Cincinnati - Enlistment period: 5 Yrs - By whom: Philip Price.

Galloway, Samuel - Corporal - Rangers - Company: James Manary - Enlistment date: 6 Apr 1812 - Enlistment period: 1 Yr - Discharged: 16 Mar 1813 - Pension: Wife Elizabeth Collins, WO-17593, WC-22721, married on 3 Apr 1828 in Xenia, OH; soldier died on 22 Dec 1851 in Xenia, OH; wife died on 29 Jan 1885; served as a corporal in Capt. James Manary's Company, OH Rangers; lived in Greene County, OH - Bounty: BLW 5344-160-50.

Galloway, William - Private - 19th Infantry - Age: 25 - Height: 5' 7" - Born: Pennsylvania - Enlistment date: 2 Apr 1814 - Enlistment place: Butler County, Hamilton - By whom: George Stall - Comments: Deserted 6 or 16 Apr 1815.

Gamble, James - Private - 1st Infantry - Company: Horatio Stark - Age: 28 - Height: 5' 6" - Born: Ireland, County Tyrone - Trade: Weaver - Enlistment date: 20 Mar 1814 - Enlistment place: Cincinnati - Enlistment period: War - By whom: Laurence Taliaferro - Died: 27 Sep 1814 - Comments: Died at Buffalo, NY, of wounds received in the sortie at Fort Erie, UC.

Gamble, William - Private - 17th Infantry - Age: 40 - Height: 5' 5" - Born: Ireland - Enlistment date: 17 Jul 1814 - Enlistment place: Cambridge - By whom: William Shang.

Gannon, Daniel - Private - 26th Infantry - Company: Benjamin Watson - Other regiment: 25th Infantry - Age: 19 - Height: 5' 6 1/2" - Born: NY, Niagara - Trade: Laborer - Enlistment date: 4 Aug 1812 - Enlistment place: Ohio - Enlistment period: 5 Yrs - By whom: Clarkson Price - Discharged: 6 Aug 1817 - Comments: Wounded.

Gano, Elijah - Private - 26th Infantry - Company: Samuel Swearingen - Other regiment: 25th Infantry - Enlistment date: 1 May 1813 - Enlistment period: 1 Yr - Discharged: 1 May 1814 - Pension: Wife Ellender Evans, WO-37302, WC-27322; served as a private in Capt. Puthoff's Company, OH Militia; married on 16 Oct 1828 in Vermilion County, IL; soldier died on 13 Oct 1834 in Vermilion County, IL; widow died on 5 Jan 1884; lived in McLean County, IL - Bounty: BLW 34177-80-50, BLW 39797-80-55.

Gardiner, James - Private - 27th Infantry - Company: George Kesling - Other regiment: 19th Infantry - Age: 24 - Height: 5' 10" - Born: Virginia - Trade: Shoemaker - Enlistment date: 26 Apr 1814 - Enlistment place: Zanesville - Enlistment period: War - Discharged: 6 Jun 1815 - Bounty: BLW 9668-160-12 (Illinois).

Gardner, Caleb - Sergeant - 19th Infantry - Company: Wilson Elliott.

Gardner, Enoch - Private - 26th Infantry - Company: Richard Talbott - Enlistment date: 2 Jan 1814 - Discharged: 23 Oct 1814 - Comments: Discharged at Greenbush, NY, because of a rupture.

Gardner, Hiram - Private - 1st Rifles - Company: Thomas Ramsey - Age: 31 - Height: 6' - Born: VA, Frederick County - Trade: Blacksmith - Enlistment date: 4 May 1814 - Enlistment place: Cincinnati - Enlistment period: War - By whom: Thomas Ramsey - Died: 17 Sep 1814 - Comments: Prisoner of War (Quebec, LC), captured at Fort Erie, UC, 17 Sep 1814, sent to Halifax, NS, 8 Nov 1814; released 25 Mar 1815.

Garmon, Daniel - Private - 19th Infantry - Company: Angus Langham - Comments: Waiter to Lieutenant Jackson.

Garnale, Abraham - Private - 19th Infantry.

Garner, James - Private - 27th Infantry - Company: Alexander Hill.

Garrard, William - Corporal - Rangers - Company: William Perry - Enlistment date: 14 Apr 1812 - Enlistment period: 1 Yr - Discharged: 14 Apr 1814 - Pension: Wife Mary Muchmore, WO-9336, WC-5962; married on 11 Jan 1810 in Hamilton County, OH; soldier died on 11 Jul 1836; in Hamilton County, OH; served as a corporal in Capt. William Perry's Company, US Rangers; lived in Hamilton County, OH; widow lived in Butler County, OH in 1871 - Bounty: BLW 15672-160-50.

Garretson, Simeon - Private - 26th Infantry - Company: George Kesling - Enlistment date: 19 May 1813 - Enlistment period: 1 Yr - Died: 17 Aug 1813.

Garrison, Jacob - Private - 26th Infantry - Company: George Kesling - Enlistment date: 19 May 1813 - Enlistment period: 1 Yr.

Garrison, Joseph - Private - 26th Infantry - Company: George Kesling - Enlistment date: 24 May 1813 - Enlistment period: 1 Yr - Died: 7 Aug 1813.

Garritson, Ebenezer - Private - 26th Infantry - Company: George Kesling - Enlistment date: 19 May 1813 - Enlistment period: 1 Yr.

Gartner, Benjamin - Private - 19th Infantry - Company: Wilson Elliott.

Gary, James - Private - 19th Infantry - Company: John Chunn - Enlistment date: 30 Mar 1813 - Enlistment period: War - Died: 24 Jan 1816 - Bounty: BLW 26194-160-12 (Arkansas) - Comments: Died at home; furloughed because of ill health on 23 Jul 1814; land bounty to William Geary, father & only heir at law of James Geary.

Gary, Peter - Corporal - 27th Infantry - Company: George Sanderson - Enlistment date: Apr 1813 - Pension: Served as a corporal in Capt. Sanderson's Company, 27th Infantry - Bounty: BLW 88-160-50.

Gasaway, Benjamin - Sergeant - 19th Infantry - Company: William Gill - Age: 30 - Height: 5' 10" - Trade:

The Enlisted Men

Carpenter - Enlistment date: 15 May 1814 - Enlistment place: Detroit - Enlistment period: War - By whom: Wynkoop Warner - Discharged: 27 May 1815 at Zanesville - Bounty: BLW 1532-160-42 (Illinois).

Gaskel, Elias - Private - 19th Infantry - Company: Carey Trimble.

Gasten, Henry - Private - 27th Infantry - Age: 19 - Height: 5' 4 1/2" - Born: Pennsylvania - Enlistment date: 27 Apr 1814 - Enlistment place: Newark.

Gaston, Hugh - Private - 1st Rifles - Company: Thomas Ramsey - Age: 35 - Height: 5' 11" - Born: PA, Fayette County - Trade: Farmer - Enlistment date: 26 Aug 1813 - Enlistment place: Cincinnati - Enlistment period: 5 Yrs - By whom: Thomas Ramsey - Died: 7 May 1814 at Newport, KY - Pension: Heirs obtained half pay for five years in lieu of military bounty land.

Gates, John - Private - 27th Infantry - Company: Alexander Hill - Other regiment: 19th Infantry - Age: 21 - Height: 5' 9" - Born: MA, Hampden County, Westfield - Enlistment date: 16 Mar 1814 - Enlistment place: Columbiana County, Warren (now Trumbull County) - Enlistment period: 1 Yr - Bounty: BLW 26828-160-12 (Arkansas) - Comments: Land bounty to Richard Gates, brother & other heirs at law of John Gates.

Gates, Matthias - Private - 27th Infantry - Company: Alexander Hill - Other regiment: 19th Infantry - Age: 40 - Height: 5' 9" - Born: CT, Middlesex County, East Haddam - Trade: Laborer - Enlistment date: 16 Mar 1814 - Enlistment place: Warren (Trumbull County) or Harpersfield - Enlistment period: 1 Yr - Discharged: 6 Jun 1815 at Chillicothe - Bounty: BLW 19189-160-12 (Illinois) - Comments: Re-enlisted until the end of the war on 7 May 1814.

Gates, William Lee - Private - 27th Infantry - Company: George Sanderson - Other regiment: 19th Infantry - Age: 18 - Height: 5' 8" - Born: New Jersey - Trade: Farmer - Enlistment date: 6 Jul 1813 - Discharged: 20 Jul 1815 at Detroit - Pension: Wife Elizabeth, WO-13868; served as a private in Capt. Wimp's Company, OH Militia, in Capt. Sanderson's Company, 27th Infantry and in Capt. Collins' Company, 19th Infantry - Bounty: BLW 9104-160-12 (Illinois), BLW 5551-160-50 - Comments: Re-enlisted until the end of the war at Detroit, MI, on 17 Mar 1814 by Lieutenant Coleman.

Gattis, Robert - Private - 19th Infantry - Company: Joel Collins - Age: 40 - Height: 5' 7" - Born: Ireland - Trade: Tailor - Enlistment date: 18 May 1814 - Enlistment place: Detroit - Enlistment period: 5 Yrs - By whom: John Patterson.

Gauldin, Thomas - Private - 2nd Artillery - Company: Daniel Cushing - Enlistment date: 29 Aug 1812 - By whom: Lieutenant Conway - Died: 16 Dec 1813 at Detroit (hospital).

Gause, Samuel - Private - 27th Infantry - Company: George Sanderson - Other regiment: 19th Infantry - Age: 18 - Height: 5' 1" - Born: North Carolina - Trade: Laborer - Enlistment date: 25 Jun 1813 - Discharged: 20 Jul 1815 at Detroit - Bounty: BLW 7275-160-12 (Illinois) - Comments: Re-enlisted until the end of the war at Detroit, MI, on 23 Apr 1814 by Lieutenant Warner.

Geary – see Gary, James

Gebhart, Anthony - Private - 27th Infantry - Company: Joseph Cairns - Enlistment date: 5 Apr 1813 - Enlistment period: 1 Yr - Discharged: 5 Apr 1814 - Pension: Wife Ellen, WO-29920, WC-21275; served as a private in Capt. Joseph Cain's Company, 27th Infantry; married on 4 Jan 1835 in Vermilion County, IL; soldier died on 21 Jul 1864 in Vermilion County, IL, widow died about 1882; lived in Georgetown, Vermilion County, IL; first wife was Elizabeth - Bounty: BLW 4975-160-50.

Gee, Joseph - Private - 26th Infantry - Company: William Puthuff - Enlistment date: 10 Apr 1813 - Enlistment period: 1 Yr.

Gee, William - Private - 26th Infantry - Company: George Kesling - Enlistment date: 11 May 1813 - Enlistment period: 1 Yr - Died: 1 Dec 1813 at Detroit.

Geeseman, John - Private - 3rd Artillery - Company: Benjamin Odgen - Age: 24 - Height: 5' 8 1/2" - Born: Pennsylvania - Trade: Farmer - Enlistment date: 12 Jan 1813 - Enlistment place: Ohio - Enlistment period: War - By whom: Lieutenant Queen - Comments: Deserted from Fort Mifflin, PA, 14 Aug 1814.

Gegave, Antonie - Private - 19th Infantry - Age: 21 - Height: 5' 7" - Born: Lower Canada - Enlistment date: 10 May 1814 - Enlistment place: Detroit - By whom: John Meldrum.

General, Lewis - Private - 19th Infantry - Company: Richard Talbott - Other regiment: 3rd Infantry - Age: 26 - Height: 6' 3" - Born: New Jersey - Trade: Farmer - Enlistment date: 5 Jul 1814 - Enlistment place: Urbana - Enlistment period: 5 Yrs - By whom: William Baird - Comments: Deserted at Detroit, MI, on 2 Feb 1816.

Geoghegan, Anthony - Musician - 19th Infantry - Company: George Kesling - Age: 40 - Height: 5' 11 3/4" - Born: Maryland - Trade: Farmer - Enlistment date: 15 Jun 1814 - Enlistment place: Lebanon - Enlistment period: War - By whom: Richard Talbott - Discharged: 27 Mar 1815 at Zanesville - Bounty: BLW 3485-160-12 (Illinois).

George, John H. - Private - 26th Infantry - Company: William Puthuff - Enlistment date: 17 Jun 1813 - Enlistment period: 1 Yr - Comments: Served aboard the US Brig Niagara on the Lake Erie Squadron.

Gerodelle, John - Private - 2nd Artillery - Company: Stanton Sholes - Other regiment: Corps of Artillery - Age: 48 - Height: 5' 5" - Born: France - Trade: Laborer - Enlistment date: 25 May 1813 - Enlistment place: OH, Cleveland - Enlistment period: 5 Yrs - By whom: Stanton Sholes - Discharged: 7 Oct 1815 at Detroit because of epilepsy and old age, unfit for service - Pension: Old War IF-1444; served in Captain Stanton Sholes and Captain John Biddle's Companies, US Art; Ohio resident - Bounty: BLW 4253-160-12 (Illinois).

Gerrard, H. - Private - Rangers - Died: 16 Jul 1814.

Gibbs, Isaac - Private - 27th Infantry - Other regiment: 19th Infantry - Age: 28 - Height: 5' 7" - Born: CT, Litchfield County - Trade: Carpenter - Enlistment date: 23 Apr 1814 - Enlistment place: Warren County - Enlistment period: War - Discharged: 22 May 1815 at Chillicothe - Bounty: BLW 8830-160-12.

Gibson, Archibald A. - Private - 1st Rifles - Company: Thomas Ramsey - Age: 29 - Height: 6' 1 1/2" - Born: New Hampshire - Trade: Carpenter - Enlistment date: 10 Jan 1814 - Enlistment place: Cincinnati - Enlistment period: 5 Yrs - By whom: Thomas Ramsey - Discharged: 1 Aug 1815 at Buffalo, NY, because of wounds received at Fort Erie, UC, on 17 Sep 1814, unit for duty - Pension: Old War IF-26100, served as a private in Capt. Ramsey's Company, US Rifles as a private.

Gibson, Burrell - Private - 19th Infantry - Company: John Chunn - Enlistment date: 1 Jul 1812 - Enlistment period: 18 Mos.

Gibson, John - Private - 19th Infantry - Company: George Kesling - Other regiment: 3rd Infantry - Age: 44 - Height: 5' 9" - Born: Ireland - Trade: Laborer - Enlistment date: 7 Sep 1814 - Enlistment place: Franklin County, Franklinton - Enlistment period: 5 Yrs - By whom: Orren Granger - Discharged: 8 Nov 1815 at Newport, KY, because of old age.

Gibson, John Jr - Private - 19th Infantry - Company: Angus Langham - Age: 27 - Height: 5' 7 1/2" - Born: PA, Fayette County - Enlistment date: 1 Jul 1812 - Enlistment period: 5 Yrs - Killed: 5 May 1813 - Bounty: BLW 27598-160-42 - Comments: Land bounty to William Gibson, surviving brother of John Gibson, junior; surviving children and grand-children of George Gibson & Henry Gibson, who were also brothers & only heirs at law of John Gibson, junior.

Gibson, John Sr - Private - 19th Infantry - Company: Joel Collins - Age: 22 - Height: 5' 11 1/2" - Born: Upper Canada - Trade: Hatter - Enlistment date: 23 Apr 1814 - Enlistment place: Detroit - Enlistment period: War - By whom: John Patterson - Discharged: 19 Jul 1815 - Bounty: BLW 27597-160-46 - Comments: Land bounty to William Gibson, surviving son of John Gibson, senior, surviving children and grand-children of George Gibson & Henry Gibson, who were also sons & only heirs at law of John Gibson.

Gibson, Joseph - Private - 27th Infantry - Company: George Sanderson - Enlistment date: 5 Jun 1813 - Died: 28 Aug 1813.

Gilbert, George - Corporal - 19th Infantry - Company: Angus Langham - Other regiment: 17th Infantry then 3rd Infantry - Enlistment date: 30 Jul 1812 - Enlistment period: 5 Yrs - By whom: Daniel Armstrong - Discharged: 24 May 1816 - Pension: Old War IF-14458 or Old War IF-14438 Rejected; served as a corporal in Capt. Langham's Company, 19th Infantry - Comments: Discharged after furnishing a substitute (Ephraim Reed).

Giles, William - Private - 2nd Artillery - Company: Daniel Cushing - Other regiment: Corps of Artillery - Age: 30 - Height: 5' 6" - Born: North Carolina - Trade: Tailor - Enlistment date: 22 Sep 1814 - Enlistment place: Lebanon - Enlistment period: 5 Yrs - By whom: Daniel Cushing - Comments: Deserted 25 Feb 1817.

Gillespie, Andrew - Private - 19th Infantry - Age: 23 - Height: 5' 9" - Born: VA, Harrison County - Enlistment date: 25 Jan 1815 - Enlistment place: Athens - Enlistment period: 5 Yrs.

Gillespie, Robert - Private - 27th Infantry - Company: Isaac Van Horne - Enlistment date: 25 Jun 1813 - Enlistment period: 1 Yr - Discharged: 24 Jun 1814 - Pension: Wife Sarah Rice, WO-9111, WC-3723; served as a private in Capt. Van Horn's Company, 27th Infantry; married on 14 Aug 1814 in Gallia County, OH; soldier died on 17 Jul 1860 in Marion County, OH; lived in Marion County, OH - Bounty: BLW 10250-160-50.

Gillett, James - Private - 19th Infantry - Company: Martin Hawkins - Other regiment: 17th Infantry - Age: 31 - Height: 5' 8 1/2" - Born: CT, Hartford County - Trade: Clothier - Enlistment date: 24 Mar 1814 - Enlistment place: Detroit - Enlistment period: 5 Yrs - By whom: George Atchison - Comments: Deserted 25 Mar 1815.

Gilman, Daniel - Private - 19th Infantry - Company: William Gill - Age: 39 - Height: 5' 10" - Born: New Hampshire - Trade: Farmer - Enlistment date: 26 Aug 1814 - Enlistment place: Cincinnati - Enlistment period: War - Discharged: 1 Jun 1815 - Bounty: BLW 24125-160-12 (Arkansas).

Gilmore, Andrew - Sergeant - 26th Infantry - Company: William Puthuff - Enlistment date: 28 Jul 1813 - Enlistment period: 1 Yr.

Givens, Robert - Private - 17th Infantry - Company: Harris Hickman - Age: 23 - Height: 5' 8 1/4" - Born: Ireland -

The Enlisted Men

Trade: Laborer - Enlistment date: 13 May 1814 - Enlistment place: Chillicothe - Enlistment period: War - By whom: James Campbell - Discharged: 9 Jun 1815 at Chillicothe - Bounty: BLW 3455-160-12.

Gladman, Michael - Private - 19th Infantry - Company: William Gill - Age: 21 - Height: 5' 8" - Born: Maryland - Enlistment date: 13 Aug 1814 - Enlistment place: Steubenville - Enlistment period: 5 Yrs - Discharged: 10 Dec 1814 - Comments: Discharged by writ of habeas corpus at St. Clairsville, OH.

Glanville, Stephen - Private - 19th Infantry - Age: 33 - Height: 5' 7" - Born: MD, Kent County - Enlistment date: 24 Mar 1814 - Enlistment place: Columbus - Enlistment period: War - By whom: Hugh Moore.

Glasburn, Peter - Private - 19th Infantry - Company: Angus Langham - Enlistment date: 20 Jul 1812 - Enlistment period: 5 Yrs - Died: 12 Jun 1813 - Bounty: BLW 24889-160-12 (Arkansas) - Comments: Land bounty to John Glasburn, brother & other heirs at law of Peter Glasburn.

Glass, John - Private - 2nd Rifles - Company: Batteal Harrison - Age: 21 - Height: 5' 7" - Born: Ireland, County Down - Trade: Blacksmith - Enlistment date: 9 Aug 1814 - Enlistment place: Cincinnati - Enlistment period: 5 Yrs - By whom: Edward Miller - Discharged: 4 Feb 1816 at Detroit on Surgeon's Certificate of Disability.

Glass, Joseph - Sergeant - 26th Infantry - Company: William Puthuff - Enlistment date: 26 Apr 1813 - Enlistment period: 1 Yr.

Glenn, Thomas - Private - 26th Infantry - Company: George Kesling - Other regiment: 25th Infantry - Enlistment date: 25 May 1813 - Discharged: 25 May 1814.

Gluffan, Thomas - Private - 19th Infantry - Company: John McDonald - Died: 22 Oct 1815 at Williamsville, NY (General Hospital), of dysentery.

Goble, John - Private - Rangers - Company: Samuel McCormick - Enlistment date: 16 Nov 1813 - Enlistment period: 1 Yr - Discharged: 22 Nov 1814 - Pension: SC-16742; soldier died circa 1879; served in Captains E. Kirtley and Samuel McCormick Companies, Ohio militia; lived in Shelby County, OH 1850-1871.

Goe, William - Private - 26th Infantry - Company: George Kesling - Enlistment date: 11 May 1813.

Gooderl, John - Private - 2nd Light Dragoons - Company: Samuel Hopkins - Enlistment date: 22 Mar 1812 - Enlistment period: 5 Yrs - Killed: 3 May 1813 at Fort Meigs, OH, by a cannon ball.

Goodrain, John R. - Private - 19th Infantry - Company: James Herron.

Goodrich, Henry - Private - 27th Infantry - Company: Absalom Martin - Born: Connecticut - Trade: Carpenter - Enlistment date: May 1813 - Enlistment place: Newark - Discharged: 30 May 1814 - Pension: Wife Ellen Jones, SO-2664, SC-15504; married in 1817 in Licking County, OH; soldier died circa 1883, served as a private in Capt. Martin's Company, 27th Infantry; lived in Cincinnati, OH, and Franklin County, OH - Bounty: BLW 3272-160-50 - Comments: Discharged at Detroit; buried at the National Military Cemetery in Dayton, OH.

Goodwin, David - Private - 17th Infantry - Company: John Chunn - Age: 43 - Height: 6' 1" - Born: VA, Bedford County - Trade: Farmer - Enlistment date: 11 May 1813 - Enlistment period: War - By whom: Hugh May - Discharged: 4 Jun 1815 at Chillicothe - Bounty: BLW 2948-160-12.

Goodwin, James - Private - 27th Infantry - Company: Absalom Martin - Other regiment: 19th Infantry - Enlistment date: 8 May 1813 - Enlistment period: 1 Yr - Discharged: 27 Jun 1814 - Pension: Wife Lucinda Chandler, WO-22668, WC-15774; married on 25 Nov 1819 in Clermont County, OH; soldier died on 26 Mar 1844 in Clermont County, OH; wife died on 4 Mar 1884; served as a private in Capt. Martin's Company, 27th Infantry; lived in Clermont County, OH - Bounty: BLW 6066-160-50 - Comments: Prisoner of War, exchanged 25 Apr 1814.

Gordon, John L. - Corporal - 27th Infantry - Company: William Gill - Other regiment: 19th Infantry - Age: 24 - Height: 5' 9 1/2" - Born: NJ, Monmouth County, Freehold - Trade: Carpenter - Enlistment date: 14 May 1814 - Enlistment period: War - By whom: Thomas Riddle - Discharged: 5 Jun 1815 at Chillicothe - Bounty: BLW 3810-160-12 (Missouri) - Comments: Prisoner of War on Parole, captured at Detroit, MI, 16 Aug 1812.

Gordon, Lewis M. - Fifer - 26th Infantry - Company: Benjamin Watson - Other regiment: 25th Infantry then 6th Infantry - Age: 31 - Height: 5' 7 1/2" - Born: PA, Philadelphia County - Trade: Laborer - Enlistment date: 14 Feb 1812 - Enlistment place: Ohio - Enlistment period: 1 Yr - 5 Yrs - By whom: Lieutenants Hovell or Caldwell - Discharged: 14 Jan 1818 at Louisville, KY - Comments: Served aboard the US Schooner Porcupine on the Lake Erie Squadron.

Gordon, Thomas - Private - 19th Infantry - Company: James Herron - Enlistment date: 27 Apr 1813 - Enlistment place: Cincinnati - Enlistment period: War.

Gossett, David - Private - 19th Infantry - Company: Joel Collins - Age: 20 - Height: 5' 10" - Born: Pennsylvania - Trade: Laborer - Enlistment date: 16 Mar 1814 - Enlistment place: Detroit - Enlistment period: War - By whom: Samuel Coleman - Discharged: 20 Jul 1815 at Detroit - Bounty: BLW 4067-160-12.

Goudling – see Gauldin, Thomas

Graham, Ebenezer A. - Sergeant - 19th Infantry - Company: Joel Collins - Age: 22 - Height: 5' 6 1/2" - Born: Vermont - Trade: Shoemaker - Enlistment date: 16 Mar 1814 - Enlistment place: Detroit - Enlistment period: War - By whom: Wynkoop Warner - Discharged: 20 Jul 1815 at Detroit - Bounty: BLW 9163-160-12 (Illinois).

Graham, Jesse - Private - 27th Infantry - Company: Alexander Hill.

Graham, Samuel - Private - 19th Infantry - Company: Richard Talbott - Age: 26 - Height: 5' 8" - Born: Virginia - Trade: Distiller - Enlistment date: 2 May 1814 - Enlistment place: Franklin County - Enlistment period: War - By whom: Robert Young - Discharged: 5 Jun 1815 at Chillicothe - Bounty: BLW 21289-160-12 (Arkansas).

Grant, William - Private - 19th Infantry - Company: Asabael Nearing - Age: 38 - Height: 5' 8" - Born: MA, Worcester County - Enlistment date: 27 Aug 1812 - Enlistment period: 5 Yrs - Pension: Wife Waty, Old War WF-14557 Rejected; served as a private in the 19th Infantry - Comments: Prisoner of War, exchanged 25 Apr 1814.

Graves, Jacob - Corporal - 2nd Rifles - Company: Batteal Harrison - Age: 35 - Height: 5' 10" - Born: NH, Grafton County, Bethlehem - Trade: Cabinet maker - Enlistment date: 28 Jul 1814 - Enlistment place: Zanesville - Enlistment period: War - By whom: William Dougherty - Discharged: 30 Jun 1815 at Detroit.

Gray, James - Private - 19th Infantry - Company: John Chunn - Enlistment date: 30 Mar 1813 - Enlistment period: War - Comments: Prisoner of War, missing 21 Jul 1813.

Gray, James - 1st Rifles - Company: Thomas Ramsey - Age: 24 - Height: 5' 8" - Born: Massachusetts - Trade: Farmer - Enlistment date: 1 Jun 1814 - Enlistment place: Cincinnati - Enlistment period: 5 Yrs - By whom: Thomas Ramsey - Comments: Deserted 13 Sep 1815.

Gray, John - 19th Infantry - Bounty: BLW 623-320-12.

Gray, Robert K. - Sergeant - 17th Infantry - Company: Harris Hickman - Age: 22 - Height: 6' - Born: PA, Northumberland County - Trade: Wheelwright - Enlistment date: 1 Jul 1813 - Enlistment place: Cincinnati - Enlistment period: War - By whom: Philip Price - Discharged: 9 Jun 1815 at Chillicothe - Bounty: BLW 11558-160-12.

Gray, Samuel - 27th Infantry - Company: Absalom Martin - Other regiment: 19th Infantry - Enlistment date: 12 Sep 1813 - Enlistment period: 1 Yr - Discharged: 11 Sep 1814 - Pension: Wife Peggy Guthridge, WC-27582; married on 2 Jun 1820 in Muskingum County, OH; soldier died on 24 Aug 1855 in OH; wife died on 7 Mar 1883; served as a private in Captains Martin's and Collins' Companies, 27th and 19th Infantries; lived in Muskingum County, OH - Bounty: BLW 1431-160-50.

Green – see Greer, John

Green, George - Private - 17th Infantry - Company: Martin Hawkins - Age: 38 - Height: 6' - Born: VA, Louisa County - Trade: Cooper - Enlistment date: 21 Jul 1814 - Enlistment place: Franklin County, Franklinton - Enlistment period: War - By whom: Lieutenant Cothran - Discharged: 9 Jun 1815 at Chillicothe - Bounty: BLW 6024-16012 (Arkansas).

Green, Henry - Corporal - 19th Infantry - Company: George Kesling - Age: 21 - Height: 5' 10" - Born: New York - Trade: Blacksmith - Enlistment date: 1 Nov 1814 - Enlistment place: Cincinnati - Enlistment period: War - By whom: William Baird - Discharged: 27 Mar 1815 at Zanesville - Bounty: BLW 11040-160-12 (Illinois).

Green, Isaac - Private - 27th Infantry - Company: Joseph Cairns - Comments: Served aboard the US Sloop Trippe on the Lake Erie Squadron, wounded during the Battle of Lake Erie.

Green, John - Private - 19th Infantry - Company: George Kesling - Age: 23 - Height: 5' 7" - Born: Ireland, County Dublin - Trade: Shoemaker - Enlistment date: 9 Jan 1815 - Enlistment place: Zanesville - Enlistment period: War - By whom: Charles Cass - Discharged: 27 Mar 1815 at Zanesville - Bounty: BLW 623-320-14 (Illinois).

Green, John - Private - 19th Infantry - Company: Richard Talbott - Age: 21 - Height: 5' 10" - Born: KY, Bourbon County - Trade: Farmer - Enlistment date: 22 Jun 1814 - Enlistment place: Urbana - Enlistment period: War - By whom: William Baird - Died: 9 Nov 1814 at Cleveland.

Green, John - Fife Major - 17th Infantry - Company: Harris Hickman - Age: 15 - Height: 4' 4" - Born: VA, Fairfax County - Trade: Barber - Enlistment date: 29 May 1814 - Enlistment place: Zanesville - Enlistment period: War - By whom: George Bryant - Discharged: 9 Jun 1815 at Chillicothe - Bounty: BLW 14304-160-12.

Green, Joseph - Private - 27th Infantry - Company: Isaac Van Horne - Enlistment date: 1 Jul 1813 - Enlistment period: 1 Yr - Discharged: 30 Jul 1814 - Pension: Wife Nancy Bowlen, WO-42303, WC-32771, SO-8155, SC-13871; married on 5 Aug 1817 in Calcutta, OH; soldier on died 21 May 1882 in Calcutta, OH; wife died on 23 Apr 1890 in Calcutta, OH; served as a private in Capt. Van Horne's Company, 27th Infantry; lived in Calcutta, Columbiana County, OH - Bounty: BLW 3671-160-50

The Enlisted Men

Green, Samuel - Private - 19th Infantry - Age: 18 - Height: 5' 10" - Born: VA, Kanawha County, Charleston (now WV) - Enlistment date: 6 Aug 1813 - Enlistment period: War - Discharged: 20 Aug 1815 at New London, CT - Comments: Prisoner of War (Halifax, NS), captured aboard a schooner on Lake Huron, 3 Sep 1814; released 17 Apr 1815.

Green, Samuel - Private - 17th Infantry - Company: Martin Hawkins - Height: 5' 11" - Born: VA, Hampshire County (now WV) - Trade: Hatter - Enlistment date: 21 Jul 1813 - Enlistment place: Chillicothe - Enlistment period: War - By whom: Asabael Nearing - Bounty: BLW 5533-160-12 (Illinois).

Green, Thomas B. - Sergeant - 19th Infantry - Company: George Kesling - Age: 23 - Height: 5' 9" - Born: Massachusetts - Trade: Carpenter - Enlistment date: 10 Feb 1815 - Enlistment place: Zanesville - Enlistment period: War - By whom: Charles Cass - Discharged: 27 Mar 1815 at Zanesville - Bounty: BLW 869-320-14 (Arkansas).

Greene, Timothy - Private - 17th Infantry - Company: Harris Hickman - Age: 35 - Height: 5' 3 1/2" - Born: PA, Dorcan - Trade: Laborer - Enlistment date: 31 May 1814 - Enlistment place: Butler County, Hamilton - Enlistment period: War - By whom: George Stall - Discharged: 9 Jun 1815 at Chillicothe - Bounty: BLW 9290-160-12 (Illinois).

Greene, William - Private - 2nd Rifles - Company: Benjamin Johnson - Age: 31 - Height: 5' 10" - Born: NC, Wake County - Enlistment date: 7 Jun 1814 - Enlistment place: Zanesville - Bounty: BLW 14162-160-12 (Missouri).

Greenly, William - Private - 26th Infantry - Company: George Kesling - Other regiment: 25th Infantry - Age: 19 - Height: 5' 7" - Enlistment date: 22 Apr 1813 - Enlistment period: 1 Yr.

Greer, John - Private - 19th Infantry - Bounty: BLW 623-160-42 (Illinois).

Greer, Thomas - Private - 26th Infantry - Company: George Kesling - Other regiment: 25th Infantry - Enlistment date: 23 May 1813 - Enlistment period: 1 Yr - Comments: Re-enlisted in the 25th Infantry on 12 Mar 1814; deserted 14 Mar 1814.

Gregg, James - Private - 17th Infantry - Company: John Chunn - Other regiment: 3rd Infantry - Age: 30 - Height: 5' 6" - Born: New Jersey - Trade: Laborer - Enlistment date: 23 Oct 1813 - Enlistment place: Cincinnati - Enlistment period: 5 Yrs - By whom: George Stall - Discharged: 1 Oct 1816 - Comments: Discharged at Fort Harrison, IN, after furnishing a substitute (Mason Johnston).

Gregory, Elnathan - Private - 27th Infantry - Company: George Sanderson - Enlistment date: 21 Jun 1813.

Gregory, William - Private - 19th Infantry - Company: John Chunn - Other regiment: 17th Infantry.

Grevis, John - Private - 26th Infantry - Died: 18 Feb 1814 - Comments: Died at Greenbush, NY (hospital).

Grey, Aronyer - Private - 1st Infantry - Company: Horatio Stark - Trade: Farmer - Enlistment date: 9 Feb 1814 - Enlistment place: Cincinnati - Enlistment period: 5 Yrs - By whom: Laurence Taliaferro - Comments: Prisoner of War, captured at Battle of Chippewa; deserted at Sackets Harbor, NY, 19 Jan 1815.

Grey, Thomas - Private - 27th Infantry - Company: Alexander Hill.

Greyhain, Samuel - Sergeant - 19th Infantry - Company: Richard Talbott.

Griffin, Thomas - 19th Infantry - Company: William MacDonald - Died: 22 Oct 1814 - Comments: Buried in the War of 1812 Cemetery in Cheektowaga, Erie County, NY.

Griffith, James - Sergeant - 26th Infantry - Company: George Kesling - Enlistment date: 19 May 1813 - Enlistment period: 1 Yr - Died: 7 Nov 1813, probably at Sackets Harbor, NY.

Grimes, Elijah - Sergeant - 2nd Dragoons - Company: Samuel Hopkins - Enlistment date: 21 Mar 1813 - Discharged: 18 Jun 1815 - Pension: Wife Nancy Lippincott, 2nd wife, WO-24320, WC-19456, SO-14205, SC-24320; married on 23 Jan 1831 in Morristown, Belmont County, OH; soldier died on 8 May 1876 in Zanesville, OH; wife died circa 1898; served as a sergeant in Captain Samuel Hopkins' Company, US Light Dragoons; lived in Zanesville, Muskingum County, OH; wife lived in Ramsey County, MN in 1887; first wife was Susan Holtz - Bounty: BLW 15617-160-12.

Grimes, Ephraim - Private - 27th Infantry - Company: George Sanderson - Enlistment date: 14 May 1813.

Grimes, Ephraim - Private - 17th Infantry - Age: 46 - Height: 5' 9" - Born: Maryland - Enlistment date: 12 Jan 1815 Enlistment place: Cincinnati - Enlistment period: War - By whom: Lieutenant Russ.

Grimes, John - Private - 26th Infantry - Company: Joel Collins - Enlistment date: 10 Aug 1813 - Enlistment period: 1 Yr.

Grimes, William - Private - 26th Infantry - Company: Samuel Swearingen - Other regiment: 25th Infantry - Enlistment date: 13 May 1813 - Enlistment period: 1 Yr - Discharged: 13 May 1814.

Gromo, Paul - Private - 2nd Artillery - Company: Stanton Sholes - Enlistment date: 1 Mar 1813 - Enlistment period: 5 Yrs - Died: 22 Oct 1813 at Cleveland, OH.

Grooms, Richard - Private - 19th Infantry - Company: Angus Langham - Enlistment date: 3 Aug 1812 - Enlistment period: 5 Yrs - By whom: James Campbell - Comments: Prisoner of War.

Grossman, Samuel - Private - 2nd Artillery - Company: Daniel Cushing - Enlistment date: 10 Aug 1812 - Died: 25 May 1813 at Fort Meigs, OH.

Groves, Lawrence - Private - 19th Infantry - Company: Carey Trimble - Other regiment: 17th Infantry - Age: 39 - Height: 5' 9 3/4" - Born: Pennsylvania - Trade: Tanner - Enlistment date: 7 Feb 1814 - Enlistment place: Chillicothe - Enlistment period: War - By whom: Lieutenant Stogeion.

Groves, Solomon - Private - 27th Infantry - Comments: Prisoner of War on Parole, captured at Detroit, MI, 16 Aug 1812.

Grubb, Daniel - Private - 17th Infantry - Company: Caleb Holder - Other regiment: 3rd Infantry - Age: 35 - Height: 5' 10 1/2" - Born: DE, Kent County - Trade: Ship's carpenter - Enlistment date: 20 Jul 1814 - Enlistment period: 5 Yrs - By whom: William Featherstone - Discharged: 27 Jun 1816 for disability.

Guard, Daniel - Private - 17th Infantry - Company: Harris Hickman - Age: 26 - Height: 5' 11" - Born: NJ, Morris County, Georgetown - Trade: Laborer - Enlistment date: 16 Apr 1814 - Enlistment place: Butler County, Hamilton - Enlistment period: War - By whom: George Stall - Discharged: 9 Jun 1815 at Chillicothe - Bounty: BLW 14857-160-12 (Illinois).

Gubby, John R. - Private - 19th Infantry - Company: James Herron.

Guitro, John Baptist - Private - 2nd Rifles - Company: Batteal Harrison - Age: 27 - Height: 5' 6 1/2" - Born: LA, Orleans Parish, New Orleans - Trade: Laborer - Enlistment date: 2 Sep 1814 - Enlistment place: Cincinnati - Enlistment period: War - By whom: Elias Langham - Discharged: 30 Jun 1815 at Detroit.

Gunn, Daniel - 2nd Rifles - Age: 26 - Height: 5' 9" - Born: Scotland - Enlistment date: 26 Jul 1814 - Enlistment place: Cincinnati.

Gunn, John - Private - 19th Infantry - Company: William Gill - Other regiment: 17th Infantry then 3rd Infantry - Age: 37 - Height: 5' 9" - Born: NY, Saratoga County - Trade: Carpenter - Enlistment date: 17 Jun 1814 - Enlistment place: Lancaster - Enlistment period: 5 Yrs - By whom: John Simons - Discharged: 27 Jun 1819 at Fort Howard, WI.

Gunyon, Daniel - Private - 26th Infantry - Company: Joel Collins - Enlistment date: 26 Aug 1813 - Enlistment period: 1 Yr.

Gunyon, Joseph - Private - 26th Infantry - Company: Joel Collins - Enlistment date: 17 Aug 1813 - Enlistment period: 1 Yr.

Guthridge, John - Private - 26th Infantry - Company: George Kesling - Enlistment date: 8 May 1813 - Enlistment period: 1 Yr - Died: 9 Sep 1813.

Guthridge, William - Private - 19th Infantry - Company: William MacDonald - Enlistment date: 15 Dec 1813 - Discharged: 6 Oct 1814 at Greenbush, NY, lost his right hand - Pension: Old War IF-1468; served as a private in the 19th Infantry in 1814.

Guy, Thomas - Private - 19th Infantry - Age: 28 - Height: 5' 8 1/3" - Born: Pennsylvania - Enlistment date: 14 May 1814 - Enlistment place: Fairfield County, New Salem.

Gwin, Richard - Private - 2nd Artillery - Company: Daniel Cushing - Enlistment date: 10 Aug 1812 - Comments: Prisoner of War.

Gwynne, Richard - Sergeant - 19th Infantry - Company: Angus Langham - Comments: Prisoner of War.

Haberson, John - Private - 27th Infantry - Company: George Sanderson - Enlistment date: 19 Jul 1813.

Haddix, Nimrod - Private - Rangers - Company: Samuel McCormick - Enlistment date: 10 Dec 1813 - Enlistment period: 1 Yr - Discharged: 9 Dec 1814.

Hadley, Smith - 27th Infantry - Company: George Sanderson - Enlistment date: 8 Jun 1813 - Enlistment period: 1 Yr - Discharged: 27 May 1814 - Pension: Wife Calista Reynolds, WO-10089, WC-30125; married on 2 Oct 1836 in Knox County, OH; solider died on 3 or 4 Mar 1863 in Centerburg, OH; served in Captains George Sanderson and John Spencer Companies, 27th Infantry; lived in Knox County, OH, and Centerburg, OH - Bounty: BLW 26369-160-55.

Hagan, James - Private - 19th Infantry - Company: John Chunn - Comments: Prisoner of War.

Hagan, Thomas - Sergeant - 19th Infantry - Company: John Chunn - Comments: Prisoner of War (Quebec, LC), captured at Fort Niagara, NY, 19 Dec 1813; exchanged 4 May 1814.

Hagan, William - Private - 17th Infantry - Age: 35 - Height: 5' 7" - Born: Pennsylvania - Trade: Shoemaker - Enlistment date: 29 Aug 1814 - Enlistment period: War - By whom: William Featherstone.

Hagerty, James - Private - 27th Infantry - Company: George Sanderson - Enlistment date: 22 Jun 1813.

Hahn, Jacob - Private - 19th Infantry - Company: Isaac Van Horn - Enlistment date: 12 Jun 1813 - Enlistment period: 1 Yr - Discharged: 13 Jun 1814 - Pension: Wife Mary Magdalena Wickert, WO-454, WC-1333; served as a private in Capt. Isaac Van Horn's Company, 19th Infantry; married on 16 Jun 1812 in

Columbiana County, OH; soldier died on 18 Nov 1870 in Stark County, OH; widow died about 1876; lived in Stark County, OH - Bounty: BLW 10697-160-50.

Haines, Solomon - Private - 19th Infantry - Company: William Gill - Enlistment date: 1 Dec 1813 - Enlistment period: 18 Mos - Discharged: 7 Jun 1814 - Pension: Wife Isabel Lowe, SO-3940, SC-5414, WO-23469, WC-16367; served as a private in Capt. William Gill's Company, 19th Infantry; married on 16 Jan 1825 in Mt. Vernon, Knox County, OH; soldier died on 16 Oct 1873 in Kirkersville, OH; widow died on 29 Oct 1878 in Kirkersville, OH; lived in Fairfield County, OH, and Licking County, OH - Bounty: BLW 3246-80-50, BLW 16723-80-55.

Haines, William - Private - 19th Infantry - Company: Richard Talbott - Age: 27 - Height: 5' 9" - Born: New Jersey - Trade: Farmer - Enlistment date: 29 Jun 1814 - Enlistment place: Urbana - Enlistment period: War - By whom: William Baird - Discharged: 5 Jun 1815 at Chillicothe.

Hale, Samuel - Private - 26th Infantry - Company: Joel Collins - Enlistment date: 24 Jul 1813 - Enlistment period: 1 Yr - Died: 1 Dec 1813 at Sandwich, UC (now Windsor, Ontario).

Hall, Bela - 19th Infantry - Company: Lt John Goode - Pension: Old War IF-14681; served in Lt. Goode's Regiment of Infantry.

Hall, Benjamin - Private - 27th Infantry - Company: Isaac Van Horne - Other regiment: 19th Infantry - Age: 25 - Height: 5' 10" - Born: Maryland - Trade: Farmer - Enlistment period: War - Discharged: 6 Jun 1815 at Chillicothe - Bounty: BLW 6036-160-12 (Illinois) - Comments: Served aboard the US Schooner Somers on the Lake Erie Squadron; re-enlisted 11 Apr 1814.

Hall, John - Private - 19th Infantry - Company: Wilson Elliott - Enlistment date: 3 Jul 1812 - Enlistment period: 5 Yrs.

Hall, John - Private - 27th Infantry - Company: George Sanderson - Other regiment: 19th Infantry - Enlistment date: 30 May 1813 - Comments: Prisoner of War on Parole, captured at Detroit, MI, 16 Aug 1812; served aboard the US Schooner Tigress on the Lake Erie Squadron.

Hall, John - Private - 2nd Artillery - Company: Daniel Cushing - Other regiment: Corps of Artillery - Age: 22 - Height: 5' 8" - Born: OH, Hamilton County - Trade: Laborer - Enlistment date: 4 Feb 1814 - Enlistment place: Lebanon - Enlistment period: 5 Yrs - By whom: Daniel Cushing - Comments: Deserted at Detroit, MI, on 30 Sep 1816.

Hall, Joseph - Private - 17th Infantry - Age: 37 - Height: 5' 11" - Born: Maryland - Trade: Farmer - Enlistment date: 4 Jan 1815 - Enlistment place: Adams County, West Union - Enlistment period: War - By whom: James Campbell - Discharged: 18 Apr 1815 at Chillicothe - Bounty: BLW 484-320-14 (Arkansas).

Hall, Samuel M. - Private - 17th Infantry - Company: Benjamin Sanders - Age: 27 - Height: 5' 6 1/2" - Born: NJ, Monmouth County - Trade: Shoemaker - Enlistment date: 2 Jul 1814 - Enlistment place: Upper Canada, Fort Malden - Enlistment period: War - By whom: Benjamin Sanders - Discharged: 10 Oct 1814 at Detroit - Pension: Wife Abigail, Old War WF-13412; served as a private in Captain Sanders' Company, 17th Infantry - Bounty: BLW 2420-160-12 (Illinois) - Comments: Wounded at Michilimackinac, MI, on 25 Aug 1814.

Hallman, Stephen - Private - 19th Infantry - Age: 25 - Height: 5' 9" - Born: Pennsylvania - Trade: Carpenter - Enlistment date: 13 May 1814 - Enlistment period: War - Died: 8 Oct 1814 at Fort Erie, UC - Pension: Heirs obtained half pay for five years in lieu of military bounty land.

Hamer, Jacob - Private - Rangers - Age: 20 - Height: 5' 11" - Born: Pennsylvania - Trade: Farmer - Enlistment date: 7 Nov 1813 - Enlistment period: 1 Yr - Discharged: 7 Nov 1814 at Fort Malden, UC.

Hamilton, Alexander - Private - 2nd Rifles - Company: Batteal Harrison - Other regiment: Rifle Regiment - Age: 24 - Height: 6' 2" - Born: PA, Chester County - Trade: Farmer - Enlistment date: 14 Jul 1184 - Enlistment place: Zanesville - Enlistment period: 5 Yrs - By whom: William Dougherty - Discharged: 14 Jul 1819 at Fort Crawford, IL - Bounty: BLW 22564-120-12 (Arkansas).

Hamilton, Andrew - Private - 17th Infantry - Company: Harris Hickman - Age: 21 - Height: 5' 8" - Born: Pennsylvania - Trade: Laborer - Enlistment date: 4 Feb 1814 - Enlistment period: 18 Mos - By whom: John Simons.

Hamilton, Charles - Private - 26th Infantry - Discharged: 18 Nov 1814.

Hamilton, James - Private - 19th Infantry - Company: James Herron - Enlistment date: 14 Sep 1812 - Enlistment period: 5 Yrs.

Hamlin, Benjamin - Sergeant - 19th Infantry - Company: George Kesling - Other regiment: 3rd Infantry - Age: 24 - Height: 5' 8 1/2" - Born: SC, Union County - Trade: Farmer - Enlistment date: 8 Sep 1814 - Enlistment place: Xenia - Enlistment period: 5 Yrs - By whom: Robert Smith - Comments: Deserted 1 Sep 1815.

Hampren, Noah - Private - 26th Infantry - Company: George Kesling - Other regiment: 2nd Light Dragoons.

Hampton, Amos - Private - 19th Infantry - Company: Wilson Elliott.

Hampton, John - Private - 26th Infantry - Company: George Kesling - Other regiment: 2nd Light Dragoons - Enlistment date: 22 May 1813 - Enlistment period: 1 Yr.

Hancock, Daniel - Private - 19th Infantry - Company: William Gill - Age: 18 - Height: 5' 7" - Born: Maryland - Trade: Farmer - Enlistment date: 9 Jun 1814 - Enlistment period: War - Discharged: 5 Jun 1815 at Chillicothe - Bounty: BLW 17630-160-12 (Illinois).

Hancock, James - Private - 17th Infantry - Company: Caleb Holder - Age: 21 - Height: 5' 9" - Born: Pennsylvania - Trade: Farmer - Enlistment date: 8 Sep 1814 - Enlistment period: War - By whom: William Featherstone - Discharged: 30 Jun 1815 at Detroit - Bounty: BLW 11493-160-12 (Illinois).

Handlin, James - Private - 17th Infantry - Company: Caleb Holder - Age: 39 - Height: 5' 7" - Born: Virginia - Trade: Tailor - Enlistment date: 15 Aug 1814 - Enlistment place: Cambridge - Enlistment period: War - By whom: Ensign Strang - Discharged: 30 Jun 1815 at Detroit.

Hanes, Charles - Private - 26th Infantry - Company: Joel Collins - Enlistment date: 8 Sep 1813 - Enlistment period: 1 Yr - Died: 11 Dec 1813 at Sandwich, UC (now Windsor, Ontario).

Haning, Aaron - Private - 2nd Artillery - Company: Daniel Cushing - Age: 29 - Height: 5' 8" - Born: New Jersey - Enlistment date: 26 Aug 1812 - Enlistment period: 18 Mos - Bounty: BLW 7810-160-12 (Illinois) - Comments: Re-enlisted.

Hannah, Robert - Private - 2nd Artillery - Company: Daniel Cushing - Age: 15 - Height: 5' 5" - Born: PA, Washington County - Enlistment date: 12 Jul 1812 - Enlistment place: Canton - Enlistment period: 5 Yrs.

Hapleton, Joseph - Private - 19th Infantry - Company: William Gill.

Harbison, John - Private - 27th Infantry - Company: George Sanderson - Pension: SO-8663, SC-17398; served in Capt. Sanderson's Company, 27th Infantry.

Hardesty, Lewis - Sergeant - 27th Infantry - Company: William Gill - Pension: SO-28650, SC-20520, served as a sergeant in Capt. William Gill's Company, 27th Infantry.

Harding, Isaac - Private - 19th Infantry - Company: Harris Hickman - Other regiment: 17th Infantry - Age: 28 - Height: 5' 5" - Born: NY, Augusta - Trade: Laborer - Enlistment date: 23 Mar 1814 - Enlistment place: Franklin County, Franklinton - Enlistment period: War - By whom: John Cochran - Discharged: 9 Jun 1815 at Chillicothe - Bounty: BLW 22523-160-12 (Illinois).

Hardy, James - Private - 19th Infantry - Age: 21 - Height: 5' 6" - Born: Pennsylvania - Enlistment date: 26 Apr 1814 - Enlistment place: Waynesville - Enlistment period: War - Comments: Re-enlisted.

Hardy, Joseph - Private - 19th Infantry - Company: Carey Trimble - Age: 24 - Height: 5' 5" - Born: PA, Greene County - Trade: Laborer - Enlistment date: 27 Feb 1814 - Enlistment place: Chillicothe - Enlistment period: War - By whom: William McDonald - Discharged: 6 Jun 1815 at Chillicothe - Bounty: BLW 15070-160-12 (Illinois).

Harland, Ishmael - Corporal - 2nd Rifles - Company: Batteal Harrison - Age: 20 - Height: 5' 6" - Born: VA, Berkeley County (now WV) - Trade: Blacksmith - Enlistment date: 13 Jun 1814 - Enlistment place: Chillicothe - Enlistment period: War - By whom: Batteal Harrison - Discharged: 30 Jun 1815 at Detroit - Bounty: BLW 19615-160-12 (Illinois).

Harley, George - Private - 19th Infantry - Company: Angus Langham - Comments: Prisoner of War (Quebec, LC), captured at Fort Niagara, NY, 19 Dec 1813; exchanged 4 May 1814.

Harper, Alexander - Private - 19th Infantry - Company: Richard Talbott - Age: 23 - Height: 5' 11" - Born: Pennsylvania - Trade: Farmer - Enlistment date: 24 Jun 1814 - Enlistment place: Urbana - Enlistment period: War - By whom: William Baird - Discharged: 5 Jun 1815 at Chillicothe - Bounty: BLW 14621-160-12 (Illinois).

Harper, Clayton - Private - 19th Infantry - Company: Carey Trimble - Age: 15 - Height: 5' 6" - Born: VA, Botetourt County - Trade: Laborer - Enlistment date: 17 Mar 1814 - Enlistment place: Franklin County, Franklinton - Enlistment period: War - By whom: Hugh Moore - Discharged: 6 Jun 1815 at Chillicothe - Pension: Old War IF-5462; served as a private in Lt. McElvain's Company, 19th Infantry - Bounty: BLW 10228-160-12.

Harper, George - Private - 19th Infantry - Company: Joel Collins - Age: 31 - Height: 5' 5" - Born: Pennsylvania - Trade: Laborer - Enlistment date: 14 May 1814 - Enlistment place: Detroit - Enlistment period: War - By whom: John Patterson - Discharged: 20 Jul 1815 at Detroit - Bounty: BLW 12133-160-12 (Illinois) .

Harrington, Harry C. (or Harvey) - Private - 27th Infantry - Company: Joel Collins - Other regiment: 19th Infantry - Age: 19 - Height: 5' 6" - Born: Connecticut - Trade: Farmer - Enlistment period: War - Discharged: 20 Jul 1815 at Detroit - Pension: Old War WF-14771 Rejected, served as a private in Capt. Spencer's Company, 27th Infantry - Bounty: BLW 18572-160-12 (Illinois) - Comments: Served aboard the US Schooner Tigress on the Lake Erie Squadron; re-enlisted on 17 Mar 1814.

The Enlisted Men

Harris, James - Private - 1st Rifles - Company: Thomas Ramsey - Other regiment: Rifle Regiment - Age: 18 - Height: 5' 7 1/2: - Born: KY, Harding County - Trade: Laborer - Enlistment date: 13 Dec 1813 - Enlistment place: Cincinnati - Enlistment period: 5 Yrs - By whom: Thomas Ramsey - Discharged: 13 Dec 1818 - Comments: Re-enlisted.

Harris, William - Private - 2nd Rifles - Company: William Adair - Other regiment: 17th Infantry - Age: 27 - Height: 5' 10 1/2" - Born: MD, Baltimore County, Baltimore - Enlistment date: 22 May 1814 - Enlistment place: Cincinnati - Comments: Joined the 17th Infantry on 1 Jul 1814, Captain Harris Hickman's Company.

Harrison, James - Private - 26th Infantry - Company: George Kesling - Enlistment date: 16 Jun 1813.

Harrison, Lewis - Private - 1st Rifles - Company: Thomas Ramsey - Age: 20 - Height: 5' 6" - Born: Kentucky - Trade: Farmer - Enlistment date: 24 Mar 1814 - Enlistment place: Cincinnati - Enlistment period: War - By whom: Thomas Ramsey - Discharged: 5 Jun 1815 at Buffalo, NY - Pension: Wife Elizabeth, WO-17391, WC-23595; served as a private in Capt. Thomas Ramsey's Company, 1st Rifles.

Harrison, Noah - Private - 26th Infantry - Company: George Kesling - Enlistment date: 19 May 1813 - Enlistment period: 1 Yr - Comments: Prisoner of War on Parole, captured at Detroit, MI, 16 Aug 1812.

Harrison, William - Musician - 19th Infantry - Company: George Kesling - Age: 39 - Height: 5' 7" - Born: Virginia - Trade: Farmer - Enlistment date: 23 Oct 1814 - Enlistment place: Xenia - Enlistment period: War - By whom: Robert Smith - Discharged: 27 Mar 1815 at Zanesville - Bounty: BLW 5863-160-12 (Arkansas).

Harrison, William B. - Musician - 19th Infantry - Company: Batteal Harrison - Age: 18 - Height: 5' 6" - Born: KY, Harrison County - Trade: Farmer - Enlistment date: 27 Jul 1814 - Enlistment place: Urbana - Enlistment period: War - By whom: William Baird - Discharged: 5 Jun 1815 at Chillicothe - Pension: Wife Rhoda, WO-44051, WC-34432, SO-3148, SC-1952; served in Capt Harrison's Company, 19th Infantry as a musician - Bounty: BLW 3168-160-12 (Illinois).

Hart, David - Private - 2nd Artillery - Company: Daniel Cushing.

Hart, James L. - Private - 2nd Rifles - Company: Batteal Harrison - Age: 30 - Height: 5' 8" - Born: CT, Farmington County - Trade: Farmer - Enlistment date: 14 May 1814 - Enlistment place: Chillicothe - Enlistment period: War - By whom: Batteal Harrison - Discharged: 30 Jun 1815 at Detroit - Bounty: BLW 2804-160-12 (Illinois).

Harter, John - Private - 27th Infantry - Company: George Sanderson - Enlistment date: 27 Apr 1813.

Hartley, Joseph - Private - 26th Infantry - Company: John Moore - Pension: Old War Invalid and Widow Rejected File 14806; served as a private in Capt. Moore's Company, 26th Infantry.

Hartman, Frederick - Private - 27th Infantry - Company: George Sanderson - Enlistment date: 30 Apr 1813 - Died: Died at Zanesville.

Hartshorn, George - Private - 19th Infantry - Company: Joel Collins - Age: 40 - Height: 5' 8" - Born: Delaware - Trade: Tailor - Enlistment date: 17 Mar 1814 - Enlistment place: Detroit - Enlistment period: War - By whom: Wynkoop Warner - Discharged: 20 Jul 1815 at Detroit - Bounty: BLW 25627-160-12 (Arkansas).

Hartzell, George - Private - 26th Infantry - Company: Samuel Swearingen - Other regiment: 25th Infantry - Age: 47 - Born: PA, Lower Sockam - Trade: Tailor - Enlistment date: 4 Jul 1813 - Enlistment period: 1 Yr - Discharged: 8 Mar 1814 at Sackets Harbor, NY, internal hernia.

Harvey, John - Private - 19th Infantry - Bounty: BLW 7096-160-12.

Harvey, Peter - Private - 19th Infantry - Company: Asabael Nearing - Age: 25 - Height: 5' 10" - Born: Virginia - Trade: Joiner - Enlistment date: 11 Jan 1813 - Enlistment period: 18 Mos - Discharged: 5 Jun 1815 - Comments: Re-enlisted 11 May 1814 at Chillicothe, OH.

Harvey, Peter - Private - 19th Infantry - Company: William Gill - Other regiment: 25th Infantry - Age: 37 - Height: 5' 9' - Born: Rhode Island - Trade: Miller - Enlistment date: 20 Aug 1812 - Enlistment period: 5 Yrs - By whom: Asabael Nearing - Died: about 30 Nov 1812 - Bounty: BLW 6164-160-12 (Illinois).

Harvey, William - Private - 19th Infantry - Company: Angus Langham - Age: 19 - Height: 5' 6" - Born: Great Britain - Enlistment date: 2 Jul 1812 - Enlistment period: 5 Yrs - Died: Died - Bounty: BLW 26018-160-12 (Arkansas) - Comments: Land bounty to Sylvia Brown, sister & heir at law of William Harvey.

Haselton, Joseph - Private - 19th Infantry - Company: William Gill - Age: 28 - Height: 5' 9" - Born: Maryland - Trade: Hatter - Enlistment date: 24 Apr 1814 - Enlistment place: Pickaway County, Jefferson (Pickaway Plains) - Enlistment period: War - By whom: John Lucas - Discharged: 5 Jun 1815 at Chillicothe.

Hasey, James - Private - 19th Infantry - Company: Wilson Elliott.

Hastings, Simeon - Private - 19th Infantry - Company: John Chunn - Enlistment date: 1 Mar 1813 - Discharged: 18 Sep 1814 - Pension: Wife Sarah Martin, WO-17398, WC-12991; served as a private in Capt Chunn's Company, 19th Infantry; married on 24 Dec 1818 in Kanawha County, WV; soldier died on 3 Dec 1869 in Kanawha County, WV; lived in Coalburg, Kanawha County, WV - Bounty: BLW 10009-160-50.

Hathaway, Abraham - Private - Rangers - Company: Samuel McCormick - Age: 27 - Height: 5' 8" - Born: Pennsylvania - Trade: Farmer - Enlistment date: 5 Nov 1813 - Enlistment period: 1 Yr - Discharged: 5 Nov 1814 at Fort Malden, UC - Died: 21 Jan 1842 - Pension: Wife Bathsheba Cox, WO-6370, WC-4832; married on 17 Apr 1810 in Miami County, OH; solder died on 21 Jan 1842 in Miami County, OH; wife died circa 1872 in Miami County, OH; served as a private in Capt. Samuel McCormick's Company, US Rangers; wife lived in Winamac, Pulaski County, IN - Bounty: BLW 4063-160-50.

Haughey, Jacob - Private - 17th Infantry - Company: David Holt - Age: 34 - Height: 5' 10" - Born: DE, Newcastle County - Trade: Laborer - Enlistment date: 23 Jun 1814 - Enlistment place: Chillicothe - Enlistment period: War - By whom: Lieutenant Huffman - Discharged: 7 Jun 1815 at Chillicothe.

Haughey, Jacob - Private - 19th Infantry - Age: 33 - Height: 5' 9" - Born: DE, New Castle County - Enlistment date: 20 Aug 1812.

Haukpal, Conrad - Private - 19th Infantry - Age: 18 - Height: 5' 5" - Born: MD, Allegeny County - Enlistment date: 13 Jul 1812 - Enlistment period: 5 Yrs.

Havens, Benjamin Jr - Private - Rangers - Company: Samuel McCormick - Age: 19 - Height: 6' - Born: Pennsylvania - Trade: Shoemaker - Enlistment date: 26 Oct 1813 - Enlistment period: 1 Yr - Discharged: 26 Oct 1814 at Fort Malden, UC - Pension: Old War Invalid and Widow Rejected File 14838; served as a private in Capt. McCormick's OH Mounted Rangers.

Hawk, Jacob - Private - 2nd Rifles - Company: Batteal Harrison - Age: 25 - Height: 5' 7" - Born: New Jersey - Trade: Farmer - Enlistment date: 28 Jul 1814 - Enlistment place: Cincinnati - Enlistment period: 5 Yrs - By whom: John Louden.

Hayes, Michael - Private - 2nd Rifles - Company: Batteal Harrison - Age: 28 - Height: 5' 11 1/2" - Born: VA, Norfolk County - Trade: Laborer - Enlistment date: 20 Oct 1814 - Enlistment place: Gallipolis - Enlistment period: 5 Yrs - By whom: Edward Miller - Comments: Re-enlisted on 24 Mar 1819.

Haymaker, John - Private - 19th Infantry - Other regiment: 3rd Infantry - Age: 33 - Height: 5' 10 3/4" - Born: Pennsylvania - Trade: Farmer - Enlistment date: 8 Feb 1815 - Enlistment place: Cincinnati - Enlistment period: 5 Yrs By whom: William Baird - Discharged: 4 Jul 1818 for disability.

Haynes – see Hanes, Charles

Haynes, Carlisle - Private - 19th Infantry - Company: David Holt - Comments: Prisoner of War, exchanged 25 Apr 1814.

Haynes, William - Private - 19th Infantry - Company: Richard Talbott - Bounty: BLW 5238-160-12 (Illinois).

Hays, Archibald - Private - 2nd Rifles - Age: 20 - Born: TN, Washington County - Enlistment date: 28 Jul 1814 - Enlistment place: TN, Warren County, McMinville - Enlistment period: 5 Yrs - By whom: George Kennedy - Died: 26 Jan 1815 at Chillicothe, OH, 26 Jan or 3 Feb 1815.

Hays, John - Private - 19th Infantry - Company: Wilson Elliott.

Hayth, Elisha - Private - 19th Infantry - Company: Lt Charles Cass - Died: 15 Oct 1814 - Comments: Buried in the War of 1812 Cemetery in Cheektowaga, Erie County, NY.

Hazen, James - Private - 26th Infantry - Company: George Kesling - Other regiment: 19th Infantry - Age: 30 - Height: 5' 3 1/2" - Born: New York - Trade: Hatter - Enlistment date: 17 Feb 1815 - Enlistment place: Cincinnati - Enlistment period: War - By whom: William Baird.

Headley, Jacob - Private - 27th Infantry - Company: George Sanderson - Enlistment date: 27 Apr 1813.

Headly, Smith - Corporal - 27th Infantry - Company: George Sanderson - Enlistment date: 8 Jun 1813.

Heaton, Joseph - Private - 27th Infantry - Company: Alexander Hill - Other regiment: 19th Infantry - Age: 44 - Height: 5' 10" - Born: Maryland - Trade: Blacksmith - Enlistment date: 24 Feb 1814 - Enlistment place: Zanesville - Enlistment period: War - By whom: Henry Northrup - Discharged: 6 Jun 1815 at Chillicothe - Bounty: BLW 11015-160-12 (Illinois).

Heaton, Samuel - Private - 2nd Artillery - Company: Daniel Cushing - Enlistment date: 23 Sep 1812 - Bounty: BLW 22217-160-12 (Arkansas).

Heavens, William - Private - Rangers - Company: Samuel McCormick - Enlistment date: 1 Nov 1813 - Enlistment period: 1 Yr - Discharged: 22 Nov 1814.

Heitt, Elisha - Private - 27th Infantry - Company: Alexander Hill.

Helms, Stephen - Private - 19th Infantry - Company: James Herron - Enlistment date: 27 Jun 1813 - Enlistment period: War.

Hemming, Samuel - Private - 19th Infantry - Company: Carey Trimble - Age: 19 - Height: 5' 7 1/2" - Born: Maryland - Enlistment date: 9 May 1814 - Enlistment place: Columbiana County, Salem - Enlistment period: War - By whom: John Carroll - Discharged: 6 Jun 1815 at Chillicothe - Bounty: BLW 18101-160-12 (Illinois).

The Enlisted Men

Hemphill, Henry - Private - 26th Infantry - Company: William Puthuff - Enlistment date: 6 May 1813 - Enlistment period: 1 Yr - Died: 14 Oct 1813 - Comments: Died at Detroit, MI; waiter to Captain Wood of the engineers.

Hemphill, James - Private - 26th Infantry - Company: William Puthuff - Enlistment date: 7 May 1813 - Enlistment period: 1 Yr.

Henderson, John - Private - 24th Infantry - Company: Caleb Holder - Other regiment: 17th Infantry - Age: 21 - Height: 5' 10 3/4" - Born: North Carolina - Trade: Farmer - Enlistment date: 27 Aug 1814 - Enlistment period: War - By whom: William Featherstone - Discharged: 30 Jun 1815 at Detroit - Pension: SC-18714; served in Capt. James Anderson's Company, 24th Infantry and in Capt. Holder's Company, 19th Infantry - Bounty: BLW 7354-160-12 (Arkansas).

Henderson, John - Private - 19th Infantry - Company: Joel Collins - Age: 34 - Height: 5' 10" - Born: Pennsylvania - Trade: Stone mason - Enlistment date: 11 July 1814 - Enlistment place: Upper Canada, Fort Malden - Enlistment period: War - By whom: Robert Smith - Discharged: 20 Jul 1815 at Detroit - Bounty: BLW 1939-160-12 (Illinois) - Comments: Re-enlisted.

Hendrick, Edmund - Private - 19th Infantry - Company: George Kesling - Enlistment date: 3 Mar 1814 - Enlistment period: War - Died: 29 Sep 1814 - Bounty: BLW 14736-160-12 (Illinois) - Comments: Died at Fort Erie, UC; land bounty to Bernard Hendrick, father & heir at law of Edmund Hendrick.

Hendrick, William - Private - Rangers - Company: Samuel McCormick - Enlistment date: 14 Nov 1813 - Enlistment period: 1 Yr - Discharged: 13 Nov 1814.

Henning, Aaron - Private - 17th Infantry - Company: John Chunn - Age: 31 - Height: 5' 10" - Born: New Jersey - Trade: Farmer - Enlistment date: 14 Jan 1814 - Enlistment place: Franklin County, Franklinton - Enlistment period: War - By whom: John Cochran - Discharged: 7 Jun 1815 at Chillicothe.

Henning, Samuel - Private - 27th Infantry - Company: Alexander Hill.

Henry, Samuel - 26th Infantry - Company: Joel Collins - Enlistment date: 13 Jun 1813 - Enlistment period: 1 Yr - Died: 1 Dec 1813 at Sandwich, UC (now Windsor, Ontario).

Henson, George - Private - 19th Infantry - Company: James Herron - Enlistment date: 17 Aug 1813 - Enlistment period: 18 Mos.

Herd, Caleb - Private - 26th Infantry - Company: George Kesling - Enlistment date: 24 Apr 1813 - Enlistment period: 1 Yr.

Herrington, Charles - Private - 19th Infantry - Company: Carey Trimble - Age: 22 - Height: 5' 7" - Born: Ireland - Trade: Joiner - Enlistment date: 23 Mar 1814 - Enlistment place: Clermont County, Williamsburg - Enlistment period: War - By whom: William McDonald Jr - Discharged: 31 May 1815 - Bounty: BLW 24806-160-12 (Arkansas).

Herrod, John - Private - 19th Infantry - Company: Asabael Nearing - Enlistment date: 17 Nov 1812.

Herron, Joseph - Sergeant - 19th Infantry - Company: Joel Collins - Age: 10 - Height: 5' 7" - Born: PA, Fayette County, Union - Trade: Clerk - Enlistment date: 9 May 1814 - Enlistment place: Upper Canada, Sandwich - Enlistment period: War - By whom: Collin McLeod - Discharged: 20 Jul 1815 at Detroit - Bounty: BLW 6535-160-12 (Illinois).

Herron, Joseph R. - Sergeant - 26th Infantry - Company: Samuel Swearingen - Other regiment: 2nd Light Dragoons - Enlistment date: 5 Jul 1812 - Enlistment period: 1 Yr - 5 Yrs - Comments: Prisoner of War, captured at the Miami Rapids, 4 May 1813; re-enlisted 6 Jul 1813.

Herron, Thomas - Private - 19th Infantry - Company: Harris Hickman - Other regiment: 17th Infantry - Age: 33 - Height: 5' 11 1/2" - Born: Tennessee - Trade: Laborer - Enlistment date: 12 Mar 1814 - Enlistment period: War - By whom: Thomas McKnight - Discharged: 9 Jun 1815 at Chillicothe - Bounty: BLW 6037-160-12 (Arkansas).

Hershberger, John - Private - 2nd Rifles - Company: Batteal Harrison - Age: 29 - Height: 5' 11" - Born: PA, Lancaster County - Trade: Rope maker - Enlistment date: 6 Jul 1814 - Enlistment place: Cincinnati - Enlistment period: War - By whom: Elias Langham - Discharged: 30 Jun 1815 at Detroit.

Hesley, Henry - Private - 26th Infantry - Company: George Kesling - Other regiment: 2nd Rifles - Enlistment date: 25 Mar 1813 - Enlistment period: 1 Yr.

Hewet, Jacob - Waiter - 19th Infantry - Company: Carey Trimble - Enlistment date: 28 Feb 1815 - Comments: Waiter for Lt McElvain.

Hewett – see Hughett, John K.

Hewitt, Thomas - Private - 26th Infantry - Company: Samuel Swearingen - Other regiment: 25th Infantry - Enlistment date: 10 Jul 1813 - Enlistment period: 1 Yr - Discharged: 22 Jun 1814.

Hewling, Samuel - Private - 26th Infantry - Company: George Kesling - Other regiment: 2nd Light Dragoons - Enlistment date: 27 May 1813 - Enlistment period: 1 Yr.

Hicks, Thomas - Private - 17th Infantry - Company: Harris Hickman - Age: 21 - Height: 5' 6" - Born: New York - Trade: Shoemaker - Enlistment date: 4 May 1813 - Enlistment place: Steubenville - Enlistment period: War - By whom: Isaac Rieley.

Hickson, Enoch - Private - 26th Infantry - Company: Samuel Swearingen - Other regiment: 25th Infantry - Enlistment date: 8 Jul 1813 - Enlistment period: 1 Yr - Discharged: 20 Jun 1814 at Buffalo, NY.

Hickson, Joel - Sergeant - 26th Infantry - Company: Carey Trimble - Other regiment: 19th Infantry - Enlistment date: 12 Oct 1813 - Enlistment period: 1 Yr - By whom: Henry Northrup - Discharged: 12 Oct 1814 - Pension: SO-14452, SC-17526; served as a private in 1st Lieutenant William McDonald's Company, 26th Infantry.

Hide – see Hyde, Charles W.

Higby, Samuel - Private - 19th Infantry - Company: Carey Trimble - Other regiment: 17th Infantry - Age: 33 - Height: 5' 5" - Born: New Jersey - Trade: Farmer - Enlistment date: 29 May 1814 - Enlistment place: Zanesville - Enlistment period: 5 Yrs - By whom: Neal McFadden - Died: 23 Apr 1815, probably at Newport, KY.

Higby, Samuel - Private - 27th Infantry - Company: John McElvain - Other regiment: 19th Infantry - Age: 23 - Height: 5' 5" - Born: New Jersey - Enlistment date: 23 Apr 1814 - Enlistment place: Zanesville.

Higgins, Daniel - Private - 19th Infantry - Company: Wilson Elliott - Age: 42 - Height: 5' 7" - Born: Ireland, County Derry - Enlistment date: 8 Aug 1812 - Enlistment period: 18 Mos.

Higley – see Higby Samuel

Higley, Elisha (or Elihu) - Private - 19th Infantry - Company: Wilson Elliott - Enlistment date: 1 Aug 1812 - Enlistment period: 18 Mos - Pension: SO-8681, SC-5605, served in Capt. James Herron's Company, 19th Infantry as a private.

Hill, Eli - Private - 26th Infantry - Company: William Puthuff - Enlistment date: 7 Jun 1813 - Enlistment period: 1 Yr - Died: 22 Nov 1813.

Hill, George S. - Private - 2nd Rifles - Company: Batteal Harrison - Age: 18 - Height: 5' 3" - Born: NY, Otsego County - Trade: Farmer - Enlistment date: 27 Sep 1814 - Enlistment place: Gallipolis - Enlistment period: 5 Yrs - By whom: Edward Miller - Discharged: 27 Sep 1819 at Fort Crawford, IL - Bounty: BLW 23628-160-12 (Arkansas).

Hill, James - Private - 26th Infantry - Company: George Kesling - Enlistment date: 28 Apr 1813 - Enlistment period: 1 Yr.

Hill, John - Private - 27th Infantry - Company: Alexander Hill - Other regiment: 19th Infantry - Age: 22 - Height: 5' 11" - Born: CT, Litchfield County - Enlistment date: 26 Apr 1814 - Enlistment place: Trumbull County, Warren.

Hill, John - Private - 19th Infantry - Company: Carey Trimble - Age: 22 - Height: 5' 10 3/4" - Born: New York - Trade: Blacksmith - Enlistment date: 27 Apr 1814 - Enlistment place: Cleveland - Enlistment period: War - By whom: James Harper - Discharged: 6 Jun 1815 at Chillicothe - Bounty: BLW 2662-16012 (Illinois).

Hill, William - Private - 26th Infantry - Company: George Will - Enlistment date: 16 Jun 1813 - Enlistment period: 1 Yr.

Hill, William B. - Private - 1st Rifles - Company: Thomas Ramsey - Age: 18 - Height: 5' 8 1/2" - Born: PA, Alleghany County - Trade: Farmer - Enlistment date: 29 Apr 1814 - Enlistment place: Columbiana County, Middleton - Enlistment period: War - By whom: Peter Albright - Bounty: BLW 15035-160-12 (Missouri) - Comments: Deserted at Erie, PA, on 1 Sep 1814.

Hill, William W. - Private - 19th Infantry - Company: Wilson Elliott - Age: 23 - Height: 5' 6 1/2" - Born: NY, Otsego County - Enlistment date: 17 Aug 1812.

Hilliard, James - Private - 19th Infantry - Company: Carey Trimble - Age: 22 - Height: 5' 8" - Born: PA, Chester County - Trade: Laborer - Enlistment date: 10 Mar 1814 - Enlistment place: Athens - Enlistment period: War - By whom: Nehemiah Gregory - Discharged: 31 Mar 1815 - Pension: Wife Kissia, WO-35723, WC-29983; served in Capt. J. Gregory's Company, Ohio Militia, and in Capt. C. A. Trimble's Company, 19th Infantry as a private - Bounty: BLW 27797-160-42.

Hillyard, James - Private - 27th Infantry - Company: Alexander Hill.

Hinkle, Ziba - Private - 26th Infantry - Company: Samuel Swearingen - Other regiment: 25th Infantry - Age: 23 - Height: 5' 8" - Enlistment date: 26 Jun 1813 - Enlistment period: 1 Yr - Discharged: Jun 1813.

Hinkley, Josiah - Private - 27th Infantry - Company: George Sanderson - Enlistment date: 17 Apr 1813 - Died: 5 Sep 1813.

Hively, John - Private - 26th Infantry - Company: George Kesling - Enlistment date: 31 May 1813 - Enlistment period: 1 Yr - By whom: George Kesling - Died: 27 Aug 1813.

The Enlisted Men

Hobson, Josiah - Private - 26th Infantry - Company: George Kesling - Other regiment: 25th Infantry - Enlistment date: 8 May 1813 - Enlistment period: 1 Yr - Discharged: 8 May 1814.

Hodge – see Hoge, William

Hoff, Benjamin - Private - 19th Infantry - Company: Carey Trimble - Age: 25 - Height: 5' 5" - Born: Maryland - Trade: Printer - Enlistment date: 5 Apr 1814 - Enlistment place: Chillicothe - Enlistment period: War - By whom: Charles Cissna.

Hogan, William - Private - 26th Infantry - Company: William Puthuff - Enlistment date: 28 May 1813 - Enlistment period: 1 Yr.

Hogan, William R. - Private - 1st Rifles - Company: Thomas Ramsey - Age: 19 - Height: 5' 7 1/2" - Born: MD, Harford County - Trade: Farmer - Enlistment date: 15 Dec 1813 - Enlistment place: Cincinnati - Enlistment period: War - By whom: Thomas Ramsey - Pension: SC-34971; served as a fifer in Capt. Thomas Ramsey's Company, OH Militia - Comments: Deserted at Cincinnati, OH, on 27 May 1814.

Hoge, William - Private - 19th Infantry - Company: William Gill - Age: 23 - Height: 5' 10" - Born: Virginia - Trade: Farmer - Enlistment date: 17 Sep 1814 - Enlistment place: Xenia - Enlistment period: War - By whom: Robert Smith - Discharged: 5 Jun 1815 at Chillicothe - Bounty: BLW 3170-160-12.

Hogues – see Hogan, William R.

Holcomb, Perlin - Private - 27th Infantry - Company: George Sanderson - Enlistment date: 18 Apr 1813 - Pension: Wife Sarah F., WO-25376, WC-21480, SO-12568,, SC-18490; served as a private in Captain George Sanderson's Company, 27th Infantry.

Holderfield, James - Private - 26th Infantry - Company: Samuel Swearingen - Comments: Prisoner of War, exchanged 25 Apr 1814.

Holliday, Andrew - Private - 27th Infantry - Company: William Gill - Comments: Served aboard the US Sloop Trippe on the Lake Erie Squadron.

Holloway, John - Corporal - 26th Infantry - Company: George Kesling - Other regiment: 25th Infantry - Enlistment date: 6 Jun 1813 - Enlistment period: 1 Yr - By whom: George Kesling - Discharged: 6 Jun 1815.

Holston, William - Private - 26th Infantry - Company: George Kesling - Enlistment date: 12 May 1813 - Enlistment period: 1 Yr - Died: 22 Dec 1813, probably at Sackets Harbor, NY.

Hood, Farmer - Private - 19th Infantry.

Hood, Henry - Private - 19th Infantry - Company: James Herron - Enlistment date: 13 Oct 1813 - Enlistment period: 18 Mos.

Hood, William - Private - 19th Infantry - Company: Carey Trimble - Age: 21 - Height: 5' 7 1/2" - Born: Pennsylvania - Trade: Printer - Enlistment date: 25 Dec 1813 - Enlistment place: Chillicothe - Enlistment period: War - By whom: Capt. Patterson - Discharged: 6 Jun 1815 at Chillicothe - Bounty: BLW 528-320-14 (Illinois).

Hood, William - Sergeant - 19th Infantry - Enlistment date: 20 Dec 1813 - Discharged: 28 Dec 1814 - Comments: Discharged at Greenbush, NY, epileptic fits.

Hook, Henry - Private - 19th Infantry - Company: Richard Talbott - Age: 32 - Height: 5' 7 1/2" - Born: PA, Lancaster County - Trade: Coppersmith - Enlistment date: 11 May 1814 - Enlistment place: Cincinnati - Enlistment period: War - By whom: Robert Anderson - Discharged: 5 Jun 1815 at Chillicothe - Bounty: BLW 2044-160-12 (Arkansas).

Hooks, Hugh - Private - 17th Infantry - Other regiment: 3rd Infantry - Age: 21 - Height: 5' 6" - Born: PA, Fayette County - Trade: Laborer - Enlistment date: 10 Aug 1814 - Enlistment place: Cambridge - Enlistment period: 5 Yrs - By whom: William Shang - Discharged: 10 Aug 1819 at Fort Howard, WI.

Hooper, John - Private - 19th Infantry - Company: William Gill - Other regiment: 3rd Infantry - Age: 27 - Height: 5' 6 1/2" - Born: England - Trade: Sawyer - Enlistment date: 8 Aug 1814 - Enlistment place: Chillicothe - Enlistment period: 5 Yrs - By whom: Carey Trimble - Comments: Deserted at Detroit, MI, on 18 Jan 1816.

Hopkins, Allen - Sergeant - 2nd Rifles - Company: Batteal Harrison - Age: 26 - Height: 5' 10 1/3" - Born: New York - Trade: Farmer - Enlistment date: 19 Jul 1814 - Enlistment place: Cincinnati - Enlistment period: War - By whom: Elias Langham - Discharged: 30 Jun 1815 at Detroit.

Hopkins, John - Private - 19th Infantry - Company: Richard Talbott - Height: 5' 10" - Born: Pennsylvania - Trade: Carpenter - Enlistment date: 18 Mar 1814 - Enlistment place: Franklin County - Enlistment period: War - By whom: Robert Young - Died: 28 Nov 1814 at Cleveland, OH - Bounty: BLW 23740-160-12 (Arkansas) - Comments: Land bounty to William Hopkins, brother & other heirs at law of John Hopkins.

Horral, Elijah - Private - 26th Infantry - Company: Samuel Swearingen - Other regiment: 25th Infantry - Enlistment date: 18 Jun 1813 - Enlistment period: 1 Yr - Discharged: 18 Jun 1814.

Hostelton, Joseph - Private - 19th Infantry - Company: William Gill - Bounty: BLW 9975-160-12 (Illinois).

Houch, John - Private - 27th Infantry - Company: Joseph Carins - Pension: Wife Barbara, WO-21518, WC-26007; served in Capt. Cairns' Company, 27th Infantry.

Hough, Jacob - Sergeant - 26th Infantry - Company: Joel Collins - Enlistment date: 12 Jul 1813 - Enlistment period: 1 Yr.

Houghley, Jacob - Sergeant - 17th Infantry - Age: 34 - Height: 5' 10" - Born: DE, New Castle County - Trade: Farmer - Enlistment date: 23 Jun 1814 - Enlistment place: Chillicothe - Enlistment period: War - By whom: Adam Hoffman.

Houseman, Abraham - Corporal - 26th Infantry - Company: George Will - Other regiment: 19th Infantry - Age: 26 - Height: 6' - Born: Virginia - Enlistment date: 11 May 1813 - Enlistment period: 1 Yr - War - Killed: 17 Sep 1814 at Fort Erie, UC - Bounty: BLW 22414-160-12 (Arkansas) - Comments: Land bounty to William Houseman, brother & other heirs at law of Abraham Houseman.

Howard, Thomas - Private - 26th Infantry - Company: George Kesling - Enlistment date: 24 Mar 1813 - Enlistment period: 1 Yr - Comments: Prisoner of War on Parole, captured at Detroit, MI, 16 Aug 1812.

Howard, William - Private - 19th Infantry - Comments: Prisoner of War, released at Fort Independence, 31 Mar 1813.

Howe, Calvin B. - Private - 1st Rifles - Company: Thomas Ramsey - Age: 19 - Height: 5' 6" - Born: NY, Ulster County - Trade: Farmer - Enlistment date: 30 Mar 1814 - Enlistment place: Cincinnati - Enlistment period: War - By whom: Thomas Ramsey - Discharged: 5 Jun 1815 at Buffalo, NY - Bounty: BLW 2882-160-12 (Arkansas) - Comments: Wounded during the Battle of Fort Erie, UC.

Howell, William - Corporal - 26th Infantry - Company: Carey Trimble - Other regiment: 19th Infantry - Age: 33 - Height: 5' 9" - Born: NY, Burlington County - Trade: Joiner - Enlistment date: 3 Mar 1814 - Enlistment place: Chillicothe - Enlistment period: War - By whom: Charles Cissna - Discharged: 6 Jun 1815 at Chillicothe - Pension: Old War IF-26165; served in Capt. Kesling's Company, US Infantry; corporal in 1814 - Bounty: BLW 1975-160-12 (Illinois).

Hoyt, Lewis - Sergeant - 17th Infantry - Company: Henry Crittenden - Age: 32 - Height: 5' 6" - Born: CT, Fairfield County - Trade: Hatter - Enlistment date: 22 Jun 1814 - Enlistment place: New Lisbon - Enlistment period: War - By whom: Thomas McKnight - Discharged: 7 Jun 1815 at Chillicothe - Bounty: BLW 2889-160-12 (Illinois).

Hubbard, Edward - Private - 2nd Light Dragoons - Company: Samuel Hopkins - Age: 22 - Height: 5' 6" - Born: Connecticut - Trade: Farmer - Enlistment date: 9 Jul 1813 - Enlistment place: Cleveland - Enlistment period: 18 Mos - By whom: Samuel Hopkins - Discharged: 9 Jan 1815.

Hubbard, John - Private - 26th Infantry - Company: Joel Collins - Other regiment: 19th Infantry - Age: 39 - Height: 5' 10" - Enlistment date: 25 Aug 1813 - Enlistment period: 1 Yr - War - Discharged: 23 Oct 1814 at Detroit, MI, on Surgeon's Certificate for disability - Bounty: BLW 19789-120-12 (Illinois) - Comments: Re-enlisted on 21 Apr 1814 at Sandwich, UC, for the war.

Hubbard, William - Private - 17th Infantry - Age: 28 - Height: 5' 8" - Born: Connecticut - Enlistment date: 24 Mar 1814 - Enlistment place: Warren - By whom: William Leavitt.

Hudson, Abraham - Private - Rangers - Company: Samuel McCormick - Pension: SO-11375, SC-6797; served as a private in Capt. Samuel McCormick's Company, US Rangers.

Hudson, Samuel - 1st Rifles - Company: Thomas Ramsey - Age: 22 - Height: 5' 8" - Born: CT, New London County - Trade: Shoemaker - Enlistment date: 18 Apr 1814 - Enlistment place: Cincinnati - Enlistment period: 5 Yrs - By whom: Thomas Ramsey - Comments: Deserted at Cincinnati, OH, on 3 Jun 1814.

Huff, Jacob J. - Sergeant - 19th Infantry - Company: George Kesling - Age: 40 - Height: 5' 9" - Born: VA, Frederick County, Winchester - Trade: Farmer - Enlistment date: 25 Oct 1814 - Enlistment place: Xenia - Enlistment period: War - By whom: Robert Smith - Discharged: 27 Mar 1815 at Zanesville - Bounty: BLW 3169-160-12 (Illinois).

Huffman, Jacob - Private - 19th Infantry - Age: 35 - Height: 5' 7" - Born: Pennsylvania - Enlistment date: 19 Apr 1814 - Enlistment place: Circleville - By whom: Jonathan Rees.

Huffman, John - Private - 19th Infantry - Company: William Gill - Age: 23 - Height: 6' - Born: Virginia - Trade: Farmer - Enlistment date: 10 Oct 1814 - Enlistment period: War - By whom: John Simons - Discharged: 5 Jun 1815 at Chillicothe - Bounty: BLW 9629-160-12 (Illinois).

Hugg, William - Private - 19th Infantry - Company: Angus Langham.

Hughes, David - Private - 27th Infantry - Company: George Sanderson - Enlistment date: 26 May 1813.

Hughes, Elias - Private - 27th Infantry - Comments: Prisoner of War on Parole, captured at Detroit, MI, 16 Aug 1812.

Hughes, John - Private - 26th Infantry - Company: George Kesling - Other regiment: 19th Infantry - Age: 19 -

Height: 5' 7" - Born: North Carolina - Enlistment date: 12 May 1813 - Enlistment period: 1 Yr - Died: 13 Jul 1814 - Bounty: BLW 23437-160-12 (Arkansas) - Comments: Land bounty to James Hughes, brother & other heirs at law of John Hughes.

Hughes, John - Private - 26th Infantry - Other regiment: 25th Infantry - Age: 21 - Height: 5' 6" - Born: Virginia - Trade: Laborer - Enlistment date: 13 Jul 1813 - Enlistment place: Ohio - Enlistment period: 18 Mos - By whom: Lieutenant Lee - Discharged: 12 May 1815 - Comments: Dishonorably discharged at Sackets Harbor, NY, for desertion.

Hughes, Levi - Private - 19th Infantry - Company: Richard Talbott - Age: 32 - Height: 5' 6 1/2" - Born: North Carolina - Trade: Weaver - Enlistment date: 21 May 1814 - Enlistment place: Montgomery County - Enlistment period: War - By whom: Philip Price - Discharged: 5 Jun 1815 at Chillicothe - Bounty: BLW 10243-160-12 (Illinois).

Hughett, John K. - Private - 19th Infantry - Company: George Kesling - Age: 19 - Height: 5' 10 1/2" - Born: Vermont - Trade: Carpenter - Enlistment date: 25 Mar 1814 - Enlistment place: Detroit - Enlistment period: War - Discharged: 27 Mar 1815 at Zanesville - Bounty: BLW 14486-160-12 (Missouri).

Hughey, Isaac H. - Private - 17th Infantry - Company: Harris Hickman - Age: 38 - Height: 5' 6" - Born: Pennsylvania - Trade: Farmer - Enlistment date: 13 May 1814 - Enlistment place: Chillicothe - Enlistment period: War - By whom: Adam Hoffman - Discharged: 9 Jun 1815 at Chillicothe - Bounty: BLW 6593-160-12 (Illinois).

Hughey, William - Private - 19th Infantry - Company: George Kesling - Age: 23 - Height: 6' 1" - Born: Maryland - Trade: Shoemaker - Enlistment date: 28 Jan 1815 - Enlistment place: Zanesville - Enlistment period: War - By whom: Charles Cass - Discharged: 27 Mar 1815 at Zanesville - Bounty: BLW 466-320-14 (Illinois).

Hulbert, Isaac - Private - 17th Infantry - Company: John Chunn - Enlistment date: 25 Nov 1813 - Enlistment period: 5 Yrs - By whom: David Carney - Discharged: 7 Nov 1814.

Hull, Henry - Private - 27th Infantry - Company: Isaac Van Horne - Enlistment date: 10 Jun 1813 - Enlistment period: 1 Yr - Discharged: 10 Jun 1814 - Pension: Wife Elizabeth Pool, WO-1729, WC-4213; served as a sergeant in Capt. Asa Hutchin's Company, OH Militia, and as a private in Capt. Isaac Van Horn's Company, 27th Infantry; married on 1 Nov 1809 in Columbiana County, OH; soldier died on 15 Aug 1869 in Meigs County, OH; lived in Wayne and Meigs Counties, OH - Bounty: BLW 12810-40-50, BLW 27035-120-55 - Comments: Served in Capt. Hutchin's Company between 29 Aug 1812 and 12 Nov 1812.

Hull, Jesse - Private - 17th Infantry - Company: David Holt - Age: 35 - Height: 5' 4" - Born: New Jersey - Trade: Farmer - Enlistment date: 15 Apr 1814 - Enlistment place: New Lisbon - Enlistment period: War - By whom: Thomas McKnight - Discharged: 4 Jun 1815 at Chillicothe - Bounty: BLW 6901-160-12.

Hull, John - Private - 19th Infantry - Bounty: BLW 27251-160-42 - Comments: Land bounty to Joseph Hull, George Hull, James Hull, Jacob Hull, Alexander Hull, Still Hull, Rachel Hull & Mary Carroll, only heirs at law of John Hull.

Humble, Martin - Private - 26th Infantry - Company: William Puthuff - Other regiment: 25th Infantry - Enlistment date: 15 May 1813 - Enlistment period: 1 Yr - By whom: Hugh Moore - Discharged: 15 May 1814.

Hungerford, John - Private - 26th Infantry - Company: Joel Collins - Enlistment date: 25 Aug 1813 - Enlistment period: 1 Yr - Discharged: 4 Jan 1814.

Hunt, John - Private - 27th Infantry - Company: George Sanderson - Enlistment date: 12 Jun 1813.

Hunter, James - Private - 26th Infantry - Company: George Kesling - Other regiment: 25th Infantry - Age: 35 - Height: 5' 11" - Enlistment date: 23 Apr 1813 - Enlistment period: 1 Yr.

Hunter, John - Private - 26th Infantry - Company: George Kesling - Other regiment: 25th Infantry - Enlistment date: 21 May 1813 - Enlistment period: 1 Yr - By whom: George Kesling - Discharged: 21 May 1814.

Hunter, Thomas - Private - 19th Infantry - Company: Joel Collins - Age: 19 - Height: 5' 2" - Born: Pennsylvania - Trade: Farmer - Enlistment date: 22 Mar 1814 - Enlistment place: Detroit - Enlistment period: War - By whom: Wynkoop Warner - Discharged: 20 Jul 1815 at Detroit - Pension: Wife Elizabeth, WO-41591, WC-32887, SO-8702, SC-8409; served in Capt. Joel Collins' Company, 19th Infantry as a private - Bounty: BLW 25506-160-12 (Arkansas).

Huntsman, Jonathan - Drummer - 17th Infantry - Age: 18 - Height: 5' 10 1/2" - Born: Pennsylvania - Trade: Drummer - Enlistment date: 30 May 1814 - Enlistment period: War - By whom: John Reeves - Discharged: 18 Apr 1815 at Chillicothe - Bounty: BLW 19318-160-12 (Illinois).

Hurd, Robert - Private - 1st Rifles - Company: Thomas Ramsey - Age: 21 - Height: 5' 9" - Born: Pennsylvania - Trade: Hatter - Enlistment date: 21 Mar 1814 - Enlistment place: America - Enlistment period: War - By whom: Thomas Ramsey - Killed: 17 Sep 1814 near Fort Erie, UC.

Hurley, Mathew - Private - 26th Infantry - Company: George Kesling - Other regiment: 25th Infantry - Enlistment date: 11 Jun 1813 - Enlistment period: 1 Yr - Discharged: 11 Jun 1814.

Huston, James Marquis - Private - 19th Infantry - Company: William Gill - Age: 18 - Height: 5' 8" - Born: VA, Frederick County - Trade: Farmer - Enlistment date: 1 Apr 1814 - Enlistment place: Portsmouth - Enlistment period: War - By whom: Lieutenant Huston - Discharged: 5 Jun 1815 at Chillicothe - Bounty: BLW 9464-160-12 (Illinois).

Hutchenson, William - Private - 19th Infantry - Company: Carey Trimble - Age: 21 - Height: 5' 9" - Born: Virginia - Trade: Farmer - Enlistment date: 21 Mar 1814 - Enlistment place: Chillicothe - Enlistment period: War - By whom: Charles Cissna - Discharged: 6 Jun 1815 at Chillicothe - Bounty: BLW 11298-160-12 (Illinois).

Hutchins, Henry - Private - 17th Infantry - Company: Henry Crittenden - Age: 22 - Height: 5' 9" - Born: MA, Hampshire County, Westfield - Trade: Hatter - Enlistment date: 25 Jul 1813 - Enlistment place: Portsmouth - Enlistment period: War - By whom: Hugh May - Discharged: 9 Jun 1815 at Chillicothe - Bounty: BLW 20543-160-12 (Missouri).

Hutchinson, Robert - Corporal - 26th Infantry - Company: George Kesling - Other regiment: 1st Rifles then 4th Rifles - Enlistment date: 17 Apr 1813 - Enlistment period: 1 Yr - Discharged: 14 Jul 1815 discharged at Canjocqueta Creek, NY - Comments: Prisoner of War (Halifax, NS); captured at Fort Erie, UC, 17 Sep 1814; released 10 Apr 1815; also Prisoner of War on Parole at Detroit.

Hutchinson, Samuel - Private - 19th Infantry - Company: William Gill - Age: 18 - Height: 5' 5" - Born: Massachusetts - Enlistment date: 27 Aug 1814 - Enlistment place: Urbana - Enlistment period: War - By whom: William Baird - Discharged: 21 Dec 1814 - Comments: Discharged for being a minor.

Hutson, Robert - Corporal - 1st Rifles - Company: Thomas Ramsey - Other regiment: 1st Infantry - Age: 21 - Height: 5' 9" - Born: PA, Huntington County - Trade: Farmer - Enlistment date: 13 May 1812 - Enlistment place: Cincinnati - Enlistment period: 5 Yrs - By whom: Thomas Ramsey - Discharged: 13 May 1815 at Fort Crawford, IL - Pension: SO-13428, SC-6745; served in Captain Thomas Ramsey's Company, and Captain John Sims' Company, US Rifles, as a private - Comments: Served with the 1st Infantry between 1 Aug 1812 and 16 Feb 1815.

Huttenhour, John - Corporal - 19th Infantry - Company: William Gill - Age: 23 - Height: 5' 6" - Born: PA, Westmoreland County - Enlistment date: 12 May 1814 - Enlistment place: Chillicothe or Circleville - Enlistment period: War - By whom: Josiah Brady - Discharged: 5 Jun 1815 at Chillicothe - Bounty: BLW 7037-160-12 (Missouri).

Hyatt, Elisha - Private - 19th Infantry - Company: Carey Trimble - Enlistment date: 26 Apr 1814 - Enlistment period: War - Died: 15 Oct 1814 - Bounty: BLW 27540-160-42 - Comments: Died in service; land bounty to Shedrick Hyatt, brother & only heir at law of Elisha Hyatt.

Hyatt, Elzy - Private - 19th Infantry - Company: William Gill - Age: 19 - Height: 6' 3" - Born: Ohio - Trade: Blacksmith - Enlistment date: 18 Sep 1814 - Enlistment period: War - By whom: Neal McFadden - Discharged: 5 Jun 1815 at Chillicothe - Pension: Wife Mary Hiatt, SO-3952, SC-5518, WO-40907, WC-31921; served as a private in Capt. William Gill's Company, 19th Infantry - Bounty: BLW 14037-160-12 (Illinois).

Hyde, Charles W. - Private - 19th Infantry - Company: Wilson Elliott - Other regiment: 17th Infantry.

Hyde, John - Private - 26th Infantry - Company: Joel Collins - Other regiment: 19th Infantry - Age: 36 - Height: 5' 6 1/2" - Born: North Carolina - Trade: Laborer - Enlistment date: 17 Jun 1813 - Enlistment period: 1 Yr - War - Discharged: 20 Jul 1815 at Detroit - Bounty: BLW 9165-160-12.

Icenogal, David - Private - 26th Infantry - Company: Benjamin Watson - Other regiment: 25th Infantry - Age: 22 - Height: 5' 7" - Born: MD, Frederick County - Trade: Farmer - Enlistment date: 3 Apr 1813 - Enlistment place: Ohio - Enlistment period: War - By whom: Isaac Reiley - Discharged: 2 Apr 1815 at Sackets Harbor, NY.

Ingerson, Benjamin - Private - 26th Infantry - Company: George Kesling - Enlistment date: 19 May 1813 - Enlistment period: 1 Yr.

Inslows, William P. - Sergeant - 19th Infantry - Company: Wilson Elliott,

Insnogle, David - Private - 19th Infantry - Company: James Herron.

Irwin, William - Private - 2nd Rifles - Company: Batteal Harrison - Age: 40 - Height: 5' 7 1/2" - Born: PA, Cumberland County - Trade: Cabinet maker - Enlistment date: 6 Jun 1814 - Enlistment place: Portsmouth - Enlistment period: War - By whom: Andrew Gilmore - Discharged: 30 Jun 1815 at Detroit - Bounty: BLW 12199-160-12 (Illinois).

Isaheart, Jacob - Private - 19th Infantry - Company: David Holt - Other regiment: 17th Infantry - Age: 27 - Height: 5' 5" - Born: PA, Northumberland County - Trade: Carpenter - Enlistment date: 7 Apr 1814 - Enlistment place: Marietta - Enlistment period: War - By whom: John Milligan - Discharged: 4 Jun 1815 at Chillicothe -

Bounty: BLW 14016-160-12 (Illinois).

Isham, George - Private - 26th Infantry - Company: William Puthuff - Enlistment date: 12 May 1813 - Enlistment period: 1 Yr - By whom: Robert Smith - Discharged: 12 May 1814, probably at Sackets Harbor, NY.

Izard, Hansel - Private - 26th Infantry - Company: Samuel Swearingen - Enlistment date: 29 Jul 1813 - Enlistment period: 1 Yr.

Jackman, Bernard - Corporal - 19th Infantry - Company: Martin Hawkins - Other regiment: 17th Infantry - Age: 20 - Height: 5' 7" - Born: PA, Fayette County, Brownsville - Trade: Laborer - Enlistment date: 24 Apr 1813 - Enlistment place: Cincinnati - Enlistment period: War - By whom: Philip Price - Discharged: 20 Aug 1815 - Bounty: BLW 13989-160-12 (Illinois) - Comments: Prisoner of War, captured on Lake Huron in a schooner, 3 Sep 1814.

Jackson, Charles - 2nd Rifles - Age: 37 - Height: 5' 7 1/2" - Born: England - Enlistment date: 30 Jul 1814 - Enlistment place: Cincinnati.

Jackson, Hugh - Private - 27th Infantry - Company: William Gill - Pension: Wife Harriet, WO-19526, WS-13426, SO-7878, SC-5303; served in Captain William Gill's Company and Captain John Spencer's company, 27th Infantry as a private.

Jackson, James - Private - 27th Infantry - Company: George Sanderson - Enlistment date: 19 May 1813.

Jackson, Jesse - Private - 26th Infantry - Company: George Kesling - Other regiment: 25th Infantry - Enlistment date: 5 Apr 1813 - Enlistment period: 1 Yr - Discharged: 5 Apr 1814.

Jackson, John - Private - 26th Infantry - Company: Joel Collins - Other regiment: 19th Infantry - Age: 24 - Height: 6' 1 1/2" - Born: Kentucky - Trade: Farmer - Enlistment date: 22 May 1813 - Enlistment period: 1 Yr - Discharged: 20 Jul 1815 at Detroit - Bounty: BLW 12378-160-12 (Illinois) - Comments: Re-enlisted in 19th Infantry 27 Apr 1814 at Sandwich, UC, by Ensign Simons, during the war enlistment.

Jackson, Robert C. - Private - 27th Infantry - Company: Carey Trimble - Other regiment: 19th Infantry - Age: 19 - Height: 5' 6 1/2" - Born: VA, Shenandoah County - Trade: Laborer - Enlistment date: 13 Apr 1814 - Enlistment place: Athens County - Enlistment period: War - By whom: John Booten - Discharged: 7 Jun 1815 at Chillicothe - Bounty: BLW 4498-160-12 (Illinois).

Jairhurst, David - 19th Infantry - Enlistment date: 10 Jul 1812 - Enlistment place: St. Clairsville - Enlistment period: 5 Yrs - By whom: Samuel Booker.

James, Isaac - Corporal - 26th Infantry - Company: George Kesling - Enlistment date: 17 May 1813 - Enlistment period: 1 Yr.

Jamison, John - Private - 19th Infantry - Company: Martin Hawkins - Other regiment: 17th Infantry - Age: 18 - Height: 5' 7" - Born: Upper Canada - Trade: Farmer - Enlistment date: 3 Apr 1814 - Enlistment place: Detroit - Enlistment period: War - By whom: George Atchison - Discharged: 31 Apr 1819 at Fort Dearborn, IL.

Jamison, William - Private - 19th Infantry - Company: James Herron - Enlistment date: Aug 1812.

Jarvis, James - Private - 27th Infantry - Company: Isaac Van Horne - Other regiment: 19th Infantry - Height: 5' 6" - Born: Virginia - Trade: Farmer - Enlistment date: 15 Mar 1814 - Enlistment period: War - By whom: Wynkoop Warner - Discharged: 21 Aug 1814 on Surgeon's Certificate of Disability, at Detroit - Pension: Old War IF-26196; served in Capt. Isaac Van Horne's Company, 27th Infantry as a private - Bounty: BLW 3771-160-12 (Arkansas).

Jefferies, Jonas - Private - 27th Infantry - Comments: Prisoner of War on Parole, captured at Detroit, MI, 16 Aug 1812.

Jeffries, James - Private - 2nd Rifles - Age: 23 - Height: 5' 8" - Born: PA, Washington County - Trade: Farmer - Enlistment date: 27 Apr 1814 - Enlistment place: Chillicothe - Enlistment period: War - By whom: Batteal Harrison - Discharged: 30 Jun 1815 at Detroit.

Jeffries, Thomas - Private - 24th Infantry - Company: Silas Stephens - Pension: Wife Mary, WO-645, WC-5561; served as a private in Captains James H. Campbell's and Silas Stephens' Companies, 24th Infantry; also in Capt. Isaac Evans' Company, OH Militia.

Jenkinson, William - Private - 19th Infantry - Company: Joel Collins - Other regiment: 17th Infantry then 3rd Infantry - Age: 29 - Height: 5' 5" - Born: England, Liverpool - Trade: Hatter - Enlistment date: 3 Mar 1813 - Enlistment place: Lancaster - Enlistment period: 5 Yrs - By whom: John Stockton - Comments: Deserted 15 May 1815.

Jennings, Edward (Ginning) - Private - 19th Infantry - Company: Asabael Nearing - Other regiment: 17th Infantry - Age: 24 - Height: 5' 8" - Born: KY, Washington County - Trade: Gunsmith - Enlistment date: 12 Feb 1813 - Enlistment period: War - By whom: Stephen Lee - Discharged: 18 Apr 1815 at Chillicothe - Bounty: BLW 13208-160-12 (Missouri) - Comments: Prisoner of War, exchanged 25 Apr 1814; transferred to 17th Infantry 12 May 1814.

Jennings, Nathan - Private - 19th Infantry - Company: Angus Langham - Pension: Wife Margaret, WO-10730, WC-6069; served in Capt. Langham's Company, 19th Infantry as a private; lived in OH.

Jenson, Joseph - Private - 17th Infantry - Company: Harris Hickman - Age: 30 - Height: 5' 8" - Born: Tennessee - Trade: Farmer - Enlistment date: 7 May 1814 - Enlistment period: War - By whom: George Stall - Discharged: 9 Jun 1815 at Chillicothe - Bounty: BLW 6589-160-12 (Illinois).

Jobes, John - Private - 1st Infantry - Company: Horatio Stark - Age: 21 - Height: 5' 7" - Born: NJ, Trenton - Trade: Millwright - Enlistment date: 25 Mar 1812 - Enlistment place: Chillicothe - Enlistment period: 5 Yrs - By whom: John Swearingen - Discharged: 25 Mar 1817 at Fort Dearborn, IL.

Johns, John - Private - 17th Infantry - Company: David Holt - Age: 23 - Height: 5' 6" - Born: Ireland - Trade: Blacksmith - Enlistment date: 5 Feb 1814 - Enlistment place: Franklin County, Franklinton - Enlistment period: War - By whom: John Cochran - Died: 25 Mar 1815 in New York; buried in the War of 1812 Cemetery in Cheektowaga, Erie County, NY.

Johnson – see Johnston

Johnson, Abel - Private - 17th Infantry - Company: Harris Hickman - Other regiment: 3rd Infantry - Age: 29 - Height: 5' 6" - Born: Maryland - Trade: Farmer - Enlistment date: 1 May 1814 - Enlistment period: 5 Yrs - By whom: Thomas McKnight - Discharged: 1 May 1819 at Fort Dearborn, IL.

Johnson, Abraham - Private - 27th Infantry - Company: William Gill - Comments: Served aboard the US Sloop Trippe on the Lake Erie Squadron.

Johnson, David - Private - 27th Infantry - Company: Carey Trimble - Other regiment: 19th Infantry - Age: 29 - Height: 6' 3" - Born: VA, Hampshire County (now WV) - Trade: Farmer - Enlistment date: 6 Apr 1814 - Enlistment place: Zanesville - Enlistment period: War - By whom: Neal McFadden - Discharged: 6 Jun 1815 at Chillicothe - Bounty: BLW 3630-160-12 (Illinois).

Johnson, Hezekiah - Private - 17th Infantry - Company: John Chunn - Other regiment: 3rd Infantry - Age: 33 - Height: 5' 6" - Born: MD, Cecil County - Trade: Laborer - Enlistment date: 27 Feb 1813 - Enlistment place: Newark - Enlistment period: 5 Yrs - By whom: George Atchison - Discharged: 2 Feb 1816 - Comments: Discharged on Surgeon's Certificate of Disability.

Johnson, Jeremiah - Private - 19th Infantry - Company: George Kesling - Other regiment: 17th Infantry - Age: 23 - Height: 5' 9" - Born: MD, Allegeny County - Trade: Farmer - Enlistment date: 10 Apr 1814 - Enlistment place: Chillicothe - Enlistment period: War - By whom: Charles Cissna - Discharged: 16 Feb 1815 - Bounty: BLW 8813-160-12 (Illinois) - Comments: Accidentally wounded after enlistment and never joined his regiment.

Johnson, John - Private - 19th Infantry - Company: Carey Trimble - Other regiment: 17th Infantry - Age: 22 - Height: 5' 7" - Born: Ireland - Trade: Joiner - Enlistment date: 19 Apr 1814 - Enlistment place: Jefferson County - Enlistment period: War - By whom: Charles Cissna - Discharged: 6 Jun 1815 at Chillicothe.

Johnson, John - Private - 17th Infantry - Company: William Adair - Age: 23 - Height: 5' 9 1/4" - Born: NJ, Salem County - Trade: Nailer - Enlistment date: 10 Feb 1815 - Enlistment period: 5 Yrs - By whom: James Campbell - Died: 22 Apr 1815 - Bounty: BLW 1067-320-14 (Arkansas) - Comments: Missing, supposed to have drown on 22 Apr 1815; land bounty to Diane Reid, late widow & only heir of John Johnson.

Johnson, John - Private - 19th Infantry - Company: Carey Trimble - Other regiment: 17th Infantry - Age: 23 - Height: 6' - Born: Maryland - Trade: Shoemaker - Enlistment date: 14 Mar 1814 - Enlistment place: Newark - Enlistment period: War - By whom: John Spencer - Discharged: 6 Jun 1815 at Chillicothe - Bounty: BLW 7416-160-12 (Illinois).

Johnson, Joseph - Private - 2nd Rifles - Company: Benjamin Desha - Age: 22 - Height: 5' 4" - Born: PA, Philadelphia County - Trade: Printer - Enlistment date: 1 Jan 1815 - Enlistment place: Cincinnati - Enlistment period: 5 Yrs - By whom: William Pritchard - Bounty: BLW 18736-160-12 (Missouri).

Johnson, Samuel - Private - 2nd Rifles - Company: Batteal Harrison - Age: 30 - Height: 6' - Born: VA, Shenandoah County - Trade: Carpenter - Enlistment date: 16 May 1814 - Enlistment place: Zanesville - Enlistment period: War - By whom: William Dougherty - Discharged: 30 Jun 1815 at Detroit.

Johnson, Samuel - Private - 17th Infantry - Company: Harris Hickman - Other regiment: 3rd Infantry - Age: 40 - Height: 6' 1" - Born: Maryland - Trade: Blacksmith - Enlistment date: 16 May 1814 at Fort Dearborn, IL - Enlistment period: 5 Yrs - By whom: George Bryant.

Johnson, Thomas S. - Private - 26th Infantry - Company: Joel Collins - Enlistment date: 1 Sep 1813 - Enlistment period: 1 Yr.

Johnson, William - Private - 19th Infantry - Died: 2 Sep 1814 at Fort Erie, UC.

Johnson, William - 2nd Rifles - Age: 44 - Height: 5' 8" - Born: New York - Enlistment date: 6 Aug 1814 - By whom: James Blair.

The Enlisted Men

Johnston – see Johnson

Johnston, Charles - 2nd Rifles - Age: 29 - Height: 5' 9" - Born: VA, Shenandoah County - Enlistment date: 19 May 1814 - Enlistment place: Zanesville.

Johnston, John - Private - 17th Infantry - Age: 23 - Height: 5' 9 1/4" - Born: NJ, Salem County - Trade: Nailer - Enlistment date: 10 Feb 1815 - Enlistment period: 5 Yrs - By whom: James Campbell.

Johnston, John - Private - 26th Infantry - Company: William Puthuff - Enlistment date: 11 Jun 1814 - Enlistment period: 1 Yr

Johnston, John - Private - 27th Infantry - Company: George Sanderson - Other regiment: 19th Infantry - Enlistment date: 1 May 1813 - Bounty: BLW 9474-160-12 (Illinois) - Comments: Prisoner of War on Parole, captured at Detroit, MI, 16 Aug 1812.

Johnston, Joseph - Private - 17th Infantry - Age: 30 - Height: 5' 8" - Born: East Tennessee - Enlistment date: 7 May 1814 - By whom: George Stall.

Johnston, Richard - Private - 26th Infantry - Company: George Kesling - Enlistment date: 30 May 1813 - Enlistment period: 1 Yr - Comments: Prisoner of War (Quebec, LC), captured at Fort Niagara, NY, 19 Dec 1813; exchanged 4 May 1814.

Johnston, Samuel - Private - 27th Infantry - Comments: Prisoner of War on Parole, captured at Detroit, MI, 16 Aug 1812.

Johnston, William - Private - 19th Infantry - Company: James Herron - Enlistment date: 3 Oct 1812 - Enlistment period: 18 Mos.

Johnston, William - Private - 17th Infantry - Company: John Chunn - Age: 26 - Height: 5' 8 1/2" - Born: Maryland - Trade: Farmer - Enlistment date: 13 Nov 1813 - Enlistment place: Chillicothe - Enlistment period: War - By whom: Charles Cass - Discharged: 7 Jun 1815 at Chillicothe - Bounty: BLW 19600-160-12 (Arkansas).

Johnston, William S. - Private - 17th Infantry - Company: Lt James Campbell - Other regiment: 3rd Infantry - Age: 23 - Height: 5' 8 1/4" - Born: KY, Bourbon County - Trade: Farmer - Enlistment date: 20 Feb 1815 - Enlistment period: 5 Yrs - By whom: James Campbell - Comments: Re-enlisted for 5 years, 21 Nov 1819.

Joice, Ambrose - Private - 27th Infantry - Company: George Sanderson - Enlistment date: 22 Jun 1813.

Joline, Anthony - Private - 2nd Artillery - Company: Daniel Cushing - Other regiment: Corps of Artillery - Age: 27 - Height: 5' 11" - Born: NY, Goshen County, Orange - Trade: Carpenter - Enlistment date: 30 Jul 1813 - Enlistment place: Chillicothe - Enlistment period: 5 Yrs - By whom: Samuel Kercheval - Discharged: 31 Jul 1817 at Detroit.

Jones, Benjamin - Private - 19th Infantry - Company: Martin Hawkins - Other regiment: 17th Infantry - Age: 22 - Height: 5' 8" - Born: PA, Philadelphia County, Philadelphia - Trade: Tanner - Enlistment date: 21 Apr 1814 - Enlistment place: Detroit - Enlistment period: War - By whom: George Atchison - Discharged: 9 Jun 1815 - Bounty: BLW 5319-160-12 - Comments: Deserted at Erie, PA, on 17 Feb 1815.

Jones, David - Private - 1st Rifles - Company: Thomas Ramsey - Age: 23 - Height: 5' 7" - Born: Georgia - Trade: Laborer - Enlistment date: 9 Apr 1814 - Enlistment place: Warren County, Middletown - Enlistment period: War - By whom: Peter Albright - Discharged: 8 Jun 1815 at Buffalo, NY- Pension: Wife Mary A., WO-28829, WC-22641, SO-553, SC-737; served in Capt. Thomas Ramsey's company, 1st Rifles, as a private.

Jones, Elijah - Corporal - 19th Infantry - Company: Joel Collins - Other regiment: 17th Infantry - Age: 20 - Height: 5' 8" - Born: Vermont - Trade: Laborer - Enlistment date: 7 May 1814 - Enlistment place: Detroit - Enlistment period: War - By whom: Wynkoop Warner - Discharged: 20 Jul 1815 at Detroit - Bounty: BLW 9821-160-12.

Jones, Isaac - Private - 2nd Rifles - Company: Benjamin Desha - Age: 42 - Height: 5' 8 3/4" - Born: New York - Trade: Laborer - Enlistment date: 5 Dec 1814 - Enlistment period: War - By whom: William Pritchard - Discharged: 11 Jul 1815 - Bounty: BLW 25006-160-12 (Arkansas) - Comments: Discharged at Chillicothe.

Jones, James - Private - 27th Infantry - Company: George Sanderson - Enlistment date: 4 Jul 1813.

Jones, Joseph - Private - 26th Infantry - Company: Samuel Swearingen - Other regiment: 25th Infantry - Age: 28 - Height: 5' 11" - Enlistment date: 9 Jul 1813 - Enlistment period: 1 Yr.

Jones, Joshua - Private - 27th Infantry - Company: Carey Trimble - Other regiment: 19th Infantry then 17th Infantry - Age: 26 - Height: 5' 10" - Born: VA, Montgomery County - Trade: Shoemaker - Enlistment date: 28 Apr 1814 - Enlistment place: Gallipolis - Enlistment period: War - By whom: John Booten - Discharged: 6 Jun 1815 at Chillicothe - Bounty: BLW 20177-160-12 (Missouri) - Comments: Joined the 27th Infantry at Athens, re-enlisted in the 19th Infantry.

Jones, Thomas - Private - 2nd Artillery - Company: Daniel Cushing.

Jones, Thomas - Private - 19th Infantry - Company: William Gill - Other regiment: 17th Infantry - Age: 30 - Height: 5' 9" - Born: Maryland - Trade: Farmer - Enlistment date: 10 May 1814 - Enlistment place:

Chillicothe - Enlistment period: War - By whom: Charles Cissna - Discharged: 5 Jun 1815 at Chillicothe - Pension: SO-19177, SC-19177, served in Capt. Birch's Company, 19th Infantry as a private - Bounty: BLW 1969-160-12 (Illinois).

Jones, William - Private - 19th Infantry - Company: Richard Talbott - Age: 19 - Height: 5' 10" - Born: PA, York County - Enlistment date: 14 Apr 1814 - Enlistment place: Xenia - Enlistment period: War - By whom: Richard Talbott.

Jones, William - Sergeant - 19th Infantry - Company: James Herron - Enlistment date: 24 Aug 1812 - Enlistment period: 18 Mos - Discharged: 24 Feb 1814 - Comments: Prisoner of War, exchanged 25 Apr 1814.

Jones, William - Sergeant - 17th Infantry - Company: Lt James Campbell - Age: 29 - Height: 5' 10" - Born: New York - Trade: Laborer - Enlistment date: 21 Jul 1814 - Enlistment period: War - By whom: William Featherstone - Discharged: 8 Jul 1815 at Chillicothe.

Jordan, Nathaniel - Private - 19th Infantry - Company: John Chunn - Other regiment: 17th Infantry - Age: 25 - Height: 5' 9" - Trade: Farmer - Enlistment date: 1 Jun 1814 - Enlistment period: War - Discharged: 8 May 1815 at Newport, KY.

Jordan, Nicholas - Private - Rangers - Company: Samuel McCormick - Age: 17 - Height: 5' 8" - Born: Pennsylvania - Trade: Farmer - Enlistment date: 20 Nov 1813 - Enlistment period: 1 Yr - Discharged: 20 Nov 1814 on Surgeon's Certificate of Disability, at Fort Malden, UC.

Jourdon, William T. - Private - 27th Infantry - Company: Absalom Martin - Enlistment date: 12 Sep 1813 - Enlistment period: 1 Yr - Discharged: 11 Sep 1814.

Judd, William - Private - 26th Infantry - Company: Samuel Swearingen - Other regiment: 25th Infantry - Enlistment date: 22 Jun 1813 - Enlistment period: 1 Yr - Discharged: 20 Jun 1814.

Justice, Griffith - Private - 19th Infantry - Company: Carey Trimble - Age: 21 - Height: 5' 9" - Born: PA, Bedford County - Trade: Farmer - Enlistment date: 20 Apr 1814 - Enlistment place: Ross County, Adelphi - Enlistment period: War - By whom: William Gill - Died: 4 Jan 1815 at Erie, PA - Bounty: BLW 25677-160-12 (Arkansas) - Comments: Land bounty to Jesse Justice, brother & other heirs at law of Griffith Justice.

Kaisey, James - Private - 19th Infantry - Company: Wilson Elliott.

Kaldwell, John - 19th Infantry - Company: Asabael Nearing - Enlistment date: 17 Aug 1813 - Enlistment period: 5 Yrs.

Kamp – see Camp, John

Kearnes, Jacob - Private - 26th Infantry - Company: William Puthuff - Enlistment date: 11 Mar 1813 - Enlistment period: 1 Yr.

Kearns, Felix - Private - 26th Infantry - Company: William Puthuff - Enlistment date: 1 Jul 1813 - Enlistment period: 1 Yr.

Keen, John - Private - 2nd Rifles - Company: Batteal Harrison - Age: 35 - Height: 5' 8" - Born: New Jersey - Trade: Coach maker - Enlistment date: 11 Sep 1814 - Enlistment place: Cincinnati - Enlistment period: War - By whom: Elias Langham - Discharged: 30 Jun 1815 at Detroit.

Keenan, William - Private - 17th Infantry - Company: Caleb Holder - Age: 25 - Height: 5' 6 1/2" - Born: Pennsylvania - Trade: Laborer - Enlistment date: 29 Jul 1814 - Enlistment place: Zanesville - Enlistment period: War - By whom: James Campbell - Discharged: 30 Jun 1815 at Detroit - Pension: Wife Sarah, SO-2449, SC-1196, WO-31525, WC-20898; served as a private in Capt. C. H. Holder's Company, 17th Infantry - Bounty: BLW 12878-160-12 (Illinois).

Kelley, Ezra - Private - 27th Infantry - Company: Joseph Cairns - Comments: Prisoner of War on Parole, captured at Detroit, MI, 16 Aug 1812; served aboard the US Sloop Trippe on the Lake Erie Squadron.

Kelly, Abraham - Private - 26th Infantry - Company: Lt William McDonald - Enlistment date: 5 Nov 1813 - Enlistment period: 1 Yr - Died: 23 Feb 1814 - Pension: Old War Minor's C-1173, served as a private in the 26th Infantry; heirs obtained half pay for five years in lieu of military bounty land - Comments: Re-enlisted until the end of the war, 18 Feb 1814.

Kelly, Barney - Private - 2nd Artillery - Company: Stanton Sholes - Enlistment date: 24 Mar 1813 - Enlistment period: 5 Yrs - Died: 2 Nov 1813 at Put-in-Bay, OH.

Kelly, Cornelius - Private - Rangers - Company: William Perry - Pension: Wife Catherine, WO-22352, WC-18189; served as a private in Capt. William Perry's Company.

Kelly, David - Private - 19th Infantry - Age: 23 - Height: 5' 9" - Born: Pennsylvania - Enlistment date: 16 Jan 1815 - Enlistment place: Cincinnati - Enlistment period: War - Comments: Deserted 17 Jan 1815.

Kelly, Francis - Private - 19th Infantry - Age: 34 - Height: 5' 8" - Born: Virginia - Enlistment date: 21 Aug 1814 - Enlistment place: Urbana.

Kelly, Jacob - Sergeant - 2nd Artillery - Company: Daniel Cushing - Enlistment date: 13 Jun 1812 - Discharged: 30

The Enlisted Men

Nov 1813.

Kelly, James - Private - 26th Infantry - Company: Samuel Swearingen - Other regiment: 25th Infantry - Enlistment date: 24 Jul 1813 - Enlistment period: 1 Yr - Comments: Deserted 23 Mar 1814.

Kelly, Jeremiah - Private - 1st Rifles - Company: Thomas Ramsey - Age: 36 - Height: 5' 5" - Born: Ireland - Trade: Farmer - Enlistment date: 24 Feb 1814 - Enlistment place: Cincinnati - Enlistment period: War - By whom: Thomas Ramsey - Comments: Deserted at Urbana, OH, on 7 Aug 1814.

Kelly, John - Private - 19th Infantry - Age: 21 - Height: 5' 8" - Born: PA, Northumberland County - Enlistment date: 20 May 1814 - Enlistment place: Ross County, Adelphi - By whom: George Will - Comments: Deserted.

Kelly, John - Private - 17th Infantry - Company: Henry Crittenden - Age: 55 - Height: 5' 7" - Born: Ireland, County Kilkenny - Trade: Laborer - Enlistment date: 27 Jul 1813 - Enlistment place: Chillicothe - Enlistment period: War - By whom: Elias Langham - Discharged: 9 Jun 1815 at Chillicothe.

Kelly, John - Private - 2nd Artillery - Company: Daniel Cushing - Enlistment date: 27 Aug 1812 - Discharged: 31 Oct 1814 - Comments: Prisoner of War, captured by Indians near Fort Meigs and paroled.

Kelly, John - Corporal - 19th Infantry - Company: Richard Talbott - Age: 18 - Height: 5' 11" - Born: Kentucky - Trade: Farmer - Enlistment date: 21 Dec 1814 - Enlistment place: Franklin County, Franklinton - Enlistment period: War - Discharged: 5 Jun 1815 at Chillicothe - Bounty: BLW 16746-160-12 (Illinois).

Kelly, John C. - Corporal - 17th Infantry - Company: William Bradford - Enlistment date: 11 Dec 1812 - Enlistment period: 18 Mos - Killed: 10 Sep 1813 during the Battle of Lake Erie - Comments: Served aboard the US Brig Lawrence on the Lake Erie Squadron.

Kennedy, William - 2nd Rifles - Age: 19 - Height: 5' 9" - Born: Ireland, County Antrim - Enlistment date: 17 Jun 1814 - Enlistment place: Cincinnati.

Kennett, George - Private - 26th Infantry - Company: Samuel Swearingen - Other regiment: 25th Infantry - Enlistment date: 15 Jul 1813 - Enlistment period: 1 Yr - Discharged: 19 Jun 1814.

Kennett, James - Corporal - 26th Infantry - Company: Samuel Swearingen - Other regiment: 25th Infantry - Enlistment date: 15 Jul 1813 - Enlistment period: 1 Yr - Discharged: 29 Jun 1814 - Pension: SC-1791; served in Capt. John Murdock's Company, 25th Infantry as a private.

Kensil, Jacob - Corporal - 26th Infantry - Company: William Puthuff - Enlistment date: 27 Apr 1813 - Enlistment period: 1 Yr.

Kerlogue, Shirley - Private - 27th Infantry - Company: Alexander Hill - Other regiment: 19th Infantry - Age: 37 - Height: 5' 10 1/2" - Born: Connecticut - Trade: Carpenter - Enlistment date: 26 May 1814 - Enlistment period: War - By whom: Lieutenant Stram - Discharged: 5 Jun 1815 at Chillicothe - Bounty: BLW 12023-160-12 (Illinois).

Kerns, James - Private - 17th Infantry - Company: Harris Hickman - Age: 21 - Height: 5' 10" - Born: Virginia - Trade: Laborer - Enlistment date: 19 Apr 1814 - Enlistment place: Marietta - Enlistment period: War - By whom: John Milligan.

Kerns, Richard - Private - 17th Infantry - Company: David Holt - Age: 30 - Height: 5' 11 1/2" - Born: Ireland, County Down - Trade: Carpenter - Enlistment date: 13 May 1814 - Enlistment place: Zanesville - Enlistment period: War - By whom: James Herron - Discharged: 4 Jun 1815 at Chillicothe - Bounty: BLW 16487-160-12 (Illinois).

Kerr, William - Private - 17th Infantry - Company: David Holt - Age: 18 - Height: 5' 4" - Born: PA, Allegheny County - Trade: Laborer - Enlistment date: 7 Apr 1814 - Enlistment place: Warren County - Enlistment period: War By whom: William Leavitt.

Kersey, Archibald - Private - 19th Infantry - Company: William Gill - Age: 27 - Height: 5' 3" - Born: Delaware - Trade: Farmer - Enlistment date: 2 Jul 1814 - Enlistment period: War - By whom: Thomas Riddle - Discharged: 5 Jun 1815 at Chillicothe - Bounty: BLW 18363-160-12 (Illinois).

Kesler, John - Private - 26th or 27th Infantry - Company: Joel Collins - Other regiment: 19th Infantry - Age: 29 - Height: 5' 10" - Born: Virginia - Trade: Millwright - Enlistment date: 16 Mar 1814 - Enlistment place: Detroit - Enlistment period: War - By whom: Samuel Coleman - Discharged: 20 Jul 1815 at Detroit - Bounty: BLW 12132-160-12 (Illinois) - Comments: Re-enlisted.

Ketlinger, Jacob - Private - 26th Infantry - Company: Samuel Swearingen - Enlistment date: 8 May 1813 - Enlistment period: 1 Yr.

Keton, Thomas - Private - 17th Infantry - Age: 30 - Height: 5' 8" - Born: Pennsylvania - Trade: Farmer - Enlistment date: 15 Sep 1814 - Enlistment period: War - By whom: William Shang.

Kiger, John - Corporal - 19th Infantry - Company: James Herron - Enlistment date: 9 Aug 1812.

Kilbourn, Benjamin - Private - 1st Rifles - Company: Thomas Ramsey - Age: 22 - Height: 6' - Born: PA, York

County - Trade: Blacksmith - Enlistment date: 12 Sep 1813 - Enlistment place: Cincinnati - Enlistment period: 5 Yrs - By whom: Thomas Ramsey - Discharged: 12 Sep 1818 at Fort Osage, MO.

Killen, James - Private - 26th Infantry - Company: Samuel Swearingen - Enlistment date: 7 Jun 1813 - Enlistment period: 1 Yr.

Kimble, Ira - Private - 26th Infantry - Company: William Puthuff - Enlistment date: 8 May 1813 - Enlistment period: 1 Yr.

Kimble, Moody - Private - 26th Infantry - Company: William Puthuff - Enlistment date: 3 May 1813 - Enlistment period: 1 Yr - Pension: SO-15194, SC-9526; served as a private in Capt Wm. H. Puthuff's Company, 26th Infantry.

Kincaid, Jonas - Private - 27th Infantry - Company: George Sanderson - Enlistment date: 9 Jun 1813.

King, Conrad - Private - 26th Infantry - Company: Samuel Swearingen - Enlistment date: 22 Jul 1813 - Enlistment period: 1 Yr - Comments: Served aboard the US Schooner Ariel on the Lake Erie Squadron.

King, James - Private - 17th Infantry - Company: Lt James Campbell - Age: 18 - Height: 5' 9" - Born: Pennsylvania - Trade: Laborer - Enlistment date: 24 Nov 1813 - Enlistment period: War - By whom: George Stall.

King, Robert - Private - 26th or 27th Infantry - Company: Joel Collins - Other regiment: 19th Infantry - Age: 20 - Height: 5' 10" - Born: Virginia - Trade: Laborer - Enlistment date: 17 Mar 1814 - Enlistment place: Detroit - Enlistment period: War - By whom: Wynkoop Warner - Discharged: 20 Jul 1815 at Detroit - Bounty: BLW 10572-160-12 (Illinois) - Comments: Re-enlisted.

King, Robert - Private - 27th Infantry - Company: Isaac Van Horne - Pension: Old War IF-15651 Rejected; served in Capt. Isaac Van Horne's Company as a private.

Kingsbury, Eleazer - Private - 19th Infantry - Company: Asabael Nearing - Enlistment date: 6 Mar 1813 - Enlistment period: War - By whom: Stephen Lee - Died: 18 Jul 1813 - Pension: Heirs obtained half pay for five years in lieu of military bounty land.

Kingsland, Daniel - Private - 19th Infantry - Company: William Gill - Age: 39 - Height: 6' - Born: New Jersey - Trade: Wheelwright - Enlistment date: 16 Apr 1814 - Enlistment place: Detroit - Enlistment period: War - By whom: Wynkoop Warner - Discharged: 19 Jul 1815 - Bounty: BLW 22841-160-12 (Arkansas) - Comments: Land bounty to Phelix Kingsland & other heirs at law of Daniel Kingsland.

Kingsland, John - Private - 19th Infantry - Company: William Gill - Age: 20 - Height: 5' 7" - Born: NY, Westchester County, East Chester - Trade: Tailor - Enlistment date: 7 May 1814 - Enlistment place: Ashtabula County, Harpersfield - Enlistment period: War - By whom: John Reeves.

Kingsley, Eli - Private - 27th Infantry - Pension: Old War Invalid and Widow Rejected File 15678; served as a private in the 27th Infantry.

Kiniman, Samuel - Private - 27th Infantry - Company: George Sanderson - Enlistment date: 30 May 1813.

Kinnett – see Kennett

Kirkendol, Moses - Private - 2nd Rifles - Company: Batteal Harrison - Age: 21 - Height: 6' - Born: NC, Brunswick County, Ash - Trade: Laborer - Enlistment date: 10 Oct 1814 - Enlistment place: Chillicothe - Enlistment period: War - By whom: Batteal Harrison - Comments: Deserted 21 Dec 1814.

Kirkpatrick, James - Private - 17th Infantry - Company: David Holt - Age: 40 - Height: 5' 7 1/2" - Born: Ireland - Enlistment date: 6 May 1814 - Enlistment place: Zanesville - Enlistment period: War - By whom: James Herron - Died: 12 Nov 1814 at Buffalo, NY - Bounty: BLW 27843-160-42 - Comments: Land bounty to John Kirkpatrick, son & only heir at law of James Kirkpatrick.

Kirkpatrick, John - Private - 17th Infantry - Company: Harris Hickman - Other regiment: 3rd Infantry - Age: 18 - Height: 5' 7" - Born: PA, Allegheny County, Pittsburgh - Trade: Laborer - Enlistment date: 1 Jun 1814 - Enlistment period: 5 Yrs - By whom: David Carney - Comments: Deserted.

Kirkpatrick, William - Private - 26th Infantry - Company: George Kesling - Other regiment: 25th Infantry - Enlistment date: 1 May 1813 - Enlistment period: 1 Yr - Discharged: 1 May 1814.

Kisler, John - Private - 27th Infantry - Company: George Sanderson - Enlistment date: 17 Apr 1813.

Kissinger, George - Private - 27th Infantry - Company: George Sanderson - Enlistment date: 23 Jun 1813.

Kittsmiller, Jonathan - Private - 27th Infantry - Company: George Sanderson - Other regiment: 19th Infantry - Enlistment date: 5 May 1813 - Enlistment period: War - Died: 17 Aug 1814 - Bounty: BLW 26592-160-12 (Arkansas) - Comments: Re-enlisted 13 Mar 1814; land bounty to Jacob Kittsmiller, brother & other heirs at law of Jonathan Kittsmiller.

Kizer, Daniel - Private - Rangers - Company: Samuel McCormick - Age: 22 - Height: 5' 9" - Born: Pennsylvania - Trade: Farmer - Enlistment date: 10 Nov 1813 - Enlistment period: 1 Yr - Discharged: 10 Nov 1814 at Fort Malden, UC.

Knapp, Jacob - Private - 7th Infantry - Company: Zachary Taylor - Enlistment date: 18 Mar 1812 - Enlistment period: 5 Yrs - By whom: Thomas Ramsey - Died: 22 Aug 1814 of wounds.

Knight, Fielding - Private - 19th Infantry - Company: James Herron - Other regiment: 17th Infantry - Enlistment date: 21 Nov 1812 - Enlistment period: 5 Yrs.

Knott, William - Private - Rangers - Company: Samuel McCormick - Enlistment date: 1 Dec 1813 - Enlistment period: 1 Yr - Discharged: 30 Nov 1814.

Kooder, David - Private - 26th Infantry - Company: William Puthuff - Enlistment date: 23 Apr 1813 - Enlistment period: 1 Yr.

Kooder, Solomon - Private - 26th Infantry - Company: William Puthuff - Enlistment date: 27 Apr 1813 - Enlistment period: 1 Yr - Pension: SO-12041, SC-8548: served in Capt. W. H. Puthuff's Company, 26th Infantry as a private.

Kottles – see Cottles Daniel

Kuder – see Kooder, Solomon

Lacey, Fielding - Private - 26th Infantry - Company: Samuel Swearingen - Enlistment date: 24 Jun 1813 - Enlistment period: 1 Yr - Comments: Prisoner of War, exchanged 25 Apr 1814.

Lacey, William - Private - 17th Infantry - Company: Caleb Holder - Age: 35 - Height: 5' 9 1/2" - Born: MD, Harford County - Enlistment date: 13 Aug 1814 - Enlistment place: Steubenville - Enlistment period: War - By whom: William Featherstone.

Lackey, Andrew - Private - 27th Infantry - Company: Batteal Harrison - Other regiment: 2nd Rifles - Age: 39 - Height: 5' 9" - Born: Ireland - Trade: Farmer - Enlistment date: 19 Jul 1814 - Enlistment place: Zanesville - Enlistment period: War - By whom: William Dougherty - Comments: Prisoner of War on Parole, captured at Detroit, MI, 16 Aug 1812.

Lackey, Hugh - Private - 27th Infantry - Comments: Prisoner of War on Parole, captured at Detroit, MI, 16 Aug 1812.

Lacy, Stephen - Private - 26th Infantry - Company: Joel Collins - Enlistment date: 17 Aug 1813 - Enlistment period: 1 Yr.

Laddle, John - Private - 2nd Artillery - Company: Daniel Cushing - Enlistment date: 16 Oct 1813 - Enlistment period: 5 Yrs - By whom: Captain Melvin.

Lafferty, Archibald - Private - 27th Infantry - Comments: Prisoner of War on Parole, captured at Detroit, MI, 16 Aug 1812.

Lafoe, Peter - Private - 19th Infantry - Company: Carey Trimble - Other regiment: 17th Infantry - Age: 22 - Height: 5' 8" - Born: Lower Canada, Montreal - Trade: Laborer - Enlistment date: 4 Feb 1814 - Enlistment place: Chillicothe or Lower Sandusky - Enlistment period: War - By whom: Charles Cissna - Discharged: 7 Jun 1815 at Chillicothe.

Laird, Benjamin - Private - 26th Infantry - Company: William MacDonald - Other regiment: 19th Infantry - Enlistment date: 11 Dec 1813 - Enlistment place: Chillicothe - Enlistment period: 1 Yr - By whom: Charles Cissna - Died: 3 Apr 1814 - Bounty: BLW 18622-160-12 (Missouri) - Comments: Re-enlisted on 18 Feb 1814, during the war enlistment, died; bounty to John Laird, et al, heirs of Benjamin Laird; land bounty to John Baird, brother & other heirs at law of Benjamin Laird.

Lamb, Richard - Private - 19th Infantry - Age: 25 - Height: 6' - Born: PA, Washington County - Enlistment date: 11 Jul 1812 - Enlistment place: St. Clairsville - Enlistment period: 5 Yrs - By whom: Samuel Booker.

Lamb, Solomon - Sergeant - 17th Infantry - Company: Harris Hickman - Age: 30 - Height: 6' 3 1/4" - Born: PA, Bedford County - Trade: Laborer - Enlistment date: 24 Feb 1814 - Enlistment place: Franklin County, Franklinton - Enlistment period: War - By whom: John Cochran – Discharged: 9 Jun 1815 at Chillicothe - Bounty: BLW 12669-160-12 (Illinois).

Lampher, Benjamin - Private - 19th Infantry - Company: James Herron - Enlistment date: 31 Mar 1813 - Enlistment period: War.

Lampson, Ebenezer K. - Private - 19th Infantry - Company: George Sanderson - Pension: Wife Olive, WO-5122, WC-4882; served as a private in Capt. Sanderson's Company, 19th Infantry.

Landroff, Andrew (alias Landroche) - Private - 19th Infantry - Company: Martin Hawkins - Other regiment: 17th Infantry then 3rd Infantry - Age: 23 - Height: 5' 7" - Born: MI, Wayne County, Detroit - Trade: Laborer - Enlistment date: 16 Mar 1814 - Enlistment place: Detroit - Enlistment period: 5 Yrs - By whom: George Atchison - Died: 28 Aug 1815 at Detroit, MI - Bounty: BLW 21318-160-12 (Missouri) - Comments: Land bounty to Pierre Landroched & other heirs of Andrew Landroff.

Lane, Elkanah - Sergeant - 17th Infantry - Company: David Holt - Age: 26 - Height: 5' 11" - Born: NH, Cheshire County, Swaney - Trade: Laborer - Enlistment date: 24 Mar 1814 - Enlistment place: Butler County, Hamilton - Enlistment period: War - By whom: John Simons - Discharged: 4 Jun 1815 at Chillicothe -

Bounty: BLW 16960-160-12 (Illinois).

Lane, Erastus - Private - 27th Infantry - Company: Isaac Van Horne - Pension: Wife Mabel, WO-18776, WC-16373; served as a private in Capt. Applegate's Company, OH Militia, and in Capt. Isaac Van Horne's Company, 27th Infantry.

Langdale, James B. - Private - 19th Infantry - Company: Angus Langham - Other regiment: 17th Infantry - Discharged: 19 May 1814 - Comments: Prisoner of War, exchanged 11 May 1814; wounded at Fort Meigs in left thigh, May 1813; discharged for disability.

Laparle, Alexander - Private - 19th Infantry - Company: Martin Hawkins - Other regiment: 17th Infantry then 3rd Infantry - Age: 35 - Height: 5' 5" - Born: Lower Canada, Montreal - Trade: Laborer - Enlistment date: 30 Mar 1814 - Enlistment place: Detroit - Enlistment period: 5 Yrs - By whom: George Atchison - Discharged: 30 Mar 1819.

Lappin, Robert - Private - 17th Infantry - Company: David Holt - Age: 33 - Height: 5' 10" - Born: Pennsylvania - Trade: Distiller - Enlistment date: 11 Jun 1814 - Enlistment place: Zanesville - Enlistment period: War - By whom: James Campbell - Discharged: 4 Jun 1815 at Chillicothe - Bounty: BLW 20413-160-12 (Missouri) - Comments: Land bounty to John Lappin, brother et al, heirs at law of Robert Lappin.

Larimer, Robert - Private - 19th Infantry - Company: Asabael Nearing - Enlistment date: 19 Nov 1813 - Enlistment period: 18 Mos.

Larimer, Robert - 2nd Rifles - Age: 22 - Height: 6' 1/2" - Born: Pennsylvania - Trade: Laborer - Enlistment date: 14 May 1814 - Enlistment place: Chillicothe - Enlistment period: War - Discharged: 14 Jun 1815 at Chillicothe - Bounty: BLW 6033-160-12 (Arkansas).

Larimore, Joseph - Private - 27th Infantry - Company: George Sanderson - Enlistment date: 24 Apr 1813.

Larrimore, Hugh - Private - 27th Infantry - Company: Isaac Van Horne - Comments: Served aboard the US Schooner Somers on the Lake Erie Squadron.

Lassen, Septemus - Private - 19th Infantry - Company: Asabael Nearing - Enlistment date: 17 Feb 1813 - Enlistment period: 18 Mos.

Lawrence, Andrew - Private - 27th Infantry - Age: 28 - Height: 5' 10" - Born: Delaware - Enlistment date: 4 Apr 1814 - Enlistment place: Zanesville.

Lawrence, Andrew - Private - 17th Infantry - Company: Lt James Campbell - Age: 28 - Height: 5' 9" - Born: PA, Delaware County - Trade: Farmer - Enlistment date: 21 Mar 1814 - Enlistment period: War - By whom: Batteal Harrison - Discharged: 11 Jul 1815 at Chillicothe - Bounty: BLW 11919-160-12 (Illinois) - Comments: Deserted about 1 Apr 1814 and returned 6 Sep 1814.

Lawrence, Andrew - Private - 2nd Artillery - Company: Daniel Cushing - Age: 25 - Height: 5' 8" - Born: Delaware - Enlistment date: 26 Aug 1812 - Enlistment period: 18 Mos.

Lawson, Isham - Private - 26th Infantry - Company: George Kesling - Other regiment: 25th Infantry - Enlistment date: 13 May 1813 - Enlistment period: 1 Yr - Discharged: 13 May 1814.

Lazar, Hirt - Private - 19th Infantry - Age: 18 - Height: 5' 11" - Born: Kentucky - Enlistment date: 16 Apr 1814 - Enlistment place: Marietta - By whom: John Milligan - Comments: Deserted before 30 Apr 1814.

Le Duc, Peter - Private - 26th Infantry - Enlistment date: 25 Apr 1814 - Enlistment period: War - Comments: Prisoner of War (Halifax, NS), captured 20 Jun 1814 at Michilimacinac, MI; released 8 Apr 1815.

Leaf, John - Drummer - 17th Infantry - Company: Harris Hickman - Other regiment: 3rd Infantry - Age: 20 - Height: 5' 5 1/4" - Born: Newfoundland, St. Johns - Trade: Tailor - Enlistment date: 26 Jun 1814 - Enlistment place: Chillicothe - Enlistment period: War - By whom: Capt Jackson - Discharged: 1 Apr 1820 - Bounty: BLW 27291-160-42 - Comments: Re-enlisted for 5 years on 1 April 1815.

Leathers, Frederick - Private - 27th Infantry - Company: George Sanderson - Enlistment date: 27 Apr 1813 - Pension: Served as a private in Capt. Sanderson's Company, 27th Infantry - Bounty: BLW 63-160-50.

Leavitt, William - Sergeant - 19th Infantry - Company: Wilson Elliott - Age: 30 - Height: 5' 10" - Born: CT, Hartford County, Suffield - Trade: Laborer - Enlistment date: 9 Jul 1812 - Enlistment place: Trumbull County, Warren - Enlistment period: 5 Yrs - By whom: Andrew Bushnell - Discharged: 22 May 1815 at Chillicothe - Bounty: BLW 25131-160-12 (Arkansas) .

Ledwick, Piere - 19th Infantry - Age: 20 - Height: 5' 9 1/2" - Born: MI, Wayne County, Detroit - Enlistment date: 4 May 1814 - Enlistment place: Detroit - By whom: John Meldrum.

Lee, Francis - Corporal - 19th Infantry - Company: Angus Langham - Age: 26 - Height: 5' 3 3/4" - Born: Ireland - Trade: Tailor - Enlistment date: 23 Jan 1813 - Enlistment period: War - Discharged: 10 Aug 1815 at Chillicothe - Pension: Old War IF-25623; served in Capt. Langham's Company, 19th Infantry as a corporal - Bounty: BLW 6124-160-12 (Illinois) - Comments: Prisoner of War, captured at Frenchtown, MI.

Lee, John - Private - 26th Infantry - Company: Samuel Swearingen - Enlistment date: 26 May 1813 - Enlistment period: 1 Yr.

Lee, John - Private - 27th Infantry - Company: George Sanderson - Enlistment date: 16 Apr 1813.

Lee, Ludwell - Private - 17th Infantry - Company: David Holt - Enlistment date: 11 Mar 1813 - Enlistment period: 5 Yrs - Died: 22 Jul 1813, probably in Ohio - Pension: Old War Minor's Pension C-499, served in Captain James Mead's Company and Captain David Holt's Company, 17th Infantry as a private; heirs obtain half pay for five years in lieu of bounty land.

Lee, Thomas - Private - 17th Infantry - Company: Henry Crittenden - Age: 45 - Height: 5' 10" - Born: Ireland, County Derry - Trade: Laborer - Enlistment date: 8 Mar 1813 - Enlistment place: Franklin County, Franklinton - Enlistment period: War - By whom: Stephen Lee - Discharged: 9 Jun 1815 at Chillicothe - Bounty: BLW 27884-160-42 - Comments: Land bounty to Nancy Ann Ferguson, the child, & Martha Lee, the grandchild, only heirs at law of Thomas Lee.

Leedele, Thomas J. - Private - 27th Infantry - Age: 27 - Height: 5' 3" - Born: England - Enlistment date: 25 Apr 1814 - Enlistment place: Zanesville.

Leeder, Thomas T. - 19th Infantry - Executed: 8 Jul 1814 at Chillicothe.

Lefoe, Peter - Private - 19th Infantry - Bounty: BLW 15553-160-12 (Arkansas).

Legenness, Antwain - Private - 26th Infantry - Company: Samuel Swearingen - Enlistment date: 2 May 1813 - Enlistment period: 1 Yr - Died: 1814 at Detroit, MI - Comments: Prisoner of War on Parole, captured at Detroit, MI, 16 Aug 1812.

Leggett, Benjamin - Private - 19th Infantry - Company: George Kesling - Age: 40 - Height: 5' 9 1/2" - Born: MD, Baltimore County - Trade: Farmer - Enlistment date: 31 Jan 1815 - Enlistment place: Lebanon - Enlistment period: War - By whom: George Kesling - Discharged: 27 Mar 1815 at Zanesville - Bounty: BLW 382-320-14 (Illinois).

Lemasters, John - Private - 17th Infantry - Company: Martin Hawkins - Other regiment: 3rd Infantry - Age: 18 - Height: 5' 6 1/2" - Born: VA, Montgomery County - Trade: Farmer - Enlistment date: 1 Aug 1812 - Enlistment place: Gallipolis - Enlistment period: 5 Yrs - By whom: Thomas Morgan.

Lemmons, Jacob - Private - 17th Infantry - Company: Caleb Holder - Age: 18 - Height: 5' 10 3/4" - Born: New Jersey - Trade: Farmer - Enlistment date: 14 Jun 1814 - Enlistment period: War - By whom: Ensign Strang - Discharged: 30 Jun 1815 at Detroit - Bounty: BLW 6163-160-12 (Illinois).

Leonard, Amos - Private - 27th Infantry - Company: George Sanderson - Enlistment date: 28 May 1813.

Leonard, Caleb - Private - 2nd Artillery - Company: Daniel Cushing - Enlistment date: 14 Jul 1812 - Enlistment period: 5 Yrs - Died: Sep 1813.

Leonard, John - Private - 26th Infantry - Company: Samuel Swearingen - Enlistment date: 8 May 1813 - Enlistment period: 1 Yr.

Leonard, John - Musician - 19th Infantry - Company: Wilson Elliott.

Leonard, Stephen - Private - 19th Infantry - Company: Joel Collins - Age: 37 - Height: 5' 7 1/2" - Born: New York - Trade: Laborer - Enlistment date: 18 Mar 1814 - Enlistment place: Detroit - Enlistment period: War - By whom: Samuel Coleman.

Lepalm, Neil - Private - 19th Infantry - Company: James Herron.

Lewis, Fielding - Artificer - 2nd Artillery - Company: Daniel Cushing - Enlistment date: 25 Aug 1812 - Enlistment period: 18 Mos.

Lewis, Joseph - Private - 2nd Artillery - Company: Daniel Cushing.

Lewis, Phineas - Private - 26th Infantry - Company: George Kesling - Other regiment: 25th Infantry - Enlistment date: 10 Jun 1813 - Discharged: 10 Jun 1814 - Pension: SO-9413, SC-19779; served as a private in Capt. George Kesling's Company, 26th Infantry and in Capt. George Howard's Company, 25th Infantry.

Lewis, Solomon - Private - 19th Infantry - Company: James Herron - Enlistment date: 29 Aug 1812 - Enlistment period: 18 Mos.

Liecester, Jonathan - Private - 19th Infantry - Comments: Prisoner of War, exchanged 25 Apr 1814.

Lief, Henry - Private - 27th Infantry - Company: George Sanderson - Enlistment date: 31 May 1813.

Lieff – see Leaf, John

Liesure, Hiat - Private - 19th Infantry - Age: 16 - Height: 6' - Born: Kentucky - Enlistment date: 22 Mar 1814 - Enlistment place: Steubenville - By whom: Ensign Jackson.

Likens, John - Private - 19th Infantry - Company: Carey Trimble - Age: 21 - Height: 6' - Born: Kentucky - Trade: Shoemaker - Enlistment date: 1 Mar 1814 - Enlistment place: Chillicothe - Enlistment period: War - By whom: Charles Cissna.

Lindsay, John - Private - 26th Infantry - Company: Joel Collins - Other regiment: 19th Infantry - Age: 45 - Height: 5' 4 3/4" - Born: Maryland - Trade: Weaver - Enlistment date: 18 Sep 1813 - Enlistment place: Upper

Canada, Sandwich - Enlistment period: War - By whom: Alexander Delerae - Discharged: 20 July 1815 at Detroit - Bounty: BLW 8319-160-12 (Illinois).

Lingar, William - Private - 19th Infantry - Age: 41 - Height: 5' 6 1/2" - Born: VA, Fauquier County - Enlistment date: 30 Aug 1814 - Enlistment place: Athens County.

Lingerall, Thomas - Private - 19th Infantry - Company: Carey Trimble - Other regiment: 17th Infantry - Age: 18 - Height: 5' 9" - Born: Maryland - Trade: Laborer - Enlistment date: 13 Apr 1814 - Enlistment place: Ross County, Adelphi - Enlistment period: War - By whom: George Will - Discharged: 7 Jun 1815 at Chillicothe - Pension: Old War IF-26705, SO-17267, SC-18720; served in Capt. Carey Trimble's Company and Lt. McElvain's Company, 19th Infantry as a private; lived in OH - Bounty: BLW 17728-160-12 (Illinois).

Link, Mathew - Private - 27th Infantry - Pension: Wife Fanny, WC-22743, SC-23964; served in Captain Joseph Bell's Company, 27th Infantry as a private.

Linsecomb, David - Private - 26th Infantry - Company: George Kesling - Enlistment date: 7 May 1813 - Enlistment period: 1 Yr - Discharged: 7 May 1814.

Linsicum, David - Private - 19th Infantry - Company: Carey Trimble - Age: 22 - Height: 5' 10" - Born: Ohio - Trade: Farmer - Enlistment date: 11 Jun 1814 - Enlistment place: Ross County, Adelphi - Enlistment period: War - By whom: George Will - Discharged: 6 Jun 1815 at Chillicothe - Bounty: BLW 24882-160-12 (Arkansas).

Linton, Zephamah - Private - 19th Infantry - Company: George Kesling - Age: 21 - Height: 5' 7" - Born: Virginia - Trade: Farmer - Enlistment date: 29 Mar 1814 - Enlistment place: Zanesville - Enlistment period: War - By whom: Neal McFadden - Bounty: BLW 12503-160-12 (Illinois).

Litterell, John - Private - 19th Infantry - Company: Asabael Nearing - Enlistment date: 26 Feb 1813 - Enlistment period: War - Died: 15 May 1813 - Pension: Heirs obtained half pay for five years in lieu of military bounty land.

Little, Alexander - Private - 19th Infantry - Company: James Herron - Enlistment date: 8 Nov 1812 - Enlistment period: 18 Mos.

Little, David - Corporal - 26th Infantry - Company: Samuel Swearingen - Other regiment: 25th Infantry - Enlistment date: 18 Jun 1813 - Enlistment period: 1 Yr - Discharged: 18 Jun 1814 - Comments: Served aboard the US Schooner Porcupine on the Lake Erie Squadron.

Little, Job - Private - 26th Infantry - Company: George Will - Enlistment date: 9 Jun 1814 - Enlistment period: 1 Yr.

Little, Martin - Private - 17th Infantry - Company: Harris Hickman - Age: 34 - Height: 5' 11" - Born: TN, Sullivan County - Trade: Carpenter - Enlistment date: 13 Mar 1814 - Enlistment place: Franklin County, Franklinton - Enlistment period: War - By whom: John Cochran - Died: 2 Mar 1815, probably at Chillicothe.

Littlejohn, Aaron - Private - 26th Infantry - Company: Joel Collins - Enlistment date: 11 Aug 1813 - Enlistment period: 1 Yr.

Littleton, John - Private - 26th Infantry - Company: George Kesling - Enlistment date: 13 May 1813 - Discharged: 13 May 1814.

Littleton, John - Private - 19th Infantry - Company: James Herron - Other regiment: 17th Infantry then 3rd Infantry - Age: 13 - Height: 5' 1 1/2" - Born: Virginia - Trade: Farmer - Enlistment date: 11 Aug 1812 - Enlistment place: Butler County, Hamilton - Enlistment period: 5 Yrs - By whom: Lewis Howell - Comments: Deserted 17 Mar 1815.

Littleton, Robert - Private - 17th Infantry - Company: John Chunn - Age: 20 - Height: 5' 8 1/2" - Born: OH, Gallia County, Gallipolis - Trade: Farmer - Enlistment date: 8 May 1813 - Enlistment period: War - By whom: Henry Crittenden.

Loar, George - Private - 27th Infantry - Company: Joseph Cairns - Pension: Wife Leah, WO-42557, WC33133, SO-792, SC-189; served in Capt. Cairne's Company, 27th Infantry as a private - Bounty: BLW 989-160-50.

Lockhart, W. M. - Private - 27th Infantry - Company: Alexander Hill.

Lofland, William - 1st Rifles - Company: Thomas Ramsey - Age: 41 - Height: 5' 8" - Born: DE, Sussex County - Trade: Shoemaker - Enlistment date: 3 Jan 1814 - Enlistment place: Cincinnati - Enlistment period: 5 Yrs - By whom: Thomas Ramsey - Comments: Deserted at Cincinnati, OH, on 14 Feb 1814.

Logue, Samuel - Private - 17th Infantry - Company: David Holt - Age: 16 - Height: 5' 6" - Born: Kentucky - Trade: Laborer - Enlistment date: 14 Feb 1814 - Enlistment place: Butler County, Hamilton - Enlistment period: War - By whom: George Stall - Discharged: 30 Mar 1815 at Erie, PA - Bounty: BLW 18008-160-12 (Missouri).

Long, Jacob - 1st Rifles - Company: Thomas Ramsey - Age: 48 - Height: 5' 7" - Born: TN, Loudon County, Philadelphia - Trade: Shoemaker - Enlistment date: 4 Nov 1813 - Enlistment place: Cincinnati - Enlistment period: War - By whom: Thomas Ramsey.

Long, Joseph - Private - 17th Infantry - Company: Benjamin Sanders - Other regiment: 3rd Infantry - Age: 18 - Height: 5' 9" - Born: OH, Hamilton County - Enlistment date: 20 Jun 1812 - Enlistment period: 5 Yrs - Discharged: 20 Jun 1817.

Long, Joseph - Private - 26th Infantry - Company: Richard Talbott - Other regiment: 19th Infantry - Age: 23 - Height: 5' 7" - Born: Virginia - Trade: Farmer - Enlistment date: 23 Feb 1814 - Enlistment place: Lebanon - Enlistment period: 1 Yr - By whom: Richard Talbott - Discharged: 22 Feb 1815 - Comments: Discharged at Erie, PA.

Long, Peter - Private - 1st Rifles - Company: Thomas Ramsey - Age: 19 - Height: 5' 5" - Born: Maryland - Trade: Farmer - Enlistment date: 4 Apr 1814 - Enlistment place: Cincinnati - Enlistment period: 5 Yrs - By whom: Thomas Ramsey - Discharged: 24 Mar 1819.

Long, William - Private - 17th Infantry - Age: 37 - Height: 6' 1" - Born: VA, Rockingham County - Enlistment date: 28 Aug 1814 - Enlistment place: Steubenville - By whom: William Featherstone.

Longwell, Robert (or Thomas) - Private - 27th Infantry - Company: Absalom Martin - Pension: Wife Martha, WO-35584, WC-23333; served as a private in Capt. Absalom Martin's Company, 27th Infantry.

Longwith, Jonathan - Private - 26th Infantry - Company: George Will - Enlistment date: 14 May 1813 - Enlistment period: 1 Yr.

Looks, Samuel - Musician - 2nd Rifles - Company: Batteal Harrison - Age: 20 - Height: 5' 5" - Born: Lower Canada, Quebec - Trade: Musician - Enlistment date: 4 Jul 1814 - Enlistment place: Chillicothe - Enlistment period: 5 Yrs - By whom: Batteal Harrison - Comments: African American.

Lott, William - Private - 19th Infantry - Company: Carey Trimble - Age: 30 - Height: 5' 8" - Born: Delaware - Trade: Laborer - Enlistment date: 2 Jan 1814 - Enlistment place: Chillicothe - Enlistment period: War - By whom: John Swearingen - Discharged: 6 Jun 1815 at Chillicothe.

Louther, William - Private - 27th Infantry - Company: George Sanderson - Enlistment date: 21 Jun 1813.

Love, James H. - Private - 19th Infantry - Company: Wilson Elliott - Other regiment: 17th Infantry - Age: 32 - Height: 5' 6" - Born: Ireland - Enlistment date: 27 Jul 1812 - Enlistment period: 5 Yrs.

Love, John K. - Private - 19th Infantry - Company: Wilson Elliott - Other regiment: 17th Infantry.

Loveland, John - Private - 27th Infantry - Company: Alexander Hill - Other regiment: 19th Infantry - Age: 33 - Height: 5' 9" - Born: CT, Litchfield County, Salesburg - Enlistment date: 21 Mar 1814 - Enlistment place: Ashtabula County, Harpersfield - Enlistment period: 5 Yrs - Died: 16 Aug 1814 - Bounty: BLW 26516-160-12 (Arkansas) - Comments: Land bounty to Hannah McKelvey, late widow, heir at law of John Loveland.

Loveland, Marinas M. - Private - 27th Infantry - Company: George Sanderson - Enlistment date: 27 Apr 1813.

Lovell, Timothy - Private - 26th Infantry - Company: Joel Collins - Enlistment date: 11 Jul 1813 - Enlistment period: 1 Yr.

Lovett, Daniel - Private - 19th Infantry - Company: Richard Talbott - Enlistment date: 14 Mar 1814 - Enlistment place: Urbana - Enlistment period: War - By whom: Christopher Wood - Discharged: 5 Jun 1815 at Chillicothe - Bounty: BLW 15676-160-12 (Illinois).

Lovett, Robert S. - Private - 17th Infantry - Company: Henry Crittenden - Other regiment: 2nd Infantry - Age: 45 - Height: 5' 7" - Born: Scotland, Sallawathan - Trade: School master - Enlistment date: 10 Mar 1813 - Enlistment place: Steubenville - Enlistment period: 5 Yrs - By whom: James Hazelton - Comments: Deserted 21 Apr 1815.

Lovewell, Timothy - Private - 2nd Rifles - Company: Batteal Harrison - Age: 19 - Height: 5' 10" - Born: Pennsylvania - Trade: Laborer - Enlistment date: 8 Sep 1814 - Enlistment place: Cincinnati - Enlistment period: War - By whom: Elias Langham - Discharged: 30 Jun 1815 at Detroit - Bounty: BLW 18360-160-12 (Illinois).

Low, David - Private - 26th Infantry - Company: Samuel Swearingen - Enlistment date: 27 Jul 1813 - Enlistment period: 1 Yr.

Lowens, Hiett - Private - 19th Infantry - Company: James Herron - Enlistment date: 11 Dec 1812 - Enlistment period: 18 Mos.

Lowry, Allen - Sergeant - 27th Infantry - Company: Carey Trimble - Other regiments: 19th Infantry then 17th Infantry - Age: 22 - Height: 5' 9" - Born: PA, Franklin County - Trade: Shoemaker - Enlistment date: 3 Mar 1814 - Enlistment place: Zanesville - Enlistment period: War - By whom: John Williby - Discharged: 6 Jun 1815 at Chillicothe - Bounty: BLW 7829-160-12 (Illinois).

Lowry, John - Private - 2nd Rifles - Company: Batteal Harrison - Age: 33 - Height: 5' 10" - Born: Pennsylvania - Trade: Laborer - Enlistment date: 23 Aug 1814 - Enlistment place: Cincinnati - Enlistment period: 5 Yrs - By whom: Elias Langham.

Lowry, John - Private - 17th Infantry - Company: David Holt - Age: 35 - Height: 5' 9" - Born: Pennsylvania - Trade: Farmer - Enlistment date: 13 Apr 1814 - Enlistment period: War - By whom: George Bryant - Discharged: 12 Jul 1815 - Pension: Wife Nancy, WO-36604, WC-27464, SO-17278, SC-11225; served in Captain David Holt's Company, 17th Infantry as a private; lived in OH - Bounty: BLW 9030-160-12 (Illinois).

Lucas, Benjamin - Private - 27th Infantry - Company: Joseph Cairns - Pension: Wife Frances, WO-12720, WC-13339, SO-3519, SC-2109; served in Capt. J. Cairne's Company, 27th Infantry as a private.

Lucas, Ephraim - Private - 27th Infantry - Company: Alexander Hill - Other regiments: 19th Infantry then 17th Infantry - Age: 49 - Height: 6' 3/4" - Born: Maryland - Trade: Farmer - Enlistment date: 5 May 1814 - Enlistment place: Zanesville - Enlistment period: War - By whom: Neal McFadden - Discharged: 6 Jun 1815 at Chillicothe - Bounty: BLW 7232-160-12 (Illinois).

Lucas, Ichabod - Private - 27th Infantry - Company: George Kesling - Other regiment: 19th Infantry - Age: 18 - Height: 5' 5" - Born: Maryland - Trade: Farmer - Enlistment date: 25 Apr 1814 - Enlistment place: Zanesville - Discharged: 27 Mar 1815 at Zanesville - Bounty: BLW 331-320-14 - Comments: Re-enlisted,.

Lucky, Abiel - Private - 19th Infantry - Company: Richard Talbott - Age: 36 - Height: 5' 8" - Born: NY, Orange County - Trade: Carpenter - Enlistment date: 16 Apr 1814 - Enlistment place: Clermont County, Williamsburg - Enlistment period: War - By whom: William McDonald Jr - Discharged: 5 Jun 1815 at Chillicothe - Bounty: BLW 3808-160-12 (Illinois).

Ludwick, John - Private - 26th Infantry - Company: Samuel Swearingen - Other regiment: 25th Infantry - Enlistment date: 6 Jul 1813 - Enlistment period: 1 Yr - Discharged: 22 Jun 1814.

Lufft, Frederick - Private - 19th Infantry - Company: John Chunn - Other regiment: 17th Infantry then 3rd Infantry - Age: 36 - Height: 5' 9" - Born: Scotland, Galloway - Trade: S. maker - Enlistment date: 14 Apr 1813 - Enlistment place: Steubenville - Enlistment period: 5 Yrs - By whom: James Hazelton - Discharged: 9 Apr 1818 at Fort Harrison, IN.

Luster, Richard - Private - 28th Infantry - Company: George Stockton - Age: 18 - Height: 5' 6" - Born: TN, Green County. - Enlistment date: 16 Feb 1814 - Enlistment place: KY, Wayne County, Monticello - Enlistment period: 1 Yr - By whom: William Haden - Died: 1 Nov 1814 - Bounty: BLW 27224-160-42 - Comments: Died at Cleveland, OH; land bounty to John Luster, William Luster, Edward Luster, Polly Garner, and Jane Smith, only surviving brothers and sisters, heirs at law of Richard Luster.

Lycgrell, Thomas - Private - 19th Infantry - Company: Lt John McElvain.

Lyles, William - Musician - 19th Infantry - Company: Wilson Elliott.

Lymming, Benjamin - Private - 17th Infantry - Age: 26 - Height: 5' 8 1/2" - Born: Pennsylvania - Enlistment date: 14 May 1814 - By whom: George Stall.

Lynch, Peter - Corporal - 17th Infantry - Age: 43` - Height: 5' 6 1/2" - Born: Ireland - Enlistment date: 28 Jan 1813 - Enlistment place: Butler County, Hamilton - Enlistment period: War - By whom: George Stall - Discharged: 18 Apr 1815 - Bounty: BLW 23087-160-12 (Arkansas).

Lynch, Samuel - Clerk - 19th Infantry - Company: Carey Trimble - Other regiment: 17th Infantry - Age: 23 - Height: 5' 11 1/2" - Born: MD, Baltimore County - Trade: Laborer - Enlistment date: 23 Feb 1814 - Enlistment place: Franklin County, Franklinton - Enlistment period: War - By whom: Hugh Moore - Discharged: 6 Jun 1815 at Chillicothe - Bounty: BLW 11111-160-12 (Illinois).

Lyons, Abraham - Private - 19th Infantry - Company: Asabael Nearing - Pension: Old War IF-26713, served in Capt. Sharp's Company, Ohio Militia, and Capt. Nearings' Company, 19th Infantry as a private.

Lyons, Abraham - Private - 17th Infantry - Company: Henry Crittenden - Other regiment: 3rd Infantry - Age: 30 - Height: 5' 8" - Born: NJ, Essex County, Newark - Trade: Shoemaker - Enlistment date: 3 Feb 1813 - Enlistment place: Zanesville - Enlistment period: 5 Yrs - By whom: James Herron - Discharged: 3 Feb 1818 at Fort Harrison, IN - Bounty: BLW 24002-160-12 (Arkansas).

Lyons, John - Corporal - 27th Infantry - Company: Carey Trimble - Other regiment: 19th Infantry - Age: 26 - Height: 5' 10" - Born: NJ, Sussex County - Trade: Farmer - Enlistment date: 8 Apr 1814 - Enlistment place: New Lisbon - Enlistment period: War - Discharged: 6 Jun 1815 at Chillicothe - Pension: Wife Mary, WO-43607, WC-34944; served in Lt. John McElvain's Company, 19th Infantry as a corporal - Bounty: BLW 18579-160-12 (Missouri).

Lyons, Michael - Private - 19th Infantry - Company: Wilson Elliott - Other regiment: 17th Infantry then 3rd Infantry - Enlistment date: 7 Jul 1812 - Enlistment period: 5 Yrs - Discharged: 1 Apr 1820 - Comments: Re-enlisted.

Lyons, William - Corporal - 27th Infantry - Company: Wilson Elliott - Other regiment: 19th Infantry - Bounty: BLW 24551-160-12 (Arkansas).

The Enlisted Men

MacKey, David - Private - 26th Infantry - Company: William Puthuff - Other regiment: Light Dragoons Regiment - Enlistment date: 31 May 1813 - Pension: Old War IF-16003 Rejected, served in Captain Puthuff's Company, 26th Infantry.

MacKey, John - Private - 26th Infantry - Company: George Kesling - Enlistment date: 5 Jun 1813 - Discharged: 5 Jul 1814.

Maddison, Thomas (or Madden) - Private - 19th Infantry - Company: Wilson Elliott - Other regiment: 25th Infantry - Age: 23 - Height: 5' 6 1/2" - Born: Ireland - Enlistment date: 28 Jul 1812 - Enlistment place: Ohio - Enlistment period: 5 Yrs - Died: 31 Jul 1815 at Brownsville Hospital, NY.

Maddox, Ebenezer H. - Fifer - 26th Infantry - Company: Samuel Swearingen - Other regiment: 3rd Infantry - Enlistment date: 12 May 1813 - Enlistment place: Detroit - Enlistment period: 1 Yr - Pension: Old War IF-26719; served in Capt. Cunningham's Company, OH militia as a fifer and in Capt. Bradley's Company, 3rd Infantry as a sergeant. - Comments: Prisoner of War on Parole, captured at Detroit, MI, 16 Aug 1812.

Magner, Edward - Private - 26th Infantry - Company: Samuel Swearingen - Enlistment date: 23 Jun 1813 - Enlistment period: 1 Yr.

Magraw, John C. - Private - 26th Infantry - Company: Samuel Swearingen - Enlistment date: 24 Jun 1813 - Enlistment period: 1 Yr.

Mahan, Archibald - Private - 19th Infantry - Company: James Herron - Enlistment date: 18 Sep 1812 - Enlistment period: 18 Mos.

Mahon, Lewis - Private - 19th Infantry - Company: Lt Campbell.

Mains, Henry - Private - 27th Infantry - Company: George Sanderson - Enlistment date: 13 Jun 1813.

Maker, Amos - Private - 26th Infantry - Company: George Will.

Mallard, Francis - Private - 1st Rifles - Company: Thomas Ramsey - Age: 35 - Height: 5' 8" - Born: Lower Canada, Montreal - Trade: Farmer - Enlistment date: 1 May 1812 - Enlistment place: Cincinnati - Enlistment period: 5 Yrs - By whom: Thomas Ramsey - Discharged: 1 May 1817.

Malona – see Molona, Simon

Malone, Thomas - Sergeant - 26th Infantry - Company: George Kesling - Enlistment date: 9 Apr 1813 - Enlistment period: 1 Yr.

Malony, Samuel - Private - 19th Infantry - Age: 26 - Height: 5' 6" - Born: PA, Philadelphia County - Enlistment date: 27 Jul 1812 - Enlistment place: St. Clairsville - Enlistment period: 18 Mos.

Malony, Simon (or Maloney) - Private - 1st Rifles - Company: Thomas Ramsey - Age: 21 - Height: 5' 6" - Born: PA, Philadelphia County - Trade: Shoemaker - Enlistment date: 29 Nov 1813 - Enlistment place: Cincinnati - Enlistment period: 5 Yrs - By whom: Thomas Ramsey - Died: 17 Sep 1814 - Comments: Prisoner of War (Halifax, NS), captured at Fort Erie, UC, 17 Sep 1814; released 10 Apr 1815.

Malure, William - Private - 17th Infantry - Company: Henry Crittenden - Other regiment: 3rd Infantry - Age: 23 - Height: 5' 6 1/2" - Born: MD, Baltimore County - Trade: Shoemaker - Enlistment date: 16 Jul 1814 - Enlistment period: 5 Yrs - By whom: John Cochran - Discharged: 16 Jul 1819.

Manett, Lewis - Corporal - 19th Infantry - Company: James Herron.

Manning, William - Private - 19th Infantry - Age: 43 - Height: 5' 6" - Born: Ireland, County Cork - Enlistment date: 7 Aug 1814 - Enlistment place: Canton.

Mannon, William - Private - 19th Infantry - Company: William Gill - Age: 56 - Height: 5' 9" - Born: Ireland - Trade: Farmer - Enlistment date: 25 Aug 1814 - Enlistment period: War - By whom: Thomas Riddle - Discharged: 29 Mar 1815 - Bounty: BLW 15846-160-12 (Illinois) - Comments: Discharged at Zanesville.

Mantany, Isaac - Private - 19th Infantry - Company: James Herron.

Manuel, John - Private - 2nd Rifles - Company: Batteal Harrison - Age: 33 - Height: 5' 8" - Born: LA, Orleans Parish, New Orleans - Trade: Laborer - Enlistment date: 7 Aug 1814 - Enlistment place: Cincinnati - Enlistment period: 5 Yrs - By whom: Elias Langham - Discharged: 7 Aug 1819 at Fort Crawford, IL - Bounty: BLW 22784-160-12 (Arkansas).

Mapes, Thomas - Private - 27th Infantry - Company: George Sanderson - Enlistment date: 28 Jun 1813.

Marble, David - Private - 26th Infantry - Company: William Puthuff - Enlistment date: 29 Apr 1813 - Enlistment period: 1 Yr.

Mare, Lewis - Private - 2nd Artillery - Company: Daniel Cushing - Other regiment: Corps of Artillery - Age: 25 - Height: 5' 8" - Born: VA, Augusta County - Trade: Farmer - Enlistment date: 2 Feb 1814 - Enlistment period: War - Discharged: 4 Jul 1815 at Fort Meigs, OH - Bounty: BLW 2276-160-12 (Arkansas).

Marfoot, Samuel - Private - 19th Infantry - Company: William Gill.

Marker, Benjamin - Private - 2nd Artillery - Company: Daniel Cushing - Age: 25 - Height: 5' 8" - Born: DE, Kent County - Trade: Farmer - Enlistment date: 6 Mar 1810 - Enlistment place: Lebanon - Enlistment period: 5

Yrs - By whom: Alexander Meek - Discharged: 7 Mar 1815 - Comments: Prisoner of War (Quebec, LC), captured at Fort Niagara, NY, 19 Dec 1813; exchanged 4 May 1814.

Marlatt, Robbins - Private - 1st Infantry - Company: Horatio Stark - Other regiment: 3rd Infantry - Age: 27 - Height: 5' 11" - Born: NJ, Sussex County - Trade: Carpenter - Enlistment date: 30 May 1812 - Enlistment place: Chillicothe - Enlistment period: 5 Yrs - By whom: Samuel Kercheval - Discharged: 30 May 1817 at Fort Crawford, IL.

Marr, James - Private - 19th Infantry - Company: Martin Hawkins - Other regiment: 17th Infantry - Age: 22 - Height: 5' 5" - Born: Pennsylvania - Trade: Laborer - Enlistment date: 10 May 1813 - Enlistment place: Cincinnati - Enlistment period: 18 Mos - War - Discharged: 9 Jun 1815 at Chillicothe - Bounty: BLW 16304-160-12 (Illinois) - Comments: Re-enlisted.

Marsac, John B. - Private - 19th Infantry - Company: James Herron - Enlistment period: War.

Marsac, Lewis - Private - 19th Infantry - Company: James Herron.

Marsh, Benjamin - Private - 1st Infantry - Other regiment: 3rd Infantry - Age: 37 - Height: 5' 8" - Born: NJ, Sussex County - Trade: Weaver - Enlistment date: 5 Sep 1812 - Enlistment place: Cincinnati - Enlistment period: 5 Yrs - By whom: Laurence Taliaferro - Discharged: 30 Nov 1816 at Newport, KY, on Surgeon's Certificate of Disability, lameness of left hip.

Marsh, Isaac - Private - Rangers - Company: William Perry - Pension: SO-16021, SC-10969; served in Capt. William Perry's Company, US Rangers.

Marsh, Joseph - Private - Rangers - Company: Samuel McCormick - Age: 22 - Height: 5' 9" - Born: New Jersey - Trade: Cabinet maker - Enlistment date: 4 Nov 1813 - Enlistment period: 1 Yr - Discharged: 3 Nov 1813 at Fort Malden, UC.

Marsh, William - Private - 7th Infantry - Company: Zachary Taylor - Enlistment date: 7 Mar 1812 - Enlistment period: 5 Yrs - By whom: Thomas Ramsey - Pension: Wife Leodica, WO-7214, WC-5748; served in Capt. Taylor's company, 7th Infantry - Comments: Prisoner of War, captured at Prairie du Chien, IL.

Marsh, William - Private - 17th Infantry - Company: Harris Hickman - Age: 33 - Height: 5' 9" - Born: Pennsylvania - Enlistment date: 15 Apr 1814 - Enlistment place: Lebanon - Enlistment period: 5 Yrs - By whom: Adam Hoffman - Died: 13 Jan 1815 - Pension: Heirs obtained half pay for five years in lieu of military bounty land.

Marshall, John - Private - 17th Infantry - Company: Harris Hickman - Age: 31 - Height: 5' 6" - Born: PA, Chester County - Enlistment date: 6 May 1814 - Enlistment place: Lancaster - Enlistment period: 5 Yrs - By whom: James Hazelton - Discharged: 29 Nov at Buffalo, NY.

Marshall, John - Private - 1st Rifles - Company: Thomas Ramsey - Age: 24 - Height: 5' 8 1/2" - Born: NC, Giueford County - Trade: Tinner - Enlistment date: 10 May 1814 - Enlistment place: Cincinnati - Enlistment period: War - By whom: Thomas Ramsey - Comments: Deserted at Cincinnati, OH, on 13 May 1814.

Marshall, Thomas - Corporal - 26th Infantry - Company: Joel Collins - Enlistment date: 3 May 1813 - Enlistment period: 1 Yr - Pension: SO-7211, SC-14877, served in Capt. Skidmore's and Capt. Joel Collins' Companies, 26th Infantry and Capt. George Gibson's Company, OH Militia.

Marshall, William - 1st Infantry - Company: Horatio Stark - Other regiment: 3rd Infantry - Age: 19 - Height: 5' 6" - Born: OH, Warren County, Hamilton - Trade: Farmer - Enlistment date: 27 Apr 1812 - Enlistment period: 5 Yrs - By whom: Thomas Ramsey - Discharged: 17 Sep 1816 for disability.

Marshall, William - Corporal - 19th Infantry - Company: Angus Langham - Other regiment: 17th Infantry - Age: 26 - Height: 5' 5 1/2" - Born: VA, Frederick County - Trade: Farmer - Enlistment date: 22 Jun 1812 - Enlistment period: 5 Yrs - Discharged: 22 Jun 1817 - Comments: Discharged at Fort Howard, WI.

Marthers, Daniel - Private - 26th Infantry - Company: William Puthuff - Enlistment date: 26 May 1813 - Enlistment period: 1 Yr.

Martin, Alexander - Private - 19th Infantry - Company: James Herron - Enlistment date: 30 Oct 1812 - Enlistment period: 5 Yrs.

Martin, Alexander - Corporal - 17th Infantry - Company: David Holt - Other regiment: 3rd Infantry - Age: 22 - Height: 5' 9" - Born: VA, Ohio County (now WV) - Trade: Laborer - Enlistment date: 23 Jun 1814 - Enlistment place: Chillicothe - Enlistment period: War - By whom: John Cochran - Discharged: 31 Mar 1815 - Pension: Wife Lucinda, WO-43324, WC-34296, SO-4446, SC-7608; served in Capt. Holt's Company, 17th Infantry and in Capt. Chunn's Company, 3rd Infantry - Bounty: BLW 27879-160-42.

Martin, Evan - Private - Rangers - Company: Samuel McCormick - Pension: SO-7213, SC-3880; served as a private in Capt. Samuel McCormick's Company, US Rangers.

Martin, James - Private - 19th Infantry - Company: Angus Langham - Bounty: BLW 26997-170-12 - Comments: Prisoner of War, captured at Frenchtown, MI; land bounty to John G. Martin, son & only heir at law of James

The Enlisted Men

Martin.

Martin, John - Private - 27th Infantry - Company: Absalom Martin - Comments: Served aboard the US Schooner Tigress on the Lake Erie Squadron.

Martin, John - Sergeant - Rangers - Company: Samuel McCormick - Age: 25 - Height: 5' 9" - Born: Kentucky - Trade: Farmer - Enlistment date: 27 Nov 1813 - Enlistment period: 1 Yr - Discharged: 17 Nov 1814 - Comments: Discharged on Surgeon's Certificate of Disability, at Fort Malden, UC.

Martin, John - Private - 19th Infantry - Company: Asabael Nearing - Enlistment date: 11 Feb 1813 - Enlistment period: 5 Yrs.

Martin, Robert - Private - 19th Infantry - Company: Richard Graham - Enlistment date: 31 Aug 1812 - Enlistment period: 18 Mos - By whom: James Campbell - Discharged: 19 Aug 1814.

Martin, Robert - Private - 26th Infantry - Company: William Puthuff - Enlistment date: 25 Apr 1814 - Enlistment period: 1 Yr.

Martin, Robert - Private - 19th Infantry - Comments: Prisoner of War, exchanged 25 Apr 1814.

Martin, Samuel - Private - 19th Infantry - Company: George Kesling - Age: 18 - Height: 5' 9" - Born: Kentucky - Trade: Farmer - Enlistment date: 13 Nov 1814 - Enlistment place: Xenia - Enlistment period: War - By whom: Robert Smith - Discharged: 27 Mar 1815 at Zanesville - Bounty: BLW 4195-160-12 (Arkansas).

Martin, Samuel - Private - 19th Infantry - Company: James Herron - Died: 22 Oct 1813.

Martin, William - Corporal - 2nd Artillery - Company: Daniel Cushing - Other regiment: Corps of Artillery - Age: 26 - Height: 5' 7 3/4" - Born: Maryland - Trade: Laborer - Enlistment date: 7 Nov 1814 - Enlistment period: War - Discharged: 25 Jul 1815 at Fort Meigs, OH.

Martin, William B. - Private - 17th Infantry - Company: Caleb Holder - Age: 24 - Height: 6' - Born: Virginia - Enlistment date: 27 May 1814 - Enlistment place: Franklin County - Enlistment period: War - By whom: John Simons.

Masco, Peter - Private - 2nd Rifles - Company: Benjamin Desha - Age: 38 - Height: 5' 5" - Born: PA, Philadelphia County - Trade: Laborer - Enlistment date: 28 Nov 1814 - Enlistment period: 5 Yrs - By whom: William Pritchard - Died: 28 Nov 1819 at Fort Crawford, IL - Bounty: BLW 23924-160-12 (Arkansas).

Mason, Benjamin - Sergeant - 1st Rifles - Company: Thomas Ramsey - Age: 25 - Height: 5' 10" - Born: MA, Cumberland - Trade: Carpenter - Enlistment date: 7 Dec 1812 - Enlistment place: Cincinnati - Enlistment period: 5 Yrs - By whom: Thomas Ramsey - Died: 22 Feb 1814, drowned in Scioto River, Ohio.

Mason, Jacob - Private - 2nd Artillery - Company: Daniel Cushing - Age: 28 - Height: 5' 6" - Born: Pennsylvania - Trade: Farmer - Enlistment date: 10 Aug 1812 - Enlistment place: Lebanon - Enlistment period: 5 Yrs - By whom: Alexander Meek - Discharged: 10 Aug 1817.

Mason, John - Private - 2nd Rifles - Company: Benjamin Desha - Age: 28 - Height: 5' 4" - Born: North Carolina - Trade: Laborer - Enlistment date: 22 Oct 1814 - Enlistment period: War - By whom: William Pritchard - Discharged: 30 Jun 1815 at Detroit.

Mason, John - Private - 26th Infantry - Died: 21 Feb 1814 - Comments: Died at Greenbush, NY (hospital), 21 or 26 Feb 1814.

Mason, Joseph S. - Corporal - 2nd Rifles - Company: John O'Fallen - Age: 21 - Height: 5' 10" - Born: VA, Frederick County - Trade: Farmer - Enlistment date: 30 Aug 1814 - Enlistment place: Chillicothe, or Lexington, KY - Enlistment period: 5 Yrs - By whom: John O'Fallon - Died: Mar 1816 at Detroit (in regiment's hospital).

Mason, Owen - Private - 17th Infantry - Company: Harris Hickman - Age: 26 - Height: 6' - Born: NC, Hyde County - Trade: Laborer - Enlistment date: 21 Jan 1814 - Enlistment place: Chillicothe - Enlistment period: War - By whom: David Carney - Discharged: 9 Jun 1815 at Chillicothe - Bounty: BLW 8265-160-12 (Illinois).

Mason, Richard - Drummer - 7th Infantry - Company: Thornton Posey - Enlistment date: 12 Jun 1809 - Enlistment period: 5 Yrs - By whom: Thomas Ramsey - Discharged: 11 Jun 1814 at Prairie du Chien, IL.

Masters, Curtis - Private - 17th Infantry - Company: Caleb Holder - Enlistment date: 23 Feb 1813 - Enlistment period: 5 Yrs - By whom: William Leavitt.

Masters, William - Private - 26th Infantry - Company: Joel Collins - Other regiment: 19th Infantry - Age: 20 - Height: 5' 19" - Born: Pennsylvania - Trade: Farmer - Enlistment date: 1 Sep 1813 - Enlistment place: Upper Canada, Sandwich - Enlistment period: 1 Yr - War - By whom: Robert Smith - Discharged: 20 Jul 1815 at Detroit - Bounty: BLW 11960-160-12 (Illinois) - Comments: Prisoner of War on Parole, captured at Detroit, MI, 16 Aug 1812; re-enlisted 17 Apr 1814, during the war enlistment, at Sandwich, UC, (now Windsor, Ontario).

Mathews, Henry - Private - 27th Infantry - Company: Joseph Carins - Pension: Wife Elizabeth, WO-33554, WC-22998, SO-5792, SC-12137; served in Capt. C. Woods' Company, OH Militia and in Capt. Joseph Cairns'

Company, 27th Infantry as a private.

Mathews, John - Private - 19th Infantry - Company: George Kesling - Age: 18 - Height: 5' 4" - Born: Virginia - Trade: Farmer - Enlistment date: 10 May 1814 - Enlistment period: War - Discharged: 27 Mar 1815 at Zanesville - Bounty: BLW 2534-160-12 (Illinois).

Matsler, John - Private - 26th Infantry - Company: Joel Collins - Enlistment date: 11 Sep 1813 - Enlistment period: 1 Yr - By whom: Robert Smith.

Matthews, Andrew - Private - 26th Infantry (new) - Company: William Bezeau - Age: 30 - Height: 5' 5" - Born: Ohio - Trade: Seaman - Enlistment date: 9 Feb 1815 - Enlistment place: PA, Philadelphia County - Enlistment period: War - By whom: William Bezeau - Comments: Colored man.

Matthews, John - Private - 19th Infantry - Age: 40 - Height: 5' 5" - Born: Pennsylvania - Enlistment date: 11 May 1814 - Enlistment place: Chillicothe - Enlistment period: War - By whom: Charles Cissna.

Matthews, John - Sergeant - 2nd Rifles - Company: Benjamin Desha - Age: 32 - Height: 6' 1" - Born: NC, Chatham County - Trade: Laborer - Enlistment date: 30 Jul 1814 - Enlistment period: War - By whom: George Kennedy - Discharged: 30 Jun 1815 at Detroit.

Maurnon, William - Private - 19th Infantry - Company: William Gill.

Maxwell, James L. - Private - 19th Infantry - Company: John Chunn - Enlistment date: 27 Apr 1813 - Enlistment period: War - Died: 19 Aug 1813 - Bounty: BLW 26333-160-12 (Arkansas) - Comments: Land bounty to Thomas P. Maxwell, son & other heirs at law of James L. Maxwell.

Maxwell, William - Private - Rangers - Company: Samuel McCormick - Enlistment date: 8 Dec 1812 - Enlistment period: 1 Yr - Discharged: 7 Dec 1814 - Pension: Wife Rebecca, WC-29054, Old War IF-11033; served in Capt. McCormick's Company, US Rangers.

Mayall, William - Private - 28th Infantry - Company: Joseph Belt - Enlistment date: 8 May 1813 - Died: 19 Jan 1814, probably at Upper Sandusky, OH (Fort Ferree).

Mayer, Francis - Private - 26th Infantry - Other regiment: 19th Infantry - Age: 22 - Height: 6' - Born: MI, Wayne County, Detroit - Enlistment date: 4 Oct 1813 - Enlistment place: Detroit - Enlistment period: 5 Yrs - By whom: Lieutenant Lee - Comments: Re-enlisted.

Mayer, George - Private - 26th Infantry - Other regiment: 19th Infantry - Age: 17 - Height: 5' 8" - Born: MI, Wayne County, Detroit - Enlistment date: 15 Oct 1813 - Enlistment place: Detroit - Enlistment period: 5 Yrs - By whom: Lieutenant Lee - Comments: Re-enlisted.

Mayhew, Mitchell - 2nd Rifles - Company: Batteal Harrison - Age: 24 - Height: 5' 6" - Born: Lower Canada - Trade: Laborer - Enlistment date: 18 Jul 1814 - Enlistment place: Cincinnati - Enlistment period: War - By whom: Elias Langham - Discharged: 30 Jun 1815 at Detroit.

Maynard, Benjamin - Corporal - 17th Infantry - Company: David Holt - Enlistment date: 5 Jun 1812 - Enlistment period: 18 Mos - By whom: Richard Davenport - Died: 14 Aug 1813, probably in Ohio.

Mays, James - Private - 19th Infantry - Company: Wilson Elliott.

Mays, John - Private - 17th Infantry - Company: John Chunn - Age: 33 - Height: 5' 11 1/2" - Born: Pennsylvania - Enlistment date: 6 Nov 1813 - Enlistment place: Butler County, Hamilton - Enlistment period: War - By whom: George Stall - Died: 24 Dec 1814 on or about 24 Dec 1814, probably in New York - Pension: Heirs obtained half pay for five years in lieu of military bounty land.

Mays, John - Private - 2nd Light Dragoons - Company: Samuel Hopkins - Enlistment date: 28 Jul 1812 - Enlistment period: 18 Mos - By whom: Edward Conway - Died: 22 Feb 1813 - Comments: Died probably at Chillicothe.

Mazner, Edward - Private - 26th Infantry - Company: Samuel Swearingen - Enlistment date: 23 Jun 1813 - Enlistment period: 1 Yr.

McAuley, James - Sergeant - 19th Infantry - Company: Richard Talbott - Age: 25 - Height: 5' 10" - Born: PA, Cumberland County, Carlisle - Trade: Shoemaker - Enlistment date: 10 Jul 1814 - Enlistment place: Urbana - Enlistment period: War - By whom: William Baird - Discharged: 5 Jun 1815 at Chillicothe - Bounty: BLW 9976-160-12 (Illinois).

McBride, John - Private - 27th Infantry - Company: George Sanderson - Enlistment date: 28 Jun 1813 - Pension: Wife Mary Williams, Old War WF-16160 Rejected; served in Captain George Sanderson's Company, 27th Infantry; widow received five year half pay under the Act of 16 Apr 1816; soldier died in service. - Comments: Widow married Charles Carter and after this death married Jacob Spealman.

McBride, Samuel - Private - 7th Infantry - Company: Zachary Taylor - Enlistment date: 30 Jan 1812 - Enlistment period: 5 Yrs - By whom: Thomas Ramsey - Discharged: 30 Jan 1817.

McCabe, William - Corporal - 26th Infantry - Company: George Kesling - Other regiment: 25th Infantry - Enlistment date: 6 Jun 1813 - Discharged: 7 Jun 1814.

McCall, Montgomery - Sergeant - 26th Infantry - Company: Joel Collins - Enlistment date: 8 May 1813 - Enlistment period: 1 Yr.

McCallem, Alexander - Private - 19th Infantry - Age: 39 - Height: 5' 6 1/2" - Born: PA, Dauphin County - Enlistment date: 25 Jun 1814 - Enlistment place: Lancaster.

McCallister, Walter - Private - 19th Infantry - Company: Wilson Elliott - Other regiment: 25th Infantry - Age: 21 - Height: 5' 9" - Born: Pennsylvania - Enlistment date: 30 Jul 1812 - Enlistment place: Trumbull County, Warren - Enlistment period: 18 Mos - Discharged: 25 Jan 1814 - Pension: Old War IF-25282; served in Capt. Elliott's Company, 19th Infantry as a private - Comments: Wounded during the Battle of Mississinewa, IN, on 18 Dec 1812.

McCarty, Hyram - Private - 17th Infantry - Company: Caleb Holder - Age: 22 - Height: 5' 8" - Born: Virginia - Trade: Shoemaker - Enlistment date: 7 Jun 1814 - Enlistment period: War - By whom: Thomas McKnight - Discharged: 30 Jun 1815 at Detroit - Bounty: BLW 6565-160-12 (Illinois).

McCarty, John - Private - 19th Infantry - Company: Joel Collins - Age: 40 - Height: 5' 6" - Born: Ireland - Trade: Farmer - Enlistment date: 5 May 1814 - Enlistment period: War - Discharged: 22 Oct 1814 at Detroit on Surgeon's Certificate of Disability, mental defect - Bounty: BLW 17358-160-12 (Missouri).

McCarty, John - Private - 27th Infantry - Company: Absalom Martin - Comments: Served aboard the US Sloop Trippe on the Lake Erie Squadron.

McCarty, Joseph - Private - 19th Infantry - Company: Wilson Elliott - Other regiment: 17th Infantry.

McCashen, John - Private - Rangers - Company: Samuel McCormick - Enlistment date: 22 Nov 1813 - Enlistment period: 1 Yr - Discharged: 22 Nov 1814 - Pension: Wife Elizabeth, WO-29294, WC-22091; served in Captain Samuel McCormick's Company, OH militia, as a private.

McCave, Peter - Private - 26th Infantry - Company: Samuel Swearingen - Other regiment: 25th Infantry - Enlistment date: 1 May 1813 - Enlistment period: 1 Yr - Comments: Deserted 15 Mar 1815.

McChritick, John - 19th Infantry - Company: John Riddle - Died: 13 Sep 1814 - Comments: Buried in the War of 1812 Cemetery in Cheektowaga, Erie County, NY.

McClain, John - Private - 2nd Rifles - Company: Batteal Harrison - Age: 32 - Height: 5' 9" - Born: Pennsylvania - Trade: Blacksmith - Enlistment date: 3 Aug 1814 - Enlistment place: Cincinnati - Enlistment period: 5 Yrs - Discharged: 3 Aug 1819.

McClain, William - Private - 27th Infantry - Company: George Sanderson - Enlistment date: 16 Jun 1813.

McClary, Archibald - Private - 19th Infantry - Company: George Kesling - Age: 43 - Height: 5' 9" - Born: Pennsylvania - Trade: Farmer - Enlistment date: 27 Nov 1814 - Enlistment place: Lebanon - Enlistment period: War - By whom: George Kesling - Discharged: 27 Mar 1815 at Zanesville - Bounty: BLW 3486-160-12 (Illinois).

McCleary, Thomas - Private - 19th Infantry - Company: Richard Talbott - Age: 41 - Height: 5' 8" - Born: Pennsylvania - Trade: Farmer - Enlistment date: 1 Mar 1814 - Enlistment place: Franklin County - Enlistment period: 1 Yr - By whom: Robert Young - Died: 16 Sep 1814 at Lower Sandusky, OH (now Fremont, OH).

McClelland, William - Private - 19th Infantry - Company: James Herron - Other regiment: 17th Infantry - Enlistment date: 19 Apr 1813 - Enlistment period: War - By whom: Isaac Rieley - Died: 1813 at Detroit, MI - Bounty: BLW 26065-160-12 (Arkansas) - Comments: Land bounty to Robert McClellend, son & other heirs of William McClellend.

McClintock, John - Private - 19th Infantry - Died: 13 Sep 1814 at Williamsville, NY (General Hospital).

McCloud, Francis - Private - 27th Infantry - Company: George Sanderson - Enlistment date: 14 Jun 1813.

McCloud, Samuel - Private - 27th Infantry - Company: Joseph Cairns - Pension: Wife Mary Ann, WO-13083, WC-12012, SO-8307, SC-8818; served in Capt. Joseph Cairn's Company, 27th Infantry as a private; lived in OH and IN.

McClung, John - Private - 27th Infantry - Company: George Sanderson - Other regiment: 19th Infantry - Age: 21 - Height: 6' - Born: Maryland - Trade: Farmer - Enlistment date: 28 Apr 1813 - Enlistment period: 1 Yr - War - Discharged: 20 Jul 1815 at Detroit - Bounty: BLW 14145-160-12 (Illinois) - Comments: Re-enlisted at Detroit, MI.

McClure, Jacob - Private - 19th Infantry - Company: Wilson Elliott.

McClure, Thomas - Private - Rangers - Company: Samuel McCormick - Enlistment date: 30 Dec 1813 - Enlistment period: 1 Yr - Discharged: 30 Dec 1814 - Pension: Wife Sarah Nealy, WO-1448, WC-646; served as a private in Capt. Samuel McCormick's Company, US Mounted Rangers; married on 13 Jan 1813 near Troy, Miami County, OH; soldier died on 20 Dec 1855 in Larmars, OH; widow died about 1879; lived in Montgomery County, OH; widow lived in Bryan, Williams County, OH - Bounty: BLW 14128-160-50.

McClurg, Joseph - Private - 27th Infantry - Company: George Sanderson - Enlistment date: 17 Jun 1813 - Enlistment period: 1 Yr - Pension: Wife Agnes; SC-9549, WO-33090; served as a private in Capt. R. Gilmore's Company, OH Militia, and as a private in Capt. Geo. W. Saunderson's Company, 27th Infantry - Bounty: BLW 9408-80-50, BLW 39334-80-55.

McComb, Jacob - Private - 27th Infantry - Company: Isaac Van Horne - Pension: Wife Polly, SO-4453, SC-5671, WO-23017, WC-28240; served as a private in Capt. Van Horn's Company, 27th Infantry.

McComb, John - Private - 19th Infantry - Company: Carey Trimble - Other regiment: 17th Infantry - Age: 24 - Height: 6' 1/2" - Born: Delaware - Trade: Farmer - Enlistment date: 4 Apr 1814 - Enlistment place: Cleveland - Enlistment period: War - By whom: Ebenezer Benedict - Discharged: 20 Oct 1815 at Newport, KY - Bounty: BLW 15848-160-12 (Illinois).

McCombs, John - Private - 27th Infantry - Company: Alexander Hill.

McCome, John - Private - 17th Infantry - Age: 25 - Height: 5' 9" - Born: Pennsylvania - Enlistment date: 29 May 1814 - Enlistment place: Columbiana County, Middleton - By whom: William Shang.

McConkey, John - Private - 27th Infantry - Company: George Sanderson - Enlistment date: 31 May 1813.

McConkin, Samuel - Private - 2nd Artillery - Company: Daniel Cushing - Born: New Jersey.

McConky, Alexander - Private - 2nd Artillery - Company: Daniel Cushing - Other regiment: Corps of Artillery - Age: 34 - Height: 5' 10" - Born: Ireland, Cleaveland - Trade: Farmer - Enlistment date: 8 Jul 1812 - Enlistment place: Chillicothe - Enlistment period: 5 Yrs - Discharged: 8 Jul 1817.

McConky, David - Private - 17th Infantry - Company: Harris Hickman - Other regiment: 3rd Infantry - Age: 28 - Height: 5' 7" - Born: Maryland - Trade: Tailor - Enlistment date: 9 Feb 1814 - Enlistment place: Steubenville - Enlistment period: 5 Yrs - By whom: Isaac Rieley - Comments: Deserted 1 Sep 1815.

McConky, Samuel - Private - 2nd Artillery - Company: Daniel Cushing.

McConley, William - Private - 2nd Artillery - Company: Stanton Sholes - Enlistment date: 22 May 1813 - Enlistment place: Cleveland - Enlistment period: 5 Yrs - By whom: Stanton Sholes.

McConnell, David - Sergeant - 26th Infantry - Company: Samuel Swearingen - Age: 24 - Height: 6' - Born: Pennsylvania - Enlistment date: 11 May 1813 - Enlistment period: 1 Yr - Discharged: 11 May 1814.

McConnell, John - Private - 27th Infantry - Company: George Sanderson - Enlistment date: 15 Jun 1813.

McConnell, John - Private - 26th Infantry - Company: Joel Collins - Enlistment date: 16 Aug 1813 - Enlistment period: 1 Yr.

McCord, Alexander - Private - 27th Infantry - Company: George Sanderson - Enlistment date: 8 Jun 1813 - Comments: Served aboard the US Schooner Tigress on the Lake Erie Squadron.

McCord, Joseph - Private - 17th Infantry - Company: Martin Hawkins - Age: 37 - Height: 6' - Born: Maryland - Trade: Farmer - Enlistment date: 28 Apr 1814 - Enlistment period: War - By whom: George Beall - Bounty: BLW 8321-160-12 (Illinois).

McCord, William - Corporal - 26th Infantry - Company: Samuel Swearingen - Enlistment date: 8 Jul 1813 - Enlistment period: 1 Yr - Comments: Prisoner of War on Parole, captured at Detroit, MI, 16 Aug 1812.

McCorkle, Isaac - Private - 17th Infantry - Age: 18 - Height: 5' 11" - Born: Virginia - Trade: Laborer - Enlistment date: 6 Sep 1814 - Enlistment period: 5 Yrs - By whom: James Campbell.

McCormick, John - Private - 27th Infantry - Born: Ireland - Enlistment date: 5 Apr 1814 - Enlistment place: St. Clairsville.

McCoy, Duncan - Private - 19th Infantry - Company: Richard Talbott - Age: 48 - Height: 5' 11" - Born: New Jersey - Trade: Shoemaker - Enlistment date: 15 Feb 1814 - Enlistment place: Chillicothe or Circleville - Enlistment period: 1 Yr - By whom: Josiah Brady - Discharged: 14 Feb 1815 at Erie, PA.

McCoy, James - Corporal - 19th Infantry - Age: 20 - Height: 5' 11" - Born: VA, Shenandoah County - Enlistment date: 22 Jun 1812 - Enlistment period: 5 Yrs.

McCoy, John - Private - 27th Infantry - Company: Isaac Van Horne - Comments: Served aboard the US Brig Niagara on the Lake Erie Squadron.

McCoy, William - Private - 19th Infantry - Company: Wilson Elliott.

McCrillis, Thomas - Private - 19th Infantry - Company: George Kesling - Other regiment: 3rd Infantry - Age: 30 - Height: 5' 9" - Born: Ireland - Trade: Shoemaker - Enlistment date: 11 Feb 1815 - Enlistment place: Zanesville - Enlistment period: 5 Yrs.

McCrum, Michael - Private - 19th Infantry - Company: Isaac Van Horn - Pension: Wife Catherine, WO-3616; served in Capt. Van Horne's Company, 19th Infantry as a private.

McCullen, Sheldon - Private - 17th Infantry - Age: 20 - Height: 5' 3" - Born: Virginia - Trade: Laborer - Enlistment date: 24 Jun 1814 - Enlistment period: War - By whom: William Shang.

McCullock, John - Private - 2nd Artillery - Company: Daniel Cushing.

The Enlisted Men

McCullough, Silas - Private - 17th Infantry - Company: David Holt - Age: 20 - Height: 5' 3" - Born: Virginia - Trade: Laborer - Enlistment date: 24 Jun 1814 - Enlistment place: Cambridge - Enlistment period: War - By whom: Ensign Strang - Discharged: 4 Jun 1815 at Chillicothe - Bounty: BLW 14305-160-12 (Illinois).

McCullum, Hugh - Private - 26th Infantry - Company: George Kesling - Other regiment: 25th Infantry - Enlistment date: 7 Apr 1813 - Discharged: 7 Apr 1814 - Pension: Wife Chloe, WO-15027, WC-24559, SO-11837, SC-16162; served in Capt. Kesling's Company, 26th Infantry as a private.

McCune, David - Private - 19th Infantry - Company: Carey Trimble - Age: 33 - Height: 5' 2 1/2" - Enlistment date: 4 Feb 1814 - Enlistment place: Lower Sandusky (now Fremont, OH) - Enlistment period: 1 Yr - Discharged: 25 Feb 1815.

McCune, Jacob - Private - 19th Infantry - Company: James Herron - Other regiment: 25th Infantry - Enlistment date: 15 Sep 1812 - Enlistment period: 18 Mos.

McCune, Jacob - Private - 19th Infantry - Company: Wilson Elliott - Other regiment: 17th Infantry - Comments: Waiter to Brigadier General Duncan McArthur.

McCurdy, James - Private - 2nd Artillery - Company: Daniel Cushing - Age: 33 - Height: 5' 9" - Born: NJ, Morris County - Trade: Shoemaker - Enlistment date: 17 Jun 1812 - Enlistment period: 5 Yrs - Discharged: 8 Nov 1813 at Detroit, disease of hip joint - Bounty: BLW 7233-160-12 (Illinois).

McDonald, Stephen - Private - 27th Infantry - Comments: Prisoner of War on Parole, captured at Detroit, MI, 16 Aug 1812.

McDonald, Thomas - Private - 17th Infantry - Company: David Holt - Age: 36 - Height: 5' 8" - Born: Scotland or Ireland - Trade: Laborer - Enlistment date: 20 Apr 1814 - Enlistment place: Adams County, West Union - Enlistment period: War - By whom: William Featherstone - Discharged: 31 May 1815 at Chillicothe - Bounty: BLW 11439-160-12 (Illinois).

McDougal, Robert - Private - 17th Infantry - Company: Henry Crittenden - Other regiment: 3rd Infantry - Age: 24 - Height: 5' 7" - Born: VA, Berkeley County (now WV) - Trade: Farmer - Enlistment date: 1 Jan 1814 - Enlistment period: 5 Yrs - By whom: Samuel Booker - Discharged: 1 Jan 1819.

McElroy, Thomas - Private - 26th Infantry - Company: George Kesling - Enlistment date: 14 May 1813 - Enlistment period: 1 Yr.

McElvain, Robert - Private - 2nd Artillery - Company: Stanton Sholes - Other regiment: Corps of Artillery - Age: 22 - Height: 5' 11" - Born: PA, Cumberland County - Trade: Farmer - Enlistment date: 26 May 1813 - Enlistment place: Cleveland - Enlistment period: 5 Yrs - By whom: Stanton Sholes - Discharged: 26 May 1818 at Detroit- Pension: SC-6801; served in Captain Stanton Sholes's Company, OH militia.

McElwayne, John - Private - 27th Infantry - Company: George Sanderson - Enlistment date: 1 Jun 1813.

McFadden, James - Private - 19th Infantry - Company: George Kesling - Other regiment: 17th Infantry - Age: 20 - Height: 5' 7" - Born: Pennsylvania - Trade: Saddler - Enlistment date: 25 Dec 1814 - Enlistment place: Cambridge - Enlistment period: War - By whom: Neal McFadden - Discharged: 27 Mar 1815 at Zanesville - Bounty: BLW 708-320-14 (Arkansas).

McGarvey, Moses (or Morris) - Private - 27th Infantry - Company: George Sanderson - Joel Collins - Other regiment: 19th Infantry - Age: 19 - Height: 5' 10" - Born: Pennsylvania - Trade: Farmer - Enlistment date: 1 Jun 1813 - Discharged: 20 Jul 1815 at Detroit - Bounty: BLW 6049-160-12 - Comments: Served aboard the US Schooner Scorpion on the Lake Erie Squadron.

McGill, James - Private - 26th Infantry - Company: William Puthuff - Other regiment: 19th Infantry then 17th Infantry - Age: 28 - Height: 5' 8" - Born: Pennsylvania - Trade: Fuller - Enlistment date: 5 May 1813 - Enlistment place: Chillicothe - Enlistment period: 1 Yr - War - By whom: Carey Trimble - Discharged: 5 Jun 1815 at Chillicothe - Bounty: BLW 16306-160-12 (Illinois).

McGill, James M. - Private - Rangers - Age: 26 - Height: 6' - Born: Kentucky - Trade: Farmer - Enlistment date: 5 May 1813 - Enlistment period: War - Discharged: 31 Aug at Detroit.

McGillam, John M. (or McGilland) - Fifer - 26th Infantry - Company: William Puthuff - Enlistment date: 9 Aug 1813 - Enlistment period: 1 Yr - Died: 15 Feb 1814 at Sandwich, UC (now Windsor, Ontario).

McGinnis, John - Private - 17th Infantry - Company: David Holt - Age: 35 - Height: 5' 11" - Born: Ireland - Trade: Laborer - Enlistment date: 4 Mar 1814 - Enlistment place: Chillicothe - Enlistment period: War - By whom: John Campbell - Discharged: 31 May 1815 at Chillicothe.

McGonegal, Charles - Private - 19th Infantry - Company: James Herron - Enlistment date: 19 Aug 1812 - Enlistment period: 18 Mos.

McGonigal, James - Private - 26th Infantry - Company: Joel Collins - Other regiment: 19th Infantry - Enlistment date: 5 Sep 1813 - Enlistment period: 1 Yr - Discharged: 5 Sep 1814.

McGowan, Levi - Private - 19th Infantry - Company: Carey Trimble - Other regiment: 17th Infantry - Age: 22 -

Height: 5' 7" - Born: Maryland - Trade: Breeches maker - Enlistment date: 23 Feb 1814 - Enlistment place: Franklin County, Franklinton - Enlistment period: 1 Yr - Discharged: 21 Apr 1815.

McGowen, James - 27th Infantry - Pension: Old War IF-16290 Rejected, served in the 27th Infantry.

McGuffin, George - Private - 2nd Artillery - Company: Daniel Cushing - Enlistment period: 18 Mos – Enlisted date: 26 Aug 1813 - Died: 28 Nov 1813 at Detroit.

McGuire, Thomas - Private - 19th Infantry - Company: Richard Talbott - Age: 56 - Height: 5' 6" - Born: Ireland or England - Trade: Weaver - Enlistment date: 26 Apr 1814 - Enlistment place: Springfield (or Redding) - Enlistment period: 5 Yrs - By whom: Lieutenant Johns - Discharged: 9 Nov 1815 at Newport, KY, in consequence of old age.

McHenney, Samuel - Private - 19th Infantry - Bounty: BLW 2537-160-12 (Illinois).

McHenry, Samuel - Private - 17th Infantry - Company: Henry Crittenden - Age: 25 - Height: 5' 11 1/2" - Born: KY, Lincoln County - Trade: Shoemaker - Enlistment date: 1 Feb 1814 - Enlistment period: War - By whom: John Cochran - Discharged: 9 Jun 1815 at Chillicothe - Bounty: BLW 6048-160-12 (Arkansas).

McIntire, Robert - Corporal - 17th Infantry - Company: Harris Hickman - Age: 22 - Height: 5' 9" - Born: PA, Luzerne County - Trade: Laborer - Enlistment date: 18 Mar 1814 - Enlistment place: Chillicothe - Enlistment period: War - By whom: Batteal Harrison - Discharged: 9 Jun 1815 at Chillicothe - Pension: Old War IF-16316 Rejected; served in Capt. Hickman's Company, 17th Infantry as a corporal - Bounty: BLW 5694-160-12 (Illinois).

McIntyre, Joseph - Private - 17th Infantry - Age: 19 - Height: 5' 7" - Born: Pennsylvania - Enlistment date: 7 Nov 1814 - Enlistment place: Steubenville - Enlistment period: War - By whom: William Featherstone - Comments: Deserter from the 22nd Regiment of US Infantry.

McKee, John - Private - 26th Infantry - Company: George Kesling - Other regiment: 25th Infantry - Enlistment date: 1 May 1813 - Enlistment period: 1 Yr - Discharged: 1 May 1814.

McKee, John - Private - 19th Infantry - Age: 36 - Height: 5' 11" - Born: Pennsylvania - Enlistment date: 15 Aug 1815 - Enlistment place: New Lisbon - Enlistment period: War - By whom: Wynkoop Warner - Died: 22 Aug 1814 - Bounty: BLW 26476-160-12 (Arkansas) - Comments: Died at New Lisbon, OH, as a recruit; land bounty to Alfred McKee, son & other heirs at law of John McKee.

McKee, John - Private - 17th Infantry - Company: Caleb Holder - Age: 40 - Height: 5' 4 1/2" - Born: Ireland - Enlistment date: 26 Jul 1814 - Enlistment place: Cambridge - Enlistment period: 5 Yrs - By whom: William Shang.

McKee, Joseph - Private - 17th Infantry - Company: Henry Crittenden - Age: 16 - Height: 5' 7" - Born: OH, Hamilton County - Trade: Tailor - Enlistment date: 25 Mar 1813 - Enlistment period: War - By whom: Lieutenant Johnston - Discharged: 9 Jun 1815 at Chillicothe - Bounty: BLW 16010-160-12 (Illinois).

McKee, William - Private - 17th Infantry - Company: Henry Crittenden - Other regiment: 3rd Infantry - Age: 52 - Height: 5' 10" - Born: VA, Berkeley County (now WV) - Trade: Laborer - Enlistment date: 28 Dec 1813 - Enlistment place: Cincinnati - Enlistment period: 5 Yrs - By whom: William Blanchard.

McKenny – see McKinney, Samuel

McKey, David - Private - 26th Infantry - Company: George Kesling - Enlistment date: 30 May 1813 - Enlistment period: 1 Yr.

McKinley, Thomas - Private - 17th Infantry - Company: Harris Hickman - Age: 26 - Height: 5' 10 1/2" - Born: Pennsylvania - Trade: Miller - Enlistment date: 6 Apr 1814 - Enlistment place: Marietta - Enlistment period: War - By whom: John Milligan - Discharged: 30 Jun 1815 at Chillicothe - Bounty: BLW 9820-160-12 (Illinois).

McKinney, Andrew - Private - 26th Infantry - Company: Samuel Swearingen - Enlistment date: 17 Jun 1813 - Enlistment period: 1 Yr - Died: 30 Aug 1813.

McKinney, Anthony W. - Private - Rangers - Company: Samuel McCormick - Age: 20 - Height: 5' 10" - Born: Kentucky - Trade: Farmer - Enlistment date: 25 Oct 1813 - Enlistment period: 1 Yr - Discharged: 25 Oct 1814 at Fort Malden, UC - Pension: Wife Catherine, WC-24042, SC-13803; served in Captain Samuel McCormick's Company, US Rangers, as a private; lived in IN and IA - Comments: Wounded on 30 September 1814 and taken prisoner on 30 Aug 1814.

McKinney, Samuel - Private - 19th Infantry - Company: Lt John McElvain - Age: 20 - Height: 5' 9 1/2" - Born: Pennsylvania - Trade: Farmer - Enlistment date: 10 Apr 1814 - Enlistment place: Chillicothe - Enlistment period: War - By whom: Charles Cissna - Discharged: 6 Jun 1815 at Chillicothe - Bounty: BLW 2537-160-12 (Illinois).

McKinney, William - Private - 26th Infantry - Company: Joel Collins - Other regiment: 19th Infantry - Enlistment date: 26 Sep 1813 - Enlistment period: 1 Yr - Discharged: 26 Sep 1814.

The Enlisted Men

McKinsey, John - Private - 19th Infantry - Age: 30 - Height: 5' 6 1/2" - Born: MD, Allegeny County - Enlistment date: 2 Jul 1812 - Enlistment period: 5 Yrs.

McKinsey, John - Private - 2nd Rifles - Company: Batteal Harrison - Age: 32 - Height: 5' 5 1/2" - Born: NY, Long Island - Trade: Farmer - Enlistment date: 21 Jul 1814 - Enlistment place: Cincinnati - Enlistment period: War - By whom: Elias Langham - Discharged: 30 June 1815 at Detroit.

McKnight, Alpheus - Private - 19th Infantry - Company: Wilson Elliott - Other regiment: 17th Infantry - Age: 18 - Height: 5' 8" - Born: CT, Hartford County, Suffield - Trade: Farmer - Enlistment date: 14 Jul 1812 - Enlistment place: Trumbull County, Warren - Enlistment period: 5 Yrs - By whom: Wilson Elliott.

McKnight, Anthony - Private - 19th Infantry - Company: Richard Talbott - Other regiment: 17th Infantry - Age: 40 - Height: 5' 11" - Born: PA, Dauphin County - Trade: Farmer - Enlistment date: 11 Mar 1814 - Enlistment place: Franklin County - Enlistment period: 1 Yr - By whom: Robert Young - Discharged: 5 Jun 1815 at Chillicothe - Bounty: BLW 13763-160-12 (Missouri) - Comments: Re-enlisted 19 Jun 1814 for War.

McKnight, John - Musician - 19th Infantry - Company: George Kesling - Age: 40 - Height: 5' 8" - Born: Virginia or Maryland - Trade: Tailor - Enlistment date: 12 May 1814 - Enlistment place: Chillicothe or Circleville - Enlistment period: War - By whom: Josiah Brady - Discharged: 10 Jun 1815 at Zanesville - Bounty: BLW 14620-160-12 (Illinois).

McLaughlin, David - Private - 19th Infantry - Company: Richard Talbott - Age: 21 - Height: 6' 4" - Born: Kentucky - Trade: Cooper - Enlistment date: 19 May 1814 - Enlistment place: Montgomery County - Enlistment period: War - By whom: Philip Price - Discharged: 5 Jun 1815 at Chillicothe - Bounty: BLW 25229-160-12 (Arkansas).

McLaughlin, George - Private - 2nd Artillery - Company: Stanton Sholes - Other regiment: Corps of Artillery - Age: 42 - Height: 5' 2" - Born: PA, Chester County - Trade: Carpenter - Enlistment date: 22 May 1813 - Enlistment place: Cleveland - Enlistment period: 5 Yrs - By whom: Stanton Sholes - Discharged: 23 May 1818.

McLaughlin, James Sr - Musician - 17th Infantry - Age: 31 - Height: 5' 9 1/2" - Born: Maryland - Enlistment date: 18 Aug 1813 - By whom: John Mershon.

McLeonold, Shase - Private - 17th Infantry - Age: 34 - Height: 5' - Born: Ireland - Trade: Laborer - Enlistment date: 22 Apr 1814 - Enlistment period: War - By whom: William Featherstone.

McMahon, Cornelius - Private - 19th Infantry - Company: Wilson Elliott - Other regiment: 25th Infantry - Age: 40 - Height: 5' 10 3/4" - Born: Ireland - Trade: Farmer - Enlistment date: 5 Aug 1812 - Enlistment place: Ohio - Enlistment period: 5 Yrs - Discharged: 24 Jul 1815 at Greenbush, NY; wounded by a musket ball at Fort Meigs, OH, on 5 May 1813.

McMahon, James - Private - 19th Infantry - Company: Wilson Elliott.

McMahon, James - Private - 2nd Artillery - Company: Daniel Cushing - Age: 31 - Height: 5' 8 1/2" - Born: Ireland - Enlistment date: 11 Jul 1812 - Enlistment place: Canton - Enlistment period: 5 Yrs.

McMannis, Joseph - Private - 19th Infantry - Company: Joel Collins - Age: 19 - Height: 5' 10" - Born: Ohio - Trade: Laborer - Enlistment date: 24 Mar 1814 - Enlistment place: Detroit - Enlistment period: War - By whom: Samuel Coleman.

McMillen, John - Private - 19th Infantry - Bounty: BLW 18364-160-12 (Illinois).

McMillen, John - Private - 27th Infantry - Age: 19 - Height: 5' 8" - Born: Pennsylvania - Enlistment date: 7 May 1814 - Enlistment place: Warren County.

McMorrow, William - Fifer - 17th Infantry - Company: William Adair - Age: 20 - Height: 5' 6 1/4" - Born: Ireland - Trade: Tailor - Enlistment date: 14 Feb 1815 - Enlistment period: 5 Yrs - By whom: John Reeves - Comments: Deserted at Herculaneum, Mississippi Territory, on 17 Jun 1815.

McMullen, John - Private - 27th Infantry - Company: Alexander Hill - Other regiment: 19th Infantry - Age: 19 - Height: 5' 10" - Born: Pennsylvania - Trade: Blacksmith - Enlistment date: 10 Mar 1814 - Enlistment place: Warren County - Enlistment period: War - By whom: Ebenezer Benedict - Discharged: 6 Jun 1815 at Chillicothe.

McMullen, Loe (or Soc) - Private - 19th Infantry - Company: George Kesling - Age: 32 - Height: 5' 7" - Born: Pennsylvania - Trade: Farmer - Enlistment date: 26 Nov 1814 - Enlistment place: Cincinnati - Enlistment period: War - By whom: William Baird - Discharged: 27 Mar 1815 at Zanesville - Bounty: BLW 27280-160-42.

McMullin, William - Private - 26th Infantry - Company: William Puthuff - Enlistment date: 12 May 1813 - Enlistment period: 1 Yr.

McMurray, Samuel - Private - 17th Infantry - Age: 25 - Height: 5' 11" - Born: KY, Lincoln County - Trade: Shoemaker - Enlistment date: 17 Feb 1814 - Enlistment place: Chillicothe - Enlistment period: War - By whom: Hugh Moore.

McNeal, Samuel - Private - 26th Infantry - Company: George Kesling - Enlistment date: 1 May 1813 - Enlistment period: 1 Yr - Comments: Served aboard the US Schooner Porcupine on the Lake Erie Squadron.

McNeeley, George - Private - 19th Infantry - Company: Richard Talbott - Age: 37 - Height: 5' 6 1/2" - Born: Ireland - Trade: Farmer - Enlistment date: 26 Feb 1814 - Enlistment place: Franklin County - Enlistment period: War - By whom: Robert Young - Died: 20 Feb 1815; drown at Erie, PA - Bounty: BLW 24533-160-12 (Arkansas) - Comments: Land bounty to John McNeely & other heirs at law of George McNeeley.

McNutt, Alexander - Private - 1st Rifles - Company: Edward Wadsworth - Age: 32 - Height: 5' 7 1/2" - Born: Ireland, County Donegal - Trade: Farmer - Enlistment date: 1 Aug 1813 - Enlistment place: Cincinnati - Enlistment period: War - Discharged: 12 Jun 1815 at Buffalo, NY - Pension: Old War IF-27166; served in Capt. Wadsworth's company, 1st Rifles.

McNutt, James - Private - 26th Infantry - Company: George Kesling - Other regiment: 25th Infantry - Enlistment date: 23 Apr 1813 - Enlistment period: 1 Yr - Discharged: 23 Apr 1814.

McNutt, John - Private - 26th Infantry - Enlistment date: 23 Apr 1813 - Enlistment period: 1 Yr.

McNutt, Robert - Private - 19th Infantry - Company: Wilson Elliott.

McPeck, Thomas - Corporal - 19th Infantry - Company: Joel Collins - Age: 21 - Height: 5' 5" - Born: Ireland - Trade: Shoemaker - Enlistment date: 18 Mar 1814 - Enlistment place: Detroit - Enlistment period: War - By whom: Wynkoop Warner - Discharged: 20 Jul 1815 at Detroit.

McRay, Allison - Private - 24th Infantry - Other regiment: 1st Rifles - Age: 23 - Height: 5' 9" - Born: VA, Alexandria - Trade: Printer - Enlistment date: 10 Aug 1812 - Enlistment period: 18 Mos - Discharged: 5 Jun 1815 at Buffalo, NY - Bounty: BLW 15359-160-12 (Illinois) - Comments: Re-enlisted for the war by Capt. Thomas Ramsey, 28 Feb 1814 at Cincinnati, OH.

McSerely, James - Private - 26th Infantry - Company: Joel Collins - Enlistment date: 18 Sep 1813 - Enlistment period: 1 Yr.

McSign, John - Private - 26th Infantry - Company: George Kesling - Enlistment date: 26 May 1813 - Enlistment period: 1 Yr - By whom: George Kesling.

McSurley, James - Private - 19th Infantry - Discharged: 17 Sep 1814.

McTuney, Samuel - Private - 19th Infantry - Company: Lt John McElvain.

McWade, Arthur - Private - 26th Infantry - Company: Samuel Swearingen - Enlistment date: 10 Jun 1813 - Enlistment period: 1 Yr - Died: 14 Dec 1813, probably at Sackets Harbor, NY.

McWilliams, Alexander - Private - 19th Infantry - Company: William Gill - Age: 32 - Height: 5' 6" - Born: Ireland - Trade: Weaver - Enlistment date: 17 Aug 1814 - Enlistment place: Franklin County, Franklinton - Enlistment period: War - By whom: Orren Granger - Discharged: 5 Jun 1815 at Chillicothe - Bounty: BLW 12514-160-12 (Illinois).

Mead, Jeremiah (or Jere) - Sergeant - 2nd Artillery - Company: Daniel Cushing - Height: 5' 9 1/2" - Born: Connecticut - Enlistment date: 2 Jul 1812 - Enlistment place: New Philadelphia - Enlistment period: 5 Yrs - Died: 22 Sep 1813 at Fort Meigs - Bounty: BLW 25501-160-12 (Arkansas) - Comments: Land bounty to Walter Mead & other heirs at law of Jere Mead.

Meddles, Joseph - Private - 19th Infantry - Company: Wilson Elliott - Age: 22 - Height: 5' 9" - Born: Pennsylvania - Enlistment date: 22 Jul 1812 - Enlistment period: 18 Mos.

Meek, Samuel - Private - 19th Infantry - Company: David Holt - Other regiment: 17th Infantry - Age: 21 - Height: 5' 8" - Born: Pennsylvania - Enlistment date: 7 Jul 1812 - Enlistment place: St. Clairsville - Enlistment period: 5 Yrs - By whom: Samuel Booker - Pension: Wife Sarah, WC-3595; served in Captains Holt and Chunn Companies, 17th Infantry.

Meeks, John – Private - 19th Infantry - Company: William Gill - Age: 21 - Height: 5' 7" - Born: Pennsylvania - Trade: Farmer - Enlistment date: 26 Jul 1814 - Enlistment place: New Lisbon - Enlistment period: War - By whom: Wynkoop Warner - Discharged: 5 Jun 1815 at Chillicothe - Bounty: BLW 16346-160-12 (Illinois).

Meldrum, John H. - Sergeant - 2nd Artillery - Company: Daniel Cushing - Discharged: 7 Nov 1813 - Pension: Wife Jane, WC-10040; served in Captain Daniel Cushing's Company, US Artillery, as a sergeant.

Mellon, Jacob - Private - 19th Infantry - Company: Carey Trimble - Other regiment: 17th Infantry - Enlistment date: 12 Feb 1814 - Enlistment period: 1 Yr - Discharged: 12 Feb 1815.

Mellon, Levi - Private - 19th Infantry - Company: Carey Trimble - Age: 23 - Height: 5' 8" - Born: New Jersey - Trade: Blacksmith - Enlistment date: 3 Apr 1814 - Enlistment place: Ross County, Adelphi - Enlistment period: War - By whom: William Gill - Discharged: 6 Jun 1815 at Chillicothe - Bounty: BLW 20564-160-12 (Missouri).

Mellow, Joshua - Private - 27th Infantry - Company: George Sanderson - Enlistment date: 4 May 1813.

The Enlisted Men

Meloy, Seth - Private - 19th Infantry - Company: James Herron - Enlistment date: 30 Apr 1813 - Enlistment period: War.

Melton, John - Private - 27th Infantry - Company: Joseph Cairns - Other regiment: 19th Infantry - Pension: SC-6477, served in Captain Joseph Carines' Company, 27th and 19th Infantries as a private.

Melvin, John - Private - 19th Infantry - Company: David Holt - Other regiment: 17th Infantry - Age: 22 - Height: 5' 10" - Born: Pennsylvania - Trade: Laborer - Enlistment date: 27 Apr 1814 - Enlistment place: Franklin County, Franklinton - Enlistment period: War - By whom: John Cochran.

Mengro, Joseph - Private - 19th Infantry - Enlistment date: Mar 1814 - Enlistment period: War - By whom: Lieutenant Cainey - Comments: Prisoner of War (Halifax, NS), captured on 2 Sep 1814; released 10 Apr 1815; reportedly killed during the Battle of Chippewa, UC.

Mercil, John - Private - 19th Infantry - Company: James Herron.

Merrill, Hosea - Private - 27th Infantry - Company: George Sanderson - Enlistment date: 13 Aug 1813.

Merris, Calvin - Private - 19th Infantry - Company: Asabael Nearing.

Merrit, James - Private - 2nd Rifles - Company: Batteal Harrison - Age: 32 - Height: 5' 11" - Born: North Carolina - Trade: Farmer - Enlistment date: 17 Aug 1814 - Enlistment place: Cincinnati - Enlistment period: War - By whom: Elias Langham - Discharged: 30 Jun 1815 at Detroit - Bounty: BLW 19472-160-12 (Missouri).

Merryon, James - Private - 19th Infantry - Company: William Gill.

Messer, John - 2nd Rifles - Company: Batteal Harrison - Age: 31 - Height: 6' - Born: PA, Monroe County, German Valley - Trade: Blacksmith - Enlistment date: 21 Jun 1814 - Enlistment place: Zanesville - Enlistment period: 5 Yrs - By whom: William Dougherty - Discharged: 29 Apr 1817 for insanity.

Messings, John - Corporal - 17th Infantry - Company: Harris Hickman - Age: 40 - Height: 5' 10" - Born: MD, Montgomery County, Fredericktown - Trade: Blacksmith - Enlistment date: 9 Apr 1814 - Enlistment place: Chillicothe - Enlistment period: War - By whom: David Carney - Discharged: 9 Jun 1815 at Chillicothe - Bounty: BLW 14023-160-12 (Illinois).

Mick, James - Private - 19th Infantry - Age: 21 - Height: 5' 8" - Born: PA, Washington County - Enlistment date: 7 Jul 1812 - Enlistment period: 5 Yrs.

Miles, Samuel - Private - 17th Infantry - Company: John Chunn - Other regiment: 3rd Infantry - Age: 21 - Height: 5' 8 1/2" - Born: Kentucky - Trade: Farmer - Enlistment date: 17 Dec 1814 - Enlistment period: 5 Yrs - By whom: James Campbell - Discharged: 17 Dec 1819 - Pension: SC-2546; served in Capt. Chunn's Company, 3rd Infantry as a private; lived in KY - Bounty: BLW 893-320-14 (Arkansas).

Milhollon, John - Corporal - 26th Infantry - Company: Samuel Swearingen - Enlistment date: 15 Jun 1813 - Enlistment period: 1 Yr.

Millan, George - Private - 1st Rifles - Company: Thomas Ramsey - Age: 25 - Height: 5' 11" - Born: OH, Marietta or Hamilton County - Trade: Farmer - Enlistment date: 16 Apr 1814 - Enlistment place: Cincinnati - Enlistment period: War - By whom: Thomas Ramsey - Discharged: 5 Jun 1815 at Buffalo, NY - Bounty: BLW 11783-160-12 (Illinois) - Comments: Prisoner of War (Quebec, LC), captured at Fort Erie, UC, 17 Sep 1814, released 13 Mar 1815.

Millburn, Andrew - Private - 27th Infantry - Company: Alexander Hill - Other regiment: 19th Infantry - Age: 20 - Height: 5' 11" - Born: VA, Frederick County, London - Trade: Laborer - Enlistment date: 5 Apr 1814 - Enlistment place: New Lisbon - Enlistment period: War - By whom: John Williby - Discharged: 6 Jun 1815 at Chillicothe - Pension: Wife Elizabeth, WO-34119, WC-27117, Old War WF-16512 Rejected, served in Capt. Cass's Company and in Lt. John McElvain's Company, 19th US Infantry as a private - Bounty: BLW 19077-160-12 (Illinois).

Miller, Andrew - Private - 27th Infantry - Company: George Sanderson - Enlistment date: 5 Jun 1813.

Miller, Benjamin T. - Private - 27th Infantry - Company: Isaac Van Horne - Other regiment: 19th Infantry - Pension: SC-7402, Old War IC-2554 File 1289; served in Captains Applegate's and Van Horne's Companies, 27th Infantry; lived in NY - Comments: Prisoner of War, exchanged 25 Apr 1814.

Miller, Chauncey - Sergeant - 27th Infantry - Company: George Sanderson - Enlistment date: 4 May 1813.

Miller, David - Private - 19th Infantry - Company: Wilson Elliott.

Miller, George - Private - 2nd Rifles - Age: 33 - Height: 5' 6 1/2" - Born: New York - Trade: Laborer - Enlistment date: 6 Sep 1814 - Enlistment place: Cincinnati - Enlistment period: War - By whom: Elias Langham - Discharged: 30 Jun 1815 at Detroit.

Miller, Isaac R. - Fifer - 17th Infantry - Company: James Herron - Age: 34 - Height: 5' 8" - Born: Pennsylvania - Trade: Blacksmith - Enlistment date: 15 Jan 1814 - Enlistment place: Xenia - Enlistment period: War - By whom: Ensign Shay - Bounty: BLW 120-320-14 (Arkansas).

Miller, Jacob - Private - 19th Infantry - Comments: Prisoner of War, exchanged 25 Apr 1814.

Miller, Jacob - Private - 2nd Rifles - Company: Benjamin Desha - Age: 28 - Height: 5' 7 1/2" - Born: Pennsylvania - Trade: Laborer - Enlistment date: 6 Jan 1815 - Enlistment place: Cincinnati - Enlistment period: War - By whom: William Pritchard - Died: 30 Jun 1815 - Bounty: BLW 22124-160-12 (Arkansas).

Miller, James - Private - 19th Infantry - Company: George Kesling - Bounty: BLW 8990-160-12 (Illinois).

Miller, James - Private - 19th Infantry - Age: 29 - Height: 5' 7 1/2" - Born: MD, Baltimore County - Trade: Carpenter - Enlistment date: 27 Aug 1813 - Enlistment period: War - By whom: Isaac Reiley - Discharged: 8 May 1815 - Comments: Prisoner of War (Quebec), captured at Fort Niagara, NY, 19 Dec 1813; exchanged 11 May 1814.

Miller, James - Private - 26th Infantry - Company: Samuel Swearingen - Enlistment date: 22 Jul 1813 - Enlistment period: 1 Yr.

Miller, John - Private - 26th Infantry - Company: George Kesling - Other regiment: 2nd Light Dragoons - Enlistment date: 24 May 1813 - Enlistment period: 1 Yr - Died: 3 Nov 1813, probably at Sackets Harbor, NY.

Miller, John - Private - 19th Infantry - Age: 40 - Height: 5' 9" - Born: PA, York County - Enlistment date: 13 Aug 1814 - Enlistment place: Xenia.

Miller, John - 1st Rifles - Company: Thomas Ramsey - Age: 17 - Height: 5' 7" - Born: OH, Hamilton County, Cincinnati - Trade: Laborer - Enlistment date: 13 Apr 1812 - Enlistment place: Cincinnati - Enlistment period: 5 Yrs - By whom: Thomas Ramsey - Discharged: 30 Apr 1817 at Bellefontaine, MO.

Miller, Joseph - Private - 1st Infantry - Company: Hugh Moore - Other regiment: 3rd Infantry - Age: 33 - Height: 5' 10" - Born: PA, Washington County - Trade: Farmer - Enlistment date: 26 Aug 1810 - Enlistment place: Cincinnati - Enlistment period: 5 Yrs - Comments: Enlistment time extended due to desertions.

Miller, Nicholas - 2nd Rifles - Company: Batteal Harrison - Age: 35 - Height: 5' 7 1/2" - Born: PA, Lancaster County - Trade: House carpenter - Enlistment date: 28 Jun 1814 - Enlistment place: Cincinnati - Enlistment period: 5 Yrs - By whom: Elias Langham.

Miller, Peter - Private - 17th Infantry - Company: Harris Hickman - Age: 29 - Height: 5' 6 1/2" - Born: Ireland - Trade: Laborer - Enlistment date: 18 Apr 1814 - Enlistment period: War - By whom: George Stall - Discharged: 9 Jun 1815 at Chillicothe - Bounty: BLW 3142-160-12 (Illinois).

Miller, Peter - Private - 19th Infantry - Company: James Herron - Enlistment date: 17 Sep 1812 - Pension: Old War IF-13924; served in Lt. Featherstone's Company, US Infantry as a private.

Miller, Peter F. - Drummer - 1st Infantry - Company: Horatio Stark - Age: 22 - Height: 5' 6" - Born: Prussia, Amden - Trade: Saddler - Enlistment date: 1 May 1812 - Enlistment place: Cincinnati - Enlistment period: 5 Yrs - By whom: Thomas Ramsey.

Miller, Samuel - Private - 17th Infantry - Company: Angus Langham - Age: 21 - Height: 5' 8 1/2" - Born: Kentucky - Enlistment date: 17 Dec 1814 - Enlistment place: Adams County, West Union - Enlistment period: 5 Yrs - By whom: James Campbell.

Millihill, Richard - Private - 26th Infantry - Company: George Kesling.

Mills, Samuel - Private - 17th Infantry - Enlistment date: 17 Dec 1814 - Enlistment place: Adams County, West Union - Enlistment period: 5 Yrs.

Milton, Isaias - Private - 26th Infantry - Company: William Puthuff - Enlistment date: 22 Aug 1813 - Enlistment period: 1 Yr - Died: 1 Feb 1814 at Sandwich, UC (now Windsor, Ontario).

Milton, William - Private - 1st Rifles - Company: Thomas Ramsey - Age: 19 - Height: 5' 6" - Born: Kentucky - Trade: Laborer - Enlistment date: 12 Apr 1814 - Enlistment place: Butler County, Middleton - Enlistment period: War - By whom: Ensign Albright - Discharged: 8 Jun 1815 near Buffalo, NY - Bounty: BLW 3141-160-12.

Minor, Moseby - Drummer - 17th Infantry - Company: David Holt - Enlistment date: 29 May 1812 - Enlistment period: 18 Mos - By whom: Richard Davenport - Died: 20 Apr 1813, probably in Ohio.

Minor, Richard - 2nd Rifles - Age: 30 - Height: 5' 6 1/2" - Born: England - Trade: Shoemaker - Enlistment date: 3 Jul 1814 - Enlistment place: Chillicothe or Circleville - Enlistment period: War - By whom: John Swearingen - Discharged: 30 Jun 1815 at Detroit.

Missings, John - Private - 19th Infantry - Age: 40 - Height: 5' 10" - Born: MD, Montgomery County - Enlistment date: 9 Apr 1814 - Enlistment place: Chillicothe - Enlistment period: War - By whom: David Carney.

Mitchell, James - Private - 19th Infantry - Company: James Herron - Enlistment date: 29 Oct 1812.

Mitchell, Richard - Private - 26th Infantry - Company: George Kesling - Enlistment date: 26 May 1813 - Enlistment period: 1 Yr.

Mitchler, David - Private - 17th Infantry - Company: Harris Hickman - Age: 37 - Height: 5' 11" - Born: North Carolina - Trade: Blacksmith - Enlistment date: 15 Mar 1814 - Enlistment period: War - By whom: George

Stall - Discharged: 9 Jun 1815 at Chillicothe - Bounty: BLW 9286-160-12 (Illinois).

Mitten, Esaias - Private - 26th Infantry - Company: William Puthuff - Enlistment date: 22 Aug 1813 - Enlistment period: 1 Yr - Died: 1 Feb 1814.

Mitten, George - Private - 26th Infantry - Company: William Puthuff - Enlistment date: 3 Sep 1813 - Enlistment period: 1 Yr.

Moles, James - Private - 19th Infantry - Company: Harris Hickman - Other regiment: 17th Infantry - Age: 24 - Height: 5' 8" - Born: VT, Chittenden County - Enlistment date: 24 Mar 1814 - Enlistment place: Franklin County, Franklinton - Enlistment period: War - Died: 26 Jan 1815 at Williamsville, NY (General Hospital).

Molona, Simon - Private - 1st Rifles - Enlistment date: 1 Sep 1814 - Enlistment period: 5 Yrs - By whom: Thomas Ramsey - Comments: Prisoner of War (Halifax, NS), captured at Fort Erie, UC, 17 Sep 1814; released 10 Apr 1815.

Monday, John M. - Private - 26th Infantry - Company: William Puthuff - Enlistment date: 17 May 1813 - Enlistment period: 1 Yr - Died: 11 Dec 1813 at Detroit.

Mondy, Jacob - Private - 26th Infantry - Company: George Kesling - Other regiment: 25th Infantry - Enlistment date: 1 Jun 1813 - Discharged: 1 Jun 1814.

Monroe, George - Private - 27th Infantry - Company: Joseph Cairns - Pension: SC-18173; served in Capt. Carnes' Company, 27th Infantry.

Monteeth, Jacob - Private - 19th Infantry - Company: William Gill - Age: 21 - Height: 5' 9 1/2" - Born: PA, Lancaster County - Trade: Blacksmith - Enlistment date: 18 May 1814 - Enlistment period: War - By whom: John Spencer - Discharged: 5 Jun 1815 - Bounty: BLW 15737-160-12 (Illinois).

Montgomery, John - Private - 17th Infantry - Company: James Meade - Age: 28 - Height: 5' 10" - Born: Pennsylvania - Trade: Laborer - Enlistment period: War - By whom: Thomas Riddle - Pension: Wife Mary, WC-30530, SC-5342; served in Captains Meade's, Bradford's and Goode's Companies, 17th Infantry.

Montgomery, John - Private - 17th Infantry - Company: David Holt - Age: 24 - Height: 5' 9" - Trade: Laborer - Enlistment date: 20 May 1813 - By whom: Thomas Riddle.

Montgomery, William - Private - 19th Infantry - Company: James Herron - Enlistment date: 14 May 1813 - Enlistment place: Cincinnati - Enlistment period: War.

Moone, Thomas - Private - 19th Infantry - Company: William Gill.

Moor, David - Private - 26th Infantry - Company: George Kesling - Other regiment: 25th Infantry.

Moore, Abraham - Private - 26th Infantry - Company: George Kesling - Enlistment date: 22 Apr 1813 - Enlistment period: 1 Yr - Comments: Prisoner of War, exchanged 25 Apr 1814.

Moore, Daniel - Corporal - 27th Infantry - Company: Alexander Hill - Other regiment: 19th Infantry - Age: 36 - Height: 5' 9 1/2" - Born: PA, Chester County - Trade: Wheelwright - Enlistment date: 11 Jan 1814 - Enlistment place: Newark - Enlistment period: War - By whom: John Spencer - Discharged: 5 Jun 1815 at Chillicothe - Bounty: BLW 8846-160-12 (Illinois).

Moore, George - Private - 26th Infantry - Company: Samuel Swearingen - Other regiment: 25th Infantry - Enlistment date: 12 Jun 1813 - Enlistment period: 1 Yr - Discharged: 12 Jun 1814.

Moore, James - Sergeant - 19th Infantry - Company: Richard Talbott - Other regiment: 17th Infantry then 3rd Infantry - Age: 26 - Height: 5' 9" - Born: Pennsylvania - Trade: Farmer - Enlistment date: 9 Jul 1814 - Enlistment place: Greenville - Enlistment period: 5 Yrs - By whom: Richard Talbott - Discharged: 9 Jul 1819.

Moore, James - 19th Infantry - Company: John Chunn - Other regiment: 25th Infantry - Pension: SC-9791; served in Capt. Chunn's Company, 19th Infantry and in Capt. Burbridge's Company, 25th Infantry.

Moore, John - Private - 19th Infantry - Company: Wilson Elliott - Age: 22 - Height: 6' 1" - Born: PA, Washington County - Enlistment date: 11 Jul 1812 - Enlistment period: 5 Yrs.

Moore, John - Private - 19th Infantry - Age: 21 - Height: 5' 10" - Born: Maryland - Enlistment date: 8 Aug 1812 - Enlistment period: 18 Mos.

Moore, John H. (or Jonathan) - Private - 26th Infantry - Company: William Puthuff - Other regiment: 25th Infantry - Age: 32 - Enlistment date: 7 Jun 1813 - Discharged: 7 Jun 1814.

Moore, Joseph - Private - 27th Infantry - Company: William Gill - Pension: Wife Rhoda R., WC-6491; served in Capt. Gill's Company, 27th Infantry as a private.

Moore, Nathan - Private - 26th Infantry - Company: George Kesling - Enlistment date: 11 Jun 1813 - Enlistment period: 1 Yr - By whom: George Kesling.

Moore, Nathaniel - Private - 19th Infantry - Company: James Herron - Enlistment date: 26 Sep 1812 - Enlistment period: 18 Mos.

Moore, Robert - Private - 26th Infantry - Company: Joel Collins - Enlistment date: 27 Aug 1813 - Enlistment period: 1 Yr.

Moore, Samuel - Sergeant - 26th Infantry - Company: Samuel Swearingen - Other regiment: 19th Infantry then 3rd Infantry - Enlistment date: 19 Apr 1813 - Enlistment period: 1 Yr - Discharged: 18 Oct 1813 - Pension: Old War IF-16576 Rejected; served in Capt. Chunn's Company, 3rd Infantry - Comments: Prisoner of War on Parole, captured at Detroit, MI, 16 Aug 1812.

Moore, Thomas - Private - 26th Infantry - Company: Joel Collins - Enlistment date: 14 Sep 1813 - Enlistment period: 1 Yr - Died: 16 Dec 1813, probably at Detroit.

Moore, Thomas - Private - 19th Infantry - Other regiment: 17th Infantry then 3rd Infantry - Age: 23 - Height: 5' 6 1/2" - Born: PA, Lancaster County - Trade: Mason - Enlistment date: 8 Aug 1814 - Enlistment place: Steubenville - Enlistment period: 5 Yrs - By whom: James Blair - Discharged: 8 Aug 1819.

Moore, Thomas P. - Private - 19th Infantry - Company: George Kesling - Age: 24 - Height: 5' 8" - Born: Pennsylvania - Trade: Tanner - Enlistment date: 14 Feb 1815 - Enlistment place: Xenia - Enlistment period: War - By whom: Robert Smith - Discharged: 27 Mar 1815 at Zanesville - Bounty: BLW 77-320-14 (Illinois).

Moore, William - Private - 2nd Rifles - Company: Benjamin Johnson - Age: 22 - Height: 5' - Born: Pennsylvania - Trade: Brick maker - Enlistment date: 8 Sep 1814 - Enlistment place: Cincinnati - Enlistment period: War - By whom: Elias Langham - Discharged: 30 Jun 1815 at Detroit - Bounty: BLW 20154-160-12 (Missouri).

Moore, William - Private - 19th Infantry - Company: William Gill - Age: 21 - Height: 5' 10" - Trade: Hatter - Enlistment date: 5 Oct 1814 - Enlistment period: War - By whom: Nehemiah Gregory - Discharged: 5 Jun 1815 at Chillicothe - Bounty: BLW 1569-160-12 (Illinois).

Moorhead, Obadiah - Musician - 17th Infantry - Age: 43 - Height: 5' 8" - Born: Pennsylvania - Trade: School master - Enlistment date: 16 Jan 1815 - Enlistment place: Adams County, West Union - Enlistment period: War - By whom: James Campbell.

Morefoot, Samuel - Private - 27th Infantry - Company: Alexander Hill - Other regiment: 19th Infantry - Age: 38 - Height: 6' 1 1/2" - Born: PA, Washington County - Trade: Shoemaker - Enlistment date: 5 May 1814 - Enlistment period: War - By whom: John Spencer - Discharged: 5 Jun 1815 at Chillicothe - Bounty: BLW 9944-160-12 (Illinois).

Morells, Anthony - Private - 1st Rifles - Age: 24 - Height: 5' 4" - Born: LA, Orleans Parish, New Orleans - Trade: Soldier - Enlistment date: 30 May 1814 - Enlistment place: Cincinnati - Enlistment period: 5 Yrs - By whom: Lieutenant Miller - Discharged: 30 May 1819 - Bounty: BLW 22549-160-12 (Arkansas).

Morgan, David - Private - 19th Infantry - Age: 30 - Height: 5' 8 1/2" - Born: New York - Enlistment date: 25 Apr 1814Enlistment place: Upper Canada, Sandwich - Enlistment period: War - By whom: Robert Smith.

Morgan, Jesse - Private - 17th Infantry - Company: David Holt - Killed: 5 May 1813.

Morgan, Moses - Sergeant - 26th Infantry - Company: William Puthuff - Other regiment: 19th Infantry - Age: 25 - Height: 5' 10" - Born: Virginia - Trade: Joiner - Enlistment date: 12 Jul 1813 - Enlistment period: 1 Yr - Discharged: 27 Mar 1815 at Zanesville - Bounty: BLW 8711-160-12 (Illinois) - Comments: Re-enlisted on 26 May 1814 at Cincinnati or Urbana with Lieutenant Baird.

Morgan, Thomas - First Sergeant - 2nd Artillery - Company: Daniel Cushing - Enlistment date: 22 Aug 1812 - Enlistment period: 18 Mos - Pension: Old War IF-16535 Rejected, served in Capt. Cushing's Company, 2nd Artillery, as a sergeant - Bounty: BLW 21439-160-12 (Missouri).

Morgan, William - Private - 27th Infantry - Company: Alexander Hill.

Morgan, William - Private - 19th Infantry - Company: Carey Trimble - Enlistment date: 14 May 1814 - Enlistment period: War - Died: Jan 1815 at Buffalo, NY.

Mosgrove - see John Musgrove

Morris, Thomas - Private - 19th Infantry - Company: Angus Langham - Age: 26 - Height: 5' 10" - Born: Pennsylvania - Trade: Farmer - Enlistment date: 23 May 1813 - Enlistment period: 5 Yrs - Killed: 5 Jul 1814 during the Battle of Chippewa, UC.

Morris, William B. - Private - 19th Infantry - Company: Asabael Nearing - Enlistment date: 8 Mar 1813 - Enlistment period: War - Died: Jul 1813 at Sandusky (now Fremont, OH).

Morris, Zadock - Private - 26th Infantry - Company: Joel Collins - Enlistment date: 2 Sep 1813 - Enlistment period: 1 Yr.

Morris, Zadock - Private - 19th Infantry - Company: William Gill - Other regiment: 3rd Infantry - Age: 19 - Height: 5' 6" - Born: VA, Monongahela County (now West Virginia) - Trade: Laborer - Enlistment date: 15 Aug 1814 - Enlistment place: Xenia - Enlistment period: 5 Yrs - By whom: Robert Smith - Discharged: 15 Aug 1819 at Fort Howard, WI.

Morrison, James - Private - 19th Infantry - Company: William Gill - Age: 21 - Height: 5' 7" - Born: Virginia - Trade: Farmer - Enlistment date: 3 Sep 1814 - Enlistment period: War - Comments: Deserted.

The Enlisted Men

Morrison, Robert - Private - 19th Infantry - Company: James Herron - Died: 2 Nov 1813 - Pension: Heirs obtained half pay for five years in lieu of military bounty land.

Morrow, Lewis - Private - 26th Infantry - Company: Joel Collins - Enlistment date: 5 Nov 1813 - Enlistment period: 1 Yr - By whom: Robert Smith

Morse, Amos - Private - 19th Infantry - Company: William Gill - Age: 45 - Height: 5' 11 1/4" - Born: Connecticut - Trade: Carpenter - Enlistment date: 1 Apr 1814 - Enlistment period: 1 Yr - Discharged: 2 Apr 1815.

Morse, Ira - 27th Infantry - Company: George Sanderson - Pension: Wife Laura D., WC-4475; served as a 3rd Lieutenant in Capt. G. Sanderson's Company, 27th Infantry.

Morse, Nehemiah - Private - 27th Infantry - Company: Alexander Hill - Other regiment: 19th Infantry then 17th Infantry - Age: 19 - Height: 5' 6" - Born: PA, Washington County - Trade: Blacksmith - Enlistment date: 23 Feb 1814 - Enlistment place: Zanesville - Enlistment period: War - By whom: Henry Northrup - Discharged: 6 Jun 1815 at Chillicothe - Bounty: BLW 6176-160-12 (Illinois).

Morton, Washington - Private - 17th Infantry - Company: Martin Hawkins - Other regiment: 3rd Infantry - Age: 21 - Height: 5' 10" - Born: Cincinnati - Trade: Tanner - Enlistment date: 3 Feb 1813 - Enlistment place: Cincinnati - Enlistment period: War - By whom: Philip Price - Discharged: 30 Jun 1815 at Detroit - Pension: Wife Rebecca, WC-33762; served in Captains Hawkins and Herron Companies, 17th Infantry as a private. - Bounty: BLW 14328-160-12 (Illinois) - Comments: Wounded.

Mose, James - Private - 27th Infantry - Company: George Sanderson - Enlistment date: 9 Apr 1813 - Died: 2 Aug 1813, executed at Fort Seneca (now Old Fort, OH).

Moslander, Sheron - Private - 19th Infantry - Company: James Herron - Enlistment date: 26 Sep 1812 - Enlistment period: 18 Mos.

Moslin, John - Private - 17th Infantry - Age: 17 - Height: 4' 6" - Born: Virginia - Enlistment date: 26 Aug 1814 - Enlistment place: Cambridge - By whom: William Shang.

Mount, James - Private - 1st Infantry - Company: Thomas Hamilton - Other regiment: 3rd Infantry - Age: 21 - Height: 5' 8" - Born: KY, Scott County - Trade: Farmer - Enlistment date: 4 Apr 1814 - Enlistment place: Cincinnati - Enlistment period: 5 Yrs - By whom: Laurence Taliaferro - Comments: Deserted 12 Nov 1815, probably at Detroit, MI.

Mounts, John - Private - 26th Infantry - Company: Samuel Swearingen - Pension: Wife Rachel, Old War WF-11828; served in Capt. Swearingen's company, 26th Infantry as a private, Ohio resident.

Mours, Henry - Private - 19th Infantry - Age: 25 - Height: 6' 1/2" - Born: Pennsylvania - Enlistment date: 22 Mar 1814 - Enlistment place: Chillicothe - Enlistment period: War.

Mowry, John - Private - 27th Infantry - Company: Alexander Hill - Age: 48 - Height: 5' 10" - Born: RI, Newport County - Enlistment date: 17 Dec 1813 - Enlistment place: Ravenna - By whom: John Reeves.

Mowry, Stephen - Private - 27th Infantry - Company: Alexander Hill.

Moyer, David - Corporal - 26th Infantry - Company: Joel Collins - Other regiment: 19th Infantry - Age: 31 - Height: 5' 10" - Born: New Jersey - Trade: Miller - Enlistment date: 26 Aug 1813 - Enlistment period: 1 Yr - Discharged: 20 Jul 1815 at Detroit - Bounty: BLW 14748-160-12 (Illinois) - Comments: Re-enlisted in 19th Infantry at Sandwich, UC, by Ensign Smith, during the war enlistment.

Moyers, William - Private - 26th Infantry - Company: William Puthuff - Enlistment date: 22 May 1183 - Enlistment period: 1 Yr - Comments: Wounded.

Muir, Thomas - Private - 17th Infantry - Age: 26 - Height: 6' - Born: VA, Frederick County - Trade: Laborer - Enlistment date: 5 Mar 1813 - Enlistment place: Franklin County, Franklinton - Enlistment period: War - By whom: Stephen Lee - Bounty: BLW 4960-160-12 (Arkansas).

Mullen, Samuel - Private - 17th Infantry - Company: Martin Hawkins - Other regiment: 3rd Infantry - Age: 22 - Height: 5' 3 1/2" - Born: OH, Columbia - Trade: Laborer - Enlistment date: 10 Jan 1813 - Enlistment place: Lebanon - Enlistment period: 5 Yrs - By whom: Lieutenant Morrow - Comments: Died, drowned near Fort Dearborn, IL, on 10 Dec 1817 (now Chicago, IL).

Mullen, William - Sergeant - 26th Infantry - Company: George Kesling - Enlistment date: 18 May 1813 - Enlistment period: 1 Yr - By whom: George Kesling - Died: 12 Jan 1814 - Pension: Wife Mary; served in Capt. George Kesling's Company, 26th Infantry as a sergeant - Bounty: BLW 27211-160-50.

Muller, Charles - Private - 19th Infantry - Company: James Herron - Enlistment date: 17 Dec 1812 - Enlistment period: 5 Yrs.

Mullica, Jesse - Private - 19th Infantry - Company: Asabael Nearing - Other regiment: 17th Infantry then 3rd Infantry - Age: 26 - Height: 5' 10" - Born: NJ, Gloucester County - Trade: Potter - Enlistment date: 28 Feb 1813 - Enlistment period: 5 Yrs - Discharged: 29 Dec 1817 at Fort Howard, WI.

Mullinix, Elijah - Private - 19th Infantry - Company: Lt Charles Cass - Enlistment date: 8 Nov 1813 - Enlistment period: War - Killed: 5 Jul 1814 during the Battle of Chippewa, UC - Bounty: BLW 22312-160-12 (Arkansas) - Comments: Land bounty to John Mullinix, brother & other heirs at law of Elijah Mullinix.

Mullinix, James - Private - 19th Infantry - Company: Lt Charles Cass - Enlistment date: 6 Nov 1813 - Enlistment period: War - Died: 5 Jul 1814, killed during the Battle of Chippewa, UC - Bounty: BLW 22311-160-12 (Arkansas) - Comments: Land bounty to John Mullinix, brother & other heirs at law of James Mullinix.

Munn, James - Private - 26th Infantry - Company: Samuel Swearingen - Enlistment date: 24 Jun 1813 - Enlistment period: 1 Yr.

Munsey, Jesse - Private - 2nd Artillery - Company: Daniel Cushing - Other regiment: Corps of Artillery - Age: 26 - Height: 6' - Born: Delaware - Trade: Armorer - Enlistment date: 8 Jun 1812 - Enlistment place: Chillicothe - Enlistment period: 5 Yrs - By whom: Samuel Kercheval - Discharged: 27 Jun 1817.

Murphy, Daniel - Fife Major - 17th Infantry - Company: Staff - Other regiment: 3rd Infantry - Age: 21 - Height: 5' 8 1/2" - Born: Ireland - Trade: Laborer - Enlistment date: 27 Jun 1814 - Enlistment place: Chillicothe - Enlistment period: 5 Yrs - By whom: John Cochran.

Murphy, James - Private - 7th Infantry - Company: Thornton Posey - Age: 25 - Born: Ohio - Trade: Carpenter - Enlistment date: 5 Mar 1814 - Enlistment period: War - Discharged: 25 Jul 1815 - Bounty: BLW 22179-160-12 (Arkansas) - Comments: Prisoner of War, captured at Prairie du Chien, IL; discharged at Bellefontaine, MO.

Murphy, Patrick - Private - 19th Infantry - Company: William Gill - Age: 40 - Height: 6' - Born: Ireland - Trade: Farmer - Enlistment date: 25 Aug 1814 - Enlistment place: Zanesville - Enlistment period: War - By whom: Neal McFadden.

Murphy, William - Private - 19th Infantry - Enlistment date: 16 Apr 1813 - Enlistment place: Cincinnati - Enlistment period: War.

Murphy, William - Private - 26th Infantry - Company: Samuel Swearingen - Enlistment date: 23 Jul 1813 - Enlistment period: 1 Yr - By whom: Hugh Moore - Died: 26 Dec 1813, probably died at Detroit, MI - Comments: Prisoner of War.

Murphy, William - Private - 2nd Rifles - Company: Batteal Harrison - Age: 40 - Height: 5' 4 1/2" - Born: Ireland - Trade: Laborer - Enlistment date: 5 Sep 1814 - Enlistment place: Cincinnati – Enlistment period: War - By whom: Elias Langham - Discharged: 30 Jun 1815 at Detroit.

Murray, William - Private - 2nd Artillery - Company: Daniel Cushing - Bounty: BLW 24700-160-12 (Arkansas).

Musgrove, John - Private - 2nd Artillery - Company: Daniel Cushing - Enlistment date: 26 Mar 1813 - Enlistment period: 5 Yrs - By whom: Alexander Meek - Died: 15 Dec 1813 at Detroit (hospital) - Bounty: BLW 25952-160-12 (Arkansas) - Comments: Land bounty to Aaron Mosgrove, brother & other heirs at law of John Mosgrove, alias Musgrove.

Muzzy, Benjamin A. - Private - 19th Infantry - Age: 21 - Height: 5' 9" - Born: Virginia - Trade: Farmer - Enlistment date: 15 Jan 1815 - Enlistment place: Franklin County, Franklinton - Enlistment period: War - By whom: Orren Granger - Discharged: 27 Mar 1815 at Zanesville - Bounty: BLW 983-320-14 (Arkansas).

Myers, Eden - Private - 19th Infantry - Company: Wilson Elliott.

Myers, Henry - 27th Infantry - Company: Isaac Van Horne - Pension: SC-9405, served in Capt. Isaac Van Horn's Company, 27th Infantry.

Myers, Jacob (Meirs) - Private - 27th Infantry - Company: Joseph Cairns - Pension: Wife Elizabeth, WC-25725; served in Capt. Joseph Cairne's Company, 27th Infantry, as a private, resided in OH and IA.

Myres, Michael - Private - 19th Infantry - Age: 36 - Height: 5' 11" - Born: PA, Lancaster County - Enlistment date: 12 Apr 1814 - Enlistment place: Chillicothe - By whom: David Carney.

Nante, John B. - Private - 19th Infantry - Company: James Herron.

Naper, William - Private - 27th Infantry - Company: George Sanderson - Enlistment date: 19 May 1813.

Neibling, John - Sergeant - 27th Infantry - Company: George Sanderson - Enlistment date: 23 Apr 1813.

Nelson, John - Musician - 17th Infantry - Age: 21 - Height: 5' 11" - Born: New York - Trade: Laborer - Enlistment date: 26 Jul 1814 - Enlistment period: War - By whom: John Reeves - Discharged: 18 Apr 1815 at Chillicothe.

Nesbit, John - Sergeant - 19th Infantry - Company: Angus Langham - Other regiment: 17th Infantry then 3rd Infantry - Age: 21 - Height: 6' - Born: Ireland, County Down, Drumore - Trade: Reed maker - Enlistment date: 10 Jul 1812 - Enlistment place: Gallipolis - Enlistment period: 5 Yrs - By whom: Ensign Morgan - Discharged: 10 Jul 1817 - Comments: Served aboard the US Schooner Porcupine on the Lake Erie Squadron; prisoner of War, captured at Frenchtown, MI.

Nesbitt, Andrew - Private - 26th Infantry - Company: William Puthuff - Enlistment date: 9 Aug 1813 - Discharged: 23 May 1814 - Died: 10 Dec 1813, probably at Sackets Harbor, NY.

Neville, Henry - Private - 28th Infantry - Company: Joseph Belt - Age: 18 - Height: 5' 6" - Born: Kentucky or Ohio - Enlistment date: 17 Mar 1814 - Enlistment place: Detroit - Enlistment period: War - By whom: Thomas Griffith - Comments: Enlisted for one year on 15 Jul 1813; re-enlisted.

Newell, Raison - Private - 2nd Rifles - Company: Benjamin Desha - Age: 30 - Height: 5 ' 9 1/2" - Born: Pennsylvania - Trade: Laborer - Enlistment date: 5 Jan 1815 - Enlistment place: Cincinnati - Enlistment period: War - By whom: William Pritchard - Discharged: 30 Jun 1815 at Detroit.

Newkirk, John - Private - 19th Infantry - Company: Richard Talbott - Age: 37 - Height: 5' 8 1/2" - Born: PA, Fayette County - Trade: Stone mason - Enlistment date: 23 Apr 1814 - Enlistment place: Springfield (or Redding) - Enlistment period: War - By whom: Abijah Johns - Discharged: 5 Jun 1815 at Chillicothe - Bounty: BLW 8883-160-12 (Illinois).

Newkirk, Robinson - Private - 26th Infantry - Company: Samuel Swearingen - Enlistment date: 25 May 1813 - Enlistment period: 1 Yr.

Newland, George W. - Private - Rangers - Age: 19 - Height: 5' 10" - Born: Kentucky - Trade: Farmer - Enlistment period: War - Discharged: 31 Aug 1815 at Detroit.

Newman, George - Private - 19th Infantry - Company: George Kesling - Other regiment: 3rd Infantry - Age: 34 - Height: 6' 1 1/4" - Born: Pennsylvania - Trade: Farmer - Enlistment date: 2 Dec 1814 - Enlistment place: Cincinnati - Enlistment period: 5 Yrs - By whom: William Baird - Comments: Deserted at Detroit, MI, on 4 Apr 1814.

Newman, Howard - Private - 17th Infantry - Company: Martin Hawkins - Other regiment: 3rd Infantry - Age: 21 - Height: 5' 4" - Born: NJ, Monmouth County - Trade: Farmer - Enlistment date: 31 Oct 1812 - Enlistment place: Hillsbury - Enlistment period: 5 Yrs - By whom: John Reeves - Discharged: 31 Oct 1817.

Newman, William - Private - Rangers - Company: Samuel McCormick - Age: 21 - Height: 5' 8" - Born: Delaware - Trade: Farmer - Enlistment date: 30 Nov 1813 - Enlistment period: 1 Yr - Discharged: 19 Nov 1814 at Fort Malden, UC.

Nice, William - Private - 19th Infantry - Company: John Chunn - Enlistment date: 3 Mar 1813 - Enlistment period: 5 Yrs - Died: 20 Jun 1813 - Bounty: BLW 26217-160-12 (Arkansas) - Comments: Land bounty to Cornelius Nice, father & only heir at law of William Nice.

Nicewinter, Frederick - Private - 19th Infantry - Company: Carey Trimble - Other regiment: 17th Infantry - Age: 25 - Height: 5' 8" - Born: Pennsylvania - Trade: Carpenter - Enlistment date: 2 Apr 1814 - Enlistment place: Columbus - Enlistment period: War - By whom: Avery Buttles - Discharged: 6 Jun 1815 at Chillicothe - Bounty: BLW 9837-160-12 (Illinois).

Nicewinter, Joseph - Private - 19th Infantry - Company: Lt John McElvain.

Nicholas, William - Private - 2nd Rifles - Company: Benjamin Desha - Age: 28 - Height: 5' 8" - Born: NJ, Monmouth County - Trade: Bloomer - Enlistment date: 23 May 1814 - Enlistment place: Highland County, Hillsboro - Enlistment period: 5 Yrs - By whom: Joseph McClain - Died: 23 May 1819 - Bounty: BLW 22301-160-12 (Arkansas).

Nichols, Joseph - Private - 1st Rifles - Company: Thomas Ramsey - Age: 23 - Height: 6' 1" - Born: PA, Philadelphia County - Trade: Farmer - Enlistment date: 10 Feb 1814 - Enlistment place: Cincinnati - Enlistment period: 5 Yrs - By whom: Thomas Ramsey - Discharged: 20 Feb 1819 at Bellefontaine, MO - Bounty: BLW 23878-160-12 (Arkansas).

Nicholson, Andrew - Private - 2nd Artillery - Company: Daniel Cushing - Enlistment date: 8 Sep 1812 - Enlistment period: 18 Mos - Died: 15 May 1813 at Fort Meigs.

Nicholson, George - Private - 19th Infantry - Age: 19 - Height: 5' 5 1/4" - Born: PA, Fayette County - Enlistment date: 27 Jul 1812 - Enlistment period: 5 Yrs.

Nickerson, Isachar - Private - 27th Infantry - Company: George Sanderson - Enlistment date: 19 Jun 1813.

Nickerson, Joseph - Private - 19th Infantry - Company: Carey Trimble - Other regiment: 17th Infantry - Age: 19 - Height: 5' 8" - Born: Pennsylvania - Trade: Hatter - Enlistment date: 18 Apr 1814 - Enlistment place: Franklin County, Franklinton - Enlistment period: War - By whom: John McElvain - Discharged: 6 Jun 1815 at Chillicothe - Pension: Wife Mary, SC-5437; served in Capt. Trimble's and Lt. McElvain's Company, 19th Infantry - Bounty: BLW 9960-160-12 (Illinois).

Nickles, James - Private - 19th Infantry - Company: Joel Collins - Age: 19 - Height: 5' 5" - Born: Massachusetts - Trade: Laborer - Enlistment date: 15 Mar 1814 - Enlistment place: Detroit - Enlistment period: War - By whom: Samuel Coleman - Discharged: 20 Jul 1815 at Detroit - Pension: SC-17778, SO-20760; served in Captain Collins' Company, 19th Infantry as a private - Bounty: BLW 7180-160-12 (Illinois).

Nicum, John - Private - 17th Infantry - Company: Harris Hickman - Age: 40 - Height: 5' 10" - Born: Maryland - Enlistment date: 23 Apr 1814 - Enlistment place: Franklin County - By whom: John Simons - Died: 2 Nov

1814 - Bounty: BLW 23025-160-12 (Arkansas) - Comments: Land bounty to John Nicum & other heirs at law of John Nicum.

Nida, Philip - Private - 17th Infantry - Company: David Holt - Age: 28 - Height: 5' 11" - Born: Pennsylvania - Trade: Laborer - Enlistment date: 28 Apr 1814 - Enlistment period: War - By whom: George Bryant - Discharged: 4 Jun 1815 at Chillicothe.

Nolen, Barnabas - Private - 26th Infantry - Other regiment: 25th Infantry - Age: 19 - Height: 5' 8" - Born: MD, Frederick County - Trade: Laborer - Enlistment date: 12 Feb 1813 - Enlistment place: Ohio - Enlistment period: War By whom: Lieutenant Lee - Discharged: 17 May 1815 at Sackets Harbor, NY.

Norman, William - Private - 19th Infantry - Company: Wilson Elliott - Enlistment date: 13 Oct 1813 - Enlistment period: 18 Mos.

Norris, Richard - Private - 26th Infantry - Company: Samuel Swearingen - Age: 21 - Height: 5' 6 1/2" - Enlistment date: 25 Jun 1813 - Enlistment period: 1 Yr - Discharged: 19 Jun 1814 - Comments: Served aboard the US Schooner Ariel on the Lake Erie Squadron.

North, Zachariah - Corporal - 19th Infantry - Company: Wilson Elliott - Enlistment date: 21 Jun 1812 - Enlistment period: 5 Yrs - Killed: 5 May 1813 - Pension: Heirs obtained half pay for five years in lieu of military bounty land.

Norton, John - Private - 2nd Artillery - Company: Daniel Cushing - Enlistment date: 18 Sep 1812 - Enlistment period: 18 Mos - Discharged: 12 May 1813 at Fort Meigs, OH, for disability - Pension: Old War IF-26313, served in Capt. Cushing's Company, Regiment of Artillery, as a private.

Norton, Robert - Private - 17th Infantry - Company: Caleb Holder - Age: 35 - Height: 6' 1" - Born: Pennsylvania - Trade: Laborer - Enlistment date: 23 Feb 1814 - Enlistment period: War - By whom: William Leavitt - Discharged: 30 Jun 1815 at Detroit - Bounty: BLW 18608-160-12 (Illinois).

Nute, Jonathan - Private - 1st Rifles - Company: Edward Wadsworth - Other regiment: 5th Infantry - Age: 24 - Height: 5' 9" - Born: NH, Strafford County, North Durham - Trade: Laborer - Enlistment date: 5 Mar 1813 - Enlistment place: Fort Meigs - Enlistment period: 5 Yrs - By whom: George Croghan - Comments: Transferred to 5th Infantry, 31 Oct 1815; deserted from Detroit, MI, 24 Nov 1815.

O'Bryan, James - 2nd Rifles - Age: 30 - Height: 5' 9" - Born: Ireland - Enlistment date: 26 Jul 1814 - Enlistment place: Cincinnati.

O'Dion, Alexander - Private - 2nd Rifles - Company: Batteal Harrison - Age: 19 - Height: 5' 3 1/4" - Born: Michigan - Trade: Sailor - Enlistment date: 1 Jul 1814 - Enlistment place: Chillicothe or Circleville - Enlistment period: War - By whom: John Swearingen - Pension: WC-35076; served in Batteal Harrison's Company, US Rifles.

O'Flackaday, John - Private - 26th Infantry - Company: William Puthuff - Enlistment date: 13 Apr 1813 - Enlistment period: 1 Yr.

Olden, George - 2nd Artillery - Company: Daniel Cushing - Other regiment: Corps of Artillery - Age: 47 - Height: 5' 10" - Born: VA, Loudoun County - Trade: Farmer - Enlistment date: 23 Aug 1813 - Enlistment place: Chillicothe - Enlistment period: 5 Yrs - Discharged: 2 Feb 1816 - Comments: Discharged after furnishing a substitute, Discharged at Detroit.

Olderfield, James - Private - 26th Infantry - Company: Samuel Swearingen - Enlistment date: 20 Jul 1813 - Enlistment period: 1 Yr.

Oldham, George - Private - 2nd Artillery - Company: Daniel Cushing - Age: 47 - Height: 5' 10" - Born: VA, Lowden County - Trade: Farmer - Enlistment date: 28 Aug 1812 - Enlistment place: Chillicothe - Enlistment period: 5 Yrs - By whom: Samuel Kercheval - Discharged: 2 Feb 1816 - Comments: Discharged at Detroit having furnished a substitute.

Oldham, James - Private - 26th Infantry - Other regiment: 25th Infantry - Enlistment date: 22 May 1813 - Enlistment period: 1 Yr - Discharged: 20 May 1814.

Olinger, Philip - Private - Rangers - Company: Samuel McCormick - Age: 20 - Height: 5' 7 1/2" - Born: Virginia - Trade: Farmer - Enlistment period: 1 Yr - Discharged: 26 Oct 1814 at Fort Malden, UC - Pension: Wife Sarah, WC-12212; served in Captain Samuel McCormick's Company, US Rangers as a private.

Oliver, John Batum - Private - 2nd Rifles - Company: Batteal Harrison - Age: 28 - Height: 5' 3" - Born: MO, St. Louis County - Trade: Laborer - Enlistment date: 19 Aug 1814 - Enlistment place: Cincinnati - Enlistment period: 5 Yrs - By whom: Elias Langham - Discharged: 19 Aug 1819 at Bellefontaine, MO.

Oliver, Robert - Private - 19th Infantry - Company: Angus Langham - Age: 30 - Height: 6' 1 1/4" - Born: PA, Chester County - Enlistment date: 1 Jul 1812 - Enlistment period: 5 Yrs - Died: 1 Mar 1814 - Pension: Wife Jane, Old War Minor C-173 in lieu of BLW; served in Capt. Booker's company, 19th Infantry; heirs obtained half pay for five years in lieu of military bounty land.

The Enlisted Men

O'Neal, John - Private - 19th Infantry - Company: Carey Trimble - Age: 19 - Height: 5' - Born: England, Guernsey Island - Trade: Farm laborer - Enlistment date: 5 May 1814 - Enlistment place: Ross County, Adelphi - Enlistment period: War - By whom: George Will - Bounty: BLW 10591-160-12 (Illinois).

O'Neal, Owen Jr - Private - 17th Infantry - Company: John Chunn - Other regiment: 3rd Infantry - Age: 39 - Height: 5' 8 1/2" - Born: Ireland - Trade: Tanner - Enlistment date: 9 Nov 1813 - Enlistment period: War - By whom: George Stall - Discharged: 7 Jun 1815 at Chillicothe - Pension: Old War IF-27280; served as a private in 17th Infantry - Bounty: BLW 8333-160-12 (Illinois).

Orns, William - Private - 26th Infantry - Company: George Kesling - Enlistment date: 17 Apr 1813 - Enlistment period: 1 Yr - Died: 12 Dec 1813.

Orwick, Samuel - Private - 17th Infantry - Company: Harris Hickman - Age: 18 - Height: 5' 5" - Born: PA, Bucks County - Trade: Farmer - Enlistment date: 2 Nov 1813 - Enlistment place: Jefferson County, Springfield Twp - Enlistment period: War - By whom: Isaac Rieley - Discharged: 9 Jun 1815 at Chillicothe - Pension: Wife Rebecca, WS-31578, SC-8800; served in Capt. Hickman's Company, 17th Infantry as a private - Bounty: BLW 16438-160-12 (Illinois).

Osborn, George - Private - 27th Infantry - Company: Alexander Hill - Enlistment date: 26 Apr 1813.

Osborn, James - Private - 26th Infantry - Company: Samuel Swearingen - Enlistment date: 14 Jun 1813 - Enlistment period: 1 Yr - Pension: Wife Alice, WC-30817; served in Capt Collin's Company, 26th Infantry.

Osborne, George - Private - 19th Infantry - Died: 17 Sep 1814 at Fort Erie, UC.

Osborne, Wilson S. - Private - 19th Infantry - Company: William Gill - Age: 23 - Height: 5' 9" - Born: NJ, Somerset County - Trade: Carpenter - Enlistment date: 29 Sep 1814 - Enlistment place: Marietta - Enlistment period: War - By whom: Samuel Coleman - Discharged: 5 Jun 1815 at Chillicothe - Bounty: BLW 19316-160-12 (Missouri).

Otterman, Lewis - Private - 19th Infantry - Company: William Gill - Age: 33 - Height: 6' 1" - Born: Pennsylvania - Trade: Farmer - Enlistment date: 20 Jul 1814 - Enlistment place: Zanesville - Enlistment period: War - By whom: Neal McFadden - Discharged: 5 Jun 1815 at Chillicothe - Bounty: BLW 21998-160-12 (Arkansas).

Owens, Benjamin - Private - 26th Infantry - Company: Joel Collins - Other regiment: 19th Infantry - Age: 22 - Height: 5' 9" - Born: Georgia - Trade: Farmer - Enlistment date: 12 Sep 1813 - Enlistment period: 1 Yr - Discharged: 20 Jul 1815 at Detroit - Bounty: BLW 11163-160-12 (Illinois) - Comments: Re-enlisted on 13 Apr 1814 at Sandwich, UC, by Lieutenant Delaroe, during the war enlistment.

Owens, James - Corporal - 19th Infantry - Age: 31 - Height: 5' 10" - Born: Virginia - Trade: Chair maker - Enlistment date: 26 Oct 1814 - Enlistment place: Xenia - Enlistment period: War - By whom: Robert Smith - Discharged: 27 Mar 1815 at Zanesville - Bounty: BLW 13991-160-12 (Illinois).

Owens, James - Private - 26th Infantry - Company: George Kesling - Other regiment: 25th Infantry - Enlistment date: 27 May 1813 - Enlistment period: 1 Yr - Discharged: 27 May 1814.

Owens, Silas - Private - 26th Infantry - Company: Joel Collins - Other regiment: 19th Infantry - Age: 27 - Height: 5' 11" - Born: Virginia - Trade: Farmer - Enlistment date: 16 Sep 1813 - Enlistment period: 1 Yr - War - Bounty: BLW 25574-160-12 (Arkansas) - Comments: Re-enlisted on 29 Apr 1814 in 19th Infantry at Sandwich, UC, by Lieutenant Delorac, during the war enlistment.

Oxley, Henry - Private - 19th Infantry - Company: Richard Talbott - Age: 30 - Height: 5' 7 1/2" - Born: Virginia - Trade: Blacksmith - Enlistment date: 29 Apr 1814 - Enlistment place: Springfield (or Redding) - Enlistment period: War - By whom: Abijah Johns - Discharged: 5 Jun 1815 at Chillicothe - Bounty: BLW 20180-160-12 (Missouri).

Pachel, John - Private - 26th Infantry - Company: George Kesling - Enlistment date: 5 May 1813 - Enlistment period: 1 Yr - Comments: Prisoner of War.

Paine, Daniel - Private - 27th Infantry - Company: Alexander Hill - Other regiment: 19th Infantry - Enlistment date: 23 Feb 1814 - Enlistment period: War - Killed: 31 Aug 1814.

Paine, Roswell - Private - 27th Infantry - Company: George Sanderson - Enlistment date: 6 Jun 1813.

Palmer, Jesse W. - Private - 17th Infantry - Company: Henry Crittenden - Age: 21 - Height: 5' 8" - Born: Connecticut - Trade: Distiller - Enlistment date: 17 Aug 1814 - Enlistment place: Cleveland - Enlistment period: War - By whom: David Carney - Discharged: 9 Jun 1814 at Chillicothe - Bounty: BLW 9444-160-12 (Illinois).

Palmer, Luther - Private - 27th Infantry - Company: George Sanderson - Enlistment date: 29 Apr 1813 - Enlistment period: 1 Yr - Died: 12 Mar 1814 at Put-in-Bay, OH.

Palmer, Richard - Private - 19th Infantry - Company: William Gill - Age: 21 - Height: 5' 10" - Born: Pennsylvania - Trade: Farmer - Enlistment date: 25 Jul 1814 - Enlistment place: New Lisbon - Enlistment period: War - By whom: Wynkoop Warner - Discharged: 5 Jun 1815 at Chillicothe - Bounty: BLW 17357-160-12 (Missouri).

Pangburn, William - Private - 19th Infantry - Company: James Herron.
Parcel, James H. - Sergeant - 19th Infantry - Company: James Herron - Age: 27 - Height: 5' 11 ½" - Born: NY, Essex County - Trade: Brick layer - Enlistment date: 17 Nov 1812 - Enlistment period: 5 Yrs - By whom: Capt Graham - Comments: Prisoner of War (Quebec, LC), captured at Fort Niagara, NY, 19 Dec 1813; exchanged 4 May 1814.
Parish, Waddy - Private - 17th Infantry - Company: David Holt - Died: May 1813
Parker, Francis - Private - 26th Infantry - Company: Samuel Swearingen - Enlistment date: 22 Jun 1813 - Enlistment period: 1 Yr - Discharged: 20 Jun 1814.
Parker, Hiram - Corporal - 26th Infantry - Company: George Kesling - Enlistment date: 27 Apr 1813 - Enlistment period: 1 Yr - Comments: Prisoner of War on Parole, captured at Detroit, MI, 16 Aug 1812.
Parkhurst, Benjamin - Private - 27th Infantry - Company: George Sanderson - Enlistment date: 5 Jun 1813Parkinson, Daniel - Private - 17th Infantry - Company: Caleb Holder - Age: 23 - Height: 5' 8" - Born: VA, Montgomery County - Trade: Laborer - Enlistment date: 1 May 1814 - Enlistment place: Columbiana County, Middleton - Enlistment period: War - By whom: William Shang - Discharged: 30 Jun 1815 at Detroit.
Parkinson, John - Private - 26th Infantry - Company: William Puthuff - Enlistment date: 13 May 1813 - Enlistment period: 1 Yr - Died: 2 Nov 1813.
Parkman, Daniel - Corporal - 17th Infantry - Company: Caleb Holder - Bounty: BLW 16486-160-12 (Illinois).
Parks, David - Private - 26th Infantry - Company: Samuel Swearingen - Enlistment date: 28 Jul 1813 - Enlistment period: 1 Yr - Discharged: 27 Jul 1814.
Parks, George - Private - 27th Infantry - Company: George Sanderson - Enlistment date: 26 May 1813 - Died: 28 Nov 1813.
Parks, Thomas - Private - 26th Infantry - Company: Joel Collins - Enlistment date: 5 Aug 1813 - Enlistment period: 1 Yr.
Parrish, John - Sergeant - 19th Infantry - Company: William Gill - Age: 23 - Height: 5' 11" - Born: Pennsylvania - Trade: Farmer - Enlistment date: 21 Mar 1814 - Enlistment period: War - By whom: Charles Cissna - Discharged: 5 Jun 1815 at Chillicothe - Bounty: BLW 6173-160-12.
Pastor, Christian - Private - 27th Infantry - Comments: Prisoner of War on Parole, captured at Detroit, MI, 16 Aug 1812
Patch, Joshua - Private - 19th Infantry - Other regiment: 25th Infantry then 6th Infantry - Age: 21 - Height: 5' 7" - Born: NH, Hillsborough County, New Berton - Enlistment date: 25 Jul 1812 - Enlistment place: Zanesville - Enlistment period: 5 Yrs - By whom: Capt Bang - Discharged: 25 Jul 1817 - Comments: Discharged at West Point, NY, from Corps of Bombardiers.
Patch, Samuel - Sergeant - 19th Infantry - Age: 23 - Height: 5' 8" - Born: NH, Hillsborough County - Enlistment date: 1 Jul 1812 - Enlistment period: 5 Yrs.
Patrick, Benjamin - Private - 27th Infantry - Company: Alexander Hill - Other regiment: 19th Infantry - Age: 39 - Height: 5' 10 1/2" - Born: Ireland, County Derry - Trade: Farmer - Enlistment date: 1 Mar 1814 - Enlistment place: Zanesville - Enlistment period: War - By whom: Neal McFadden - Discharged: 15 Jun 1815 at Chillicothe - Bounty: BLW 6028-160-12 (Illinois).
Patterson, Joseph - Private - 2nd Artillery - Company: Daniel Cushing - Age: 22 - Height: 5' 8 3/4" - Born: PA, Washington County - Enlistment date: 24 Aug 1812 - Enlistment period: 18 Mos - Discharged: 24 Feb 1814 - Comments: Prisoner of war, taken by the Indians on 8 Apr 1813 in Ohio, paroled.
Patterson, Robert M. - Private - 27th Infantry - Company: Absalom Martin - Pension: Old War IF-9805, served in Captain Absalom Martin's Company, 27th Infantry as a private.
Patterson, Samuel R. - Sergeant - 2nd Artillery - Company: Daniel Cushing - Other regiment: Corps of Artillery - Age: 23 - Height: 6' 1" - Born: Kentucky - Trade: Farmer - Enlistment date: 28 Dec 1814 - Enlistment period: War - Discharged: 25 Jul 1815 at Fort Meigs, OH.
Patton, John - Private - 1st Infantry - Company: Horatio Stark - Other regiment: 3rd Infantry - Age: 21 - Height: 6' - Born: Maryland - Trade: Laborer - Enlistment date: 26 Jun 1812 - Enlistment place: Lebanon - Enlistment period: 5 Yrs - By whom: Ensign Meeks - Discharged: 26 Jun 1817 at Fort Dearborn, IL.
Patton, Thomas - Corporal - 19th Infantry - Company: James Herron - Enlistment date: 17 Sep 1812 - Enlistment period: 18 Mos.
Patton, William R. - Private - 19th Infantry - Discharged: 17 Sep 1814.
Paul, Jesse - Private - 24th Infantry - Company: William Allen - Other regiment: Rifle Regiment - Age: 19 - Height: 5' 5 1/2" - Born: OH, Hamilton County, Cincinnati - Trade: Farmer - Enlistment date: 25 Jul 1812 - Enlistment place: AL, Fort Mines - Enlistment period: 5 Yrs - By whom: Walter Wilkinson - Discharged: 25

Jul 1817 - Comments: Transferred to Rifle Regiment, 30 June 1816.

Paul, John - Private - 2nd Rifles - Company: John O'Fallon - Age: 35 - Height: 5' 8" - Born: Maryland - Trade: Farmer - Enlistment date: 18 Aug 1814 - Enlistment place: OH or Newport, KY - Enlistment period: 5 Yrs - By whom: Elias Langham - Discharged: 23 Sep 1815 at Detroit on Surgeon's Certificate of Disability.

Paulin, David - Private - 19th Infantry - Company: Wilson Elliott - Age: 44 - Height: 5' 11" - Born: New Jersey - Enlistment date: 21 Jul 1812 - Enlistment period: 5 Yrs.

Payne, Colston - Sergeant - 19th Infantry - Company: Richard Talbott - Age: 44 - Height: 5' 11" - Born: Virginia - Trade: Cooper - Enlistment date: 19 Jun 1814 - Enlistment place: Lebanon - Enlistment period: War - By whom: John Goode - Discharged: 5 Jun 1815 at Chillicothe - Bounty: BLW 7815-160-12 (Illinois).

Payne, Roswell - Private - 27th Infantry - Company: George Sanderson - Other regiment: 19th Infantry - Enlistment date: 6 Jun 1813 - Enlistment period: 1 Yr - Discharged: Jun 1814 at Detroit - Pension: Wife Hopey, WO-2893; served in Capt. Sanderson's Company, 19th Infantry as a private, lived in OH.

Pearson, Robert (Parsons) - Private - 2nd Artillery - Company: Daniel Cushing - Age: 19 - Height: 5' 7 1/2" - Born: VA, Hardy County (now WV) - Enlistment date: 22 Aug 1812 - Enlistment period: 5 Yrs - Died: 26 Mar 1813 - Bounty: BLW 26684-160-12 (Arkansas) - Comments: Died at Fort Meigs; land bounty to Ann Buckley, sister & other heirs at law of Robert Pearson.

Peck, Jacob - Private - 26th Infantry - Company: George Kesling - Other regiment: 19th Infantry then 3rd Infantry - Age: 27 - Height: 5' 5 1/2" - Born: PA, Bedford County - Trade: Shoemaker - Enlistment date: 8 May 1813 - Enlistment period: 1 Yr - 5 Yrs - Comments: Prisoner of War on Parole, captured at Detroit, MI, 16 Aug 1812, re-enlisted 31 Dec 1818.

Peck, Joseph - Private - 26th Infantry - Company: William Puthuff.

Peck, Thomas M. - Corporal - 19th Infantry - Company: Joel Collins - Bounty: BLW 8487-160-12 (Illinois).

Peeples, Alexander - Private - 19th Infantry - Company: Richard Talbott - Age: 24 - Height: 5' 7" - Born: Maryland - Trade: Farmer - Enlistment date: 11 Jun 1814 - Enlistment place: Urbana - Enlistment period: War - By whom: William Baird - Discharged: 5 Jun 1815 at Chillicothe - Bounty: BLW 3503-160-12 (Missouri).

Pelham, Bine - Private - 2nd Artillery - Company: Daniel Cushing.

Peltz, M. - Drummer - 19th Infantry - Company: Wilson Elliott - Other regiment: 25th Infantry.

Pennell, James - Private - 2nd Rifles - Company: John O'Fallon - Enlistment date: 7 Nov 1814 - Enlistment place: Ohio - Enlistment period: 5 Yrs - By whom: John Swearingen - Comments: Deserted 4 Jun 1815.

Pense, Isaac - Private - 27th Infantry - Company: William Gill - Other regiment: 19th Infantry - Pension: SC-16643; served in Capt. John Spencer's Company, OH Militia and in Capt. Gill's Company, 27th and 19th Infantries.

Peoples, Seymore - Private - 17th Infantry - Company: William Bradford - Age: 26 - Height: 5' 9" - Born: PA, Chester County - Trade: Carpenter - Enlistment date: 30 May 1814 - Enlistment place: Franklin County, Franklinton - Enlistment period: War - By whom: John Cochran - Discharged: 4 Jun 1815 at Chillicothe.

Perkins, William B. - Private - 19th Infantry - Company: John Stockton - Comments: Served aboard the US Brig Lawrence on the Lake Erie Squadron; slightly wounded during the Battle of Lake Erie.

Perry, Samuel - Private - 26th Infantry - Company: Joel Collins - Enlistment date: 2 Aug 1813 - Enlistment period: 1 Yr.

Peters, Ebenezer - Private - 19th Infantry - Enlistment date: 8 May 1813 - Enlistment place: Cincinnati - Enlistment period: War.

Peters, Thomas - Private - 19th Infantry - Company: James Herron.

Petitt, Charles - Private - 19th Infantry - Company: James Herron.

Petitt, Jonas - Private - 19th Infantry - Company: Carey Trimble - Age: 26 - Height: 5' 5 1/2" - Born: Maryland - Trade: Farmer - Enlistment date: 15 Feb 1814 - Enlistment place: Chillicothe - Enlistment period: War - By whom: John Stockton - Discharged: 6 Jun 1815 at Chillicothe - Bounty: BLW 7824-160-12.

Pettee, Hira - Private - 27th Infantry - Company: Alexander Hill.

Pettet, Benjamin - Musician - 28th Infantry - Company: Joseph Belt - Age: 14 - Height: 4' 8" - Born: Ohio - Trade: Farmer - Enlistment date: 6 Sep 1814 - Enlistment place: KY, Grayson County, Sandy Salt Works - Enlistment period: War - By whom: John Kouns - Discharged: 31 Mar 1815 at Olympian Springs, KY.

Pettit, Alexander - Private - 19th Infantry - Company: Wilson Elliott.

Pettit, Joseph - Private - 27th Infantry - Comments: Prisoner of War on Parole, captured at Detroit, MI, 16 Aug 1812.

Pettit, Mathew - Private - 2nd Artillery - Company: Daniel Cushing - Age: 20 - Height: 5' 9" - Born: Pennsylvania - Trade: Laborer - Enlistment date: 28 Jun 1814 - Enlistment period: War - Discharged: 25 Jan 1815 at Lower Sandusky (now Fremont, OH).

Petts, Michael - Drummer - 27th Infantry.

Petty, Hira - Private - 19th Infantry - Company: Carey Trimble - Other regiment: 17th Infantry - Age: 19 - Height: 5' 9" - Born: VT, Franklin County, Georgia - Trade: Laborer - Enlistment date: 21 Feb 1814 - Enlistment place: Zanesville - Enlistment period: War - By whom: Henry Northrup - Discharged: 6 Jun 1815 at Chillicothe - Bounty: BLW 7179-160-12 (Illinois).

Pew, James - Corporal - 19th Infantry - Company: Wilson Elliott - Age: 24 - Height: 5' 10" - Born: New York - Enlistment date: 18 Jul 1812 - Enlistment period: 18 Mos - Pension: Wife Ashsa, WC-31227; served in Captain Wilson Elliott's Company, 19th Infantry as a corporal.

Pewtherer, John - Private - 17th Infantry - Company: Caleb Holder - Age: 39 - Height: 5' 8" - Born: Scotland - Trade: Laborer - Enlistment date: 22 Sep 1813 - Enlistment period: War - By whom: Hugh May.

Phelps, David - Private - 26th Infantry - Company: George Kesling - Enlistment date: 11 Jun 1813 - Enlistment period: 1 Yr - Discharged: 11 Jun 1814.

Phares – see Farris, Joseph H.

Phelps, H. K. - Private - 19th Infantry - Age: 22 - Height: 5' 8" - Born: Connecticut - Enlistment date: 12 Aug 1814 - Enlistment place: Lancaster - Enlistment period: War - By whom: John Simons.

Philbrick, Gideon (Philbeck) - Private - 19th Infantry - Company: George Kesling - Age: 23 - Height: 5' 10" - Born: Maine - Trade: Shoemaker - Enlistment date: 12 Jan 1815 - Enlistment place: Zanesville - Enlistment period: War - By whom: Charles Cass - Discharged: 27 Mar 1815 at Zanesville - Bounty: BLW 633-320-14 (Illinois).

Philips, Benjamin - Private - 2nd Light Dragoons - Company: Samuel Hopkins - Died: 30 May 1813, probably in Ohio.

Phillips, Alexander - Private - 19th Infantry - Company: George Kesling - Other regiment: 3rd Infantry - Age: 39 - Height: 5' 10" - Born: Pennsylvania - Trade: Tanner - Enlistment date: 2 Feb 1815 - Enlistment place: Zanesville - Enlistment period: 5 Yrs - By whom: Charles Cass.

Phillips, Daniel - Private - 19th Infantry - Company: Joel Collins - Other regiment: 3rd Infantry - Age: 19 - Height: 5' 6" - Born: VA, Frederick County - Trade: Laborer - Enlistment date: 15 Mar 1814 - Enlistment place: Detroit - Enlistment period: 5 Yrs - By whom: Wynkoop Warner - Discharged: 14 Mar 1819 at Fort Howard, WI.

Phillips, Daniel - Private - 27th Infantry - Company: Isaac Van Horne - Pension: Wife Sarah, Old War IF-17077 Rejected; served in Capt. Van Horn's Company, US Infantry as a private.

Phillips, Philip - Private - 17th Infantry - Age: 25 - Height: 5' 11" - Born: Kentucky - Enlistment date: 4 May 1814 - Enlistment place: Franklin County - Enlistment period: War - By whom: John Simons - Comments: Deserted 5 May 1814.

Phinney, James H. - Sergeant - 19th Infantry - Other regiment: 25th Infantry - Enlistment date: 15 Aug 1812 - Enlistment period: 18 Mos - By whom: Asabael Nearing - Discharged: 15 Feb 1814.

Piatt, John - Private - 17th Infantry - Company: Caleb Holder - Age: 19 - Height: 5' 8" - Born: VA, Ohio County (now WV) - Trade: Farmer - Enlistment date: 4 Sep 1814 - Enlistment period: War - By whom: James Herron - Discharged: 30 Jun 1815 at Detroit - Pension: Wife Elizabeth, SC-31153; served in Capt. Herron's Company, 17th Infantry.

Pickle, Joseph - Private - 19th Infantry - Company: Joel Collins - Age: 31 - Height: 5' 10" - Born: Lower Canada - Trade: Cooper - Enlistment date: 5 Apr 1814 - Enlistment place: Detroit - Enlistment period: War - By whom: Wynkoop Warner.

Pickle, Mathias - Private - 27th Infantry - Company: Isaac Van Horne - Pension: Served in Capt. Van Horne's Company, 27th Infantry as a private - Bounty: BLW 3683-160-50.

Pierce, Arzel - Private - 27th Infantry - Company: George Sanderson - Enlistment date: 3 May 1813.

Pierce, Enoch - Private – 2nd Artillery - Company: Henry Craig - Other regiment: Corps of Artillery - Age: 17 - Height: 5' 6" - Born: Ohio - Trade: Blacksmith - Enlistment date: 16 Feb 1814 - Enlistment place: PA, Allegheny County, Pittsburgh - Enlistment period: 5 Yrs - By whom: Henry Craig - Comments: Deserted at Detroit, MI, on 5 Nov 1816.

Pierce, James - Private - 26th Infantry - Company: William Puthuff - Other regiment: 19th Infantry - Age: 38 - Height: 5' 8 1/2" - Born: Pennsylvania - Trade: Tailor - Enlistment date: 15 May 1813 - Enlistment period: 1 Yr - War - By whom: Hugh Moore - Discharged: 20 Jul 1815 at Detroit - Bounty: BLW 7125-160-12 (Arkansas).

Pierce, Joshua - Sergeant - 27th Infantry - Company: George Sanderson - Enlistment date: 24 May 1813 - Pension: Wife Martha, WC-22292; served in Captain George Sanderson's Company, 27th Infantry.

Piggott, Solomon - Private - 17th Infantry - Company: Henry Crittenden - Other regiment: 3rd Infantry - Age: 15 - Height: 5' 3" - Born: Ohio - Trade: Laborer - Enlistment date: 12 May 1814 - Enlistment period: 5 Yrs - By whom: David Carney.

Piles, Thomas (Pyles) - Private - 19th Infantry - Company: Angus Langham - Enlistment date: 19 Feb 1813 - Enlistment period: 18 Mos - Died: 31 Aug 1813 - Pension: Wife Deborah Ruth, Old War WF-11193; served in Capt. Bonnett's Company, VA Militia and in Capt. Langham's Company, 19th Infantry as a private - Bounty: BLW 98870-160-55 - Comments: Died probably at Lower Sandusky (now Fremont, OH), about 31 Aug 1813 ; had re-enlisted for the war.

Pitcher, Shederick - Corporal - 17th Infantry - Age: 42 - Height: 5' 11 1/2" - Born: VA, Culpeper County - Trade: Laborer - Enlistment date: 16 Feb 1815 - Enlistment period: War - By whom: John Reeves - Discharged: 17 Apr 1815 at Chillicothe - Bounty: BLW 256-320-14 (Illinois).

Pixley, Elijah - Musician - 19th Infantry - Discharged: 28 Jan 1815.

Place, Daniel - Private - 26th Infantry - Company: George Will - Enlistment date: 26 May 1813 - Enlistment period: 1 Yr.

Plangher, John - Private - 26th Infantry - Company: George Kesling - Enlistment date: 13 May 1813 - Enlistment period: 1 Yr.

Plank, Jacob - Private - 19th Infantry - Company: George Kesling - Enlistment date: 9 Jul 1814 - Enlistment period: War - By whom: Charles Cissna - Comments: Captured or deserted 22 Oct 1814.

Plankes, Jacob - Private - 19th Infantry - Age: 17 - Height: 5' - Born: Ohio - Enlistment date: 11 Jul 1814 - Enlistment place: Zanesville.

Plummer, William - Private - 2nd Rifles - Company: Batteal Harrison - Age: 27 - Height: 5' 7 1/2" - Born: Lower Canada, Quebec - Trade: Shoemaker - Enlistment date: 2 Jul 1814 - Enlistment place: Chillicothe - Enlistment period: 5 Yrs - By whom: Batteal Harrison - Discharged: 31 Dec 1818 after furnishing a substitute.

Pollock, Samuel - Private - 27th Infantry - Age: 38 - Height: 5' 8 1/2" - Born: Holland - Enlistment date: 5 Apr 1814 - Enlistment place: New Lisbon.

Polson, Philip - Private - 1st Rifles - Company: Thomas Ramsey - Age: 21 - Height: 5' 7" - Born: Maryland - Trade: Cooper - Enlistment date: 6 Dec 1813 - Enlistment place: Cincinnati - Enlistment period: War - By whom: Thomas Ramsey - Comments: Deserted 5 Aug 1814 at Camp Springfield.

Pomeroy, Joseph - Private - 19th Infantry - Company: John Chunn - Enlistment period: 18 Mos - Comments: Served aboard the US Schooner Tigress on the Lake Erie Squadron.

Pore, James (or Poor) - Private - 2nd Artillery - Company: Daniel Cushing - Pension: SC-20516, served in Capt. Cushing's Company, 2nd Artillery as a private.

Porter, James - Private - 26th Infantry - Company: Samuel Swearingen - Enlistment date: 16 Jul 1813 - Enlistment period: 1 Yr - Died: 17 Nov 1813 - Comments: Died probably at Sackets Harbor, NY.

Porter, James - 1st Rifles - Company: Thomas Ramsey - Age: 38 - Height: 5' 11" - Born: MD, Baltimore County - Trade: Farmer - Enlistment date: 17 May 1814 - Enlistment place: Cincinnati - Enlistment period: War - By whom: Thomas Ramsey - Comments: Deserted at Cincinnati, OH, on 20 May 1814.

Porter, Randall - Private - 19th Infantry - Company: Carey Trimble - Other regiment: 17th Infantry - Age: 18 - Height: 5' 5" - Born: Virginia - Trade: Farmer - Enlistment date: 24 May 1814 - Enlistment place: Urbana - Enlistment period: War - By whom: William Baird - Discharged: 6 Jun 1815 at Chillicothe - Bounty: BLW 6129-160-12 (Illinois).

Post, Cornelius - Private - 27th Infantry - Comments: Prisoner of War on Parole, captured at Detroit, MI, 16 Aug 1812.

Potten, John - Corporal - 19th Infantry - Company: Lt John McElvain - Bounty: BLW 5381-160-12 (Illinois).

Potts, John - Private - 27th Infantry - Company: Alexander Hill - Other regiment: 19th Infantry - Age: 19 - Height: 5' 6" - Born: Pennsylvania - Trade: Farmer - Enlistment date: 27 May 1814 - Enlistment place: Columbiana County, Salem - Enlistment period: War - By whom: John Carroll - Discharged: 6 Jun 1815 at Chillicothe - Bounty: BLW 26401-160-12 (Arkansas).

Power, Thomas - Musician - 19th Infantry - Company: James Herron - Enlistment date: 6 Aug 1812 - Enlistment period: 18 Mos.

Powers – see Pore, James

Powers, Daniel - Drummer - 19th Infantry - Company: George Kesling - Age: 33 - Height: 5' 8" - Born: Virginia - Trade: Farmer - Enlistment date: 29 Dec 1814 - Enlistment place: Xenia - Enlistment period: War - By whom: Robert Smith.

Powers, Ebenezer - Private - 17th Infantry - Company: Caleb Holder - Age: 37 - Height: 5' 8" - Born: DE, New Castle County - Trade: Hatter - Enlistment date: 26 Sep 1814 - Enlistment period: War - By whom: James Herron - Discharged: 23 Jun 1815 - Bounty: BLW 14443-160-12 (Illinois).

Powers, William D. - Corporal - 2nd Artillery - Company: Daniel Cushing.
Pratt, George - Private - 1st Rifles - Company: Thomas Ramsey - Enlistment date: 22 Jul 1813 - Enlistment period: War - Died: Sep 1813, probably at Fort Seneca, OH - Bounty: BLW 26033-160-12 (Arkansas) - Comments: Land bounty to Mary Pratt, daughter & other heirs at law of George Pratt.
Pratt, Joseph - Private - 19th Infantry - Company: Richard Talbott - Age: 21 - Height: 5' 10" - Born: VA, Campbell County - Trade: Farmer - Enlistment date: 7 May 1814 - Enlistment place: Xenia - Enlistment period: War - By whom: Jacob Leslie - Discharged: 5 Jun 1815 at Chillicothe - Bounty: BLW 23945-160-12 (Arkansas).
Pratt, Lemuel - Private - 27th Infantry - Company: George Sanderson - Enlistment date: 29 Apr 1813.
Pratt, Robert - Private - 2nd Rifles - Age: 23 - Height: 5' 9" - Born: Massachusetts - Trade: Laborer - Enlistment date: 20 Oct 1814 - Enlistment place: Cincinnati - Enlistment period: War - By whom: William Pritchard - Discharged: 14 Apr 1815.
Price, John - Private - 19th Infantry - Company: James Herron - Enlistment date: 16 Dec 1812 - Enlistment period: 5 Yrs - Died: 5 Oct 1813.
Price, John L. - Private - 26th Infantry - Company: Joel Collins - Enlistment date: 27 Aug 1813 - Enlistment period: 1 Yr - Died: 7 Jan 1814, probably at Detroit.
Price, Joseph - Private - 19th Infantry - Company: Lt John McElvain.
Price, William - 2nd Rifles - Age: 18 - Height: 5' 2" - Born: Virginia - Enlistment date: 27 Apr 1814 - Enlistment place: Portsmouth.
Pride, Joseph - Private - 26th Infantry - Company: George Kesling - Other regiment: 25th Infantry - Age: 18 - Height: 5' 2" - Enlistment date: 27 May 1813 - Enlistment period: 1 Yr - Discharged: 27 May 1814 - Pension: SC-17425; served in Capt. Thomas Reed's Company, 25th Infantry.
Primrose, William - Private - 17th Infantry - Company: John Chunn - Age: 21 - Height: 5' 11" - Born: MI, Wayne County, Detroit - Trade: Tailor - Enlistment date: 22 Apr 1813 - Enlistment place: Franklin County, Franklinton - Enlistment period: War - By whom: John Cochran - Discharged: 9 Jun 1815 at Chillicothe - Bounty: BLW 5821-160-12 (Illinois).
Pritchard, Carvall - 1st Rifles - Company: Thomas Ramsey - Age: 40 - Height: 5' 9" - Born: MD, Cecil County - Trade: Hatter - Enlistment date: 29 Jan 1814 - Enlistment place: Cincinnati - Enlistment period: 5 Yrs - By whom: Thomas Ramsey - Died: 12 Jul 1814, probably at Newport, KY.
Pritchard, James - Private - 27th Infantry - Company: Alexander Hill - Other regiment: 19th Infantry - Bounty: BLW 13637-160-12 (Arkansas).
Probus, Henry - Private - 1st Infantry - Company: John Symmes - Age: 21 - Height: 5' 11" - Born: Maryland - Trade: Farmer - Enlistment date: 4 Apr 1814 - Enlistment place: Cincinnati - Enlistment period: War - By whom: Laurence Taliaferro - Comments: Wounded during the Battle of Bridgewater, UC, on 25 Jul 1814.
Prophet, James - Private - 19th Infantry - Enlistment date: 9 Apr 1813 - Enlistment place: Cincinnati - Enlistment period: 5 Yrs.
Prouse, Thomas - Private - 19th Infantry - Company: Wilson Elliott - Enlistment date: 26 Aug 1812 - Enlistment period: 18 Mos.
Purdue, James - Private - 19th Infantry - Age: 21 - Height: 5' 6" - Born: MD, Cumberland County - Enlistment date: 11 Apr 1814 - Enlistment place: Portsmouth - By whom: Hugh May.
Purl, John - Private - 19th Infantry - Company: James Herron - Enlistment date: 22 Dec 1812 - Enlistment period: 18 Mos.
Purwine, Symmering O. - Private - 19th Infantry - Company: Wilson Elliott - Enlistment date: 8 Feb 1813 - Enlistment period: 18 Mos.
Quick, Aaron - Private - 19th Infantry - Company: James Herron - Enlistment date: 13 Sep 1812 - Enlistment period: 18 Mos.
Quick, Martin - Private - 19th Infantry - Comments: Possible 17th Infantry.
Quick, William - Private - 26th Infantry - Company: Samuel Swearingen - Enlistment date: 9 Jul 1813 - Enlistment period: 1 Yr.
Quimby, John - Private - 7th Infantry - Company: Zachary Taylor - Enlistment date: 28 Jan 1812 - Enlistment period: 5 Yrs - By whom: Thomas Ramsey - Died: 28 Apr 1814.
Radcliff, John - Private - 19th Infantry - Company: William Gill - Age: 14 - Height: 5' - Born: OH, Delaware County, Berkshire - Trade: Shoemaker - Enlistment date: 4 Jun 1814 - Enlistment period: War - By whom: Charles Cissna - Discharged: 5 Jun 1815 Battle of Bridgewater - Bounty: BLW 14401-160-12 (Illinois).
Rader, Abraham - Private - 2nd Rifles - Company: Batteal Harrison - Age: 19 - Height: 5' 9" - Born: Virginia - Trade: Farmer - Enlistment date: 5 May 1814 - Enlistment place: Zanesville - Enlistment period: War - By whom: William Dougherty - Discharged: 30 Jun 1815 at Detroit - Pension: SO-2674, SC-7394; served in

The Enlisted Men

Captain Batteal Harrison's Company, 2nd Rifles, as a private.

Ragan, William - Private - 19th Infantry - Company: Carey Trimble - Age: 41 - Height: 5' 8" - Born: Maryland - Trade: Farmer - Enlistment date: 1 Jan 1814 - Enlistment period: War - Discharged: 7 Jun 1815 Battle of Bridgewater, UC - Bounty: BLW 17043-160-12 (Illinois).

Raider, Charles G. - Private - 2nd Rifles - Company: Batteal Harrison - Age: 20 - Height: 5' 6" - Born: Germany, Geneva - Trade: Hatter - Enlistment date: 6 Aug 1814 - Enlistment place: Highland County, Hillsboro - Enlistment period: 5 Yrs - By whom: Joseph McClain - Discharged: 16 Aug 1819 at Fort Crawford, IL - Bounty: BLW 24378-160-12 (Arkansas).

Ramsay, Daniel A. - Private - 17th Infantry - Company: David Holt - Age: 31 - Height: 5' 10" - Born: New Jersey - Trade: Brick maker - Enlistment date: 4 May 1814 - Enlistment place: Trumbull County, Warren - Enlistment period: War - By whom: Wilson Elliott - Discharged: 4 Jun 1815 at Chillicothe.

Ramsay, James - Private - 19th Infantry - Age: 22 - Height: 5' 11" - Born: Kentucky - Enlistment date: 8 Apr 1814 - Enlistment place: Franklin County - Enlistment period: War - By whom: John Simons - Comments: Deserted 9 Apr 1814.

Ramsbottom, Simeon - Private - 19th Infantry - Company: Carey Trimble - Other regiment: 17th Infantry - Age: 18 - Height: 5' 5 1/2" - Born: Virginia - Trade: Laborer - Enlistment date: 14 Jan 1814 - Enlistment place: Chillicothe - Enlistment period: War - By whom: Charles Cissna - Discharged: 6 Jun 1814 at Chillicothe - Bounty: BLW 14332-160-12 (Illinois).

Ramsey, John - Private - 27th Infantry - Age: 26 - Height: 5' 8" - Born: Maryland - Enlistment date: 25 Apr 1814 - Enlistment place: Steubenville.

Ramsey, John - 26th Infantry - Company: Joel Collins - Died: 7 Jan 1814 at Greenbush, NY.

Ramsey, Lasley - Sergeant - 17th Infantry - Company: Henry Crittenden - Age: 27 - Height: 5' 11" - Born: PA, Center County - Trade: Boatman - Enlistment date: 19 Apr 1814 - Enlistment place: Portsmouth - Enlistment period: War - By whom: Hugh May - Discharged: 9 Jun 1814 at Chillicothe - Bounty: BLW 3143-160-12 (Illinois).

Randall, Benjamin - Private - 19th Infantry - Company: Richard Graham - Enlistment date: 17 Sep 1812 - Enlistment period: 18 Mos.

Randles, John - Private - 26th Infantry - Company: Joel Collins - Other regiment: 19th Infantry - Age: 24 - Height: 6' - Born: North Carolina - Enlistment date: 24 Jul 1813 - Enlistment period: 1 Yr - Comments: Re-enlisted on 28 Apr 1814, during the war enlistment, at Sandwich, UC, by Ensign Smith.

Rankins, James - Private - 19th Infantry - Company: Carey Trimble - Other regiment: 17th Infantry - Age: 40 - Height: 5' 6" - Born: Delaware - Trade: Laborer - Enlistment date: 30 Mar 1814 - Enlistment place: Chillicothe - Enlistment period: War - By whom: Charles Cissna - Discharged: 6 Jun 1815 at Chillicothe - Pension: Old War IF-5343; served in Lt. McElvain's Company, 19th Infantry as a private - Bounty: BLW 8058-160-12 (Illinois).

Rankins, John - Private - 19th Infantry - Company: William Gill - Age: 33 - Height: 5' 8" - Born: Pennsylvania - Trade: Farmer - Enlistment date: 16 Aug 1814 - Enlistment place: Urbana - Enlistment period: War - By whom: William Baird - Discharged: 27 Mar 1815 at Zanesville - Bounty: BLW 16423-160-12 (Illinois).

Raredon, Daniel - Private - 19th Infantry - Company: Carey Trimble - Other regiment: 17th Infantry - Age: 28 - Height: 5' 8" - Born: PA, York County - Trade: Boatman - Enlistment date: 27 May 1814 - Enlistment place: Portsmouth - Enlistment period: 5 Yrs - By whom: John Brown - Discharged: 18 Apr 1816 at Greenbush, NY, on Surgeon's Certificate of Disability - Pension: Old War IF-24346; served in Capt. Stockton's Company, 19th Infantry as a private - Bounty: BLW 20109-160-12 (Missouri) - Comments: Wounded in the left ankle during the Battle of Fort Erie.

Rasher, Daniel - Private - 19th Infantry - Company: William Gill - Age: 18 - Height: 5' 10" - Born: Pennsylvania - Trade: Carpenter - Enlistment date: 11 Sep 1814 - Enlistment period: War - By whom: Thomas Riddle - Discharged: 31 May 1815.

Rawl, William - Private - 27th Infantry - Comments: Prisoner of War on Parole, captured at Detroit, MI, 16 Aug 1812.

Ray, James - Private - 17th Infantry - Company: David Holt - Other regiment: 3rd Infantry - Age: 20 - Height: 5' 7" - Born: Newfoundland - Trade: Blacksmith - Enlistment date: 7 Jul 1814 - Enlistment place: Chillicothe - Enlistment period: 5 Yrs - By whom: John Cochran - Comments: Re-enlisted.

Ray, John - Private - 27th Infantry - Company: George Sanderson - Enlistment date: 28 Apr 1813.

Reader, Charles - Private - 26th Infantry - Company: George Kesling - Enlistment date: 6 May 1813 - Comments: Prisoner of War.

Reardon, John W. - Corporal - 19th Infantry - Company: Thomas Read - Other regiment: 25th Infantry - Age: 21 -

Height: 5' 8" - Born: Maryland - Enlistment date: 28 Aug 1812 - Enlistment place: Ohio - Enlistment period: 18 Mos Discharged: 25 Oct 1814 - Comments: Wounded.

Redburn, James T. - Private - 17th Infantry - Company: David Holt - Age: 39 - Height: 5' 8" - Born: Maryland - Trade: Laborer - Enlistment date: 11 May 1814 - Enlistment place: Zanesville - Enlistment period: War - By whom: James Herron - Discharged: 30 Jun 1815 at Detroit - Pension: Wife Jemima, WO-39501, WC-30636; served in Capt. Holder's Company, 17th Infantry - Bounty: BLW 9423-160-12 (Illinois).

Redding, Elijah - Private - 19th Infantry - Company: Richard Talbott - Age: 35 - Height: 5' 9 1/2" - Born: Kentucky - Trade: Laborer - Enlistment date: 15 Apr 1814 - Enlistment place: Franklin County - Enlistment period: War - By whom: Robert Young - Discharged: 5 Jun 1815 at Chillicothe - Bounty: BLW 11955-160-12 (Illinois).

Redding, Joseph - Private - 19th Infantry - Age: 21 - Height: 5' 9" - Born: KY, Mason County, Limestone - Enlistment date: 17 Apr 1814 - Enlistment place: Adams County, West Union - By whom: William Featherstone.

Redding, Lewis - Private - 2nd Rifles - Company: Batteal Harrison - Age: 31 - Height: 5' 9 1/2" - Born: Upper Canada - Trade: Boatman - Enlistment date: 28 May 1814 - Enlistment place: Cincinnati - Enlistment period: 5 Yrs - By whom: Elias Langham.

Redman, John - 26th Infantry - Company: George Kesling - Enlistment date: 23 May 1813 - Enlistment period: 1 Yr.

Redman, John L. - Private - 26th Infantry - Enlistment date: 27 Aug 1813 - Enlistment period: 1 Yr.

Redman, Joseph - Private - 1st Rifles - Company: Daniel Appling - Other regiment: Rifle Regiment - Age: 21 – Height: 5' 2" - Born: Ohio - Trade: Blacksmith - Enlistment date: 25 May 1810 - Enlistment place: KY, Washington County - Enlistment period: War - By whom: Henry Graham - Discharged: 11 Jun 1815 at Conjocquita Creek, NY - Pension: Old War IF-25768; served in Captains Appling'and Capt. Gray Companies, 1st Rifles, as a private.

Reed, Charles - Private - 19th Infantry - Company: Richard Talbott - Age: 18 - Height: 5' 5" - Born: VA, Berkeley County (now WV) - Trade: Carpenter - Enlistment date: 27 Feb 1814 - Enlistment place: Franklin County - Enlistment period: War - By whom: Robert Young - Discharged: 5 Jun 1815 at Chillicothe.

Reed, Elias - Private - 17th Infantry - Age: 24 - Height: 5' 10" - Born: Virginia - Trade: Blacksmith - Enlistment date: 20 Jul 1814 - Enlistment place: Cambridge - Enlistment period: War - By whom: William Shang - Discharged: 5 Jul 1815 at Chillicothe - Bounty: BLW 6595-160-12 (Illinois).

Reed, Frederick - Private - 19th Infantry - Company: James Herron - Enlistment date: 16 Sep 1812 - Enlistment period: 18 Mos.

Reed, John - Private - 27th Infantry - Company: Isaac Van Horne - Other regiment: 19th Infantry - Age: 27 - Height: 5' 9" - Born: Pennsylvania - Enlistment date: 24 Mar 1814 - Enlistment period: War - Died: 2 May 1814 - Pension: Old War Minor's C-1117 in lieu of BLW; served in Capt. Van Horne's Company, 19th Infantry as a private.

Reed, John - Sergeant - 19th Infantry - Company: George Kesling - Age: 22 - Height: 5' 11 1/2" - Born: DE, New Castle County - Trade: Chair maker - Enlistment date: 18 May 1814 - Enlistment place: Franklin County, Franklinton - Enlistment period: War - By whom: Hugh Moore - Discharged: 27 Mar 1815 at Zanesville - Bounty: BLW 5983-160-12.

Reed, John - Private - 2nd Artillery - Company: Daniel Cushing - Pension: SO-8048, SC-14412, served in Capt. D. Cushing's Company, US Artillery and Capt. Samuel Price's Company, Corps of Artillery - Bounty: BLW 24903-160-12 (Arkansas).

Reed, Reasin - Sergeant - 26th Infantry - Company: William Puthuff - Enlistment date: 22 Apr 1813 - Enlistment period: 1 Yr - Pension: SO-14745, SC-9481, served as a sergeant in Captain W. H. Puthoff's Company, 26th Infantry and as a private in Captain John Jones' Company, OH Volunteers - Bounty: BLW 20219-160-50 - Comments: Prisoner of War on Parole, captured at Detroit, MI, 16 Aug 1812.

Reed, William - Private - 27th Infantry - Company: Absalom Martin - Enlistment date: 16 May 1813 - Comments: Served aboard the US Schooner Scorpion on the Lake Erie Squadron.

Reeder, Benjamin - Private - Rangers - Company: Samuel McCormick - Enlistment date: 28 Oct 1813 - Enlistment period: 1 Yr - Discharged: 22 Nov 1814.

Reeder, Levi - Private - 26th Infantry - Company: William Puthuff - Enlistment date: 6 May 1813 - Enlistment period: 1 Yr - Pension: No claim for pension; served in Capt. Puthoff's Company, 26th Infantry - Bounty: BLW 3656-160-50.

Reese, Aaron - Sergeant - 27th Infantry - Company: Isaac Van Horne - Pension: Served in Captain Rowland's Company, Ohio Volunteers, and in Captain Van Horne's Company, 27th Infantry as a sergeant - Bounty:

BLW 134-160-50.

Reeves, Asa - Private - 7th Infantry - Company: Horatio Stark - Age: 21 - Height: 6' - Born: Maryland - Enlistment date: 22 Apr 1812 - Enlistment period: 5 Yrs - By whom: Thomas Jessup - Died: 27 Dec 1814 - Comments: Died at Sachets Harbor, NY.

Reeves, Daniel - Private - 19th Infantry - Company: Asabael Nearing - Other regiment: 17th Infantry - Enlistment date: 12 Mar 1813 - Enlistment period: 18 Mos.

Reeves, William - Private - 19th Infantry - Discharged: 8 Sep 1814.

Reilly, Hugh - Private - 19th Infantry - Company: Richard Talbott - Age: 37 - Height: 5' 7 1/2" - Born: Ohio - Enlistment date: 7 May 1814 - Enlistment place: Butler County, Hamilton - Enlistment period: War - By whom: John Hall.

Repiley, Alexander - Private - 19th Infantry - Company: George Kesling - Age: 25 - Height: 5' 4" - Born: Maryland - Enlistment date: 11 Jul 1814 - Enlistment place: Urbana - Discharged: 27 Mar 1815 at Zanesville.

Reyburn, William M. - Private - Rangers - Company: William Perry - Pension: Wife Ann S., WO-32861, WC-20871; served as a private in Capt. William Perry's Company, US Rangers.

Reynolds, James - Sergeant Major - 19th Infantry - Commissioning date: 6 Jul 1812 - Killed: 16 Aug 1812.

Reynolds, John - Private - 19th Infantry - Age: 39 - Height: 5' 5" - Born: Virginia - Trade: Hatter - Enlistment date: 1 Dec 1814 - Enlistment place: Zanesville - Enlistment period: War - By whom: Charles Cass - Bounty: BLW 8910-160-12 (Illinois).

Reynolds, William L. - Private - 27th Infantry - Company: Carey Trimble - Other regiment: 19th Infantry - Height: 5' 2 1/2" - Born: CT, Litchfield County - Trade: Laborer - Enlistment date: 21 Feb 1814 - Enlistment place: Newark - Enlistment period: War - By whom: John Spencer - Pension: Wife Diadama, WO-11906, WS-9650, SO-15837, SC-20195; served as a private in Captain C. A. Trimble's Company, 27th and 19th Infantries.

Rheam, Adam - Corporal - 17th Infantry - Company: Martin Hawkins - Age: 21 - Height: 5' 10" - Born: PA, Dauphin County - Trade: Hatter - Enlistment date: 13 Jan 1813 - Enlistment place: Portsmouth - Enlistment period: War - By whom: Hugh May - Discharged: 7 Jun 1815 at Chillicothe.

Rhoads, Conway - Private - 19th Infantry - Company: Richard Talbott - Age: 23 - Height: 6' 2" - Born: KY, Mason County - Trade: Farmer - Enlistment date: 29 Mar 1814 - Enlistment place: Urbana - Enlistment period: War - By whom: Christopher Wood - Discharged: 5 Jun 1815 at Chillicothe - Bounty: BLW 6347-160-12 (Illinois).

Rhoads, John - Private - 2nd Rifles - Company: John O'Fallon - Age: 29 - Height: 5' 11" - Born: Massachusetts - Trade: Farmer - Enlistment date: 24 Jul 1814 - Enlistment place: Ohio - Enlistment period: War - By whom: Elias Langham - Bounty: BLW 22384-160-12 (Arkansas).

Rhoads, Sanford - Private - 19th Infantry - Company: Richard Talbott - Age: 25 - Height: 6' - Born: Pennsylvania - Enlistment date: 8 Mar 1814 - Enlistment place: Urbana - Enlistment period: War - By whom: Christopher Wood - Discharged: 5 Jun 1815 at Chillicothe - Bounty: BLW 5858-160-12 (Illinois).

Rhodes, Francis - Private - 2nd Rifles - Company: Benjamin Johnson - Age: 28 - Height: 5' 11" - Born: MA, Hampshire County, Pellum - Trade: Farmer - Enlistment date: 21 Jul 1814 - Enlistment place: Cincinnati - Enlistment period: War - Discharged: 30 Jun 1815 at Detroit.

Rice, John - Private - 19th Infantry - Company: James Herron - Enlistment date: Dec 1812 at Detroit - Enlistment period: 5 Yrs - Died: 5 Oct 1813 - Pension: Heirs obtained half pay for five years in lieu of military bounty land.

Rice, John - Private - 19th Infantry - Company: Richard Graham - Enlistment date: 26 Dec 1812 - Enlistment period: 18 Mos.

Rice, Moses - Corporal - 17th Infantry - Company: Henry Crittenden - Age: 23 - Height: 5' 9 1/2" - Born: MA, Middlesex County - Trade: Clothier - Enlistment date: 4 Jul 1814 - Enlistment period: War - By whom: David Carney.

Rice, Russell - Fifer - 17th Infantry - Company: John Chunn - Other regiment: 3rd Infantry - Age: 14 - Height: 4' 10" - Born: CT, New Haven County, Wallingsford - Trade: Farmer - Enlistment date: 4 Jun 1813 - Enlistment place: Dayton - Enlistment period: 5 Yrs - By whom: Abraham Edwards - Pension: SC-25981 Rejected, served in Captain Mountjoy, Captain Chunn and Captain Stockton's Companies, 17th Infantry as a private - Comments: Deserted at Newport, KY, 20 May 1815.

Rice, Silas - Drummer - 17th Infantry - Company: John Chunn - Age: 18 - Height: 5' 8" - Born: CT, New Haven County, Wallingsford - Trade: Wagon maker - Enlistment date: 11 Jun 1813 - Enlistment place: Dayton - Enlistment period: War - By whom: Abraham Edwards - Discharged: 7 Jun 1815 at Chillicothe - Pension: Wife Esher, WO-9321, WC-7138; served in Capt. John F. Chunn and Capt. Edwards' Companies, 17th

Infantry - Bounty: BLW 17614-160-12 (Illinois).

Richards, Christopher - Private - 26th Infantry - Other regiment: 25th Infantry then 22nd Infantry - Age: 25 - Height: 5' 7 1/2" - Born: PA, York County, Little York - Trade: Tailor - Enlistment date: 12 Jan 1813 - Enlistment place: Ohio - Enlistment period: War - Discharged: 17 May 1815 at Sackets Harbor, NY.

Richardson, Jesse - Sergeant - 19th Infantry - Comments: Prisoner of War, exchanged 11 May 1814.

Richardson, Thomas - Private - 26th Infantry - Died: 26 Feb 1814 - Comments: Died at Greenbush, NY (hospital), in Mar 1814 or 26 Feb 1814.

Richie, John - Private - 1st Rifles - Company: Thomas Ramsey - Age: 20 - Height: 5' 10" - Born: Pennsylvania - Trade: Laborer - Enlistment date: 24 Aug 1813 - Enlistment place: Cincinnati - Enlistment period: War - By whom: Thomas Ramsey - Comments: Deserted at Erie, PA, 4 Sep 1814.

Richter, Frederick - Private - 26th Infantry - Company: William Puthuff - Enlistment date: 9 May 1813 - Enlistment period: 1 Yr.

Riddle, James - Private - Rangers - Company: William Perry - Samuel McCormick - Pension: Wife Isabella, WO-10427, WC-5764; served as a private in Capt. William Perry's Company, US Rangers, and as a private in Capt. McCormick's Company, OH Rangers.

Ridengam, John - Private - 19th Infantry - Age: 38 - Height: 5' 5" - Born: VA, Beatland - Enlistment date: 20 May 1814 - Enlistment place: Athens County.

Ridgeway, Paul S. - Private - 19th Infantry - Company: William Gill - Age: 34 - Height: 5' 9" - Born: PA, Philadelphia County - Trade: Tailor - Enlistment date: 10 Apr 1814 - Enlistment place: Lancaster - Enlistment period: War - By whom: John Simons - Discharged: 5 Jun 1815 at Chillicothe - Pension: Old War IF-1331; served as a private in the War of 1812 - Bounty: BLW 11874-160-12 (Illinois).

Ridingour, John - Private - 27th Infantry - Company: Alexander Hill.

Ridinour, David - Private - 27th Infantry - Company: George Sanderson - Enlistment date: 30 Apr 1813.

Rife, Christopher - Private - 19th Infantry - Company: James Herron - Enlistment date: 25 Jul 1813 - Enlistment period: 5 Yrs - Died: 29 Dec 1813 - Bounty: BLW 26908-160-12 (Arkansas) - Comments: Died at Sackets Harbor, NY; land bounty to Abraham Rife, brother and heir at law of Christopher Rife.

Riggle, Abraham - Private - 19th Infantry - Company: Carey Trimble - Other regiment: 17th Infantry - Age: 34 - Height: 5' 9" - Born: Pennsylvania - Trade: Carpenter - Enlistment date: 6 Apr 1814 - Enlistment place: Ross County, Adelphi - Enlistment period: War - By whom: George Will - Discharged: 6 Jun 1815 at Chillicothe - Pension: Old War IF-26368; served in Capt. McElvain's Company, 19th Infantry as a private - Bounty: BLW 14622-160-12 (Illinois).

Riley, John - Private - 2nd Artillery - Company: Daniel Cushing - Other regiment: Corps of Artillery - Age: 39 - Height: 6' 1" - Born: Virginia - Trade: Laborer - Enlistment date: 6 Jan 1815 - Enlistment period: War - Discharged: 25 Jul 1815 at Lower Sandusky (now Fremont, OH).

Risher, Daniel - Private - 19th Infantry - Company: William Gill - Age: 19 - Height: 5' 10" - Born: KY, Bourbon County - Enlistment date: 11 Sep 1814 - Enlistment place: Canton - Bounty: BLW 27573-160-42 - Comments: Land bounty to Daniel Risher, Isabella Shires and Julia Jackson, the children & only heirs at law of Daniel Risher.

Risley, Eli - Private - Rangers - Company: Samuel McCormick - Enlistment date: 23 Oct 1813 - Enlistment period: Yr - Discharged: 22 Oct 1814 at Newport, KY.

Ritter, Jacob - Private - 1st Infantry - Company: Horatio Stark - Other regiment: 3rd Infantry - Age: 27 - Height: 5' 8" - Born: PA, Berks County - Trade: Coppersmith - Enlistment date: 5 May 1812 - Enlistment place: Cincinnati - Enlistment period: 5 Yrs - By whom: Thomas Ramsey - Discharged: 5 May 1817 at Fort Dearborn, IL.

Roach, Ebenezer A. - Private - 17th Infantry - Company: Caleb Holder - Age: 19 - Height: 5' 6" - Born: Virginia - Trade: Farmer - Enlistment date: 15 Jul ???? - Enlistment period: War - By whom: William Featherstone - Discharged: 30 Jun 1815 at Detroit - Pension: Wife Mary, WO-7711, WC-24374; served in Capt. C. H. Holder's Company, US Infantry – Bounty: BLW 25094-160-12 (Arkansas).

Roach, Reuben - Private - 19th Infantry - Age: 21 - Height: 5' 8" - Born: VA, Monroe County - Enlistment date: 27 May 1814 - Enlistment place: Athens County.

Roath, Joseph - Private - 19th Infantry - Company: John Chunn - Enlistment date: 30 Mar 1813 - Enlistment period: 18 Mos.

Robb, Andrew - Private - 26th Infantry - Company: William Puthuff - Other regiment: 25th Infantry - Enlistment date: 27 Apr 1813 - Enlistment period: 1 Yr - Discharged: 27 Apr 1814.

Robb, Andrew - Private - 17th Infantry - Company: Henry Crittenden - Other regiment: 3rd Infantry - Age: 24 - Height: 5' 5" - Born: Massachusetts - Enlistment date: 17 Aug 1814 - Enlistment period: 5 Yrs - By whom:

The Enlisted Men

David Carney - Discharged: 17 Aug 1819 at Fort Gratiot, MI - Pension: Served in Capt. Chunn's Company as a private - Bounty: BLW 24361-160-12.

Robb, John - Private - 19th Infantry - Age: 36 - Height: 5' 11" - Born: New Hampshire - Enlistment date: 18 Apr 1814.

Robbe, John - Private - 2nd Rifles - Company: Batteal Harrison - Age: 36 - Height: 5' 8 1/2" - Born: NH, Petersburg - Trade: Shoemaker - Enlistment date: 16 May 1814 - Enlistment place: Chillicothe - Enlistment period: War - By whom: Batteal Harrison - Discharged: 30 Jun 1815 at Detroit.

Robbins, Alexander - Private - 17th Infantry - Other regiment: 3rd Infantry - Age: 35 - Height: 5' 5 1/2" - Born: RI, Washington County, Kingston - Trade: Farmer - Enlistment date: 10 Dec 1814 - Enlistment place: Cincinnati - Enlistment period: 5 Yrs - By whom: John Reeves - Discharged: 1 Feb 1816 on Surgeon's Certificate of Disability for epileptic fits.

Roberts, Aaron - Sergeant - 26th Infantry - Company: George Kesling - Enlistment date: 19 May 1813 - Enlistment period: 1 Yr - By whom: George Kesling - Comments: Prisoner of War (Quebec, LC), captured at Fort Niagara, NY, 19 Dec 1813; exchanged 4 May 1814.

Roberts, Henry - Corporal - 19th Infantry - Company: Wilson Elliott - Comments: Served aboard the US Schooner Porcupine on the Lake Erie Squadron.

Roberts, Peter - Private - 1st Rifles - Company: Thomas Ramsey - Age: 20 - Height: 5 11 1/2" - Born: NY, Rensselaer County, Stephentown - Trade: Farmer - Enlistment date: 1 May 1814 - Enlistment place: Cincinnati - Enlistment period: 5 Yrs - By whom: Thomas Ramsey - Died: 30 Nov 1814 - Pension: Wife Margaret, WO-20548, WC-18834, SO-7511, SC-8342, served in Captain Thomas Ramsey's Company, 1st Rifles as a private - Bounty: BLW 16598-160-12 (Illinois) - Comments: Land bounty to Zopher Roberts, father & heir at law of Peter Roberts.

Roberts, Robert - Private - 19th Infantry - Company: George Kesling - Age: 21 - Height: 5' 8" - Born: Pennsylvania - Enlistment date: 23 May 1814 - Enlistment place: Chillicothe - Enlistment period: War - By whom: Charles Cissna.

Robertson, John - Private - 19th Infantry - Company: Harris Hickman - Age: 36 - Height: 5' 10" - Born: PA, Chester County - Trade: Tailor - Enlistment date: 4 Apr 1814 - Enlistment place: Lancaster - Enlistment period: War - By whom: Batteal Harrison - Discharged: 9 Jun 1815 - Comments: Discharged at Chillicothe.

Robertson, John - Private - 19th Infantry - Company: Richard Talbott - Age: 32 - Height: 5' 5 1/2" - Born: DE, New Castle County - Trade: Hatter - Enlistment date: 3 May 1814 - Enlistment place: Cincinnati - Enlistment period: War - By whom: Robert Anderson - Discharged: 5 Jun 1815 at Chillicothe - Bounty: BLW 20181-160-12 (Missouri).

Robinson, Aaron - Corporal - 19th Infantry - Company: William Gill - Age: 38 - Height: 5' 11" - Born: Delaware - Trade: Joiner - Enlistment date: 15 Aug 1814 - Enlistment place: New Lisbon - Enlistment period: War - By whom: Wynkoop Warner - Discharged: 5 Jun 1815 at Chillicothe - Bounty: BLW-8832-160-12 (Illinois).

Robinson, Archibald - Private - 19th Infantry - Company: Harris Hickman - Other regiment: 17th Infantry - Age: 38 - Height: 5' 8 1/2" - Born: Ireland - Enlistment date: 8 Apr 1814 - Enlistment place: Marietta - Enlistment period: War - By whom: John Milligan - Died: 12 Nov 1814 at Buffalo, NY - Pension: Wife Jane, Old War 11188, served as a private in the US Infantry.

Robinson, Elijah - Private - 19th Infantry - Age: 18 - Height: 5' 4 1/2" - Born: VA, Harrison County - Enlistment date: 14 Apr 1814 - Enlistment place: Chillicothe - By whom: James Campbell.

Robinson, Francis S. - Sergeant - 2nd Rifles - Company: Batteal Harrison - Age: 24 - Height: 5' 10 3/4" - Born: Maryland - Trade: House joiner - Enlistment date: 8 Aug 1814 - Enlistment place: Cincinnati - Enlistment period: War - By whom: Edward Miller - Discharged: 20 Jun 1815 - Pension: SO-17685, SC-8464; served in Capt. Batteal Harrison's Company, 2nd Rifles - Bounty: BLW 27124-160-42 (Iowa).

Robinson, Harry B. (or Harvey) - Musician - 19th Infantry - Company: George Kesling - Age: 14 - Height: 5' - Born: Vermont or Pennsylvania - Trade: Laborer - Enlistment date: 12 Dec 1814 - Enlistment place: Franklin County, Franklinton - Enlistment period: War - By whom: Orren Granger - Discharged: 27 Mar 1815 at Zanesville - Bounty: BLW 266-320-14.

Robinson, John - Private - 19th Infantry - Company: William Gill - Age: 18 - Height: 5' 9" - Born: Pennsylvania - Trade: Shoemaker - Enlistment date: 28 Jul 1814 - Enlistment place: St. Clairsville - Enlistment period: War - By whom: William Gill - Comments: Deserted at St. Clairsville, OH, 1 Aug 1814.

Robinson, Otis - Private - 19th Infantry - Company: George Kesling - Age: 38 - Height: 5' 11' - Born: Vermont - Trade: Shoemaker - Enlistment date: 12 Dec 1814 - Enlistment place: Franklin County, Franklinton - Enlistment period: War - By whom: Orren Granger - Discharged: 27 Mar 1815 at Zanesville - Bounty: BLW 265-320-14.

Robinson, Thomas - Private - 19th Infantry - Enlistment date: 26 Apr 1813 - Enlistment place: Cincinnati - Enlistment period: 5 Yrs.
Robinson, William - Private - 19th Infantry - Company: George Kesling - Other regiment: 17th Infantry - Enlistment date: 31 May 1814 - Enlistment period: War - Died: 26 Oct 1814.
Robison, William - Private - 17th Infantry - Company: David Holt - Age: 21 - Height: 5' 8" - Born: Pennsylvania - Enlistment date: 11 May 1814 - Enlistment place: Franklin County, Franklinton - Enlistment period: War - By whom: John Cochran - Died: 12 Nov 1814 at Buffalo, NY.
Roderick, Lewis - Private - 27th Infantry - Company: Joseph Cairns - Pension: SO-4004, SC-2125, served in Captain Joseph Cairne's Company, 27th Infantry.
Roders, Isaac - Private - 19th Infantry - Company: Carey Trimble - Other regiment: 17th Infantry - Enlistment date: 1 Jan 1814 - Enlistment period: 1 Yr - Died: 1 Jan 1815.
Rodgers, Hugh - Private - 19th Infantry - Company: Carey Trimble - Other regiment: 17th Infantry - Age: 30 - Height: 5' 8" - Born: VA, Berkeley County, Martinsburg (now WV) - Trade: Millwright - Enlistment date: 25 Feb 1814 - Enlistment place: Chillicothe - Enlistment period: War - By whom: Charles Cissna.
Rodgers, John - Private - 26th Infantry - Company: George Kesling - Other regiment: 25th Infantry - Enlistment date: 7 May 1813 - Enlistment period: 1 Yr - Discharged: 7 May 1814 - Comments: Served aboard the US Schooner Porcupine on the Lake Erie Squadron; re-enlisted 8 May 1814.
Rogers, Elijah - Private - 27th Infantry - Company: George Sanderson - Enlistment date: 25 May 1813.
Rogers, Isaac - Private - 27th Infantry - Age: 19 - Height: 5' 8" - Born: Pennsylvania - Enlistment date: 11 Jan 1814 - Enlistment place: Newark - By whom: John Spencer.
Rogers, Joel - Sergeant - 19th Infantry - Age: 40 - Height: 5' 8 1/2" - Born: New Jersey - Trade: Farmer - Enlistment date: 2 Jun 1814 - Enlistment period: War - Discharged: 27 Mar 1815 at Zanesville - Bounty: BLW 14307-160-12 (Illinois).
Rogers, Joseph - Sergeant - 19th Infantry - Company: Asabael Nearing - Enlistment date: 3 Mar 1812 - Enlistment period: 18 Mos.
Roland, Thomas - Sergeant - 26th Infantry - Company: William Puthuff - Enlistment date: 10 May 1813 - Enlistment period: 1 Yr.
Rollings, John - Private - 2nd Rifles - Company: Batteal Harrison - Age: 23 - Height: 5' 8" - Born: LA, Orleans Parish, New Orleans - Trade: Laborer - Enlistment date: 5 Jul 1814 - Enlistment place: Chillicothe - Enlistment period: 5 Yrs - By whom: Batteal Harrison - Discharged: 6 Mar 1819.
Roof, Samuel - Private - 26th Infantry - Company: George Kesling - Other regiment: 19th Infantry - Height: 5' 10" - Born: Pennsylvania - Enlistment date: 1 May 1813 - Enlistment place: Xenia - Enlistment period: 1 Yr - War - Comments: Served aboard the US Schooner Porcupine on the Lake Erie Squadron; prisoner of war left at Detroit.
Rook, James - Private - 17th Infantry - Company: David Holt - Age: 23 - Height: 5' 8" - Born: Maryland - Trade: Laborer - Enlistment date: 14 Jun 1812 - Enlistment place: Zanesville - Enlistment period: War - By whom: James Herron - Discharged: 4 Jun 1815 at Chillicothe - Bounty: BLW 2659-160-12 (Illinois).
Root, Charles - Private - 17th Infantry - Age: 24 - Height: 5' 10 1/2" - Born: Massachusetts - Enlistment date: 29 May 1814 - By whom: John Cochran.
Root, Gabriel - Private - 27th Infantry - Company: Alexander Hill - Other regiment: 19th Infantry - Age: 18 - Height: 5' 11" - Born: CT, Tolland County - Enlistment date: 27 May 1814 - Enlistment place: Ashtabula County, Harpersfield - Enlistment period: War - Died: 15 Aug 1814 at Fort Erie, UC - Bounty: BLW 27298-160-42 - Comments: Land bounty to Henry, Edward, David, Benjamin B. & Gabriel Root; Humphrey, Julius, Quinton, Josephine & John Heater; Henry, Edward & Frederick Allen; and Sally Beckley, only heirs at law of Gabriel Root.
Root, Marion - Sergeant - 27th Infantry - Company: Alexander Hill - Other regiment: 19th Infantry then 17th Infantry - Age: 30 - Height: 5' 4 1/4" - Born: Connecticut - Trade: Joiner - Enlistment date: 26 Apr 1814 - Enlistment place: New Lisbon - Enlistment period: War - By whom: Thomas McKnight - Discharged: 6 Jun 1815 at Chillicothe - Bounty: BLW 6026-160-12 (Illinois).
Rophy, George - Private - 27th Infantry - Company: George Sanderson - Enlistment date: 27 Apr 1813 - Died: 2 Dec 1813.
Rose, Asa - Private - 27th Infantry - Company: George Sanderson - Enlistment date: 15 Jul 1813.
Rose, Jason - Private - 27th Infantry - Company: Absalom Martin - Enlistment date: 11 Aug 1813 - Enlistment period: 1 Yr - Died: 28 Mar 1814.
Ross, Alexander - Private - 17th Infantry - Company: David Holt - Age: 33 - Height: 5' 5" - Born: Scotland - Trade: Cooper - Enlistment date: 6 Jul 1814 - Enlistment place: Cincinnati - Enlistment period: 5 Yrs - By whom:

Philip Price.

Ross, Job - Private - Rangers - Company: Samuel McCormick - Pension: Old War IF-17539 Rejected, SO-18660, SC-16282; served in Capt. Samuel McCormick's Company, 12-month Rangers as a private.

Ross, John - Private - 17th Infantry - Company: John Chunn - Other regiment: 3rd Infantry - Age: 43 - Height: 5' 11 3/4" - Born: Ireland - Trade: Mason - Enlistment date: 28 Oct 1813 - Enlistment period: 18 Mos - By whom: George Stall - Discharged: 5 May 1815.

Ross, Martin - Private - Rangers - Company: Samuel McCormick - Age: 21 - Height: 5' 9" - Born: North Carolina - Trade: Farmer - Enlistment date: 11 Nov 1813 - Enlistment period: 1 Yr - Discharged: 11 Nov 1814 at Fort Malden, UC.

Ross, Robert - Private - 1st Rifles - Company: Thomas Ramsey - Age: 26 - Height: 5' 7" - Born: PA, Fayette County - Trade: Farmer - Enlistment date: 31 Mar 1814 - Enlistment place: Cincinnati - Enlistment period: War - By whom: Thomas Ramsey - Discharged: 8 Jun 1815 at Buffalo, NY - Bounty: BLW 8173-160-12 (Illinois).

Rossell, Abednigo - Private - 19th Infantry - Age: 18 - Height: 5' 8" - Born: Kentucky - Enlistment date: 15 Apr 1814 - Enlistment place: Franklin County - Enlistment period: War - By whom: Robert Young - Comments: Deserted.

Rossell, Meshack - Private - 19th Infantry - Company: Richard Talbott - Age: 20 - Height: 5' 7" - Born: Kentucky - Trade: Laborer - Enlistment date: 14 Mar 1814 - Enlistment place: Franklin County - Enlistment period: War - By whom: Robert Young - Discharged: 5 Jun 1815 at Chillicothe - Bounty: BLW 12402-16-12.

Rothe, Thomas - Private - 1st Rifles - Company: Thomas Ramsey - Age: 39 - Height: 5' 9" - Born: PA, Cumberland County - Trade: Stone mason - Enlistment date: 10 Jun 1811 - Enlistment place: Cincinnati - Enlistment period: 5 Yrs - By whom: Thomas Ramsey - Discharged: 12 Feb 1816 probably at Detroit on Surgeon's Certificate of Disability.

Routh, Joseph - Private - 19th Infantry - Enlistment date: 30 Mar 1813 - Enlistment place: Cincinnati - Enlistment period: 18 Mos.

Rozekilde, John - Private - 19th Infantry - Company: Angus Langham.

Rucker, Wisdom - Private - 19th Infantry - Company: Joel Collins - Age: 45 - Height: 6' 3" - Born: Virginia - Trade: Farmer - Enlistment date: 12 Jul 1814 - Enlistment place: Upper Canada, Fort Malden - Enlistment period: War - By whom: Robert Smith.

Rude, Felix - Private - 2nd Artillery - Company: Daniel Cushing - Enlistment date: 29 Aug 1812 - Enlistment period: 18 Mos - Killed: 8 Apr 1813 near Fort Meigs, OH.

Rudicilly, Jacob - Private - 19th Infantry - Discharged: 13 Dec 1814.

Rudolph, Titan K. - Private - 17th Infantry - Company: David Holt - Age: 21 - Height: 5' 10" - Born: Maryland - Trade: Shoemaker - Enlistment date: 26 May 1814 - Enlistment place: Trumbull County, Warren - Enlistment period: War - By whom: Wilson Elliott - Discharged: 4 Jun 1815 at Chillicothe - Bounty: BLW 7230-160-12 (Illinois).

Rudrow, Spicer - Private - 26th Infantry - Company: George Kesling - Other regiment: 25th Infantry - Enlistment date: 6 Jul 1813 - Discharged: 6 Jul 1814 after furnishing a substitute.

Ruggles, Michael - Corporal - 26th Infantry - Company: George Kesling - Other regiment: 25th Infantry - Enlistment date: 26 May 1813 - Enlistment period: 1 Yr - Discharged: 26 May 1814 - Bounty: BLW 20752-160-12 (Missouri).

Ruggles, Nicholas - Private - 17th Infantry - Age: 25 - Height: 6' - Born: Kentucky - Trade: Laborer - Enlistment date: 1 Jul 1814 - Enlistment place: Chillicothe - Enlistment period: War - By whom: John Cochran.

Rumsey, Samuel A. - Private - 17th Infantry - Age: 31 - Height: 5' 11" - Born: New Jersey - Trade: Brick maker - Enlistment date: 4 May 1814 - Enlistment place: Warren County - Enlistment period: War - By whom: Ensign Austin - Bounty: BLW 14399-160-12 (Illinois).

Runden, Daniels - Private - 19th Infantry - Company: Lt John McElvain.

Rush, Garrett - Private - 27th Infantry - Company: Absalom Martin - Comments: Served aboard the US Sloop Trippe on the Lake Erie Squadron.

Russell, James - Private - 2nd Rifles - Company: Batteal Harrison - Age: 22 - Height: 5' 4" - Born: Tennessee - Trade: Farmer - Enlistment date: 21 Aug 1814 - Enlistment place: Cincinnati - Enlistment period: War - By whom: Elias Langham - Discharged: 20 Jun 1815 at Detroit - Bounty: BLW 9977-160-12 (Illinois).

Russell, John - Private - 19th Infantry - Company: William Gill - Age: 19 - Height: 5' 2" - Born: Pennsylvania - Trade: Farmer - Enlistment date: 23 Jul 1814 - Enlistment place: Zanesville - Enlistment period: War - By whom: Neal McFadden - Discharged: 5 Jun 1815 at Chillicothe - Bounty: BLW 8251-160-12 (Illinois).

Russell, Joshua - Private - 19th Infantry - Company: James Herron - Enlistment date: 4 May 1813 - Enlistment period: War - By whom: Samuel Booker - Bounty: BLW 27414-160-42 - Comments: Land bounty to Henry Johnston, sole heir of Joshua Russell.

Russell, William - Private - 26th Infantry - Company: Samuel Swearingen - Enlistment date: 3 Jun 1813 - Enlistment period: 1 Yr.

Ryan, John - Private - 19th Infantry - Other regiment: 25th Infantry - Age: 30 - Height: 5' 10" - Born: Maryland - Trade: Farmer - Enlistment date: 24 Mar 1813 - Enlistment place: Ohio - Enlistment period: 5 Yrs - Discharged: 20 Mar 1815 at Sackets Harbor, NY, because of scrotal hernia.

Ryan, Patrick - Private - 17th Infantry - Company: Henry Crittenden - Age: 18 - Height: 5' 5" - Born: Ireland - Trade: Laborer - Enlistment date: 15 Apr 1813 - Enlistment period: 18 Mos - By whom: Adam Hoffman - Comments: Re-enlisted 28 Jul 1814 by Lieutenant Hoffman for the War, OH, Jefferson County, Steubenville; absent without leave on 31 May 1815.

Ryan, William - Private - 17th Infantry - Company: John Chunn - Other regiment: 3rd Infantry - Age: 21 - Height: 5' 5 1/2" - Born: Virginia - Trade: Carpenter - Enlistment date: 27 Jun 1812 - Enlistment place: Gallipolis - Enlistment period: 5 Yrs - By whom: Thomas Morgan - Discharged: 27 Jun 1817 at Fort Harrison, IN - Bounty: BLW 10592-160-12 (Illinois).

Rynearson, Joacum - Private - 19th Infantry - Company: Richard Talbott - Age: 35 - Height: 5' 10" - Born: New Jersey - Trade: Carpenter - Enlistment date: 27 Apr 1814 - Enlistment place: Springfield - Enlistment period: War - By whom: Abijah Johns - Discharged: 5 Jun 1815 at Chillicothe - Bounty: BLW 23260-160-12 (Arkansas).

Sackett, Almerson - Private - 19th Infantry - Company: George Kesling - Age: 40 - Height: 5' 7" - Born: Connecticut - Trade: Cooper - Enlistment date: 20 Dec 1814 - Enlistment place: Zanesville - Enlistment period: War - By whom: Charles Cass - Discharged: 27 Mar 1815 at Zanesville - Bounty: BLW 600-320-14 (Illinois).

Sackett, David - Corporal - 19th Infantry - Company: George Kesling - Age: 19 - Height: 5' 5" - Born: New York - Trade: Farmer - Enlistment date: 21 Jan 1815 - Enlistment place: Zanesville - Enlistment period: War - By whom: Charles Cass - Discharged: 27 Mar 1815 at Zanesville - Bounty: BLW 603-320-14 (Illinois).

Sackett, Elisha - Private - 19th Infantry - Company: George Kesling - Age: 21 - Height: 5' 7" - Born: Pennsylvania - Trade: Farmer - Enlistment date: 9 Jan 1815 - Enlistment place: Zanesville - Enlistment period: War - By whom: Charles Cass - Discharged: 27 Mar 1815 at Zanesville - Bounty: BLW 604-320-14 (Illinois).

Salliday, Samuel - Private - 19th Infantry - Company: Richard Talbott - Age: 34 - Height: 5' 11 1/2" - Born: PA, Fayette County - Trade: Laborer - Enlistment date: 10 Apr 1814 - Enlistment place: Montgomery County - Enlistment period: War - By whom: Philip Price - Discharged: 5 Jun 1815 at Chillicothe.

Sally, Jack M. - Private - 17th Infantry - Company: David Holt - Pension: Old War IF-1348; served as a private in Capt. Holt's Company, 17th Infantry - Bounty: BLW 18875-160-50.

Salmon, Henry - Private - 26th Infantry - Company: George Kesling - Enlistment date: 18 May 1813 - Enlistment period: 1 Yr.

Saltsgiver, Adam - 19th Infantry - Born: PA, Adams County - Enlistment date: 27 Jul 1812 - Enlistment period: 5 Yrs.

Saltsgiver, Jacob - Private - 19th Infantry - Company: Wilson Elliott - Age: 21 - Height: 5' 7" - Born: PA, Adams County - Enlistment date: 27 Jul 1812 - Enlistment place: Trumbull County, Warren - Enlistment period: 5 Yrs - By whom: Wilson Elliott - Died: 31 May 1813 - Bounty: BLW 27793-160-42 - Comments: Land bounty to Eve Thomas, sister & only heir at law of Jacob Saltsgiver.

Snar – see Saner, Adam

Sanborn, John - Private - 19th Infantry - Company: William Gill - Age: 24 - Height: 5' 8" - Born: New Hampshire - Trade: Farmer - Enlistment date: 25 Jul 1814 - Enlistment place: Marietta - Enlistment period: War - Discharged: 5 Jun 1815 - Bounty: BLW 18365-160-12 (Illinois) - Comments: Discharged at Chillicothe.

Sanders, Isaac - Private - 19th Infantry - Company: Richard Talbott - Age: 23 - Height: 5' 8" - Born: Kentucky - Enlistment date: 29 Apr 1814 - Enlistment place: Lebanon - Enlistment period: War - By whom: Richard Talbott - Pension: SO-9911, SC-6000; served in Capt R. C. Talbott's Company, 19th Infantry - Bounty: BLW 24362-160-12 (Arkansas).

Sanders, Isaac - Private - 19th Infantry - Company: Richard Talbott - Age: 23 - Height: 5' 8" - Born: Kentucky - Trade: Carpenter - Enlistment date: 24 Feb 1814 - Enlistment place: Clermont County, Dunhantown - Enlistment period: War - By whom: Josiah Brady - Discharged: 5 Jun 1815 at Chillicothe - Pension: SC-6000; served in Capt. Talbott's Company, 19th Infantry as a private.

Sanderson, Robert - Sergeant - 27th Infantry - Company: George Sanderson - Enlistment date: 28 Apr 1813 - Pension: Wife Hannah, WO-17696, WC-17049; served in Captain George Sanderson's Company, 27th

Infantry.

Saner, Adam - Private - 19th Infantry - Company: Joel Collins - Age: 21 - Height: 5' 4" - Born: Germany - Trade: Blacksmith - Enlistment date: 31 Mar 1814 - Enlistment place: Detroit - Enlistment period: War - By whom: Samuel Coleman - Died: 19 Jul 1815 - Bounty: BLW 27654-160-42.

Sardon, Jonathan - Private - 27th Infantry - Company: George Sanderson - Enlistment date: 27 Apr 1813.

Sartain, Lewis - Private - 19th Infantry - Enlistment date: 30 Jul 1813 - Enlistment period: War - Died: Oct 1813 - Bounty: BLW 27155-160-12 - Comments: Died in service; land bounty to John Sartain, Fanny Davis, Thomas Sartain, Sarah Sartain, Lewis Sartain, Henry Sartain, Mary Sartain & Elizabeth Sartain, only children & heirs at law of Lewis Sartain.

Saunders, Edward - Private - 17th Infantry - Other regiment: 3rd Infantry - Age: 35 - Height: 5' 9" - Born: NJ, Cumberland County - Trade: Carpenter - Enlistment date: 16 Aug 1814 - Enlistment place: Coshocton County, Coshocton - Enlistment period: 5 Yrs - By whom: John Reeves.

Saunders, Moses - Private - Rangers - Company: William Perry - Killed: 5 Sep 1812.

Saxton, Edward - Private - 2nd Artillery - Company: Stanton Sholes - Enlistment date: 5 Dec 1812 - Enlistment period: 5 Yrs - Died: 21 Sep 1813 - Bounty: BLW 27400-160-42 - Comments: Died probably in Ohio; land bounty to Elizabeth Conner, Benjamin Saxton and Ann Lenox, only heirs at law of Edward Saxton.

Schaffner, Jacob - Private - 1st Infantry - Company: Horatio Stark - Age: 22 - Height: 5' 7" - Born: Pennsylvania - Trade: Weaver - Enlistment date: 22 Apr 1812 - Enlistment period: 5 Yrs - By whom: Thomas Ramsey - Died: 1 Oct 1814 at Fort Erie, UC, of fever.

Schloeman, Francis H. - Private - 1st Rifles - Company: Thomas Ramsey - Age: 22 - Height: 5' 2 1/2" - Born: Germany - Trade: Printer - Enlistment date: 25 Mar 1814 - Enlistment place: Cincinnati - Enlistment period: War - By whom: Thomas Ramsey - Discharged: 5 Jun 1815 at Buffalo, NY.

Schofield, George - Private - 28th Infantry - Company: Nimrod Moore - Enlistment date: 17 May 1813 - Enlistment period: 1 Yr - Died: 20 Sep 1813 - Comments: Served aboard the US Brig Niagara on the Lake Erie Station; died at Bass Island, OH (Put-in-Bay, OH) from wounds received during the Battle of Lake Erie, 10 Sep 1813.

Schooley, James - Private - 17th Infantry - Other regiment: 3rd Infantry - Age: 22 - Height: 5' 7" - Born: Pennsylvania - Trade: Stone mason - Enlistment date: 14 Jan 1814 - Enlistment place: Xenia - Enlistment period: 5 Yrs - By whom: Ensign Shay - Discharged: 12 Jan 1820.

Scott, Alexander - Private - 1st Infantry - Company: Hugh Moore - Other regiment: 3rd Infantry - Age: 40 - Height: 5' 9 1/2" - Born: Ireland - Trade: Weaver - Enlistment date: 1 Jan 1813 - Enlistment place: IN, Fort Wayne - Enlistment period: 5 Yrs - By whom: Hugh Moore - Pension: Old War IF-17702 Rejected; enlisted in OH; later lived in PA; served in the 1st and 3rd Infantries - Bounty: BLW 16199-160-12 - Comments: Discharged 5 Nov 1817 and re-enlisted.

Scott, James - Private - 17th Infantry - Company: David Holt - Age: 36 - Height: 5' 11" - Born: PA, York County, York - Trade: Clerk - Enlistment date: 17 May 1814 - Enlistment place: Marietta - Enlistment period: War - By whom: John Milligan - Discharged: 15 Jun 1815 - Bounty: BLW 6694-160-12.

Scott, James - Private - 1st Infantry - Company: Horatio Stark - Age: 18 - Height: 5' 7" - Born: Pennsylvania - Trade: Farmer - Enlistment date: 21 Apr 1812 - Enlistment period: 5 Yrs - By whom: Thomas Ramsey - Discharged: 21 Apr 1817 - Comments: Discharged probably at Fort Mackinaw, MI.

Scott, John - Private - 19th Infantry - Company: Richard Talbott - Age: 20 - Height: 5' 11" - Born: New York - Trade: Farmer - Enlistment date: 24 Mar 1814 - Enlistment place: Urbana - Enlistment period: War - By whom: Christopher Wood - Discharged: 5 Jun 1815 at Chillicothe - Pension: SO-6519, SC-5307; served in Capt. R. C. Talbott's Company, 19th Infantry; lived in OH - Bounty: BLW 17725-160-12 (Illinois).

Scott, Joseph - Private - 19th Infantry - Company: Carey Trimble - Age: 21 - Height: 5' 5" - Born: KY, Campbell County - Trade: Hatter - Enlistment date: 5 Jun 1814 - Enlistment place: Athens - Enlistment period: War - By whom: Nehemiah Gregory.

Scott, Joseph M. - Private - 19th Infantry - Company: Wilson Elliott – Comments: Prisoner of War (Quebec), captured at Fort Niagara, NY, 19 Dec 1813; exchanged 11 May 1814.

Scott, Robert - 17th Infantry - Age: 21 - Height: 5' 8" - Born: New Jersey - Enlistment date: 3 Nov 1814 - Enlistment place: Adams County, West Union - Enlistment period: 5 Yrs - By whom: James Campbell.

Scudder, Thomas - Private - 19th Infantry - Company: Henry Crittenden - Other regiment: 17th Infantry - Age: 19 - Height: 5' 6" - Born: New Jersey - Trade: Laborer - Enlistment date: 27 Apr 1814 - Enlistment place: Butler County, Hamilton - Enlistment period: War - By whom: George Stall - Discharged: 9 Jun 1815 at Chillicothe - Bounty: BLW 9287-160-12 (Illinois).

Searls, Sweetland - Private - 19th Infantry - Company: Harris Hickman - Other regiment: 17th Infantry - Age: 21 - Height: 5' 8" - Born: NY, Addison County or Harrison County - Trade: Laborer - Enlistment date: 28 Mar

1814 - Enlistment place: Franklin County, Franklinton - Enlistment period: War - By whom: John Cochran - Discharged: 9 Jun 1815 at Chillicothe - Bounty: BLW 8641-160-12 (Illinois).

Seiting, Frederick M. - Private - 19th Infantry - Age: 32 - Height: 5' 2 1/1" - Born: Germany - Enlistment date: 22 Jan 1815 - Enlistment place: Cambridge - Enlistment period: 5 Yrs.

Selare, Baptist - Private - 19th Infantry - Company: Martin Hawkins - Other regiment: 17th Infantry then 3rd Infantry - Age: 21 - Height: 5' 11" - Born: Michigan - Trade: Farmer - Enlistment date: 17 Mar 1814 - Enlistment place: Detroit - Enlistment period: 5 Yrs - By whom: George Atchison.

Sells, William - Private - 19th Infantry - Bounty: BLW 6032-160-12 (Illinois).

Selwood, Henry - Corporal - 17th Infantry - Company: Harris Hickman - Age: 20 - Height: 5' 7 1/2" - Born: Virginia - Trade: Shoemaker - Enlistment date: 16 Mar 1814 - Enlistment place: Steubenville - Enlistment period: War - By whom: Lieutenant Mitchell - Discharged: 9 Jun 1815 at Chillicothe - Bounty: BLW 11581-160-12 (Arkansas).

Serow, Leonard - Private - 19th Infantry - Enlistment date: 3 May 1813 - Enlistment place: Cincinnati - Enlistment period: War.

Serrin, Ezekiel - Private - 17th Infantry - Company: Henry Crittenden - Other regiment: 3rd Infantry - Age: 28 - Height: 5' 10" - Born: NY, Dutchess County - Trade: Shoemaker - Enlistment date: 13 Jun 1814 - Enlistment period: War - By whom: John Reeves - Discharged: 30 Jun 1815 - Bounty: BLW 9285-160-12 (Illinois).

Severs, David - Private - 27th Infantry - Company: George Sanderson - Enlistment date: 19 May 1813.

Severs, John - Private - 27th Infantry - Company: George Sanderson - Other regiment: 19th Infantry then 17th Infantry - Age: 23 - Height: 5' 9" - Born: New Jersey - Trade: Laborer - Enlistment date: 27 Apr 1814 - Enlistment place: Detroit - Enlistment period: War - By whom: George Atchison - Discharged: 9 Jun 1815 at Chillicothe.

Seward, John T. - Sergeant - 17th Infantry - Company: David Holt - Age: 19 - Height: 5' 7 1/2" - Born: PA, Fayette County - Trade: Laborer - Enlistment date: 20 Jul 1813 - Enlistment place: Lebanon - Enlistment period: War - By whom: Ensign Seward - Discharged: 4 Jun 1815 at Chillicothe - Pension: Wife Polly, WO- 34667, WC-29086, IF-4816, IC-1161; served in Captains John Good's and David Holt's Companies, 17th Infantry as a sergeant - Bounty: BLW 25373-160-12 (Arkansas).

Seward, William - Fifer - 19th Infantry - Other regiment: 3rd Infantry - Age: 16 - Height: 5' 5" - Born: Ohio - Trade: Farmer - Enlistment date: 4 Sep 1814 - Enlistment place: Urbana - Enlistment period: 5 Yrs - Comments: Re-enlisted on 30 Jun 1819.

Seymore, Sanford - Private - 2nd Rifles - Company: Batteal Harrison - Age: 22 - Height: 5' 5" - Born: NH, Cheshire County, Walpole - Trade: Farmer - Enlistment date: 30 Jun 1814 - Enlistment place: Portsmouth - Enlistment period: War - By whom: Andrew Gilmore - Discharged: 30 Jun 1815 at Detroit.

Seymore, Stanford - Private - 26th Infantry - Company: William Puthuff - Enlistment date: 8 May 1813 - Enlistment period: 1 Yr.

Shackley, Clement - Private - 19th Infantry - Discharged: 4 Jan 1815.

Shadley, Henry - Private - 27th Infantry - Company: George Sanderson - Enlistment date: 8 Jun 1813 - Died: Died at Fort Ball, OH (now Tiffin, OH) - Comments: Prisoner of War on Parole, captured at Detroit, MI, 16 Aug 1812.

Shadwick, George - Private - 27th Infantry - Company: George Sanderson - Enlistment date: 25 Sep 1813 - Pension: Wife Elizabeth, WO-35217, WC-25834, SO-23184, SC-18405; served in Captain George Sanderson's Company, 27th Infantry as a private.

Shaffer, Archibald - Private - 19th Infantry - Company: Carey Trimble - Age: 32 - Height: 5' 11" - Born: Pennsylvania - Trade: Shoemaker - Enlistment date: 28 Feb 1814 - Enlistment place: Lancaster - Enlistment period: 1 Yr - By whom: Lieutenant Collins - Discharged: 28 Feb 1815 - Comments: Discharged at Erie, PA.

Shane, John - Private - 19th Infantry - Company: Wilson Elliott.

Shaner, Solomon - Private - 19th Infantry - Company: Joel Collins - Age: 21 - Height: 5' 8" - Born: Pennsylvania - Trade: Hatter - Enlistment date: 29 Apr 1814 - Enlistment place: Detroit - Enlistment period: War - By whom: Samuel Coleman - Discharged: 20 Jul 1815 at Detroit - Bounty: BLW 18316-160-12 (Illinois).

Shank, Jacob - Sergeant - 19th Infantry - Company: Richard Talbott - Age: 23 - Height: 5' 9" - Born: Virginia - Trade: Laborer - Enlistment date: 23 Mar 1814 - Enlistment place: Lebanon - Enlistment period: War - By whom: Richard Talbott - Discharged: 5 Jun 1815 Fort Ball, OH (now Tiffin, OH)- Bounty: BLW 13764-160-12 (Missouri).

Shankling, Robert - Private - 19th Infantry - Company: William MacDonald - Enlistment date: 15 Dec 1813 - Enlistment period: War - Killed: 25 Jul 1814 - Bounty: BLW 23266-160-12 (Arkansas) - Comments: Land bounty to William Shankling, son & other heirs at law of Robert Shankling.

The Enlisted Men

Sharp, Thomas - Private - 19th Infantry - Age: 34 - Height: 5' 6 1/2" - Born: Ireland, County Dublin - Trade: Hairdresser - Enlistment date: 4 Jan 1815 - Enlistment place: Franklin County, Franklinton - Enlistment period: War - By whom: Orren Granger - Discharged: 27 Mar 1815 at Zanesville - Bounty: BLW 653-320-14 (Illinois).

Sharp, Thomas - Private - 27th Infantry - Company: George Sanderson - Enlistment date: 4 Jul 1813.

Shaver, Simon - Sergeant - 19th Infantry - Company: Angus Langham - Comments: Prisoner of War, captured at Frenchtown, MI, 22 Feb 1813.

Shaver, Thomas - Private - 19th Infantry - Company: James Herron - Enlistment date: 14 May 1813 - Enlistment period: 5 Yrs.

Shaw, Andrew - Private - 19th Infantry - Company: John Chunn - Other regiment: 17th Infantry.

Shaw, Elisha - Private - 17th Infantry - Company: Henry Crittenden - Age: 28 - Height: 5' 10" - Born: NY, Dutchess County - Trade: Shoemaker - Enlistment date: Jun 1814 - Enlistment period: War - By whom: John Reeves - Discharged: 9 Jun 1815 at Chillicothe.

Shaw, Freeman - Private - 19th Infantry - Company: Wilson Elliott.

Shaw, James - Private - 26th Infantry - Company: Joel Collins - Enlistment date: 3 Aug 1813 - Enlistment period: 1 Yr.

Shaw, John - Private - 19th Infantry - Company: Wilson Elliott - Age: 28 - Height: 5' 8 1/2" - Born: Pennsylvania - Trade: Farmer - Enlistment date: 2 Mar 1814 - Enlistment place: Franklin County, Franklinton - Enlistment period: War - By whom: Hugh Moore - Discharged: 1 Aug 1816 at Washington, DC, on Surgeon's Certificate of Disability, wounded in right leg by bursting shell - Pension: Old War IF-25821; served in Lt. Donald's Company, 19th Infantry as a private - Bounty: BLW 7085-160-12 (Illinois).

Sheanor, Solomon - Private - 27th Infantry - Company: George Sanderson - Enlistment date: 4 Jul 1813.

Shearer, William - Private - 17th Infantry - Company: Harris Hickman - Age: 44 - Height: 6' - Born: Pennsylvania - Trade: Farmer - Enlistment date: 3 Jan 1814 - Enlistment period: War - By whom: Isaac Rieley - Discharged: 6 Jun 1815 at Chillicothe - Bounty: BLW 26757-160-12 - Comments: Land bounty to Jane Smith, daughter & other heirs at law of William Shearer.

Shears, William - Private - 19th Infantry - Company: Joel Collins - Age: 33 - Height: 5' 11" - Born: Virginia - Trade: Farmer - Enlistment date: 17 Mar 1814 - Enlistment place: Detroit - Enlistment period: War - By whom: Samuel Coleman.

Sheers, Mynder - Private - 27th Infantry - Company: George Sanderson - Enlistment date: 19 May 1813.

Sheets, Jacob - Private - 19th Infantry - Died: 20 May 1813.

Sheets, Jacob - Private - 17th Infantry - Company: David Holt - William Bradford - Enlistment date: 26 Feb 1813 - Enlistment period: War - Died: 29 May 1813, probably in Ohio - Pension: Old War IF-17806 Rejected, served in Colonel Miller's Regiment, US Infantry as a private.

Sheets, William - Private - 19th Infantry - Company: James Herron.

Sheiter – see Skeiter, Joseph

Shelhour, Jacob (or Shelhouse) - Private - 17th Infantry - Other regiment: 3rd Infantry - Age: 21 - Height: 5' 8" - Born: North Carolina - Trade: Laborer - Enlistment date: 12 Jan 1815 - Enlistment place: Adams County, West Union - Enlistment period: 5 Yrs - By whom: James Campbell - Comments: Re-enlisted 20 Oct 1819.

Shepherd, Joseph - Private - 7th Infantry - Company: Zachary Taylor - Enlistment date: 16 Mar 1812 - Enlistment period: 5 Yrs - By whom: Thomas Ramsey - Killed: 21 Jul 1814.

Sherman, Joel - Corporal - 19th Infantry - Comments: Prisoner of War, exchanged 25 Apr 1814.

Sherrard, William - Private - 17th Infantry - Company: Henry Crittenden - Age: 26 - Height: 5' 10" - Born: VA, Berkeley County (now WV) - Trade: Laborer - Enlistment date: 3 May 1814 - Enlistment period: War - By whom: James Harper.

Shery, John - Private - 19th Infantry - Pension: Old War IF-1374; served in Lt McDonald's Company, 19th US Infantry private.

Sheward, John - Private - 26th Infantry - Company: Samuel Swearingen - Enlistment date: 18 Jun 1813 - Enlistment period: 1 Yr.

Shickle, Richard - Private - 26th Infantry - Company: Samuel Swearingen - Other regiment: 25th Infantry - Enlistment date: 27 Jul 1813 - Enlistment period: 1 Yr - Discharged: 14 Jun 1814.

Shields, Patrick - Private - 19th Infantry - Company: Richard Talbott - Age: 26 - Trade: Baker - Enlistment date: 27 Apr 1814 - Enlistment place: Clinton County, Wilmington - Enlistment period: War - By whom: John Noel - Discharged: 10 May 1815 - Bounty: BLW 16301-160-12 (Missouri) - Comments: Discharged at Newport, KY.

Shields, William - Private - 19th Infantry - Company: George Kesling - Age: 18 - Height: 5' 7" - Born: Kentucky -

Trade: Farmer - Enlistment date: 14 Feb 1815 - Enlistment place: Zanesville - Enlistment period: War - By whom: Charles Cass - Discharged: 27 Mar 1815 at Zanesville- Bounty: BLW 327-320-14 (Arkansas).

Shields, William - Private - 19th Infantry - Company: Lewis Bissells - Other regiment: 3rd Infantry - Age: 19 - Height: 5' 7" - Trade: Farmer - Enlistment date: 27 Mar 1815 - Enlistment period: 5 Yrs - By whom: Robert Smith - Comments: Deserted at Newport, KY, 13 Sep 1815.

Shields, William - Private - 17th Infantry - Company: Caleb Holder - Age: 38 - Height: 5' 9" - Born: Ireland - Trade: Stone mason - Enlistment date: 17 Jul 1814 - Enlistment period: War - By whom: William Featherstone.

Shields, William - Corporal - Rangers - Company: Samuel McCormick - Age: 23` - Height: 5' 9 1/2" - Born: Pennsylvania - Trade: Farmer - Enlistment date: 5 Nov 1813 - Enlistment period: 1 Yr - Discharged: 4 Nov 1814 at Fort Malden, UC.

Shields, William - Private - 2nd Artillery - Company: Daniel Cushing.

Shiely, David - Private - 19th Infantry - Company: Richard Talbott - Other regiment: 17th Infantry - Age: 33 - Height: 5' 10" - Born: VA, Jefferson County - Trade: Shoemaker - Enlistment date: 2 Mar 1814 - Enlistment place: Xenia - Enlistment period: 5 Yrs - By whom: Richard Talbott - Comments: Deserted at Detroit, MI, on 30 Nov 1815.

Shiller, Samuel - Private - 2nd Artillery - Company: Daniel Cushing - Other regiment: Corps of Artillery - Age: 21 - Height: 5' 5 1/2" - Born: PA, Lancaster County - Trade: Farmer - Enlistment date: 5 Jul 1812 - Enlistment place: Canton - Enlistment period: 5 Yrs - By whom: Lieutenant Lowell - Comments: Prisoner of War; deserted 14 Sep 1815.

Shipley, Peter - Private - 19th Infantry - Company: Carey Trimble - Age: 33 - Height: 5' 9" - Born: Maryland - Trade: Laborer - Enlistment date: 8 Jun 1814 - Enlistment place: Portsmouth - Enlistment period: War - By whom: John Brown - Discharged: 6 Jun 1815 at Chillicothe - Pension: Old War IF-1369; served in Lt. McElwain's Company, 19th Infantry as a private - Bounty: BLW 6559-160-12 (Illinois).

Shipman, Jacob - Private - 26th Infantry - Company: Joel Collins - Enlistment date: 17 Aug 1813 - Enlistment period: 1 Yr.

Shipman, John - Private - 26th Infantry - Company: Joel Collins - Enlistment date: 31 Jul 1813 - Enlistment period: 1 Yr.

Shirley, John - Private - 27th Infantry - Company: Absalom Martin - Pension: Wife Maria, WO-17273, WC-8983; served in Capt. Absalom Martin's Company, 27th Infantry as a private.

Shisler, Paul - Private - 17th Infantry - Company: Caleb Holder - Age: 33 - Height: 5' 8" - Born: Germany - Trade: Tailor - Enlistment date: 5 Jul 1814 - Enlistment place: Cambridge - Enlistment period: War - By whom: William Shang - Discharged: 30 Jun 1815 at Detroit - Bounty: BLW 16484-160-12 (Illinois) -.

Shockley, Clement - Private - 19th Infantry - Company: Carey Trimble - Other regiment: 17th Infantry - Enlistment date: 4 Jan 1814 - Enlistment period: 1 Yr - Discharged: 4 Jan 1815 - Pension: Wife Elizabeth, WO-29036, WC-24547; served in Lieutenant C. A. Trimble's Company, 19th Infantry.

Shoemaker, David - Private - 19th Infantry - Age: 18 - Height: 5' 10 1/2" - Born: Pennsylvania - Enlistment date: 4 Apr 1814 - Enlistment place: Clermont County, Williamsburg - Enlistment period: War.

Shoemaker, Thomas - Private - 19th Infantry - Company: James Herron - Enlistment date: 15 Sep 1812 - Enlistment period: 18 Mos - Died: 30 Dec 1813.

Shourd, John - Private - 26th Infantry - Company: Samuel Swearingen - Enlistment date: 18 Jun 1813 - Enlistment period: 1 Yr.

Shouts, Henry - Private - 26th Infantry - Company: George Kesling - Other regiment: 25th Infantry - Age: 32 - Height: 5' 8" - Enlistment date: 1 Jun 1813 - Enlistment period: 1 Yr - Discharged: 1 Jun 1814.

Shrader, John - Private - 17th Infantry - Company: Harris Hickman - Age: 40 - Height: 5' 9" - Born: MD, Frederick County - Trade: Farmer - Enlistment date: 27 Oct 1813 - Enlistment place: Butler County, Hamilton - Enlistment period: War - By whom: George Stall - Discharged: 9 Jun 1815 at Chillicothe - Bounty: BLW 3139-160-12 (Illinois).

Shriver, James - Private - 19th Infantry - Age: 22 - Height: 5' 7" - Born: MD, Prince Georges County, Georgetown - Enlistment date: 25 Jul 1812 - Enlistment place: Zanesville - Enlistment period: 5 Yrs.

Shrose, Emanuel - Private - 19th Infantry - Company: Carey Trimble - Age: 41 - Height: 5' 11 1/2" - Born: Pennsylvania - Trade: Millwright - Enlistment date: 3 Feb 1814 - Enlistment place: Clermont County, Williamsburg - Enlistment period: War - By whom: Charles Cissna - Bounty: BLW 25889-160-12 (Arkansas).

Shroup, Jacob - Private - 27th Infantry - Company: George Sanderson - Enlistment date: 22 May 1813.

Shulk, John - Private - 19th Infantry - Company: Angus Langham.

Shultz, Henry - Private - 1st Rifles - Company: Thomas Ramsey - Other regiment: 17th Infantry - Age: 17 - Height: 5' 2" - Born: PA, Bedford County, Bedford - Trade: Laborer - Enlistment date: 21 Nov 1813 - Enlistment place: Cincinnati - Enlistment period: 5 Yrs - By whom: Thomas Ramsey - Pension: SO-10813, SC-15270, served in Capt. M. L. Hawkins' Company, 17th Infantry as a private - Bounty: BLW 25647-160-12 (Arkansas) - Comments: Transferred to 17th Infantry on 6 Jan 1814, Capt. Martin Hawkins' Company.

Shupe, Jonathan C. - Drummer - 27th Infantry - Company: George Sanderson - Enlistment date: 8 May 1813.

Shutz, Jacob - Private - 19th Infantry - Died: 20 May 1813 - Pension: Heirs obtained half pay for five years in lieu of military bounty land.

Shyhawk, Christian - Private - 27th Infantry - Company: George Sanderson - Enlistment date: 17 Jun 1813 - Died: 18 Nov 1813.

Siberall, William - Private - 19th Infantry - Company: Carey Trimble - Age: 23 - Height: 6' - Born: Virginia - Trade: Farmer - Enlistment date: 2 Apr 1814 - Enlistment place: Chillicothe - Enlistment period: War - By whom: Charles Cissna - Discharged: 6 Jun 1815 at Chillicothe - Pension: Wife Elizabeth B., WO-11607, WC-6727, Old War IF-1472; served in Lt. J. McElvain's Company, 19th Infantry as a private - Bounty: BLW 4105-160-12 (Illinois).

Sickle, George M. - Private - 27th Infantry - Comments: Prisoner of War on Parole, captured at Detroit, MI, 16 Aug 1812.

Sickman, Presley (or Sigman) - Private - 17th Infantry - Company: David Holt - Age: 25 - Height: 5' 9" - Born: Pennsylvania - Trade: Laborer - Enlistment date: 18 Jun 1814 - Enlistment place: Cambridge - Enlistment period: War - By whom: William Shang - Discharged: 4 Jun 1815 at Chillicothe - Pension: Wife Sophia, WO-30520, WC-28597; served in Capt. Benjamin's Company, OH Militia, and in Capt. Holt's Company and Lieutenant John Good's Company, 17th Infantry - Bounty: BLW 6177-160-12, BLW 34053-40-50, BLW 39618-120-55.

Silvers, John - Private - 27th Infantry - Company: Alexander Hill - Other regiment: 19th Infantry - Age: 20 - Height: 5' 6" - Born: Pennsylvania - Trade: Shoemaker - Enlistment date: 5 May 1814 - Enlistment place: Zanesville - Enlistment period: War - By whom: Neal McFadden - Discharged: 6 Jun 1815 at Chillicothe - Pension: Served as a private in Lieutenant McElvain's Company, 19th Infantry - Bounty: BLW 6591-160-12.

Simason, John - Private - 26th Infantry - Company: Joel Collins - Enlistment date: 27 Jul 1813 - Enlistment period: 1 Yr.

Simcox, Michael (Simcock) - Private - 19th Infantry - Company: Carey Trimble - Pension: Old War IF-17844 Rejected; served as a private in Capt. Trimble's Company, 19th Infantry; lived in OH.

Simmonds, Joseph - Private - 2nd Artillery - Company: Daniel Cushing - Pension: Old War IF-6106, served in Capt. Birdsall's Company, US Artillery, as a private.

Simmons – see Lemmons, Jacob

Simmons, George - Private - 19th Infantry - Age: 21 - Height: 5' 10 1/2" - Born: Kentucky - Enlistment date: 22 Mar 1814 - Enlistment place: Columbiana County - By whom: Thomas McKnight.

Simmons, Ira - Private - 27th Infantry - Age: 24 - Height: 5' 5" - Born: VA, Brook County - Enlistment date: 9 May 1814 - Enlistment place: Athens.

Simmons, Ira - Private - 19th Infantry - Company: Carey Trimble - Other regiment: 17th Infantry - Age: 30 - Height: 5' 9" - Born: Maryland - Trade: Blacksmith - Enlistment date: 7 May 1814 - Enlistment place: Ross County, Adelphi - Enlistment period: War - By whom: Hugh Moore - Discharged: 6 Jun 1815 at Chillicothe - Pension: Wife Minta, WO-7504; served in Capt C. A. Trimble's Company, 19th Infantry and in Capt Adair's Company, 17th Infantry - Bounty: BLW 23562-160-12.

Simmons, John - Private - 17th Infantry - Company: Harris Hickman - Age: 24 - Height: 5' 8" - Born: VA, Frederick County - Trade: Laborer - Enlistment date: 14 Mar 1814 - Enlistment place: Franklin County, Franklinton - Enlistment period: War - By whom: John Cochran.

Simmons, Richard - Private - 17th Infantry - Company: William Adair - Height: 5' 5" - Born: SC, Fairfield County - Trade: Shoemaker - Enlistment date: 2 Jun 1814 - Enlistment period: War - By whom: David Carney - Discharged: 4 Jun 1815 at Chillicothe - Bounty: BLW 5630-160-12 (Illinois).

Simmons, Thomas - Private - 17th Infantry - Company: David Holt - Age: 21 - Height: 5' 6" - Born: VA, Frederick County - Trade: Laborer - Enlistment date: 14 Mar 1814 - Enlistment place: Franklin County, Franklinton - Enlistment period: War - By whom: John Cochran - Discharged: 4 Jun 1815 at Chillicothe - Bounty: BLW 9930-160-12 (Illinois).

Simms, James - Private - 19th Infantry - Company: Wilson Elliott.

Simons, Faulkner - Private - 19th Infantry - Company: Carey Trimble - Age: 21 - Height: 5' 5" - Born: South Carolina - Trade: Laborer - Enlistment date: 19 Feb 1814 - Enlistment place: Chillicothe - Enlistment period:

War - By whom: Charles Cissna - Discharged: 6 Jun 1815 at Chillicothe - Pension: Old War IF-1471; served as a private in Company H, 19th Infantry in 1814 - Bounty: BLW 10910-160-12 (Illinois).

Simpson, Jeremiah - Private - 19th Infantry - Company: Wilson Elliott.

Simpson, John - Sergeant - 17th Infantry - Company: Henry Crittenden - Age: 27 - Height: 5' 9" - Born: Ireland - Trade: Sailor - Enlistment date: 7 Jun 1814 - Enlistment place: Cincinnati - Enlistment period: War - By whom: David Carney - Discharged: 9 Jun 1815 at Chillicothe - Bounty: BLW 23942-160-12 (Arkansas).

Simpson, Jonathan - Private - 19th Infantry - Pension: Old War WF-9879; served as a private in the 19th Infantry.

Simson, Isaac - Private - 2nd Artillery - Company: Daniel Cushing.

Siner, Adam - Private - 27th Infantry - Company: George Sanderson - Enlistment date: 23 Jun 1813.

Singer, Thomas - Private - 19th Infantry - Age: 18 - Height: 5' 7" - Born: Maryland - Enlistment date: 13 Apr 1814 - Enlistment place: Ross County, Adelphi.

Siseman, James - Private - 2nd Rifles - Company: Batteal Harrison - Age: 23 - Height: 6' 1" - Born: North Carolina - Trade: Laborer - Enlistment date: 18 Oct 1814 - Enlistment place: Chillicothe - Enlistment period: War - By whom: Batteal Harrison - Comments: Deserted 2 Dec 1814.

Skeels – see Skills, Henry

Skeiter, Joseph - Private - 1st Rifles - Company: Edward Wadsworth - Age: 15 - Height: 5' 3" - Born: KY, Fayette County - Trade: Farmer - Enlistment place: Ohio - Enlistment period: War - Discharged: 3 Jun 1815 at Buffalo, NY.

Skidmore, William - Private - 28th Infantry - Company: Nimrod Moore - Enlistment date: 13 May 1813 - Enlistment period: 1 Yr - Died: 24 Sep 1813 at Fort Seneca (now Old Fort, OH).

Skills, Henry - Private - 27th Infantry - Company: George Sanderson - Enlistment date: 22 May 1813 - Comments: Prisoner of War on Parole, captured at Detroit, MI, 16 Aug 1812.

Slater, Titus - Private - 17th Infantry - Company: Caleb Holder - Age: 32 - Height: 5' 9" - Enlistment date: 1 Apr 1813 - Enlistment period: War - By whom: James Hazelton - Discharged: 20 Jun 1815 at Chillicothe on Surgeon's Certificate of Disability - Bounty: BLW 1660-160-12 (Illinois).

Slaughter, Jonathan - Private - 2nd Artillery - Company: Daniel Cushing - Other regiment: Corps of Artillery - Age: 22 - Height: 5' 8" - Born: Delaware - Trade: Coach maker - Enlistment date: 31 Jul 1812 - Enlistment place: Chillicothe - Enlistment period: 5 Yrs - By whom: Lieutenant Couchwell - Discharged: 31 Jul 1817 - Comments: Prisoner of War.

Sloan, Samuel - Private - 19th Infantry - Company: James Herron.

Sloop, Michael - Private - 17th Infantry - Company: Caleb Holder - Other regiment: 3rd Infantry - Age: 40 - Height: 5' 7" - Born: Virginia - Trade: Barber - Enlistment date: 25 Jul 1814 - Enlistment place: Cambridge - Enlistment period: 5 Yrs - By whom: William Shang - Discharged: 25 Jul 1819.

Small, Nicholas - Private - Rangers - Company: William Perry - Killed: 5 Sep 1812.

Smalls, Jacob - Private - 19th Infantry - Company: Wilson Elliott.

Smarr, John - Private - 2nd Rifles - Company: Batteal Harrison - Age: 18 - Height: 5' 10" - Born: Pennsylvania - Trade: Laborer - Enlistment date: 24 May 1814 - Enlistment place: Lancaster - Enlistment period: 5 Yrs - By whom: John Stockton - Discharged: 24 May 1819 - Bounty: BLW 22293-160-12 (Arkansas).

Smartsfeller, Adam - Private - 17th Infantry - Age: 28 - Height: 5' 7" - Born: Pennsylvania - Trade: Carpenter - Enlistment date: 29 Jun 1814 - Enlistment place: Cincinnati - Enlistment period: War - By whom: David Carney.

Smiley, William - Private - 19th Infantry - Company: George Kesling - Age: 18 - Height: 5' 9" - Born: Pennsylvania - Trade: Carpenter - Enlistment date: 25 Dec 1814 - Enlistment place: Xenia - Enlistment period: War - By whom: Robert Smith - Discharged: 27 Mar 1815 - Pension: Wife Nancy, WO-11029, WC-10039, SO-1075, SC-669; served in Capt. Kesling's Company, 19th Infantry as a private - Bounty: BLW 14168-160-12 (Illinois), BLW 26973-160-12.

Smith, Benjamin - Private - 19th Infantry - Company: Wilson Elliott.

Smith, Charles - Private - 27th Infantry - Company: George Sanderson - Age: 22 - Height: 5' 7" - Born: Ireland, County Donegal - Trade: Laborer - Enlistment date: 20 Apr 1813 - Comments: Prisoner of War, exchanged 25 Apr 1814; re-enlisted on 18 Jul 1814 for 5 years by Lieutenant Brown.

Smith, Christian P. - Drum Major - 27th Infantry - Company: Alexander Hill - Other regiment: 19th Infantry - Age: 27 - Height: 5' 8" - Born: MD, Frederick County, Summitburg - Trade: Shoemaker - Enlistment date: 28 Jun 1813 - Discharged: 27 Mar 1815 at Zanesville- Bounty: BLW 11360-160-12 (Missouri) - Comments: Enlisted 18 Apr 1814 for War by Capt Spencer at Newark, OH; George Kesling's Company.

Smith, Daniel - 26th Infantry - Company: Benjamin Watson - Other regiment: 25th Infantry - Age: 19 - Height: 5' 6" - Born: VA, Loudoun County - Trade: Laborer - Enlistment date: 15 Mar 1813 - Enlistment place: Ohio -

Enlistment period: 5 Yrs - By whom: George Baskerville - Comments: Discharged at Plattsburgh, NY, died on 15 Mar 1818.

Smith, Eccleston - Private - 19th Infantry - Company: William Gill - Age: 27 - Height: 5' 11" - Born: Delaware - Trade: Joiner - Enlistment date: 11 May 1814 - Enlistment place: Pickaway County, Jefferson (Pickaway Plains) - Enlistment period: War - By whom: John Lucas - Discharged: 5 Jun 1815 at Chillicothe - Bounty: BLW 9523-160-12 (Illinois).

Smith, Eli - Private - 19th Infantry - Company: George Kesling - Other regiment: 17th Infantry then 3rd Infantry - Age: 18 - Height: 5' 8" - Born: VA, Jersey - Trade: Farmer - Enlistment date: 8 Dec 1814 - Enlistment place: Washington County - Enlistment period: 5 Yrs - By whom: Lieutenant Hully - Discharged: 4 Jul 1818 for disability.

Smith, Henry - Private - Rangers - Company: Samuel McCormick - Enlistment date: 10 Dec 1813 - Enlistment period: 1 Yr - Discharged: 9 Dec 1814.

Smith, Jacob - Private - 26th Infantry - Company: Samuel Swearingen - Enlistment date: 19 Jul 1813 - Enlistment period: 1 Yr.

Smith, James - Private - Rangers - Company: William Perry - Pension: SO-9106, SC-18453; served in Capt. William Perry's Company, OH Militia.

Smith, James - Private - Rangers - Company: Samuel McCormick - Age: 20 - Height: 5' 11" - Born: Kentucky - Trade: Farmer - Enlistment date: 27 Oct 1813 - Enlistment period: 1 Yr - Discharged: 26 Oct 1814 at Fort Malden, UC - Pension: SO-9103, SC-4916; served in Captain Samuel McCormick's Company, US Rangers; lived in OH.

Smith, James - Private - 1st Infantry - Company: Silas Owens - Age: 21 - Height: 5' 9 1/2" - Born: VA, Botetourt County - Trade: Hatter - Enlistment date: 11 Mar 1812 - Enlistment period: 5 Yrs - By whom: James Swearingen - Killed: 25 Jul 1814 at Niagara Falls, UC.

Smith, Joel - Private - 19th Infantry - Company: Martin Hawkins - Other regiment: 17th Infantry - Age: 26 - Height: 6' 1" - Born: PA, Northampton County - Enlistment date: 24 Mar 1814 - Enlistment place: Detroit - Enlistment period: War - By whom: George Atchison - Died: 24 Dec 1814 at Buffalo, NY; buried in the War of 1812 Cemetery in Cheektowaga, Erie County, NY.

Smith, John - Private - 17th Infantry - Company: David Holt - Age: 30 - Height: 5' 10" - Born: TN, Hawkins County - Trade: Laborer - Enlistment date: 3 Apr 1814 - Enlistment place: Cleveland - Enlistment period: War - By whom: William Leavitt - Discharged: 4 Jun at Chillicothe.

Smith, John - Private - 19th Infantry - Company: John Chunn - Enlistment date: 19 Mar 1813 - Enlistment period: 18 Mos.

Smith, John - Private - 19th Infantry - Company: William Gill - Age: 23 - Height: 5' 7" - Born: Canada - Trade: Farmer - Enlistment date: 26 Aug 1814 - Enlistment place: Franklin County, Franklinton - Enlistment period: War - By whom: Nehemiah Gregory - Discharged: 5 Jun 1815 at Chillicothe - Bounty: BLW 6251-160-12 (Illinois).

Smith, John - Private - 19th Infantry - Company: Henry Crittenden - Other regiment: 17th Infantry - Age: 19 - Height: 5' 9" - Born: Maryland or Pennsylvania - Trade: Shoemaker - Enlistment date: 3 Apr 1813 - Enlistment place: Mount Vernon - Enlistment period: War - By whom: John Milligan - Discharged: 6 Apr 1815 at Erie, PA - Bounty: BLW 9887-160-12 (Illinois).

Smith, John - Sergeant - 17th Infantry - Company: Caleb Holder - Other regiment: 3rd Infantry - Age: 25 - Height: 5' 10 1/2" - Born: PA, Mifflin County - Trade: Farmer - Enlistment date: 28 Oct 1812 - Enlistment period: 5 Yrs - By whom: William Leavitt - Discharged: 28 Oct 1817.

Smith, John - Private - 27th Infantry - Company: George Sanderson - Enlistment date: 4 Jul 1813 - Comments: Served aboard the US Schooner Somers on the Lake Erie Squadron.

Smith, John - Corporal - 17th Infantry - Company: John Chunn - Age: 22 - Height: 5' 8 1/2" - Born: Ireland - Trade: Laborer - Enlistment date: 5 Feb 1814 - Enlistment place: Franklin County, Franklinton - Enlistment period: War - By whom: John Cochran - Discharged: 1 Apr 1815 at Erie, PA - Bounty: BLW 4391-160-12 (Missouri).

Smith, John 1st - Private - 19th Infantry - Company: Joel Collins - Age: 20 - Height: 6' - Born: Pennsylvania - Trade: Laborer - Enlistment date: 15 Mar 1814 - Enlistment place: Detroit - Enlistment period: War - By whom: Wynkoop Warner - Discharged: 20 Jul 1815 at Detroit - Bounty: BLW 4792-160-12 (Illinois).

Smith, John 2nd - Private - 19th Infantry - Company: Joel Collins - Age: 24 - Height: 5' 9" - Born: Maryland - Trade: Blacksmith - Enlistment date: 30 Apr 1814 - Enlistment place: Detroit - Enlistment period: War - By whom: Wynkoop Warner - Discharged: 20 Jul 1815 at Detroit - Bounty: BLW 3811-160-12 (Illinois).

Smith, John D. - Private - 27th Infantry - Company: Carey Trimble - Other regiment: 19th Infantry - Age: 20 -

Height: 5' 8" - Born: NY, Sarasota County - Trade: Hatter - Enlistment date: 9 May 1814 - Enlistment place: Trumbull County, Warren or Portage County, Ravenna - Enlistment period: War - By whom: John Reeves - Discharged: 6 Jun 1815 at Chillicothe - Bounty: BLW 14400-160-12 (Illinois).

Smith, John W. - Private - 27th Infantry - Company: Alexander Hill - Other regiment: 19th Infantry - Age: 23 - Height: 5' 9" - Born: NH, Harwick - Trade: Farmer - Enlistment date: 6 May 1814 - Enlistment place: Ashtabula County, Harpersfield - Enlistment period: War - Died: 9 Mar 1815 at Erie, PA - Bounty: BLW 25240-160-12 (Arkansas) - Comments: Land bounty to William Smith, brother & other heirs at law of John W. Smith.

Smith, Joseph D. - Private - 19th Infantry - Company: William Gill - Age: 40 - Height: 5' 10 1/2" - Born: MD, Harford County - Trade: Shoemaker - Enlistment date: 17 Mar 1814 - Enlistment period: War - By whom: John Simons - Discharged: 5 Jun 1815 at Chillicothe - Bounty: BLW 13651-160-12 (Illinois).

Smith, Joshua - Private - 1st Infantry - Company: Horatio Stark - Age: 21 - Height: 5' 11" - Born: KY, Harrison County - Trade: Farmer - Enlistment date: 15 Feb 1814 - Enlistment place: Cincinnati - Enlistment period: 5 Yrs - By whom: Laurence Taliaferro - Discharged: 15 Feb 1819 at Fort Howard, IA - Comments: Prisoner of War.

Smith, Lyman - Private - 1st Rifles - Company: Thomas Ramsey - Age: 25 - Height: 6' - Born: MA, Berkshire County - Trade: Farmer - Enlistment date: 28 May 1814 - Enlistment place: Cincinnati - Enlistment period: War - By whom: Thomas Ramsey - Discharged: 5 Jun 1814 at Buffalo, NY - Bounty: BLW 13062-160-12 (Illinois).

Smith, Richard - Private - 17th Infantry - Other regiment: 3rd Infantry - Age: 21 - Height: 5' 5" - Born: MD, Queen Anne's County - Enlistment date: 18 Jul 1812 - Enlistment place: St. Clairsville - Enlistment period: 5 Yrs - By whom: Samuel Booker - Discharged: 17 Jul 1817 at Fort Howard, WI - Bounty: BLW 15591-160-12 - Comments: Prisoner of War (Halifax, NS); captured 12 Jun 1813; exchanged on 31 Mar 1814.

Smith, Richard - Private - 19th Infantry - Company: Angus Langham - Comments: Prisoner of War, captured at Frenchtown, MI.

Smith, Roswell W. - Private - 17th Infantry - Company: Caleb Holder - Other regiment: 3rd Infantry - Age: 30 - Height: 5' 9 1/2" - Born: New York - Trade: Cabinet maker - Enlistment date: 20 Apr 1813 - Enlistment period: War - By whom: John Cochran.

Smith, Samuel - Private - 2nd Artillery - Company: Daniel Cushing - Age: 25 - Height: 5' 10" - Born: NH, Grafton County - Trade: Cordwainer - Enlistment date: 20 Feb 1813 - Enlistment place: Lebanon - Enlistment period: 5 Yrs - By whom: Alexander Meek - Bounty: BLW 25410-160-12 (Arkansas).

Smith, Samuel - Private - 26th Infantry - Company: Samuel Swearingen - Other regiment: 25th Infantry - Enlistment date: 9 May 1813 - Enlistment period: 1 Yr - Discharged: 9 May 1814.

Smith, Simon - Musician - 19th Infantry - Company: Wilson Elliott.

Smith, Thomas - Private - 17th Infantry - Company: Henry Crittenden - Other regiment: 3rd Infantry - Age: 35 - Height: 5' 8" - Born: VA, Shenandoah County - Trade: Farmer - Enlistment date: 1 Jan 1814 - Enlistment period: 5 Yrs - By whom: Samuel Booker - Bounty: BLW 27350-160-42 - Comments: Land bounty to William Smith, son & other heirs of Thomas Smith.

Smith, William - Private - 17th Infantry - Age: 22 - Height: 5' 7" - Born: Virginia - Enlistment date: 1 Dec 1814 - Enlistment place: Xenia - Enlistment period: War - By whom: William Shang.

Smith, William - Sergeant - 26th Infantry - Company: Samuel Swearingen - Other regiment: 25th Infantry - Enlistment date: 20 Jun 1813 - Enlistment period: 1 Yr - Pension: Old War IF-48509; served in Lt Swearingen's Company, 26th Infantry as a private; lived in OH - Comments: Served aboard the US Schooner Ariel on the Lake Erie Squadron, deserted at Geneva, NY, on 23 Mar 1814.

Smith, William - Corporal - 1st Infantry - Company: Thomas Hamilton - Other regiment: 3rd Infantry - Age: 22 - Height: 6' - Born: OH, Muskingum County - Trade: Miller - Enlistment date: 5 Mar 1814 - Enlistment place: Cincinnati - Enlistment period: War - By whom: Laurence Taliaferro - Discharged: 17 Jul 1815 at Buffalo, NY - Bounty: BLW 6035-160-12 (Arkansas).

Smith, William - Private - 17th Infantry - Age: 22 - Height: 5' 4 1/2" - Born: VA, Frederick County - Trade: Carpenter - Enlistment date: 13 Aug 1814 - Enlistment place: Steubenville - Enlistment period: War - By whom: William Featherstone.

Smith, William B. - Private - 19th Infantry - Company: Angus Langham - Enlistment date: 20 Jul 1812 - Enlistment period: 18 Mos.

Smith, Wilson - Private - 19th Infantry - Company: William Gill - Age: 23 - Height: 5' 9" - Born: Ireland, County Derry - Trade: Sailor - Enlistment date: 6 Oct 1814 - Enlistment period: War - By whom: Samuel Coleman - Comments: Deserted at Zanesville, OH, on 26 Oct 1814.

The Enlisted Men

Smoot, Jeremiah - Private - 2nd Artillery - Company: Daniel Cushing - Died: 20 Dec 1813 at Detroit, MI.

Smoots, Leonard - Private - 2nd Rifles - Company: Batteal Harrison - Age: 39 - Height: 5' 9" - Born: PA, Bucks County - Trade: Carpenter - Enlistment date: 10 Jul 1814 - Enlistment place: Chillicothe - Enlistment period: 5 Yrs - By whom: Batteal Harrison - Discharged: 10 Jul 1819 at Fort Crawford, IL - Bounty: BLW 23104-160-12 (Arkansas).

Smooty, Joseph - Private - 27th Infantry - Born: New Jersey - Enlistment date: 8 Apr 1814 - Enlistment place: New Lisbon.

Snapp, Abraham - Sergeant - 26th Infantry - Company: George Kesling - Other regiment: 19th Infantry - Enlistment date: 16 May 1813 - Enlistment period: 1 Yr.

Snider, Adam - Private - 19th Infantry - Company: George Kesling - Age: 19 - Height: 5' 10" - Born: Maryland - Trade: Laborer - Enlistment date: 3 Jan 1815 - Enlistment place: Franklin County, Franklinton - Enlistment period: War - By whom: Orren Granger - Discharged: 27 Mar 1815 at Zanesville - Bounty: BLW 465-320-14 (Missouri).

Snider, Henry - Private - 27th Infantry - Age: 21 - Height: 5' 10" - Born: Pennsylvania - Enlistment date: 25 May 1814 - Enlistment place: Zanesville.

Sniff, Martin - Private - 27th Infantry - Company: Joseph Cairns - Comments: Served aboard the US Sloop Trippe on the Lake Erie Squadron.

Snodgrass, James - Private - 17th Infantry - Other regiment: 3rd Infantry - Age: 29 - Height: 5' 6" - Born: Virginia - Enlistment date: 13 Jan 1815 - Enlistment place: Xenia - Enlistment period: 5 Yrs - By whom: William Shang - Discharged: 11 Jan 1820 at Fort Howard, WI.

Snodgrass, Samuel - Private - 19th Infantry - Company: George Kesling - Other regiment: 3rd Infantry - Age: 18 - Height: 5' 7" - Born: Virginia - Trade: Farmer - Enlistment date: 2 Feb 1815 - Enlistment place: Xenia - Enlistment period: 5 Yrs - By whom: Robert Smith - Discharged: 2 Feb 1820.

Snyder, Benjamin - Private - 27th Infantry - Company: Alexander Hill - Other regiment: 19th Infantry - Age: 21 - Height: 5' 8" - Born: PA, Berks County - Enlistment date: 28 Jan 1813 - Enlistment place: Ravenna - By whom: John Reeves - Discharged: 8 Feb 1815.

Snyder, Jacob (Snider) - Private - 17th Infantry - Company: Henry Crittenden - Age: 21 - Height: 5' 8" - Born: VA, Whyte County - Trade: Laborer - Enlistment date: 22 Jun 1814 - Enlistment place: Cincinnati - Enlistment period: War - By whom: David Carney - Discharged: 9 Jun 1815 at Chillicothe - Bounty: BLW 23606-160-12 (Arkansas).

Snyder, William - Private - 27th Infantry - Company: Alexander Hill - Other regiment: 19th Infantry - Age: 30 - Height: 5' 8" - Born: PA, Bucks County - Trade: Blacksmith - Enlistment date: 26 Apr 1814 - Enlistment place: Warren County - Enlistment period: War - By whom: John Reeves - Discharged: 6 Jun 1815 at Chillicothe - Pension: Wife Elizabeth, WO-18051, WC-13156, Old War IF-1491; served in Captains Hill, Trimble and Lt. McEvain's Companies, 19th Infantry as a private; lived in OH - Bounty: BLW 20110-160-12 (Missouri).

Sockrider, Jacob - Private - 26th Infantry - Company: William Puthuff - Enlistment date: 8 May 1813 - Enlistment period: 1 Yr - Died: 22 Dec 1813 - Comments: Died probably at Sackets Harbor, NY.

Sourd, William - Private - 19th Infantry - Company: Joel Collins - Age: 18 - Height: 5' 5" - Born: Ohio - Trade: Farmer - Enlistment date: 9 Sep 1814 - Enlistment place: Urbana - Enlistment period: 5 Yrs - By whom: William Baird.

Southerland, John - Private - 19th Infantry - Company: Wilson Elliott.

Spalding, Jesse - Private - 27th Infantry - Company: Alexander Hill.

Sparks, John - Private - 26th Infantry - Company: Samuel Swearingen - Other regiment: 25th Infantry - Enlistment date: 3 Jul 1813 - Enlistment period: 1 Yr - Discharged: 22 Jun 1814.

Sparks, John - Private - 27th Infantry - Company: Absalom Martin - Pension: Old War IF-18061 Rejected; served in Capt. Martin's Company, 27th Infantry as a private.

Spaulding, Jesse - Private - 19th Infantry - Age: 29 - Height: 5' 10" - Born: NY, Saratoga County, Charlton - Enlistment date: 10 May 1814 - Enlistment place: Ashtabula County, Harpersfield - Enlistment period: 5 Yrs - Killed: 15 Aug 1814.

Spence, Peter - Private - 26th Infantry - Company: George Kesling - Enlistment date: 31 May 1813 - Enlistment period: 1 Yr - Died: 21 Dec 1813.

Spencer, David - Private - 26th Infantry - Company: William Puthuff - Other regiment: 19th Infantry - Age: 22 - Height: 5' 9 1/2" - Born: Virginia - Trade: Laborer - Enlistment date: 19 Apr 1813 - Enlistment place: Upper Canada, Sandwich - Enlistment period: 1 Yr - War - By whom: Collin McLeod - Discharged: 20 Jul 1815 at Detroit - Bounty: BLW 16713-160-12 (Illinois).

Spiceman, Michael - Corporal - 2nd Artillery - Company: Daniel Cushing.
Spicer, Joseph - 19th Infantry - Company: John Chunn - Enlistment date: 17 Dec 1812 - Enlistment period: 5 Yrs - Comments: Deserted 15 May 1813 and Jul 1813; discharged.
Spires, William - Private - 26th Infantry - Company: George Kesling - Enlistment date: 2 May 1813 - Enlistment period: 1 Yr.
Sprague, Ephraim - Private - 17th Infantry - Company: Harris Hickman - Enlistment date: 30 Nov 1813 - Enlistment period: War - By whom: Thomas McKnight - Died: 25 Jan 1815 at Williamsville, NY (General Hospital), of natural death - Pension: Heirs obtained half pay for five years in lieu of military bounty land - Comments: Buried in the War of 1812 Cemetery in Cheektowaga, Erie County, NY.
Sprague, John - Private - 27th Infantry - Company: Carey Trimble - Other regiment: 19th Infantry - Age: 33 - Height: 5' 10" - Born: Tuscarawas County, New Philadelphia - Enlistment date: 25 Mar 1814 - Enlistment period: War - Discharged: 20 Nov 1814 at For Erie, UC - Pension: Old War IF-1387; served in Lt. Trimble's Company, 19th Infantry as a private - Bounty: BLW 7229-160-12 (Illinois) - Comments: Wounded in left arm on 15 Aug 1814.
Spry, Perry - Private - 27th Infantry - Company: George Sanderson - Enlistment date: 4 Jun 1813 - Pension: Wife Mary, SC-24009; served in Captain George Sanderson's Company, 2nd Infantry and Captain William Douglass' Company, OH Militia.
Spurgeon, Nathan - Private - 17th Infantry - Company: Martin Hawkins - Age: 30 - Height: 6' 1" - Born: PA, Bedford County - Trade: Laborer - Enlistment date: 2 Feb 1813 - Enlistment place: St. Clairsville - Enlistment period: 5 Yrs - By whom: Samuel Booker - Bounty: BLW 25435-160-12 (Arkansas) - Comments: Land bounty to James Spurgeon, brother & other heirs at law of Nathan Spurgeon.
Spurgeon, William - Fifer - 27th Infantry - Company: Alexander Hill - Other regiment: 19th Infantry - Age: 21 - Height: 5' 9 1/2" - Born: VA, Monongahela County (now West Virginia) - Trade: Farmer - Enlistment date: 18 Apr 1814 - Enlistment place: Newark - Enlistment period: War - By whom: John Spencer - Discharged: 6 Jun 1815 at Chillicothe - Bounty: BLW 19800-160-12 (Illinois).
Sroffe, Emanuel - Private - 19th Infantry - Died: 6 Jan 1815 - Pension: Old War IF-18251; served as a private in the 19th Infantry.
Stackpole, Conrad - Private - 19th Infantry - Age: 18 - Height: 5' 5" - Born: MD, Allegeny County - Enlistment date: 13 Jul 1812 - Enlistment period: 5 Yrs.
Stadler, Joseph - Private - 27th Infantry - Comments: Prisoner of War on Parole, captured at Detroit, MI, 16 Aug 1812.
Staley, Alexander - Private - 17th Infantry - Company: Henry Crittenden - Other regiment: 3rd Infantry - Age: 37 - Height: 5' 11" - Born: Pennsylvania - Trade: Carpenter - Enlistment date: 11 Sep 1813 - Enlistment period: 18 Mos - By whom: John Mershon.
Stalia, Joseph - Musician - 17th Infantry - Company: Henry Crittenden - Age: 29 - Height: 5' 6" - Born: Lower Canada - Trade: Carpenter - Enlistment date: 17 Mar 1812 - Enlistment period: 5 Yrs - By whom: James Herron.
Stall, John - Drummer - 26th Infantry - Company: William Puthuff - Enlistment date: 26 Apr 1813 - Enlistment period: 1 Yr.
Stanard, John - Private - 19th Infantry - Company: John Chunn.
Stancliff, John - Private - 26th Infantry - Company: William Puthuff - Enlistment date: 12 May 1813 - Enlistment period: 1 Yr.
Standsburg, Christian - Private - 27th Infantry - Company: Alexander Hill - Other regiment: 19th Infantry - Enlistment date: 8 Mar 1814 - Enlistment period: 5 Yrs - Died: Jan 1815 at Williamsville, **NY.**
Stanley, James - Private - 19th Infantry - Company: Wilson Elliott - Enlistment date: 8 Sep 1812 - Enlistment period: 18 Mos - Killed: 5 May 1813.
Stanley, John - Private - 27th Infantry - Company: Alexander Hill - Age: 18 - Height: 5' 5 1/2" - Born: PA, Fayette County - Enlistment date: 19 Apr 1814 - Enlistment place: Cambridge.
Stansberry, James - Private - 19th Infantry - Died: 17 Sep 1814 at Fort Erie, UC.
Starks, Samuel - Sergeant - 26th Infantry - Company: George Kesling - Enlistment date: 19 May 1813 - Enlistment period: 1 Yr.
Starn, George - Private - 17th Infantry - Company: Caleb Holder - Age: 23 - Height: 5' 7" - Born: Pennsylvania - Trade: Farmer - Enlistment date: 12 Oct 1813 - Enlistment period: War - By whom: Isaac Reiley - Discharged: 30 Jun 1813 at Detroit - Bounty: BLW 16401-160-12 (Illinois).
Starr, Adam - Private - 19th Infantry - Company: Angus Langham - Enlistment date: 4 Jul 1812 - Enlistment period: 5 Yrs - Killed: 4 Apr 1813 by Indians - Bounty: BLW 26723-160-12 (Arkansas) - Comments: Land

bounty to Riley Barber, half brother & other heirs at law of Adam Starr.

Stead, Peter - Private - 19th Infantry - Age: 16 - Height: 5' 9" - Born: VA, Wood County (now West Virginia) - Enlistment date: 22 Mar 1814 - Enlistment place: Steubenville - By whom: Ensign Jackson.

Stearnes, Luther - Private - 19th Infantry - Company: Henry Crittenden - Other regiment: 17th Infantry - Age: 27 - Height: 5' 9" - Born: VT, Addison County - Trade: Laborer - Enlistment date: 4 Jun 1813 - Enlistment place: Cleveland - Enlistment period: War - By whom: George Atchison - Discharged: 9 Jun 1815 at Chillicothe - Pension: Old War IF-18187 Rejected, served in Capt. Murray's Company, OH Militia, and Capt. Gray's Company, Company, 19th Infantry - Bounty: BLW 25943-160-12 (Arkansas).

Stedman, Abel - Sergeant - 19th Infantry - Company: George Kesling - Age: 29 - Height: 5' 9 1/2" - Born: Vermont - Trade: Laborer - Enlistment date: 6 Apr 1814 - Enlistment period: War - Discharged: 27 Mar 1815 at Zanesville - Bounty: BLW 16416-160-12 (Illinois).

Steed, Peter - Private - 19th Infantry - Age: 17 - Height: 5' 9" - Born: Virginia - Enlistment date: 6 Apr 1814 - Enlistment place: Marietta - By whom: John Milligan - Comments: Deserted before 30 Apr 1814.

Steel, John - Private - 26th Infantry - Company: Samuel Swearingen - Enlistment date: 30 Jul 1813 - Enlistment period: 1 Yr.

Steel, Joseph - Private - Rangers - Company: Samuel McCormick - Enlistment date: 8 Dec 1813 - Enlistment period: 1 Yr – Discharged: 7 Dec 1814.

Steelman, James - Private - 17th Infantry - Company: William Whistler - Other regiment: 3rd Infantry - Age: 22 - Height: 5' 5 1/2" - Trade: Blacksmith - Enlistment date: 13 Jan 1814 - Enlistment place: Xenia - Enlistment period: 5 Yrs - By whom: Ensign Shay - Discharged: 11 Jan 1820 at Fort Howard, WS - Bounty: BLW 955-320-14 (Arkansas).

Steinberg, Christian - Private - 27th Infantry - Age: 27 - Height: 5' 6 1/2" - Born: NY, Schoharie County - Enlistment date: 8 Mar 1814 - Enlistment place: Cambridge.

Stephens, Daniel - Private - 2nd Artillery - Company: Stanton Sholes - Other regiment: Corps of Artillery - Age: 45 - Height: 5' 10" - Born: CT, Windham County - Trade: Blacksmith - Enlistment date: 22 May 1813 - Enlistment place: Cleveland - Enlistment period: 5 Yrs - By whom: Stanton Sholes - Discharged: 22 May 1818 at Detroit.

Stephens, Drury - Private - 24th Infantry - Died: 3 Aug 1813 at Fort Meigs.

Stephens, John - Private - 19th Infantry - Company: Carey Trimble - Age: 23 - Height: 6' - Born: Virginia - Trade: Blacksmith - Enlistment date: 2 Mar 1814 - Enlistment place: Franklin County, Franklinton - Enlistment period: War - By whom: Hugh Moore - Discharged: 6 Jun 1815 at Chillicothe - Bounty: BLW 5629-160-12 (Illinois).

Stephens, Richard - Private - 26th Infantry - Company: William Puthuff - Enlistment date: 3 May 1813 - Enlistment period: 1 Yr.

Sterret, Alexander - Private - 19th Infantry - Company: Richard Talbott - Age: 23 - Height: 5' 8 3/4" - Born: PA, Franklin County - Trade: Laborer - Enlistment date: 22 Apr 1814 - Enlistment place: Cincinnati - Enlistment period: War - By whom: Robert Anderson - Discharged: 5 Jun 1815 at Chillicothe - Bounty: BLW 11126-160-12 (Illinois).

Steth, John - Private - 19th Infantry - Company: Lt John McElvain.

Stevens – see Stephens, Daniel

Stevenson, Arthur - Private - 19th Infantry - Company: Harris Hickman - Other regiment: 17th Infantry then 3rd Infantry - Age: 27 - Height: 5' 5 1/2" - Born: PA, Philadelphia County - Trade: Cordwainer - Enlistment date: 2 Feb 1813 - Enlistment place: Chillicothe - Enlistment period: 5 Yrs - By whom: Stephen Lee - Discharged: 2 Feb 1818.

Steward, John - Corporal - 19th Infantry - Company: Wilson Elliott.

Stewart, Aaron - Private - 19th Infantry.

Stewart, Alexander - Private - 19th Infantry - Age: 37 - Height: 5' 10" - Born: VA, Gloucester County - Enlistment date: 28 May 1814 - Enlistment place: Athens.

Stewart, Isaac - Private - 19th Infantry - Company: George Kesling - Age: 19 - Height: 5' 7" - Born: Virginia - Trade: Farmer - Enlistment date: 4 Feb 1815 - Enlistment place: Cincinnati - Enlistment period: 5 Yrs - By whom: William Baird - Discharged: 27 Mar 1815 at Zanesville - Bounty: BLW 677-320-14 (Illinois).

Stewart, James - Private - 19th Infantry - Company: Harris Hickman - Age: 30 - Height: 5' 11" - Born: Ireland - Trade: Silversmith - Enlistment date: 22 Apr 1814 - Enlistment place: Lebanon - Enlistment period: War - By whom: Adam Hoffman.

Stewart, James - Private - 19th Infantry - Company: William Gill - Other regiment: 3rd Infantry - Age: 31 - Height: 5' 10" - Born: PA, York County - Trade: Farmer - Enlistment date: 8 Oct 1814 - Enlistment period: 5 Yrs -

By whom: Wynkoop Warner - Comments: Deserted 16 May 1816.

Stewart, John - Private - 19th Infantry - Enlistment date: 26 Mar 1813 - Enlistment place: Cincinnati - Enlistment period: 18 Mos.

Stewart, Levi - Private - 19th Infantry - Company: George Kesling - Age: 45 - Height: 5' 10" - Born: Connecticut - Trade: Laborer - Enlistment date: 4 Sep 1814 - Enlistment place: Franklin County, Franklinton - Enlistment period: 5 Yrs - By whom: Orren Granger - Discharged: 18 Mar 1815.

Stewart, William - Private - 7th Infantry - Age: 19 - Height: 5' 8" - Born: OH, Hamilton County, Cincinnati - Enlistment date: 4 Jun 1814 - Enlistment place: Shawansetown - By whom: Henry Helm - Comments: Taken off by his father because he was a minor, 6 Aug 1814.

Sticker, Jacob - Private - 26th Infantry - Company: Joel Collins - Other regiment: 19th Infantry - Enlistment date: 7 Aug 1813 - Enlistment period: 1 Yr - Bounty: BLW 7447-160-12 (Illinois) - Comments: Re-enlisted.

Stillman – see Steelman, James

Stith, John M. - Private - 27th Infantry - Company: Carey Trimble - Other regiment: 19th Infantry - Age: 25 - Height: 6' - Born: VA, Booth - Trade: Shoemaker - Enlistment date: 15 Apr 1814 - Enlistment place: Athens - Enlistment period: War - By whom: Samuel Booker - Discharged: 6 Jun 1815 at Chillicothe - Bounty: BLW 23795-160-12 (Arkansas).

Stitt, Samuel - Private - 19th Infantry - Company: Carey Trimble - Pension: Wife Margaret, WO-30489, WC-24103, Old War IF-24384; served in Capt. C. A. Trimble's Company and in Capt. Jones' Company, 19th Infantry - Bounty: BLW 8991-160-50.

Stockings, Oliver - Private - 27th Infantry - Company: Alexander Hill - Other regiment: 19th Infantry - Age: 41 - Height: 5' 4" - Born: Connecticut - Trade: Farmer - Enlistment date: 25 Dec 1813 - Enlistment place: Newark - By whom: John Spencer - Comments: Re-enlisted until the end of the war on 14 Mar 1814 at Newark, OH.

Stockum, John - Private - 26th Infantry - Company: George Kesling - Other regiment: 25th Infantry - Enlistment date: 4 May 1813 - Comments: Deserted 27 Mar 1814.

Stoddard, Avery - Musician - 17th Infantry - Company: Henry Crittenden - Other regiment: 3rd Infantry - Age: 15 - Height: 4' 8" - Born: Connecticut - Enlistment date: 11 Nov 1813 - Enlistment place: Steubenville - Enlistment period: 5 Yrs - By whom: Ensign Riley - Pension: Wife Sarah A., WC-11198, WO-21278; served as a musician in Capt. Henry Crittenden's Company, 17th Infantry in Capt. Chunn's Company, 3rd Infantry and in Capt. Green's Company, 8th Infantry.

Stonn, George - Private - Rangers - Company: James Manary - Pension: Wife Kansy, WO-33302, WC-21343; served as a private in Capt. James Manary's Company, OH Militia.

Storm, John - Private - Rangers - Company: James Manary - Pension: SO-18745, SC-17937; served as a private in Capt. James Manary's Company, US Rangers.

Stout, George W. - Drummer - 26th Infantry - Company: George Kesling - Enlistment date: 14 May 1813 - Enlistment period: 1 Yr - Pension: Wife Hannah, Old War WF-13005; served as a drummer in the 26th Infantry.

Stout, James - Private - 26th Infantry - Company: Joel Collins - Enlistment date: 30 May 1813 - Enlistment period: 1 Yr.

Straight, Henry C. - Private - 27th Infantry - Company: George Sanderson - Enlistment date: 17 Apr 1813 - Pension: Served in Capt. George Sanderson's Company, 27th Infantry - Bounty: BLW 26567-160-50.

Strang, William - Private - 17th Infantry - Company: John Chunn - Age: 22 - Height: 5' 8" - Born: NC, Rockingham County - Trade: Laborer - Enlistment date: 25 Feb 1814 - Enlistment place: Franklin County, Franklinton - Enlistment period: War - By whom: John Cochran - Discharged: 7 Jun 1815 at Chillicothe - Bounty: BLW 5982-160-12.

Stratler, Joseph - Private - 27th Infantry - Company: George Sanderson - Enlistment date: 22 May 1813.

Stratton, Charles - Private - 19th Infantry - Age: 19 - Height: 5' 11" - Born: New Jersey - Enlistment date: 19 May 1814 - Enlistment place: Chillicothe - Enlistment period: War - By whom: Charles Cissna.

Stratton, Hosea - 1st Rifles - Company: Batteal Harrison - Age: 38 - Height: 5' 8 1/2" - Born: New Jersey - Trade: Laborer - Enlistment date: 21 May 1814 - Enlistment place: New Lisbon or Lancaster - Enlistment period: War - By whom: William Pritchard - Bounty: BLW 17702-160-12 (Missouri).

Strawbrige, John - Private - 19th Infantry - Company: James Herron - Other regiment: 17th Infantry - Enlistment date: 15 Sep 1812 - Enlistment period: 18 Mos - By whom: Lewis Howell.

Strickland, William - Private - 19th Infantry - Company: Richard Talbott - Age: 35 - Height: 5' 6" - Born: Maryland - Trade: Tailor - Enlistment date: 4 Feb 1814 - Enlistment place: Xenia - Enlistment period: War - By whom: Jacob Leslie.

Strong, Benjamin - Private - 17th Infantry - Company: Caleb Holder - Age: 26 - Height: 5' 9" - Born: MD, Kent

County - Trade: Tailor - Enlistment date: 10 Jul 1814 - Enlistment period: War - By whom: William Featherstone - Discharged: 30 Jun 1815 - Bounty: BLW 4099-160-12 (Illinois) - Comments: Discharged at Detroit.

Strong, William A. - Private - 27th Infantry - Company: Alexander Hill - Other regiment: 19th Infantry - Age: 31 - Height: 5' 8 1/2" - Born: CT, Middlesex County, Durham - Enlistment date: 10 May 1814 - Enlistment place: Ashtabula County, Harpersfield - Enlistment period: War - Died: 30 Nov 1814 - Bounty: BLW 26727-160-12 - Comments: Land bounty to Alonzo Strong & other heirs at law of William A. Strong.

Struple, John - Private - 19th Infantry - Company: Wilson Elliott - Other regiment: 17th Infantry then 3rd Infantry - Age: 18 - Height: 5' 6" - Born: PA, Chester County - Trade: Carpenter - Enlistment date: 30 Jul 1812 - Enlistment place: New Lisbon - Enlistment period: 5 Yrs - By whom: Henry Frederick - Discharged: 30 Jul 1817 at Fort Harrison, IN - Pension: Old War IF-26405; served in Capt. Elliott's Company, 19th Infantry as a private - Bounty: BLW 15629-160-12 (Arkansas).

Stuart, James - Private - 26th Infantry - Company: William Puthuff - Enlistment date: 7 May 1813 - Enlistment period: 1 Yr.

Stull, Henry - Private - Rangers - Company: Samuel McCormick - Enlistment date: 3 Dec 1813 - Enlistment period: 1 Yr - Discharged: 2 Dec 1814 at Newport, KY - Pension: SO-2730, SC-1221; served in Captain Samuel McCormick's Company, US Rangers.

Stultz, Adam - Private - 19th Infantry - Company: Wilson Elliott - Age: 28 - Height: 5' 8" - Born: PA, Northampton County - Enlistment date: 19 Jun 1812 - Enlistment period: 5 Yrs - Killed: 5 May 1813 - Pension: Wife Fanny, C-435, heirs obtained half pay for five years in lieu of military bounty land; served as a private in Captain Elliott's Company, 19th Infantry.

Stultz, Jacob - Private - 19th Infantry - Company: George Kesling - Enlistment date: 22 Jun 1814 - Enlistment period: War - Died: 29 Nov 1814 - Pension: Heirs obtained half pay for five years in lieu of military bounty land.

Stultz, John - Private - 19th Infantry - Company: Benjamin Watson - Other regiment: 25th Infantry - Age: 20 - Height: 5' 8" - Born: PA, Northampton County - Trade: Laborer - Enlistment date: 19 Jan 1812 - Enlistment place: Ohio - Enlistment period: 5 Yrs - By whom: Lieutenant Armstrong - Discharged: 19 Jun 1817.

Stutsman, Daniel - Musician - 19th Infantry - Company: Richard Talbott - Age: 22 - Height: 5' 4 1/2" - Born: MD, Washington County - Trade: Sickle maker - Enlistment date: 11 Apr 1814 - Enlistment place: Franklin County - Enlistment period: War - By whom: Robert Young - Discharged: 5 Jun 1815 at Chillicothe - Bounty: BLW 15444-160-12 (Illinois).

Sullivan, Adores S. - Private - 17th Infantry - Other regiment: Corps of Artillery - Age: 24 - Height: 5' 9" - Born: VA, Loudon County, Granville - Trade: Weaver - Enlistment date: 3 May 1814 - By whom: George Bryant - Comments: Deserted from the 17th Infantry; died from smallpox on 28 Jul 1816.

Sullivan, William - Private - 19th Infantry - Company: Carey Trimble - Age: 28 - Height: 5' 7 3/4" - Born: Delaware - Trade: Farmer - Enlistment date: 1 Apr 1814 - Enlistment place: Ross County, Adelphi - Enlistment period: War - By whom: George Will - Discharged: 6 Jun 1815 at Chillicothe - Bounty: BLW 9978-160-12 (Illinois).

Summers, Alexander - Private - 26th Infantry - Company: George Kesling - Other regiment: 25th Infantry - Enlistment date: 3 May 1813 - Enlistment period: 1 Yr - Discharged: 3 May 1814.

Summers, Ephraim - Private - 27th Infantry - Company: George Sanderson - Enlistment date: 23 Apr 1813.

Summers, Jesse C. - Corporal - 19th Infantry - Company: John Chunn - Enlistment date: 14 Mar 1813 - Enlistment period: 5 Yrs - Died: 31 Aug 1813 - Bounty: BLW 26141-160-12 (Arkansas) - Comments: Died on or about 31 Aug 1813; land bounty to Jesse C. Summers, son & other heirs at law of Jesse C. Summers.

Summons, Frederick - Private - 19th Infantry - Bounty: BLW 24920-160-12 (Arkansas).

Sunderland, John - Private - 27th Infantry - Company: George Sanderson - Enlistment date: 5 Jun 1813.

Surber, Jacob - Private - 26th Infantry - Company: William Puthuff - Enlistment date: 20 Apr 1813 - Enlistment period: 1 Yr.

Surgeon, Nathan - Private - 19th Infantry - Company: Asabael Nearing - Enlistment date: 2 Feb 1813 - Enlistment period: 5 Yrs.

Surhill, Edward - Private - 26th Infantry - Company: George Kesling - Enlistment date: 24 May 1813 - Enlistment period: 1 Yr - Died: 11 Sep 1813.

Sutton, Amariah - Private - 19th Infantry - Company: Martin Hawkins - Other regiment: 17th Infantry - Age: 20 - Height: 5' 5 1/2" - Born: Pennsylvania - Trade: Laborer - Enlistment date: 30 Apr 1814 - Enlistment place: Detroit - Enlistment period: War - By whom: George Atchison - Discharged: 9 Jun 1815 at Chillicothe - Pension: Old War IF-18298 Rejected; served in Captain Herron's Company, 19th Infantry as a private -

Bounty: BLW 4959-160-12 (Illinois).

Sutton, Ezra - Private - Rangers - Company: Samuel McCormick - Enlistment date: 8 Jan 1814 - Enlistment period: 1 Yr - Discharged: 2 Jan 1815 at Newport, KY - Pension: Wife Lydia, WO-7556, WC-2709; served in Captain Samuel McCormick's Company, OH militia.

Sutton, James - Private - 26th Infantry - Company: Samuel Swearingen - Other regiment: 25th Infantry - Enlistment date: 24 May 1813 - Enlistment period: 1 Yr.

Sutton, Jesse - Private - Rangers - Company: Samuel McCormick - Enlistment date: 14 Dec 1813 - Enlistment period: 1 Yr - Discharged: 12 Dec 1814.

Sutton, John - Private - 26th Infantry - Company: Samuel Swearingen - Other regiment: 25th Infantry - Enlistment date: 15 Jul 1813 - Enlistment period: 1 Yr - Discharged: 20 Jun 1814 at Buffalo, NY.

Swaggart, Philip - Private - 27th Infantry - Company: Alexander Hill - Other regiment: 19th Infantry - Age: 29 - Height: 5' 9" - Born: PA, Bedford County - Enlistment date: 17 Feb 1814 - Enlistment place: Zanesville - Enlistment period: War - By whom: Henry Northrup - Discharged: 6 Jun 1815 at Chillicothe - Pension: Served as a private in 19th Infantry - Bounty: BLW 8252-160-12 (Illinois).

Swails, Benjamin - Private - 19th Infantry - Company: Wilson Elliott.

Swales, Isaac - Private - 19th Infantry - Company: Wilson Elliott.

Swan, Hezekiah - Private - 2nd Rifles - Company: Batteal Harrison - Age: 39 - Height: 5' 10 3/4" - Born: Virginia - Trade: Farmer - Enlistment date: 18 Aug 1814 - Enlistment period: War - By whom: William Pritchard - Discharged: 20 Jun 1815 at Detroit.

Swaney, Frederick - Private - 2nd Artillery - Company: Daniel Cushing - Height: 5' 5 1/2" - Born: PA, Washington County - Enlistment date: 19 Jul 1812 at Franklinton, OH - Enlistment place: Canton - Enlistment period: 5 Yrs - Died: 2 Feb 1813.

Swar, Samuel - Sergeant - 26th Infantry - Company: Joel Collins - Enlistment date: 19 Apr 1813 - Enlistment period: 1 Yr.

Swartzfeller, Adam - Private - 17th Infantry - Company: Henry Crittenden - Age: 28 - Height: 5' 7 1/2" - Born: Pennsylvania - Trade: Carpenter - Enlistment date: 29 Jun 1814 - Enlistment period: War - By whom: David Carney.

Sweem, Eyer - Private - 26th Infantry - Company: Lt William McDonald - Pension: Wife Mary, WO-3412, WC-649; served in Lt. McDonald's Company, 26th Infantry.

Sweet, Ona - Private - 26th Infantry - Company: Joel Collins - Other regiment: 19th Infantry - Age: 25 - Height: 5' 9" - Born: Rhode Island - Trade: Farmer - Enlistment date: 30 Jun 1814 - Enlistment place: Detroit - Enlistment period: War - By whom: John Patterson - Bounty: BLW 20107-160-12 (Missouri) - Comments: Re-enlisted.

Swift, John - Private - 27th Infantry - Company: Alexander Hill.

Swiler, John - Sergeant - 19th Infantry - Company: George Kesling - Age: 22 - Height: 5' 8" - Born: Maryland - Trade: Potter - Enlistment date: 9 May 1814 - Enlistment period: War - By whom: John Spencer - Discharged: 27 Mar 1815 at Zanesville - Bounty: BLW 19703-160-12 (Illinois).

Sworth, Aaron - Private - 1st Infantry - Company: Hugh Moore - Age: 22 - Height: 5' 9" - Born: OH, Warren County - Trade: Laborer - Enlistment date: 8 Jun 1810 - Enlistment place: IN, Fort Wayne - Enlistment period: 5 Yrs By whom: James Rhea.

Sykes, Ethelred - Private - 19th Infantry - Company: John Chunn - Killed: 10 Sep 1813 during the Battle of Lake Erie - Comments: Served aboard the US Brig Lawrence on the Lake Erie Squadron.

Symrell, William - Private - 1st Rifles - Company: Thomas Ramsey - Age: 21 - Height: 6' - Born: SC, Fairfield County - Trade: Farmer - Enlistment date: 13 Apr 1812 - Enlistment place: Cincinnati - Enlistment period: 5 Yrs - By whom: Thomas Ramsey.

Taggart, Samuel - Private - 26th or 27th Infantry - Company: William Gill - Other regiment: 19th Infantry - Enlistment date: 24 Apr 1813 - Enlistment period: 1 Yr - Pension: Wife Margaret, WO-989, WC-32680; served in Capt. William Gill's Company, 19th Infantry as a private; lived in IN - Bounty: BLW 6172-160-12 (Illinois) - Comments: Re-enlisted.

Taliaferro, Zachariah - Sergeant - 1st Rifles - Company: Thomas Ramsey - Age: 26 - Height: 5' 9" - Born: KY, Bourbon County - Trade: Farmer - Enlistment date: 23 Apr 1814 - Enlistment place: Cincinnati - Enlistment period: War - By whom: Thomas Ramsey - Discharged: 5 Jun 1815 at Buffalo, NY - Bounty: BLW 23779-160-12 (Arkansas).

Tanner, Samuel B. - Corporal - 17th Infantry - Company: Henry Crittenden - Age: 23 - Height: 5' 8" - Born: CT, Litchfield County - Trade: Laborer - Enlistment date: 8 Mar 1814 - Enlistment period: War - By whom: William Leavitt - Discharged: 31 May 1815 at Chillicothe - Bounty: BLW 2658-160-12 (Illinois).

The Enlisted Men

Tanner, William - Private - 19th Infantry - Company: James Herron - Enlistment date: Oct 1812 - Enlistment period: 18 Mos.

Taylor, David - Private - 27th Infantry - Company: George Sanderson - Enlistment date: 9 Jun 1813.

Taylor, Hastings - Private - 19th Infantry - Company: James Herron - Enlistment date: 29 Aug 1812 - Enlistment period: 18 Mos.

Taylor, Jacob - Private - 17th Infantry - Company: John Chunn - Age: 26 - Height: 5' 7" - Born: PA, Franklin County - Trade: Shoemaker - Enlistment date: 6 Feb 1814 - Enlistment period: War - Discharged: 7 Jun 1815 at Chillicothe - Pension: Wife Barbara, WO-37734; served in Capt. Chunn's Company, 17th Infantry lived in OH - Bounty: BLW 8366-160-12 (Missouri).

Taylor, John - Private - 27th Infantry - Company: Alexander Hill - Other regiment: 19th Infantry - Age: 18 - Height: 5' 2" - Born: Pennsylvania - Trade: Laborer - Enlistment date: 24 Mar 1814 - Enlistment place: Athens - Enlistment period: War - By whom: Nehemiah Gregory.

Taylor, John C. - Private - 1st Rifles - Company: Thomas Ramsey - Age: 21 - Height: 5' 8" - Born: KY, Scott County - Trade: Farmer - Enlistment date: 17 May 1814 - Enlistment place: Cincinnati - Enlistment period: War - By whom: Thomas Ramsey - Died: 2 Oct 1814 at Fort Erie, UC, of fever.

Taylor, Joseph - Private - 17th Infantry - Company: Caleb Holder - Other regiment: 3rd Infantry - Age: 41 - Height: 5' 8" - Born: MD, Washington County - Trade: Farmer - Enlistment date: 23 Sep 1814 - Enlistment place: Dayton - Enlistment period: 5 Yrs - By whom: Asher Phillips - Discharged: 9 Jun 1816 on Surgeon's Certificate of Disability.

Taylor, Sharp H. - Private - 17th Infantry - Company: Harris Hickman - Age: 20 - Height: 5' 10" - Born: PA, Philadelphia County - Trade: Carpenter - Enlistment date: 27 Jan 1814 - Enlistment place: Chillicothe - Enlistment period: War - By whom: Adam Hoffman - Discharged: 9 Jun 1815 at Chillicothe - Bounty: BLW 3147-160-12.

Taylor, Thomas - Private - 19th Infantry - Company: Lt John McElvain - Bounty: BLW 14090-160-12 (Illinois).

Taylor, Townly - Waiter - 19th Infantry - Company: Carey Trimble - Enlistment date: 1 Jul 1814 - Comments: Waiter for Lieutenant Cessa.

Taylor, William - Private - 26th Infantry - Company: Samuel Swearingen - Enlistment date: 26 Jul 1813 - Enlistment period: 1 Yr - Discharged: 10 Jun 1814 discharged on Surgeon's Certificate of Disability because of wounds - Comments: Prisoner of War (Quebec), captured at Fort Niagara, NY, 19 Dec 1813; exchanged 11 May 1814.

Teal, Nicholas - Private - 2nd Artillery - Company: Daniel Cushing - Age: 49 - Height: 6' - Born: MD, Baltimore County - Enlistment date: 19 Aug 1812 - Enlistment period: 18 Mos.

Teel, Nicholas - Private - 27th Infantry - Company: Alexander Hill - Other regiment: 19th Infantry - Age: 40 - Height: 6' - Born: Maryland - Trade: Millwright - Enlistment date: 22 Apr 1814 - Enlistment place: Steubenville - Enlistment period: War - By whom: John Carroll - Discharged: 6 Jun 1815 at Chillicothe - Bounty: BLW 6990-160-12 (Illinois).

Tennant, Alexander - Private - Rangers - Company: Samuel McCormick - Age: 25 - Height: 6' 1/2" - Born: Virginia - Trade: Laborer - Enlistment date: 18 Nov 1813 - Enlistment period: 1 Yr - Discharged: 18 Nov 1814 at Fort Malden, UC - Pension: Old War IF-18398; served in Captain Samuel McCormick's Company, US Rangers, as a private - Bounty: BLW 19872-160-50.

Tenney, John - Private - Rangers - Company: Samuel McCormick - Age: 42 - Height: 5' - Born: England - Trade: Farmer - Enlistment date: 7 Nov 1813 - Enlistment period: 1 Yr - Discharged: 7 Nov 1814 at Fort Malden, UC.

Tennis, John - Private - 19th Infantry - Company: Carey Trimble - Age: 38 - Height: 5' 8" - Born: Pennsylvania - Trade: Laborer - Enlistment date: 5 Apr 1814 - Enlistment place: Adams County, West Union - Enlistment period: War - By whom: John Williby - Discharged: 6 Jun 1815 at Chillicothe - Bounty: BLW 25093-160-12 (Arkansas).

Terrel, Roswell - Private - 19th Infantry - Company: Carey Trimble - Age: 18 - Height: 5' 6" - Born: CT, Litchfield County, New Milford - Trade: Farmer - Enlistment date: 7 May 1814 - Enlistment place: Warren or Harpersfield - Enlistment period: War - By whom: Andrew Bushnell - Discharged: 6 Jun 1815 at Chillicothe - Pension: SC-5739; served in Capt. C. A. Trimble's Company, 19th Infantry.

Tesh, Peter - Private - 19th Infantry - Company: William Gill - Age: 18 - Height: 5' 5 1/2" - Born: Maryland - Trade: Farmer - Enlistment date: 17 Aug 1814 - Enlistment period: War - By whom: Wynkoop Warner - Discharged: 5 Jun 1815 at Chillicothe - Pension: SO-8122, SC-15357; served in Capt. Wm. Gill's Company, 19th Infantry as a private - Bounty: BLW 5891-160-12 (Illinois).

Test, Joseph - Private - 26th Infantry - Company: George Kesling - Other regiment: 25th Infantry - Age: 21 -

Height: 5' 8" - Enlistment date: 30 May 1813 - Enlistment period: 1 Yr - Discharged: 31 May 1814.

Tester, Frederick - Private - 27th Infantry - Company: George Sanderson - Enlistment date: 27 Apr 1813.

Thatcher, Joseph - Private - 1st Infantry - Company: Hugh Moore - Other regiment: 3rd Infantry - Age: 19 - Height: 6' 1 3/4" - Born: Ohio - Trade: Laborer - Enlistment date: 19 Dec 1814 - Enlistment place: IN, Fort Wayne - Enlistment period: 5 Yrs - By whom: John Whistler - Discharged: 19 Dec 1819 at Fort Howard, IA.

Thatcher, Samuel - Private - 26th Infantry - Company: Samuel Swearingen - Other regiment: 25th Infantry - Enlistment date: 21 May 1813 - Enlistment period: 1 Yr - Discharged: 21 May 1814.

Therman, Job - Private - 19th Infantry - Company: Wilson Elliott.

Thomas, Jacob - Private - 1st Rifles - Company: Thomas Ramsey - Age: 16 - Height: 5' 3" - Born: NH, Grafton County - Trade: Farmer - Enlistment date: 2 May 1814 - Enlistment place: Cincinnati - Enlistment period: War - By whom: Thomas Ramsey - Discharged: 5 Jun 1815 at Buffalo, NY - Pension: SO-13299, SC-16686; served in Captain T. Ramsay's Company, 1st Rifles.

Thomas, John - Private - 27th Infantry - Company: Isaac Van Horne - Enlistment date: 13 May 1813 - Enlistment period: 1 Yr - Died: 15 Jun 1815 at Detroit.

Thomas, John - Private - 26th Infantry - Company: John McDonald - Died: 24 Mar 1814 - Comments: Died or discharged on 24 Mar 1814.

Thomas, John - 2nd Rifles - Company: Batteal Harrison - Age: 28 - Height: 5' 8" - Born: Ireland - Trade: Carpet weaver - Enlistment date: 26 Jul 1814 - Enlistment place: Chillicothe - Enlistment period: 5 Yrs - By whom: Batteal Harrison.

Thomas, John - Private - 19th Infantry - Company: Wilson Elliott.

Thomas, Joseph - Private - 19th Infantry - Company: George Kesling - Other regiment: 3rd Infantry - Age: 24 - Height: 6' 1 1/4" - Born: Pennsylvania - Trade: Brick layer - Enlistment date: 18 Feb 1815 - Enlistment place: Cincinnati - Enlistment period: 5 Yrs - By whom: William Baird - Discharged: 18 Feb 1820.

Thomas, Whittey - 2nd Rifles - Age: 27 - Height: 5' 7" - Born: Delaware - Enlistment date: 14 Jun 1814 - Enlistment place: Lancaster.

Thomberg, Thomas - Private - 19th Infantry - Age: 36 - Height: 5' 7" - Born: Ireland, County Armagh - Enlistment date: 23 Jul 1813 - Enlistment period: War - Discharged: 20 Aug 1815 at New London, CT - Bounty: BLW 14908-160-12 (Illinois) - Comments: Prisoner of War (Halifax, NS), captured at Fort Niagara, NY, 19 Dec 1813; released 8 Apr 1815.

Thombury, George - Private - Rangers - Company: Samuel McCormick - Enlistment date: 6 Dec 1813 - Enlistment period: 1 Yr - Discharged: 5 Dec 1814.

Thompson, David - Private - 27th Infantry - Comments: Prisoner of War on Parole, captured at Detroit, MI, 16 Aug 1812.

Thompson, Isaiah - Private - 17th Infantry - Company: Caleb Holder - Age: 38 - Height: 5' 10" - Born: Ireland - Trade: Laborer - Enlistment period: War - By whom: William Featherstone - Discharged: 30 Jun 1815 at Detroit - Bounty: BLW 2871-160-12 (Illinois).

Thompson, James - Private - 2nd Artillery - Company: Stanton Sholes - Other regiment: Corps of Artillery - Enlistment date: 24 Jun 1813 - Enlistment place: Cleveland - Enlistment period: 5 Yrs - By whom: Stanton Sholes - Died: 15 Jun 1815 at Detroit - Bounty: BLW 7130-160-12 (Arkansas) or BLW 18573-160-12 (Arkansas).

Thompson, James - Private - 2nd Artillery - Company: Daniel Cushing - Enlistment date: 19 Jun 1812 - Enlistment period: 18 Mos - Discharged: 19 Dec 1813.

Thompson, James - Private - 17th Infantry - Enlistment date: 6 Oct 1813 - Enlistment period: War - By whom: Hugh May - Bounty: BLW 4288-160-12 (Illinois) - Comments: Prisoner of War (Halifax, NS), captured on 2 Sep 1814; released 10 Apr 1815.

Thompson, John - Private - 26th Infantry - Company: Samuel Swearingen - Enlistment date: 5 Jul 1813 - Enlistment period: 1 Yr - Discharged: 5 Jul 1814.

Thompson, John - Private - 19th Infantry - Company: James Herron - Other regiment: 17th Infantry - Enlistment date: 28 Aug 1812 - Enlistment period: 18 Mos - 5 Yrs - Discharged: 10 Oct 1814 - Pension: Old War IF-26454; served in Capt. Herron's Company, 17th Infantry as a private - Bounty: BLW 6349-160-12 (Illinois) - Comments: Re-enlisted.

Thompson, John - Private - 19th Infantry - Age: 36 - Height: 5' 6" - Born: England, Somerset County - Enlistment date: 3 Apr 1813 - Enlistment place: Mount Vernon - Enlistment period: 5 Yrs - By whom: John Milligan.

Thompson, John - Private - 17th Infantry - Company: Martin Hawkins - Age: 30 - Height: 5' 8" - Born: NY, Gallion or Goshen County - Trade: Brick layer - Enlistment date: 29 Apr 1813 - Enlistment place: Cincinnati - Enlistment period: War - By whom: Philip Price - Discharged: 9 Jun 1815 at Chillicothe.

The Enlisted Men

Thompson, Lewis - Private - 19th Infantry - Company: William Gill - Other regiment: 3rd Infantry - Age: 21 - Height: 5' 7" - Born: VA, Berkeley County (now WV) - Trade: Farmer - Enlistment date: 14 Aug 1814 - Enlistment place: Lancaster - Enlistment period: 5 Yrs - By whom: John Simons - Discharged: 31 Aug 1819.

Thompson, Smith - Private - 26th Infantry - Company: Samuel Swearingen - Enlistment date: 16 Jun 1813 - Enlistment period: 1 Yr - Discharged: 15 Jun 1814.

Thompson, Thomas - Private - 1st Rifles - Company: Joshua Hamilton - Age: 27 - Height: 6' - Born: PA, Fayette County, Brownsville - Trade: Laborer - Enlistment date: 19 Jun 1813 - Enlistment place: Ohio - Enlistment period: 5 Yrs - By whom: William Armstrong - Discharged: 1 Jun 1818 at Bellefontaine, MO - Bounty: BLW 19726-160-12 (Missouri).

Thompson, William - Private - 19th Infantry - Company: Wilson Elliott - Enlistment date: 18 Jun 1812 - Enlistment period: 5 Yrs - Killed: 5 May 1813 at Fort Meigs, OH - Pension: Wife Hannah, Old War Widow File 13978; heirs obtained half pay for five years in lieu of military bounty land; served as a private in the 19th Infantry - Bounty: BLW 24459-160-12 Cancelled - Comments: Land bounty (cancelled) to William Harvey Thompson, son & others heirs at law of William Thompson.

Thompson, William - Private - 17th Infantry - Company: Henry Crittenden - Age: 22 - Height: 5' 8 1/2" - Born: PA, Lancaster County - Trade: Farmer - Enlistment date: 22 Jun 1813 - Enlistment place: Butler County, Hamilton - Enlistment period: War - By whom: George Stall - Discharged: 9 Jun 1815 at Chillicothe - Pension: Served in Lt. Gray's Company, 17th Infantry as a private - Bounty: BLW 9126-160-12 (Illinois).

Thorn, Martin - Private - 2nd Rifles - Company: Batteal Harrison - Age: 31 - Height: 6' 1" - Born: Connecticut - Trade: Farmer - Enlistment date: 5 Jul 1814 - Enlistment place: Portsmouth - Enlistment period: War - By whom: Andrew Gilmore - Discharged: 30 Jun 1815 - Bounty: BLW 26670-160-12 - Comments: Discharged at Detroit; land bounty to William Thorn, son & other heirs at law of Martin Thorn.

Thorn, Martin - Private - 26th Infantry - Company: George Kesling - Enlistment date: 5 May 1813 - Enlistment period: 1 Yr.

Thornbury – see Thomberg, Thomas

Thorne, Thomas - Private - 27th Infantry - Company: Isaac Van Horne - Enlistment date: 24 Jun 1813 - Enlistment period: 1 Yr - Comments: Deserted 26 Jun 1813.

Thorp, Benjamin - Private - 27th Infantry - Company: George Sanderson - Enlistment date: 19 Apr 1813.

Thorp, John - Private - 27th Infantry - Company: George Sanderson - Enlistment date: 10 May 1813.

Throckmorton, Lewis - Corporal - 17th Infantry - Company: John Chunn - Age: 40 - Height: 5' 10" - Born: PA, Fayette County - Trade: Millwright - Enlistment date: 20 Sep 1813 - Enlistment period: 18 Mos - By whom: Hugh May - Pension: Old War IF-18422 Rejected, served in Captain Chinn's Company, 17th Infantry as a private.

Throckmorton, Peter - Private - 27th Infantry - Company: Isaac Van Horne - Enlistment date: 22 May 1813 - Enlistment period: 1 Yr - Died: 29 Nov 1813 at Detroit.

Throgmorton, William - Private - 19th Infantry - Discharged: 19 Sep 1814.

Thurman, Joel - Sergeant - 19th Infantry - Company: Wilson Elliott - Other regiment: 17th Infantry then 3rd Infantry - Age: 25 - Height: 5' 10 3/4" - Born: Virginia - Trade: Farmer - Enlistment date: 1 Aug 1812 - Enlistment period: 5 Yrs - Discharged: 31 Jul 1817 - Pension: SO-7172, SC-3385, served in Captain Whistler's Company, 17th Infantry as a sergeant, lived in OH - Bounty: BLW 10531-160-12 - Comments: Prisoner of War.

Timmons, Edmund - Private - 26th Infantry - Company: Joel Collins - Other regiment: 25th Infantry - Enlistment date: 6 May 1813 - Enlistment period: 1 Yr - Died: 12 May 1814 at Buffalo, NY - Pension: Wife Rachel, WO-1636, WC-5095, served in Captain Collins' Company, 26th Infantry.

Timmons, Elijah - Private - 19th Infantry - Company: Wilson Elliott - Age: 43 - Height: 5' 11" - Born: DE, Sussex County - Trade: Laborer - Enlistment date: 27 Apr 1814 - Enlistment place: Franklin County, Franklinton - Enlistment period: War - By whom: Hugh Moore - Died: 24 Feb 1815 at Erie, PA.

Tinsely, Joseph - Corporal - 2nd Artillery - Company: Daniel Cushing.

Tod, Edward - Private - 19th Infantry - Company: Wilson Elliott.

Todd, Edward - Private - 19th Infantry - Company: Edward White - Other regiment: 25th Infantry - Age: 28 - Height: 5' 10 1/2" - Enlistment date: 26 Feb 1813 - Enlistment period: 18 Mos - By whom: James Herron - Comments: Transferred to 25th Infantry 28 Feb 1814.

Todd, John - 19th Infantry - Company: Capt Williams - Pension: SC-22135; served in Capt. Williams' Company, 19th Infantry.

Toline, Anthony - Private - 2nd Artillery - Company: Daniel Cushing.

Toncray, James H. - Private - 1st Rifles - Company: Thomas Ramsey - Age: 24 - Height: 5' 6" - Born: NY, Albany

County - Trade: Silversmith - Enlistment date: 14 Apr 1814 - Enlistment place: Cincinnati - Enlistment period: War - By whom: Thomas Ramsey - Discharged: 5 Jun 1815 at Buffalo, NY - Bounty: BLW 8944-160-12 (Arkansas).

Tonett, Charles - 19th Infantry - Died: 8 Jul 1814, executed at Chillicothe.

Tool, Arthur - Private - 2nd Rifles - Company: Batteal Harrison - Age: 40 - Height: 5' 9" - Born: Delaware - Trade: Cooper - Enlistment date: 8 Sep 1814 - Enlistment place: Cincinnati - Enlistment period: War - By whom: Elias Langham - Discharged: 30 Jun 1815 at Detroit.

Tool, Michael - Drummer - 17th Infantry - Company: David Holt - Other regiment: 3rd Infantry - Age: 22 - Height: 5' 7 3/4" - Born: Canada, Nova Scotia, Halifax - Trade: Soldier - Enlistment date: 28 Mar 1814 - Enlistment place: Chillicothe - Enlistment period: 5 Yrs - Comments: Deserted at Detroit, MI, on 15 Nov or 9 Dec 1815.

Toomar, Thomas - Private - 2nd Rifles - Company: Batteal Harrison - Age: 25 - Height: 5' 7" - Born: Great Britain - Trade: Laborer - Enlistment date: 18 Aug 1814 - Enlistment place: Cincinnati - Enlistment period: War - By whom: Elias Langham.

Topping, Zopher - Private - 19th Infantry - Company: William MacDonald - Died: 27 Sep 1814 at Williamsville, NY (hospital); buried in the War of 1812 Cemetery in Cheektowaga, Erie County, NY.

Totten, John - Corporal - 19th Infantry - Company: Carey Trimble - Age: 29 - Height: 5' 11" - Born: PA, Washington County - Trade: Farmer - Enlistment date: 21 Feb 1814 - Enlistment place: Franklin County, Franklinton - Enlistment period: War - By whom: John McElvain - Discharged: 6 Jun 1815 at Chillicothe.

Trader, Moses - Private - 26th Infantry - Company: George Kesling - Other regiment: 19th Infantry - Enlistment date: 16 Jun 1813 - Enlistment period: 1 Yr - Bounty: BLW 29701-160-12 (Arkansas) - Comments: Land bounty to John Trader & other heirs at law of Moses Trader.

Trapnell, Joshua - Private - 17th Infantry - Company: William Bradford - Enlistment date: 6 Jul 1812 - Enlistment period: 18 Mos - By whom: Parry Hawkins - Killed: 10 Sep 1813 during the Battle of Lake Erie - Pension: Wife Elizabeth, Navy Old Act WF-1196; served as a private in the US Marine Corps aboard the US Brig Niagara; mortally wounded - Comments: Served aboard the US Brig Niagara on the Lake Erie Squadron.

Treat, Amaziah - Private - 19th Infantry - Age: 23 - Height: 5' 10" - Born: MA, Berkshire County - Enlistment date: 29 Apr 1814 - Enlistment place: Franklin County, Franklinton - Enlistment period: War - By whom: Hugh Moore.

Trimble, Daniel - Corporal - 19th Infantry - Company: Carey Trimble - Enlistment date: 5 Mar 1814 - Enlistment period: War - Died: 24 Oct 1814 at Fort Erie, UC.

Trimble, John - Corporal - 19th Infantry - Company: Alexander Hill - Bounty: BLW 24055-160-12 (Arkansas) - Comments: Land bounty to Anna Ream & other heirs at law of John Trimble.

Trobridge, Ammy D. - Private - 19th Infantry - Age: 25 - Height: 5' 2 1/2" - Born: Connecticut - Enlistment date: 25 Apr 1814 - Enlistment place: New Lisbon - By whom: Thomas McKnight

Trovinger, Jacob - Private - 27th Infantry - Company: George Sanderson - Enlistment date: 2 Jun 1813.

Truman, Noah - Private - 19th Infantry - Age: 23 - Height: 6' - Born: Massachusetts - Enlistment date: 17 Aug 1814 Enlistment place: Franklin County, Franklinton.

Trumble, Daniel - Private - 27th Infantry - Company: Alexander Hill.

Tucker, Frederick - Private - 27th Infantry - Company: George Sanderson - Enlistment date: 21 May 1813 - Comments: Prisoner of War on Parole, captured at Detroit, MI, 16 Aug 1812..

Tucker, Thomas - Private - 19th Infantry - Company: Asabael Nearing - Bounty: BLW 26705-160-12 (Arkansas) - Comments: Land bounty to John R. Tucker, son & other heirs at law of Thomas Tucker.

Tull, Solomon - Private - 19th Infantry - Age: 21 - Height: 5' 11 1/2" - Born: England, Wilkshire - Enlistment date: 4 Apr 1814 - Enlistment place: Columbus - Enlistment period: War - By whom: Hugh Moore.

Tullus, David R. - Private - Rangers - Company: Samuel McCormick - Enlistment date: 1 Nov 1813 - Enlistment period: 1 Yr - Discharged: 20 Nov 1814.

Turk, Ephraim - Private - 2nd Artillery - Company: Daniel Cushing.

Turwillizer, John - Private - 26th Infantry - Company: Samuel Swearingen - Other regiment: 19th Infantry - Enlistment date: 1 Jul 1813 - Enlistment period: 1 Yr - Pension: Wife Catharine McKown, Old War Widow File 9552; served as a private in the 19th Infantry.

Tuttle, Jabez - Private - 19th Infantry - Company: James Herron - Other regiment: 17th Infantry - Age: 28 - Height: 5' 8" - Born: NJ, Morris County, Morristown - Trade: Tanner - Enlistment date: 27 Apr 1814 - Enlistment place: Detroit - Enlistment period: War - By whom: George Atchison - Discharged: 9 Jun 1815 at Detroit - Bounty: BLW 13136-160-12 (Illinois) - Comments: Re-enlisted.

Twaddle, Joseph - Private - 27th Infantry - Company: George Sanderson - Enlistment date: 16 Apr 1813.

Tyler, Seymour - Private - 27th Infantry - Company: George Sanderson - Enlistment date: 29 Jul 1813.

The Enlisted Men

Tyroder, James - Private - 19th Infantry - Age: 37 - Height: 5' 7" - Born: England, Guernsey Island - Enlistment date: 15 Jul 1812 - Enlistment period: 5 Yrs.

Tyrrell, Roswell - Private - 27th Infantry - Company: Carey Trimble - Age: 18 - Height: 5' 6" - Born: PA, Cumberland County - Enlistment date: 16 Mar 1814 - Enlistment place: Warren County - Enlistment period: 1 Yr - Pension: SO-7981, SC-5739; served as a private in Capt. C. A. Trimble's Company, 19th Infantry; lived in IL - Bounty: BLW 20730-160-12 (Missouri).

Ulery, Nicholas - Private - 26th Infantry - Company: William Puthuff - Enlistment date: 13 May 1813 - Enlistment period: 1 Yr.

Ulry, Jacob - Private - Rangers - Company: William Perry - Discharged: 5 Oct 1812.

Ulry, John - Private - 26th Infantry - Company: William Puthuff - Enlistment date: 7 May 1813 - Enlistment period: 1 Yr.

Uppenhouse, Frederick - Private - 19th Infantry - Company: Wilson Elliott.

Usher, John - Private - 27th Infantry - Other regiment: 19th Infantry - Age: 29 - Height: 5' 5" - Born: Maryland - Trade: Shoemaker - Enlistment date: 16 Apr 1814 - Enlistment place: Zanesville - Enlistment period: War - Bounty: BLW 9669-160-12 (Arkansas) - Comments: Deserted 28 Sep 1814.

Vail, Samuel - Private - 19th Infantry - Company: William Gill - Age: 40 - Height: 5' 7" - Born: New York - Trade: Millwright - Enlistment date: 8 Aug 1814 - Enlistment place: Franklin County, Franklinton - Enlistment period: War By whom: Nehemiah Gregory - Discharged: 31 May 1815 - Bounty: BLW 24364-160-12.

Van Camp, Moses - Private - 26th Infantry - Company: Joel Collins - Enlistment date: 18 Sep 1813 - Enlistment period: 1 Yr - Died: 14 Dec 1813, probably at Detroit.

Van Fosson, John - Private - 27th Infantry - Company: William Gill - Other regiment: 19th Infantry - Age: 22 - Height: 5' 8" - Born: PA, Philadelphia County - Trade: Farmer - Enlistment date: 19 Aug 1814 - Enlistment place: OH, Louisville - Enlistment period: War - By whom: William Gill - Discharged: 5 Jun 1815 at Chillicothe - Pension: SO-23578, SC-18744; served in Captain William Gill's Company, 27th Infantry and in Captain Van Horne's Company, 19th Infantry; lived in Marion, Linn County, IA in 1854 and in Newcomerstown, Tuscarawas County, OH, in 1871 - Bounty: BLW 13660-160-12 (Illinois); BLW 26787-160-50.

Van Meter, John - Sergeant - 27th Infantry - Company: George Sanderson - Enlistment date: 3 Jun 1813 - Comments: Prisoner of War on Parole, captured at Detroit, MI, 16 Aug 1812.

Van Osdoll, Robert - Corporal - 26th Infantry - Company: Samuel Swearingen - Other regiment: 25th Infantry - Enlistment date: 3 May 1813 - Enlistment period: 1 Yr - Discharged: 30 Apr 1814.

Van Winkle, James - Private - 27th Infantry - Comments: Prisoner of War on Parole, captured at Detroit, MI, 16 Aug 1812.Vance, Daniel - Private - 19th Infantry - Age: 18 - Height: 5' 7 1/2" - Born: KY, Green County - Enlistment date: 31 Jul 1812 - Enlistment period: 18 Mos.

Vance, Henry M. - 1st Rifles - Company: Thomas Ramsey - Age: 28 - Height: 5' 7 1/2" - Born: New Jersey - Trade: Whitesmith - Enlistment date: 7 Feb 1815 - Enlistment place: Cincinnati - Enlistment period: 5 Yrs - By whom: William Pritchard - Discharged: 29 Feb 1816 - Comments: Discharged at Bellefontaine, MO.

Vandorn, Hezekiah - Corporal - 26th Infantry - Company: William Puthuff - Other regiment: 25th Infantry - Enlistment date: 18 Apr 1813 - Enlistment period: 1 Yr - Discharged: 18 Apr 1814 - Pension: SO-1974, SC-1098; served in Captains Puttoff and John B. Murdock Companies, 25th Infantry.

Vantile, Isaac - Private - 19th Infantry - Company: William Gill - Other regiment: 17th Infantry then 3rd Infantry - Age: 25 - Height: 5' 10 1/2" - Born: NJ, Morris County - Trade: Laborer - Enlistment date: 17 Jul 1814 - Enlistment place: Steubenville - Enlistment period: 5 Yrs - By whom: James Blair - Discharged: 17 Jul 1819 at Fort Howard, WI.

Vanway, Lewis - Private - 27th Infantry - Company: George Sanderson - Died: 27 Oct 1813 - Comments: Served aboard the US Schooner Tigress on the Lake Erie Squadron.

Varner, Henry - Private - 19th Infantry - Company: John Chunn - Other regiment: 17th Infantry - Age: 18 - Height: 5' 6 1/2" - Born: PA, Westmoreland County - Trade: Farmer - Enlistment date: 5 Dec 1813 - Enlistment period: War - By whom: David Carney - Discharged: 7 Jun 1815 at Chillicothe - Bounty: BLW 18891-160-12 (Missouri).

Vince, James - Private - 19th Infantry - Company: James Herron - Other regiment: 25th Infantry - Age: 35 - Height: 5' 9" - Enlistment date: 4 Nov 1812 - Discharged: 4 May 1814 - Comments: Transferred to 25th Infantry 26 Feb 1814.

Vince, James - Private - 2nd Rifles - Company: Batteal Harrison - Age: 35 - Height: 5' 9" - Born: VA, Culpepper County - Trade: Farmer - Enlistment date: 9 Jul 1814 - Enlistment place: Highland County, Hillsboro - Enlistment period: War - By whom: Joseph McClain - Discharged: 30 Jun 1815 at Detroit - Bounty: BLW

13159-160-12 (Illinois)

Vince, John - Sergeant - 19th Infantry - Company: Richard Graham - Enlistment date: 11 Aug 1812 - Enlistment period: 5 Yrs - Died: 26 Jul 1813.

Violet, Sampson - Private - 26th Infantry - Company: William Puthuff - Enlistment date: 7 Jun 1813 - Enlistment period: 1 Yr - Pension: Wife Eve; served in Capt. Lucas' Company, OH Militia as a private - Bounty: BLW 21594-160-50.

Virgin, Mathew - Corporal - 2nd Rifles - Company: Benjamin Johnson - Age: 25 - Height: 5' 10" - Born: Ohio - Trade: Hatter - Enlistment date: 3 May 1814 - Enlistment place: KY, Fayette County, Lexington - Enlistment period: War - By whom: Hugh Innes.

Voorhees, Isaac - Private - 1st Infantry - Company: Horatio Stark - Other regiment: 3rd Infantry - Age: 29 - Height: 5' 9" - Born: MD, Kent County - Trade: Saddler - Enlistment date: 24 Mar 1812 - Enlistment place: Chillicothe - Enlistment period: 5 Yrs - By whom: Swearingen - Discharged: 24 Mar 1817.

Vulgermett, Joseph - Private - 19th Infantry - Company: Carey Trimble - Age: 46 - Height: 6' - Born: VA, Frederick County - Trade: Laborer - Enlistment date: 25 Apr 1814 - Enlistment place: Canton - Enlistment period: War - By whom: Abraham Shane - Discharged: 6 Jun 1815 at Chillicothe - Bounty: BLW 7231-160-12 (Illinois).

Waggoner, Ephraim - Private - 2nd Artillery - Company: Daniel Cushing.

Wagner, John H. - Private - 27th Infantry - Age: 22 - Height: 5' 10" - Born: PA, Montgomery County - Enlistment date: 2 Apr 1814 - Enlistment place: New Lisbon.

Walbridge, James - Private - 26th Infantry - Company: Samuel Swearingen - Other regiment: 2nd Light Dragoons - Enlistment period: 1 Yr.

Walk, John D. - Sergeant - 17th Infantry - Age: 23 - Height: 5' 10" - Born: PA, Fayette County - Trade: Chair maker - Enlistment date: 7 Mar 1814 - Enlistment place: Franklin County, Franklinton - Enlistment period: War - By whom: John Cochran.

Walker, Alexander - Private - 27th Infantry - Company: George Sanderson - Enlistment date: 15 May 1813.

Walker, Gideon - Quartermaster Sergeant - 26th Infantry - Company: George Kesling - Other regiment: 19th Infantry - Enlistment date: 3 Jun 1813 - Enlistment period: 1 Yr - Died: 9 Dec 1813 - Pension: Wife Barbara, Old War WF-5163; quartermaster sergeant in the 19th Infantry; resided in NY - Bounty: BLW 66956-160-55.

Walker, Henry V. - Private - 19th Infantry - Company: Richard Talbott - Age: 28 - Height: 5' 8" - Born: New York - Trade: Farmer - Enlistment date: 4 Jan 1815 - Enlistment place: Cleveland - Enlistment period: War - By whom: Richard Talbott.

Walker, James B. - Private - 19th Infantry - Company: William Gill - Age: 23 - Height: 5' 6" - Born: Ireland, County Down - Trade: Blacksmith - Enlistment date: 20 Sep 1814 - Enlistment place: Marietta - Enlistment period: War - By whom: Samuel Coleman - Bounty: BLW 25578-160-12 (Arkansas).

Walker, John D. - Sergeant - 17th Infantry - Company: David Holt - Age: 23 - Height: 5' 10" - Born: PA, Franklin County - Trade: Chair maker - Enlistment date: 7 Mar 1814 - Enlistment place: Franklin County, Franklinton - Enlistment period: War - By whom: John Cochran - Discharged: 4 Jun 1815 at Chillicothe - Bounty: BLW 5861-160-12 (Illinois).

Walker, Joseph - Corporal - 19th Infantry - Company: James Herron - Enlistment date: 15 Sep 1812 - Enlistment period: 18 Mos.

Walker, Philip - Private - 19th Infantry - Company: David Holt - Other regiment: 17th Infantry - Age: 26 - Height: 5' 10" - Born: Pennsylvania - Enlistment date: 27 Apr 1814 - Enlistment place: Franklin County, Franklinton - By whom: John Cochran - Died: 30 Nov 1814 at Buffalo, NY.

Walker, Samuel - Sergeant - 19th Infantry - Company: Carey Trimble - Age: 40 - Height: 5' 11" - Born: NY, Albany County, Linsonburg - Trade: Farmer - Enlistment date: 18 Apr 1814 - Enlistment place: Zanesville - Enlistment period: War - By whom: Neal McFadden - Pension: Old War IF-18758 Rejected; served as a sergeant in the 19th Infantry; born in NY; lived in OH - Bounty: BLW 12149-160-12 (Illinois).

Walker, Samuel - Private - 27th Infantry - Age: 38 - Height: 5' 8" - Born: New York - Enlistment date: 1 May 1814 - Enlistment place: Zanesville,

Wallace, Aaron - Private - 17th Infantry - Company: Caleb Holder - Age: 34 - Height: 5' 10" - Born: Virginia - Trade: Tailor - Enlistment date: 26 Jul 1814 - Enlistment period: War - By whom: George Stall - Discharged: 30 Jun 1815 at Detroit - Bounty: BLW 20901-160-12 (Missouri).

Wallace, Allen - Private - 27th Infantry - Company: Carey Trimble - Other regiment: 19th Infantry - Age: 17 - Height: 5' 8" - Born: Virginia - Trade: Laborer - Enlistment date: 18 Mar 1814 - Enlistment place: Worthington - Enlistment period: War - By whom: Lieutenant Pinney - Discharged: 6 Jun 1815 at Chillicothe

- Pension: Wife Phebe J., WO-13929, WC-11742 Rejected; served in Lt. John Elvain's Company, 19th Infantry as a private; lived in IL - Bounty: BLW 15835-160-12 (Illinois) - Comments: Prisoner of War on Parole, captured at Detroit, MI, 16 Aug 1812, also wounded at Fort Erie, UC, 15 Aug 1815.

Wallace, Austin - Musician - 19th Infantry - Company: Henry Crittenden - Other regiment: 17th Infantry then 3rd Infantry - Age: 17 - Height: 5' 4" - Born: VT, Addison County, Shorcham - Trade: Musician - Enlistment date: 30 Mar 1814 - Enlistment place: Worthington - Enlistment period: War - By whom: John Cochran - Discharged: 9 Jun 1815 - Bounty: BLW 9473-160-12 (Illinois) - Comments: Discharged at Chillicothe.

Wallace, David - Private - 17th Infantry - Company: Caleb Holder - Age: 26 - Height: 5' 8" - Born: Connecticut - Trade: Wheelwright - Enlistment date: 4 Jul 1814 - Enlistment period: War - By whom: John Simons - Discharged: 30 Jun 1815 at Detroit - Bounty: BLW 11273-160-12 (Illinois).

Wallace, James - Sergeant - 19th Infantry - Company: John Chunn - Comments: Prisoner of War, arrived at Plattsburgh, NY, 15 Apr 1814.

Wallace, Ross - Private - 17th Infantry - Company: William Adair - Other regiment: 3rd Infantry - Age: 25 - Height: 5' 6 1/2" - Born: Pennsylvania - Trade: Laborer - Enlistment date: 11 Sep 1814 - Enlistment place: Dayton - Enlistment period: 5 Yrs - By whom: David Carney - Discharged: 28 Feb 1816 at Detroit on Surgeon's Certificate of Disability - Pension: Wife Elizabeth, Old War IF-10263; served in Capt. Adair's Company, 3rd Infantry - Bounty: BLW 25104-160-12 (Arkansas).

Wallace, William - Sergeant - 17th Infantry - Company: David Holt - Age: 35 - Height: 5' 10" - Born: Virginia - Trade: Tailor - Enlistment date: 26 Jul 1814 - Enlistment place: Cincinnati - Enlistment period: War - By whom: George Stall - Discharged: 4 Jun 1815 at Chillicothe - Bounty: BLW 19152-160-12 (Illinois).

Wallace, William - Corporal - 27th Infantry - Company: Alexander Hill - Other regiment: 19th Infantry - Age: 30 - Height: 5' 6" - Born: PA, Westmoreland County - Trade: Joiner - Enlistment date: 12 Mar 1814 - Enlistment period: 1 Yr - War - By whom: John Spencer - Discharged: 5 Jun 1815 at Chillicothe - Bounty: BLW 4339-160-12 (Illinois).

Waller, Henry - Private - 19th Infantry - Company: Wilson Elliott.

Walling, William - Private - 26th Infantry - Company: George Kesling - Other regiment: 25th Infantry - Enlistment date: 19 Apr 1813 - Enlistment period: 1 Yr - Discharged: 19 Apr 1814.

Walsh, Frederick - Private - 19th Infantry - Company: Carey Trimble - Age: 27 - Height: 5' 6" - Born: Pennsylvania - Trade: Brick layer - Enlistment date: 21 Jul 1814 - Enlistment place: Franklin County, Franklinton - Enlistment period: 1 Yr - By whom: John McElvain - Discharged: 22 Feb 1815.

Walsinger, John - Private - 2nd Rifles - Company: Batteal Harrison - Age: 22 - Height: 5' 11" - Born: VA, Bath County - Trade: Laborer - Enlistment date: 5 Jul 1814 - Enlistment place: Portsmouth - Enlistment period: War - By whom: Andrew Gilmore - Discharged: 30 Jun 1815 at Detroit - Bounty: BLW 20613-160-12 (Missouri).

Walters, David - Private - 27th Infantry - Company: George Sanderson - Enlistment date: 27 Apr 1813.

Walters, George - Private - 17th Infantry - Company: Harris Hickman - Age: 21 - Height: 5' 11" - Born: Pennsylvania - Trade: Laborer - Enlistment date: 7 May 1814 - Enlistment period: War - By whom: John Stockton.

Walters, Henry - Musician - 19th Infantry - Company: Wilson Elliott - Other regiment: 25th Infantry - Age: 24 - Height: 5' 8 1/2" - Born: Maryland - Trade: Farmer - Enlistment date: 30 Jul 1812 - Enlistment place: Trumbull County, Warren - Enlistment period: 5 Yrs - By whom: Lieutenant Frederick - Pension: Old War IF-18788 Rejected; served in Capt. Elliott's Company, 19th Infantry as a private - Comments: Wounded during the Battle of Mississinewa, IN, on 18 Dec 1812.

Walters, Joseph L. - Private - 19th Infantry - Company: Wilson Elliott - Enlistment date: 30 Aug 1812 - Enlistment period: 18 Mos.

Wamble, Edward - Private - 19th Infantry - Company: Joel Collins - Discharged: 11 Aug 1814 - Pension: Served in Capt. Collins' Company, 19th Infantry as a private - Bounty: BLW 55-160-50.

Ward, Ashabel - Private - Rangers - Company: William Perry - Pension: Wife Mary A., WO-22165, WC-20445; served in Captain William Perry's Company, US Rangers, as a private; lived in OH.

Ward, Calvin - Sergeant - Rangers - Company: Samuel McCormick - Enlistment date: 5 Nov 1813 - Enlistment period: 1 Yr - Discharged: 4 Nov 1814.

Ward, Joseph - Private - 17th Infantry - Company: Henry Crittenden - Other regiment: 3rd Infantry - Age: 25 - Height: 5' 5" - Born: OH, Hamilton County - Trade: Laborer - Enlistment date: 1 Jan 1814 - Enlistment period: War - By whom: Samuel Booker - Bounty: BLW 25237-160-12 - Comments: Land bounty to Isaac Ward, son & other heirs at law of Joseph Ward.

Ward, Samuel - Corporal - 2nd Rifles - Company: Batteal Harrison - Age: 23 - Height: 5' 10" - Born: Pennsylvania

- Trade: Farmer - Enlistment date: 3 Apr 1814 - Enlistment place: Highland County, Hillsboro - Enlistment period: War - By whom: Joseph McClain - Discharged: 30 Jun 1815 at Detroit - Bounty: BLW 13160-160-12 (Missouri).

Ward, Solomon - Private - 2nd Rifles - Company: Batteal Harrison - Age: 24 - Height: 5' 8" - Born: South Carolina - Trade: Farmer - Enlistment date: 5 Aug 1814 - Enlistment place: Cincinnati - Enlistment period: War - By whom: Elias Langham - Discharged: 30 Jun 1815 at Detroit - Bounty: BLW 11582-160-12 (Arkansas).

Warfield, Silvanus - Private - 26th Infantry - Company: William Puthuff - Enlistment date: 9 Apr 1813 - Enlistment period: 1 Yr.

Warman, Joshua - Corporal - 2nd Artillery - Company: Daniel Cushing - Enlistment date: 25 Aug 1812 - Enlistment period: 18 Mos - Died: 6 Mar 1813 at Fort Meigs.

Warren, Benny W. - Private - 27th Infantry - Age: 23 - Height: 5' 9 1/2" - Born: Maryland - Enlistment date: 25 Apr 1814 - Enlistment place: Newark.

Wartimber, Francis A. - Private - 2nd Artillery - Company: Daniel Cushing - Age: 30 - Height: 5' 4 3/4" - Born: New Jersey - Enlistment date: 30 Aug 1812 - Enlistment period: 18 Mos.

Waters, Jacob - Private - 27th Infantry - Company: George Kesling - Other regiment: 19th Infantry - Age: 19 - Height: 5' 6" - Born: PA, Fayette County - Enlistment date: 21 Feb 1814 - Enlistment place: Marietta - Enlistment period: War - By whom: Nehemiah Gregory.

Watkins, Perigrine (or Perry) - Private - 3rd Artillery - Company: William Parker - Other regiment: Corps of Artillery - Age: 37 - Height: 5' 6" - Born: DE, Kent County - Trade: Farmer - Enlistment date: 24 Sep 1814 - Enlistment place: Ohio - Enlistment period: 5 Yrs - By whom: Lieutenant Scott - Discharged: 23 Sep 1819.

Watkins, Thomas - Private - 19th Infantry - Company: William Gill - Age: 43 - Height: 5' 9" - Born: Delaware - Trade: Farmer - Enlistment date: 20 Mar 1814 - Enlistment period: War - By whom: George Paull - Discharged: 5 Jun 1815 at Chillicothe - Bounty: BLW 15878-160-12 (Illinois).

Watrons, William - Private - 19th Infantry - Other regiment: 17th Infantry - Age: 27 - Height: 5' 10 1/2" - Born: Connecticut - Trade: Laborer - Enlistment date: 10 Apr 1814 - Enlistment place: Marietta - Enlistment period: War - By whom: John Milligan - Discharged: 4 Jun 1815 at Chillicothe - Bounty: BLW 4006-160-12 (Arkansas); BLW 6668-160-12 (Illinois).

Watson, Archibald - Private - 19th Infantry - Company: George Kesling - Other regiment: 3rd Infantry - Age: 19 - Height: 5' 6" - Born: Maryland - Trade: Farmer - Enlistment date: 4 Feb 1815 - Enlistment place: Zanesville - Enlistment period: 5 Yrs - By whom: Charles Cass - Discharged: 4 Feb 1820 - Pension: Wife Cassandra, Old War IF-18829 Rejected, WO-11477, WC-27889, SO-18339, SC-21692; served in Capt. Thos. Mountjoy's Company, OH Militia and in Captains Daniel Baker's, George Kesling's and Bissell's Companies, 19th and 3rd Infantries; lived in IN.

Watson, David - Private - 26th Infantry - Company: George Kesling - Other regiment: 25th Infantry - Enlistment date: 26 May 1813 - Enlistment period: 1 Yr - By whom: Richard Talbott - Comments: Deserted 23 Mar 1814.

Watson, James C. - Private - 27th Infantry - Company: Joseph Cairns - Pension: Old War IF-18824 Rejected; SO-10545, SC-13340; served in Capt. Cairne's Company, 27th US Infantry Regiment, lived in IL.

Watson, John - Private - 19th Infantry - Company: Carey Trimble - Age: 40 - Height: 5' 9" - Born: Pennsylvania - Trade: Farmer - Enlistment date: 17 Feb 1814 - Enlistment period: War - By whom: Lieutenant Patterson - Discharged: 6 Jun 1815 at Chillicothe.

Watson, William - Private - 27th Infantry - Company: George Sanderson - Enlistment date: 28 Apr 1813 - Enlistment period: 1 Yr.

Watson, William - Private - 17th Infantry - Company: David Holt - Age: 26 - Height: 6' - Born: Pennsylvania - Trade: Hatter - Enlistment date: 11 Jun 1814 - Enlistment place: Youngstown - Enlistment period: War - By whom: Ensign Rue - Discharged: 4 Jun 1815 at Chillicothe.

Watsworth, Daniel - Private - Rangers - Company: Samuel McCormick - Age: 19 - Height: 5' 6" - Born: New York - Trade: Farmer - Enlistment date: 30 Oct 1813 - Enlistment period: 1 Yr - Discharged: 30 Oct 1814 at Fort Malden, UC.

Watt, Daniel - Sergeant - 19th Infantry - Company: Joel Collins - Age: 25 - Height: 5' 10" - Born: Pennsylvania - Trade: Blacksmith - Enlistment date: 28 Feb 1814 - Enlistment place: Detroit - Enlistment period: War - By whom: Samuel Coleman - Discharged: 2 Jul 1815 t Detroit - Bounty: BLW 23121-160-12 (Arkansas).

Wayman, James - Private - 19th Infantry - Enlistment date: 1 Feb 1814 - Enlistment period: War - Died: 9 Jun 1814 - Bounty: BLW 26756-160-12 (Arkansas) - Comments: Land bounty to John Wayman & other heirs at law of James Wayman.

Weaver, Adam - Sergeant - 19th Infantry - Company: Wilson Elliott - Age: 28 - Height: 6' 2" - Born: PA, Dauphin

County - Trade: Hatter - Enlistment date: 1 May 1813 - Enlistment place: Cincinnati - Enlistment period: War - By whom: Philip Price - Discharged: 7 Jun 1815 at Chillicothe - Bounty: BLW 25107-160-12 (Arkansas).

Weaver, Jacob - Private - 27th Infantry - Company: George Sanderson - Enlistment date: 28 May 1813.

Webb, David - Sergeant - 17th Infantry - Company: Harris Hickman - Age: 54 - Height: 5' 11" - Born: CT, Fairfield County - Trade: Tailor - Enlistment date: 20 Jun 1814 - Enlistment place: Chillicothe - Enlistment period: War - By whom: Stephen Lee - Discharged: 9 Jun 1815 at Chillicothe - Bounty: BLW 7226-160-12 (Illinois).

Webb, James - Private - 26th Infantry - Company: William Puthuff - Enlistment date: 27 May 1813 - Enlistment period: 1 Yr.

Webb, Joseph – Private - 19th Infantry - Discharged: 9 Jun 1814 - Comments: Discharged at Newport, KY.

Webb, Joseph - Private - 26th Infantry - Company: William Puthuff - Enlistment date: 10 May 1813 - Enlistment period: 1 Yr - Comments: Prisoner of War, exchanged 25 Apr 1814.

Webb, Joseph S. - Sergeant - 19th Infantry - Company: George Kesling - Other regiment: 3rd Infantry - Age: 33 - Height: 5' 8" - Born: Ireland, County Londonderry - Trade: Farmer - Enlistment date: 22 Feb 1815 - Enlistment place: Chillicothe - Enlistment period: 5 Yrs - By whom: Charles Cissna - Discharged: 5 Jun 1816 on Surgeon's Certificate of Disability.

Webster, William - Corporal - 27th Infantry - Company: William Gill - Enlistment date: 15 May 1813 - Enlistment period: 1 Yr - Comments: Served aboard the US Schooner Tigress on the Lake Erie Squadron.

Weir, James - Private - 19th Infantry - Company: Carey Trimble - Age: 21 - Height: 6' - Born: PA, Westmoreland County - Trade: Farmer - Enlistment date: 18 Mar 1814 - Enlistment place: Athens - Enlistment period: War - By whom: Nehemiah Gregory - Discharged: 6 Jun 1815 at Chillicothe - Bounty: BLW 16415-160-12 (Illinois).

Welch, James - Private - 2nd Artillery - Company: Daniel Cushing - Other regiment: Corps of Artillery - Age: 33 - Height: 6' 1" - Born: VA, Wythe County - Trade: Farmer - Enlistment date: 26 Jul 1812 - Enlistment place: Chillicothe - Enlistment period: 5 Yrs - By whom: Samuel Kercheval - Discharged: 26 Jul 1817.

Welch, Thomas - 2nd Rifles - Age: 23 - Height: 6' 1" - Born: Pennsylvania - Enlistment date: 18 Jul 1814 - Enlistment place: New Lisbon.

Welch, Thomas - Private - 19th Infantry - Company: Harris Hickman - Age: 29 - Height: 5' 10" - Born: Pennsylvania - Enlistment date: 30 Mar 1814 - Enlistment place: Butler County, Hamilton - Enlistment period: War - By whom: George Stall - Died: 25 Feb 1815 at Erie, PA, of natural death - Bounty: BLW 25377-160-12 (Arkansas) - Comments: Land bounty to James Welch & other heirs at law of Thomas Welch.

Wellington, Thomas - Private - 19th Infantry - Company: Wilson Elliott - Age: 20 - Height: 5' 9" - Born: Virginia - Enlistment date: 30 Jul 1812 - Enlistment place: Trumbull County, Warren - Enlistment period: 18 Mos - Discharged: 25 Jan 1814 - Pension: Wife Eliza, SO-18597, SC-13810, WO-41503, WC-32318; served in Capt. W. Elliott's Company, US Infantry - Comments: Wounded during the Battle of Mississinewa, IN, on 18 Dec 1812.

Wells, James - Private - 19th Infantry - Age: 19 - Height: 5' 3" - Born: MD, Allegeny County - Enlistment date: 26 Jul 1812 - Enlistment period: 5 Yrs.

Wells, John - Private - 27th Infantry - Comments: Prisoner of War on Parole, captured at Detroit, MI, 16 Aug 1812.

Wells, Robert - Private - 2nd Rifles - Company: Batteal Harrison - Age: 20 - Height: 5' 9" - Born: England - Trade: Laborer - Enlistment date: 27 Aug 1814 - Enlistment place: Cincinnati - Enlistment period: War - By whom: Elias Langham - Discharged: 30 Jun 1815 at Detroit - Bounty: BLW 8368-160-12 (Missouri).

Wells, Thomas - Sergeant - 19th Infantry - Age: 36 - Height: 5' 10" - Born: Virginia - Enlistment date: 15 Jul 1812 - Enlistment period: 18 Mos.

Wells, William - Private - 27th Infantry - Company: Joseph Carins - Enlistment date: 15 Apr 1813 - Enlistment period: 1 Yr.

Welsh, Robert - Private - Rangers - Company: Samuel McCormick - Enlistment date: 6 Dec 1813 - Enlistment period: 1 Yr - Discharged: 5 Dec 1814 - Pension: Old War IF-14823; served in Captain Samuel McCormick's Company, US Rangers as a private in 1813.

Welshaus, John - Private - 27th Infantry - Company: George Sanderson - Enlistment date: 25 May 1813.

Welshon, Jacob - Private - 19th Infantry - Company: Carey Trimble - Age: 22 - Height: 5' 3" - Born: PA, York County - Trade: Miller - Enlistment date: 7 Jun 1814 - Enlistment place: Ross County, Adelphi - Enlistment period: War - By whom: John Booten - Discharged: 6 Jun 1815 at Chillicothe - Bounty: BLW 9630-160-12 (Illinois).

Welson, William - Private - 19th Infantry - Company: Lt John McElvain.

Wertz, Francis - Private - 17th Infantry - Age: 24 - Height: 5' 7" - Born: Virginia - Enlistment date: 7 Nov 1814 -

Enlistment place: Steubenville - Enlistment period: War - By whom: William Featherstone - Comments: Deserted from the 22nd Infantry and reinstated in the 17th Infantry.

Wesley, Archibald - Private - 19th Infantry - Company: William Gill.

West, David - Private - 19th Infantry - Company: William Gill - Other regiment: 17th Infantry then 3rd Infantry - Age: 17 - Height: 5' 4" - Born: MD, Harford County - Trade: Laborer - Enlistment date: 19 Oct 1814 - Enlistment period: 5 Yrs - By whom: Wynkoop Warner - Pension: Wife Lydda, WO-40099, WC-31394, SO-20403, SC-9876; served in Captains William Gill, J. Adair and George Gray companies, 17th and 3rd Infantries as a private.

West, James - Private - 26th Infantry - Company: George Kesling - Enlistment date: 14 May 1813 - Enlistment place: Adams County, West Union - Enlistment period: 1 Yr - Discharged: 14 May 1814.

West, Richard - Private - 19th Infantry - Company: Asabael Nearing - Comments: Waiter to Colonel John Miller.

West, Thomas - Private - 19th Infantry - Company: Carey Trimble - Enlistment date: 23 Jan 1814 - Enlistment period: 1 Yr - Discharged: 25 Jan 1815.

Westcoat, James (Westcott) - Private - 19th Infantry - Company: William Gill - Age: 20 - Height: 5' 6" - Born: Massachusetts - Trade: Farmer - Enlistment date: 19 Sep 1814 - Enlistment period: War - By whom: Neal McFadden - Discharged: 31 Mar 1815 - Pension: Wife Sarah (alias Mercy), WC-44267, SO-11587, SC-7261; served in Capt. W. Gill's Company, 19th Infantry as a private; lived in OH and PA - Bounty: BLW 27033-160-55.

Wheatley, Thomas - Private - 27th Infantry - Company: George Sanderson - Enlistment date: 12 Apr 1813.

Wheatley, Thomas (Whitley) - Private - 2nd Rifles - Company: Batteal Harrison - Age: 27 - Height: 5' 7" - Born: Delaware - Trade: Tailor - Enlistment date: 14 Jun 1814 - Enlistment place: Lancaster - Enlistment period: War - By whom: John Stockton - Discharged: 30 Jun 1815 at Detroit.

Wheeland, Joseph - Private - 19th Infantry - Company: Asabael Nearing - Enlistment date: 6 Feb 1813 - Enlistment period: 18 Mos - By whom: Lieutenant Morrow.

Wheeler, Jacob - Private - 27th Infantry - Company: George Sanderson - Enlistment date: 25 May 1813.

Wheeler, William - Private - 19th Infantry - Company: Carey Trimble - Other regiment: 17th Infantry - Enlistment date: 2 Feb 1814 - Enlistment period: 1 Yr - Discharged: 2 Feb 1815.

Wheelon, William - Private - 19th Infantry - Company: Angus Langham - Pension: SO-21701, SC-18561; served as a private in Capt. Langham's Company, 19th Infantry.

Weightman – see Wightman, James

Whelan, Thadeus - Private - 1st Rifles - Company: Thomas Ramsey - Age: 23 - Height: 5' 6" - Born: OH, Hamilton County - Trade: Cooper - Enlistment date: 3 Apr 1814 - Enlistment place: Cincinnati - Enlistment period: War - By whom: Thomas Ramsey - Discharged: 5 Jun 1815 at Buffalo, NY - Bounty: BLW 8327-160-12 (Illinois).

Whelpley, David - Private - 2nd Rifles - Company: Benjamin Desha - Age: 37 - Height: 5' 8" - Born: New York - Trade: Hatter - Enlistment date: 10 Nov 1814 - Enlistment place: Cincinnati - Enlistment period: War - By whom: William Pritchard - Discharged: 10 Jun 1815 at Plattsburgh, NY.

Whetsone, Jasper - Private - 19th Infantry - Other regiment: 25th Infantry then 6th Infantry - Age: 18 - Height: 5' 7" - Born: OH, Hamilton County - Trade: Farmer - Enlistment date: 16 Apr 1813 - Enlistment place: Cincinnati - Enlistment period: 5 Yrs - By whom: Lieutenant Price - Discharged: 3 Oct 1815 at Fort Columbus, NY, on Surgeon's Certificate of Disability.

Whitacre, Thomas - Private - 17th Infantry - Company: Henry Crittenden - Age: 28 - Height: 5' 8" - Born: Virginia - Trade: Laborer - Enlistment date: 10 Jan 1814 - Enlistment period: War - By whom: Samuel Booker - Discharged: 9 Jun 1815 at Chillicothe - Bounty: BLW 3456-160-12 (Illinois).

Whitaker, John - 27th Infantry - Pension: Old War IF-18983 Rejected, served in the 27th Infantry - Bounty: BLW 806.

Whitaker, Joseph - Private - 19th Infantry - Discharged: 2 Dec 1814.

Whitaker, Josiah - Private - 29th Infantry - Company: John McDonald - Other regiment: 19th Infantry - Pension: Wife Lydia, WO-12374, WC-29745; served as a private in Capt McDonald's Company, 26th and 19th Infantries; Capt Randolph's Company, 26th US Infantry; lived in OH.

Whitcraft, Joseph - Private - 28th Infantry - Company: Johnston Magowan - Enlistment date: 26 Jun 1813 - Enlistment period: 1 Yr - Discharged: 27 Oct 1813 at Bass Island, OH (Put-in-Bay, OH).

White, Ansel - Private - 27th Infantry - Company: George Sanderson - Enlistment date: 20 Apr 1813.

White, Henry - Private - 26th Infantry - Company: William Puthuff - Enlistment date: 7 May 1813 - Enlistment period: 1 Yr.

White, John - Private - 19th Infantry - Age: 18 - Height: 5' 4" - Born: Kentucky - Trade: Farmer - Enlistment date:

11 May 1814 - Enlistment place: Chillicothe - Enlistment period: War - By whom: Charles Cissna - Discharged: 6 Jun 1815 at Chillicothe - Bounty: BLW 9525-160-12 (Illinois).

White, John - Private - 19th Infantry - Company: Carey Trimble - Age: 27 - Height: 5' 6 3/4" - Born: England, Devonshire - Trade: Tailor - Enlistment date: 18 Mar 1814 - Enlistment place: Chillicothe - Enlistment period: War - By whom: Charles Cissna.

White, Joseph - Private - 17th Infantry - Company: John Chunn - Age: 19 - Height: 5' 4 1/2" - Born: Connecticut - Trade: Laborer - Enlistment date: 20 Jan 1814 - Enlistment place: Franklin County, Franklinton - Enlistment period: War - By whom: John Cochran - Bounty: BLW 9526-160-12 (Illinois).

White, Matthew - Private - 19th Infantry - Company: Carey Trimble - Age: 29 - Height: 5' 10" - Born: Pennsylvania - Trade: Laborer - Enlistment date: 25 Feb 1814 - Enlistment place: Zanesville - Enlistment period: War - By whom: Neal McFadden.

White, Peter - Private - 17th Infantry - Age: 18 - Height: 5' 8" - Born: Kentucky - Enlistment date: 1 Nov 1814 - Enlistment place: Lancaster - Enlistment period: War - By whom: William Shang.

White, William - Private - 26th Infantry - Company: William Puthuff - Enlistment date: 2 Jun 1813 - Enlistment period: 1 Yr.

White, William W. - Corporal - 1st Rifles - Company: Thomas Ramsey - Age: 22 - Height: 5' 3" - Born: NC, Burke County - Trade: School master - Enlistment date: 12 Jun 1814 - Enlistment place: Cincinnati - Enlistment period: War - By whom: Thomas Ramsey - Discharged: 5 Jun 1815 at Buffalo, NY - Bounty: BLW 25245-160-12 (Arkansas).

Whitehead, James - Private - 19th Infantry - Company: James Herron - Enlistment date: 15 Sep 1812 - Enlistment period: 18 Mos.

Whitehouse, John - Private - 19th Infantry - Company: Asabael Nearing - Enlistment date: 19 Mar 1813 - Enlistment period: War.

Whiteright, Jacob - Private - 17th Infantry - Company: John Chunn - Other regiment: 3rd Infantry - Age: 34 - Height: 5' 10 1/4" - Born: PA, York County - Trade: Blacksmith - Enlistment date: 23 Oct 1814 - Enlistment period: 5 Yrs - By whom: James Campbell - Discharged: 23 Oct 1819.

Whiting, Leonard - Corporal - 19th Infantry - Company: Asabael Nearing - Age: 45 - Height: 5' 11" - Trade: Carpenter - Enlistment date: 29 Aug 1812 - Enlistment period: 18 Mos - Discharged: 18 Oct 1814 at Detroit - Pension: Old War IF-7887; served in Capt Nearing's Company, 19th Infantry as a corporal - Bounty: BLW 17506-160-12 (Illinois) - Comments: Wounded at Fort Meigs, OH, on 5 May 1813.

Whitman, William - Sergeant - 17th Infantry - Company: Henry Crittenden - Age: 20 - Height: 5' 5" - Born: PA, Philadelphia County - Trade: Laborer - Enlistment date: 17 Jan 1814 - Enlistment place: Warren County - Enlistment period: War - By whom: William Leavitt - Discharged: 9 Jun 1815 at Chillicothe.

Whitney, Mathias - Private - 19th Infantry - Company: Wilson Elliott.

Whitson, Joseph - Private - 27th Infantry - Company: William Gill - Other regiment: 19th Infantry - Age: 29 - Height: 5' 7" - Born: PA, Buck County or Berk County - Trade: Laborer - Enlistment date: 1 May 1814 - Enlistment place: Newark - Enlistment period: War - By whom: John Spencer - Discharged: 5 Jun 1815 at Chillicothe - Bounty: BLW 9979-160-12.

Whittlesey, Joseph - Private - 26th Infantry - Company: Richard Talbott - Other regiment: 19th Infantry - Age: 41 - Height: 5' 8" - Born: Connecticut - Trade: Laborer - Enlistment date: 28 Feb 1814 - Enlistment place: Franklin County - Enlistment period: 1 Yr - By whom: Robert Young - Discharged: 5 Jun 1815 at Chillicothe - Bounty: BLW 13767-160-12 (Missouri) - Comments: Re-enlisted 27 Jul 1814 for War.

Wieley, Jonas - Private - 27th Infantry - Age: 24 - Height: 6' - Born: PA, Westmoreland County - Enlistment date: 20 May 1814 - Enlistment place: Athens.

Wienro, Thomas - Private - 1st Rifles - Enlistment date: 7 Feb 1814 - Enlistment period: 5 Yrs - Discharged: 1 Oct 1814 - Killed near Fort Erie, UC.

Wightman, James - Private - 19th Infantry - Company: George Kesling - Age: 21 - Height: 5' 7" - Born: New York - Enlistment date: 4 May 1814 - Enlistment place: Franklin County, Franklinton - Enlistment period: War - By whom: Hugh Moore - Died: 15 Aug 1814 - Bounty: BLW 27292-160-42 - Comments: Land bounty to Sylvia & George Bardsley, Elizabeth Clark, Ruth Richards and Alexander Wightman, sole heirs at law of James Wightman, alias Weightman.

Wilcox, Daniel - Private - 19th Infantry - Company: Carey Trimble - Age: 18 - Height: 6' 2 1/2" - Born: PA, Washington County - Trade: Tailor - Enlistment date: 25 Feb 1814 - Enlistment place: New Lisbon - Enlistment period: 5 Yrs - By whom: James Harper - Discharged: 25 Feb 1819 at Fort Howard, WI.

Wilcox, William H. - Sergeant - 17th Infantry - Company: David Holt - Age: 28 - Height: 5' 8" - Born: Massachusetts - Trade: Laborer - Enlistment date: 26 Feb 1814 - Enlistment place: Butler County, Hamilton -

Enlistment period: War - By whom: George Stall - Discharged: 4 Jun 1815 at Chillicothe - Bounty: BLW 6063-160-12 (Illinois).

Wiley, James - Private - 19th Infantry - Company: Angus Langham - Age: 28 - Height: 5' 10" - Born: PA, Fayette County - Trade: Wheelwright - Enlistment date: 27 Jul 1812 - Enlistment period: 5 Yrs - By whom: Lieutenant Jackson - Discharged: 27 Jul 1817.

Wiley, James - Private - 28th Infantry - Company: Nimrod Moore - Enlistment date: 13 May 1813 - Enlistment period: 1 Yr - Died: 31 Dec 1813.

Wiley, John - Private - 19th Infantry - Age: 28 - Height: 5' 10" - Born: PA, Fayette County - Enlistment date: 27 Jul 1812 - Enlistment place: Zanesville - Enlistment period: 5 Yrs.

Wiley, William - Private - 26th Infantry - Company: George Kesling - Enlistment date: 19 Jun 1813 - Enlistment period: 1 Yr - Discharged: 26 Jun 1814 - Comments: Prisoner of War (Quebec), captured at Fort Niagara, NY, 19 Dec 1813; exchanged 11 May 1814.

Wilkinson, Thomas B. - Private - 19th Infantry - Company: Richard Talbott - Age: 27 - Height: 5' 10" - Born: VA, Chester County - Trade: Laborer - Enlistment date: 19 Jan 1814 - Enlistment place: Lebanon - Enlistment period: War - By whom: Philip Price - Discharged: 5 Jun 1815 at Chillicothe - Bounty: BLW 13871-160-12 (Illinois).

Willey, Frederick - Private - 17th Infantry - Company: Henry Crittenden - Age: 35 - Height: 5' 3" - Born: Germany, Saxony - Trade: Laborer - Enlistment date: 21 May 1813 - Enlistment place: Cleveland - Enlistment period: War - By whom: George Tod - Discharged: 9 Jun 1815 - Comments: Discharged at Chillicothe.

Williams – see Fickle, Michael F.

Williams, Benjamin - Private - 26th Infantry - Company: George Kesling - Other regiment: 2nd Light Dragoons - Enlistment date: 24 Apr 1813 - Enlistment period: 1 Yr - Discharged: 24 Apr 1814.

Williams, Biram - Private - 26th Infantry - Enlistment date: 9 Sep 1813 - By whom: Alexander Delerae - Comments: Prisoner of War on Parole, captured at Detroit, MI, 16 Aug 1812.

Williams, Charles - Private - 19th Infantry - Company: James Herron - Other regiment: 25th Infantry - Age: 24 - Height: 5' 11" - Born: PA, Philadelphia - Trade: Farmer - Enlistment date: 27 Jun 1813 - Enlistment place: Cleveland - Enlistment period: 5 Yrs - By whom: Lieutenant Exeter - Discharged: 27 Jun 1818.

Williams, Flavel - Private - 27th Infantry - Company: George Sanderson - Enlistment date: 31 May 1813 - Pension: Wife Martha, Old War WF-19158 Rejected; served in Captain Harper's Company, 27th Infantry as a private.

Williams, Isaac - Private - 26th Infantry - Company: William Puthuff - Enlistment date: 9 May 1813 - Enlistment period: 1 Yr.

Williams, James - Private - 1st Rifles - Company: Thomas Ramsey - Age: 16 - Height: 5' - Born: SC, Martin County - Trade: Laborer - Enlistment date: 10 Nov 1813 - Enlistment place: Cincinnati - Enlistment period: War - By whom: Thomas Ramsey - Discharged: 5 Jun 1815 at Buffalo, NY - Bounty: BLW 4235-160-12 (Missouri).

Williams, John 1st - Private - 19th Infantry - Company: Joel Collins - Age: 22 - Height: 5' 8" - Born: Ohio - Trade: Farmer - Enlistment date: 19 Apr 1814 - Enlistment place: Upper Canada, Sandwich - Enlistment period: War - By whom: Robert Smith - Discharged: 20 Jul 1815 at Detroit - Bounty: BLW 25024-160-12 (Arkansas).

Williams, John 2nd - Private - 19th Infantry - Company: Joel Collins - Age: 38 - Height: 5' 8" - Born: Pennsylvania - Trade: Laborer - Enlistment date: 14 Sep 1814 - Enlistment place: Detroit - Enlistment period: War - By whom: John Patterson - Bounty: BLW 22519-160-12 (Arkansas).

Williams, John M. - Corporal - 26th Infantry - Company: Samuel Swearingen - Other regiment: 25th Infantry - Enlistment date: 26 Jul 1813 - Enlistment period: 1 Yr - Discharged: 22 Jun 1814.

Williams, John P. - Private - 26th Infantry - Company: Joel Collins - Enlistment date: 19 Apr 1813 - Enlistment period: 1 Yr.

Williams, Joseph - Private - 26th Infantry - Company: Joel Collins - Enlistment date: 6 Sep 1813 - Enlistment period: 1 Yr - Died: 1 Dec 1813 at Sandwich, UC (now Windsor, Ontario).

Williams, Linus - Sergeant Major - 27th Infantry - Enlistment date: 5 May 1813.

Williams, Linzar - Private - 19th Infantry - Company: William Gill - Age: 41 - Height: 5' 6 1/2" - Born: VA, Farquhar County - Trade: Farmer - Enlistment date: 30 Aug 1814 - Enlistment period: War.

Williams, Mathew - Private - Rangers - Company: Samuel McCormick - Age: 18 - Height: 5' 8" - Born: Virginia - Trade: Farmer - Enlistment date: 7 Nov 1813 - Enlistment period: 1 Yr - Discharged: 6 Nov 1814 at Fort Malden, UC - Pension: SO-2778, SC-1276; served in Captain Samuel McCormick's Company, OH militia as a private.

Williams, Nathan - Private - 27th Infantry - Other regiment: 19th Infantry - Age: 22 - Height: 5' 10" - Born: CT,

The Enlisted Men

Litchfield County, North Hartford - Enlistment date: 8 Apr 1814 - Enlistment place: Marietta - By whom: John Milligan - Comments: Deserted.

Williams, Remembrance - Private - 19th Infantry - Company: James Herron - Enlistment date: 27 Apr 1812 - Enlistment period: War.

Williams, Samuel - Private - 19th Infantry - Company: George Kesling - Other regiment: 3rd Infantry - Age: 28 - Height: 5' 8" - Born: Virginia - Trade: Shoemaker - Enlistment date: 19 Feb 1815 - Enlistment place: Cincinnati - Enlistment period: 5 Yrs - By whom: William Baird.

Williams, Thomas - Private - Rangers - Company: Samuel McCormick - Enlistment date: 1 Nov 1813 - Enlistment period: 1 Yr - Discharged: 22 Nov 1814.

Williams, William - Private - 19th Infantry - Company: Carey Trimble - Enlistment date: 25 Feb 1814 - Enlistment period: War - Died: 2 Sep 1814 from wounds - Bounty: BLW 27314-160-42 - Comments: Land bounty to Mary McMonigle, Daniel McMonigle, Thomas McMonigle, Sarah Jacobs and Catherine Applegate, only heirs of William Williams.

Williamson, John - Private - 19th Infantry - Company: William Gill - Age: 23 - Height: 5' 9" - Born: Virginia - Trade: Farmer - Enlistment date: 21 Oct 1814 - Enlistment period: War - By whom: John Simons - Discharged: 5 Jun 1815 at Chillicothe - Bounty: BLW 13664-160-12 (Illinois).

Willibey, Andrew - Private - 27th Infantry - Age: 31 - Height: 5' 7 1/2" - Born: New Jersey - Enlistment date: 2 May 1814 - Enlistment place: New Lisbon.

Willis, Amos - Private - 19th Infantry - Died: Died at Fort Erie, UC, date unknown.

Willis, John - Private - 19th Infantry - Company: James Herron - Enlistment date: 5 Nov 1812.

Wills, John S. - 8th Military District - Company: Staff - Commissioning date: 7 May 1813 - Discharged: 15 Jun 1815 - Comments: Judge Advocate from 7 May 1813 to 15 Jun 1815.

Willson, Thomas - Private - 17th Infantry - Age: 21 - Height: 6' 1" - Born: KY, Fayette County - Enlistment date: 9 Jun 1814 - Enlistment place: Cincinnati - Enlistment period: War - By whom: David Carney.

Willson, William - Private - 19th Infantry - Company: Carey Trimble - Other regiment: 17th Infantry - Age: 17 - Height: 5' 3" - Born: Ohio - Trade: Laborer - Enlistment date: 23 May 1814 - Enlistment place: Urbana - Enlistment period: War - By whom: William Baird - Comments: Re-enlisted for 5 years, 12 Apr 1815.

Wilmoth, Benson - Private - 19th Infantry - Company: Carey Trimble - Age: 19 - Height: 5' 8" - Born: Pennsylvania - Trade: Farmer - Enlistment date: 11 Mar 1814 - Enlistment place: Chillicothe - Enlistment period: War - By whom: Charles Cissna - Discharged: 31 May 1815 - Pension: Old War IF-19089 Rejected, served in 19th Infantry as a private - Bounty: BLW 27501-160-42.

Wilson, Archibald - Private - 27th Infantry - Company: George Sanderson - Pension: Wife Hannah, WO-34044, WC-18182; served in Captain Spencer's Company, 27th Infantry.

Wilson, Chester - Sergeant - 19th Infantry - Company: Asabael Nearing.

Wilson, Earl - Musician - 17th Infantry - Company: Lt James Campbell - Age: 22 - Height: 5' 10 1/2" - Born: Massachusetts - Trade: Laborer - Enlistment date: 22 Dec 1814 - Enlistment place: Xenia - Enlistment period: War - By whom: William Shang - Discharged: 25 Jul 1815 at Lower Sandusky (now Fremont, OH)- Bounty: BLW 569-320-14 (Illinois) or BLW 567-320-14 (Illinois).

Wilson, James - Private - 19th Infantry - Company: Wilson Elliott - Other regiment: 17th Infantry - Age: 19 - Height: 5' 10 1/2" - Born: PA, Allegheny County - Enlistment date: 3 Sep 1812 - Enlistment period: 18 Mos.

Wilson, James - Sergeant - 19th Infantry - Company: George Kesling - Age: 29 - Height: 5' 11 1/2" - Born: NJ, Sussex County - Trade: Farmer - Enlistment date: 1 Sep 1814 - Enlistment place: Lebanon - Enlistment period: War - By whom: George Kesling - Discharged: 27 Mar 1815 at Zanesville - Bounty: BLW 8904-160-12 (Illinois).

Wilson, John - Private - 19th Infantry - Company: George Kesling - Age: 41 - Height: 5' 10" - Born: Ireland - Trade: Tailor - Enlistment date: 10 Jan 1815 - Enlistment place: Lebanon - Enlistment period: War - By whom: George Kesling - Died: 27 Mar 1815 - Bounty: BLW 499-320-14 (Missouri) - Comments: Land bounty to Thomas Wilson, et al, heirs at law of John Wilson.

Wilson, John - Private - 19th Infantry - Bounty: BLW 4834-160-12 (Arkansas).

Wilson, John - Sergeant - 28th Infantry - Company: Joseph Belt - Age: 16 - Height: 5' 2" - Born: Ohio - Trade: Farmer - Enlistment date: 2 Mar 1815 - Enlistment place: KY, Newport - Enlistment period: 5 Yrs - By whom: Johnston Magowan - Discharged: 2 Mar 1820.

Wilson, Joseph - Private - 27th Infantry - Company: George Sanderson - Enlistment date: 19 Jun 1813 - Discharged: 15 Sep 1813.

Wilson, Moses - Private - 19th Infantry - Company: John Chunn - Enlistment date: 19 Jul 1812 - Enlistment period: 5 Yrs.

Wilson, Simeon - Private - Rangers - Company: Samuel McCormick - Enlistment date: 20 Nov 1813 - Enlistment period: 1 Yr - Discharged: 2 Nov 1814.

Wilson, Thomas - Private - 17th Infantry - Company: Henry Crittenden - Age: 21 - Height: 6' 1" - Born: KY, Fayette County - Trade: Brick layer - Enlistment date: 9 Jun 1814 - Enlistment period: War - By whom: David Carney - Discharged: 9 Jun 1815 at Chillicothe - Bounty: BLW 17127-160-12 (Illinois).

Wilson, William - Private - 27th Infantry - Company: James Applegate - Other regiment: 19th Infantry - Enlistment date: 3 May 1813 - Enlistment period: 1 Yr - Bounty: BLW 10590-160-12 (Illinois) - Comments: Re-enlisted.

Wilt, George - Private - 19th Infantry - Company: Carey Trimble - Age: 39 - Height: 5' 8 1/2" - Born: Pennsylvania - Trade: Farmer - Enlistment date: 17 Mar 1814 - Enlistment place: Newark - Enlistment period: War - By whom: John Spencer - Discharged: 6 Jun 1815 at Chillicothe - Bounty: BLW 7111-160-12 (Illinois).

Winans, Benjamin - Private - Rangers - Company: Samuel McCormick - Age: 29 - Height: 5' 9" - Born: New Jersey - Trade: Farmer - Enlistment date: 9 Nov 1813 - Enlistment period: 1 Yr - Discharged: 8 Nov 1814 at Fort Malden, UC.

Windel, James - Private - 19th Infantry - Enlistment date: 30 Jan 1813 - Enlistment place: Cincinnati - Enlistment period: 18 Mos.

Winders, Thomas - Private - 17th Infantry - Company: Henry Crittenden - Age: 38 - Height: 5' 10" - Born: Maryland - Trade: Laborer - Enlistment date: 14 Jun 1812 - Enlistment period: War - By whom: John Reeves - Discharged: 9 Jun 1815 - Bounty: BLW 8616-160-12 (Illinois).

Wingard, James C. - Sergeant - 17th Infantry - Company: Martin Hawkins - Age: 34 - Height: 5' 11" - Born: Maryland - Trade: Carpenter - Enlistment date: 11 May 1813 - Enlistment period: War - By whom: Chesteen Scott - Discharged: 10 May 1815 at Newport, KY - Pension: Wife Elizabeth Klink, Old War WF-12042; served as a sergeant in the US Infantry - Bounty: BLW 21047-160-12 (Arkansas) - Comments: On furlough at Cincinnati, OH; recovering from a wound.

Wingate, Archibald - Private - Rangers - Company: Samuel McCormick - Enlistment date: 12 Nov 1813 - Enlistment period: 1 Yr - Discharged: 22 Nov 1814 - Pension: Old War Widow File 19163 Rejected; served as a private in Capt. McCormick's Company, Rangers.

Wingo, James - Private - 26th Infantry - Company: Joel Collins - Enlistment date: 3 Aug 1813 - Enlistment period: 1 Yr - Died: 4 Dec 1813 at Sandwich, UC (now Windsor, Ontario).

Winner, John - Private - 27th Infantry - Comments: Prisoner of War on Parole, captured at Detroit, MI, 16 Aug 1812.

Winstead, Samuel - Private - 1st Infantry - Company: Horatio Stark - Age: 21 - Height: 6' - Born: VA, Shenandoah County - Trade: Blacksmith - Enlistment date: 15 Mar 1812 - Enlistment period: 5 Yrs - By whom: Capt Swearenger - Discharged: 15 Mar 1817 at Fort Dearborn, IL.

Winter, Thomas - Private - 19th Infantry - Age: 22 - Height: 5' 8" - Born: Pennsylvania - Enlistment date: Nov 1814 - Enlistment place: Lebanon - Enlistment period: War - By whom: George Kesling - Discharged: 23 Nov 1814 by writ of habeas corpus.

Wiseheart, Adam - Private - 19th Infantry - Company: Angus Langham - Enlistment date: 19 Oct 1812 - Enlistment period: 5 Yrs.

Wisely, Archibald - Private - 19th Infantry - Company: William Gill - Age: 40 - Height: 5' 7" - Born: PA, York County - Trade: Farmer - Enlistment date: 23 Apr 1814 - Enlistment place: Xenia - Enlistment period: War - By whom: George Kesling.

Wisgaver, John - Private - 26th Infantry - Company: William Puthuff - Enlistment date: 7 Jun 1813 - Enlistment period: 1 Yr.

Witing, Leonard - Corporal - 19th Infantry.

Wittington, Thomas - Private - 19th Infantry - Company: Wilson Elliott - Comments: Wounded during the Battle of Mississinewa, IN, on 18 Dec 1812.

Wolcott, Robert - Private - 27th Infantry - Company: George Sanderson - Pension: SO-34887; served in Capt. Sanderson's Company, 27th Infantry.

Wolcott, William - Private - 27th Infantry - Age: 53 - Height: 6' 1 1/2" - Born: Maryland - Enlistment date: 27 Dec 1813 - Enlistment place: Newark - By whom: Anderson Spencer.

Wolf, Charles - Private - 17th Infantry - Age: 30 - Height: 6' 1" - Born: Virginia - Enlistment date: 1 May 1814 - By whom: James Hazelton.

Wolff, Jacob - Sergeant - 19th Infantry - Company: Richard Talbott - Age: 22 - Height: 5' 6" - Born: Virginia - Trade: Laborer - Enlistment date: 24 Apr 1814 - Enlistment place: Franklin County - Enlistment period: War - By whom: Robert Young - Discharged: 5 Jun 1815 at Chillicothe - Bounty: BLW 17637-160-12 (Illinois).

The Enlisted Men

Wolfley, Coonrod - Private - 27th Infantry - Company: George Sanderson - Enlistment date: 31 May 1813.

Wolverton, Daniel - Private - 26th Infantry - Company: Samuel Swearingen - Enlistment date: 27 Apr 1813 - Enlistment period: 1 Yr.

Womble, Edward - Private - 26th Infantry - Company: Joel Collins - Enlistment date: 12 Apr 1813 - Enlistment period: 1 Yr - By whom: Richard Talbott.

Wood, Benjamin - Private - 19th Infantry - Company: James Herron - Enlistment date: 10 Jul 1812 - Enlistment period: War.

Wood, Charles - Private - 26th Infantry - Company: George Kesling - Enlistment date: 25 May 1813 - Enlistment period: 1 Yr - Died: 17 Nov 1813.

Wood, Frederick - Sergeant - 19th Infantry - Company: John Chunn - Other regiment: 17th Infantry - Age: 21 - Height: 5' 6" - Trade: Shoemaker - Enlistment date: 29 Jan 1814 - Enlistment period: War - By whom: Adam Hoffman - Discharged: 18 Apr 1815 at Chillicothe - Bounty: BLW 6187-160-12 (Illinois).

Wood, James M. - Private - 27th Infantry - Comments: Prisoner of War on Parole, captured at Detroit, MI, 16 Aug 1812.

Wood, Joshua - Private - 19th Infantry - Company: Harris Hickman - Other regiment: 17th Infantry - Age: 19 - Height: 6' 1" - Born: Ohio - Enlistment date: 25 Apr 1814 - Enlistment place: Marietta - By whom: John Milligan.

Wood, Michael - Private - 19th Infantry - Died: died in Charleston - Comments: Prisoner of War on Parole, captured at Detroit, MI, 16 Aug 1812.

Woodcock, Aaron - Private - 1st Rifles - Company: Thomas Ramsey - Age: 25 - Height: 6' 2" - Born: New Hampshire - Trade: Farmer - Enlistment date: 26 Jul 1814 - Enlistment place: Greenville - Enlistment period: War - By whom: Thomas Ramsey - Discharged: 5 Jun 1815 at Buffalo, NY - Bounty: BLW 3714-160-12 (Missouri).

Wooden, Eri - Private - 27th Infantry - Company: William Gill - Enlistment date: 22 Jun 1813 - Enlistment period: 1 Yr - Killed: 4 Mar 1814.

Woodruff, Elisha - Private - 26th Infantry - Company: Samuel Swearingen - Enlistment date: 24 Jul 1813 - Enlistment period: 1 Yr.

Woodruff, John - Private - 26th Infantry - Company: Samuel Swearingen - Enlistment date: 15 Jul 1813 - Enlistment period: 1 Yr.

Woods, Andrew - Private - 26th Infantry - Company: George Kesling - Other regiment: Light Dragoons Regiment - Enlistment date: 20 May 1813 - Enlistment period: 1 Yr.

Woods, William - Private - 27th Infantry - Company: Joseph Cairns - Other regiment: 19th Infantry then 3rd Infantry - Age: 19 - Height: 5' 7" - Born: Virginia - Trade: Shoemaker - Enlistment date: 12 May 1813 - Enlistment period: 1 Yr - 5 Yrs - Discharged: 14 Mar 1819 - Comments: Served aboard the US Sloop Trippe on the Lake Erie Squadron; re-enlisted.

Woolford, Daniel - Private - 17th Infantry - Company: John Chunn - Other regiment: 3rd Infantry - Age: 45 - Height: 5' 10 1/2" - Born: VA, Culpepper County - Trade: Carpenter - Enlistment date: 8 Aug 1813 - Enlistment place: Portsmouth - Enlistment period: 5 Yrs - By whom: Hugh May - Discharged: 8 Aug 1818 - Pension: Old War IF-19225 Rejected; served in Capt. Chunn's Company, 17th Infantry as a private.

Worthington, Joshua - Private - 19th Infantry - Company: James Herron - Enlistment date: 1 Dec 1812 - Enlistment period: 18 Mos.

Worthington, Stephen - Sergeant - 27th Infantry - Company: Alexander Hill.

Wortsbough, John - Private - 19th Infantry - Company: Joel Collins - Age: 18 - Height: 5' 7" - Born: Germany - Trade: Tanner - Enlistment date: 15 Mar 1814 - Enlistment place: Detroit - Enlistment period: War - By whom: Wynkoop Warner - Discharged: 20 Jul 1815 at Detroit - Bounty: BLW 9631-160-12 (Illinois).

Wrengan, William - Private - 19th Infantry - Company: George Kesling - By whom: Charles Cissna.

Wright, Alexander - Private - 26th Infantry - Company: George Kesling - Enlistment date: 1 May 1813 - Enlistment period: 1 Yr - Discharged: 1 May 1814 - Comments: Served aboard the US Brig Niagara on the Lake Erie Squadron.

Wright, John - Private - 19th Infantry - Company: Wilson Elliott.

Wright, John - Private - 2nd Rifles - Company: Benjamin Desha - Age: 36 - Height: 5' 5" - Born: Ireland, County Tryone - Trade: Laborer - Enlistment date: 24 Oct 1814 - Enlistment place: Cincinnati - Enlistment period: 5 Yrs - By whom: William Pritchard - Discharged: 24 Oct 1819 at Fort Crawford, IL.

Wright, Joseph - Private - 27th Infantry - Company: George Sanderson - Enlistment date: 30 Jun 1813 - Comments: Served aboard the US Schooner Somers on the Lake Erie Squadron.

Wright, Robert B. - 27th Infantry - Pension: Wife Margaret Barber, Old War WF-12256; served as a private in the

27th Infantry.

Wright, William - Private - 27th Infantry - Company: William Gill - Enlistment date: 15 Jun 1813 - Enlistment period: 1 Yr - Died: 28 Aug 1813.

Writson, Joseph - Private - 19th Infantry - Company: William Gill.

Wyant, John - Private - 19th Infantry - Company: Richard Talbott - Age: 34 - Height: 5' 9" - Born: Pennsylvania - Trade: Farmer - Enlistment date: 13 Sep 1814 - Enlistment place: Lower Sandusky (now Fremont, OH) - Enlistment period: War - By whom: Richard Talbott - Discharged: 5 Jun 1815 at Chillicothe - Bounty: BLW 17171-160-12 (Illinois).

Wyatt, Elisha - 27th Infantry - Age: 21 - Height: 5' 8" - Born: PA, Washington County - Enlistment date: 25 Jan 1813 - Enlistment place: Ravenna - By whom: John Reeves.

Yarnell, Abraham - Private - 17th Infantry - Company: David Holt - Age: 24 - Height: 5' 9" - Born: New York - Trade: Hatter - Enlistment date: 22 May 1813 - Enlistment place: OH, Yorktown - Enlistment period: War - By whom: George Tod - Discharged: 4 Jun 1815 at Chillicothe - Bounty: BLW 18893-160-12 (Missouri).

Yeoman, Samuel - Private - 27th Infantry - Other regiment: 19th Infantry - Pension: Old War IF-19300 Rejected; served as a private in the 27th and the 19th Infantries and in the Ohio Militia.

Young, Alexander - Sergeant - 19th Infantry - Company: James Herron - Enlistment date: 3 Aug 1812 - Enlistment period: 18 Mos.

Young, Andrew - Private - 19th Infantry - Company: Carey Trimble - Age: 22 - Height: 5' 6" - Born: Virginia - Trade: Laborer - Enlistment date: 12 Mar 1814 - Enlistment place: Franklin County, Franklinton - Enlistment period: 1 Yr - By whom: John McElvain - Discharged: 12 Mar 1815.

Young, James - Private - 26th Infantry - Other regiment: 25th Infantry - Enlistment date: 24 Jul 1813 - Enlistment period: 1 Yr - Discharged: 24 Jul 1814 at Buffalo, NY.

Young, Matthias - Private - 19th Infantry - Company: Richard Talbott - Age: 23 - Height: 5' 9 1/2" - Born: Maryland - Trade: Tanner - Enlistment date: 28 Jan 1814 - Enlistment place: Franklin County, Franklinton - Enlistment period: 1 Yr - By whom: Robert Young - Discharged: 23 Jan 1815.

Young, Philip - Private - 19th Infantry - Company: James Herron - Enlistment date: 22 May 1812 - Enlistment period: 18 Mos.

Young, Soloman - Private - 19th Infantry - Company: Wilson Elliott.

Young, Thomas - Private - 1st Rifles - Company: Thomas Ramsey - Age: 25 - Height: 5' 6" - Born: PA, Washington County - Trade: Laborer - Enlistment date: 15 Nov 1813 - Enlistment place: Cincinnati - Enlistment period: War - By whom: Thomas Ramsey - Discharged: 31 Jul 1815 near Buffalo, NY, on Surgeon's Certificate of Disability, wounded at Fort Erie, UC, on 17 Sep 1814 - Pension: Old War IF-10306, served in Capt Ramsey's Company, 1st US Rifles as a private - Bounty: BLW 7167-160-12 (Arkansas) - Comments: Prisoner of War (Quebec, LC), captured at Fort Erie, UC, 17 Sep 1814; released 13 Mar 1815.

Ziegley, Benjamin - Private - 17th Infantry - Company: David Holt - Other regiment: 3rd Infantry - Age: 35 - Height: 5' 10" - Trade: Laborer - Enlistment date: 25 Feb 1814 - Enlistment place: Steubenville - Enlistment period: 5 Yrs - By whom: Isaac Reiley - Discharged: 4 Mar 1815 after furnishing a substitute.

Zimmerman, Frederick - Private - 17th Infantry - Company: Harris Hickman - Age: 30 - Height: 6' 2" - Born: Maryland - Trade: Laborer - Enlistment date: 14 Mar 1814 - Enlistment place: Dayton - Enlistment period: War - Discharged: 9 Jun 1815 at Chillicothe - Bounty: BLW 8258-160-12 (Missouri).

Zimmerman, Henry (or Peter) - Private - 27th Infantry - Company: George Sanderson - Enlistment date: 7 Jun 1813 - Pension: Old War IF-19341 Rejected, served in Captain Sanderson's Company, 27th Infantry.

Zipler, Daniel - Private - 27th Infantry - Company: George Sanderson - Enlistment date: 6 Jul 1813.

The Enlisted Men

The Bibliography

Adjutant and Inspector General's Office, **Military Laws and Rules and Regulations for the Army of the United States**, September 1816, (E. De Krafft, Printer: Washington, DC).

Allen, Jeremiah C., **Subject Index of the General Orders of the War Department from January 1, 1809 to December 31, 1860**, (Adjutant General's Department: Government Printing Office, Washington, DC, 1886).

Altoff, Gerard T., **Deep Water Sailors, Shallow Water Soldiers, Manning the United States Fleet on Lake Erie 1813**, (The Perry Group, Put-in-Bay, OH: 1993).

Andrews, Martin R., M.A., **History of Marietta and Washington County, Ohio, and Representative Citizens**, (Biographical Publishing Company, Chicago, Illinois: 1902), page 560.

Baker, Harrison Scott II, **American Prisoners of War Held at Halifax During the War of 1812**, (Heritage Books, Inc.: Westminster, MD, 2004), volumes 1 and 2.

Clift, G. Glenn, **Remember the Raisin!**, (Kentucky Historical Society, Frankfort, Kentucky: 1961), page 177.

"Clothing, arms, Accoutrements and camp equipage for Major Tod's detachment," 2 January 1814, **George Tod Collection**, Western Reserve Historical Society Archives Library, Cleveland, OH, manuscript section, call number MS-3202, container 21B, folder 3.

"Clothing issue roster for Captain Harris Hickman's company," 15 August 1814, **George Tod Collection**, Western Reserve Historical Society Archives Library, Cleveland, OH, manuscript section, call number MS-3202, container 2, folder 4.

"Clothing issue roster for Captain Wilson Elliott's Company," 14 August 1812, **George Tod Collection**, Western Reserve Historical Society Archives Library, Cleveland, OH, manuscript section, call number MS-3202, container 1B, folder 3.

"Clothing issue roster for Captain Wilson Elliott's Company," 25 January 1813, **George Tod Collection**, Western Reserve Historical Society Archives Library, Cleveland, OH, manuscript section, call number MS-3202, container 2.

"Clothing issue roster for Captain Wilson Elliott's Company," 12 March 1813, **George Tod Collection**, Western Reserve Historical Society Archives Library, Cleveland, OH, manuscript section, call number MS-3202, container 2.

"Clothing issue roster for Captain Wilson Elliott's Company," May-June 1813, **George Tod Collection**, Western Reserve Historical Society Archives Library, Cleveland, OH, manuscript section, call number MS-3202, container 2.

"Clothing issue roster for Ensign William Featherton's detachment," July, August, September 1814, **George Tod Collection**, Western Reserve Historical Society Archives Library, Cleveland, OH, manuscript section, call number MS-3202, container 2, folder 4.

"Compete muster roll of a detachment of recruits," 9 August 1812, **George Tod Collection**, Western Reserve Historical Society Archives Library, Cleveland, OH, container 2a.

"Compete muster roll of a detachment of recruits," 18 September 1812, **George Tod Collection**, Western Reserve Historical Society Archives Library, Cleveland, OH, container 2a.

"Complete muster roll from Lieutenant Joseph H. Larwill," 28 October 1812, manuscript section, call number MS-3202, container 2a, **George Tod Collection**, Western Reserve Historical Society Archives Library, Cleveland, OH.

"Death of Michael Duffy," **George Tod Papers 1783-1834**, Western Reserve Historical Society Archives Library, Cleveland, OH, manuscript section, call number MS-3202, container 1B, folder 5.

The Bibliography

"Discharge roster," **George Tod Collection**, Western Reserve Historical Society Archives Library, Cleveland, OH, manuscript section, call number MS-3202, container 2, folder 6.

"Discharge muster and payroll muster of Lieutenant John McElvain's Company, 19th Regiment of Infantry," **Adjutant General's Militia Records**, Series 88, Payroll, Folder 2, Ohio Historical Society's Library, Columbus, OH.

Duncan McArthur Papers, Library of Congress, 1922, Microfilm 47, reel 2, volumes 4-5, 22 September 1813 – 4 March 1814, Ohio Historical Society, Columbus, OH.

Duncan McArthur Papers, Library of Congress, 1922, Microfilm 47, reel 4, volumes 9-11, 21 May 1814-21 July 1814, Ohio Historical Society, Columbus, OH.

Fredriksen, John C., **The United States Army in the War of 1812**, (McFarland & Company, Inc.: Jefferson, NC, 2009).

Graves, Donald E., **Red Coats & Grey Jackets: The Battle of Chippawa, 5 July 1814**, (Dundurn Press Limited, Toronto, Canada: 1994), Appendices, American Regulars, Militia and Native Warriors killed at Chippawa, page 173.

Graves, Donald E., **Where right and Glory Lead! The Battle of Lundy's Lane, 1814**, (Robin Brass Studio: Toronto, Canada, 1993).

Heitman, Francis B., **Historical Register and Dictionary of the United States Army From Its Organization, September 29, 1789, to March 2, 1903**, Volume I and II, (Genealogical Publishing Company, Baltimore, Maryland: 1994).

History of Franklin and Pickaway Counties, Ohio, (Williams Brothers, Evansville, Indiana: 1880), chapter XIX Military Record, Captain George Sanderson's Company, pp. 107-108.

Index to War of 1812 Pension Files, (National Historical Publishing Company, Waynesboro, Tennessee: 1992).

Johnson, Eric Eugene, **American Prisoners of War Held at Quebec During the War of 1812**, (Heritage Books, Inc.: Westminster, MD, 2011).

Knopf, Richard C., **Document Transcriptions of the War of 1812 in the Northwest, Volume VII Part 3, Letters to the Secretary of War 1812 Relating to the War of 1812 in the Northwest,** (Anthony Wayne Parkway Board, Ohio State Museum, Columbus, OH: 1957), page 122, Effects of Deceased Soldiers, 13 Dec 1813.

Lindley, Harlow, **Fort Meigs and the War of 1812, Orderly Book of Cushing's Company, 2nd U.S. Artillery April 1813 – February 1814**, (The Ohio Historical Society, Columbus, OH: 1975), pp. 80-82.

"List of artillery men sent to Chillicothe," 29 October 1812, **George Tod Papers 1783-1834**, Western Reserve Historical Society Archives Library, Cleveland, OH, manuscript section, call number MS-3202, container 2a.

"Listing of Officers from Ohio," 1 December 1814, **George Tod Collection**, Western Reserve Historical Society Archives Library, Cleveland, OH, manuscript section, call number MS-3202, military papers.

Malcomson, Robert, **Historical Dictionary of the War of 1812**, (Scarecrow Press, Inc.: Lanham, MD, 2006).

Medert, Patricia Fife, **Raw Recruits & Bullish Prisoners, Ohio's Capital in the War of 1812**, Ross County Historical Society Publication, (Jackson Publishing Company, Jackson, OH: 1992), page 131.

"Monthly report of Captain Wilson Elliott's company, November 1814," **George Tod Papers 1783-1834**, Western Reserve Historical Society Archives Library, Cleveland, OH, manuscript section, call number MS-3202, container 2, folder 3.

"Monthly recruiting report from Lieutenant Joseph H. Larwill," 8 August 1812, **George Tod Collection**, Western Reserve Historical Society Archives Library, Cleveland, OH, manuscript section, call number MS-3202, container 2a, folder 1.

"Monthly recruiting report from Lieutenant Joseph H. Larwill," For August 1812, **George Tod Collection**, Western Reserve Historical Society Archives Library, Cleveland, OH, manuscript section, call number MS-3202, container 2a.

"Monthly report of Lieutenant Joseph H. Larwill," 14 September 1812, **George Tod Collection**, Western Reserve Historical Society Archives Library, Cleveland, OH, manuscript section, call number MS-3202, container 2a.

"Muster roll of Captain James Herron's company," 31 August 1813 to 31 October 1813, **George Tod Collection**, Western Reserve Historical Society Archives Library, Cleveland, OH, manuscript section, call number MS-3202, container 2, folder 3.

"Muster roll of Captain James Herron's company, 31 Oct 1814," **George Tod Papers 1783-1834**, Western Reserve Historical Society Archives Library, Cleveland, OH, manuscript section, call number MS-3202.

National Archives and Records Administration. **Index to the Compiled Military Service Records for the Volunteer Soldiers Who Served During the War of 1812**. Washington, D.C.: National Archives and Records Administration. M602, 234 rolls.

Naveaux, Ralph, **Invaded on All Sides**, (Walsworth Publishing Company: Marcelie, MO, 2008).

"Payroll Muster of Captain Richard C. Talbott's Company, 19th Regiment of Infantry," **Adjutant General's Militia Records**, Series 88, Payroll, Folder 2, Ohio Historical Society's Library, Columbus, OH.

"Payroll Muster of Captain William Gill's Company, 19th Regiment of Infantry," **Adjutant General's Militia Records**, Series 88, Payroll, Folder 2, Ohio Historical Society's Library, Columbus, OH.

Peterson, Clarence Joseph, **Known Military Dead During the War of 1812**, (Baltimore, Maryland: April 1955).

Powell, Colonel William H. (US Army), **List of Officers of the Army of the United States from 1779-1900**, (L. R. Hamersly & Co.: New York 1900).

"Quarterly enlistment report from Major George Tod," November 1811, manuscript section, call number MS-3202, container 2a, folder 2, **George Tod Collection**, Western Reserve Historical Society Archives Library, Cleveland, OH.

Quimby, Robert S., **The U.S. Army in the War of 1812: An Operational and Command Study**, (Michigan State University Press; East Lansing, MI, 977), volumes 1 and 2.

Records Relating to War of 1812 Prisoners of War, 1812; (National Archives Microfilm Publication M2019); Records of the Adjutant General's Office, 1780's-1917; Record Group 94, compiled by Clair Prechtel-Kluskens; National Archives, Washington, D.C.

"Recruit's accounts at St. Clairsville," 30 July 1812, **George Tod Collection**, Western Reserve Historical Society Archives Library, Cleveland, OH, manuscript section, call number MS-3202, container 2a.

"Recruiting accounts from Lieutenant Samuel P. Booker," July 1812, **George Tod Collection**, Western Reserve Historical Society Archives Library, Cleveland, OH, container 2a.

The Bibliography

"Recruiting accounts Major George Tod," 11 August 1812, **George Tod Collection**, Western Reserve Historical Society Archives Library, Cleveland, OH, container 2a.

"Recruiting account from Lieutenant Samuel P. Booker, 17th Regiment of Infantry," August-September 1812, **George Tod Collection**, Western Reserve Historical Society Archives Library, Cleveland, OH, manuscript section, call number MS-3202, container 2a.

"Recruiting returns of the 17th Regiment of Infantry," August 1814, manuscript section, call number MS-3202, container 2, folder 4, **George Tod Collection**, Western Reserve Historical Society Archives Library, Cleveland, OH.

"Recruiting returns for the 17th Regiment of Infantry," December 1814, manuscript section, call number MS-3202, container 2, folder 5, **George Tod Collection**, Western Reserve Historical Society Archives Library, Cleveland, OH.

"Recruiting account from Lieutenant C. H. Holder, 17th Regiment of Infantry," December 1813 to May 1814, **George Tod Collection**, Western Reserve Historical Society Archives Library, Cleveland, OH, manuscript section, call number MS-3202, container 2, folder 4.

"Recruiting account from Lieutenant James Campbell, 17th Regiment of Infantry," December 1814, **George Tod Collection**, Western Reserve Historical Society Archives Library, Cleveland, OH, manuscript section, call number MS-3202, container 2, folder 4.

"Recruiting account from Lieutenant James Campbell, 17th Regiment of Infantry," January 1815, **George Tod Collection**, Western Reserve Historical Society Archives Library, Cleveland, OH, manuscript section, call number MS-3202, container 2, folder 5.

"Recruiting account from Ensign William H. Shaug, 17th Regiment of Infantry," December 1814 to January 1815, **George Tod Collection**, Western Reserve Historical Society Archives Library, Cleveland, OH, manuscript section, call number MS-3202, container 2, folder 5.

Register of Enlistments in the U.S. Army, 1798-1914; (National Archives Microfilm Publication M233, 81 rolls); Records of the Adjutant General's Office, 1780's-1917, Record Group 94; National Archives, Washington, D.C.

Report from the Secretary of War in Obedience to the Resolutions of the Senate of the 5th and 30th of June, 1834, and the 3rd of March, 1835, in Relation to the Pension Establishment of the United States (1835 Pension Rolls), (Duff Green, Washington, D.C.: 1835).

"2nd Lieutenant James S. Gray's detachment," 1 June 1815, **George Tod Collection**, Western Reserve Historical Society Archives Library, Cleveland, OH, manuscript section, call number MS-3202, container 2, folder 5.

"2nd Lieutenant John Goode's detachment," 1815, **George Tod Collection**, Western Reserve Historical Society Archives Library, Cleveland, OH, manuscript section, call number MS-3202, container 2, folder 5.

United States. Bureau of Land Management, General Land Office Records. Automated Records Project; **Federal Land Patents**, State Volumes. http://www.glorecords.blm.gov/. Springfield, Virginia: Bureau of Land Management, Eastern States, 2007.

Volkel, Lowell M., **War of 1812 Bounty Lands in Illinois**, (Heritage House, Thompson, Illinois: 1977).

War of 1812 Military Bounty Land Warrants, 1815-1858; National Archives Microfilm Publication M848; Records of the Bureau of Land Management, Record Group 49; National Archives, Washington, D.C.

War of 1812 Pension Applications; National Archives Microfilm Publication M313; Records of the Department of Veterans Affairs, Record Group Number 15; National Archives, Washington D.C.

"Weekly enlistment report from Captain Wilson Elliott," 28 July 1812, manuscript section, call number MS-3202, container 1B, folder 3, **George Tod Collection**, Western Reserve Historical Society Archives Library, Cleveland, OH.

"Weekly recruiting report from Captain James Herron," 27 July 1812, container 2a, **George Tod Collection**, Western Reserve Historical Society Archives Library, Cleveland, OH.

"Weekly enlistment report from 1st Lieutenant Samuel Booker," 13 July 1812, manuscript section, call number MS-3202, container 1B, folder 9, **George Tod Collection**, Western Reserve Historical Society Archives Library, Cleveland, OH.

"Weekly enlistment report from Captain Wilson Elliott," 11 Aug 1812, manuscript section, call number MS-3202, container 1B, folder 3, **George Tod Collection**, Western Reserve Historical Society Archives Library, Cleveland, OH.

"Weekly enlistment report from Lieutenant John Milligan," Apr 1813, manuscript section, call number MS-3202, container 2, folder 3, **George Tod Collection**, Western Reserve Historical Society Archives Library, Cleveland, OH.

Whitehorne, Joseph, **While Washington Burned: The Battle of Fort Erie 1814**, (Nautical & Aviation Publishing Company of America: Baltimore, MD 1992).

Wilder, Minnie S., **Kentucky Soldiers of the War of 1812**, (Genealogical Publishing Company: Baltimore, MD 1969).

The Bibliography

www.ingramcontent.com/pod-product-compliance
Lightning Source LLC
Chambersburg PA
CBHW082121230426
43671CB00015B/2764